CORPORATIONS

Examples and Explanations

CORPORATIONS

Examples and Explanations
Second Edition

Lewis D. Solomon

Professor of Law
George Washington University

Alan R. Palmiter

Professor of Law
Wake Forest University

Little, Brown and Company
Boston   New York   Toronto   London

Library of Congress Catalog Card No. 94-75304

ISBN 0-316-80371-5

CCP

Second Edition

Published simultaneously in Canada
by Little, Brown & Company (Canada) Limited

Printed in the United States of America

To our families, who in their own ways
continue to labor with us

Contents

Preface   *xv*
Acknowledgments   *xvii*
Special Notice   *xix*

PART ONE
Introduction to Corporate Law

Chapter 1: The Corporation — An Introduction   **3**
 §1.1 Basics of the Corporation   3
 §1.2 Sources of Corporate Law   8
 §1.3 The Corporation as a Constitutional Entity   10

Chapter 2: Choice of Organizational Form   **19**
 §2.1 The Range of Organizational Choices   19
 §2.2 Choosing between a Partnership and a Corporation   21
 §2.3 Taxation — A Critical Element in the Choice   24

PART TWO
Formation of the Corporation

Chapter 3: Incorporation — How and Where   **35**
 §3.1 The Process of Incorporation   35
 §3.2 Choosing Where to Incorporate   39

**Chapter 4: Corporate Powers — The Rise and Fall
    of the Ultra Vires Doctrine**   **45**
 §4.1 Decline of the Ultra Vires Doctrine   45
 §4.2 Modern Ultra Vires Doctrine — A Limited Planning
    Device   47
 §4.3 Distinguishing the Ultra Vires Doctrine
    from Corporate Duties   47
 §4.4 Corporate Largesse and the Ultra Vires Doctrine   48

Chapter 5: The Duties of Promoters   53
§5.1   Promoter's Liability on Preincorporation Contracts   53
§5.2   Liability for Defective Incorporation   60
§5.3   Promoter's Liability for Early Dealings with the Corporation   65

Chapter 6: Piercing the Veil of Limited Liability   69
§6.1   General Rule of Limited Liability   69
§6.2   Traditional Piercing Factors   71
§6.3   Distilling a Principle — Solving the Piercing Conundrum   81

Chapter 7: Statutory Recognition of the Corporate Form   87
§7.1   Statutory Recognition of Corporation   87
§7.2   Equitable Subordination Doctrine   89

PART THREE
Financial Structure of the Corporation

Chapter 8: Capital Structure of the Corporation   95
§8.1   Equity Financing   96
§8.2   Debt Financing   111
§8.3   Choosing a Debt-Equity Mix   114

Chapter 9: Limitations on Corporate Distributions   119
§9.1   Distributions — Transferring Assets to Shareholders   119
§9.2   Limitations on Distributions   121
§9.3   Contractual Limitations on Distributions   129
§9.4   Liability of Directors for Authorizing Illegal Distributions   129

Chapter 10: Federal Regulation of Securities Offerings   139
§10.1   The 1933 Act's Disclosure Mandate   140
§10.2   Exemptions — Tempering the Breadth of §5   141
§10.3   Civil Liability under the 1933 Act   152
§10.4   The Definition of a Security   160

PART FOUR
The Structure of Corporate Governance

Chapter 11: Statutory Model of Corporate Governance   167
§11.1   Basic Elements of the Corporate Governance Structure   168
§11.2   Analyzing the Traditional Model of Corporate Governance   168

Contents

Chapter 12: The Corporate Electorate — The Shareholders' Role in Corporate Governance   **171**
   §12.1   The Nature of the Shareholders' Limited Role   171
   §12.2   The Mechanics of Shareholders' Meetings   175

Chapter 13: The Center of Corporate Governance — The Board of Directors   **181**
   §13.1   Election of Directors   181
   §13.2   Removal of Directors   185
   §13.3   Board Decision-Making   186

Chapter 14: The Corporate Bureaucracy — Officers' Authority to Bind the Corporation   **195**
   §14.1   Corporate Authority   195
   §14.2   Respondeat Superior — Corporate Liability for Employee Torts   199

PART FIVE
Management of the Closely Held Corporation

Chapter 15: The Control Dilemma in the Close Corporation — An Introduction   **205**
   §15.1   Special Problems in the Close Corporation   205
   §15.2   Planning for the Close Corporation   207

Chapter 16: Control Devices in the Close Corporation   **211**
   §16.1   Supermajority Requirements — Minority Veto Power   211
   §16.2   Vote-Pooling Agreements — Shareholder Coalitions   214
   §16.3   Voting Trusts — Locking In Shareholders   220
   §16.4   Different Classes of Stock — Building Control into the Capital Structure   223
   §16.5   Irrevocable Proxies — Voting Power "Coupled with an Interest"   224
   §16.6   Transfer Restrictions and Liquidity Rights   231
   §16.7   Restraints on Directors' Discretion — Planner Beware!   237
   §16.8   Close Corporation Statutes — Certainty and Guidance for the Planner   240

Chapter 17: Dispute Resolution in the Close Corporation   **249**
   §17.1   An Overview   249
   §17.2   Judicial Protection of Minority Shareholders   252
   §17.3   Deadlocks   258

Contents

PART SIX
Shareholder Action in Public Corporations

**Chapter 18: Shareholders' Role in Publicly
Held Corporations**   **265**

§18.1   Shareholder Voting in Public Corporations   265
§18.2   Public Trading of Corporate Securities   269

Chapter 19: Proxy Regulation   **275**

§19.1   State Proxy Regulation   275
§19.2   Federal Proxy Regulation — An Introduction   277
§19.3   Reach of the SEC Proxy Rules   278
§19.4   Formal Requirements of the SEC Proxy Rules   281
§19.5   Shareholder Initiatives   288
§19.6   Private Action to Challenge Proxy Fraud   297

PART SEVEN
*Fiduciary Duties of Management
and Controlling Shareholders*

Chapter 20: Corporate Fiduciary Duties — An Introduction   **311**

§20.1   The Corporate Fiduciary — A Unique Relationship   312
§20.2   Two Broad Fiduciary Duties — Care and Loyalty   314
§20.3   Fiduciary Duties — Fitting Corporate
and Market Realities   316
§20.4   Enforcing Fiduciary Duties   317

Chapter 21: Duty of Care and the Business Judgment Rule   **319**

§21.1   Standards of Care — General, but Misleading,
Guidance   319
§21.2   Business Judgment Rule   321
§21.3   Overcoming the Business Judgment Presumption   323
§21.4   Remedies for Breaching the Duty of Care   332
§21.5   Limitations on Directors' Liability   332

Chapter 22: Duty of Loyalty — Self-Dealing Transactions   **343**

§22.1   The Danger and Forms of Self-Dealing   344
§22.2   Judicial Suspicion of Self-Dealing Transactions   345
§22.3   The "Fairness" Test   347
§22.4   "Safe Harbors" — Informed Approval
by Disinterested Directors or Shareholders   351
§22.5   Remedies for Self-Dealing   353

Contents

Chapter 23: Executive Compensation   361
    §23.1 Forms of Executive Compensation   361
    §23.2 Judicial Review of Executive Compensation   362
    §23.3 Directors' Compensation   365
    §23.4 Reform Initiatives   365

Chapter 24: Corporate Opportunities and Unfair Competition   369
    §24.1 The Corporate Opportunity Doctrine   369
    §24.2 Definition of "Corporate Opportunity"   370
    §24.3 Corporate Consent and Incapacity   373
    §24.4 Competition with the Corporation   374

Chapter 25: Indemnification and Insurance   381
    §25.1 Indemnification — Reimbursement by the Corporation   381
    §25.2 Insurance   386

Chapter 26: Responsibilities of Controlling Shareholders   395
    §26.1 Who Are Controlling Shareholders?   395
    §26.2 Dealings between the Corporation and Controlling
           Shareholders   396
    §26.3 Squeeze-out Transactions — Eliminating
           Minority Interests   399

Chapter 27: Sale of Control   411
    §27.1 Sale of Office   411
    §27.2 Limitations on Sale of Controlling Stock   411

PART EIGHT
Dealings in Securities

Chapter 28: Common Law Prohibitions on Insider Trading   423
    §28.1 An Introduction to Insider Trading   423
    §28.2 State Fiduciary Law on Insider Trading   424
    §28.3 Liability to the Corporation for Insider Trading   427
    §28.4 Liability for Outsider Trading under State Law   429

Chapter 29: Rule 10b-5   433
    §29.1 An Introduction to Rule 10b-5   433
    §29.2 Rule 10b-5 — An Overview   435
    §29.3 Rule 10b-5 — The Basic Elements   437
    §29.4 Limits of Rule 10b-5 — Pruning the Oak   443
    §29.5 Rule 10b-5 and Insider Trading   453

Chapter 30:   Section 16(b) — Disgorging Short-Swing Profits   465

§30.1   Coverage of §16   465
§30.2   Disgorging Short-Swing Profits under §16(b) —
    The Mechanical Test   466
§30.3   Special Interpretive Issues   467

PART NINE
Shareholder Litigation

Chapter 31:   Shareholder Litigation   479

§31.1   The Nature of Derivative Litigation   479
§31.2   Distinguishing between Derivative, Direct, and Class
    Action Suits   482

Chapter 32:   Procedural Restrictions on Derivative Litigation   489

§32.1   The Distorted Incentives Created by Derivative Litigation   489
§32.2   Procedural Requirements   490
§32.3   Derivative Litigation in Federal Courts   495

Chapter 33:   Dismissal of Derivative Litigation — Finding
a Corporate Voice   501

§33.1   The Self-Appointed Derivative Suit Plaintiff   501
§33.2   The Unwieldy Body of Shareholders   502
§33.3   Board of Directors — The Voice of Central
    Corporate Governance   502
§33.4   Special Litigation Committees   506

PART TEN
Organic Changes

Chapter 34:   Internal Organic Changes — Charter Amendments,
Recapitalizations, and Dissolution   517

§34.1   Amendments to Articles of Incorporation   517
§34.2   Dissolution   520

Chapter 35:   External Organic Changes — Corporate
Combinations   525

§35.1   The Combination Choices — Some Basics   525
§35.2   Mergers and Consolidations   526
§35.3   Sales of Assets   533
§35.4   De Facto Merger and Successor Liability Doctrines   536

Chapter 36:   Dissenters' Appraisal Rights   **543**

§36.1   The Appraisal Remedy — Protection against Majority
Tyranny   543

§36.2   The Appraisal Proceeding   545

§36.3   Exclusivity of Appraisal   548

PART ELEVEN
Takeover Contests

Chapter 37:   Takeover Contests — An Introduction   **555**

§37.1   The Hostile Choices — Proxy Contest or
Tender Offer   555

§37.2   A Garden-Variety Takeover Drama   557

§37.3   An Epilogue — Is the Takeover Phenomenon
Healthy?   565

Chapter 38:   Proxy Contests   **569**

§38.1   The Insurgent's Uphill Battle in a Proxy Contest   569

§38.2   Federal Regulation of Proxy Contests   570

§38.3   State Fiduciary Regulation of Proxy Contests   571

Chapter 39:   Federal Securities Regulation of Tender Offers   **579**

§39.1   Disclosure of Foothold Position   540

§39.2   Federal Tender Offer Rules   540

§39.3   Standing to Sue for Williams Act Violations   585

Chapter 40:   Takeover Defenses   **593**

§40.1   The Dilemma of Takeover Defenses —
The Proper Role of the Target's Board   593

§40.2   State Fiduciary Law — An Evolving Response
to the Takeover Dilemma   595

§40.3   The Lurking Question of the Board's Power —
A Mild Revival of the Ultra Vires Doctrine   605

§40.4   State Takeover Statutes — Protection for Whom?   611

Index   *621*

Preface

For many students corporate law is a cold, uninviting mystery. Notions such as debt/equity ratios, stock markets, bylaws, leveraged buyouts, and cumulative preferred stock cause many to freeze.

In addition to its unfamiliar business setting, corporate law presents a jumble of topics from the first year of law school — some civil procedure, a good dose of contracts and agency, tort concepts in the form of fiduciary rules, a bit of constitutional and property law, and even some criminal law. The methods of analysis are equally varied — pervasive statutory interpretation, heavy case synthesis, moderate regulatory analysis, and goodly policy debates.

Although the corporations casebooks increasingly show sympathy to the student's plight, they often still fail to offer a context: What problems do the statutory rules address? How do the cases fit with the statutes? What are the underlying social and business issues?

This book is meant to help students understand the workings of corporate law and the nature of the legal relationships among the corporate constituents. It covers the areas of the standard corporations and business organizations casebooks but is neither a study outline nor a treatise.

Our purpose is to provide a context for the cases and the statutes and an opportunity for students to probe their own understanding. Textual material offers an analytical framework, and follow-up examples and explanations reinforce and illuminate the text.

Further, the book covers some topics that professors often gloss over in class, such as the ultra vires doctrine, the legal capital regime, the public offering of securities, the common law of insider trading, the disgorgement of short-swing insider profits, merger and appraisal procedures, and federal tender offer regulation.

We have strived to make the book accessible to students without a business background. Students will find that reading the relevant chapter and writing out answers to the questions, before comparing their answers to ours, will go a long way in helping prepare for class and for the exam.

Acknowledgments

We have greatly appreciated the assistance of our students in and out of class. Their questions and comments have inspired much of this book.

We owe special thanks to a cadre of Wake Forest student assistants whose research and editorial suggestions on this second edition were invaluable — in particular, Anne Lee ('94), Brian McGinn ('94), and William Pleasant ('94). We also are indebted to Barbara Rappaport of Little, Brown for her excellent work in moving us through the re-editing process.

Finally, we thank the many professors who have suggested our book to their students, for their many useful comments to us, and for their kind words of encouragement.

Special Notice

To reduce the distraction of citations, the book departs from standard citation form in a number of ways:

1. Dates. References to statutory sources and SEC rules are usually undated. All such references are to compilations as of 1993, unless we give a different date.

2. State statutes. We abbreviate the citations to corporation statutes:

RMBCA §8.50	Revised Model Business Corporation Act, Section 8.50 (as approved June 1984)
Cal. Corp. §317	California Corporations Code, Section 317
Del. GCL §145	Delaware General Corporation Law, Section 145
N.Y. BCL §721	New York Business Corporation Law, Section 721

3. State cases. We cite only to the West regional reporters. An unadorned abbreviation of the state's name means the decision was by the state's highest court. For example, "493 A.2d 946 (Del. 1985)" cites to a decision of the Delaware Supreme Court; "316 A.2d 599 (Del. Ch. 1974)" cites to a decision of the Delaware Chancery Court.

4. Securities law statutes and rules. We cite only to the section numbers of the Securities Act of 1933, compiled at 15 U.S.C. §§77a et seq., and the Securities Exchange Act of 1934, compiled at 15 U.S.C. §§78a et seq. Likewise, we cite only to the numbers of the rules promulgated under the 1933 Act, found at 17 C.F.R. §230.____, and under the 1934 Act, found at 17 C.F.R. §240.____.

CORPORATIONS

Examples and Explanations

PART ONE

Introduction to Corporate Law

1

The Corporation — An Introduction

What is a "corporation"? There are many answers, some of which you already know from your first year of law school. A corporation is a structuring device for conducting modern business. It is a framework — a legal person — through which a business can enter into contracts, own property, sue in court, and be sued. It is a taxable entity subject to property, sales, income, and other taxes. It can range in size from a one-person business to a multi-national conglomerate. It is a capitalist invention for the pooling of capital (from shareholders and lenders), management (from executives), and other factors of production (from suppliers and employees). It is a creature of state law; its formation and existence depend on state enabling statutes.

A "corporation" is an artifice. Nobody (not even your law professor) has ever seen one. A business conducted as a corporation looks much the same as one conducted in a noncorporate form. In the end, a corporation is a construct of the law — a set of legal relationships. It is what the law defines it to be.

In this chapter we consider the principal attributes and constituents of the modern business corporation, the reasons for the corporate form, the purpose and the sources of corporate law, and the status of the corporation as a "person" under the Constitution.

§1.1 Basics of the Corporation

§1.1.1 Four Basic Attributes

The paradigmatic corporation has four basic attributes:

Separate existence. The corporation has an independent, perpetual existence. It is an entity distinct from those who contribute capital

3

(shareholders and lenders) and those who manage the business (directors and officers). The corporation owns the assets of the business and is liable for any business debts.

Centralized management.   Management power lies in the board of directors, which often delegates its power to officers. Shareholders elect the directors but cannot control specific board decisions.

Transferability of ownership interests.   Shareholders' ownership interests (their shares) are freely transferable.

Limited liability.   The corporation is liable for its own debts and obligations but is otherwise a "nonconductor" of liability. The corporation insulates directors, officers, lenders, and shareholders (except to the extent of their investment) from liability.

You should not be surprised to learn that there are exceptions to these tenets. For example, in special circumstances courts may hold shareholders personally liable for corporate debts beyond their investment; lenders may require shareholders to give personal guarantees before they extend credit to the corporation; and, in closely held corporations, shareholders can agree to manage the business and to limit their ability to transfer their stock. Because of this malleability, corporate law places a premium on the lawyer's role as creative planner.

§1.1.2   *Corporate Constituents*

Who is interested in a corporation? We all are. Consider the following range of corporate constituents:

Managers (directors and officers) — business executives who supply their labor (human capital) to run the business.

Shareholders — investors who contribute money in the hope of a return on their investment: discretionary dividends, liquidation rights, and market appreciation. Shareholders can be individual investors or institutions who invest others' money.

Lenders (debtholders) — investors who lend money to the corporation on the promise of interest payments and the repayment of principal. Loans to the corporation can take many forms: secured bank loans, unsecured bonds, short-term notes, suppliers' trade credit.

Employees — those who supply their labor (human capital) to the business, subject to the direction of the corporate managers.

Customers and suppliers — buyers and sellers of goods and services. Some dealings are conducted through long-term contracts and others through market transactions.

Contract creditors — suppliers and customers who in their dealings with the corporation obtain contract and payment rights.

Tort creditors — customers and members of the public to whom the corporation becomes obligated because of losses caused by its business activities.

Tax authorities — federal, state, and local government revenue collectors.

Government regulators — government agencies charged with regulating business: environmental, antitrust, banking, health, product safety; you name it.

The lines between these categories are in some respects artificial. From an economic standpoint, the capital provided by shareholders, debtholders, and contract creditors may be difficult to distinguish. It is possible to view the corporation's capital-providers, managers, employees, and suppliers as being involved in a joint economic activity.

Nonetheless, corporate law generally draws its boundaries around the relationship between shareholders and managers — the two constituent groups usually understood to comprise the internal organization of the corporation. Outside relationships with creditors, suppliers, customers, employees, and government authorities usually are subject to legal norms that treat the corporation as a person — such as the laws of contract, debtor-creditor, antitrust, labor, and tax.

§1.1.3 Theory of the Corporation

The corporation separates the functions of funding and managing the business, thus creating a mechanism for operating large enterprises and raising large amounts of capital. In a business where only managers contribute capital, the firm's horizons are limited by the personal wealth of the managers. If the risk of business failure is high, lenders will demand an exorbitant interest rate to compensate for the risk. Borrowing large sums will be out of the question. The corporation seeks to solve the problem of capital formation by using three techniques to re-allocate risk:

Shareholders as residual claimants. The corporation establishes a hierarchy of claims on the business assets. Shareholder claims come behind all others. The corporation compensates shareholders for assuming this last-in-line position by offering them an "ownership" interest with the possibility of large returns if the business is successful. By comparison, lenders stand ahead of shareholders but can only hope to earn interest.

Limited management liability. The corporation shifts the risk of business failure away from a small number of capital-poor managers to many capital-rich shareholders. Shareholders (compared to full-time managers) are better able to bear risk because they can invest their money in several diversified investments; full-time managers can "invest" their human capital in only one business at a time.

Limited shareholder liability. The corporation limits shareholders' liability to the amount of their investment. This leaves the risk of loss with the firm's voluntary and involuntary creditors. It is argued that these creditors (such as lenders, suppliers, and tort victims) are better able than shareholders to appraise the risk of loss and protect themselves. The firm's creditors can either stop dealing with the firm, demand contract protections, or purchase insurance to protect themselves against the risk that business assets will be inadequate to meet their claims.

By separating the functions of shareholders and managers, the corporation becomes a breeding ground for conflicting interests — and opportunism. Although shareholders and managers ideally should want their efficient specialization to maximize returns for the business as a whole, each constituent will have its own separate agenda. Once shareholders have invested their money in the business, managers will want ever more compensation, and they may become lazy and be reluctant to take business risks that threaten their job security. Once managers have committed their human capital to the business, shareholders will want the managers to be ever more self-denying and hard-working. The shareholders may want to have the profits paid to them rather than reinvested in the business and have the managers take risks if the expected value of return is high. Despite these conflicts, the premise of the corporation is that neither shareholders nor managers can exist without the other.

Corporate law allocates risks between shareholders and managers in an attempt to minimize shareholder-manager conflicts and to maximize the firm's overall success. In some contexts, corporate law assumes legal intervention is too costly and leaves the risk with shareholders: For example, the judicially created business judgment rule gives directors broad discretion to run the business without interference (see §22.2). In other contexts, corporate law intervenes to regulate conflicts: For example, a majority of shareholders must approve the board's decision to merge the corporation into another corporation (see §35.2).

Over the last decade, some legal theorists have described the corporation as a "nexus of contracts." Contractarians view the corporation as a set of voluntary relationships among corporate constituents who are bound together by formal contracts, statutory norms, implicit understandings, and market constraints. The corporation serves as a convenient organizing tool for all their relationships.

The contractarian vision of the corporation contrasts with the traditional notion of the corporation as a control device. To traditionalists, the corporation organizes capital and labor in a way that creates dangerous opportunities for managers to exploit shareholders and other constituents. Traditionalists maintain that in public corporations, active management "control" dominates passive shareholder "ownership." Even in close corporations that lack centralized management, controlling participants can unfairly take advantage of minority participants.

Traditionalists thus place great emphasis on corporate law to regulate manager opportunism. They urge greater shareholder voting powers, broad disclosure rights, and strong fiduciary protection. On the other hand, contractarians believe that market forces (like an invisible hand) keep managers from becoming too opportunistic. Contractarians argue that if managers fail to ensure investors a fair governance structure, investors either will not invest or they will sell their shares. Falling prices of corporate shares in capital markets will make it harder for managers to raise capital and to compete in product and service markets. Eventually, a corporation in which managers exploit shareholders will become a takeover target or go bankrupt.

Compare the views of traditionalists and contractarians:

Traditionalists	Contractarians
1. The corporation is a creature of law; no real bargaining occurs in the modern public corporation	1. The corporation (like a contract) is a device, recognized by law, to organize specialized business activity
2. Managers can use "control" to exploit shareholders and other constituents	2. Managers do not exploit "control" because of market constraints that align their interests with shareholders'
3. Many shareholders can be exploited because they are unsophisticated or undiversified	3. Most public shareholders are diversified; close corporation participants can protect themselves by contract
4. Capital (and other) markets are not always efficient; markets act slowly and unevenly to discipline poor managers	4. Capital markets operate so that stock prices of public corporations reflect publicly-available information
5. Corporate law should mandate rules to promote fairness and efficiency	5. Corporate law should seek to infer and enforce the parties' bargain, whether explicit or implicit
6. Judges should actively enforce managers' fiduciary duties to shareholders	6. Judges should intervene with caution, only to fill gaps in the parties' bargain and to ensure the vitality of market constraints
7. Weakened fiduciary protection will drive investors away from equity, toward debt; high leverage is dangerous	7. Managers who face high debt are more motivated; leverage may make business more efficient

§1.2   Sources of Corporate Law

§1.2.1   *A Historical Sketch of the Corporation*

The modern corporation did not rise up in one blazing moment of inspiration. Instead, we can trace its current attributes to various earlier times and forms. The idea of an amalgamation of persons with a separate juridical personality moved from Greece, to Rome, to the continent, and to England. The idea of perpetual separate existence conferred by a grant of the sovereign derives from early English ecclesiastical, municipal, and charitable bodies. The idea of common ownership by a body of passive investors originates from joint-stock trading companies, such as the East India Company (a monopoly franchise) in the early 1600s. A combination of continuity of life, central management, transferability of shares, and limited liability existed in the 1700s in the form of complex deeds of settlement — an unincorporated association.

These concepts came to the American colonies. At first private corporations, like political municipalities, had to receive a special charter from the state legislature. Legislatures granted charters on a case-by-case basis to non-commercial associations (such as churches, universities, and charities) that wanted the convenience of perpetual existence and to commercial associations (such as banks, navigation companies, canals, and turnpikes) with special public purposes and large capital needs. As the needs for capital (and thus incorporation) increased during the early 1800s, states began to enact general incorporation statutes for specified, usually capital-intensive, businesses. Eventually, the corporation evolved into a legal form available to all, subject only to state statutory restrictions.

During the late 1800s two major trends, leading in opposite directions, shaped modern corporate regulation. The first trend led to restraints on business activities. In the 1880s Congress created the Interstate Commerce Commission to regulate the railroad monopolies; in 1890 and 1916 Congress passed antitrust legislation (the Sherman and Clayton acts) to combat consolidations of corporate economic power; in the early 1900s states enacted "blue sky" laws to deal with fraud in the sale of corporate securities; and in the 1930s Congress passed a series of securities laws aimed at abusive management practices in interstate securities markets.

The other trend led to a liberalization of state corporation statutes. In the late 1800s, to attract incorporation revenues, some states amended their statutes to lift limits on the amount of capital that a corporation could raise, to permit corporate ownership of other corporations, and generally to increase the flexibility available to corporate management. Eventually Delaware won this race, which some have called a scurrilous "race to the bottom" and others an efficiency-producing "race to the top." Today most large, publicly traded corporations are incorporated in Delaware.

§1.2.2 Modern State Business Corporation Statutes

Each state specifies the basic elements of the corporation in its corporation statutes. The statutes

- describe how to form a corporation;
- define the rights and duties of shareholders, directors, and officers;
- specify how to conduct directors' and shareholders' meetings; and
- allow for structural changes such as charter amendments, mergers, and dissolution.

Some of the statutory terms are mandatory, such as annual election of directors and shareholder voting on mergers. Others, such as the removal of directors without cause or majority voting on mergers, are default terms that apply unless the parties choose different terms. Contractarians often view corporate statutes as providing standardized "off the rack" terms that apply unless the parties (usually in the charter) choose different, firm-specific terms. Under the internal affairs rule, the law of the state of incorporation governs all shareholder-manager matters in multistate corporations (see §3.2).

Although no two state corporation statutes are alike, there has been a trend toward greater uniformity and modernization. In 1950 the American Bar Association's committee on corporate laws published the first Model Business Corporation Act (MBCA). The MBCA, and its many revised versions, served as the basis for the corporation statutes in 36 states. In 1984 the ABA committee substantially reorganized and rewrote the model act. As of 1993, 16 states have enacted corporate statutes based on this 1984 revision, referred to as the Revised Model Business Corporation Act (RMBCA); a number of states have used its provisions as models for specific changes.

Not all states, however, have enacted a version of the model acts. In fact, the most prominent corporate law states — Delaware, California, and New York — have their own idiosyncratic corporation statutes. Delaware's statute is particularly important in corporate law because of the sophistication of the state's corporate bar and judiciary and because most large, public corporations are incorporated in Delaware.

State corporation statutes often treat all corporations the same. Corporations with numerous, widely dispersed shareholders (publicly held corporations) generally are subject to the same statutory rules as corporations with a small group of shareholders who do not have a public market for their shares (closely held corporations).

§1.2.3 Role of Common Law

Corporation statutes are not all-encompassing; court decisions clarify and fill in the statutory gaps in the statutes and the parties' constitutive documents.

The most important judicial gap-filling involves the fiduciary duties of directors, officers, and controlling shareholders. Common law fiduciary principles that regulate abuse by those who control the corporation's decision-making machinery lie at the heart of corporate law.

§1.2.4   ALI Corporate Governance Project

In 1977 the American Law Institute embarked on a long-term project to describe and unify the basic standards of corporate governance and structure, particularly in those areas not addressed by state corporation statutes. Tentative drafts of Principles of Corporate Governance were controversial and have not received the same reception as have other ALI documents, such as the ALI Restatements. Although some courts have embraced portions of the ALI Principles as useful statements of corporate law, other courts have given them little attention or have refused to follow them. In 1993, after more than 15 years, the project came to a conclusion when the ALI approved a final version of the Principles.

§1.2.5   Federal Law

There is no federal corporation statute, although some commentators have recommended a uniform national law applicable to large public corporations. Nonetheless, federal law adds a significant layer of corporate regulation. Raising capital in public markets (whether by selling stock or taking on debt) is subject to disclosure regulation under the federal Securities Act of 1933 (see Chapter 10). Corporations whose stock is publicly traded are subject to periodic reporting and proxy voting requirements under the Securities and Exchange Act of 1934 (see Chapter 19). In addition, the 1934 Act regulates the trading of securities in public (and private) markets, including the use of confidential corporate information to buy or sell stock (insider trading) (see Chapters 29 and 30).

§1.3   The Corporation as a Constitutional Entity

The corporation as "person" is a powerful metaphor. Corporate personality makes possible the aggregation of capital and management as a business entity capable of contracting, owning property, suing, and being sued — just like natural persons. For commercial purposes, state and federal law largely respect the corporation-as-person metaphor. Most commercial statutes either specifically define corporations to be persons subject to the statute or have been so interpreted.

But there are many noncommercial contexts in which the law does not treat corporations as natural persons, such as laws on intestacy, adoption, and political voting. This makes perfect sense. It would be ludicrous if a corporation could be an adopted child or if the courts recognized a rule of "one-corporation-one-vote."

This returns us to a variant of our earlier question: When does the corporation have constitutional rights normally associated with natural persons?

§1.3.1 Broad Commercial Rights under the Constitution

According to the Supreme Court, the constitutional status of the corporation varies depending on the constitutional right at issue. The corporation is a constitutional "person" only for some purposes. As to those constitutional provisions that can be seen as protecting *commercial interests,* the Supreme Court has had no trouble finding that corporations have constitutional rights.

Commerce clause.   Corporations are protected against state restrictions that burden interstate commerce. *Allenberg Cotton Co., Inc. v. Pittman,* 419 U.S. 20 (1974).

Equal protection.   Corporations are persons under the Equal Protection Clause of the Fourteenth Amendment. *Munn v. Illinois,* 94 U.S. (4 Otto) 113 (1877).

Due process (property interests).   Corporate property is protected against governmental deprivation under the Due Process Clauses of the Fifth and Fourteenth Amendments. *Oklahoma Press Publishing Co. v. Walling,* 327 U.S. 186 (1946).

Commercial speech.   Corporations have a limited First Amendment right to express themselves as to commercial matters — such as advertising their products. *Virginia State Board of Pharmacy v. Virginia Citizens Consumer Council,* 425 U.S. 748 (1976).

The one exception to the commercial-interest analysis has been the Supreme Court's refusal to treat the corporation as a "citizen" protected by the Privileges and Immunities Clause of Article IV. *Paul v. Virginia,* 75 U.S. (8 Wall.) 168 (1868). This allows states to regulate "foreign" corporations (those incorporated in another state) doing in-state business differently from its own "domestic" corporations, though in practice the differences in regulation have been minor.

§1.3.2 Limited Noncommercial Rights under the Constitution

As to the corporation's *noncommercial interests,* the Supreme Court has been far less willing to extend constitutional protection:

Self-incrimination. Corporations cannot claim a Fifth Amendment privilege against self-incrimination. *Bellis v. United States,* 417 U.S. 85 (1974). Nonetheless, where the corporation's interests are closely linked to an individual's interests — such as in a one-person corporation — some lower courts have suggested that the individual's privilege against self-incrimination may extend to the corporation.

Unreasonable searches and seizures. Corporations have a limited Fourth Amendment right to be free from unreasonable searches and seizures. *G.M. Leasing Corp. v. United States,* 429 U.S. 338 (1977). But because business privacy is less compelling than personal privacy, the right may be narrower than that afforded individuals.

Due process (life and liberty). For some constitutional provisions, the corporation-as-person metaphor does not work. For example, it is difficult to imagine a corporation's "liberty" or "life" interest under the Due Process Clause.

Political (noncommercial) speech. A corporation has some free-speech protection under the First Amendment as to noncommercial speech. In a 5-4 decision, the Supreme Court held that a state cannot forbid a corporation from expressing its views on a state referendum, even when the referendum does not materially affect the corporation's business. *First National Bank of Boston v. Bellotti,* 435 U.S. 765 (1978).

EXAMPLES

1. Alexa and George want to open a new bank. They have studied the Uniform Partnership Act (UPA) and have concluded that a partnership structure presents problems for them. According to the UPA, a partnership dissolves whenever any partner dies or withdraws (§31(4)); each partner must contribute new capital (as needed) equally with other partners (§18(a)); each partner is jointly liable for any business debts (§15(b)); every partner votes on partnership matters (§18(e)); and new partners can be added only by unanimous vote (§18(g)).
   a. How does a corporation solve these problems?
   b. Assuming that state and federal regulation allows a bank in to operate in partnership form, can a partnership have corporate attributes?

2. Alexa and George incorporate their bank as First Bank of New Columbia, Inc. New Columbia has adopted a statute modeled on the RMBCA. Alexa and George each becomes a director and officer; to get the bank started, they raise money from a varied and dispersed group of shareholders.
   a. First Bank accepts cash deposits from depositors, the principal source of capital for its lending business. The RMBCA mandates that holders of voting shares elect the board of directors annually. RMBCA

§8.03(d). Can depositors, instead, elect the corporation's directors?

b. New Columbia's corporation statute, unlike the RMBCA, specifies that directors are never liable to shareholders if they exercise good-faith judgment. By its terms, the RMBCA is not as generous. It says directors must exercise their functions in good faith, with the care of a prudent person in a like position under similar circumstances, and in a manner reasonably believed to be in the best interests of the corporation. RMBCA §8.30. Prior court decisions in New Columbia had adopted the RMBCA formulation. Which standard applies?

c. First Bank loses money because the directors, in approving construction loans, rely on overly optimistic projections about the real estate market. Are the directors liable to the shareholders?

3. The Federal Election Campaign Act (FECA) prohibits corporations from spending general corporate funds in connection with any political election. 2 U.S.C. §441b. Comparable limits do not apply to individuals, who may independently support candidates or issues without dollar limitation.

a. First Bank's business is faltering, and its managers use corporate funds to make a substantial contribution to "Save the Banks," a political action committee that promotes candidates who support a federal bailout of frail financial institutions. Such a bailout would greatly benefit First Bank's shareholders. Is FECA, as applied to First Bank's contribution, constitutional under the First Amendment?

b. New Columbia is in the middle of a heated senatorial race. One of the candidates, an outspoken critic of the banking industry and its managers, is seeking reelection. She has proposed increasing criminal sanctions for bank managers who engage in "willful mismanagement." Alexa and George are aghast. They have First Bank fund a newspaper ad campaign to discredit the incumbent's candidacy. Is FECA, as applied to First Bank's political advertising, constitutional under the First Amendment?

EXPLANATIONS

1a. The corporation creates an immortal juridical entity that exists beyond the lives of its participants. Unlike a classic partnership, a corporation can have participants who manage the bank business but who need not contribute capital (directors and officers) and participants who provide capital but whose only significant voice in the bank's management is to elect directors (shareholders). The directors, officers, and shareholders are not liable for business debts except to the extent of their financial investment. Shareholders can transfer their shares without first obtaining the approval of other participants, thus greatly increasing the liquidity of their investment (the ease with which their shares can be sold).

1b. More or less. In many respects, the modern partnership can be made to have the attributes of a corporation. Except for partners' joint liability to third parties, the UPA provisions are not binding, and the parties can "agree otherwise." Thus, a partnership agreement can provide for *continuation* after any partner's death or withdrawal; it can provide for *centralized management* in which some partners vote on how the business is run and others have only limited voting rights; it can make nonmanaging partners' interests *freely transferable;* it can specify that *partnership property* is transferable only in the name of the partnership; and it can specify that nonmanaging partners are *not liable* to contribute any capital beyond their initial capital contribution.

It is even possible to create by contract a structure having the semblance of *limited liability.* Voluntary creditors — such as banks, customers, and suppliers — can be required to agree to indemnify partners (whether acting as managers or capital providers) and look only to partnership assets to satisfy their claims against the business. Liability to involuntary creditors — tort victims — can be minimized through insurance, as well as through internal liability allocation among the partners. But achieving this through the partnership form requires "custom tailoring." The advantage of a corporation is that these attributes are "off the rack."

2a. The depositors don't vote unless they own shares. As is true under all corporation statutes, the RMBCA reserves the voting right to shareholders. The theory is that depositors and other contract providers of capital to the corporation have rights fixed by their contract (to be paid interest, to make withdrawals, and to receive account information). Their contractual rights are senior to (come before) the shareholders' dividend and liquidation rights. Shareholders generally cannot withdraw their investment or receive specified periodic payments — their rights are residual. To protect their precarious position, shareholders receive voting rights.

2b. The New Columbia statutory standard applies. The RMBCA is merely a model statute that a group of lawyers and law professors — members of an ABA committee — have recommended for adoption by state legislatures. No legislature has adopted a version of the model act wholesale without modifications. Corporate common law, like all other state common law, is subject to statutory revision. Courts will be bound by the statute, although they may use judge-made doctrines to interpret the statute's open-ended meaning.

2c. Corporate law says no. First Bank's losses can be seen as resulting from two kinds of risks: external risks beyond the control of the firm's managers (real estate market) and internal risks within their control (monitoring, evaluation, and reaction to external risks by management). Corporate law assumes that shareholders are more efficient bearers of risk. Efficient enterprise organization will be advanced if dispersed investors, each with a small stake in the firm, bear the risk of firm losses. Shareholders are better able than managers to diversify their investment, thus dampening the impact of a particular firm's loss, whether arising from external or internal risk. Rarely will a small group of managers, even if individually wealthy, be able to risk sufficient resources to provide the necessary capital for a large, modern business. Moreover, by having shareholders bear internal risks, corporate law facilitates management specialization and rational risk-taking. If manager-specialists were required to bear the loss of their poor decisions, they might be reluctant to become managers in the first place (choosing a career in law instead) or they might become overly cautious (shunning positive net-value, high-risk projects).

But this does not mean that shareholders should (or do) bear all internal risks. There are some internal risks — such as embezzlement by managers — which if borne by shareholders would hardly encourage investment. But as to internal risks that turn on the honest and informed judgment of corporate managers, corporate law places the burden of loss on shareholders.

When are managers' decisions unreviewable? Traditionalists argue that judges should readily inquire into managers' honesty and efforts to become informed. Corporate law, through fiduciary duties, should cast a watchful eye on exploitative managers. Contractarians, on the other hand, argue that markets will discipline bad decisions and compel managers to be careful. Judges are prone to second-guessing mistakes; corporate law should only step in when markets are not functioning.

3a. FECA's constitutionality may well depend on how we view the corporation. If we regard it as a "creature of law," corporate regulation can be seen as an inherent consequence of the governmental concession. That is, "the state giveth and the state taketh away." This way of seeing the corporation, first articulated in the early 1800s, was at the heart of the Supreme Court's recent decision upholding a Michigan campaign finance law that prohibits corporations from using general funds to support specific candidates to state office. *Austin v. Michigan Chamber of Commerce*, 494 U.S. 652 (1990). The Court found compelling the state's interest in preventing "the unique state-conferred corporate structure that facilitates the amassing of large treasuries" to obtain an "unfair advantage in the political marketplace." Under this view, federal FECA (like state corporate law) can be seen as a constitutional condition on the corporate form.

If we regard the corporation as a natural entity whose rights extend beyond those conceded by the state, corporate rights (exercised by management) may approximate those of individuals. The Supreme Court adopted this viewpoint in *First National Bank of Boston v. Bellotti* (see

§1.3.2) when it held Massachusetts could not interfere with corporate free-speech rights in a state referendum. In a similar vein, the Court has viewed the corporation from management's perspective in cases that invalidate state regulation of management-written inserts accompanying monthly utility bills. *Consolidated Edison v. Public Service Commission of New York,* 447 U.S. 530 (1980) (state ban of such inserts); *Pacific Gas & Electric Co. v. Public Utilities Commission of California,* 475 U.S. 1 (1986) (plurality) (state requirement that management include messages by consumer group). Under the perspective reflected in these cases, FECA unconstitutionally infringes on the right of First Bank (really, management) to speak.

If we regard the corporation as a "nexus of contracts," the rights of each constituent group who form the nexus are relevant. The Supreme Court seemed to adopt this viewpoint when it recently invalidated FECA's application to a nonprofit corporation formed solely to promote political ideas. *FEC v. Massachusetts Citizens for Life, Inc. (MCFL),* 479 U.S. 238 (1986). The Court held that the nonbusiness organization had "features more akin to a voluntary political association," and that the First Amendment prohibits the administrative burden imposed by the government requirement that political expenditures come only from earmarked, segregated funds. Under this view, if First Bank's shareholders and other corporate constituents support management's contributions to "Save the Banks," FECA interferes with the corporate constituents' collective First Amendment rights and cannot be justified as protecting them from becoming "captive political speakers."

3b. This question is more difficult because shareholders' and managers' interests are not necessarily aligned, as they seemed to be in the previous question. Shareholders may favor the idea of greater management accountability or support the Senate candidate for other reasons.

A "creature of law" analysis suggests, as before, that FECA is constitutional in this regard. The Supreme Court's decision in *Austin* may well have been aimed at confirming the constitutionality of FECA, as applied to for-profit business corporations. The accumulation of capital permitted by the corporate form is also subject to government regulation.

A "natural entity" theory suggests FECA is unconstitutional. If the First Amendment prohibits limits on individual political expenditures, the government cannot limit corporate political expenditures. As an aggregate greater than the sum of its parts, the corporation has the right to participate in political discourse. Any internal conflicts within the corporation would be subject to existing corporate remedies. In *Bellotti,* the Supreme Court suggested shareholders could elect new directors or hold the managers accountable under state law in a shareholder derivative suit (see Chapter 31).

A "nexus of contracts" approach suggests that FECA is unconstitutional in this conflict-of-interest situation. Shareholders may not have intended that their capital contributions would be used to advance management's political agenda. In *MCFL* the Supreme Court seemed to say the First Amendment would not protect collective speech that does not accurately reflect shareholders' political views. The conflict between the First Bank shareholders and managers assumes constitutional importance.

2

Choice of Organizational Form

Given the advantages of incorporation, it is strange that a corporate lawyer often will advise her clients, "When in doubt, don't incorporate." There is a common lay perception that no business can be successful without the mystique of being a CORPORATION. But choosing what organizational form best suits the needs of the business and its participants is more complicated. This chapter presents a cursory introduction to the tax and nontax implications of the choice.

§2.1   The Range of Organizational Choices

Suppose Rudy and Bud plan a flower shop. Bud will run the shop; Rudy will put in money. The organizational forms that they can use to structure their for-profit business exist along a continuum. Each form can be manipulated to approximate the characteristics of the others. Keep in mind that whatever structure Rudy and Bud choose, it will not significantly affect how they conduct the business of selling flowers. The organizational form determines their legal relationship, their responsibilities for business debts, and their tax liability.

The more common choices available to them are:

Sole proprietorship.   A single individual, Rudy, owns the business assets and is liable for any business debts; Bud would be her employee. (Or Bud could be the proprietor and Rudy would lend him money.) Proprietorships usually are small, with few capital needs that cannot be met from the owner's resources and from lenders.

General partnership.   If Rudy and Bud arrange to carry on the business while sharing control and profits, they automatically create a partnership. As partners, they are each individually liable for partnership debts. Partnerships are prevalent in service industries — such as law, accounting, and medicine — where trust must exist among the participants and capital needs are not great.

Limited partnership.   Rudy and Bud can form a limited partnership in which so-called limited partners provide capital and are liable only to the extent of their investment. General partners run the business and are fully liable for partnership debts. Since limited partners need not be general partners, Bud could be the general partner and both of them can be limited partners. Limited partnerships combine tax advantages and limited liability.

Limited liability company.   In a growing number of states, Rudy and Bud could form a limited liability company — an entity that is a hybrid between a corporation and a partnership. Like a partnership, the members of the LLC provide capital and manage the business according to their agreement; their interests are not freely transferable. Like a corporation, members are not personally liable for debts of the LLC entity. (As of 1994, there are no model or uniform LLC statutes; Wyoming adopted the first LLC statute in 1977.)

Corporation.   Rudy and Bud can form a legal entity called a corporation. Shareholders provide capital, and directors and officers manage the business. Unless there is fraud or inequity that justifies "piercing the corporate veil" (see Chapter 6), corporate participants are not personally liable for corporate debts; only the corporation is liable. Corporations are the principal means of organizing businesses with complex organizational structures and large capital needs. The corporate form, however, works for any size business, including a one-person "incorporated proprietorship."

There are other variants. A *joint venture* is basically a partnership with a defined, closed-end objective. Examples include two law professors writing a student study book or three corporations developing a new chemical process. In a *business trust* (or *Massachusetts trust*) investors transfer property to a trustee who manages and controls the property for their benefit. The investors' beneficial interests are freely transferable, and the beneficiaries generally are not liable for trust debts. A *professional corporation* allows certain professionals — doctors, lawyers, and accountants — to obtain some advantages of incorporation without running afoul of ethical rules that prohibit professionals from limiting their liability through use of the traditional corporate form.

§2.2   Choosing between a Partnership and a Corporation

If Rudy and Bud want to share in the control and profits of the flower shop, they would likely choose between a partnership, limited liability company, or a corporation. Although a business planner can adapt each form to suit particular needs, some characteristics are relatively immutable — formation, liability, and tax. Others require planning — duration, management, and transfer of ownership interests.

§2.2.1   *Life Span — Formation and Duration*

General Partnership. A general partnership is created any time two or more persons associate to carry on a business as co-owners to share profits and control. It requires no legal documentation. UPA §6. Unless agreed otherwise, a general partnership dissolves upon the death, bankruptcy, or withdrawal of any partner. UPA §31. Without planning, there is no assurance that a partner will not withdraw and demand that the business be liquidated. UPA §38(1).

Limited Partnership. A limited partnership arises when a certificate is filed with a state official. RULPA §201. A limited partnership lasts as long as the parties agree or, absent agreement, until a general partner withdraws. RULPA §801.

Limited Liability Company. An LLC arises when two members file articles of organization with a state official. By statute, an LLC dissolves upon the death or withdrawal of any member.

Corporation. A corporation arises when articles of incorporation are filed with a state official. RMBCA §2.03. Corporate existence is perpetual, regardless of what happens to shareholders, directors, or officers. RMBCA §3.02.

§2.2.2   *Management — Authority to Bind and Control the Business*

General Partnership. Each partner is an agent of all other partners and can bind the partnership, either by transacting business as agreed by the partners (actual authority) or by appearing in the eyes of third parties to carry on partnership business (apparent authority). UPA §9. Unless otherwise agreed, a majority vote of the partners decides ordinary partnership matters, but anything that is extraordinary or contravenes the agreement requires unanimity. UPA §18(h).

Limited Partnership.   General partners have authority to bind the partnership as to ordinary matters. RULPA §403. Limited partners have voting authority over specified matters. RULPA §302.

Limited Liability Company.   Most LLC statutes give broad authority to bind the LLC in much the same way as partners. Management of the LLC business is decided in proportion to the members' capital contributions, unless the members agree to centralize decision-making by electing managers.

Corporation.   The corporation has a centralized management structure. Its business is under the management and supervision of the board of directors. RMBCA §8.01. Officers carry out the policies formulated by the board. RMBCA §8.41. Shareholders elect the board, RMBCA §8.03, and decide specified fundamental matters; they cannot bind the corporation.

§2.2.3   Transfer of Ownership Interests — Free or Restricted

General Partnership.   A partner cannot transfer her interest in the partnership unless all the remaining partners agree or the partnership agreement permits it. UPA §18(g).

Limited Partnership.   A general partner cannot transfer its interest unless all the other general and limited partners agree or the partnership agreement permits it. RULPA §401. Limited partner interests are freely assignable. RULPA §702.

Limited Liability Company.   An LLC member cannot transfer her LLC interest unless all the other members consent. Some LLC statutes suggest that under specified circumstances, the articles of organization can provide standing consent to new members.

Corporation.   Corporate shares are freely transferable unless there are specific written restrictions. RMBCA §6.27.

§2.2.4   Liability — Unlimited or Limited

General Partnership.   Partners have unlimited liability. Their personal assets are at risk for all partnership obligations, whether they are contractual or arise because of misconduct (torts) of the partners or partnership employees. UPA §15.

Limited Partnership.   At least one partner must be a general partner, with unlimited liability. Limited partners are liable only to the extent of their investment, so long as they do not "participate in the control" of the business. RULPA §303. Older statutes did not define "participation," and courts construed the term broadly. Limited partners were said to participate in control if they shared in operational decisions, retained control of financial matters, and decided the general partner's tenure. See *Holzman v. de Escamilla,* 195 P.2d 833 (Cal. App. 1948). Modern statutes clarify that some activities do not constitute participation in control. Limited partners do not lose their limited liability merely by being officers, directors, or shareholders of a corporate general partner, voting on major business matters, or advising the general partner. RULPA §303.

Limited Liability Company.   In both their capacities as capital contributors and managers, LLC members are not liable for LLC obligations beyond their investment. Some statutes, however, state that LLC members can become liable for LLC obligations by reason of their own acts.

Corporation.   Shareholders have limited liability for corporate obligations. RMBCA §6.22. This is true also for directors and officers acting on behalf of the corporation. Corporate participants can lose only what they have invested unless there is fraud or an inequity that justifies "piercing the corporate veil." Often, large creditors of small corporations will demand that corporate participants personally guarantee the corporation's obligations, thus reducing the significance of corporate limited liability.

§2.2.5   *Tax — Flow-Through or Double Tax*

General Partnership.   A partnership is not a taxable entity under the federal income tax laws. The partnership acts as a tax conduit. Its income, deductions, and credits *flow through* to its partners, who must pay tax, whether or not they actually receive these items. The partnership files an informational tax return disclosing relevant financial information.

Limited Partnership.   A limited partnership is treated as a partnership for tax purposes. Flow-through tax treatment may be lost, however, if the limited partnership *is structured like* a corporation. The Internal Revenue Service uses a multi-factor test for determining when an entity is an "association" and thus subject to corporate tax treatment, regardless of its nominal form. IRS Reg. §301.7701. The four critical attributes the IRS uses to distinguish a corporation from a partnership are the same four that characterize a corporation (see §1.1.1): (1) continuity of life, (2) centralized management, (3) liability for business debts limited to corporate property, and (4) free transferability of interests. For example, if limited partners cannot remove a general partner and the general partner has no substantial assets, the IRS might see the limited partnership as having the attributes of unlimited duration, centralized management, and limited liability — thus making it taxable as a corporation.

Limited Liability Company.   An LLC is an ingenious hybrid that the IRS treats as a flow-through partnership for tax purposes if the LLC avoids at least two of the "association" factors, such as (1) and (4). IRS Rev. Ruling 88-76. If the LLC dissolves upon the withdrawal of any member and the interests of LLC members are not freely transferable, the LLC is not subject to corporate tax.

C Corporation.   Under Subchapter C of the Internal Revenue Code, a corporation is a taxable entity. The Code also taxes shareholders on any dividends or other distributions they receive. Because dividends are not deductible at the corporate level, there is a *double tax* when earnings (taxed at the corporate level) are distributed to shareholders as dividends (taxed again at the shareholder level).

S Corporation.   Under Subchapter S of the Internal Revenue Code, shareholders of a closely held corporation may elect flow-through tax treatment so the corporation is treated as a tax conduit. The S corporation's income, losses, deductions, and credits pass through to the shareholders' tax returns. See more on this in §2.3 below.

§2.3   Taxation — A Critical Element in the Choice

Because Rudy and Bud are in business to make money, their reasons for choosing an organizational form will be largely financial. Tax considerations will loom large. We provide a cursory introduction to this complex area, which is treated more fully in advanced tax courses.

§2.3.1   *Flow-Through Tax Treatment versus the Corporate Double Tax*

To illustrate the basic structure of federal income taxation and its effect on the organizational choice, consider the following two cases.

Case 1: Rudy's and Bud's flower shop generates $150,000 in revenues and $110,000 in tax-deductible expenses during the first year — leaving $40,000 in taxable income. They share equally in after-tax earnings; they each are subject to tax rates for married individuals filing jointly; and they have no other income.

Case 2: The same as Case 1, except the flower shop generates $800,000 in revenues and $600,000 in tax-deductible expenses, leaving taxable income of $200,000.

The Tax Reform Act of 1986 substantially lowered the federal tax rates applicable to individual and corporate taxpayers but increased the relative impact of the double corporate tax. As the table on the next page* shows, there is a significant advantage in achieving flow-through tax treatment and avoiding "C corporation" status.

The table shows that in each case taxes make the corporate form more expensive than the partnership form. Look at the *effective rate* — that is, the total tax bite stated as a percentage of taxable income. Whether taxable income is $40,000 or $200,000, the IRS takes almost twice as much when the business is a corporation that distributes its dividends to shareholders as when there is flow-through tax treatment. The result is similar when you compare the *marginal rates* — that is, the tax bite on each additional $1 of taxable income. Consider what would happen if Rudy and Bud had gone to the trouble of earning another taxable dollar. In case 2, 31.00 percent of that dollar would be taxed if the business is a partnership and 56.08 percent would be taxed if it is a C corporation. Knowing the marginal rates helps them decide whether it is worth the trouble.

§2.3.2 Avoiding Double Taxation

How do business planners avoid the harshness of the double-tax rule without giving up limited liability?

---

* In our two cases, we have disregarded the effect of personal exemptions and other deductions. We have used the tax rules that would apply for tax year 1993:

Married individuals filing jointly are taxed at different rates depending on their taxable income —

15% on taxable income up to $36,900;
$5,535 + 28% of taxable income over $36,900;
$20,165 + 31% of taxable income over $89,150;
$35,928.50 + 36% of taxable income over $140,000;
$75,528.50 + 39.6% of taxable income over $250,000.

Corporations are also taxed at graduated rates —

15% on taxable income up to $50,000;
25% on taxable income over $50,000 but less than $75,000;
34% on taxable income over $75,000 but less than $100,000;
35% on taxable income over $100,000 remainder.

Corporations may also be subject to an additional 5% tax if their taxable income exceeds $100,000, or an additional 3% tax if their income exceeds $15,000,000.

Case 1

	Partnership, LLC, or S Corporation	Corporation
Taxable income	$40,000	$40,000
Entity tax	no entity tax	
rate		15%
entity tax		$6,000
amount for		
distribution	$40,000	$34,000
Individual tax	flow-through	on dividends
amount distrib-		
uted to each	$20,000	$17,000
rate	15%	15%
tax	$3,000	$2,550
after-tax		
income	$17,000	$14,450
Total tax	$6,000	$11,100
Rates of tax		
effective rate	15%	27.75%
marginal rate	15%	27.75%

Case 2

	Partnership, LLC, or S Corporation	Corporation
Taxable income	$200,000	$200,000
Entity tax	no entity tax	
rate		15% ($50,000) +
		25% (next $25,000) +
		34% (over $75,000) +
		5% (over $100,000)
entity tax		$61,250
amount for		
distribution	$200,000	$138,750
Individual tax	flow-through	on dividends
amount distrib-		
uted to each	$100,000	$69,375
rate	$20,165 +	$5,535 +
	31% (over $89,150)	28% (over $36,900)
tax	$23,528	$14,628
after-tax		
income	$76,472	$54,747
Total tax	$47,057	$90,506
Rates of tax		
effective rate	23.53%	45.25%
marginal rate	31.00%	56.08%

Electing Subchapter S.   A popular stratagem has been to elect S corporation status. An S corporation, incorporated under state law, retains all of its corporate attributes (including limited liability) but is not subject to an entity tax. All corporate income, losses, deductions, and credits flow through to the shareholders. To be eligible, the S corporation must be a domestic corporation with no more than 35 individual shareholders and only one class of stock. When heavy losses are anticipated, the Subchapter S form may not be as desirable as a partnership. S corporation shareholders can only write off losses up to the amount of capital they invested (though the loss can be carried forward and recognized in future years). In addition, rules on the deductibility of passive-activity losses may limit deductions for shareholders in S corporations, just like deductions for partners in a partnership.

Forming a Limited Liability Company.   An LLC combines corporate-type limited liability and partnership-type tax treatment, but there are some disadvantages. Not all states have LLC statutes, and operating a business as an LLC outside the state of formation may expose LLC members to partner-like personal liability. States without an LLC statute may refuse to recognize foreign LLCs. Even in those states with LLC statutes, judges may craft exceptions to the rule of limited liability for LLC members beyond those for piercing the corporate veil. In addition, the IRS may deny flow-through tax treatment if the LLC sets up mechanisms to facilitate investment by new members.

Forming a Limited Partnership with a Corporate General Partner.   A limited partnership with a corporation as general partner combines flow-through tax treatment and limited liability. Limited partner investors have limited liability; those who participate as shareholders, directors, or officers of the corporation have limited corporate liability. The only uncertainty, clarified in RULPA §303, is whether limited partners who take on roles in corporate management "participate in control" by virtue of their corporate positions. Some courts interpreted earlier limited partnership statutes (ULPA §7) to make limited partners liable if they acted as directors and officers of a corporate general partner. See *Delaney v. Fidelity Lease Ltd.*, 526 S.W.2d 543 (Tex. 1975).

Paying Deductible Compensation to Shareholders.   Corporate tax in a small, closely held C corporation can be zeroed out by paying shareholder-employees salaries, bonuses, and contributions to profit-sharing plans. "Reasonable compensation" is deductible by the corporation from gross income in computing taxable income; dividends are not. The effect is that tax is paid only at the shareholder-employee level. But there can be too much of a good thing: If compensation in whatever form is not reasonable — that is, if it is not related to the value of the services — the IRS can treat excess compensation as "constructive dividends," and the corporation loses its deduction.

Paying Deductible Interest to Shareholders.   If the capital contributions of investors in a C corporation can be characterized as debt rather than equity, payments to investors are treated as deductible interest rather than as non-deductible dividends. But again there can be too much of a good thing: The IRS will recharacterize debt as equity if it appears the contributions were at "the risk of the business" (see §8.2.3).

Accumulating Earnings and Liquidating Assets Tax-Free.   Under federal income tax law there is no double tax if corporate earnings are not distributed to shareholders but instead are reinvested in the business. Before the Tax Reform Act of 1986, it was possible to reinvest earnings and to wait until a major capital transaction (for example, a liquidation of the firm's assets) to distribute the appreciated assets without tax liability at the corporate level. This rule, known as the *General Utilities* doctrine, was repealed in 1986. Under current tax law, any gains from selling assets that have increased in value are taxed at the corporate level before the proceeds are distributed to shareholders, where they are taxed again.

EXAMPLES

1. Brigg has operated a landscaping business, Good Earth Landscaping, as a sole proprietorship. He has done most of the work himself and financed the business out of his pocket. Brigg wants to expand by taking on regular employees and purchasing new equipment. His sister, Pearl, is willing to put up some money, but she wants to be sure she won't have to pay in any more than the money she invests.
   a. If Pearl invests on the understanding that she will share in the profits and will help Brigg run the business, is her liability exposure limited to her investment?
   b. What forms of business organization might accommodate Pearl's interests?
   c. Is Pearl assured of limited liability if she is a limited partner? A member of a limited liability company? A corporate shareholder?
   d. For Pearl, what is the difference between being a shareholder in a corporation, an LLC member, and a limited partner in a limited partnership?
2. Pearl agrees to contribute money to Good Earth Landscaping. She wants to help run the business with Brigg but avoid personal liability for Good Earth's debts and obligations. Brigg and Pearl conclude that flow-through tax treatment will be advantageous to them.
   a. Can they accomplish their purposes with a corporation?
   b. Brigg has grand designs for the business and hopes to seek capital

from many other investors. Will an S corporation provide limited liability and flow-through tax treatment? Will a limited partnership? Will a limited liability company?

3. Brigg forms "Good Earth Landscaping, a Limited Partnership," and GEL Management, Inc., a corporation that will act as its general partner. Brigg and Pearl are the only shareholders, directors, and officers of the corporation. They and 40 other investors (including some corporations) will invest in the partnership.

   a. Will this structure accomplish their purpose of limited liability for all participants in the business?

   b. Brigg and Pearl consider either having the partnership pay the corporation a large management fee or taking larger limited partner interests for themselves. Which is more advantageous from a tax standpoint?

   c. Brigg and Pearl consider having the corporation make no investment in the limited partnership and receive only a nominal portion of the profits. Will this affect flow-through tax treatment for the limited partnership?

EXPLANATIONS

1a. No. When Brigg and Pearl agreed to "carry on as co-owners a business for profit," they formed a general partnership. UPA §6. As a partner, Pearl is liable for the business's debts and obligations, even if they exceed the amount of her investment. UPA §15.

1b. Pearl wants limited liability. She can be a limited partner in a limited partnership, a member of a limited liability company, or a shareholder in a corporation. In each case, she will be shielded against personal liability if business debts exceed business assets. She will be "liable" only to the extent that she may lose her investment. Each organizational form requires a filing with state officials.

1c. No. These organizational forms provide some, but not complete, assurance that participants can limit their losses to the amount they invested. As a limited partner, Pearl will not be liable for business debts and obligations beyond her investment unless she "participates" in the management of the business. Although ULPA §7 provides little guidance as to when a limited partner participates in control, RULPA §303 offers a safe-harbor list of permissible activities. Pearl would risk becoming personally liable if she helps Brigg run the business.

As an LLC member or corporate participant, Pearl will not be liable for business debts or obligations beyond her investment unless the company or corporate veil is "pierced." Some LLC statutes suggest that LLC members may become personally liable "by reason of their own acts," a formulation similar to that under corporate statutes. See RMBCA §6.22 (b). When and whether courts disregard corporate limited liability is a vexing question of corporate law. This subject is dealt with in Chapter 6. Normally, Pearl would not become liable for corporate debts and obligations merely by being active in the management of the business. Piercing typically happens only when a corporate participant defrauds or confuses creditors about limited liability or engages in activities that frustrate creditors' expectations to be paid ahead of shareholders.

1d. As the previous answer illustrates, limited liability is somewhat similar in a corporation, LLC, and limited partnership, but the tax implications can be markedly different. Under a corporate structure, there may be double taxation, which will reduce the amount of profits that are available to distribute to Pearl. Unless the corporate participants can elect Subchapter S status, corporate earnings are taxed first at the corporate level and then a second time at the shareholder level when distributed as dividends.

Business earnings in a qualifying LLC or partnership (including a limited partnership) are taxed only once at the member or partner level, whether or not the earnings are distributed. This flow-through tax treatment leaves available more earnings to distribute to Pearl.

2a. Yes. Although a C corporation will be subject to double taxation, Brigg and Pearl can elect to have the corporation treated as an S corporation. This election affects only the corporation's tax treatment, not its nontax attributes. In this way Brigg and Pearl can obtain the limited liability afforded by the corporate form while enjoying the benefits of flow-through tax treatment. The corporation easily can be made to qualify: It must be incorporated in the United States; it must have fewer than 35 individual shareholders (none may be a nonresident of the United States); and it must have only one class of stock.

2b. An S corporation is not possible if there will be more than 35 shareholders. A limited partnership is a problem because of Pearl's insistence on participating in the management of the business. If she does, she will be subject to liability as a general partner. UPA §7; RULPA §303. A limited liability company accomplishes the multiple purposes of permitting varied investors, flexible management structures, flow-through tax treatment, and limited participant liability. The LLC agreement can provide that Brigg and Pearl are the sole managers, so long as it also provides for LLC dissolution upon the death or withdrawal of any investing member and places limits on the transferability of investment interests. The LLC agreement can ameliorate the hardship of such provisions by providing for a process to continue the business after dissolution and to give permission to investors to transfer their investment interests. The IRS has accepted flow-through tax treatment in such cases.

3a. Yes. By forming a limited partnership with a corporate general partner, Brigg and Pearl have created a structure that provides limited liability to all participants. As limited partners, the outside investors will not be liable for any business debts or obligations beyond their investment. In their capacities as limited partners and participants in a corporation, Brigg and Pearl are not liable for the limited partnership's or the general partner's obligations.

There is, however, some case law under ULPA §7 that limited partners who participate in the management of a corporate general partner are deemed to participate in the control of the limited partnership — their limited liability is lost. RULPA §303, on the other hand, specifically allows such a structure without the limited partners becoming subject to partnership liabilities. Unless they obtain personal guarantees, those dealing with the partnership can look only to the credit of the corporate general partner.

3b. To avoid double taxation, it is advantageous not to pass earnings through a C corporation. Any management fee to the corporation will be taxed at the corporate level and then again when distributed to the shareholders. This concern is irrelevant if the corporate general partner chooses S corporation status. Although an S corporation must have no more than 35 shareholders and all must be individuals, these restrictions apply only to those who invest in the general partner, not in the limited partnership.

3c. Yes. If the corporate general partner does not invest any money but merely manages the business, the IRS might see the structure as having the attributes of a traditional corporation. The general partner can be analogized to central corporate management, and because of its corporate limited liability, liability for partnership debts is effectively limited to partnership property. The limited partnership thus might be seen as having three important characteristics of a corporation: unlimited duration, centralized management, and limited liability. Although formed as a limited partnership, the entity runs the risk that the IRS will treat it as a corporation for tax purposes.

PART TWO

Formation of the Corporation

3

Incorporation — How and Where

Forming a corporation under modern state corporation statutes is quick and straightforward. The process creates a public record of incorporation; it binds the parties to the corporate law scheme of the state in which they incorporate; and it documents any additional, optional terms the parties may wish to specify. For the corporate planner, there are three significant questions:

- What provisions must be in the articles of incorporation?
- What optional provisions should be in the articles?
- In what state should the corporation be incorporated?

Corporate existence and the attributes of "corporateness" begin with the filing of articles of incorporation or, in some states, when a state official issues a certificate of incorporation.

§3.1 The Process of Incorporation

Forming a corporation involves three essential steps:

(1) preparing articles of incorporation (in some states called the charter or the certificate of incorporation) according to the requirements of state law (RMBCA §2.02);

(2) signing of the articles by one or more incorporators (RMBCA §1.20(f)); and

(3) submitting the signed articles to the state's secretary of state for filing (RMBCA §2.01).

Corporation service companies perform many of the routine tasks of forming a corporation. For a modest fee these companies will prepare articles, bylaws, stock certificates, and organizational minutes; and they will file the proper documents and act as a registered agent in the state of incorporation and in other states where the corporation is qualified to do business.

§3.1.1 Articles of Incorporation

Modern statutes prescribe the standard information that the articles must contain.

Name of the Corporation.   The statutes require that the articles state the corporation's complete name and include a reference to its corporate status — a word such as "Corporation," "Incorporated," or "Inc." The name must also be different from any other corporate name in the state. How different? Some statutes say it must be "distinguishable upon the records" of the secretary of state from other names already in use or reserved for use. RMBCA §4.01. Other statutes require it not be "deceptively similar" to an existing name. The "distinguishable upon the records" test simply assures each corporate name will be unique and easy to identify. The "deceptively similar" test has a further aim to prevent unfair competition.

Many states allow businesses to *reserve* a corporate name (for a fee) during the preincorporation process. RMBCA §4.02 (nonrenewable reservation good for 120 days). In some states a corporation incorporated in another state (a "foreign corporation") may register its name with the secretary of state to keep local firms from using it. RMBCA §4.03 (registration renewable annually).

Registered Office and Agent.   The statutes require that the articles state the corporation's address for service of process and for sending official notices. RMBCA §2.02. Often the articles also must name a registered agent at that office on whom process can be served. RMBCA §§2.02, 5.01. Changes in the registered office or registered agent must be filed with the secretary of state. RMBCA §5.02.

Capital Structure of the Corporation.   The statutes require that the articles specify the securities (or shares) the corporation will have authority to issue. The corporation will raise capital by issuing its shares. The articles must describe the various classes of authorized shares, the number of shares of each class, and the privileges, rights, limitations, and preferences of each class. RMBCA §6.01. Some states continue to require a minimum amount of capital, such as $1000, before the corporation commences business, but most states have eliminated this requirement.

Purpose and Powers of the Corporation.   Modern statutes permit, but do not require, that the articles state the corporation's purposes and powers. With the decline of the ultra vires doctrine (see Chapter 4), a "purposes" clause has far less prominence than it once did. The modern trend is to assume the corporation can engage in any lawful business. RMBCA §3.01.

Most state statutes also contain an all-inclusive list of the activities a corporation may engage in. The articles need not state these powers. RMBCA §3.02 (corporation has the "same powers as an individual . . . to carry out its business and affairs").

Size and Composition of the Board of Directors.   Most modern statutes have abandoned earlier requirements that the articles name the initial directors, that the board be composed of at least three directors, or that the articles specify the number of directors. RMBCA §8.03 (requiring only that the board be composed of "one or more individuals").

Optional Provisions.   The articles can contain a broad range of other provisions to "customize" the corporation. RMBCA §2.02(b). Such provisions are often important in closely held corporations where the participants want specific protections. These optional provisions might include:

- *voting provisions* that call for greater-than-majority approval of certain corporate actions, such as mergers or charter amendments;
- *membership requirements* that directors be shareholders or that shareholders in a professional corporation be members of a specified profession; or
- *management provisions* that require shareholders to approve certain matters normally entrusted to the board, such as executive compensation.

In some situations, provisions that deviate too far from the normal corporate structure may not be enforceable (see Chapter 16).

§3.1.2   *Incorporators*

The role of incorporators, as such, is purely mechanical. They sign the articles and arrange for their filing. If the articles do not name directors, the incorporators select them at an organizational meeting. After incorporation, the incorporators fade away and need not have any continuing interest in the corporation. Employees of corporation service companies, legal secretaries, and paralegals often serve as incorporators. In some states the incorporators must be natural persons, although the trend is that a corporation may act as an incorporator of another corporation. RMBCA §§2.01, 1.40(16).

§3.1.3   The Filing Process

Filing the articles is today a simple ministerial task. Older statutes, drawn from a time when the legislature chartered corporations, gave the secretary of state significant discretion to reject articles of incorporation for technical or other perceived defects. Modern statutes, particularly the RMBCA, remove much of that discretion. The RMBCA *requires* that state officials accept articles for filing if (1) they contain the minimal information required by the statute, (2) the document is typed or printed, (3) sufficient copies are submitted, (4) appropriate fees and franchise taxes are paid, and (5) the corporate name is distinguishable on the secretary of state's records. RMBCA §1.25. In some states the filing fee is a flat amount; in other states it depends on the number of authorized shares or the aggregate legal capital of the corporation (see Chapter 8).

Once the articles are filed, they become public documents. Those interested in the corporation's existence can confirm it in several ways:

- a certificate of existence (sometimes called a certificate of incorporation) obtained from the secretary of state (RMBCA §1.28);
- a receipt returned by the secretary of state when the articles of incorporation are filed;
- a copy of the articles with an original acknowledgment stamp by the secretary of state (RMBCA §1.25);
- a certified copy of the original articles obtained from the secretary of state for a nominal fee (RMBCA §1.27).

§3.1.4   The Organizational Meeting

Filing the articles merely brings the corporation into existence. It is the first step in its formation. For the corporation to function, the corporate planner must create a working structure. This is done at an organizational meeting of the incorporators or the board of directors named in the articles. The meeting, called upon written notice, usually follows a script already devised by the corporate planner.

The first item of business at the meeting will be to elect directors, unless the initial directors named in the articles are to remain in office. Once the board is constituted, other items on the agenda will include approving bylaws to govern the internal structure of the corporation, electing officers, adopting preincorporation promoters' contracts (including the lawyers' fees for setting up the corporation), designating a bank for the deposit of corporate funds, authorizing the issuances of shares, and setting the consideration for the shares. RMBCA §2.05.

The Bylaws. As the articles have become more sketchy and the statutes more open-ended under modern corporate practice, the bylaws have assumed greater importance as an organic corporate document. The bylaws describe such matters as the functions of each corporate office, how shareholders' and directors' meetings are called and conducted, the formalities of shareholder voting (including voting by proxy), the qualifications of directors, the formation of board committees (such as executive or audit committees), and procedures for and limits on issuing and transferring shares.

State law does not require that the bylaws be filed. The bylaws must be consistent with the articles. RMBCA §2.06. Like the articles, the bylaws are not enforceable if they deviate too far from the traditional corporate model (see §16.7).

§3.2 Choosing Where to Incorporate

In the United States a corporation can be formed in any state, no matter where the corporation does business. That is, the parties can choose the governing law for their corporate relationship. The question of where to incorporate requires balancing the benefits of incorporating in a state that provides flexibility in managing the business against the costs of incorporating in one state and then qualifying to do business as a foreign corporation (see below) in other states where business is to be conducted. The decision often comes down to a choice between the home state and Delaware.

§3.2.1 Internal Affairs Doctrine

In the United States the law of the state of incorporation, with limited exceptions, governs the relationships among the parties in the corporation. This choice-of-law rule, known as the *internal affairs doctrine,* permits the parties through the incorporation process to fix the law that applies to their corporate relationship, wherever litigation is brought. The corporation's "internal affairs" are those that relate to the legal relationships between the traditionally regarded corporate participants, including the rights of shareholders, the fiduciary duties of directors, and the procedures for corporate action.

A few states have changed this choice-of-law rule and purport to regulate the internal affairs of corporations — sometimes called "pseudo-foreign" corporations — that have substantial operations in the state but are incorporated in another jurisdiction. For example, California subjects foreign corporations to California corporate law if more than 50 percent of the corporation's property, sales, payroll, and outstanding voting shares are in the state. Cal.

Corp. Code §2115. A recent Supreme Court decision suggests the certainty of the internal affairs doctrine may have constitutional dimensions for publicly held corporations. *CTS Corp. v. Dynamics Corp. of America,* 481 U.S. 69 (1987) (see §40.4.1). The Supreme Court commented, "No principle of corporation law and practice is more firmly established than a State's authority to regulate domestic corporations."

§3.2.2 Qualification of Foreign Corporations

A business incorporated in one state may conduct *intrastate* operations in another state if "qualified" to do business in the other state. To "qualify," the corporation must file a certified copy of its articles, pay a filing fee, and appoint a local agent to receive service of process in that state. RMBCA §15.01. Corporations that conduct only *interstate* business (such as mail-order catalog companies) need not qualify because of the constitutional prohibition against interference with interstate commerce.

What are the penalties for doing business without being qualified? Some states fine the corporation and its officers for failing to qualify or treat the business as unincorporated, thus subjecting corporate officers to individual liability for contracts made in that state. Until a foreign corporation is qualified, it cannot bring lawsuits in local court. RMBCA §15.02.

§3.2.3 The Choice — Why Delaware for National Businesses?

The general rule of thumb is that a business that will operate locally should be incorporated locally because doing so is easier and less costly. If the business will operate throughout the United States, the corporation will be be incorporated in one state and qualified as a foreign corporation elsewhere.

Most large publicly held corporations have chosen Delaware as their state of incorporation. There are a number of explanations for this: Delaware's statute is designed to give management flexibility in structuring and running the business; the Delaware courts and corporate bar are sophisticated in corporate law matters; a large body of case law interprets the Delaware statute, thus providing certainty to corporate planners; and the statute is amended often as new needs and problems arise. Some academics have criticized Delaware for having a promanagement slant in an incorporation "race to the bottom." Empirical studies, however, indicate that reincorporating in Delaware does not adversely affect a corporation's stock prices. Recent Delaware decisions favoring shareholder interests also cast doubt on the criticism.

EXAMPLES

1. Xenon, Yentl, and Zebekiah want to incorporate their palm-reading business. They have filed articles in New Columbia, an RMBCA jurisdiction:

   ### Articles of Incorporation

   A. The name of the corporation is XYZ, Inc.

   B. The corporation is authorized to issue 3000 shares of common stock.

   C. Any shareholder of the corporation must be a cosmologist certified by the Universal Association of Cosmologists.

   D. All voting by shareholders must be unanimous.

   E. The corporation will have a term of ten years.

   F. The corporation's registered address is 13 East-West Highway, North Point, New Columbia, and the registered agent at that address is Abner Zebekiah.

   G. The incorporator is Abner Zebekiah, 13 East-West Highway, North Point, New Columbia.

   Abner Zebekiah

   Abner Zebekiah, Incorporator

   a. Are these articles sufficient?

   b. The secretary of state's records show that two other New Columbia corporations have similar names: "XYZ Universal, Inc." (a well-known health spa chain) and "X-Y-Z Palm Reading, Inc." Can the state official reject the articles?

   c. Xenon, Yentl, and Zebekiah have been sued for defrauding bereaved widows who they promised would communicate with their deceased husbands. Can the state official reject the filing on this basis?

   d. Another "XYZ, Inc." operates a chain of camera shops in adjoining states, though this corporation has not reserved its name or qualified as a foreign corporation in New Columbia. Can the official reject the filing on this basis?

   e. New Columbia cases hold that requirements of unanimous shareholder approval (such as article D) are invalid. If the secretary of state's office accepts the XYZ articles for filing, does this assure Article D's validity?

   f. Can the XYZ, Inc. articles specify a term of ten years (article E)?

2. Xenon, Yentl, and Zebekiah want a bank loan for their business. The bank is willing to extend credit if a bank representative sits on the XYZ board and the shareholders pledge their shares to the bank. The bank does not want any public record that it holds pledged shares in a palm-reading business or that it has a representative on the XYZ board. How can this be accomplished?

3. New Columbia prohibits individuals (but not corporations) from charging usurious interest rates. Can XYZ, Inc. charge usurious interest?

4. Assume XYZ, Inc. is incorporated in Delaware, even though it conducts its palm-reading business in New Columbia. New Columbia's corporation statute, unlike the RMBCA, permits the removal of directors *only for cause*. Delaware's statute allows for removal *with or without cause*. Del. GCL §141(k). Xenon and Zebekiah call a special shareholders' meeting and remove Yentl from the XYZ board.

   a. Assume New Columbia's statute states: "This act does not authorize the state to regulate the organization or internal affairs of [an authorized] foreign corporation." See RMBCA 15.05(c). Should Yentl sue in Delaware or in New Columbia to get back his seat?

   b. Assume New Columbia has followed California's lead and regulates "pseudo-foreign" corporations under New Columbia corporate standards. Does New Columbia's "for cause only" standard apply?

   c. The XYZ articles state that directors can never be removed. Now what law governs: the articles, Delaware law, or New Columbia law?

EXPLANATIONS

1a. Yes. The articles are sufficient. RMBCA §2.02 requires only a name for the corporation (article A), a description of its capital structure (article B), a registered address and agent (article F), and the incorporator's address (article G). Further, the articles must be signed by the incorporator; one incorporator is enough. RMBCA §1.20.

1b. Probably not in this RMBCA jurisdiction. Under RMBCA §1.25 the articles can be rejected if they do not comply with statutory requirements. See RMBCA §1.20. According to RMBCA §2.02(a)(1), the articles must comply with RMBCA §4.01, which requires that the corporate name be "distinguishable upon the records of the secretary of state" from other names of corporations incorporated in the state. "XYZ Universal, Inc." and "X-Y-Z Palm Reading, Inc." are distinguishable from "XYZ, Inc." for purposes of identifying the corporations and sending notice.

   If the jurisdiction applied a "deceptively similar" standard, the name "XYZ, Inc." for a corporation that will engage in the palm-reading business may confuse consumers seeking the services of "X-Y-Z Palm Reading, Inc."

1c. No. Under RMBCA §1.25, state officials have no discretion to reject articles that comply with the technical filing requirements. Even though Xenon, Yentl, and Zebekiah may be trying to create a corporate veil to limit their liability and may be defrauding customers, the RMBCA does not make this the concern of the secretary of state. Private plaintiffs may be able to pierce the corporate veil (see Chapter 6), or the state's consumer affairs agency may close down the business. The incorporation rules under the RMBCA do not serve these functions.

1d. No. Under RMBCA §4.01, the articles can be rejected only if the name "XYZ, Inc." is reserved or registered, or is the name of a corporation incorporated in the state, or is a fictitious name of a qualified foreign corporation.

1e. No. Although accepting articles for filing is ministerial and not discretionary, the proper filing of a document does not affect its validity. RMBCA §1.25.

1f. Yes. Although the RMBCA §3.02 assumes the corporation will have perpetual duration, RMBCA §2.02(b)(2)(iii) permits limitations on corporate powers, including duration. A limited duration acts as an agreement to dissolve the company after ten years.

2. The directors do not have to be named in the articles, which is the only corporate document that need be filed. RMBCA §2.02. State law requires that the articles specify the types and number of authorized shares but does not require disclosure about their ownership.

The incorporators can elect directors (including the bank representative) in the organizational meeting; the board can then issue shares. The only record will be the minutes of the meeting. In a jurisdiction that requires that initial directors be named in the articles, "dummy" directors can be named who can elect replacements at the organizational meeting. The bank can condition extending a loan on the election of its representative.

3. RMBCA §3.02's specification of corporate powers — "same powers as an individual" — was meant to be as broad as possible. But there may be instances, as here under the usury laws, in which corporations have powers beyond those of individuals. XYZ's articles should be drafted to allow it to charge any interest rate.

4a. Even though New Columbia's "for cause" standard is more favorable to Yentl, it shouldn't matter where suit is brought. Under the internal affairs doctrine, Delaware's "with or without cause" standard will apply. Both Delaware and New Columbia courts (federal and state) will apply the law of the state of incorporation to this shareholder-management dispute. This assures predictability and certainty in structuring internal corporate relationships.

4b. The choice of venue now makes a difference. A New Columbia court would be bound to apply the New Columbia standard. Not surprisingly, Delaware courts have declared the virtual inviolacy of the internal affairs doctrine. See *McDermott Inc. v. Lewis,* 531 A.2d 206 (Del. 1987) (applying Panamanian law to a Panamanian corporation, even though at odds with Delaware's statute). This means two courts might answer the same corporate law question in two different ways. For example, the

Second Circuit recently applied New York's broad statute on shareholder inspection rights to a Maryland corporation, whose statute would not have permitted the inspection sought by a New York shareholder. *Sadler v. NCR*, 928 F.2d 48 (2d Cir. 1991).

For public corporations, where legal predictability is important in pricing publicly traded shares, a choice-of-law rule that varies depending on where suit is brought may frustrate expectations in a multistate public corporation and run afoul of the Constitution. This concern is less compelling for a closely held corporation, where private choice is today the rule.

4c. The choice between Delaware and New Columbia law raises the same issues as in the previous questions. The additional wrinkle is the parties' choice of a removal standard that neither Delaware nor New Columbia contemplates. Recently, the Delaware Supreme Court applied Delaware law to a Delaware corporation, disregarding an agreement among the parties to be bound by New Jersey law. *Rosenmiller v. Bordes*, 607 A.2d 465 (Del. 1991). On the other hand, a non-Delaware court has upheld the parties' agreement to waive application of the law of Delaware, the state of incorporation. *Yates v. Bridge Trading Co.*, 1992 Mo. App. LEXIS 1629.

As the leading state for incorporation, Delaware has a vested interest in an all-encompassing internal affairs doctrine. That is, parties that incorporate in Delaware are bound exclusively by Delaware law and cannot choose to substitute other state or private provisions for their off-the-rack Delaware provisions. Non-Delaware courts may not feel so constrained and may deviate from the internal affairs doctrine to promote party choice or to remedy perceived gaps in Delaware protection.

4

Corporate Powers — The Rise and Fall of the Ultra Vires Doctrine

In the nineteenth century, state legislatures chartered American corporations for narrow purposes and with limited powers. Concerned with the economic power the capitalist invention could wield, early courts fashioned the "ultra vires doctrine" to invalidate corporate transactions beyond the powers stated in the corporation's charter.

As corporations became an accepted part of the economic landscape, state enabling statutes came to authorize "general purpose" clauses and virtually unlimited powers. See RMBCA §§3.01, 3.02. Today the ultra vires doctrine has limited relevance. It applies when (1) corporate parties create restrictions in the articles, or (2) the corporation engages in activities not directly related to profit seeking, such as charitable giving.

§4.1 Decline of the Ultra Vires Doctrine

§4.1.1 Early Common Law — Weaseling Out of Contracts

Early corporations were formed to run capital-intensive businesses such as canals, railroads, and banks. To attract investors and legislative approval, managers drafted the articles of incorporation to limit the scope of the business. Early courts applied the ultra vires doctrine with vigor. Whenever a transaction was beyond the corporation's limited purposes or powers, either party to the contract could disaffirm it, even after the other party's full or partial performance. Courts construed purposes and powers clauses narrowly, and the ultra vires doctrine invited parties to weasel out of contracts whenever a deal went sour.

Consider a typical "powers" clause of an early railroad corporation:

> To purchase, hold and use . . . real estate and other property as may be necessary for the construction and maintenance of its road and canal and the stations and other accommodations necessary to accomplish the objects of its incorporation . . . .

Suppose the corporation leased a summer hotel at its seaside terminus. If leasing and operating a seaside hotel did not fall within the corporations's powers, the railroad or the lessor could have raised an ultra vires defense to avoid its obligations under the lease.

§4.1.2   Erosion of the Doctrine

Around the turn of the last century, courts recognized the commercial uncertainty created by the ultra vires doctrine and modified the doctrine in two respects. First, courts permitted an ultra vires defense only if the contract was still *executory*. In our example, neither the railroad nor the lessor could have disaffirmed the lease once the hotel began operations. Second, courts interpreted charter provisions flexibly to authorize transactions reasonably incidental to the business. For instance, seaside hotels were interpreted to be within the *implied powers* of railway companies. *Jacksonville, Mayport, Pablo Railway & Navigation Co. v. Hooper*, 160 U.S. 514 (1896).

At about the same time, state legislatures limited the doctrine by passing enabling statutes that authorized a wide variety of corporate purposes and powers. Drafters of corporate articles accepted the invitation and drafted voluminously, enumerating multiple business purposes and specifying powers to cover virtually every imaginable business transaction. Later, legislatures passed modern enabling statutes that authorized "general purpose" clauses and specified a long laundry list of corporate powers. Detailed drafting is today no longer necessary. In many jurisdictions, the articles need not recite even that the corporation has the purpose of engaging in any lawful business and has the power to engage in any lawful transaction — both are implicit. RMBCA §§3.01, 3.02.

§4.2 Modern Ultra Vires Doctrine — A Limited Planning Device

Modern statutes, including the RMBCA, seek to eliminate the vestiges of inherent corporate incapacity. Neither the corporation nor any party doing business with the corporation can avoid its contractual commitments — whether executory or not — by claiming the corporation lacked capacity. RMBCA §3.04(a).

What if the articles state a limitation? To protect the expectations that arise from such a limitation, the RMBCA specifies three *exclusive* means of enforcement:

(1) Shareholder suit.   Shareholders can sue to enjoin the corporation from entering into or continuing in an unauthorized transaction. A court can issue an injunction only if "equitable" and only if all of the parties, including the third party, are present in court. The official comment to RMBCA §3.04 states an injunction is equitable as against a third party only if the party knew about the corporate incapacity. Other statutes go further and provide that there can be no injunction if the contract has already been entered into.

(2) Corporate suit against directors and officers.   The corporation, on its own or by another on its behalf, can sue directors and officers (whether current or former) for taking the unauthorized action. The officers and directors can be enjoined or held liable for damages. RMBCA §3.04(b)(2).

(3) Suit by state attorney general.   The state attorney general can seek involuntary judicial dissolution if the corporation has engaged in unauthorized transactions. This authority harkens back to the "state concession" theory of the corporation. RMBCA §§3.04(b)(3), 14.30.

The modern ultra vires doctrine thus provides only limited assurance that charter provisions restricting the scope of the corporation's business will work.

§4.3 Distinguishing the Ultra Vires Doctrine from Corporate Duties

The ultra vires doctrine concerns corporate *powers*. It often is confused with corporate *duties* — specifically, the corporation's duty not to engage in illegal conduct and management's fiduciary duties. Consider a couple examples:

Illegality.   An incorporated waste-disposal business dumps toxic wastes in violation of state and federal environmental law. If the corporation has a general-purpose clause, has it acted ultra vires? Although some courts describe illegal behavior as ultra vires, the characterization is misleading. As a matter of corporate law, the corporation has the *power* to dump wastes, including toxic wastes, but as a matter of environmental law it has a *duty* not to.

Fiduciary breaches. The corporation enters into a contract with a director. Unless the articles disable the corporation from entering into self-dealing transactions, the corporation has the *power* to do this; the transaction is not ultra vires. The corporation, however, may avoid the transaction if its terms are unfair and the director has breached her fiduciary *duties*.

§4.4   Corporate Largesse and the Ultra Vires Doctrine

A for-profit corporation's primary purpose is to make money. Does such a corporation have the power to make charitable contributions, to give money to the founder's orphans, or to guarantee a shareholder's loan? Are these ultra vires?

Courts generally have accepted that corporations have implicit powers to make charitable gifts that in the long run may benefit the corporation. Most state statutes specifically permit the corporation to make charitable donations. See RMBCA §3.02(13). Gifts cannot be for unreasonable amounts and must be for a proper purpose. In general, if the gift is tax deductible (currently not more than 10 percent of the corporation's taxable income), it is a reasonable exercise of corporate powers.

If corporate largesse is unrelated to corporate benefits — such as when a gift is excessive — the transaction may be attacked as ultra vires. Such corporate altruism may also constitute corporate waste — a fiduciary breach (see §21.3.2).

EXAMPLES

1. In 1960 Sam and Tom opened a small printing shop, which they incorporated as S-T Printing, Inc., in a jurisdiction that has now adopted the RMBCA. When they incorporated, Tom worried that Sam's plans were too grandiose, so he insisted on the following provision in the articles:

   The Corporation shall engage only in the business of printing, unless all the shareholders agree otherwise.

   By 1990 both Sam and Tom had retired, leaving all their shares to their children, who continue to run the shop. The business has been dragging. Last month the board of directors decided to change direction: S-T Printing is to enter into a ten-year joint venture to sell computer printing systems to commercial customers. The board authorized its president, Sid, to sign the agreement with Desktop Corp.

    a. Sara, an S-T Printing shareholder, objects to the joint venture. She says the corporation has no power to be a joint venturer and the charter forbids this particular agreement. Is either view tenable?

    b. If the articles can be construed to prohibit this particular venture, can Sara prevent Sid from signing the agreement?

2. Sara files suit, but after the joint venture agreement is signed.

    a. Assume Desktop management did not know about the charter limitation but could easily have found out. Can Sara prevent further performance?

    b. If Desktop management did not know about the charter limitation, does Sara have any other recourse?

    c. Assume Desktop management knew about the charter limitation, and the court enjoins the venture. Can Desktop recover the profits it would have made had the venture gone forward?

3. The joint venture uses printing software it bought from a copyright pirate.

    a. When Sara learns of this, she wants to sue to enjoin the agreement as ultra vires. Can she?

    b. The state attorney general investigates the joint venture's use of pirated software. Can the state prevent S-T Printing's participation in the joint venture?

4. The computer printing business proves to be highly profitable.

    a. The S-T Printing board considers getting out of the joint venture. Can it use an ultra vires theory?

    b. Desktop Corp. also considers abandoning the joint venture. Can it avoid the agreement?

    c. The S-T Printing board authorizes a large cash "Christmas gift" to Sara. Maybe she will stop being so critical. Is the gift ultra vires?

EXPLANATIONS

1a. Corporations have broad, general powers under modern enabling statutes, including the power to be a joint venturer. RMBCA §3.02(9). If nothing in S-T Printing's articles limits this power, Sara cannot attack the joint venture on this basis. The S-T charter, however, does limit the corporation to the "business of printing." How should this limitation be construed?

    Modern courts are reluctant to limit corporate flexibility under the ultra vires doctrine. The provision could be construed broadly to encompass the business of retailing printing equipment. The joint venture is a reaction to a change in market conditions in the printing industry. A modern court is unlikely to confine the corporate majority under a vague limitation.

1b. Yes, if Sara can show an injunction would be equitable. RMBCA §3.04(b)(1) and (c). The S-T board could argue that an injunction would be inequitable because the charter proviso is no longer relevant and frustrates the majority will. The statutory requirement that any injunction be equitable provides a second line of defense against a vague or unduly broad charter restriction.

At this stage, Desktop Corp. need not be made a party to the proceeding, and its awareness of the limitation on corporate powers would be irrelevant. Any injunction would affect only the S-T Printing board and Sid.

2a. No. Under the RMBCA, once the parties enter into the transaction, the third-party Desktop must be made a party to the proceeding, and any injunction must also be equitable as to it. RMBCA §3.04(b)(1), (c). This means Desktop would have to have actually been aware of the "printing business" limitation. The RMBCA comments make clear that persons dealing with a corporation need not "inquire into limitations on its purposes or powers." Some state statutes go further in rejecting the vestiges of the ultra vires doctrine and only allow an injunction before the contract is signed.

2b. Yes, but it won't be easy. Sara can sue the directors who approved the transaction in a derivative action. RMBCA §3.04(b)(2). A claim of fiduciary breach may be difficult. If there was no conflict of interest and if there was a rational business purpose for the transaction, the business judgment rule (see §21.2) may shield the directors from liability. It is unclear whether the directors' knowing disregard of a charter limitation would be tantamount to bad faith.

2c. No. Although the RMBCA allows a court to award damages for losses caused by enjoining an ultra vires transaction, RMBCA §3.04(b)(1), the damages are meant only to put the parties into the position they would have been in had the transaction not occurred. Anticipated profits are specifically disallowed. RMBCA §3.04(c).

3a. No. If entering into the joint venture agreement is within the corporation's lawful purposes and powers, it cannot be enjoined as ultra vires. The ultra vires doctrine only enforces limitations in the articles. Whether Sara can enjoin the venture on copyright grounds depends on whether she has standing under the copyright laws.

3b. Yes. Nothing in the corporate statutes meant to ensure the validity of corporate action challenged as ultra vires affects the action's legality under other laws. If the state can forbid participation in a copyright pirating scheme, it makes no difference what the corporate articles say.

4a. No. Modern statutes make clear that the corporation cannot challenge the validity of corporate action on the theory it lacks power. RMBCA

§3.04(a). This evisceration of the ultra vires doctrine prevents precisely the kind of contract weaseling that the S-T directors are contemplating.

Although the board might enlist a shareholder to seek to enjoin the corporation, the injunction would have to be equitable. Avoiding contracts through the artifice of a shareholder suit hardly seems equitable.

4b. No. The third party can no more avoid its obligations on an ultra vires theory than can the corporation.

4c. Probably not. Although some courts continue to frame the issue as one of corporate power, the real issue is one of fiduciary duty and corporate waste. If the payment involves a remote benefit to the corporation, the business judgment rule shields it from review. A shareholder or creditor challenging this transaction would have to show extremely poor business judgment or a tainting conflict of interest.

5

The Duties of Promoters

Incorporation creates a structure for conducting a business but does not make the business operational. Contractual arrangements must be made with employees, suppliers, and customers; and capital must be obtained from investors and lenders. The people who perform these functions are called "promoters," but they often continue to run the business after the initial setup.

Unlike incorporators (see §3.1), promoters have significant responsibilities and run the risk of incurring heavy liabilities. During the critical initial phase of a new business, promoters can become liable for:

- preincorporation contracts they sign before the business is incorporated (§5.1);
- contracts they sign for a business that was not properly incorporated (§5.2);
- transactions they enter into with the corporation(§5.3).

§5.1 Promoter's Liability on Preincorporation Contracts

As we have seen, incorporation under modern corporation statutes is painless. Nonetheless, promoters sometimes enter into contractual arrangements for the to-be-incorporated business before the magic moment when the corporation comes into existence and with it limited liability for the corporate actors. Who is liable on preincorporation contracts when both parties know there is no corporation: the promoter, the corporation once it is formed, neither of them, or both of them?

At the time of the transaction, the to-be-formed corporation does not yet exist and cannot be a principal or a party to a contract. Traditional theories of contract and agency law are therefore unsatisfactory. Some nineteenth century cases, for example, held that under agency principles a newly formed corporation could not ratify preincorporation contracts because no corporation existed when the contract was entered into. Although courts have abandoned this formalistic approach, the question of who is liable remains.

Consider a well-known example of this problem: D. J. Geary bids to build a bridge for O'Rorke across the Allegheny River. Before Geary incorporates Bridge Company, he signs a contract for the work: "D. J. Geary, for a bridge company to be organized and incorporated." Since no corporation exists, who is liable under the contract? Modern courts often look to the Restatement (Second) of Agency §326, which states that (unless agreed otherwise) a purported agent acting for a nonexistent principal becomes a party to the contract. Comment *b* to §326 describes some of the relationships Geary and O'Rorke might have agreed to:

(A) Promoter as nonrecourse agent. Geary is a mere messenger who carries O'Rorke's offer to Bridge Company. There is no contract unless Bridge Company is incorporated and adopts the contract. O'Rorke has no recourse against Geary, even if Bridge Company never accepts the offer, for whatever reason.

(B) Promoter as "best efforts" agent. Geary agrees to use his "best efforts" to bring Bridge Company into existence and have it accept O'Rorke's offer. There is no contract until Bridge Company is incorporated and it adopts the contract. Geary is not personally liable on the contract unless he fails to use his best efforts to incorporate Bridge Company and have it accept the offer.

(C) Promoter as interim contracting party. Geary accepts liability to O'Rorke under the contract until Bridge Company is incorporated, adopts the contract, and is substituted in Geary's place. Under this "novation" view, O'Rorke discharges Geary after the substitution of parties.

(D) Promoter as additional contracting party. Geary accepts liability under the contract even if Bridge Company adopts the contract. Under this view, Geary remains severally liable on the contract with the corporation. His liability is "primary" if O'Rorke can look to him first, or "secondary" if O'Rorke must first exhaust recourse to Bridge Company. Bridge Company, however, may be obligated to indemnify Geary.

Do promoters and third parties have the foresight to make clear which of these alternatives they have chosen? Often they do not. See *O'Rorke v. Geary,*

56 A. 541 (Pa. 1903). Instead, courts must infer the parties' *intentions* from the circumstances.

Liability on preincorporation contracts can arise in three ways: (1) the third party sues the promoter; (2) the third party sues the newly formed corporation; and (3) the corporation or promoter sues the third party.

§5.1.1   Promoter's Presumed Liability on Preincorporation Transactions

The general rule in the cases (and the one espoused by the Restatement (Second) of Agency §326) is that the promoter is personally liable on the contract unless there is a contrary intent. That is, alternative (D) reflects the parties' intentions unless shown otherwise.

Discerning parties' contrary intentions. How can the promoter show a contrary intention? Often the promoter will have signed the contract "for a corporation to be formed." This alone, however, does not clarify whether the parties agreed to a "nonrecourse" status for the promoter. Further evidence of intent must be found in the contract document itself or in the surrounding circumstances.

Consider a couple representative cases:

In *Quaker Hill, Inc. v. Parr,* 364 P.2d 1056 (Colo. 1961), the salesman for a supplier of nursery stock insisted on closing a supply contract before the buyers incorporated their business. The court held the promoters were not liable because the nursing stock seller, by its agent's actions, had agreed to look only to the corporation for payment.

In *Stanley J. How & Associates, Inc. v. Boss,* 222 F. Supp. 936 (S.D. Iowa 1963), the court held a hotel promoter liable on an architectural contract. The contract contemplated the architect would partially perform before the promoter formed the corporation. Although the promoter had signed as agent for "a corporation to be formed who will be the obligor," the court decided the parties had intended that the promoter would pay the architect if the corporation did not.

Even when the promoter cannot show a "nonrecourse" intention, she still might get off the hook if she can show the parties intended a discharge once the corporation adopted the contract. That is, if the parties intended a novation in which the corporation replaces the promoter, the promoter is discharged from any further obligation.

An intention that the corporation's adoption will act as a novation can be shown from the circumstances. For example, if the third party looks first to the promoter and then exclusively to the corporation, a novation intention might be inferred. But just because the corporation performs under the contract does not necessarily establish a novation. Such action is also consistent with dual obligors. Furthermore, even if the parties intended a substitution, a novation requires corporate authorization, and courts have held that mere formation of the new corporation is not enough to constitute a novation. There must be an affirmative act evidencing consent before the corporation is bound and the promoter discharged (see below).

Liability for misrepresenting corporate existence.   Thus far, we have assumed that both the promoter and the third party knew that no corporation existed. If, however, the promoter creates the false impression that a corporation exists, the promoter may be liable for breaching an implied warranty that the corporate principal exists and that the promoter was acting pursuant to proper authority. If such a breach injures a third party, modern courts have held the promoter personally liable on the contract.

§5.1.2   Corporation's Adoption of Liability on the Contract

The outside party may also want to hold the corporation liable on preincorporation contracts. A newly formed corporation, however, is not automatically liable for contracts made by promoters before incorporation. To protect the new shareholders from surprise corporate liability, the corporation must adopt the contract. (Some courts describe this as "ratification," but technically a corporation cannot ratify acts that occurred before its existence.)

What constitutes a binding adoption? Although the clearest evidence would be a formal corporate resolution by the board of directors approving the contract (see §14.1), this is not necessary. Adoption can be implicit. It is sufficient that the corporate directors or officers with power to enter into the contract for the corporation knew of and acquiesced to the contract.

In *McArthur v. Times Printing Co.,* 51 N.W. 216 (Minn. 1892), the court inferred the adoption of a preincorporation employment contract because all the shareholders and officers knew about the contract and none attempted to repudiate it. Later acts by the corporation consistent with or in furtherance of the contract — such as making payments under the contract — also provide evidence of adoption.

If a corporation does not adopt a promoter's contract but accepts its benefits, the third party may be able to recover on a quasi-contract or restitution theory.

§5.1.3   Third-Party Liability

Promoter liability is a two-way street. If the promoter is liable under the contract to the third party, so too is the third party to the promoter. Likewise, if the parties contemplated that the newly formed corporation could adopt the contract, such an adoption binds the third party to the corporation. One way of testing whether a promoter or corporation is liable on the contract is to ask whether the third party is conversely bound.

EXAMPLES

1. Bascomb Smythe decides to start a new business to offer moonlit carriage rides. He learns that if he hurries, he can buy ten antique carriages from Old Plantation, an antique dealer. Bascomb has not yet incorporated his business but plans to. He enters into a contract with Old Plantation that calls for installment payments over 12 months. Bascomb signs the contract as "agent for Antebellum, a corporation to be formed which will become party to this contract."

   a. Before Antebellum is incorporated, Bascomb picks up the carriages. When the first installment comes due, is Bascomb liable on the contract?

   b. After Antebellum is incorporated, Bascomb uses the carriages in the business. When Old Plantation does not get paid, it asks Bascomb for payment. Is Bascomb liable?

   c. Bascomb had suggested to Old Plantation's manager that he wait to sign the contract until Antebellum's articles were filed. The manager had said, "Go ahead and sign now. This is a deal with the corporation, anyway." Does this affect Bascomb's liability?

   d. Bascomb had made four payments on Antebellum's checks before the payments stopped. Does this affect Bascomb's liability?

   e. Bascomb sells his Antebellum shares to Carolyn. Carolyn repudiates the Old Plantation contract. She refuses to make any more payments and tries to return the carriages. Can Old Plantation hold Antebellum liable?

2. The Old Plantation contract states: "This contract is between Old Plantation and Antebellum, Inc. once it is formed. Bascomb is obligated only to use his best efforts to form a corporation that will duly accept the contract."

   a. Bascomb does not incorporate Antebellum. Is he liable?

   b. Bascomb incorporates Antebellum, but its board never acts on the contract. Instead, Bascomb accepts delivery of the carriages and uses them in the business. In light of the contract provision, is Antebellum or Bascomb liable?

3. The Old Plantation contract reads as follows:

   It is understood by the parties hereto that it is the intention of the Purchaser to incorporate. Upon condition that such incorporation be completed by closing, all agreements, covenants, and warranties contained herein shall be construed to have been made between Seller and the resultant corporation and all documents shall reflect the same.

     a. Does this provision assure a novation once Antebellum adopts the contract?

     b. How should this provision be redrafted?

4. After Antebellum is incorporated, Bascomb wants to make clear that there is a novation. Old Plantation's manager agrees to tear up the original contract and sign a new one with Antebellum. Bascomb plans to sign as follows:

Bascomb Smythe

Bascomb Smythe
President, Antebellum, Inc.

Does this signature accomplish Bascomb's purpose?

EXPLANATIONS

1a. Most likely. As a general rule, courts presume that a promoter is personally liable on any preincorporation contract unless a contrary intention can be shown from the documents or the circumstances. Since incorporation is so easy, the promoter's failure to incorporate suggests the parties were dealing with each other on a "full recourse" basis. In this case Bascomb might argue that his signature as "agent for" the to-be corporation indicates that the parties did not intend a contract until the corporation was formed and adopted the contract. But Old Plantation's partial performance under the contract by delivering the carriages to Bascomb belie this argument. The phrasing of the signature line does not rule out the possibility of joint promoter-corporate liability.

1b. Most likely. If Bascomb was initially liable, his liability continues after incorporation, unless there is a novation. There are two problems with a novation theory here. First, it is not clear that the parties intended a substitution of parties after the corporation was formed and adopted the contract. The statement in the signature line that Antebellum would "become party to this contract" is ambiguous as to whether the corporation would be the only party. Bascomb's picking up the carriages before incorporation is inconsistent with corporation-only liability. Second, even if the parties intended a novation, there is no indication that Antebellum adopted the contract — its incorporation is not enough.

1c. Probably. The events surrounding the signing of the contract indicate that Old Plantation intended to look only to the corporation. Bascomb was an agent of the corporation to-be. Even if Old Plantation looks to Bascomb after Antebellum's adoption and breach, the intentions must be gauged as of the initial transaction.

1d. Probably not. Bascomb's personal liability, suggested by his preincorporation partial performance, continues until there is a novation. That Old Plantation accepted payments from Antebellum allows an inference of adoption but not necessarily a novation. Bascomb would have to show some further evidence that the parties intended Antebellum's adoption would discharge Bascomb.

1e. Yes, but not on the contract. Antebellum's incorporation does not automatically result in an adoption of the contract, and Carolyn's repudiation made clear that Antebellum was not adopting it. Nonetheless, because it kept the carriages, Antebellum may be liable on a quasi-contract theory.

2a. Perhaps, but not on the contract. The contract provision seems sufficient to establish the parties' intention that no contract was to exist until incorporation occurred and Antebellum adopted the contract. The transaction creates an option to Antebellum. But Bascomb promised to use his best efforts to incorporate Antebellum and to induce the corporation to accept the offer. If Bascomb shirked this duty, he could be liable on that promise.

2b. Antebellum is liable, but Bascomb is not. By its actions, Antebellum has adopted the contract. Adoption need not be formal; it can be inferred from the acquiescence of those who would have power to accept the contract. The use of the carriages constitutes implicit adoption. Bascomb is not liable because his only duty was to form a corporation and to have it adopt the contract, which he did.

3a. Maybe not. The provision is ambiguous. It fails to specify whether the promoter's liability ends with incorporation or whether the corporation simply becomes a co-obligor on the contract along with the promoter. A court has read the second sentence to mean that the promoter was a co-obligor. See *RKO-Stanley Warner Theaters, Inc. v. Graziano*, 355 A.2d 830 (Pa. 1976).

3b. The provision should make clear that the third party will look only to the corporation after incorporation and adoption. Something along the following lines might work:

> The parties understand that Bascomb Smythe intends to organize a corporation that upon adoption of this contract will become the sole obligor. Bascomb Smythe will be liable on this contract only until the corporation adopts the contract. Adoption by the corporation will operate as a novation, releasing Bascomb Smythe from all personal liability under this contract.

4. No. Some courts have held that such a signature does not indicate that Bascomb signed in his corporate capacity alone. The signature can be interpreted to indicate that he is signing for himself and simply noting

that he is also a corporate officer, or that he is signing both for himself and for the corporation. To do it right, the signature should be *precisely* as follows (no less and no more):

Antebellum, Inc.

By: *[signature]*

Bascomb Smythe, President

This makes clear that the corporation is signing through its officer-agent, Bascomb. It insulates Bascomb from liability by making clear that he is acting in his corporate capacity.

§5.2   Liability for Defective Incorporation

In our discussion of a promoter's liability on preincorporation contracts, we assumed the promoter and the third party knew that no corporation had yet been formed. What happens when both the promoter and the third party mistakenly believe that a corporation has been formed? One reaction might be: "Tough luck! Only actual incorporation gets you limited liability."

Such a reaction is unfair if the failure to incorporate properly was due to some minor or technical defect — such as improper notarization, failing to compute the filing fee correctly, or not filing in the county where the principal office is located (a requirement in some states). It is particularly unfair if the third party believed she was dealing with a corporation and treated the promoter as a nonrecourse agent. Placing full liability on an unwitting investor or manager who in good faith thought he was shielded by corporate limited liability would not advance any rational corporate law purpose — other than precise compliance with the formalities of incorporation.

§5.2.1   *Softening the Blow of Defective Incorporation — The De Jure, De Facto, and Estoppel Doctrines*

Equity courts developed the concepts of *de jure* and *de facto* corporations and *corporations by estoppel* to take the bite out of the harsh consequences of improper incorporation. Modern courts continue to imply the attributes of corporateness — particularly limited liability — when there is an innocent defect in the incorporation process or the parties assume there is a corporation.

A *de jure corporation* arises when the promoter complies completely or substantially with the incorporation guidelines. A promoter is in substantial compliance if his failure to comply involves only discretionary or relatively unimportant matters, such as not filing articles with the county or spelling incorrectly the name of the corporation's registered agent. Courts treat a de jure corporation as having all corporate attributes; its existence cannot be attacked by anyone, including the state.

A *de facto corporation* arises when there was (1) some colorable, good-faith attempt to incorporate; and (2) actual use of the corporate form, such as carrying on the business as a corporation or contracting in the corporate name. Although the state can challenge the existence of a de facto corporation, third parties cannot. As to third parties, a de facto corporation creates for the corporate parties all the attributes of a de jure corporation, including limited liability.

A *corporation by estoppel* arises when there has been no colorable or good-faith attempt to incorporate but courts impute corporateness if the parties have dealt with each other on the assumption that a corporation existed. Third parties who rely on representations that a corporation exists and act accordingly are estopped from denying the existence of the corporation. (This is an estoppel theory stood on its head; estoppel normally prevents *the person who makes a representation* on which others rely from denying the representation.)

Whether a court uses one of these theories to impute a nonrecourse relationship depends on two factors. First, does the state corporate statute permit the court to impute corporateness even without incorporation? Second, do the circumstances surrounding the defective incorporation warrant it?

§5.2.2   Modern Abolition of the De Facto and Estoppel Doctrines?

Because incorporation under modern corporate statutes is so easy, forgiving a promoter's or investor's failure to incorporate properly may be unnecessarily protective. Many statutes, such as RMBCA §2.03(a) and the previous MBCA §50, specify that corporate existence begins when the articles of incorporation are filed. Some statutes also specify the effect of purporting to act as a corporation without proper incorporation. Under the previous MBCA §139, persons "who assume to act as a corporation without authority" are personally liable.

In *Robertson v. Levy,* 197 A.2d 443 (D.C. App. 1964), the court interpreted the provisions of the D.C. corporate statute modeled after MBCA §§50 and 139 to abolish the de facto corporation and corporation by estoppel doctrines. The case involved the following chronology:

December 23 -Levy agrees to purchase Robertson's business.

December 27 -Levy submits articles of incorporation for a corporation that would be the buyer.

> January 2 -The articles are returned to Levy as defective.
>
> January 8 -Robertson transfers the business assets to Levy's "corporation," which gives a note in exchange.
>
> January 17 -After Levy refiles the articles, he is issued a certificate of incorporation.

The court held Levy personally liable on the note, even though Robertson assumed he was dealing with a corporation. The court concluded that MBCA §§50 and 139 operated to create limited liability only by incorporation and thus eliminated the de jure, de facto, and estoppel concepts. The result might seem harsh because it provided Robertson with a windfall pocket he had not expected. Nonetheless, Levy may have signed the notes knowing there was no incorporation. The decision ensures the integrity of the incorporation process.

Most other courts have been more sanguine. For example, in *Cantor v. Sunshine Greenery*, 398 A.2d 571 (N.J. Super. Ct. 1979), the court applied the de facto corporation theory to deny recovery in circumstances very similar to *Robertson*. Cantor agreed to lease commercial space to Brunetti, who had 13 days before mailed articles to incorporate the new business. Because of administrative bungling, the articles were actually filed two days after Brunetti signed the lease on behalf of the nonexistent corporation. When Brunetti's corporation later repudiated the lease, Cantor sought to recover from him personally. The court accepted that the elements of a de facto corporation had been shown: Brunetti made a colorable, good-faith attempt to incorporate and used the corporate form in his dealings with Cantor. The court concluded that to impose personal liability on Brunetti when the parties assumed a corporation, and thus a nonrecourse relationship, would be "unjust and inequitable." New Jersey's statute, unlike the D.C. statute in *Robertson*, did not specify that personal liability results for those assuming to act as a corporation.

While getting caught by incorporation technicalities may be excusable, not even trying would seem a different story. Nonetheless, even in this age of easy incorporation, some courts have continued to apply an estoppel theory when both parties believe there is a corporation, even though there was no attempt to incorporate. In *Cranson v. International Business Machines Corp.*, 200 A.2d 33 (Md. 1964), the court shielded an attorney who inadvertently failed to file a certificate of incorporation. The attorney told investor Cranson that he had formed a corporation, and Cranson purchased eight IBM typewriters on credit as president of the nonexistent corporation. When the business stopped making payments, IBM sued Cranson. Although there could be no de facto corporation since there was no attempt to incorporate, the court accepted that there was a corporation by estoppel. IBM had extended credit on the basis that Cranson's business was incorporated.

How does the RMBCA handle this quagmire? RMBCA §2.04 states: "All persons purporting to act as or on behalf of a corporation, knowing there was no incorporation . . . are jointly and severally liable for all liabilities." This seems simple enough — deceptive parties become liable. But is there liability when the parties do not know about a defect in incorporation? A strong argument might be made that, given the simplicity of incorporation, nothing short of incorporation creates limited liability. The official comment to RMBCA §2.04, however, indicates the section creates a negative inference: There is liability only when a person knows of the incorporation defect, and no liability if he does not. The RMBCA forgives unwitting business people who act on the mistaken assumption the business is incorporated.

§5.2.3. Defective Incorporation When None of the Doctrines Works

When the de jure, de facto, and estoppel concepts are not available, courts impose liability as if no corporation exists. The luckless promoter who signs a contract may become individually liable as an agent for a nonexistent principal, and anyone who participates with the signer may become liable as a principal or partner. But an incorporation defect does not necessarily subject nonsignatory participants to liability. Some courts have excused passive investors who did not act on behalf of the business or when the third party knew they had not authorized the transaction. See *Frontier Refining Co. v. Kunkel's, Inc.*, 407 P.2d 880 (Wyo. 1965).

EXAMPLES

1. Bascomb enters into a contract with Rebel Threads to purchase Confederate Army uniforms for Antebellum's carriage drivers. He signs the contract properly as president of Antebellum, Inc. When Rebel Threads delivers the uniforms, Bascomb decides they are not what he wants and refuses to pay. Rebel Threads sues Bascomb on the contract.

   a. Suppose Bascomb mailed articles of incorporation for Antebellum to the secretary of state two weeks before signing the contract. Postal employees, now under indictment, threw away the mailing. How might Bascomb argue he is not liable under the contract?

   b. Suppose Bascomb asked his lawyer to create a corporation, Antebellum, Inc. The lawyer forgot to file the articles. As Bascomb's new attorney, how would you argue Bascomb is not liable on the contract?

   c. Antebellum was to have been incorporated in a jurisdiction that has two relevant provisions: One states that "a corporation's existence begins with the filing of the articles of incorporation"; the other states that "any person who assumes to act as a corporation that does not exist is liable for all debts arising as a result." Is the de facto corporation or estoppel doctrine available to Bascomb?

2. When Bascomb signed the Rebel Threads contract for nonexistent Antebellum, his sister Elizabeth had contributed money and thought she

was a shareholder of the corporation. She, however, had nothing to do with Bascomb's dealings with Rebel Threads. Is she liable to Rebel Threads on the contract?

EXPLANATIONS

1a. De facto corporation doctrine. Bascomb made a colorable, good-faith attempt to incorporate and contracted in the name of the corporation. The de facto corporation theory shields Bascomb from liability to the same extent the corporate form limits the liability of officers acting for the corporation.

The RMBCA accepts this theory. In an RMBCA jurisdiction, §2.04 would shield Bascomb from liability if he contracted not knowing of the defect in incorporation.

1b. Corporation by estoppel. The lawyer's failure to try to incorporate eliminates a de facto corporation theory. Nonetheless, if Bascomb believed there was a corporation and led Rebel Threads to believe it too, Rebel Threads may be estopped from denying the existence of a corporation.

The RMBCA accepts a modified version of the estoppel theory. In an RMBCA jurisdiction, §2.04 would shield Bascomb if *he* did not know about the lawyer's possible malpractice, apparently even if Rebel Threads knew of the incorporation defect.

1c. Perhaps not. These two provisions evince a legislative intent that only actual incorporation assures limited liability. By imposing liability on any who assume to act as a corporation, regardless of intent or knowledge, the statute creates a strong incentive for precise compliance with the state's incorporation procedures. This may seem harsh, and it might be argued that the second provision ("assumes to act") implicitly conditions liability on the promoter's knowledge of the incorporation defect. Otherwise, the third party receives a windfall when both parties believe that only the business's assets are at risk and the third party forswears recourse to the promoter individually.

2. Not necessarily. Rebel Threads must establish a basis for holding Elizabeth liable. There can be no direct liability because she did not sign the contract. Since she did not act for the business, a statutory basis, such as that found in RMBCA §2.04, also seems unavailable. The only possible basis of liability is as a principal or partner of Bascomb in an inadvertent agency or partnership relationship.

Elizabeth has a number of separate lines of defense. First, she can argue that she had not consented to Bascomb acting as her agent and that they had no agreement to carry on a business as co-owners (see UPA §6). She anticipated being only a shareholder, never a full-liability principal or partner/co-owner. Second, she can argue that even if Bascomb was her agent or partner, he did not have authority: He did not have *actual* authority to sign the contract (or do anything for the business) until it was incorporated, and any *apparent* authority would be negated if Rebel Threads did not know of Elizabeth or knew of this limitation on Bascomb's authority. Third, Elizabeth could assert the equitable doctrines of de facto corporation or corporation by estoppel, if available (see discussion above). Fourth, if the action arises in an RMBCA jurisdiction, §2.04 creates liability in cases of defective incorporation only as to those persons who purport to act for a nonexistent corporation and who know the corporation does not exist. A passive investor such as Elizabeth, who did not act and did not know of the defect, cannot be liable. This makes sense because Rebel Threads was not counting on her credit.

§5.3   Promoter's Liability for Early Dealings with the Corporation

During a corporation's start-up process, promoters often have absolute control of the corporate governance machinery. In the absence of disclosure requirements or other constraints, promoters can put themselves in an advantaged position with respect to future shareholders and creditors.

Consider the case of two promoters, Lewisohn and Bigelow, who sold mining rights and property to a corporation they formed. They had purchased the assets a few weeks earlier for $1 million, the assets' fair market value. As consideration for these assets, the corporation gave the promoters notes for $3.25 million. This was not difficult because the promoters, as the corporation's only shareholders, controlled the board of directors. Later, when outside shareholders bought the promoters' stock and came to control the board of directors, they discovered the promoters' rip-off and sought to rescind the notes.

In general, self-dealing in a corporation is governed by a set of fiduciary duties that directors, officers, and controlling shareholders owe to the corporation. (See Chapters 22 and 26.) Promoter self-dealing, however, is a subset that presents a special conceptual problem: To whom do promoters owe duties when they enter into a transaction with the corporation before there are other shareholders or creditors?

Courts have used two theories for inferring promoters' duties and, in our example, for imposing liability on promoters like Lewisohn and Bigelow. The first theory is based on the promoters' fiduciary duties to the corporation; the second is based on the promoters' disclosure duties to subsequent investors and creditors.

§5.3.1 Promoter Self-Dealing as a Breach of a Fiduciary Duty

Under the first theory, promoters breach a fiduciary duty to the corporation by engaging in a self-dealing transaction whose unfairness was not fully disclosed. The problem with this theory is that *at the time* of the transaction the promoters' interest was known by the corporation's decision-makers. The promoters were the only shareholders and controlled the board. The promoters can argue that the board's fully informed approval immunized the transaction from attack. The U.S. Supreme Court accepted the argument in a case involving the facts of our example, *Old Dominion Copper Mining & Smelting Co. v. Lewisohn,* 210 U.S. 206 (1908).

The *Lewisohn* approach disregards the fact that the victims of the transaction — the outside shareholders — never agreed to it. To overcome this, the outside shareholders might argue that approval and disclosure of the transaction must await their arrival and that the promoters stand in a fiduciary position as to shareholders who are expected to be brought in after the transaction. The Massachusetts Supreme Court accepted this argument in a case involving the same facts, *Old Dominion Copper Mining & Smelting Co. v. Bigelow,* 89 N.E. 193 (Mass. 1909).

Which argument is more persuasive? — In a sense, neither is persuasive. The real problem is the failure to tell corporate newcomers what they are getting into. The newcomers' real complaint is lack of disclosure. Nonetheless, a majority of courts have come to accept *Bigelow* (the "Massachusetts rule") rather than *Lewisohn* (the "federal rule"). Courts have inferred duties to the corporation to ease enforcement of deception claims and to avoid the complicated issues of individual proof. Under this approach, the promoter has a duty not to engage in unfair self-dealing where subsequent investors or creditors are contemplated. Although perhaps conceptually contorted, the theory protects corporate newcomers who would not have invested or extended credit on the terms they did if they had known of the unfair self-dealing.

A modern example of the *Bigelow* approach is *Frick v. Howard,* 126 N.W.2d 619 (Wis. 1964). Preston incorporated a business to run a motel. He purchased land for $240,000 and resold it to the corporation for $350,000. At the time of the transaction, Preston was the only shareholder and dominated the corporation's board. Part of the consideration for the sale was a note and mortgage for $110,000, which Preston later assigned to Frick. When the corporation defaulted, Frick (who knew of the note's questionable origins) sought to foreclose on the mortgage.

The receiver for the corporation, as representative of the corporation's creditors, argued that Preston had breached a fiduciary duty to the corporation by taking a quick and undeserved $110,000 profit, that the mortgage was infirm because of the self-dealing, and that Frick had no right to foreclose. The court agreed that Preston's transaction constituted "a fraud on creditors, existing and subsequent." No independent board had ratified the self-dealing transaction. The *Bigelow* approach provided a theory of creditor protection.

§5.3.2 Promoter's Duty to Disclose Self-Dealing

The real problem in cases like that of Lewisohn and Bigelow is that the promoters induced outsiders to invest in the company without disclosing prior self-dealing. Lewisohn and Bigelow had led new investors to believe the corporation owned mining assets worth $3.25 million (the value of the notes), when in fact they were worth far less. Since the enactment of the federal securities laws, a fraud on subsequent investors and creditors might be handled in a couple of ways.

Issuance of stock or bonds to public investors is subject to the registration and disclosure requirements of the Securities Act of 1933. New investors could recover from directors Lewisohn and Bigelow if the registration statement (the disclosure document mandated by the 1933 Act) did not fully disclose the self-dealing transactions with promoters. 1933 Act §11 (see §10.3.2).

Even if registration liability were unavailable, the investors could seek recovery under the antifraud provisions of the federal securities laws, in particular §12(2) of the 1933 Act (see §10.3.3) and the famous Rule 10b-5 of the Securities Exchange Act of 1934 (see Chapter 29).

The securities laws are of limited use when promoters deceive creditors whose transactions with the corporation are not "securities" transactions. Traditional deceit law, which requires a showing of an affirmative and intentional misrepresentation, might not be useful. In such cases, a receiver or bankruptcy trustee may want to use the concept of a promoter's fiduciary duty to the corporation.

EXAMPLES

1. Bascomb is the sole shareholder of Antebellum, Inc. The only directors are his nephews, Jerry Lee and Jimmy. Bascomb proposes a five-year employment contract for himself, fixed at $30,000 a year, plus 40 percent of all net profits. The board approves the contract. One year later, Antebellum takes on additional investors. Can a new Antebellum board rescind Bascomb's employment contract on a theory that he breached a fiduciary duty to the corporation?

2. After the original board approved the employment contract, Antebellum bought uniforms for its drivers, rented a stable for its horses, and took out an unsecured bank loan to cover operating expenses. When the business fails, the bankruptcy trustee seeks to recover Bascomb's excessive salary payments. How should the receiver proceed?

EXPLANATIONS

1. Perhaps, if the new investors did not know of the deal and Bascomb is indeed overcompensated. Under the *Bigelow* approach, when Bascomb contemplated subsequent investors, he had a fiduciary duty either to abstain from unfair self-dealing or to have the transaction approved by an independent board. If Jerry Lee and Jimmy were not independent, Bascomb is liable to the corporation and indirectly to the new investors. The *Lewisohn* view — that he breached no duty to the corporation because a fully informed board approved the employment contract — is today at best a minority view. If the new investors knew of the deal, it could be argued they ratified Bascomb's employment contract by their investment.

2. The trustee, who acts for the bank and other creditors, cannot claim securities fraud because none of these creditors sold or bought securities (see §§10.3, 29.4.2). Instead, the receiver can claim Bascomb breached a fiduciary duty to the corporation. The trustee will sue on behalf of the corporation, thus avoiding the difficulty of proving individual claims of deception on behalf of individual creditors.

6

Piercing the Veil of Limited Liability

The corporate form promises shareholders and managers limited liability. When can a corporate creditor ask a court to disregard this promise and "pierce the corporate veil" to hold shareholders, directors, and officers personally liable for corporate obligations? This is one of the most perplexing questions in corporate law. The piercing cases are rich in metaphors — "alter ego," "dummy," "instrumentality," "sham" — but are short on principled analysis, and their results are often irreconcilable.

Piercing the corporate veil differs from asserting promoter liability, which arises when a transaction occurs before incorporation or when there has been a defect in incorporation (see §5.1). In a piercing case, the corporation has been formed properly, but creditors seek to have the court disregard the corporate attribute of limited liability and to have it impose unlimited personal liability on shareholders and managers.

In this chapter, we consider the rationale for corporate limited liability (see §6.1) and the factors that courts have articulated in deciding to pierce the corporate veil (see §6.2). We then suggest a principled basis for weighing these factors (see §6.3).

§6.1 General Rule of Limited Liability

The corporation separates the risks and assets of business from those of its investors and managers. Under modern corporate law, this separation implies the rule of limited liability: A shareholder (equity investor) is not liable for corporate obligations beyond the shareholder's investment. RMBCA §6.22.

69

This rule also applies to other corporate participants, such as managers, employees, and lenders. Creditors may look only to the corporation's assets. Courts recognize limited liability even if it is the motivating reason for incorporation.

Why the rule of limited liability? There are a number of explanations:

(1) Limited liability facilitates capital formation.   The corporation, which limits investment risk to the amount invested, allows investors to finance a business without risking their other assets. It encourages capital formation, making investors more likely to invest in desirable, though risky, enterprises.

(2) Limited liability facilitates desirable management risk-taking.   Without the promise of limited liability, managers would be discouraged from undertaking high-risk ventures, even when the venture offers net positive returns (that is, expected gains exceed expected losses).

(3) Limited liability facilitates broad-based investment diversification. Limited liability encourages investors to invest in many businesses — to diversify — without exposing their other assets to unlimited liability with each new investment. Diversification stimulates capital formation when it is easier to raise capital by seeking many small investments rather than a few large investments. Diversification spreads out the investment risk, thus reducing the need for investors to investigate their investment choices and to monitor closely the business in which they invest. Diversification thus reduces the costs of investing.

(4) Limited liability facilitates public stock trading markets.   Stock trading markets are important for modern business. They make capital formation easier, reveal enterprise value by establishing market prices, and provide a place to buy corporate control. How does limited liability make trading markets possible? If limited liability did not exist, wealthy investors (with more to lose) would assign lower value to identical securities than poor investors (with less to lose), because the greater risk of liability would reduce the securities' value to the wealthy investor. The limited liability rule shields all corporate investors equally, and the price at which they are willing to invest does not depend on their individual capacity to risk other assets. Limited liability makes securities fungible regardless of who owns them, thus enabling public trading markets to operate.

Limited liability does not operate in a vacuum. Corporate law also seeks to protect the expectations of those who deal with the corporation. When a court decides to pierce the corporate veil, it in effect decides that creditor expectations outweigh shareholders' expectations in limited liability. Courts do not take this step lightly. Piercing the veil chills capital formation and desirable risk-taking. Furthermore, those who have consensual dealings with the company can protect themselves by contract. Nonconsensual creditors — such as tort victims — often are protected by insurance or government regulation.

§6.2   Traditional Piercing Factors

The traditional tests articulated by courts for piercing the corporate veil are to "prevent fraud, oppression or illegality" and to "achieve equity." These tests provide little guidance. In addition, the courts often refer to particular considerations and factors, yet no one factor emerges as determinative. Piercing cases leave an unavoidable feeling that the courts merely use these factors to justify results reached on other, unarticulated grounds.

§6.2.1   *Closely Held Corporations*

Courts pierce the corporate veil only in closely held corporations with one or a few shareholders. A recent study of modern piercing cases found no reported case of piercing in a publicly traded corporation. Thompson, Piercing the Corporate Veil: An Empirical Study, 76 Cornell L. Rev. 1036 (1991) (looking at all piercing cases on WESTLAW through 1985). Shareholders in a closely held business usually manage it and are responsible for the risks it takes and the level of asset coverage of those risks. Moreover, investment diversification and stock trading markets — two of the reasons for limited liability — are far less important to investors in a closely held business.

Just because a business is closely held does not automatically subject shareholders to unlimited liability. Although courts often refer to shareholder "domination" or "absolute control" as factors in piercing cases, this is the usual state of affairs in most closely held corporations. Other reasons must support piercing, because encouraging capital formation and rational risk-taking remain valid reasons for limited liability in a closely held business.

§6.2.2   *Involuntary Creditors — Protecting Guileless Risk Bearers*

Courts often seem less willing to pierce the corporate veil for creditors whose dealings with the corporation were voluntary — such as suppliers, employees, customers, and lenders — than they are for involuntary creditors. As long as the voluntary creditors are not deceived, they usually can anticipate the corporation's "no recourse" structure and provide for it contractually by obtaining either personal guarantees, assurances on how the business will be conducted, or higher prices. For example, in *Brunswick Corp. v. Waxman*, 599 F.2d 34 (2d Cir. 1979), the court denied recovery to a supplier from shareholders who had set up a no-asset "straw" corporation for the sole purpose of making payments under the supply contract. The supplier, which knew the corporation had minimal capitalization and was incorporated to assure limited liability for its shareholders, was not misled and assumed the risk. The court refused to pierce the corporate veil.

Involuntary creditors — such as tort victims and retail customers — generally cannot protect themselves contractually, nor do they knowingly assume the risk of dealing with a "no recourse" business. But courts do not necessarily pierce the veil whenever an involuntary creditor suffers a loss that exceeds corporate assets. The rule of limited liability is meant to shift the risks of the business to outside creditors, whether voluntary or involuntary. To encourage corporations to buy liability insurance and to manage business risks better, some commentators have urged a rule of pro rata liability (liability assessed per share) in cases of tort creditors. In practice, however, courts continue to pierce only when other factors are present.

§6.2.3 Enterprise Liability Doctrine — Disregarding Multiple Incorporations of the Same Business

Courts are more willing to hold a corporation responsible for the liabilities of related corporations than to hold individual shareholders responsible. Often a single business is incorporated as separate corporations to isolate business assets and risks. For example, risky underinsured operations can be placed in a manufacturing "subsidiary" while the profits of the business flow to a marketing "parent" corporation. (A parent corporation is one that owns a majority, or all, of the stock of the subsidiary corporation.) Or the business can be split into a number of separate "brother-sister" corporations, each owned by the same investors. This separation isolates the assets of each "affiliate" corporation from the risks of the others.

Courts sometimes use the *enterprise liability doctrine* to disregard multiple incorporations of the same business. In cases brought by *involuntary* creditors, courts treat corporations under common ownership as one pool of assets if: (1) the corporations are essentially parts of a single business, and (2) separate incorporation merely isolates risk. Enterprise liability is more likely when the managers who run the "asset" corporation also run the "risk" corporation. In cases brought by *voluntary* creditors, enterprise liability is less likely because these creditors (unless they are deceived or purposefully confused) can assess and contract around the separation of risk and assets. In a well-planned business arrangement, the separation of assets from risk with multiple incorporations often is used legitimately by parties to allocate risk.

The intra-enterprise doctrine does not expose individual shareholders to unlimited liability; it simply pools together business assets to meet the liabilities of any part of the enterprise. Nonetheless, courts are reluctant to invoke the enterprise liability doctrine. Even though tort creditors often seek to recover the assets of related corporations, courts combine these assets in only a small portion of such cases.

Consider the famous case of *Walkovsky v. Carlton,* 223 N.E.2d 6 (N.Y. Ct. App. 1966). Carlton had set up ten wholly owned cab corporations in which he was the controlling and dominant shareholder. Following a common practice in New York City's taxi business, each corporation had two cabs and employed its own taxi drivers. A taxi driver of one of the corporations ran over Walkovsky, who sued the corporation that owned the offending cab, Carlton's nine other corporations, the corporations that owned the central garage, and Carlton himself. As required by statute, each cab corporation carried insurance in the amount of $10,000, but no more. The cabs were heavily mortgaged, and the only other assets of value, the licenses authorizing taxi operation in New York City, were judgment-proof by law.

Walkovsky sued on two theories: (1) Carlton's whole taxi enterprise was liable, making all the affiliated assets available on an enterprise liability theory, and (2) Carlton was liable in his personal capacity. The court readily accepted the enterprise liability theory because each company was part of a single enterprise fragmented artificially into separate corporations. But the court rejected the argument that Carlton's using multiple corporations or his barely satisfying the minimum insurance requirement justified imposing personal liability. The court remanded for the plaintiff to allege that Carlton had conducted the business in his "individual capacity," suggesting Carlton would be liable if he had "siphoned off" assets by taking wrongful dividends and distributions.

§6.2.4 *Failure to Observe Corporate Formalities*

One of the most common, and most criticized, factors that courts mention in piercing the corporate veil is whether the corporate participants have observed corporate formalities — issuing stock, electing directors and officers, holding shareholders' and directors' meetings, passing resolutions authorizing payments, and keeping corporate minutes. When formalities are not observed, courts often pierce on the theory that shareholders have used the corporation as their "alter ego" or as a conduit for their own personal affairs.

The emphasis on corporate formalities is hard to explain. Rarely do the unobserved formalities relate to the creditor's claim; their introduction at trial often seems little more than an afterthought. Nonetheless, the importance courts give to corporate formalities can be explained at a few levels. First, it can be argued — perhaps simplistically — that anyone who disregards the corporate form should not be allowed to claim the privilege of limited liability. Second, it can be argued — more meaningfully — that the failure to observe formalities may indicate that creditors were confused or misled about who they were dealing with. Third, it can be argued — perhaps most meaningfully — that a lack of formalities suggests that shareholders systematically have disregarded legitimate claims of actual or potential creditors. That is, lack of formalities provides indirect evidence of shareholder abuse and siphoning.

§6.2.5   *Commingling of Assets and Affairs*

Courts also justify piercing when shareholders fail to keep corporate assets and personal assets separate. Using a corporate bank account to pay for personal expenses, for example, is a sure way to risk piercing. As with the emphasis on corporate formalities, the theory is that corporate creditors have a valid expectation that company assets will be available to meet their claims. The commingling of assets, often accomplished by corporate participants who "completely dominated" corporate affairs, allows an inference that the participants disregarded creditor claims.

Courts often cite confusion of a subsidiary's affairs with those of the parent corporation, or among subsidiaries, as a reason for disregarding separate incorporation in cases of enterprise liability. Creditors may be confused about which entity they are dealing with, whose credit is on the line, and which corporation is responsible for accidents. Mixing assets, failing to observe formalities, having officers who do not identify in which capacity they are acting, and using the same trade name or stationery are common indiscretions used to justify enterprise liability.

§6.2.6   *Undercapitalization and Purposeful Insolvency*

Courts are more willing to pierce the corporate veil if the business is formed or operated without capital adequate to meet expected business risks. Courts occasionally justify piercing when there is nominal capitalization or a purposeful failure to insure. But simply organizing or running a business that has little or no capital is, standing alone, generally not sufficient to pierce the corporate veil. In a largely discredited decision by the California Supreme Court, *Minton v. Cavaney,* 364 P.2d 473 (Cal. 1961), the piercing doctrine reached its furthest extension. The court suggested that the undercapitalization of a corporation set up to run a swimming pool was sufficient grounds for holding a director personally liable when a young girl drowned soon after the pool opened. Justice Traynor reasoned that piercing is proper when a corporation's capital is "trifling" compared to its business risks and when the defendant actively participated in the conduct of corporate affairs. Courts in other jurisdictions, as well as more recent California decisions, have rejected this broad undercapitalization rule.

Undercapitalization can also be significant if the corporation is run so that it can never make a profit or is always insolvent. In general, creditors expect that the business will be run to be profitable and that those running the business set aside reserves to meet corporate obligations as they become due and payable. Purposeful insolvency caused by a shareholder's undisclosed practice of siphoning whatever corporate assets become available can justify piercing. In *DeWitt Truck Brokers, Inc. v. W. Ray Flemming Fruit Co.,* 540

F.2d 681 (4th Cir. 1976), Flemming had set up a one-man corporation to run a fruit brokerage, selling growers' produce and arranging for its transportation to buyers. Flemming collected the sales price from the buyers, took out his selling commission plus an amount to cover transportation charges, and remitted the balance to the growers. He paid himself a salary that often included amounts withheld as transportation charges. When one of the transporters sued for unpaid charges, Flemming claimed the company was insolvent and that his liability was limited. The court pierced the corporate veil and held Flemming personally liable. By surreptitiously pocketing transportation charges, he had operated the business to abuse the transporters' extension of credit.

§6.2.7 Active Corporate Participation

Piercing the corporate veil does not disregard the corporate existence for all purposes. Often piercing — and hence personal liability — is appropriate for some of the corporate participants but not for others. Shareholders who are not active in the business and have not acted to disadvantage creditors are less likely to be personally liable than those whose actions resulted in a depletion of assets. See RMBCA §6.22 (shareholder "may become personally liable by reason of his own acts or conduct").

One implication of this is procedural. A shareholder sued on a piercing theory has a due process right to litigate the underlying issue of corporate liability. Even if the corporation has been held liable, there is no res judicata or collateral estoppel effect if the shareholder is not a party to the suit against the corporation.

§6.2.8 Deception

Perhaps the most critical factor in piercing cases is the presence of a misrepresentation. In Thompson's exhaustive study of piercing cases, piercing happened in 92 percent of the cases in which the court also found some misrepresentation but in only 1.7 percent of the cases where the court explicitly stated there was no misrepresentation. Thompson, Piercing the Corporate Veil: An Empirical Study, 76 Cornell L. Rev. 1036 (1991).

Corporate limited liability creates a default "no recourse" rule that those who deal with the corporation should look only to business assets. Unless they obtain personal guarantees, the personal assets of corporate participants are not available to satisfy corporate obligations. Participants who create the appearance of sufficient business assets, thus misleading creditors to believe that they need not obtain personal guarantees or take other protective steps, should not be able to claim a no-recourse understanding.

§6.2.9   *Distinguishing Piercing from Direct Personal Liability*

Many cases that hold shareholders liable are not piercing cases at all. If a shareholder has personally obligated herself for debts of the corporation, liability arises not from disregarding the corporate entity but from the shareholder's personal guarantee. Some courts have extended this idea and have held that the statute of frauds is not an impediment to a creditor who extends credit to the corporation on the basis of a shareholder's oral guarantee. The creditor, induced to deal with the corporation by a false promise, can sue the shareholder personally. *Weisser v. Mursam Shoe Corp.*, 127 F.2d 344 (2d Cir. 1942). Other courts simply use the piercing doctrine as a safety valve to avoid the problems of enforcing an oral personal guarantee.

Likewise, if a shareholder or corporate manager commits a tort in the course of corporate business, she is liable under traditional tort and agency rules. Piercing the corporate veil is unnecessary to reach the tortfeasor's personal assets.

EXAMPLES

1. Five years ago Don incorporated a watch and clock repair business, Timend, Inc. He signed a ten-year lease with Metro Realty to rent a downtown shop. The lease was between Metro and Timend. During the first few years, Don's business did modestly well. Don drew a salary that approximated net earnings (revenues less expenses). He kept meticulous records of receipts and payments, but did not observe any corporate formalities. He did not hold shareholders' or directors' meetings; he did not adopt corporate resolutions approving his salary. Last year the business began to struggle, and Don's salary began to shrink.

   a. Last month Don closed the shop. He told Metro Realty that Timend could no longer make payments under the lease. Is Don personally liable under the lease?

   b. Can Metro Realty pierce the corporate veil and recover from Don personally under the lease?

   c. Don had told Metro Realty when he signed the lease that he would stand behind it. Metro did not get Don's guarantee in writing. Does the statute of frauds prevent Metro from suing on the guarantee?

   d. Before Don closed the business, Howard (one of the shop's employees) drove the company truck over Thelma's prize poodle, Fifi. Assume Timend is liable to Thelma because Howard was acting within the scope of his employment. Can Thelma recover from Don if insurance doesn't cover her loss?

   e. Roger brought his priceless grandfather clock to Don's shop for repairs. Howard ruined it, and insurance covers only part of the loss. Don admits that he incorporated the business precisely to shield himself from liability in such circumstances. Can Roger pierce the corporate veil and recover from Don personally?

f. Suppose that Don, anticipating the possibility of uninsured damage to valuable clocks, set up the business as two corporations, Heirloom Clocks Corp. and Timend Inc. Don sets up a separate counter and invoice forms for Heirloom, which handles all repairs of clocks valued at more than $500. Heirloom is a sublessee of Timend and hires the same employees. If Roger had brought his grandfather clock to the Heirloom counter and the clock was damaged, can Roger look to Timend's assets for recovery?

2. In 1989 Rupert and Olive incorporate a mail-order business, Exquisite Time Corp., to sell "designer" watches through television advertisements. The business gets off to a good start. But Rupert and Olive draw salaries that exceed the margin between receipts and operating costs. They do this by buying merchandise to fill back orders using money that comes in with new orders. They keep meticulous records and observe corporate formalities to a tee. Board resolutions appoint them as officers and approve every payment to them. After one year, there is a $50,000 backlog of unfilled watch orders.

a. Rupert writes expectant customers that the corporation is suffering a "cash flow problem" and is unable to fill their orders. Can the customers pierce the corporate veil?

b. One of Exquisite Time's early customers, Dora, writes complaining that her watch has a corrosive backing that has turned her skin purple. Assuming Exquisite Time would be liable in tort, can Dora recover from Rupert and Olive by piercing the corporate veil?

c. Aside from piercing the corporate veil, can Rupert and Olive be held liable on any other theory?

d. Suppose Rupert and Olive had enticed Laura to invest as a shareholder in Exquisite Time. Laura did not take a salary or participate in running the business. If the corporate veil is pierced because of Rupert's and Olive's activities, is Laura also liable to the company's tort and contract creditors?

e. Suppose that Exquisite Time was one of a number of mail order businesses set up by Rupert and Olive. The businesses were all held as separate subsidiaries of a holding company, Mail-Order Possibilities, Inc. (MOP). Each subsidiary — one for watches, another for records, another for gold jewelry, another for vegematics — flowed through its profits to MOP, the parent. Can MOP and other subsidiaries be liable for Exquisite Time's debts?

EXPLANATIONS

1a. Don is not liable under the lease. Even though he was the person who signed the lease and stopped making payments, he acted on behalf of the corporation and is not himself obligated to pay under the lease. The corporate form provides limited liability to managers, employees, and agents who act on behalf of the corporation and to shareholders who invest in the corporation. Unless Don obligated himself through a personal guarantee or a court uses the piercing factors to disregard corporate limited liability, the creditor Metro Realty can look only to corporate assets for repayment. This is the essence of limited liability.

1b. Many of the factors that courts cite in piercing cases (see §6.2) don't look good for Don: (factor 1) Timepiece Repair is a closely held corporation and Don as sole shareholder dominated the business; (factor 4) Don did not observe corporate formalities; (factor 6) the business was operated on a no-profit basis and did not have sufficient capital to meet its ten-year lease commitment; (factor 7) Don was an active participant. But other factors argue against piercing: (factor 2) Metro Realty is a voluntary creditor and could have sought a personal guarantee but did not; (factor 3) Don is an individual manager/shareholder and imposing personal liability on him may discourage socially useful but risky businesses; (factor 5) Don kept corporate and personal assets separate and paid himself a salary only after covering expenses; (factor 8) Don did not deceive Metro Realty or give any personal guarantees.

The score is 4-4. The piercing factors do not provide a terribly useful guide either for planning or in litigation. Nonetheless, Don's case is not a good candidate for piercing the corporate veil: It seems to be little more than a case of a garden-variety failed business. If piercing is appropriate here, it will apply in virtually every case, and limited liability would become an empty promise. Don never deceived or systematically avoided creditors. His failure to observe corporate formalities does not provide indirect evidence that he purposefully avoided creditor expectations. Other records make clear that he paid his salary after paying current expenses. By failing to get personal guarantees or security interests in particular business assets, Metro Realty assumed the full risk of Timend's business failure.

1c. No. The statute of frauds is not a bar. Metro may be able to hold Don to his promise or even to recover on a piercing theory. Some courts have held that an oral promise made before or at the time that a debt is created and that induces the creditor to extend credit is an "original promise" and thus is not within the statute of frauds. Other courts have avoided the statute of frauds simply by piercing the corporate veil to protect creditor expectations. Given Don's guarantee, Metro did not assume the risk of Timend's failure.

1d. Maybe. Piercing in Thelma's tort case will depend on many of the same factors discussed above in Metro Realty's contract case. The only significant differences are that Thelma, unlike Metro, is an involuntary creditor and the corporation did not carry sufficient insurance to cover her loss — both factors adding weight to a piercing argument.

Nonetheless, courts remain reluctant to pierce in tort cases unless there are other factors that support piercing. In fact, a recent study indicates that piercing occurs less frequently in tort cases compared to contract cases. Thompson, Piercing the Corporate Veil: An Empirical Study, 76 Cornell L. Rev. 1036 (1991) (finding that piercing happened in 42 percent of contract cases and 31 percent of tort cases). This study, however, may reflect only that disappointed contract creditors, compared to injured tort victims, are more selective about the cases in which they seek piercing.

Don't forget that Don may also be liable on other theories besides piercing. If he had hired Howard knowing that Howard had a miserable driving record or if he had told Howard to speed as he made deliveries, Don might be liable to Thelma in tort, regardless of piercing.

1e. Although the corporation is also liable on a respondeat superior theory, piercing will again depend on much the same factors discussed above with respect to Metro Realty. A significant question is whether Roger should be treated as a voluntary or involuntary creditor. Presumably, he could have sought personal guarantees or demanded higher insurance coverage before he left his clock at the shop. On the other hand, requiring that retail customers make such demands would significantly increase the costs of retail transactions, so the threat of piercing may be a more efficient way of assuring responsibility to creditors. But if Don did not make any personal guarantees, mislead Roger about insurance, or violate any minimum insurance requirements, piercing seems inappropriate. That Don incorporated solely to avoid personal liability makes no difference; corporate law's promise of limited liability is meant to be an important incentive for doing business in the corporate form.

1f. This is not a typical case of piercing — that is, of shareholder or manager liability — but of redrawing the boundaries of the enterprise's assets. Courts have accepted a theory of enterprise liability when a business artificially separates assets from risks to avoid claims by involuntary creditors. In our case, liability of the combined enterprises may depend on whether Roger was aware of the fragmentation. If Roger did not know he was dealing with an assetless shell, a court might well aggregate the assets of the two corporations as though they were a single entity. The actual enterprise — as evidenced by its location, its shared employees, and the nature of its business — was essentially one. But if Roger was aware of this separation, perhaps because of the separate counter and invoice forms, he might be seen as a voluntary creditor who assumed the risk of dealing with a corporate shell.

2a. As with Don's failed business, the relevance of the piercing factors is less than clear. Some indicate piercing is appropriate: Exquisite Time is a closely held corporation; the mail-order customers hardly were able to demand personal guarantees or impose contract restraints; the business was operated so that eventually orders could not be filled; Rupert and Olive were active participants. But other factors argue against piercing: Rupert and Olive are individual shareholders; they observed corporate formalities; they kept corporate and personal assets separate; and they never personally guaranteed that the orders would be filled.

The score is 4-4. But unlike in Don's case, Rupert and Olive were abusing creditor expectations by taking salaries based on receipts, not on after-expense earnings. Mail-order customers assumed their payments would be used to buy and ship their merchandise. Piercing seems likely. Their case smells of fraud.

2b. Probably. Dora is an involuntary creditor, and the factors favoring piercing discussed in the previous answer also favor piercing in her case. The self-induced insolvency that resulted from the way Rupert and Olive ran the business, besides violating the expectations of contract creditors, also undermines tort deterrence and compensation goals. The business was run so that there would be no assets to satisfy legitimate claims.

2c. Perhaps. Through their television ads, Rupert and Olive implicitly represented to customers that the payments for their watches would be used to fill the orders. Even though customers purchased watches from the corporation, Rupert and Olive may be individually liable for intentionally misrepresenting material facts on which others relied to their detriment — the tort of deceit. Privity is not necessary.

2d. Probably not. The corporation does not cease to exist because some of its shareholders are subject to personal liability. Piercing the corporate veil — disregarding the rule of limited liability — is determined shareholder by shareholder. Only those shareholders whose actions are related to the piercing factors, particularly those who "dominated" the business and participated in draining corporate assets, may be held personally liable for the corporation's debts and obligations.

2e. The question of disregarding corporate structures — whether the division is "horizontal" (parent-subsidiary corporations), "vertical" (brother-sister corporations) or, as here, both — is one of the most vexing piercing problems. Much will depend on the traditional piercing factors, including whether the plaintiff acceded to the no-recourse structure and whether there was confusion as to the separateness of the many corporations.

Beyond this, the principal reason for limited liability — promoting capital formation — provides a useful springboard for analysis. If the reasons for the multiple corporate structures suggest that desirable investment will be discouraged by amassing the entire bulk of assets together, vertically or horizontally, piercing may be inappropriate. Putting all the assets into one pot for creditors would put companies whose capital is provided by a holding company at a competitive disadvantage compared to those companies whose capital is provided by individual or widely dispersed investors. The holding company and its affiliates would all bear risks that other limited-liability investors do not. Because of this, the holding company would demand higher returns for assuming the greater risk, and the affiliates would be forced to buy more insurance or set aside greater reserves to cover their greater exposure.

If MOP's mail-order subsidiaries operate separately, so that it can be said they represent separate investment decisions, the rule of limited liability teaches that a no-recourse structure deserves presumptive respect. The mail-order creditors would have to show more than the existence of related businesses.

§6.3 Distilling a Principle — Solving the Piercing Conundrum

Is it possible — on some *principled* basis — to distinguish between Don's failed business and Rupert's and Olive's mail-order fast shuffle? Counting factors and giving various weights to them is an unpredictable game with potentially high costs to efficient capital formation. General principles of creditor protection, of which the piercing cases represent a subset, provide some useful insights into the piercing conundrum.

§6.3.1 *The Uniform Fraudulent Transfer Act*

The concept of limiting the discretion of debtors and protecting the expectations of creditors beyond the terms of their contract has a long history in the law. The notion that debtors cannot use sham transactions to hide their assets from creditors — whether or not the matter is addressed explicitly in the contract — is as old as Roman law and in England was codified in the Statute of Elizabeth (1571). Today it is embodied in the Uniform Fraudulent Transfer Act (UFTA). The UFTA helps explain many of the piercing factors and when they are (or are not) relevant.

The UFTA, like its predecessor the Uniform Fraudulent Conveyance Act, is relatively straightforward. It defines certain debtor transactions as fraudulent and allows creditors with matured or maturing claims to void such transactions or to claim the property fraudulently conveyed. UFTA §7.

The UFTA defines three categories of "fraudulent" transfers:

(1) any transfer that the debtor made with the actual intent to hinder, delay, or defraud present or future creditors — particularly when the transfer is to an insider or relative of the debtor (UFTA §4(a)(1));

(2) any transfer for which the debtor does not receive reasonably equivalent value and that leaves the debtor with unreasonably small assets in relation to her actual or anticipated needs (UFTA §4(a)(2)(i)); and

(3) any transfer for which the debtor does not receive reasonably equivalent value and that the debtor knew or should have known would render him insolvent (UFTA §4(a)(2)(ii)).

In short, even when a creditor cannot show the debtor is purposefully trying to avoid her creditors, a transfer by the debtor is "constructively" fraudulent if it is for questionable value and threatens the debtor's ability to pay her other debts as they become due. For example, suppose that Patty Jo bought a sports car from Sam for $15,000 and promised to pay for it over two years, and that Sam foolishly failed to perfect a security interest in the car. If Patty Jo becomes unable to make the installment payments and sells the car to her brother Billy Joe for $500, the UFTA will permit Sam to sue to have the transaction set aside as fraudulent and to attach the car.

§6.3.2 Applying the UFTA to the Piercing Conundrum

The UFTA, and its philosophy of protecting creditor expectations, is a useful starting point for considering the piercing conundrum. It helps explain in our two problems why piercing the corporate veil seems a bad idea in Don's case but eminently proper in Rupert's and Olive's.

Don's Case: No Fraudulent Transfers. Although Don continued to draw a salary, that salary seemed to have a relationship to the value of his services. The corporation's inability to meet its obligations under the lease was not because of Don's siphoning away assets from the business for himself in transactions of questionable value. He had not intentionally avoided paying on the lease. Disregarding limited liability in the case of a failed business would dampen the incentive to invest or take rational business risks.

Rupert's and Olive's Case: Fraudulent Transfers. Rupert's and Olive's salaries are more easily characterized as lacking fair value because they were based on the business's receipts, without regard to other expenses. They necessarily jeopardized the company's ability to fill customer orders. As a result, the high salaries left the company with unreasonably small assets in relation to its business and eventually rendered it insolvent. UFTA §4(a)(2). Moreover, the salary payments to insiders suggest an intent to hinder customers from receiving their watches as promised. UFTA §4(a)(1). Imposing personal liability does not discourage desirable risk-taking, but it does protect reasonable creditor expectations.

In this light, it is easier to see the relevance of corporate formalities and the intermingling of corporate and personal assets or affairs in deciding piercing cases. Disregarded formalities provide indirect evidence of fraudulent transfers, and intermingling may provide direct evidence.

Both the UFTA and corporate veil-piercing doctrine create for corporate participants implicit duties (similar to fiduciary duties) to consider creditor expectations and to place them ahead of their own expectations. This is inherent in the promise that creditor claims are senior to shareholder residual claims.

§6.3.3   Limits of the UFTA

Why haven't courts used fraudulent transfer doctrine — whether the UFTA, the UFCA, or their common law analogues — instead of the vague piercing doctrine? Fraudulent transfer law depends on identifying *specific transactions* lacking fair equivalent value. In a business where corporate records are sketchy or corporate formalities are not followed, evidence of specific fraudulent transfers may be hard to find. Also, where funds are siphoned from the business as they become available, it may be difficult to identify all the transactions that operated to defraud creditors. The broader piercing doctrine avoids these problems of proof. Unlimited liability is imposed regardless of specific proof of transactions that lacked reasonably equivalent value.

EXAMPLES

1. Fred is the sole shareholder and president of Penultimate Inc., a construction company that specializes in high-rise construction projects. Fred set up the company with $1000 in capital. Fred owns all of the scaffolding, machinery, and cranes used by the corporation, which he leases to the corporation at a high annual rent. Because of these heavy rent obligations, the corporation has rarely run a profit after expenses. Although Fred generally does not follow corporate procedures, the rental arrangement was specifically approved by the company's three-person board.

   a. Penultimate borrows money from Irwin Trust for the construction of a high-rise hotel. Construction costs are more than expected, and Penultimate defaults on the loan. Can Irwin Trust recover from Fred under the UFTA?

      b. Patrick, a passerby at one of Penultimate's job sites, is badly hurt when a beam falls to the ground. The corporation has some insurance, but it does not cover the judgment Patrick obtains against Penultimate, which is virtually assetless. Can Patrick recover from Fred under the UFTA?

  2. Should there be piercing liability:
     a. In Irwin Trust's case?
     b. In Patrick's case?

EXPLANATIONS

1a. Perhaps. Irwin Trust can recover from Fred, as the first transferee, the excess of the rental payments over market value if they were "fraudulent transfers." UFTA §8(b)(1). If Fred intentionally set up the rental arrangement to avoid creditors, the rental payments would constitute fraudulent transfers. The UFTA suggests that above-market transfers to insiders, especially when concealed, are badges of fraud. Comment to UFTA §4(b). Nonetheless, actual intent may be difficult to show if Penultimate had been operating this way for some time.

The rental payments would be constructively fraudulent if they were not for "reasonably equivalent value" — that is, if they were significantly above market rates — and the rent left Penultimate with insufficient assets for its business or Fred should have known Penultimate would incur debts (like the construction loan) it could not pay back. UFTA §4(b).

A constructive fraud theory has some difficulties. Even though the rental payments were above market, it is not clear that they led Penultimate to be unable to repay its loan. Presumably, Irwin Trust extended credit knowing of the rental arrangement and believing it did not leave Penultimate with assets insufficient for its business. Moreover, Penultimate's inability to pay the construction loan may have been due not to the high rentals but to cost overruns on the project. But if Penultimate could not repay its construction loan because of the drain of the rental payments, the UFTA would treat the payments to Fred as fraudulent.

1b. Probably. Like any other creditor, Patrick can recover from Fred if the rental payments were fraudulent transfers. UFTA §8(b)(1). Penultimate did not receive "reasonably equivalent value" in the above-market rental arrangement, and it could be argued its resulting assets were unreasonably small given its dangerous construction business. The high rental in effect avoided creditor claims that Penultimate should have anticipated.

Patrick became a creditor of Penultimate when his claim against the company matured — that is, when he obtained a judgment against the corporation. Under the UFTA it makes no difference that Patrick's claim matured after the rental payments.

2a. Perhaps. The piercing analysis is similar to that of the UFTA. Applying the piercing factors, it will be relevant that Irwin Trust is a voluntary creditor that could have inquired, and presumably did, into Fred's rental arrangement. If Fred disclosed the arrangement, Irwin Trust could have protected itself against the corporation's insolvency by seeking personal guarantees or by demanding that Fred charge market-rate rentals. A principal reason for corporate limited liability — to encourage socially desirable risk-taking — argues against piercing liability. The UFTA also recognizes this by not imposing liability if the above-market transfers did not undermine the business.

2b. Piercing is more likely, although again the piercing analysis is similar to that under the UFTA. As the piercing factors suggest, Patrick (an involuntary creditor) was unable to protect himself against Fred's above-market rental arrangement. Fred's practice of effectively depleting the corporation of working capital was something against which Patrick could not protect himself. The UFTA's prohibition against above-market transactions that leave the corporation with "unreasonably small" assets provides a framework for considering whether Fred owed a duty to Patrick (and other potential tort victims) not to siphon away assets.

On the one hand, the arrangement had been going on for quite a while, apparently without hurting other creditors. The argument would be buttressed if the excess rental payments legally could have been paid to Fred as dividends or other distributions (see Chapter 9). Moreover, unless Fred had failed to comply with mandatory insurance requirements applicable to construction companies, state policy would seem to favor corporations' engaging in the construction business rather than in creating capital reserves to satisfy potential tort claims. Fred's rental arrangement created a no-recourse company that insulated business risks from personal assets.

7

Statutory Recognition of the Corporate Form

The recognition of corporate attributes arises in a number of contexts. In piercing cases, courts seek to fit the corporate attribute of limited liability with state contract and tort law. Conceptually related to the piercing cases, though sometimes confused with them, corporate recognition also is an issue in cases interpreting state and federal statutes. This chapter considers the recognition of such attributes as corporate personality, limited liability, and central decision-making under particular regulatory schemes.

§7.1 Statutory Recognition of the Corporation

§7.1.1 The Corporation as a Separate Entity

Most modern regulatory schemes explicitly visit on corporations the same regulatory burdens and benefits as apply to any other person or entity. Recognition of corporate personality, however, becomes an issue when a constitutional provision, statute, or regulation refers to a "person" without specifying whether corporations are included in the reference. As we have seen, corporations are treated as persons for most economic purposes but receive only limited recognition in matters involving individual rights (see §1.3).

Corporate personality also is relevant when an individual attempts to use a corporation to create transactions with a separate entity to obtain benefits under a statute. For example, many regulatory schemes provide benefits — such as unemployment compensation and retirement benefits — to individuals employed by another person. Although most schemes recognize the legal personality of the corporation, particular issues arise where a corporation is used to create employment relationships (and benefits) that otherwise do not exist. For example, in *Stark v. Flemming,* 283 F.2d 410 (9th Cir. 1960), an elderly woman who was not otherwise entitled to Social Security benefits set up a one-person corporation to hold real estate from which she derived rental income. Then, to qualify her for Social Security benefits, the corporation "employed" her at a "salary" equal to the rental income. The court construed the Social Security statute to respect the employment relationship, provided the salary was reasonable. Other courts, construing other statutes, have refused to respect similar use of the corporate form. See, e.g., *Baker v. Caravan Moving Corp.,* 561 F. Supp. 337 (N.D. Ill. 1983) (sham corporation cannot be used to escape obligations under the Employee Retirement Income Security Act).

§7.1.2 *Corporate Limited Liability*

In general, regulatory schemes respect corporate limited liability. For example, individual shareholders are not liable to users of the corporation's unsafe products, and managers are not typically liable on government contracts. Nonetheless, a number of statutory schemes override corporate limited liability to serve the imperative purposes of the statute. Under federal discrimination laws, a parent corporation can be liable for claims by an employee of an insolvent subsidiary if the parent is linked to the subsidiary's discriminatory policies. Under federal law, officers and shareholders can be liable for trademark and parent infringements if they "actively assisted" in the infringement. Limited liability is thus a matter of statutory interpretation.

Sometimes courts have difficulty ascertaining whether a particular statutory scheme incorporates traditional notions of corporate separateness and limited liability. This has been true of the federal Superfund statute, which imposes liability on former and present "owners or operators" of hazardous waste sites. Federal courts interpreting the Superfund statute have taken different tacks. Some federal courts have refused to look to traditional veil-piercing criteria — such as active participation and lack of corporate formalities — and have imposed liability on individual officers who "could have prevented" the hazardous discharge. In a like vein, courts have imposed liability if a parent corporation was "actively involved" or exercised "pervasive control" of the subsidiary and its hazardous waste operations. Other federal courts, however, have said that absent a contrary congressional intent "limited liability is the rule, not the exception" and have exonerated parent corporations when traditional piercing factors were absent.

In the end, the Superfund statute's "owner or operator" language raises the question whether the statutory purposes of cleaning up hazardous waste sites and identifying parties responsible for deficient disposal practices are best advanced by readily imposing liability on those who could have prevented the harm or only on those who actually participated in it. Whether there was commingling of assets, siphoning of funds, or failure to follow corporate formalities — traditional veil-piercing issues — may well be irrelevant in this inquiry.

§7.2 Equitable Subordination Doctrine

The malleable corporate form permits its participants to enter into corporate transactions that adjust the relationships between corporate insiders and creditors. Recognition of such corporate transactions may sometimes be inconsistent with the creditor-protection purposes of the Bankruptcy Code. When corporate insiders claim rights superior to those of other creditors based on a corporate transaction, the Bankruptcy Code dictates whether the transaction should be respected, recharacterized, or disregarded to protect creditors.

Under the doctrine of *equitable subordination,* bankruptcy courts can subordinate claims by corporate insiders — that is, they lower the normal priority of such claims — if the claim arose from a transaction that constituted a breach of a fiduciary duty (see Chapter 20). The doctrine, now codified in the Bankruptcy Code, was first articulated in *Taylor v. Standard Gas & Electric Co.,* 306 U.S. 307 (1939). There, a parent corporation caused its subsidiary, Deep Rock, to enter into a series of transactions with the parent and affiliated companies on terms that were highly disadvantageous to Deep Rock. Because these transactions violated the parent's fiduciary duties to the subsidiary, the Court subordinated the parent's claims to those of preferred shareholders of the subsidiary. This process of subordination came to be known as the "Deep Rock doctrine."

The most famous case of equitable subordination is *Pepper v. Litton,* 308 U.S. 295 (1939). Dixie Splint Coal Company had failed to pay Pepper royalties under a coal lease, and Pepper sued. Litton, Dixie Splint's sole shareholder and dominant director, recognized that the suit would leave the company penniless and sought to grab what he could. Litton caused the company to confess a judgment for back salary that he claimed. Next he executed on his confessed judgment, and at the execution sale he "purchased" the company's assets, using the sale proceeds to "pay" his salary claims. In effect, Litton acquired the company's assets in exchange for his salary claims. Dixie Splint, now assetless, filed for voluntary bankruptcy.

Meanwhile, Pepper had obtained a judgment against Dixie Splint on his claim for back royalties, but nothing was left for him to collect. The issue: Could the bankruptcy trustee (on behalf of Pepper) disregard or subordinate Litton's salary claims and the company's confession of judgment? The effect would be to move Pepper ahead of Litton in the line of creditors. The Supreme Court held that Litton's judgment for back salary was properly disallowed or subordinated to Pepper's judgment for back royalties. Justice Douglas wrote that a one-person corporation cannot be used to defraud creditors and that as a director Litton had a fiduciary obligation to the corporation and its creditors not to engage in unfair self-dealing (see Chapter 22).

This would all be simple enough except that bankruptcy courts often use piercing factors to justify subordination: whether the insider dominated the corporation without regard to corporate formalities, whether the insider commingled corporate and personal assets, and whether paid-in capital was nominal or the corporation was undercapitalized. Two things should be kept in mind. First, the issue is not whether the corporate form should be disregarded and the insider held liable personally for the corporation's obligations but whether the insider's claims should be disregarded or subordinated to those of other creditors. Second, these factors (as in the piercing cases) rest on the broad principle of creditor protection embodied in the Uniform Fraudulent Transfer Act (see §6.3) that in part imposes on debtors a duty not to prefer some creditors, including themselves, at the expense of others — a debtor's fundamental duty to treat creditors evenhandedly.

EXAMPLES

1. Lone Star Air, Inc. is the holding company for a number of regional airline companies. One of them, Orient Airlines, Inc., has a miserable safety record and faces a number of workers' compensation claims, which state law authorizes against dangerous employers. Orient, always thinly capitalized by Lone Star, does not have enough assets to satisfy all the claims against it. It turns out that Lone Star often paid Orient's workers' compensation taxes. Is Lone Star liable for the workers' compensation claims against Orient?

2. Lone Star Air holds much of Orient's preferred stock. Anticipating Orient's bankruptcy, Lone Star has its executives who make up the Orient board of directors approve a resolution authorizing an exchange of preferred stock for debentures (unsecured debt obligations). The normal bankruptcy rule is that creditors (including unsecured creditors) have priority over preferred shareholders, but among unsecured creditors (including debenture holders) there is pro rata participation. Will Lone Star's debentures share with other unsecured debt claims in bankruptcy?

EXPLANATIONS

1. It depends on what the statute says. Some of the traditional piercing factors — such as commingling of the companies' finances, undercapitalization, and perhaps the parent's direct participation in the operations of the subsidiary — suggest that Lone Star should be liable for its sub-

sidiary's obligations. Nonetheless, the statutory scheme need not adhere to the piercing doctrine. Under a workers' compensation scheme, the question is likely to be whether Lone Star is an "employer" of its subsidiary's employees. This depends on an interpretation of the statutory purposes. In similar circumstances, some courts have said that the parent corporation should be treated as the employer if its executives controlled the activities of the subsidiary's employees and the dangers to which they were exposed. See *Joyce v. Super Fresh Food Markets, Inc.*, 815 F.2d 943 (3d Cir. 1987). Thus, more information about Lone Star's relationship to Orient would be needed.

2. Probably not. Lone Star's claims may be equitably subordinated to those of other unsecured creditors if the exchange was a breach of the board's fiduciary duties. Because the transaction was a self-dealing transaction by a controlling shareholder, it will be subject to a "fairness" review (see §22.3). Fairness involves a twofold inquiry: (1) Did the exchange approximate a transaction that would have occurred in an arm's length transaction?; and (2) Was the exchange one that made financial sense for the corporation under the circumstances? In this light, the exchange faces a difficult road. The value of the debentures cannot exceed the value of the preferred stock, and some corporate purpose for the exchange must have existed.

PART THREE

Financial Structure of the Corporation

8

Capital Structure of the Corporation

The corporation provides a structure for financing business operations. Corporate financing can come from three sources:

Equity financing. The corporation can issue shares of stock — equity financing. Shareholders pay the corporation for their shares, each of which represents an ownership interest in the corporation and gives the shareholder a bundle of rights and powers. Shareholders acquire rights to dividends and to a portion of the corporate assets on liquidation and, in some instances, the power to elect directors and vote on important corporate transactions (see Chapter 12). Equity securities broadly fall into two general categories: common stock and preferred stock.

Debt financing. The corporation can borrow money. Corporate debt obligations (debt securities) are usually fixed by contract and can be issued to third persons (outside debt financing) or to shareholders (inside debt financing). Unlike equity, debt obligates the corporation to repay its lenders the debt principal, along with a specified rate of interest. Unless provided by contract, debtholders do not acquire ownership rights to participate in earnings or to vote.

Corporate earnings. The corporation can use funds generated internally by its business.

The mix of financing sources varies depending on the business's stage of growth. During the start-up stage, entrepeneurs often rely on equity and internal debt financing. As the business becomes more established, it develops a credit history and outside debt financing becomes more available. For a business that has sold its equity shares to the public, there is often a wide variety of private and public sources for financing. Nonetheless, corporate earnings typically represent the largest source of corporate financing for publicly held firms.

For a corporate planner organizing the corporation's financial structure, the important questions are what kinds and what mix of equity and debt financing to use. The planner can be seen as a chef putting together dishes (securities) for a banquet (capital structure). In preparing each dish, the chef has many ingredients to choose from — the rights, powers, limitations, and preferences of which all securities are made up. The ingredients usually are combined according to recipes, with an accepted nomenclature for each dish. But the chef can, and often does, add or vary the ingredients to give the dish its own special flavor. Moreover, each dish must be carefully chosen to complement the other dishes — the mix of common and preferred stock and the debt-equity ratio.

§8.1   Equity Financing

§8.1.1   The Creation of Equity Securities

The fountainhead of all equity securities is the articles of incorporation. The articles prescribe the classes (or types) of equity securities, the number authorized for each class, and the preferences, limitations, and relative rights of each class. RMBCA §§2.02, 6.01. When the articles empower the board to issue equity securities, they are said to be "authorized." They are "issued" when sold to shareholders and "outstanding" when held by shareholders. RMBCA §6.03. Stock authorized and issued in accordance with the articles, usually by resolution of the board of directors, is "validly issued." Stock that is "issued, but no longer outstanding" because it has been repurchased by the corporation is commonly known as "treasury stock." Cf. RMBCA §6.31(a) (eliminates use of term).

Beyond the basic rule that the articles must provide for one or more classes of shares that together have voting power and final liquidation rights, modern statutes permit the rights and powers represented by equity securities to be more or less whatever the corporate planner decides. RMBCA §6.01.

§8.1.2   The Basic Equity Ingredients

Equity shares have a variety of recipes, although the ingredients are relatively standardized:

Dividends are payments by the corporation to equity shareholders based on an apportionment of earnings. Dividend payments can take many forms: cash, property, common stock, preferred stock, debt, even rights to whiskey during wartime liquor controls. Under American corporate law, the declaration of dividends is within the discretion of the board of directors, subject to limitations based on the corporation's financial ability to pay (see Chapter 9).

Rights on dissolution (sometimes known as *liquidation rights*) are distributions in cash or in kind by the corporation to equity shareholders based on an apportionment of assets on dissolution. The articles can specify the amount to be paid in liquidation and the priority of payment. "Senior" shares receive payment before "junior" shares.

Voting rights empower shareholders to vote on a variety of matters, including the election of directors and the approval of certain corporate transactions proposed by the board, such as the amendment of the articles, the creation of new classes of stock, mergers, and sales of all the corporation's assets (see Chapters 34 and 35). Voting rights usually are in proportion to the number of shares, although they are sometimes disproportionate or conditional. Sometimes shares have voting rights limited to certain matters, such as voting for two of five directors. RMBCA §7.21.

Conversion rights give shareholders an option to convert their stock into another security of the corporation. The option, granted by the corporation, can be limited so it is exercisable only upon certain events and during certain periods. RMBCA §6.01(c)(2). For example, conversion rights sometimes are exercisable only during a short period after stock is issued or if the corporation does not pay dividends for a specified number of consecutive years.

Redemption rights give shareholders an option to force a redemption by other shareholders (or repurchase by the corporation) of the shares. The right, whether granted by other shareholders or by the corporation, may be made exercisable at the discretion of the option holder or only upon certain events and during certain periods. The redemption price can be specified in the articles or set by the board if not in the articles. RMBCA §6.01(c)(2).

Preemptive rights allow shareholders to acquire stock when the corporation issues new stock so that the new stock does not dilute the shareholders' proportional interests (voting and ownership) in the corporation's stock that is already issued and outstanding. For example, if a shareholder owns 300 of 1000 outstanding common shares and the corporation proposes to issue 200 more common shares, a preemptive right would entitle the shareholder to acquire 60 more shares at the issue price, thus preserving the shareholder's 30 percent position.

Once viewed as an inherent aspect of stock ownership, preemptive rights are now generally a matter of statutory right. RMBCA §6.30. In some states they exist automatically unless the articles specifically state otherwise (an "opt out" scheme). In others, including the RMBCA, they do not exist unless the parties provide for them in the articles (an "opt in" scheme). Preemptive rights make issuing new stock cumbersome, particularly if the firm's stock is publicly held. Even when they do exist, preemptive rights do not arise in all situations. Common exceptions include when stock is issued in consideration for management services or for noncash property. RMBCA §6.30(b)(3).

Other ingredients are possible, including rights to disclosure, limitations on transferability, and a right to name directors to the board.

§8.1.3   Varieties of Equity Securities — Common Stock and Preferred Stock

The equity ingredients can be mixed in many ways. Recipes range from plain vanilla "common stock" to exotic "nonvoting nonparticipating cumulative convertible redeemable preferred stock." Each separate dish, whose recipe is specified in the articles of incorporation, is known as a class of stock. Within a class, each share has the same rights and powers unless the class is divided into subclasses known as series. Each series has a separate designation, and the rights, limitations, and preference of each series deviate from the class only to the extent specified.

Often the articles will give the board of directors a "blank check" to fix the rights and powers of a series (or even a class) without shareholder action. The board, in effect, fills in the blanks left by the articles. This provides the corporation with the flexibility to sell stock — particularly preferred stock — at prevailing market rates without going through the lengthy process of amending the articles. RMBCA §6.02.

The two generally accepted categories of equity securities are common stock and preferred stock, although the RMBCA (§6.01) does away with this categorization.

Common Stock.   Common stock represents the corporation's residual ownership interests — that is, what is left over after all other claims by creditors, bondholders, and preferred shareholders have been satisfied. Common shareholders enjoy only standby, last-in-line status. Dividends on common stock are not guaranteed: If the board does not declare them in a given year, there is no continuing right to receive any later. If the corporation is dissolved, common stockholders have *liquidation rights* only as to the liquidated assets left over after the "senior" claims of creditors, debtholders, and preferred shareholders have been satisfied. Common shareholders make up for their precarious "junior" position through *voting rights* and their residual claims to dividends and liquidation rights, which may become highly prized in a successful business.

Some state statutes limit the scope of *conversion rights* and *redemption rights* of common stock. The theory behind these statutes is that common shareholders, who are likely through their voting power to have access to inside information and the corporate governance machinery, ought not to be able to advance from the back of the line and avoid their nonpreferred status through "up stream" conversion into more senior securities or forced corporate redemption. RMBCA §6.01 eliminates these restrictions; fiduciary protection is deemed sufficient.

Common stock can be issued in multiple classes. Some classes can have special dividend rights, such as the right to receive twice as many dividends as the basic class of common stock. Nonvoting common stock allows for participation in earnings without affecting the voting power of common stock.

Common stock can be issued to insiders (the usual case in closely held corporations), to a few private outside investors (a frequent phenomenon in start-up businesses), or to many outside investors who trade their stock on public trading markets. Lately, spurred by tax incentives from Congress, many firms have issued some of their common stock to employee stock ownership plans (ESOPs). Under an ESOP, the employer sets up a trust for the benefit of employees and then makes annual payments to the trust so the trust can purchase the company's stock. An ESOP accomplishes a number of things. It gives employees a stake in the company; the employer's contributions to the ESOP are tax deductible; and the higher level of employee ownership may make employees more loyal to the company and may make it harder for shareholders to oust current management.

Preferred Stock. Preferred stock is a hybrid between debt and common stock. It earns fixed dividends and is entitled to fixed liquidation rights. It has priority over and is "senior" to common stock as to dividends and liquidation rights but is behind and is "junior" to the claims of debtholders and creditors. The decision to pay dividends on preferred shares is within the board's discretion, and nonpayment is not an act of default.

The *dividend preference* often is stated in the stock's name: "$10 preferred" is entitled to receive $10 per share each year before any dividends on the common stock are paid, and "15 percent preferred" means that 15 percent of the preferred stock's par value (described below) or stated value must be paid first. The *liquidation preference* is usually a fixed price per share (generally equal to par or stated value, though sometimes including a small liquidation premium) that must be paid in dissolution before any amounts are paid on the common stock.

Normally dividends on preferred stock, like those on common stock, are a matter of board discretion, although some cases have construed provisions in the articles to mandate payment of dividends. Even if dividends are not mandatory, preferred shareholders can have "carry-forward" rights to receive dividends if the board does not declare them in a given year. This depends on whether the preferred stock is *cumulative, noncumulative,* or *partially cumulative.* If the preferred stock is "cumulative" and the board decides in one year not to declare dividends, the corporation assumes a continuing, accumulating obligation to pay the unpaid dividends before it pays any other dividends in the future. For example, if dividends are not paid on "$10 cumulative preferred" in Year 1 and Year 2, no dividends (on preferred or common) can be paid in Year 3 or any year thereafter until the corporation first pays the accumulated $20 to the preferred shareholders. If the preferred stock is "noncumulative," the corporation has no further obligation for unpaid dividends; noncumulative dividends are lost for any year in which they are not declared. In between the two is "partially cumulative" preferred, for which unpaid dividends accumulate only to the extent there were sufficient earnings in the year that was passed over.

In addition to establishing dividend preferences, the articles or provisions setting up the preferred stock can establish *participation rights* — that is, the right of preferred stock to participate with the common stock in any dividends declared on the common stock.

Although preferred stock generally does not have *voting rights,* such rights can be granted by statute or in the articles. State statutes often grant preferred stock a right to vote on certain fundamental transactions, such as mergers or amendments to the articles that eliminate or dilute the stock's seniority. In addition, provisions authorizing preferred often specify that voting rights vest in the preferred stock if, for example, the corporation fails to pay dividends for two consecutive years.

Preferred stock can have *conversion rights* that give preferred shareholders the option to convert their preferred into other stock of the corporation, usually common stock. In effect, preferred shareholders can exchange fixed dividend rights for voting and broad residual rights, which may become more valuable if the business has strong earnings. Besides specifying the ratio at which the conversion is to take place, the provisions setting up the preferred stock often will contain antidilution provisions to take into account changes that have occurred in the amount of common stock outstanding since the preferred stock was issued.

At the option of either the corporation or the shareholder, preferred stock can allow for *redemption.* The corporation often will retain the redemption option (a "call") when the corporate planner anticipates that dividends on preferred stock may become more expensive than other forms of financing. When it is the shareholder who holds the redemption option (a "put"), the corporation often will secure its repurchase obligation by setting up a *sinking fund* into which the corporation sets aside earnings to redeem the stock. The sinking fund may not be used to pay dividends or make other distributions.

EXAMPLES

1. Bacchanalia Banquets, Inc. is in the catering business. Its articles authorize one class of common stock with 100,000 shares. There are 20,000 shares issued and outstanding.

a. Most of the Bacchanalia shares are owned by the firm's managers, who have invested their life savings in the business. What are the advantages and disadvantages of their investment in the common stock?

b. The Bacchanalia board declares a stock dividend that entitles each shareholder to receive one additional common share for every common share she holds. This will double the number of shares each shareholder owns. Are these new shares "validly issued"?

c. An amendment to Bacchanalia's articles authorizes 50,000 shares of new convertible preferred, each share convertible into two shares of common stock. Are there any problems?

d. Another amendment to Bacchanalia's articles authorizes a new class of nonvoting redeemable common stock, under which holders can redeem their stock for $25 a share at any time. Are there any problems?

2. Suppose Bacchanalia has two classes of stock outstanding: 100,000 shares of common stock and 6,000 shares of 10 percent cumulative preferred stock (stated value $100). In Year 1 Bacchanalia has sufficient earnings only to pay $100,000 in dividends.

a. The board chooses in Year 1 not to pay any dividends. Can it?

b. The board declares dividends in Year 1 of $50,000 on the cumulative preferred and $20,000 on the common. Can it?

c. The board does not declare dividends in Year 1 or Year 2. In Year 3 the board declares $60,000 in dividends for Year 1 and $60,000 for Year 2. It does not pay any interest on these arrearage payments. Are there any problems?

d. In Year 1 the board declares $30,000 in dividends on the cumulative preferred. In Year 2 the board does not declare any dividends. In Year 3 there are $100,000 in distributable assets, and the board declares dividends of $60,000 on the preferred and $40,000 on the common stock. Can it?

e. In Years 1 and 2 the board does not, and could not, declare dividends on the cumulative preferred. In Year 3 Bacchanalia has $200,000 in distributable assets. The board wants to declare $20,000 in dividends for the long-suffering common shareholders. Can it?

3. All of Bacchanalia's 100,000 authorized common shares are family-owned. The family decides to bring in new investors but does not want to share in voting control. A group of venture capitalists are willing to invest $1 million. They want a high fixed return on their investment but also want to share in profits if the business is highly successful. To protect their investment, they want to take control if the corporation stops paying a fixed return. The family agrees but wants to be able to buy out the investors (at a premium) if the business becomes wildly successful. Draft an appropriate provision.

EXPLANATIONS

1a. Being a common shareholder has its pluses and minuses. As common shareholders, the Bacchanalia insiders are residual claimants of the firm's income stream. Any return on their investment comes only after the firm's creditors and senior shareholders are paid. They do not have a fixed right to dividends or other payments. As compensation for standing "last in line" behind the firm's other sources of financing, shareholders receive broad participation and voting rights. If the firm succeeds, their rights to dividends and to distributions on liquidation can make their shares extremely valuable. To protect and maximize these rights, the shareholders elect the board and must approve any fundamental corporate changes.

1b. Yes. Shares are "validly issued" if the articles authorize them when the board approves their issue. Bacchanalia's articles of incorporation authorize the board to issue up to 100,000 shares. As a result of the stock dividend, the corporation will have 40,000 shares issued and outstanding, well within the limit.

1c. Yes. There is insufficient authorized common stock to handle all of the possible conversions, up to 100,000 common shares. Before issuing the new convertible preferred, the articles must be amended to authorize additional common shares.

1d. Yes. The redemption right (a put option) will have much the same effect as a forced dividend payment. Just as there are statutory limits on when dividends can be paid, there are limits on a corporation's repurchase of its own stock, including insolvency and balance sheet tests (see §§9.2, 9.3). The right of redemption must be made contingent on meeting the relevant test for corporate repurchases. Moreover, the possibility of a massive redemption might make business planning difficult. A sinking fund would alleviate some of the uncertainty.

2a. Yes. The declaration of dividends on common and preferred stock generally is within the discretion of the corporation's board of directors. Equity securities, unlike debt, do not obligate the corporation to pay dividends, even if it is financially and legally able to pay.

2b. No. All dividends payable on the preferred stock, both current and in arrears, must be paid before any are paid on the common. This is the effect of preferred stock's dividend preference. Assuming there are no accumulated unpaid dividends, the dividend preference requires that the corporation pay $60,000 ($10 per share times 6,000 shares) on the preferred before any dividends are paid to the common.

2c. No. Payments on preferred stock are largely a matter of contract. If the articles or the provisions setting up the preferred stock do not mandate the payment of interest on unpaid cumulative dividends, the corporations need not pay interest. This may create an incentive for the board not to pay preferred dividends and receive in effect a no-interest loan, but preferred rights arise from the provisions setting up the stock. Preferred shareholders protect against this opportunism by specifically providing for interest payments, by securing voting rights or representation on the board if dividends fall into arrears, or by acquiring rights to resell their stock to the corporation (puts).

2d. No. The board must declare and pay a total of $150,000 in dividends to the preferred ($30,000 accumulated from Year 1 and $60,000 from Year 2, plus the current $60,000 preference) before any dividends are declared on the common stock. Thus, no dividends can be paid in Year 3 on the common stock.

2e. Yes, unless the preferred is participating. After paying the preferred dividends, both in arrears and current, the board can declare up to $20,000 in dividends. If the preferred stock is participating, it would be entitled to participate in any additional dividends declared by the board in the proportion specified in the articles or in the provisions setting up the preferred stock. This participation would be in addition to any regular dividends to which the preferred is entitled.

3. Insert into the articles the following provision:

ARTICLE XXX: The corporation has authority to issue 10,000 shares of Preferred Shares ($100 face value). The Preferred Shares will have the following preferences, limitations, and relative rights:

A. *Dividends.* Holders of Preferred Shares will be entitled annually to receive (1) cumulative dividends at the rate of no more than five percent (5%) of face value [well above prevailing market rates], and (2) dividends equal share for share to any dividends paid on the Common Shares. Dividends will be paid only when, as, and if declared by the board of directors out of legally available funds. Cumulative dividends commence to accrue, whether or not earned or declared, from the date of issuance.

B. *Dividend preference.* No dividend may be paid on the Common Shares, nor may any Common Shares be acquired by the Corporation, unless all dividends on any outstanding Preferred Shares are paid (or have been declared and set apart for payment).

C. *Liquidation preference.* If there is a liquidation, dissolution, or winding up of the affairs of the Corporation, holders of Preferred Shares are entitled (1) to be paid in cash $150.00 per share, plus any unpaid dividends, and (2) to participate share for share with the Common Shares in any further distribution.

D. *Voting rights.* Unless provided for by law, the Preferred Shares are nonvoting. If the Corporation fails to pay holders of Preferred Shares earned cumulative dividends for two consecutive years, the Preferred Shares may elect four directors [a majority of the board]. This voting right continues until all earned cumulative dividends have been fully paid.

E. *Redemption.* The Corporation may at any time (in the discretion of the board of directors) redeem all or any part of the outstanding Preferred Shares by paying $150.00 per share, plus any accrued unpaid dividends. If less than all the Preferred Shares are redeemed, the Corporation will redeem the shares pro rata. Notice of redemption must be mailed, postage prepaid, to the holder of record at least fifteen (15) days but no more than sixty (60) days before the date of redemption.

F. *Fractional shares.* There may be fractional Preferred Shares.

This amendment accomplishes the family's and investors' purposes. It creates participation rights for the investors, yet the family retains voting control. Issuing common shares to the investors would not have done this. The preferred stock provisions give the investors contingent control rights and an incentive for the family to pay regular dividends. Yet the investors acquire voting rights only if dividends could have been paid, but were not, for two consecutive years. It caps the extent of investor participation by allowing the family to buy out the investors, although the buyout is at a 50 percent premium. The family can dissolve the corporation or redeem the preferred shares — the price is the same in either case. Although participation is "share for share," the significantly greater number of common shares (100,000 compared to 10,000 preferred shares) means that common participates in a 10:1 ratio.

§8.1.4 *Issuing Equity Securities*

Corporate statutes once mandated minimum initial financing for the corporation. Although a few state statutes continue to impose a minimum capital requirement (at most $1000), the requirement provides little assurance that the business will have enough assets to start up or later to meet creditor claims.

Instead, the important question in issuing equity securities — a question on which new investors often seek a legal opinion — is whether the stock is "fully paid and nonassessable." That is, have investors paid enough for their stock? The answer depends on how much the investors paid and the quality of consideration paid for the stock.

Amount of Consideration — Par Value versus No-Par. Whether investors paid enough depends on whether the stock has "par value." Par value is simply an artificial value attached to shares and specified in the articles of incorporation. It represents the amount that must be paid before shares can be issued as "fully paid and nonassessable." Par value, a concept of diminishing importance, has no relationship to the market value of the shares and, in modern practice, usually is set far below the issuance price — for example, at $1 or even $.01.

The history of par value reveals its intended purposes. During the nineteenth century, the nascent period of the modern corporation, legislatures and judges grappled with how best to protect investors and creditors from unscrupulous practices. To prevent free-riding insiders from issuing themselves stock at prices below those paid by outside investors, par value set a price floor that in theory assured shareholder parity. In addition, to assure creditors that they would have an equity cushion that shareholders could not siphon, the par value system placed aggregated par values (known as "stated capital") out of reach of shareholders through a system of primitive accounting rules. (In Chapter 9, we take up the limits on shareholder distributions under this system of legal capital.)

Consider an example of how the par value system theoretically worked to protect both investors and creditors. Car Company issues 1000 shares of common stock with a par value of $100. Under the par value system, each and every investor must pay par — at least $100 per share. The aggregated par tells creditors that the company in theory has at least $100,000 in assets that cannot be distributed to shareholders. But even during its heyday, par value was not absolute. Courts developed an exception to the par value rule if the market value of the stock fell below par. For example, if Car Company's stock (par $100) was trading at $60, courts accepted that the corporation could sell stock for $60 without new investors incurring liability for the $40 difference between the issuance price and par. Otherwise, strict enforcement of the par value rule would have effectively prevented companies — in the name of protecting shareholders and creditors — from raising new money in times of financial difficulty.

The par value system also had to deal with stock issued for less than par — *watered stock*.* To illustrate, suppose the promoters of Car Company issued themselves preferred stock with an aggregated par value of $2.3 million for assets that they (as the board) had valued at $2.3 million and also issued themselves for no consideration common stock with an aggregated par value of $1.5 million. (These are essentially the facts in the famous case of *Hospes v. Northwestern Manufacturing & Car Co.*, 50 N.W. 1117 (Minn. 1892).) This raises two issues: (1) When investors pay for stock with noncash consideration, should courts defer to the board's valuation?; and (2) Are shareholders liable when they buy watered stock, and, if so, for how much?

On the first question, whether the $2.3 million valuation creates watered-stock liability, courts and corporate statutes have increasingly deferred to the board. Originally, courts required that the board valuation reflect "true value," and courts imposed watered-stock liability on any shareholder who received

---

*Although stock issued for less than par is generically known as "watered stock," it can take one of three forms: (1) shares issued for no consideration — *bonus stock;* (2) shares issued for less than par value — *discount stock;* or (3) shares issued for property whose value is overstated — technically, *watered stock.*

stock for assets that a judge in hindsight decided was overvalued. Although courts later relaxed this test to require that the valuation be made in "good faith" and reflect "reasonable prudence," it continued to create uncertainty for directors, investors, and corporate planners.

Today many statutes make the board's valuation conclusive "in the absence of fraud." The test provides greater certainty, although it leaves open the question whether a challenger must show actual fraud (intentional deception) or merely constructive fraud (such as a breach of fiduciary duty). The RMBCA makes the board's valuation "conclusive" and purposefully does not address whether "fraud or bad faith" constitutes grounds for cancelling validly issued shares. See Official Comment to RMBCA §6.21(c).

On the second question, whether the issuance of $1.5 million in bonus stock creates shareholder liability, the statutes and cases have created a conceptual jumble:

Contract liability.   If shareholders are bound under a subscription agreement to pay par, creditors in insolvency proceedings or shareholders in a derivative action can enforce the corporation's contractual rights to full payment.

Statutory liability.   Regardless of the contract price, corporate statutes may obligate shareholders to pay par value to the corporation. For example, the older MBCA §18 requires that stock having par value be issued for consideration "not less than the par value thereof," and MBCA §25 requires that shareholders pay the corporation "the full consideration for which such shares were . . . to be issued." Courts have interpreted these two provisions as creating a statutory obligation to pay par.

Liability under "trust fund" theory.   In the absence of contractual or statutory liability, early courts devised the theory that the corporation's stated capital (the aggregated par value) was a "trust fund" for creditors. If the corporation went bankrupt and shareholders had not paid full par value, creditors could compel shareholders who received watered stock to ante up the shortfall. The theory, however, was a fiction. No fund or segregated pool of assets existed, and creditors did not have to show they had relied on stated capital. Shareholders were liable to make additional capital contributions even if the creditors had not been misled or had extended credit before shareholders had taken their watered stock.

Liability under "holding out" theory.   Responding to the conceptual deficiencies of the trust fund theory, the *Hospes* court and others adopted a misrepresentation or "holding out" theory. The theory creates a rebuttable presumption that creditors rely on the corporation's stated capital as an implicit representation of the company's creditworthiness. To protect these presumed creditor expectations, the theory relaxes the elements of a common law fraud action. Creditors can recover without showing a misrepresentation of stated capital or their actual reliance on stated capital, but only creditors who extended credit after the watering of the stock and who did not know about it can recover.

Par value is a thorn in the side of corporate planners, and its use is diminishing. Many modern statutes permit shares to be issued without par (RMBCA §2.02(b)(2)(iv)), and low par stock has gained universal acceptance. Although no-par stock avoids the problem of watered-stock liability, limits on distributions to shareholders continue to apply (see Chapter 9).

When stock is issued without par, shareholders are liable to the corporation or its creditors only to the extent they have not paid "the consideration for which the shares were authorized to be issued . . . or specified in their subscription agreement." RMBCA §6.22(a). Liability may be asserted by shareholders on behalf of the corporation in a derivative action or by creditors in insolvency proceedings. Parity among shareholders is dealt with by contract and disclosure requirements, and creditors are protected only after insolvency to the extent shareholders had not paid the contract or authorized price.

Quality of Consideration.   To be "fully paid and nonassessable," stock must also be issued for the proper kind of consideration. Typically, statutes require that stock be issued for money paid, services performed, or tangible or intangible property actually received. The RMBCA broadly permits any "tangible or intangible property or benefit to the corporation." RMBCA §6.21(b).

Many statutes, however, continue to prohibit the use of unsecured promissory notes or promises of future services. MBCA §19. These statutes proceed on the premise that cash in hand is worth more than a promise, and consideration for stock should represent solid assets with realizable value to assure shareholder parity and to provide a measure of creditor protection.

Issuing stock for ineligible consideration can result in two possible things: (1) the stock is treated as not being fully paid, and the shareholder can be assessed for the shortfall as in the case of watered or unpaid stock; or (2) the stock is treated as voidable. Courts differ on whether the choice between the assessment or cancellation remedy belongs to the corporation or the shareholder.

These limitations severely restrict planning flexibility, and the RMBCA eliminates them. The RMBCA requires only that (1) the board determine that the consideration is adequate, §6.21(c); and (2) shareholders are advised before the next shareholders' meeting if shares are issued for future services or promissory notes, §16.21(b). Shareholders are left to their contractual and fiduciary remedies, and creditors are expected to evaluate the soundness of the corporation's business and assets in extending credit.

EXAMPLES

1. The articles of Bacchanalia Banquets, Inc. specify that the common stock has a par value of $5.00 per share. At the beginning of Year 1 the board approves the issuance of common stock for $10 per share. It issues shares as follows: Anna pays $10,000 for 1000 shares; Benny pays $7000 for 1000 shares; and Chris pays $3000 for 1000 shares.
   a. After Year 1 the business is still solvent. Is any shareholder liable? To whom?
   b. After Year 2 the business is insolvent. Is any shareholder liable? To whom?

2. The articles of Bacchanalia Banquets specify that the common stock has no par value. At the beginning of Year 1 the board approves the issuance of 20,000 shares of common stock to Anna and 10,000 to Benny. Anna pays $50,000 in cash, and Benny agrees to work for the corporation for two years. The board values the agreement with Benny at $50,000.
   a. Is Anna liable for having paid $2.50 per share while Benny paid $5.00 per share?
   b. After Year 1 Anna and Benny have a falling out. Using her control position, Anna has the corporation sue Benny to pay for his shares. Can the corporation recover?
   c. In Year 2, Anna and Benny reconcile. Benny has not yet finished his two years of promised service. There is an election of directors, and the board declares dividends on the stock. Can Benny vote and receive dividends on his 10,000 shares?

3. Instead of promising future services, Benny offers a sketchy business plan for his 10,000 shares. He assures the board he will know how to carry it out. The board determines the plan has a value of $50,000 but does not seek an independent valuation. The board issues the shares to Benny and carries the plan on the corporation's financial statements as an asset worth $50,000.
   a. In Year 1 Anna sells some of her shares to David, who later finds out how Benny got his shares. Can David sue to have the shares canceled because Benny paid for them with ineligible consideration?
   b. David is also furious that the board was so naive as to think that Benny's business plan was worth $50,000. David has found a number of experts who say the plan was essentially worthless. Can David sue to have Benny's shares canceled because the board acted improvidently?

c. In Year 3 Benny's business plan fails, and the business becomes insolvent. Creditors sue Benny to compel him to pay for his stock. Is Benny liable?

EXPLANATIONS

1a. Benny and Chris might be liable to the corporation. Even though Anna overpaid for her stock, thus diluting her interest in the corporation, she cannot recover personally. The harm was to the corporation, and she must sue on behalf of the corporation in a derivative suit to recover any shortfall from Benny and Chris.

Anna paid an amount ($10.00 per share) greater than par and equal to the price set by the board. She does not have watered-stock liability.

Benny bought stock ($7.00 per share) above par but below the authorized price. Benny may be contractually liable if he agreed to pay a $10.00 price. Even if there was no contract, some statutes make Benny liable for the difference between the authorized price and the purchase price. See RMBCA §6.22 ("consideration for which the shares were authorized to be issued"); MBCA §25 ("full consideration for which such shares were . . . to be issued").

Chris bought stock ($3.00 per share) below par and below the authorized price. In addition to any contract or statutory liability, Chris may be liable for the difference between the purchase price and par value. Although the RMBCA abandons the notion, par value may have continuing vitality as a matter of charter interpretation. As in this example, par value serves to ensure shareholder parity. RMBCA §6.21(a) states that the powers of the board to issue stock (including to determine what is adequate consideration) "may be reserved to the shareholder by the articles of incorporation." A par value provision in the charter arguably prevents the board from issuing stock below the stated floor unless the shareholders agree to amend the par value provisions.

1b. The liability and theories for recovery are the same as before, but upon insolvency any corporate recovery is for the corporation's creditors.

2a. Without par value, there is no requirement that the board issue stock for a particular price. Even in a par value regime, the board can issue stock (so long as it is above par) for different prices and types of consideration.

Benny may have some protection against the dilutive half-price issue to Anna under federal disclosure rules. Bacchanalia (and Anna) may not mislead Benny about the price or value of his shares, and the dilutive issue to Anna might be considered a material omission entitling Benny to remedies under §12(2) of the Securities Act of 1933 and Rule 10b-5 under the Securities Exchange Act of 1934. See chapters 10 and 29.

2b. It depends on the jurisdiction. Under the RMBCA, Benny's contract for future services constitutes eligible consideration for his shares, and the board's valuation of the contract is conclusive. RMBCA §6.21(b), (c). The RMBCA recognizes that many other contingent assets (such as promissory notes given by others) are eligible, even though they may be equally illusory. If Benny is not performing his contract, any liability to finish paying or to return the shares arises under contract law, not corporate law.

Under other statutes, Benny's promise of future services is considered too uncertain and is not eligible consideration. MBCA §19. The corporation can seek to cancel his shares or assess him for any shortfall in consideration. Cases are split on whether Benny can choose whether to pay or to return the shares. Nonetheless, a good argument can be made that the choice should be the corporation's. If we view his original promise as inadequate, giving him the option to invest at a price he was originally unwilling to pay provides him an investment choice unavailable to the corporation's other investors.

2c. Yes. Benny is a full-fledged shareholder, although (depending on the jurisdiction) the validity of his shares may be subject to attack by the corporation or, upon insolvency, by creditors. Even if Benny's consideration is statutorily ineligible, courts generally view such shares to be voidable, not void.

One way that corporate planners deal with Benny's contingent investment is to set up an escrow arrangement. The shares (and distributions made with respect to the shares) are released from escrow as services are performed under the employment contract. Failure to perform allows the corporation to cancel the shares. See RMBCA §6.21(e).

3a. Probably no. If David sues derivatively on behalf of the corporation to cancel Benny's shares, he will have to argue that the business plan is ineligible consideration under the statute. Under the RMBCA the board can accept any "tangible or intangible property or benefit to the corporation." RMBCA §6.21(b). In jurisdictions that limit eligible consideration, it will be difficult to argue that the business plan should be recharacterized as a promise for future services. Although this argument is plausible, courts increasingly permit greater flexibility in corporate financing. Cases read the prohibition against future services narrowly and have refused to void such transactions when all the shareholders had consented.

3b. No. The board's valuation of the business plan is conclusive under most statutes, absent fraud or bad faith. See Official Comment to RMBCA §6.21(c).

There is nothing to indicate that the valuation was meant to deceive investors or creditors. The board carried it on the company's books, which David could have asked about. Even if the consideration was paltry, the board's valuation should not be lightly disregarded. Only if the directors acted with tainted motives — such as if Benny had bribed them to buy stock for less than fair value — should a court question the board's valuation. Otherwise, it should be unassailable and conclusive.

3c. No. Although upon insolvency creditors can enforce shareholder payment obligations, the creditors will run into the same problems as if the corporation were suing. Without more, the board's valuation is conclusive.

§8.2   Debt Financing

While equity financing is infested with arbitrary and often archaic notions of par value and legal capital, debt financing — borrowing money to finance business operations — is by comparison a model of clarity. A debt security represents the corporation's promise to repay a loan made by the debtholder. The corporation is bound by contract to make payments of principal and interest on a fixed schedule. Corporations can borrow money in many ways — by making short-term commercial notes, taking shareholder loans, accepting bank lines of credit, taking trade creditors' extensions of credit, and issuing debt securities traded in public debt markets.

§8.2.1   Debt Securities

Debt securities include both short-term and long-term debt obligations. Short-term debt (to be paid within a year) usually consists of loans or notes to finance day-to-day operations of the business. Long-term debt is often freely transferable and is a more permanent part of the capital structure. Common kinds of long-term debt securities are bonds (usually secured by specific corporate assets, such as a new hospital wing) and debentures (unsecured debts).

As a general matter, debt securities do not have the participation, voting, conversion, and redemption rights (see §8.1) that constitute the fundamental ingredients of equity securities, but it is possible to incorporate such rights into a debt security. It is not uncommon for a corporation to issue bonds that are convertible at the holder's option into specified equity securities or that are redeemable at the holder's option ("put" bonds). To the extent the debt securities are assigned voting rights, they must be authorized in the articles. Otherwise, the issuance of debt securities (like entering into any other contractual arrangement) is a matter within the board's discretionary power.

§8.2.2   *Leverage*

Using debt to finance the corporation creates *leverage*. Leverage means simply that debt financing is providing some of the capital. The greater the ratio of debt to equity, the greater the leverage. High outside debt financing increases the potential for large returns (and losses) on the insiders' equity investment. Because the debt obligation is fixed, high earnings will produce a high return on equity; low earnings will do just the opposite.

The following two examples illustrate this:

Case 1: Debt-Equity Ratio — 1:1. Assume a total investment of $100,000 in which debt and equity participate equally.

Debt (10% interest rate)	$ 50,000
Equity	50,000
Total investment	$100,000

After one year, assume the following range of earnings on the $100,000 investment, and then subtract the fixed debt obligation to calculate the return on equity.

Earnings	$2,000	$10,000	$20,000
Return on investment	2%	10%	20%
Interest payments (at 10%)	$5,000	$ 5,000	$ 5,000
Return on equity ($)	− $3,000	$ 5,000	$15,000
Return on equity (%)	− 6%	10%	30%

Case 2: Debt-Equity Ratio — 4:1. Assume again a total investment of $100,000, but now debt is four times greater than equity.

Debt (10% interest rate)	$ 80,000
Equity	20,000
Total investment	100,000

Assume the same range of earnings after one year on the $100,000 investment, and then subtract the fixed debt obligation to calculate the return on equity.

Earnings	$2,000	$10,000	$20,000
Return on investment	2%	10%	20%
Interest payments (at 10%)	$8,000	$ 8,000	$ 8,000
Return on equity ($)	− $6,000	$ 2,000	$12,000
Return on equity (%)	− 30%	10%	60%

The different returns on equity shown in these tables demonstrate that greater leverage accentuates both the good and the bad for equity, assuming the debt is from outsiders. The effect of leverage is meaningless if the debt is held by insiders — that is, the same persons who hold the equity. Putting aside any tax effects or the higher priority in insolvency, the *overall* return to insiders who hold debt and equity will be simply the business's return on investment. The financial advantages and dangers of leverage are created by outside debt financing.

Leverage also allows an equity investor to put up less money and still retain full management control of the business. But greater leverage also increases the risk of loss for the debt investor because the equity cushion is proportionately thinner. A highly leveraged company is said to be "thinly capitalized."

§8.2.3 Tax Advantages of Debt

Interest payments by a corporation are tax-deductible; dividend payments are not. I.R.C. §163. Interest deductions keep more money in the corporate treasury and hence out of the public treasury. For this reason, an investor considering whether to make a debt or equity investment will prefer debt, all other things being equal. The IRS is not blind to this tax avoidance preference. Merely characterizing an investment as debt is not enough. The courts use a number of factors to distinguish real debt from equity masquerading as debt. The principal factors are:

(1) *Is there a payment schedule?* Debt must be paid when due; equity payments are never due. Failure to repay obligations as they mature is a sure way to risk losing debt characterization.

(2) *Is the rate of return fixed or does it fluctuate?* Debt is fixed; equity fluctuates. Variable payments are a sign of equity, not debt.

(3) *Are payments made only from earnings?* Debt must be paid, regardless of whether there are earnings; dividends on equity are paid from earnings.

(4) *Do the investors also manage the company?* Investments made by outsiders are easier to characterize as debt than those made by insiders. Inside debt will tend to be viewed as "at the risk of the business," particularly when the debt-equity ratio is high.

(5) *Is the corporation thinly capitalized?* The higher the debt-equity ratio (particularly the ratio of inside debt to equity), the more likely it is that some of the debt will be recharacterized as equity.

The tax effect of recharacterizing debt as equity is twofold: (1) payments to the putative debtholder are not deductible by the corporation, often resulting in back-tax liability; and (2) that part of the payment to the putative debtholder characterized as a return of principal (normally not taxable when received) may be treated as a taxable dividend payment.

§8.2.4 Debt's Priority over Equity

When the corporation becomes insolvent or dissolves, creditors — that is, debtholders — are entitled to payment before equity shareholders. For this reason, investors prefer that their investment be characterized as debt rather than equity.

Courts do not always respect this preference. If the corporation has an insufficient equity cushion to satisfy all inside and outside creditor claims, outside creditors will seek to have the inside debt recharacterized as equity. This is essentially an equitable subordination question (see §7.2), which involves an inquiry into whether there was fraud or a fiduciary breach justifying the recharacterization. Courts also consider factors used in piercing the corporate veil (see §6.2), such as whether the corporation was undercapitalized, whether corporate formalities were followed, and whether the asserted debt was treated as such.

§8.3   Choosing a Debt-Equity Mix

Creating a capital structure — a debt-equity mix — is an art that balances the parties' relative desires:

(1) *Do investors want to participate in profits?* Debt generally does not participate. Equity participates and with different preferences.

(2) *Do investors want control rights?* Debt generally does carry voting rights. Control over management provides protection for equity's last-in-line status.

(3) *Do investors want fixed payments?* Debt must be repaid, with interest. Equity payments depend on earnings, subject to stated preferences.

(4) *Do investors want corporate-level taxes?* Interest payments, but not dividends, are deductible by the corporation. In a flow-through S corporation, shareholders are taxed on corporate earnings, even if the earnings are not distributed.

(5) *Do investors want leverage?* Greater debt levels increase the risks for equity investors as well as debt investors.

(6) *Do investors want priority in insolvency and on dissolution?* Debt and preferred equity have priority when the business is wound up.

Determining the proper mix of common and preferred stock — and their relative voting and participation rights — will be largely a matter of the parties' relative desires and bargaining strength. But if the mix is weighted too heavily toward debt (particularly inside debt), the advantages of tax deductibility of interest payments and debt's priority over equity may be jeopardized.

It might seem that — to a point — debt financing would tend to reduce the cost of capital for a firm. That is, when debt is "cheaper" than equity, a business would do better to issue more debt than equity. A widely recognized thesis (first advanced by two economists, Modigliani and Miller) rejects the view that a firm has an optimal capital structure. Rather, M-M assert that no matter what a firm's mix of debt and equity, the firm's total investment value remains constant. A highly leveraged firm, for example, presents higher risks for equity investors, who demand a higher return on their investment; "cheap" debt thus is offset by the increased cost of "expensive" equity. M-M further assert that whenever the risk-adjusted costs of equity and debt are not the same, investors will buy one or the other to bring them back to equilibrium. More recent economists argue that a number of imperfections distort this theoretical equilibrium: the double taxation of equity dividends, the bankruptcy costs borne by debt of winding up a failed business, the efficiency of monitoring by equity rather than debt, and informational defects in capital trading markets that lead to higher valuation of debt than equity. For each firm, there may indeed be a particular capital structure that is optimal.

EXAMPLES

Lina and Maurice want to start a construction business, which will be incorporated. Lina has equipment (with an appraised value of $60,000) and some cash ($30,000). Maurice has a little cash ($10,000) and will manage the business with Lina. Each wants an equal voice in the company. To reflect her larger contribution, Lina wants a larger return and priority over Maurice. Lina also wants to get her investment back if the business fails, a common occurrence in the construction industry. On one thing the two agree: Lina and Maurice each will receive 10,000 shares of common stock at $1 per share. How should the remaining $80,000 contributed by Lina be handled?

a. If Lina receives an $80,000 unsecured note from the corporation, must this be authorized in the articles of incorporation?

b. What are the advantages and disadvantages of Lina taking an unsecured note for $80,000? Consider the debt-equity ratio.

c. What are the advantages and disadvantages of Lina taking 8000 shares of nonvoting common stock at $10 per share?

d. What are the advantages and disadvantages of Lina taking 800 shares of nonvoting preferred stock at $100 per share?

e. What are the advantages and disadvantages of Lina taking a combination of 300 shares of nonvoting preferred stock at $100 per share and a $50,000 unsecured note? Consider the debt-equity ratio.

EXPLANATIONS

a. No. Only equity securities need be authorized in the articles (see §8.1). The corporation's issuance of debt (its borrowing) is within the discretion of the board of directors. Unless the note calls for voting rights (which notes rarely do), it need not be mentioned in the articles.

b. *Advantages*: Interest on notes is deductible by the corporation, and noteholders are not taxed on repayments of principal; noteholders share with other unsecured creditors on insolvency; debtholders have an enforceable contractual claim to payments of principal and interest; for Maurice, the note will be like outside debt, so that his equity investment will be subject to the upside (and downside) effects of leverage.

Disadvantages: The inside debt-equity ratio is 4:1, and it is possible the IRS might seek to recharacterize the note as a capital contribution, making interest on the note nondeductible and payments to Lina taxable dividends; Lina will not participate in profits to the same relative degree because her return under the note is fixed; Maurice's investment is at greater risk because of the company's heavy debt burden; outside lenders may be reluctant to lend money to a company so thinly capitalized; Lina's claim as an unsecured creditor may be equitably subordinated to those of other unsecured creditors because of the business's thin capitalization.

c. *Advantages*: Lenders will flock to such a well-capitalized company; if the corporation is successful, Lina will participate fully in the success (while she would not in the case of preferred stock or debt).

Disadvantages: Any payments to Lina will be subject to double taxation; Lina will have no assured return (as would be the case for debt); Lina will have no dividend or liquidation preference (as would be the case for preferred stock); Lina will have no priority with or over creditors on insolvency (as would be the case for debt).

d. *Advantages*: Lenders will flock to such a well-capitalized company; Lina will be assured of being paid before Maurice.

Disadvantages: Any dividends paid to Lina will be subject to double taxation; Lina will have no assured return (as would be the case for debt); Lina will have no priority with or over creditors on insolvency (as would be the case for debt); Lina will not participate fully if the company is successful (unless the preferred stock is participating).

e. *Advantages*: With an inside debt-equity ratio of 1:1, the IRS would probably not challenge interest deductibility on the note; Lina probably also would have unsecured creditor status on the note in a bankruptcy or insolvency proceeding; the note would provide Lina enforceable contract rights; Lina would have payment and liquidation preferences over Maurice on both the note and the preferred stock; Lina's assumption of debt gives Maurice some leverage; the capital structure provides lenders a pretty decent equity cushion.

Disadvantages: More debt would have been better, but then more debt would have been less likely to withstand tax and insolvency-priority scrutiny.

9

Limitations on Corporate Distributions

Shareholders, like other investors, expect a return on their investment. The return comes in two forms: market appreciation — an increase in what others are willing to pay for the shares — and distributions from the corporation. When shares appreciate in market value, everyone is happy. Shareholders can sell and earn a favorable return on their investment; purchasers acquire an attractive new investment; the corporation has a healthy market in which to raise new capital; and the corporation's creditors (although not directly affected) are reassured they will be paid. But corporate distributions are a different story. When the corporation declares dividends or otherwise distributes its assets to shareholders, there is a potential conflict between the interests of creditors and the interests of shareholders. Creditors want assurances that no claimants who rank junior to them (shareholders and subordinated debtholders) are paid before them.

In this chapter we describe corporate distributions and the elaborate legal apparatus erected to protect creditors from the risk of shareholders' emptying the corporate treasury.

§9.1 Distributions — Transferring Assets to Shareholders

The corporation can distribute its assets to shareholders in a variety of ways: dividends, capital (or liquidating) distributions, stock redemptions, and corporate repurchases.

119

§9.1.1 Dividends

Dividends are periodic payments by the corporation, usually made in relation to past or current corporate earnings, to shareholders in proportion to their share ownership. In the United States, declaration of dividends — that is, the decision to pay them — generally is within the discretion of the board of directors and protected by the business judgment rule (see §21.3).

Dividends may be paid in cash or property, including the corporation's own shares. A *stock dividend* is the pro rata distribution of additional shares of the corporation among existing shareholders. Its effect is simply to divide ownership among a greater number of shares. (Because no assets are transferred to shareholders, RMBCA §1.40(b) does not treat a stock dividend as a distribution.) As with any issuance of new shares, there must be sufficient authorized but unissued shares for a stock dividend to be declared.

Once the board declares a *cash dividend,* shareholders (as of the record date specified by the board) obtain rights as creditors for the amount of the dividend. The board has no discretion to rescind a cash dividend once declared, unless the dividend is not legally authorized or an intervening catastrophe (such as a fire at the manufacturing plant) makes payment imprudent. Stock dividends, on the other hand, may be rescinded at any time before being issued.

In a *stock split,* outstanding shares are converted into (and replaced by) additional new shares. For example, in a three-for-one stock split each outstanding share is extinguished and replaced by three new shares, which must be authorized. Most corporate statutes allow the board on its own initiative to authorize a stock split, although some also require shareholder approval. From an economic standpoint, a stock split is identical to a stock dividend: Shareholders receive additional shares without paying any consideration to the corporation. But, as we will see, there may be significant differences in how each affects the legal ability of the corporation to pay subsequent dividends.

§9.1.2 Capital Distributions (Partial Liquidations)

Capital distributions are payments made in relation to capital, not earnings. Many statutes, including pre-1980 versions of the Model Business Corporation Act, allow capital distributions in circumstances in which dividends would not be permissible. MBCA §46.

§9.1.3 Redemption and Repurchase

The corporation also can distribute assets to shareholders by acquiring outstanding shares through redemption or repurchase. A *redemption* usually refers to a forced sale initiated by the corporation in accordance with a contract or the articles of incorporation. A *repurchase* is a voluntary buy-sell transaction between the corporation and a shareholder.

Although repurchases were once a great conundrum of corporate law — "How can the corporation buy itself?" — all corporate statutes now recognize the power of the corporation to repurchase its own shares. RMBCA §6.31.

§9.2   Limitations on Distributions

The effect of a corporate distribution, whatever its form, is to transfer assets from the corporation to its shareholders, thus jeopardizing creditor claims. Creditors want to limit distributions to shareholders, while shareholders (standing last in line) want periodic payments to reduce their ultimate risk. The creditors' position is especially unenviable because the power to declare dividends resides with the board of directors, who are elected by and accountable to the shareholders. To protect creditors (and sometimes preferred shareholders) who may be counting on corporate assets to satisfy their claims against the corporation, corporate law imposes a variety of rules for when distributions are legally authorized.

§9.2.1   The "Equity Insolvency" Test

All corporation statutes forbid distributions that would render the corporation unable to pay its debts as they become due in the ordinary course of business. RMBCA §6.40(c)(1). This common-sense "equity insolvency" test is concerned with liquidity — the ability of the corporation to cope with its bills — not the excess of asset value over liabilities. (It is called "equity" because it was a test used in equity courts to determine a debtor's solvency; it should be distinguished from the use of the word "equity" to refer to shareholders' ownership interest.)

In practice, the equity insolvency test reflects what primarily concerns creditors: that the business will not have enough assets after a distribution to pay its debts. The test is similar to that of the Uniform Fraudulent Conveyance Act §4, which deems any transaction without fair consideration to be fraudulent as to a debtor's creditors if it renders the debtor insolvent (see §6.3). Stock dividends are not subject to the equity insolvency test because they do not involve the transfer of cash or other corporate property to shareholders. Stock dividends can be made even when the corporation is insolvent.

§9.2.2   "Balance Sheet" Tests

In addition to the equity insolvency test, nearly all corporation statutes also impose a system of accounting rules to decide when distributions are legally authorized. The rules use accounting entries made on the corporation's balance sheet to test whether specified accounts are sufficiently large for a particular distribution to be made.

Keep in mind that the "balance sheet" tests are completely separate from whether the corporation in fact has the cash or assets to make a distribution. Although courts, lawyers, and law professors often speak of whether dividends or other distributions can "come out" of surplus (or some other account), this is only metaphorical. There is no bank vault into which money is deposited for each account; the balance sheet accounts are merely accounting entries. It is entirely possible that a corporation with a substantial amount in its "earned surplus" account might have no cash and be unable to pay its debts as they come due.

Many of the balance sheet tests continue to use a conceptual framework based on par value (see §8.1.3) to account for capital contributions and earnings of the corporation. These tests — intended to provide creditors with an inviolable financial cushion known as "legal capital" — rely on highly conceptual and often meaningless accounting conventions that often have nothing to do with the economic condition of the corporation. The RMBCA and a growing number of modern state statutes eliminate many of the legal capital concepts — such as par value, stated capital, capital surplus, earned surplus, and treasury stock. But it is small comfort to today's law students that legal capital is on its deathbed. The concept of legal capital survives in many jurisdictions — most notably Delaware — and promises to torment at least one more generation of corporate lawyers.

The Balance Sheet and the "Shareholders' Equity" Accounts.   The balance sheet tests are essentially formulas into which you plug numbers derived from accounting entries on the corporation's balance sheet. Before discussing the tests, we provide a basic primer on balance sheet accounting and the three "shareholders' equity" accounts referred to by the legal capital regime.

A *balance sheet* is an accountant's snapshot of a corporation's financial status at a given moment. One side of a ledger shows the nominal value of the corporation's *assets* (usually based on historical cost); the other side shows the corporation's *liabilities* and the *shareholders' equity*. Shareholders' equity is the amount by which assets exceed liabilities — the corporation's net worth. (In a corporation with one class of stock, the *book value* of each share is shareholders' equity divided by the number of shares.)

Balance Sheet	
Assets	Liabilities
	Shareholders' equity

Whenever an item is entered on one side of the ledger, an equal amount must be entered on the other side — always a balanced sheet. The equation "Assets = Liabilities + Shareholders' Equity" always holds true. For example, if assets increase after a new stock issue, shareholders' equity increases by the same amount; if assets increase when a bank lends the corporation money, liabilities increase; if assets decrease because the firm loses money, shareholders' equity decreases.

The legal capital regime (and the accounting profession) use shareholders' equity accounts to show capital contributions and corporate earnings.

Stated (or paid-in) capital. Equity capital contributions are allocated to the *stated capital* (or *paid-in capital*) account. The amount in this account represents the aggregated par value of the corporation's outstanding equity securities. If there is no par, the board by resolution establishes a "stated value" for each share.

Suppose immediately after its incorporation Corporation X issued 2000 common shares (par $100). According to the legal capital regime, the corporation has $200,000 (2000 times $100) in its stated (or paid-in) capital account. This financial state of affairs can be represented by accounting entries on the balance sheet:

Balance Sheet
(after initial full-par capitalization)

Assets		Liabilities	$ 0
Cash	$200,000		
		Shareholders' equity	
		Stated capital:	$100 ·
		par common, 2000	
		shares	200,000
	$200,000	Total	$200,000

Capital surplus (or paid-in surplus). As we have seen, the corporation can issue low-par stock to avoid exposing shareholders to watered stock liability (see §8.1.3). If the corporation issues low-par stock, the amount paid for the stock in excess of its par value is reflected in the *capital surplus* (or *paid-in surplus*) account. (Modern accountants favor the term "capital contributed in excess of par.")

Suppose Corporation X issues 2000 common shares at a par value of $10. It receives $100 per share, for a total of $200,000. Because assets increase by $200,000, and "stated capital" (the number of shares times par) is only $20,000, a "capital surplus" is created:

Shareholders' equity

Stated capital: $10		
par common, 2000 shares	$ 20,000	
Capital surplus	180,000	
TOTAL	$200,000	

If the corporation issues no-par stock, the full issue price is allocated to stated capital unless the board allocates some to capital surplus. Suppose Corporation X issues 2000 common shares, no-par, for $100 per share (total $200,000), and the board allocates $150,000 to capital surplus:

Shareholders' equity

Stated capital: no-par		
common, 2000 shares		$ 50,000
Capital surplus		150,000
	TOTAL	$200,000

Earned surplus (or accumulated retained earnings).   After its initial capitalization, the corporation's financial affairs do not remain static. If all goes well, assets will increase faster than liabilities, and the business will show a profit; if not, assets will fall faster than liabilities, and the business will show a loss. In either event, adjustments will have to be made in the shareholders' equity accounts. *Earned surplus* (or, among accountants, *accumulated retained earnings*) represents accumulations of earnings (or losses) from earlier periods, less any dividends and other distributions paid in earlier years.

Suppose after one year assets of our Corporation X exceed liabilities by $230,000. Stated capital and capital surplus remain unchanged, and the new surplus in shareholders' equity is reflected as earned surplus:

Shareholders' equity

Stated capital: no-par		
common, 2000 shares		$ 50,000
Capital surplus		150,000
Earned surplus		30,000
	TOTAL	$230,000

Legal Capital Balance Sheet Tests — Dipping into the Shareholders' Equity Accounts.   The legal capital tests limit corporate distributions according to the amounts in the various shareholders' equity accounts. There is no one legal capital test; each depends on the language of the incorporating state's statute.

Surplus (capital impairment) test.   Most statutes allow distributions to come from surplus, which Delaware defines as the amount by which "net assets [assets minus liabilities] exceed capital stock [stated capital]." Del. GCL §§154, 170 (dividends), 160 (repurchases). See also N.Y. BCL §§102(13), 510(b). (Older statutes specified essentially the same test, permitting dividends to the extent "capital is not impaired.") The "capital impairment" test is meant to keep the corporation's stated capital beyond the shareholders' reach on the simplistic assumption creditors will look to it as a measure of how much shareholders have paid into the corporate treasury since the corporation was formed.

Earned-surplus test. Some statutes employ a more demanding test and allow dividends (and corporate repurchases of shares) to come only from earned surplus. Pre-1980 MBCA §45(a) (dividends); MBCA §6 (repurchases). Many of these statutes, however, permit redemptions — forced sales to the corporation — regardless of earnings, a possibility often revealed to creditors in the articles. MBCA §6(d).

Some statutes with earned-surplus tests also permit distributions to come from capital (paid-in) surplus, even when earned surplus is unavailable. Such "capital distributions" are subject to a variety of requirements, among them that they be authorized in the articles of incorporation or by shareholder vote, that there be no unpaid cumulative dividends, that remaining net assets not be reduced below preferred shares' liquidation preference, and that such distributions be identified as coming from capital surplus. MBCA §46.

Nimble dividends. Some statutes allow dividends to come from current earnings, even when surplus (capital or earned) is unavailable. MBCA §45(a) [alternative]. Such dividends are known as *nimble dividends* — current earnings are nimbly applied to dividends rather than to the deficit in the earned-surplus account. Nimble dividends allow corporations with large accumulated deficits and unpaid debts to attract new capital, because these corporations have no chance of obtaining credit. Thus, a deeply indebted corporation that earns a profit in the current year can distribute this profit to its shareholders before repaying its outstanding debts. Nimble dividend statutes offer little or no protection to creditors, and some statutes even allow nimble dividends from earnings of both the current and preceding year. Del. GCL §170(a).

Modern Balance Sheet Tests — Doing Away with Shareholders' Equity Accounts. The RMBCA and a growing number of modern statutes do away with the legal capital concepts of stated capital, capital surplus, and earned surplus — rendering these accounts irrelevant for purposes of distributions. The RMBCA balance-sheet test merely requires that, after a distribution, assets must exceed (1) liabilities plus (2) the total amount that would have to be paid on liquidation to any senior preferred shares. RMBCA §6.40(c)(2). That is, the distribution may not be greater than shareholders' equity less any liquidation preferences. (This test is a strict interpretation of the historical "bankruptcy sense" of insolvency applied by law courts and is sometimes referred to as the bankruptcy insolvency test.)

In 1977 California established the pattern for abolishing concepts of stated capital and surplus. The California statute allows dividends if total assets exceed 125 percent of total liabilities (and "current" assets exceed "current" liabilities) and the payment does not endanger any liquidation preference. Cal. Corp. §§500(b), 502.

Effect of Distribution on Balance Sheet. Normally, a distribution reduces both assets and shareholders' equity, but some transactions require special treatment.

Treatment of stock dividends and stock splits.   Stock dividends increase the number of shares outstanding without affecting the corporation's assets or liabilities. Suppose the following shareholders' equity:

Shareholders' equity		
Stated capital: $100 par		
common, 500 shares		$50,000
Earned surplus		30,000
	TOTAL	$80,000

A stock dividend of one share for each two outstanding will add 250 new shares to the 500 already outstanding. By accounting convention, a stock dividend increases stated capital to reflect the new shares and decreases earned surplus:

Shareholders' equity		
Stated capital: $100 par		
common, 750 shares		$75,000
Earned surplus		5,000
	TOTAL	$80,000

Stock splits, on the other hand, do not affect stated capital or surplus. Structuring the same transaction as a two-for-three stock split will increase the number of shares to 750 and will reduce par to $66.67 (the ratio of the stock split), but it will not affect the shareholders' equity accounts.

Treatment of repurchases and redemptions.   Stock repurchases and redemptions reduce the corporation's assets and shareholders' equity. Under the legal capital regime, shareholders' equity is changed to reflect that repurchased or redeemed stock becomes treasury stock — technically issued, but no longer outstanding. Earned surplus is restricted until treasury stock is either resold, restored as authorized (but unissued), or cancelled. Suppose the corporation *repurchases* 10 shares for $200 per share. Such a $2000 repurchase would change the shareholders' equity shown above:

Shareholders' equity		
Stated capital: $100 par		
common, 550 shares		$55,000
(100 shares in treasury)		
Earned surplus		
Unrestricted	$ 5,000	
Restricted	20,000	
		25,000
Less: 100 shares		
treasury stock		−20,000
	TOTAL	$60,000

Under the legal capital regime, stock *redeemed* pursuant to the articles does not become treasury stock, but instead is automatically cancelled or reverts to the status of authorized (but unissued) stock. The effect is to reduce stated capital by the par (or stated value) of the redeemed stock and to reduce the surplus account, if any, from which the redemption was made.

The RMBCA does away with treasury stock and this elegant silliness — repurchased and redeemed stock reverts to authorized, but unissued, stock. Under the RMBCA, the corporation can reacquire its stock so long as assets exceed liabilities (and any liquidation preferences). RMBCA §6.40(c)(2). For example, if our Corporation X has shareholders' equity of $80,000, it may repurchase up to $80,000 of its stock — regardless of stated capital, capital surplus, earned (restricted or unrestricted) surplus, current earnings, or treasury stock.

§9.2.3 *Manipulating the Balance Sheet to Increase Shareholders' Equity*

Although the balance sheet tests have an air of plausibility, in practice they are porous. Based as they are on accounting entries, they recall the refrain that "figures never lie, but liars figure." By manipulating the amounts recorded as assets, liabilities, or shareholders' equity, it is possible to create legal capital on paper. Whether and when this can be done raises a host of complex accounting issues, many beyond the scope of this book. For example —

On the assets side of the ledger: When should business expenditures be "expensed" and when should they be "capitalized" as an asset? When should historical asset values be adjusted to reflect current market values? When should losses be recognized and written off? Should goodwill be capitalized and treated as an asset? Can research and development expenses be capitalized?

On the liabilities side of the ledger: When should contingent liabilities be recognized and treated as liabilities? How should long-term contingencies (such as pension obligations) be treated? How should debts in foreign currencies be accounted for?

In the shareholders' equity accounts: What should be the effect on stated capital when shareholders receive a stock dividend? What should be the effect of stock that is not fully paid when issued? What should be the accounting for convertible shares (such as $100 par preferred convertible into $1 par common)? What should be the effect of the corporation repurchasing its stock?

We consider only two of the more common methods by which boards can increase distributions to shareholders: (1) "writing up" the value of appreciated assets and (2) reducing stated capital.

Revaluation (or Reappraisal) Surplus.   Because assets must equal liabilities plus shareholders' equity, any upward revaluation of assets increases shareholders' equity. In general, the value assigned to assets shown on the balance sheet is historical cost (less any depreciation), an amount that often will be less than the actual market value of the assets.

Some statutes and court decisions specifically allow good-faith revaluation of assets by the board. RMBCA §6.40(d) ("fair valuation . . . reasonable under the circumstances"); Del. GCL §172; *Randall v. Bailey,* 43 N.E.2d 43 (N.Y. 1942). Some statutes expressly forbid it. If assets are revalued above historical cost, the legal capital regime refers to the surplus account that results as *revaluation surplus.*

Reduction Surplus.   Under the legal capital regime, surplus can be created simply by reducing stated capital and making a corresponding increase in a new surplus account, often known as *reduction surplus.* (Some statutes do not have a separate label for this; they simply add this surplus to capital surplus. MBCA §70.)

Reduction surplus can be created in a number of ways, including: (1) an amendment to the articles of incorporation approved by the shareholders reducing the par value (or stated value) and a board resolution transferring a specified amount from stated capital to reduction surplus (Del. GCL §242); or (2) in the case of no-par stock, a board resolution approved by the shareholders transferring the amount from stated capital to reduction surplus. Some statutes also require the filing of a certificate disclosing such reductions. Del. GCL §§242, 244. Others, however, impose restrictions on using reduction surplus similar to those imposed on stated capital.

§9.2.4   *Timing of Insolvency and Balance Sheet Tests*

Normally, the legality of a distribution is tested at the time the distribution is made, not when the board authorizes it. Cf. RMBCA §6.40(e) (dividends measured on authorization date, unless dividend is to be paid more than 120 days after authorization). Thus, a dividend declared when the corporation is solvent (and has a surplus) cannot be paid if the corporation later becomes insolvent before payment.

This rule creates a problem when the corporation makes a distribution by giving a promissory note that calls for installment payments to the shareholder. In such a case, do the relevant limits on distributions apply when each payment is made or only at the time the note was originally given? Some statutes treat the installment note as an ordinary debt of the corporation if full payment was legally authorized when the note was given. See RMBCA §6.40(f); Del. GCL §160; MBCA §45; *Williams v. Nevelow,* 513 S.W.2d 535 (Tex. 1974). But some courts have held otherwise, subordinating the former shareholder's note to claims of other creditors.

§9.3 Contractual Limitations on Distributions

Given the gaping holes in the legal capital regime, it should not surprise you that creditors and preferred shareholders rarely rely on legal capital when deciding whether to extend credit or to invest their money. Instead, many preferred shareholders and long-term creditors (particularly bank lenders and bondholders) demand contractual limits on dividends and distributions, contained in an indenture agreement or sometimes incorporated into the articles of incorporation.

§9.4 Liability of Directors for Authorizing Illegal Distributions

Corporate distributions involve a conflict between shareholders and creditors, and directors were once strictly liable for approving an illegal distribution. Modern statutes are not as exacting: They impose liability on directors who assent to an illegal distribution only if they did not act in good faith. RMBCA §§8.33(a), 8.30(a). Liability is to the corporation, or to creditors upon dissolution, and is joint and several. Some statutes allow for directors who are held liable to seek contribution from other directors who assented to the illegal distribution and from shareholders who accepted the distribution knowing it was illegal. RMBCA §8.33(b).

Under some statutes, shareholders who receive an illegal distribution may be liable to the corporation, along with directors, if the shareholders knew the distribution was illegal. Cal. Corp. §316. A distribution by an insolvent debtor may also constitute a fraudulent conveyance, allowing creditors to recover from the shareholders directly.

EXAMPLES

1. Bacchanalia Banquets, Inc., has one class of common stock, with 3000 shares authorized and 1500 shares issued and outstanding. The board of directors is considering authorizing a dividend of $1.50 per share.

    a. Bacchanalia's articles of incorporation prohibit total annual dividends greater than $2000 unless approved by a majority of the shareholders. The requirement is not found in New Columbia's statute, which otherwise would authorize the dividend as proposed. Can the board declare the $1.50 dividend?

b. Bacchanalia's shareholders approve the $1.50 dividend, and on September 15 the board fixes a record date of October 1 for the payment of dividends. Benny owns 500 shares of Bacchanalia stock on October 1 but plans to sell his shares to Chris on October 10. Dividends are to be paid on October 31. Who will be entitled to receive the $750 in dividends on these shares?

c. On October 10, after the record date of October 1, the directors learn that the corporation's current earned surplus is smaller than they originally thought. The board rescinds the $1.50 dividend. Do Bacchanalia's shareholders nonetheless have a right to receive the dividend?

2. Bacchanalia is incorporated in New Columbia, a state that still has a legal capital regime and imposes a surplus (capital impairment) test. Bacchanalia's three shareholders, Anna, Benny, and Chris, each plan to contribute $50,000 in cash and assets as the corporation's initial capitalization.

a. Each shareholder receives 500 shares, par $100. What does the corporation's initial balance sheet look like?

b. If there is no other corporate activity, can the board pay dividends? If so, how much?

c. After this initial capitalization, a bank lends the corporation $90,000. What does the balance sheet look like now? Can the shareholders now have the corporation repurchase some of their shares? If so, how much can they be paid?

d. How might Anna, Benny, and Chris provide themselves greater access to the corporation's assets?

3. Suppose Bacchanalia's initial capitalization was $150,000 no-par common. The board allocated $100,000 to capital surplus. In its first year the corporation lost $100,000; in the second year it made $10,000; in the third year it made $55,000; and in the current year there are already $20,000 in earnings. There have been no distributions or other stock issues. As of the end of the last fiscal year, the corporation's assets and liabilities are as follows:

Balance Sheet
(after three years of operations)

Assets		Liabilities	
Cash	$ 10,000	Bank loan	$ 90,000
Accounts		Accounts payable	44,000
receivable	60,000	Total	134,000
Inventory	50,000	Shareholders' equity	
Warehouse	100,000		
Patents	29,000		
	$249,000	Total	$249,000

    a. Compute for the balance sheet the amounts in the shareholders' equity accounts.

    b. Can the board declare a dividend in the form of the right to receive a pro rata amount of the corporation's accounts receivable?

    c. Using this balance sheet, can the board declare a $60,000 dividend? Consider the statutory limits on distributions.

4. Bacchanalia's fortunes continue to rise. Earnings for the fourth year are $60,000.

    a. Using the shareholders' equity accounts in question 3a and assuming no distributions, what would the shareholders' equity accounts look like at the end of four years?

    b. Using this balance sheet, what is the maximum distribution the board can make under an earned-surplus statute that allows for nimble dividends and capital distributions?

    c. Bacchanalia's shareholders want even more. Can they receive a further distribution from stated capital?

    d. Bacchanalia bought a warehouse for $100,000 four years ago. Because of increased land values, the warehouse today is worth $175,000. Does this increase in asset value increase the amount that the corporation can distribute?

5. Anna, one of Bacchanalia's founding shareholders, wants the corporation to repurchase her shares. An investment banker, using the earnings potential of the business, values the corporation at $600,000. Anna wants one-third, or $200,000.

    a. Using the statement of shareholders' equity in question 4d above, what is the book value of Anna's shares?

    b. Benny and Chris, the two other shareholders, are willing to have the corporation borrow $200,000 to fund the repurchase. Would the repurchase be legal under the RMBCA?

    c. The corporation cannot borrow enough money to repurchase Anna's stock, although she is willing to take a note under which the corporation would pay her $50,000 a year for the next five years. Would such payments be legal under the RMBCA?

6. Two years after giving Anna a $250,000 note to buy her shares, Bacchanalia becomes insolvent. The bankruptcy trustee sells the corporation's warehouse for a mere $50,000 and sues Benny and Chris for the distribution to Anna, claiming that their revaluation of the warehouse (writing up the $100,000 cost to $175,000) was improper. The court agrees the revaluation was unreasonable and the distribution illegal.

    a. Are Benny and Chris strictly liable for approving an illegal distribution?

    b. Benny and Chris assert that they relied on an appraiser's report stating that commercial buildings in the area of the warehouse had increased in value by 80 percent since Bacchanalia's original purchase. Is this enough to exonerate them under modern statutes?

 c. If Benny and Chris are liable, how much are they liable for under an RMBCA standard? (Remember that before revaluation, shareholders' equity was $175,000.)

 d. Is Anna liable? To whom, and for how much?

7. The bankruptcy trustee resuscitates Bacchanalia's business. New owners approach a bank for a loan. The bank, wary of porous legal capital protection, demands restrictions on corporate distributions to the new owners. Draft a contractual restriction for the bank.

EXPLANATIONS

1a. No. Even though the dividend is legally authorized by statute, additional restrictions can be imposed by contract or in the corporation's organic documents. The $1.50 per share dividend would result in total dividends of $2250, requiring shareholder approval. In a closely held corporation, shareholders may not want dividends paid because of double taxation (see §2.2.5). It may be desirable for corporate profits to reach shareholders not in relation to share ownership but instead as deductible salaries and other non-share payments.

1b. Benny, as record owner of the shares on the record date of October 1. By setting a record date, the board simplifies the problem of identifying who is paid dividends (see §8.1.2). Because of this rule, sellers in stock sales agreements often will assign to the buyer any unpaid stock dividends.

1c. Probably not, but it might depend on the statute. Although a declared dividend creates an obligation of the corporation to pay, it is weaker than a fixed debt obligation. Courts have allowed corporations to rescind a dividend if the payment would be illegal or if circumstances change.

  Under the RMBCA, the dividend's legality would be determined when it was authorized, if paid (as here) within 120 days. RMBCA §6.40(e)(3). Other statutes are not as precise and may permit the board to rescind a dividend that, although legal when declared, would be illegal when paid — as might happen if the corporation suddenly becomes unable to pay its debts as they come due.

  Even if payment would not be illegal, a court (whether or not in an RMBCA jurisdiction) might well respect the board's good-faith determination to rescind the dividend if there was a valid business purpose. This is consistent with the rule that payment of dividends is within the board's discretion. Nonetheless, shareholders often rely on dividends when they are declared, and this expectation interest might force the board to have a compelling (not just rational) business reason for rescinding a dividend once declared. Although perhaps no longer controlling, early cases state that shareholders acquire rights as creditors once the board declares a dividend.

2a. Remember that "assets = liabilities + shareholders' equity":

Balance Sheet
(after initial capitalization)

Assets		Liabilities	
Cash	$100,000		$0
Other assets	50,000	Shareholders' equity	
		Stated capital: $100	
		par common, 1500	
		shares	$150,000
	$150,000	Total	$150,000

2b. No, even though cash is available. Legal capital would be impaired because net assets minus stated capital equals zero — there is no surplus. Conceivably, noncash assets could be revalued to create a surplus, but it would seem difficult because the board only recently valued them at $50,000 in connection with the initial capitalization.

Stated capital is supposed to represent the long-term investment of shareholders. In theory, stated capital provides creditors the assurance that assets equal to shareholder investment are available to satisfy their claims.

2c. The new liability ($90,000 loan) will be balanced by new assets ($90,000 in cash):

Balance Sheet
(after bank loan)

Assets		Liabilities	
Cash	$190,000		$90,000
Other assets	50,000	Shareholders' equity	
		Stated capital: $100	
		par common, 1500	
		shares	150,000
	$240,000	Total	$240,000

Even though the business is awash in cash, the corporation cannot repurchase any shares. Repurchases generally are subject to the same legal capital limits as are dividends (MBCA §6; RMBCA §1.40(6); Del. GCL §160), and Bacchanalia is in no better "legal capital" shape to make a distribution than it was before the bank loan. Net assets (assets minus liabilities) less stated capital is still zero — there is no surplus.

2d. The three should change the $100 par common to low-par or no-par shares. For example, if the three shareholders approved an amendment to the articles so that par is restated as $1, the shareholders' equity account would look like this:

Shareholders' equity

Stated capital	$ 1,500
Capital surplus	148,500
TOTAL	$150,000

Under a surplus (capital impairment) test, the corporation can now pay *dividends* totaling $148,500. Moreover, even under an earned-surplus statute, the corporation could make a *capital distribution* of $148,500, provided certain formalities were adhered to — although, notably, notice to creditors is not among them. Creditors who naively rely on stated capital as an inviolable equity cushion might be surprised at how easily shareholders can thin the cushion.

The only meaningful protection for creditors is the equity insolvency test, which requires that the corporation after the distribution remain able to meet its debts (such as the bank loan) as they come due.

3a. Most statutes respect the board's allocation of the no-par stock, $100,000 to capital surplus and $50,000 to stated capital. Earned surplus can be calculated: the sum of accumulated earnings for the prior years (a negative $35,000) less any distributions (none). Current earnings will show up once the end-of-year balance sheet is prepared. Shareholders' equity, as of the end of three years, would be as follows:

Shareholders' equity

Stated capital	$ 50,000
Capital surplus	100,000
Earned surplus (deficit)	− 35,000
TOTAL	$115,000

Notice that assets ($249,000) = liabilities ($134,000) + shareholders' equity ($115,000), as must always be the case.

3b. Yes. Dividends can be in the form of cash or other property. The dividend must, however, meet the equity insolvency and relevant balance sheet test.

3c. Whatever balance sheet test applies, corporate statutes uniformly require that the corporation be able to continue to pay its debts as they come due. RMBCA §6.40(c)(1). If the equity insolvency test is met, the legality of the dividend depends on which balance sheet test applies:

Stated-capital test. There is sufficient surplus — capital surplus plus earned-surplus total $65,000. Del. GCL §170.

Earned-surplus test. Earned surplus is negative and therefore not a legal source for dividends. MBCA §45. Nonetheless, under some statutes, the board can declare a $60,000 dividend by calling it a capital distribution. Capital or paid-in surplus ($100,000) can be the source for such a distribution if permitted in the articles or approved by the shareholders. MBCA §46.

Nimble-dividends test. Even though earned surplus is insufficient, the board might be able to declare "nimble dividends" using earnings from both the current year ($20,000) and the previous year ($55,000). Some statutes allow this, Del. GCL §170(a); others limit nimble dividends to the current year's earnings. MBCA §45 [alternative]. As you can see, the exceptions nearly engulf the earned-surplus test.

Modern bankruptcy insolvency test. The board can declare a $60,000 dividend because assets minus liabilities — that is, shareholders' equity — exceeds $60,000, provided the dividend does not endanger any liquidation preference. RMBCA §6.40(c)(2). If, for example, preferred shareholders have rights to receive $70,000 in liquidation, the board could not declare a $60,000 dividend because, after the dividend, assets would be less than the sum of (i) liabilities plus (ii) liquidation preferences ($189,000 is less than $134,000 + $70,000).

4a. The only change is an increase in earned surplus from a negative $35,000 to a positive $25,000:

Shareholders' equity	
Stated capital	$ 50,000
Capital surplus	100,000
Earned surplus (deficit)	25,000
TOTAL	$175,000

4b. The maximum distribution: $125,000. Earned surplus can be a source for $25,000, and capital surplus can be a source for $100,000. Nimble dividends cannot be paid because there is earned surplus.

4c. Yes. Under some statutes, the shareholders could approve a reduction of stated capital. MBCA §69. If shareholders reduce stated capital from $50,000 to $1,000, the excess $49,000 can be added to capital surplus or become reduction surplus (depending on how the statute defined such surplus):

Shareholders' equity	
Stated capital	$ 1,000
Capital surplus	100,000
Reduction surplus	49,000
Earned surplus (deficit)	25,000
TOTAL	$175,000

However described, this additional surplus can be used as a legal source for dividends under a surplus (capital impairment) test or under earned-surplus statutes that allow capital distributions. The effect would be that $174,000 in assets can be distributed to shareholders.

In Delaware the same result could be accomplished if the board approves a corporate repurchase or redemption of shares and reduces capital by the amount represented by those shares. Del. GCL §244(a)(2).

4d. Perhaps, by revaluing the warehouse on the balance sheet. The effect will be to increase shareholders' equity by $75,000, reflected in revaluation surplus:

Shareholders' equity	
Stated capital	$ 1,000
Capital surplus	100,000
Reduction surplus	49,000
Revaluation surplus	75,000
Earned surplus (deficit)	25,000
TOTAL	$250,000

A number of jurisdictions permit use of revaluation surplus as a legal source for distributions. The RMBCA requires that any revaluation be reasonable in the circumstances. RMBCA §6.40(d). This may undermine the creditor-protection policy of the balance sheet tests and deviate from the modern accounting penchant to value assets at historical cost. But revaluation may more accurately reflect present value of the corporation's assets.

5a. The book value of each share is shareholders' equity ($250,000) divided by the number of outstanding shares (1500), or $166.67 per share. Anna's 500 shares have a book value of $83,333.33. It is frequently true that book value is less than appraised (or market) value. Book value represents the amount that would be realized if the business assets were liquidated at historic cost and all liabilities were paid. In a going concern, such as Bacchanalia's catering business, earnings provide a better guide to the value of an ownership interest than do net assets.

5b. Yes, assuming no liquidation preferences and no insolvency. Under RMBCA §140(6), distributions include share repurchases. The repurchase satisfies the RMBCA's bankruptcy insolvency test: assets exceed liabilities by $250,000 (shareholders' equity). RMBCA §6.40(c)(2).

5c. Yes, because there is currently sufficient legal capital, and assuming the corporation will be able to continue to pay its debts. The RMBCA measures the validity of the repurchase when the corporation incurs the debt to Anna, not as of the time each payment comes due. RMBCA §6.40(f). If the business declines, Anna would be in the same position as any other unsecured creditor of the corporation. Her sale of stock moved her residual equity claim ahead in line to that of a debt claim.

In some jurisdictions, the validity of payments for the repurchase of shares is measured at the time of each payment. Thus, if the corporation lacked legal sources or would be rendered insolvent when it made any future payment, Anna's note might be subordinated to other creditors' claims against the corporation.

6a. No, not under most modern statutes. Although some statutes prohibit revaluation surplus, most statutes make directors who approve an illegal distribution liable only if they did not act in good faith. Del. GCL §172 (directors "fully protected in relying in good faith" upon corporate records and professional reports); RMBCA §§8.33(a). This suggests that the presumptions of the business judgment rule apply, and Benny's and Chris's liability may well turn on whether they were personally interested, grossly negligent, or knew the revaluation was unjustified. See RMBCA §8.30(a).

6b. Perhaps. The report will undermine any argument that they were grossly uninformed. Nonetheless, they might still be liable if they stood to gain personally from the repurchase or if they knew the revaluation would seriously weaken creditor claims. It is telling that they did not seek to also sell their shares to the corporation and that the corporation did not become insolvent until two years after the repurchase.

6c. The RMBCA specifies that directors are liable only for the amount of the distribution that exceeds that which could have been distributed legally. RMBCA §8.33(a). (Other statutes are not as clear.) Under the RMBCA standard, a valuation of the warehouse of $100,000 (its historic cost, as opposed to its lower market value) would be consistent with usual "accounting practices and principles." Shareholders' equity (the excess of assets over liabilities) would then have been $175,000. This means $75,000 of the $250,000 distribution to Anna was not from a legal source. Benny and Chris would each be jointly and severally liable for this amount.

6d. In many jurisdictions, Anna is liable if she knew the repurchase was illegal. RMBCA §8.33(b)(2). This is an even more protective standard than applies to directors. Even if Anna sought to protect herself to the detriment of the firm's creditors — arguably not in good faith — Anna would be liable only if she knew that the revaluation was excessive.

Some statutes, such as Del. GCL §174(c) and RMBCA §8.33(b), make shareholders liable in contribution only to directors who are themselves liable for approving an unlawful distribution. Other statutes allow the corporation to recover directly from knowing shareholders. In either case, Anna would be liable in proportion to the amount she received. In our example (according to problem 6.c), Anna would be liable for her share of the excess $75,000.

7. A provision along the following lines could be inserted in an indenture agreement.

Section X. Restrictions on Distributions

(a) The Corporation may not make any distribution in respect of Common Shares, unless the Corporation's annual income in the preceding fiscal year was at least $50,000. If so, distributions are permitted only as follows:

(1) $1.00 per share per fiscal quarter if income for the immediately preceding quarter was at least $10,000;

(2) $1.50 per share per fiscal quarter if income for the immediately preceding quarter was at least $20,000;

(3) $2.00 per share per fiscal quarter if income for the immediately preceding quarter was at least $30,000.

Distributions in excess of $2.00 per share per fiscal quarter are permitted if authorized by the Bank in writing.

(b) For purposes of this section, a distribution is a direct or indirect transfer of money or other property (except the Corporation's own shares) or incurrence of indebtedness by the Corporation to or for the benefit of its shareholders in respect of Common shares. A distribution includes (i) a declaration or payment of a dividend, (ii) a purchase, redemption, or other acquisition of shares, and (iii) a distribution of indebtedness.

(c) The Corporation will cause its articles of incorporation to be amended to contain the restrictions of subsections (a) and (b) of this Section.

Further, the indenture should specify that failing to abide by any of these restrictive covenants will be an "event of default" and that on default the lender may step in to protect its loan.

10

Federal Regulation of Securities Offerings

Corporate investors are protected not only by the undertakings implicit in the corporation's capital structure (see Chapter 8); federal securities law also protects investors by mandating disclosure when the corporation raises capital in public offerings of equity and debt securities. Congress enacted these disclosure requirements in the Securities Act of 1933, as part of the New Deal program to address the perceived causes of the Great Depression. One explanation for the stock market crash of 1929 and the ensuing collapse of the U.S. financial markets was rampant speculation during the 1920s in the stock of new, financially unsound companies. Congress chose a system of mandatory disclosure to investors about new stock offerings as the appropriate antidote.

To ensure adequate disclosure by issuers when they offer their securities, the 1933 Act creates a complex regulatory structure. This chapter gives an overview of the act's significant elements:

- registration and disclosure requirements (§10.1), as well as the principal exemptions from these requirements (§10.2);
- civil liability for violating the registration requirements and for making false or misleading statements in a securities sale (§10.3); and
- definition of a security — the linchpin on which the registration, disclosure, and liability provisions all hinge (§10.4).

The Securities Act of 1933 is different from the Securities Exchange Act of 1934, which deals primarily with stock *trading* — that is, the buying and selling of securities after their original issuance — and the regulation of securities professionals and organized stock markets. Ongoing disclosure is

139

required under the 1934 Act by "public" or "reporting" companies — companies with more than 500 shareholders and $5 million in assets (see §19.3.1).

§10.1   The 1933 Act's Disclosure Mandate

§10.1.1   *Public Offerings — Issuers, Underwriters, Dealers, and Investors*

To understand the 1933 Act's operation, it is necessary to have some understanding of the way in which securities are generally sold to the public. In a typical "firm commitment" public offering, the marketing of securities occurs much as the marketing of most consumer products. The securities are created by the issuer (the manufacturer), which sells them to "underwriters" (wholesalers), which in turn sell them to "dealers" (retailers), which then sell them to investor-shareholders (consumers). The process of getting securities from the issuer to the investing public is known as a *public distribution*.

The issuer can be any person or entity selling an investment interest — usually it is a corporation selling equity or debt securities. Underwriters and dealers are generally securities firms, which specialize in evaluating, recommending, buying, and selling securities. Well-known securities firms involved both in the business of underwriting (known as "investment banking") and the retail business include such firms as Merrill Lynch and Shearson Lehman. Sometimes securities firms act as agents for sellers and investors; when acting in this capacity they are known as "brokers." Investors come in many sizes and varieties. Some are unsophisticated grandparents; others are enormous pension funds with sophisticated investment counselors.

§10.1.2   *Registration and Mandated Disclosure — The Broad Prohibitions of §5*

The 1933 Act accomplishes its purpose of full disclosure to investors in public offerings principally by requiring the filing and dissemination of disclosure documents. The centerpiece of the 1933 Act is §5, which broadly prohibits the sale of *any* security using the mails or other interstate means of communication unless (1) the issuer has filed a disclosure document (known as a "registration statement") with the Securities and Exchange Commission (SEC), and (2) the registration statement has become effective.

Section 5 also requires that investors receive specified information contained in a disclosure document, known as a "prospectus." The prospectus forms the main part of the registration statement and contains information about the company, its financial performance, its management, its capital structure, the securities being offered, and the purpose of the particular offering.

§10.2 Exemptions — Tempering the Breadth of Section 5

Extremely broad exemptions temper the enormous sweep of §5's prohibition against unregistered securities sales. Market trading, nonpublic offerings, intrastate offerings, and certain small offerings all are exempted from the registration and mandated disclosure requirements of the 1933 Act. Registering securities for public sale is expensive and intrusive and, for most securities lawyers, helping clients avoid the act's coverage is a more significant part of practice than helping them comply with the act's registration and disclosure requirements. None of the exemptions discussed below, however, exempts sellers from the antifraud provisions of either the 1933 Act or the 1934 Act (in particular, Rule 10b-5; see Chapter 29).

§10.2.1 Intrastate Offerings

To permit local offerings that could be regulated by state securities law, Congress exempted from the registration and disclosure requirements of the 1933 Act any offering made and sold only to residents within a single state. §3(a)(11). The exemption is narrow and strict, and relying on it is risky:

(1) *The issuer must reside in and be doing business in the state of the offering.* A corporation "resides" in the state of its incorporation. An issuer "does business" in a state if its revenues, assets, and principal office, as well as use of the proceeds of the offering, are principally in-state.

(2) *The offering can be made only to in-state residents — actual residence and domiciliary intent controls.* The statutory exemption is lost if any sale *or* offer (even one that does not result in a sale) is made to an out-of-state resident. The exemption is also lost if any in-state purchaser acts as an underwriter by purchasing securities with a view to offering them or reselling them to out-of-state investors; the issuer cannot rely on representations by in-state purchasers.

(3) *The intrastate offering cannot be part of a larger offering in which there are out-of-state investors.* Sales of securities that are close in time and have similar purposes may be *integrated*, requiring that all sales satisfy the statutory exemption.

The SEC has attempted to clarify and ease some of these requirements in Rule 147, one of its many exemptive "safe harbor" rules under the 1933 Act. Rule 147 qualifies the issuer if at least 80 percent of the issuer's revenues, assets, and proceeds are in-state; it defines residence without reference to domiciliary intent; it allows resales to out-of-state investors beginning nine months after the initial offering; it forgives offers by in-state purchasers to out-of-state residents so long as the offer does not result in a sale during the nine-month holding period; it clarifies when an intrastate offering is considered part of a larger offering. But, as with the statutory exemption, any sale to an out-of-state investor or resale by an in-state purchaser to an out-of-state investor during the nine-month holding period destroys the entire exemption.

§10.2.2   Nonpublic (Private) Offerings

One of the most important 1933 Act exemptions for securities offerings is the "private placement" exemption of §4(2). The 1933 Act exempts any offering "by an issuer not involving any public offering." Without it, virtually every effort to raise capital, regardless of who the investors are, would be subjected to the expense and burden of the Act's registration and disclosure process.

The private-placement exemption exists in two forms: (1) the statutory exemption that provides a complete exemption from the disclosure and registration requirements of the 1933 Act, and (2) a regulatory exemption (Rule 506 of Regulation D) created by the SEC to provide greater certainty to issuers but that sometimes compels disclosure to given investors.

Section 4(2) Statutory Exemption.   Courts have interpreted the §4(2) statutory exemption to be available if the offering meets the following criteria:

(1) The securities can be sold only to investors who are "able to fend for themselves."   Each investor must meet a sliding-scale test that factors both her ability to evaluate the investment (given her business and investment sophistication) and the availability of information (based on both her access to it and its actual disclosure). The less sophisticated the investor, the more disclosure required; the more sophisticated the investor, the less disclosure required. If *all* the investors meet the test, mandated disclosure is unneeded. But if *any* investor fails to meet the test, the exemption is lost for all.

In *SEC v. Ralston Purina Co.,* 346 U.S. 119 (1953), the Supreme Court defined the scope of the §4(2) exemption. The case involved Ralston Purina's policy of selling its stock to employees who on their own initiative sought to buy the stock; hundreds of employees in a variety of positions in the company (chow-loading foreman, stock clerk, stenographer) had purchased unregistered stock. The Court held that the exemption applies when the offerees and investors, regardless of how many there are, are "able to fend for themselves." The Court gave as an example "executive personnel" with access to the same kind of information as would be available in a registration statement. In the case, many of the employees lacked this access, and the Court held that registration under the Act was required.

(2) The securities cannot be resold in a secondary distribution to investors who lack the requisite sophistication and access to information. The §4(2) exemption is lost if qualified purchasers in a private placement turn around and resell the securities to investors who cannot "fend for themselves." For this reason securities sold in a private placement are known as *restricted securities,* and issuers will often seek to preserve their exemption by placing contractual restrictions on the transferability of the securities. Transfer limits are noted on the security certificates, and the issuer will instruct any transfer agent (usually a bank that keeps records on shareholder ownership) not to record any transfer unless it is shown that the resale is not subject to the act's registration requirements.

(3) The securities can be offered only to those with the requisite sophistication and access to information. An *offer* to just one unqualified investor (or to the public at large) causes the entire exemption to be lost.

There is no numerical maximum either on the dollar size of a private offering or the number of offerees and purchasers. In fact, it is not uncommon for issuers to use the §4(2) statutory exemption for private placements that raise many millions of dollars and are sold to hundreds of sophisticated institutional investors. Nonetheless, the larger the group to whom offers or sales are made, the more likely that some will not meet the sophistication and information requirements, thus putting the entire exemption at risk.

Regulation D — SEC Regulatory Exemption. The SEC has created a set of rules under the 1933 Act, known as Regulation D, or affectionately as "Reg D," which (1) provides detailed guidance on when an offering qualifies for the private placement exemption of §4(2) (Rule 506), and (2) contains exemptions for "small offerings" as authorized by §3(b) of the 1933 Act (Rules 504 and 505).

The exemptions under Reg D's Rules 504-506 turn on

- the dollar amount of the offering,
- the number and kinds of investors (as opposed to offerees) who participate in the offering,
- whether the Reg D offering is part of a larger offering,
- the kind of advertisement used,
- the kind of information provided investors.

Regulation D exempts three categories of offerings, subject to certain conditions that the SEC periodically revises. The discussion below represents conditions as of 1993:

Rule 504 — small offerings subject to state blue-sky law. Nonpublic companies can sell up to $1 million in securities in any one year. There is no limit on the number or kinds of investors. The issuer may use general advertising and solicitations, and there are no restrictions on resales.

This broad exemption for small offerings is based on the assumptions that state securities laws will provide sufficient protection to investors and that the burden of SEC regulation is unwarranted.

Rule 505 — medium-sized offerings subject to SEC conditions. Companies, regardless of their size, can sell up to $5 million in any one year. No general advertising or solicitations may be used. The offering can be made to an unlimited number of "accredited" investors, but to no more than 35 "nonaccredited" investors. All nonaccredited investors must receive specified written disclosure and an opportunity to ask questions of the issuer. Securities acquired pursuant to this exemption become "restricted securities."

Rule 506 — private offerings subject to SEC safe-harbor conditions. Companies can sell an unlimited amount of securities under the same conditions as Rule 505, with one additional condition. If any sale is made to nonaccredited investors, the issuer must reasonably believe that each nonaccredited investor (alone or with her purchaser representative) has knowledge and experience in business and financial matters so that she can evaluate the merits and risks of the investment. Securities acquired pursuant to this exemption become "restricted securities."

The Rule 505 and Rule 506 exemptions thus depend on whether particular investors are accredited and how many are nonaccredited. Rule 501 of Reg D defines various categories of accredited investors, which include:

- *institutional investors* — banks, savings institutions, brokerage firms, insurance companies, mutual funds, and certain ERISA employee benefit plans;
- *big organizations* — tax-exempt organizations and for-profit corporations with more than $5 million in assets;
- *key insiders* — the directors, executive officers, and general partners of the issuer;
- *fat cats* — individuals who (along with a spouse) have a net worth of over $1 million;
- *doctors* — individuals who have an annual income of $200,000 (or $300,000 with a spouse);
- *sophisticated trusts* — trusts that have over $5 million in assets and are run by someone with the knowledge and experience to evaluate the merits and risks of the investment.

Reg D assumes that investors falling into these categories either have the sophistication to fend for themselves or the financial resources to seek the help of a sophisticated investment advisor.

Reliance on any of the Reg D exemptions requires that notice be filed with the SEC within 15 days after the first sale. Rule 503(a). Even if an issuer fails to comply with Reg D, the exemption is not lost if the issuer shows that the failures are insignificant. The issuer must show (1) the noncompliance did not undermine the protection available to the particular investor seeking to avoid the exemption; (2) the noncompliance did not involve the ban on general solicitations, the Rule 504 and 505 dollar limits, or the Rule 505 and 506 limits on the number of nonaccredited investors; and (3) the issuer made a good-faith and reasonable attempt to comply with the rule. Rule 508(a).

§10.2.3 Small Offering Exemptions

Under §3(b) of the 1933 Act, the SEC has authority to exempt offerings of less than $5 million. In addition to Reg D's exemptions in Rules 504 and 505, the SEC has adopted Regulation A pursuant to this authority, which exempts offerings of up to $1 million provided the issuer follows a simplified registration-type process. The SEC revised the exemption in 1992 to permit the use of a simplified question-and-answer disclosure document.

An exemption under §4(6) of the 1933 Act also is available for offerings of less than $5 million if made *only* to accredited investors, provided there is no general advertising or solicitations. Only a very small number of sales exempted by §4(6) are not also exempted by Reg D's Rule 505.

§10.2.4 Exemption for Postdistribution Market Trading

Ordinary trading transactions — such as on stock exchanges or between investors — are exempted from the 1933 Act's registration and disclosure requirements. Under §4(1) the exemption extends to any transaction by a person *other than* an issuer, an underwriter, or a dealer (during the initial distribution of an offering). The effect of this exemption — along with the exemptions for postdistribution market transactions by dealers in §4(3) and for broker transactions in §4(4) — is that only transactions that are part of the *distribution* of securities are subject to the Act's registration and disclosure requirements.

Defining a Distribution. The §4(1) exemption has some hidden catches because of the way the Act defines a statutory "underwriter." An underwriter is defined under §2(11) to include any person —

(1)   who purchases shares from an issuer "with a view to" their further distribution;

(2)   who offers or sells shares "for an issuer" in connection with a distribution;

(3)   who purchases shares from a *control person* "with a view" to further distribution;

(4)   who offers or sells shares for a *control person* in connection with a distribution.

A control person is anyone who because of his position or shareholdings has access to confidential corporate information and the power to have the corporation register shares under the 1933 Act.

As a result of this definition of "underwriter," the distribution of securities becomes a surprisingly broad concept. The §4(1) market trading exemption does not apply to a shareholder who owns *restricted securities* (see §10.2.2 above) and resells them into a public trading market. If the securities were purchased with "a view to public distribution," their resale in a public trading market is known as a *secondary distribution,* and the selling shareholder is deemed a statutory underwriter. The holder of restricted shares must wait until the shares have "come to rest" with him, so their subsequent resale is not viewed as part of a distribution.

In addition, sales by a *control person* into a public trading market with the assistance of another person, such as a brokerage firm, are treated as issuer distributions. Under §2(11), the brokerage firm becomes a statutory underwriter, and the control person's sale is a nonexempt transaction. To prevent abuses by control persons, whose unregistered sales pose the same dangers as sales by an issuer, the §2(11) definition forces controlling shareholders and executives to have the corporation register their shares before selling them in a public trading market.

Rule 144 — A Safe Harbor.   Under the SEC's Rule 144, secondary distributions and sales by control persons into public markets are permitted without violating the registration requirements if each of the following conditions is met:

(1)   Current public information about the issuer must be available. Rule 144(c).

(2)   The seller must have held the securities for at least two years after they were purchased. Rule 144(d).

(3)   The securities must be sold through a broker who receives no more than a normal commission and does not solicit orders. Rule 144(f).

(4)   The seller must "trickle" the securities into the market; no more than 1 percent of the issuer's outstanding securities or the average weekly trading volume (whichever is greater) may be sold in any three-month period. Rule 144(e).

(5) The seller must give notice to the SEC whenever more than 500 shares are sold or the sales price exceeds $10,000. Rule 144(h).

There are a couple important exceptions to these conditions. A control person who does not hold restricted securities is not subject to the two-year holding period. Rule 144(d)(1). A noncontrol holder of restricted securities who has held them for *more than three years* may sell without condition. Rule 144(k).

For control persons, Rule 144 is the exclusive means by which they can sell their stock into a *public* trading market without registration. Noncontrol holders of restricted securities who sell into a public trading market can either use Rule 144 or argue that their shares had "come to rest" and had not been acquired with a view to public distribution.

EXAMPLES

1. Adam, Boone, and Carver are friends, ardent outdoorsmen, and weekend chefs. They fix on a new concept in dining — a rustic outdoor restaurant offering a menu that includes muskrat steaks, squirrel sausage, and hickory ale. They form Outdoor Cafes, Inc., incorporated in the state of Mayflower, to operate the business in Mayflower. Each invests $100,000 and receives 100,000 shares of stock. Adam will manage the restaurant; Boone and Carver will be passive investors.
   a. Has Outdoor Cafes violated §5 by issuing stock to Adam, Boone, and Carver?
   b. Adam and Boone are Mayflower residents; Carver lives in the adjoining state of New Columbia, though he covenants to be subject to Mayflower jurisdiction. Is Outdoor Cafes's issuance of stock exempted from registration by §3(a)(11)?
   c. After learning that Carver is from New Columbia, Adam and Boone decide that each will buy $150,000 of stock and then resell $50,000 of stock to Carver. Is the intrastate offering exemption available, and does Rule 147 help?
   d. Adam has little wealth but some experience running an eating establishment. Boone is a well-to-do physician who enjoys hunting and investing in start-up restaurants. Carver is a struggling securities lawyer who, while waiting for work to pick up in New Columbia, makes ends meet with his modest investment portfolio. Is the issuance of Outdoor Cafes stock to them exempted from registration by §4(2)?

2. After five years Outdoor Cafes becomes a success and opens new restaurants throughout New England. Adam, Boone, and Carver figure that they will need to raise about $3 million for their plans. The company will issue 300,000 new shares ($10 each) not only to sophisticated investors (known as *venture capitalists*) who look for these kinds of start-up companies, but also to some of the three founders' personal and

147

business acquaintances. Many of the prospective investors will be from outside Mayflower.

a. Can Outdoor Cafes rely on the statutory §4(2) exemption?

b. Outdoor Cafes expects to raise the $3 million by selling to about 40 investors: Ten each have a net worth of over $1 million; another ten have incomes of over $200,000; another ten are intimately familiar with the restaurant business; the last ten are relatives of Adam, Boone, and Carver. Can Outdoor Cafes rely on any of the exemptions of Regulation D? Which ones?

c. Zeb, who knows Adam because they have gone on hunting trips together, is a cross-country truck driver with minimal investment and business experience. He nonetheless has a net worth of $750,000. Can Outdoors Cafe sell stock to Zeb under Rule 506?

3. Outdoor Cafes uses Rule 505 to avoid the 1933 Act's registration requirements.

a. It places an advertisement in *Outdoor Life,* a national publication, soliciting interest in the company's offering. No sales are made through this advertisement except to accredited investors. Is the advertisement permitted?

b. Adam, Boone, and Carver talk to Jane, who works for an investment firm that advises start-up businesses on how to raise money from venture capitalists. She agrees to help in the offering, and the investment firm's next mailing to its venture capitalist clients includes a reference to the Outdoor Cafes offering. Is this mailing permitted?

c. Adam, Boone, and Carver send a total of 60 letters to squirrel sausage-loving friends and acquaintances who in the past have inquired about investing in their business. Of those who receive the letters, 50 do not satisfy the definition of an accredited investor. Is this mailing permitted?

d. Adam, Boone, and Carver have identified exactly 35 nonaccredited friends and family members who are interested in buying stock. The men also consider whether to sell to Michelle, a Hollywood producer, who has a current personal net worth of over $2 million but who has fallen on hard times. Michelle has not earned a dime for the last two years and is quickly squandering her fortune. Can they sell to Michelle?

4. The Outdoor Cafe issue takes place under Rule 505 in July 1994 and is a complete (and legal) success.

a. In December 1994 Michelle, who purchased 10,000 shares, wants to sell 5000 to her gardener, George. Can Michelle sell?

b. In December 1994 Michelle wants to sell her 10,000 shares to Adam, who is still the company's president. Can Michelle sell?

    c. In December 1996 Michelle wants to sell 5000 shares to George, her still unsophisticated gardener. Outdoor Cafes is still owned by only 50 shareholders and does not make public reports of its financial condition. Can Michelle sell?

5. In August 1997 Outdoor Cafes makes a public, registered offering of 1 million shares of its stock. After this registered offering, a trading market in Outdoor Cafes stock develops and Outdoor Cafes becomes subject to and complies with the periodic reporting requirements of the Securities Exchange Act of 1934 (see §19.3.1). The price of Outdoor Cafes's stock rises from its initial public offering price of $20 to $28 in March 1994.

    a. Adam, who acquired his stock in 1988, wants to sell 20,000 of his 100,000 shares through his stockbroker at the current market price. Can he?

    b. Michelle, who purchased 10,000 shares pursuant to Rule 505 in 1994, wants to sell immediately all of her shares through her broker. Can she?

EXPLANATIONS

1a. Possibly. It depends on (1) whether the mails or other interstate means of communication were used during the issuance, and (2) whether there is an exemption. It is virtually impossible to avoid using the mails in a securities transaction. If the parties transact a check, which will be cleared through the mails, §5 prohibits the sales to Adam, Boone, and Carver unless Outdoors Cafes registers the stock with the SEC or there is an exemption. To know whether an exemption applies, we must know much more.

1b. No. The intrastate offering exemption requires that each investor be from the same state as the issuer — in this case, Mayflower. Because Carver is a New Columbia resident, regardless of any representation or covenant to the contrary, the entire offering (including the sales to Adam and Boone) fails the intrastate offering exemption.

1c. No, under the statute; perhaps, under the safe-harbor rule. The statutory exemption is not available because Adam and Boone purchased their stock "with a view" to reselling to an out-of-state resident. See 1933 Act §2(11). They become statutory underwriters, and their resales to Carver — no matter when they occur — would be viewed as part of the original distribution, thus disqualifying the entire offering under the statutory §3(a)(11) exemption.

    If Adam and Boone held on to their stock for nine months despite their resale intention, Rule 147 would provide a safe harbor for their resales. But there is a twist. If Carver had agreed to this arrangement from the outset, it might be possible to characterize his original agreement as one to purchase from the company through Adam and Boone. If so, it would be an out-of-state sale, occurring during the nine-month holding period.

1d. Probably. The nonpublic offering exemption of §4(2) requires that each investor meet a sliding-scale test that factors in both their ability to evaluate the investment and the availability of information (both their access to it and its actual disclosure). As manager of the business, Adam would seem to satisfy the test because his business knowledge and access to inside information makes him able to fend for himself.

Boone and Carver may also qualify. Their status as "weekend chefs," their personal relationship to Adam (and hence their indirect access to investment information), their investing experience, and their wealth (and hence their ability to bear the risk and to afford sophisticated representation) indicates they are able to evaluate (or have someone else evaluate) the investment and its risks. Nonetheless, if either Boone or Carver fails the test, the private-offering exemption is lost as to the whole issue.

2a. Probably not. The statutory exemption is risky. If any purchaser *or person to whom an offer is made* fails to satisfy the investor qualification test, the entire exemption is lost. It seems likely that at least some of the personal and business acquaintances do not satisfy the standards, in which case the entire statutory exemption would be lost.

2b. Yes. Rule 505 allows for issues of up to $5 million each year; Rule 506 has no dollar limit. Because Outdoor Cafes plans to raise more than $1 million, Rule 504 is unavailable. Both Rules 505 and 506 allow for the sale to up to 35 nonaccredited investors. Twenty of the investors (the millionaire "fat cats" and $200,000 "doctors") are accredited under Reg D and do not count against this limit. The other twenty, on the facts, are nonaccredited. If any sales are made to these nonaccredited investors, they must be provided with specified disclosure, often known in a Reg D offering as an "investment circular."

2c. Probably not, unless Zeb has an investment representative. Rule 506 presents a significant disadvantage compared to Rule 505. The issuer must reasonably believe that each nonaccredited investor (alone or with his purchaser representative) has knowledge and experience in business and financial matters so he can evaluate the merits and risks of the investment.

Because its source is the small-offering exemption of §3(b) of the 1933 Act, Rule 505 has no such requirement, unlike Rule 506, which is a safe-harbor rule for the private-offering exemption of §4(2).

3a. No. General advertising is not allowed under a Rule 505 or 506 offering. See Rule 502(c). The idea is that information about the offering should be controlled to prevent the market from being softened or Reg D being used to sell speculative schemes, which generally depend on widespread advertising or solicitations.

3b. Yes. Inclusion in a mailing to venture capitalists *who are clients of the firm* is not a general solicitation. According to the SEC, if the issuer or its representative has a "preexisting relationship" with the solicited investors, it is not a general solicitation. Those who receive the mailing have shown an interest in such investments; Jane is not softening the market or widely touting a speculative scheme; and many of the recipients will probably qualify as accredited investors.

3c. Probably not. This mailing does not seem to be a general solicitation because it is directed to those who had before expressed an interest in buying the company's stock — a "preexisting relationship." There seems little risk of creating a "speculative mania." Further, Rules 505 and 506, unlike the §4(2) statutory exemption, allow offers to nonaccredited investors as long as the final number of nonaccredited *purchasers* does not exceed 35. Unlike the statutory exemption, an offer to nonaccredited investors (even if they have no investment representative when they receive the offer) does not undermine the Reg D exemption.

3d. Yes. Rule 505 (like Rule 506) places no limit on the number of *accredited* investors who can purchase under the rule. Michelle satisfies the Reg D criteria for a "fat cat" — a person whose personal net worth exceeds $1 million. Even though she may not be able to appreciate the investment or its risks and would not meet the sophistication requirements of Rule 506 if she were unaccredited, this makes no difference because she fits one of the "accredited investor" categories. Reg D is a safe harbor.

4a. Almost certainly no. All securities acquired under Rule 505 are treated as restricted securities and cannot be sold unless their resale is itself registered or an exemption is available. See Rule 502(d). But no exemption seems to be available. The intrastate offering exemption of §3(a)(11) and the private placement exemption of §4(2) are available only to issuers, and Michelle would not be selling for the issuer when she resells to George.

The market trading exemption of §4(1), which at first blush seems might apply, is unavailable because Michelle is probably a statutory underwriter. The definition of an underwriter includes anyone who buys stock "with a view" to its distribution to the public. Because of the short time she has held the securities, Michelle probably will be viewed as having purchased her shares with a view to reselling them. The sale to George is a public "distribution" because George does not appear to be an investor who can fend for himself.

4b. Probably. The market trading exemption of §4(1) seems to apply. In her sale to Adam, Michelle fails the definition of a statutory underwriter. Although her quick resale to Adam might indicate that she purchased her shares with a view to their resale, the sale is not a *public* "distribution" that the 1933 Act is meant to regulate. Adam qualifies as an investor who can fend for himself, and Michelle's sale to Adam would not be a "transaction by an issuer, underwriter or dealer" and thus would be exempt under §4(1).

4c. Perhaps. The market trading exemption of §4(1) depends on Michelle's intentions when she originally bought the stock. If Michelle originally purchased with "a view to" reselling them, they remain restricted. Any sale to an unsophisticated investor (or in a public market) would be a prohibited public distribution no matter how long Michelle holds on to the shares. Nonetheless, original intentions are rarely clear. Michelle has held the stock for more than two years, negating a resale intention. Securities lawyers would say that the stock had "come to rest" with Michelle, and she may now resell without being considered a statutory underwriter.

The safe harbor of Rule 144, however, is not available, even though Michelle has held her "restricted shares" for more than two years. The issuer Outdoor Cafes does not make information about itself available to the public — one of the Rule 144 requirements.

5a. Yes, but he must comply with the conditions of Rule 144. As a control person, Adam cannot sell into a public stock market using an intermediary unless he complies with the conditions of Rule 144. He must "trickle" his stock into the market — selling no more in any three-month period than 1 percent of Outdoor Cafes's outstanding shares or its average weekly trading volume. Because he will sell more than 500 shares, Adam must also provide notice to the SEC. Otherwise the conditions of Rule 144 appear to be met: Current public information about Outdoor Cafes is available, and Adam has held his "restricted stock" for more than two years.

5b. Yes. Rule 144 permits noncontrol holders of "restricted stock" to resell without conditions if they have held their stock for more than three years. Michelle is not subject to any "trickle" or filing requirements.

§10.3 Civil Liability under the 1933 Act

Civil liability under the 1933 Act is structured along three themes:

(1) Protecting the integrity of the act's mandatory disclosure system by allowing investors to rescind their investment if there was any violation of the §5 registration and disclosure requirements. §12(1).

(2) Imposing broad liability on specified participants for misrepresentations in *registered* offerings, thus providing protection to investors

and creating incentives for full and honest disclosure in the registration statement. §11.

(3) Imposing liability on "sellers" for misrepresentations in unregistered securities offerings, whether or not exempt from registration, §12(2), and imposing broad liability enforced by the SEC for misrepresentations in any offering, registered or exempt. §17.

Sale of unregistered securities in violation of §5, or the fraudulent sale of securities, is also subject to administrative and criminal sanctions.

§10.3.1 Section 12(1) — Rescission for Violations of §5

Section 12(1) is a simple and powerful provision to enforce the registration and prospectus dissemination requirements of §5. A purchaser of a security may rescind the transaction and get her money back with interest (or to recover damages if she has resold the stock) whenever the stock was offered or sold in violation of §5. Section 12(1) imposes strict liability for violations of §5 and represents a significant private enforcement tool against the sale of unregistered securities for which no exemption applies.

§10.3.2 Section 11 — Damages for Deceptive Registration Statements

Section 11 allows the purchaser of a *registered* security to recover damages from the issuer and others involved in the distribution of the securities if the registration statement contains any falsehoods or half-truths concerning any material fact — that is, one that a reasonable investor would consider important in deciding to invest. Section 11 creates a complex liability scheme that specifies enumerated defendants, convoluted "due diligence" defenses, limits on damages, allocation of liability among defendants, intricate rules for computing damages, and a carefully crafted limitations period. We discuss only who may be sued, the elements of liability, and the "due diligence" defenses.

Section 11 Defendants. As we have seen, the public offering of securities generally takes place in much the same way as the distribution of a consumer product — from issuer (or manufacturer) to wholesaler, retailer, and final customer. Just as modern products liability law cuts through old privity requirements, §11 specifies a list of potential defendants, many of whom will not be in a privity relationship with the purchasing investor: the issuer, directors, officers who signed the registration statement, the underwriters of the offering, and any expert whose opinion is used in the registration statement (for example, an accounting firm that audited the company's financial statements). Section 11 is purposefully meant to put fear in the hearts of potential defendants in hopes of creating a diligent group of watchdogs to ensure full and honest disclosure for investors.

Section 11 Expansion of Common Law Fraud Rules.   Section 11 changes the common law fraud and contract rescission rules in a number of important respects:

(1) There is no privity requirement.   A shareholder who purchases stock that is part of a registered offering can sue any of the specified defendants regardless of whom the shareholder purchased from.

(2) The shareholder can make out a prima facie case merely by showing material untruths or omissions of material facts.   Silence is not a defense.

(3) The shareholder need not show that she actually relied on the untruths or omissions.   Defendants have a reliance defense only if the issuer provides shareholders with financial information for the year following the issuance or if the defendants can show the investor knew of the untruths or omissions when she bought the securities.

(4) The shareholder need not show that the defendants knew of the false or misleading statements.   Intent or scienter is not an element of §11 liability. Nonetheless, each defendant (except the issuer) is provided a defense based on the defendant's knowledge and diligence in ascertaining the veracity of the registration statement. These complex defenses, known as "due diligence" defenses, are described below.

(5) The shareholder need not show false or misleading statements actually caused her investment to fall in value.   Nonetheless, the defendants have a "comparative causation" defense that allows them to limit their liability if they can show the investor's losses were due to factors other than the false or misleading statements. In addition, underwriters are generally liable only to the extent of the amount of stock they sold or helped sell in the offering.

(6) Damages are limited.   To provide some balance for defendants, shareholders who establish a claim under §11 cannot recover more than the total amount of the offering, even if their damages are larger.

"Due Diligence" — a Flexible Defense.   Very few cases actually have imposed liability under §11. (Most cases are settled.) Nonetheless, the section's staggering *potential* liability and its due diligence defenses mold the way in which participants in registered offerings behave.

What is "due diligence" — besides something that junior securities lawyers are told they will enjoy? Due diligence is the potential defendants' investigation of the information contained in the registration statement and prospectus. The investigation task is usually delegated to outside law firms and, within those firms, often to junior associates. The level of diligence due varies according to who prepared (or audited) the information that at some point might be attacked as false or misleading.

Those portions of the registration statement certified by an expert — such as financial information audited by an accounting firm or legal opinions given by lawyers — are referred to as "expertised." As to expertised portions, experts must show they made a reasonable investigation and had reasonable grounds to believe (and did believe) that the expertised portions were true and not misleading — ignorance is not an excuse. §11(b)(3)(B). As to expertised portions, nonexperts need only show that they had no reasonable ground to believe (and did not believe) that the expertised portions were not true or misleading — good-faith ignorance is an excuse. §11(b)(3)(C).

Those portions of the registration statement not prepared or reviewed by an expert — usually most of the information in the registration statement — are referred to as "nonexpertised." To establish a due diligence defense, both experts and nonexperts must show that they made a reasonable investigation and had reasonable grounds to believe (and did believe) that the nonexpertised portions were true and not misleading — ignorance is not an excuse. §11(b)(3)(A). Although the statute does not explicitly create different standards for different defendants, courts have created a sliding scale to judge when the various defendants' investigation is sufficient.

To understand how these due diligence defenses apply to the various §11 defendants and affect the investigation by potential defendants and their counsel, it is useful to consider an illustrative case. The most famous is *Escott v. BarChris Construction Co.*, 283 F. Supp. 643 (S.D.N.Y. 1968). The case involved a bowling alley construction company that suffered a significant downturn in its business during the early 1960s after the bowling industry became overbuilt. In an attempt to raise additional money, insiders misstated the company's financial position and its exposure to losses in a registration statement for a new issue of debentures. There was little question that the false and misleading information in the registration statement was material. The case turned on whether the individual defendants had made out their §11 due diligence defenses.

The *BarChris* court interpreted the requirements of "reasonable investigation" and "reasonable belief" as varying depending on whether the defendant was employed by the company (an insider) and on the defendant's role in the offering.

Inside directors and officers — how inside? The court held that those insiders (Vittolo, the company's founder and president, and Russo, the executive vice-president) who perpetrated — and obviously knew about — the cover-up of the company's faltering financial position had no defense with respect to either the *expertised* or *nonexpertised* portions.

Another insider (Kirchner, the company treasurer) who claimed ignorance also was denied the defense as to *expertised* portions because he was thoroughly familiar with the company's financial affairs and knew relevant facts underlying the inaccuracies in the financial statements. The court also held that Kirchner, as an insider with intimate knowledge of the company, "must have known" of the *nonexpertised* inaccuracies as well. Like the perpetrators of the fraud, Kirchner became a virtual guarantor of the accuracy of the registration statement.

But another insider (Birnbaum, the company's in-house counsel, who was also a director) was held not liable as to the *expertised* portions because he was generally ignorant of the company's accounts. But as to the *nonexpertised* portions, Birnbaum had failed to make any investigation despite his position and access to information in the company. Complete verification was not required, but some was, and the court held him liable on this basis.

Outside directors — how involved? The court viewed outside directors, who did not have an employment relationship with the company, as having a less demanding duty of investigation. The court held that one outside director (Auslander, the chairman of the company's bank) justifiably relied on the reputation of the accounting firm as to the *expertised* audited financial information. But Auslander could not rely on the assurances of Vittolo and Russo (company president and vice-president) and lost his due diligence defense as to the *nonexpertised* portions by failing to read or familiarize himself with the information in the registration statement.

Another outside director (Grant, the company's outside lawyer and drafter of the registration statement) was held to a somewhat different standard, one approximating that applying to an insider. Although he was allowed to rely on the accuracy of the *expertised* portions, he failed to sufficiently investigate the letters, contracts, and corporate minutes that would have revealed the inaccuracies of the *nonexpertised* portions. He was held liable on this basis.

Underwriters — the principal outside watchdogs. The due diligence investigation of the principal underwriter for the offering (Drexel & Co.) was performed by a Drexel partner and a law firm that represented Drexel. For want of asking for them, that inquiry failed to turn up the minutes and contracts that Grant also had failed to examine. Drexel was held liable as to the *nonexpertised* portions because of the laxity of its outside lawyer-agents, who were not entitled to rely on the company's insiders and had a duty to ensure veracity. The other underwriters, which were represented by Drexel, were bound by Drexel's failure to make a reasonable investigation as to the *nonexpertised* portions. None of the underwriters, however, was liable for the *expertised* portions for which they could rely on the accounting firm.

A Drexel partner (Coleman, who was also a BarChris director) was held to a standard comparable to Drexel and Grant — to inquire and independently verify all material information. Although the court stated that Coleman could delegate his due diligence duty, he was bound by its inadequacies as to the *nonexpertised* portions to the same extent as Drexel.

Accounting firm (expert). BarChris's financial statements in the registration statement were audited by an accounting firm (Peat, Marwick). Peat, Marwick's due diligence inquiry was conducted by a non-CPA who was in charge of an audit for the first time. As to the *expertised*-audited figures, the court seemed to require that the auditor verify the "raw" information on which the financial figures were based (such as specific entries concerning accounts-receivable and costs). The court held Peat, Marwick liable because the auditor failed to notice certain discrepancies in the files and accepted information from insiders at face value. Peat, Marwick also was held liable as to the *nonexpertised* portions because the auditor failed to read certain minutes and contracts and failed to investigate danger signals about the company's cash position.

The case indicates that the §11 responsibility to become informed and to track down leads varies along a continuum in which "inside" insiders assume the role of virtual guarantors of a registration statement's accuracy and "outside" outsiders must only read the registration statement and follow up on any obvious problems.

§10.3.3 Section 12(2) — Rescission for Fraud

Section 12(2) is an antifraud provision that picks up where §11 leaves off. Under §12(2) the purchaser of any security in an exempt offering not subject to registration can rescind the transaction and get her money back if the security was sold by means of any materially false or misleading statements, whether written or oral. (Although some commentators have urged that §12(2) apply to after-market trading as well, recent courts have uniformly rejected this expansion.)

Like §11, §12(2) significantly modifies the common law deceit and contract rescission elements:

(1) Courts have not required strict privity. In addition to the actual seller who passes title, those who actively solicit the purchaser (and who do so for gain) also can be held liable. See *Pinter v. Dahl,* 486 U.S. 622 (1988). This "statutory seller" liability can encompass collateral participants in a securities offering, such as lawyers and investment advisers.

(2) Liability can be based not only on material untruths but also on failure to state material facts. Half-truths and silence can be actionable.

(3) The plaintiff-purchaser need not show that she actually relied on the misstatement. However, the defendants can assert a reliance defense if the plaintiff knew of the untruths or omissions.

(4) The plaintiff need not show that the defendants knew of the falsity or misleading nature of their statements. Intent or scienter is not a necessary element of §12(2) liability. Nonetheless, there is a "reasonable care" defense that in effect forces the defendant to prove he was not negligent.

(5) The plaintiff need not show that the false or misleading statements were related to any loss. Courts do not require a showing of reliance or causation. The plaintiff is entitled simply to a return of the purchase price.

EXAMPLES

1. Soon after Adam, Boone, and Carver form Outdoor Cafes — each investing $100,000 — Carver becomes disenchanted with his investment. Adam (the restaurant manager) had given him a pro forma income statement before he invested. The statement optimistically forecasted that the restaurant would have monthly revenues of $40,000. In fact, they have averaged only $25,000. Carver has come to you for some litigation advice.

   a. You conclude an exemption from registration was unavailable. Can Carver get his money back without having to litigate the accuracy of the income statement?

   b. You conclude a private offering exemption applies to the offering and the sale to Carver. Is there another route by which Carver can get his money back?

   c. Who can Carver sue?

   d. Adam approaches Carver to purchase his shares. Adam knows that a national restaurant chain is about to offer to buy Outdoor Cafes at a significant premium but does not tell Carver. Can Carver sue under the 1933 Act?

2. Outdoor Cafes opens new restaurants in other states. To raise capital it sells its stock in a registered offering in compliance with §5. The prospectus states that the concept of a "rustic outdoor restaurant" has been tried successfully in other states besides Mayflower. The statement is false: The only such restaurants are in Mayflower. Michael buys some of the stock a couple months after the public issue. Within a year the price of the stock plummets.

   a. Can Michael sue Outdoor Cafes to recover damages? What must he show?

   b. Joseph, Outdoor Cafes's outside counsel, had drafted the prospectus. Is he liable to Michael?

EXPLANATIONS

1a. Yes. Carver can seek rescission of his stock purchase under §12(1). If the sale was made using the mails or some means of interstate communication — a virtual certainty — the sale to Carver violated §5 because (1) no exemption was available, and (2) no registration statement was filed or became effective. Section 12(1) provides for strict liability and rescission.

1b. Yes. Carver can seek rescission under §12(2), which will require him to show the income statement was materially false or misleading. (There can be no liability under §11 because there was no registration statement.)

Seeking rescission under §12(2) presents a number of obstacles not presented by §12(1). Carver must show that the misstatement was material — that is, that it would be important to a reasonable investor in making an investment decision. The defendants can defend that the misstatement was one of opinion, not of fact, or that they exercised reasonable care in preparing the statements, or even that Carver knew $40,000 was an overly optimistic misstatement.

1c. Outdoor Cafes (the issuer) and Adam are both potential defendants under §12(2). Outdoor Cafes was the privity seller, and Adam actively solicited Carver's investment, acted for the issuer, and stood to gain by bringing in another investor.

1d. No. The 1933 Act only regulates fraud in the *sale* of securities, not in their purchase, as here. (Michael, however, can sue for this insider trading under the 1934 Act's antifraud Rule 10b-5; see Chapter 29.)

2a. Yes. Michael can sue to recover damages from Outdoor Cafes under §11. To recover against the issuer, which has no due diligence defense under §11, Michael need only show the prospectus contained a materially false or misleading statement. The "other states" statement was false. Its materiality depends on whether a reasonable investor would consider it important in deciding whether to invest. Because the offering was meant to raise money to expand to other states, the success of a "rustic outdoor restaurant" in other states would seem to have a significant bearing on the success of the expansion plans. The falsehood seems material.

Once Michael has made such a showing, the burden switches to Outdoor Cafes to show that (1) some or all of Michael's loss was caused by factors other than the deception in the prospectus, such as a general decline in restaurant stock prices (comparative causation); or (2) Michael knew that the "other states" statement was false.

Michael does not have any burden to show reliance because he acquired his shares before Outdoor Cafes could have supplied an earnings statement to shareholders covering the 12 months beginning after the registration statement's effective date. See §11(a).

2b. Probably not. Joseph is liable under §11 only if he fits within one of the categories of §11 defendants. Unless he was a director, or was a statutory underwriter by actively soliciting investors, or was an expert by providing *expertised* information used in the registration statement, he cannot be liable under §11. (For this reason, lawyers are well-advised not to accept positions as directors of corporate clients or to assist in the solicitation of investors.) Moreover, even if a court were to apply §12(2) to a registered offering, Joseph would not be liable as a "statutory seller" under §12(2) unless he actively participated in the promotion of the offering.

If, however, Joseph fits into one of the §11 categories, he could be liable with respect to the "other states" statement. If the falsehood was contained in a *nonexpertised* portion of the prospectus, Joseph would have the burden of showing he reasonably believed the statement was true after a reasonable investigation — ignorance would not be a defense. Like outside lawyer Grant in *BarChris,* as the drafter of the prospectus, Joseph would be held to a higher standard of investigation or due diligence than if he had not been the drafter. He will have to show that he had reviewed materials that supported the statement and followed up any suspicious leads.

§10.4   The Definition of a Security

All of the prohibitions and liability created by the 1933 Act turn on whether a transaction can be characterized as the sale of a security. What is a security?

§10.4.1   The Statutory Definition

Section 2(1) of the 1933 Act, like the definition section of the other federal securities laws, contains a long list of financial instruments that qualify as securities: stock, bonds, debentures, notes, transferable shares. The section also contains some catch-all terms that qualify as securities: evidences of indebtedness, investment contracts, and certificates of interest in profit-sharing agreements. In most cases, there is no question about whether a transaction involves the sale of a security. For example, a company's issuance of stock or the sale of limited partnership interests are unquestionably subject to the 1933 Act; the sale of a car, a house, or the assets of a business are not. But many investment schemes fall in-between. The marginal case often turns on whether the scheme involves an "investment contract."

§10.4.2   Definition of an Investment Contract

The Supreme Court has defined *investment contract* as any transaction in which (1) a person invests money (2) in a common enterprise and (3) is led to expect profits (4) solely from the efforts of others. *SEC v. W. J. Howey Co.,* 328 U.S. 293 (1946). The Court's definition has taken on a quasi-statutory quality. Since it was first pronounced, courts have clarified the contours of the *Howey* test:

- the investment can be other than that of money;
- there must be a number of investors in a common pool (horizontal commonality), although some courts have held a single investor who

allows another to manage his investment is enough (vertical commonality);
- the expected return must come from earnings, not merely additional contributions; and
- "solely from the efforts of others" means that someone other than the investor has contributed the *predominant* effort in the common enterprise.

Basically, the *Howey* test attempts to identify transactions in which investors are counting on others to manage enterprises that will produce returns on their investment. This definition is consistent with the purpose of the 1933 Act: to ensure that capital used in the production of goods and services in the U.S. economy goes to those ventures where a well-informed market dictates it should go.

The investment contract definition has been used in surprising ways. Courts have held each of the following schemes to involve such a contract and hence the sale of a security:

- The sale of interests in rows of orange trees where the cultivation, harvesting, and marketing of the fruit was handled by the seller — the facts in the *Howey* case.
- The sale of earthworms where the seller promised to buy back all the worms (after they reproduced at geometric rates) for a guaranteed price and market them to fishermen.
- The sale of a "piece" in a pyramid scheme where the seller conducted promotional meetings and the buyer was paid a commission for each new person brought into the scheme.
- The sale of beachfront condominiums where the seller managed the condos and pooled the rentals from the condo units, and the buyer's right to occupy her unit was limited.

In each of these cases, people had put money into a scheme in which the expected returns derived predominantly from the efforts of others. The enticement was not in the property ostensibly being sold to the investor but rather in a return on the investment created by others' management or marketing efforts.

EXAMPLES

Outdoor Cafes turns out to be a roaring success. Adam, the company's president, decides to expand the business by selling "muskrat dogs" from pushcarts in downtown business districts throughout the Northeast. Adam has devised an ingenious way to finance the new venture. Under his plan, Outdoor Cafes will purchase the pushcarts and then sell them to Pushcart Owners, who will agree to buy their muskrat dogs and related supplies from Outdoor Cafes. Pushcart Owners either can operate the carts themselves or can enter into an operator's agreement with Outdoor Cafes under which the company will select, train, and supervise an operator who the Owner will hire to push the cart and sell the muskrat dogs. Outdoor Cafes advertises the sale of Pushcart Owners interests in area newspapers, and Adam assures prospective purchasers that they will earn significant returns on the sale of muskrat dogs (after paying for supplies and any operator fees).

a. Owen buys a muskrat dog cart from Outdoor Cafes and opts to pay a fee to have Outdoor Cafes provide an operator for the cart. After a few months, Owen discovers that his cart is losing money. The cost of supplies and his monthly operator fee to Outdoor Cafes exceed revenues. Owen wants his money back. How might he use the 1933 Act?

b. Has Outdoor Cafes sold Owen a security?

c. Oprah buys a muskrat dog cart from Outdoor Cafes but decides to operate the cart herself, even though she must buy all her supplies from Outdoor Cafes. After a few months, Oprah is losing money on the cart and wants to get her money back. Can she under the 1933 Act?

EXPLANATIONS

a. Owen can argue that the sale of the cart with the operator agreement was the sale of a security. If so, he can seek rescission both under §§12(1) and 12(2). Owen could rescind the transaction under §12(1) if the Pushcart Owners interests were securities sold in a nonexempt offering without registration. In addition, even if the offering was exempt from registration, Owen could seek rescission under §12(2) if the interests were securities sold by means of materially misleading statements of significant returns.

b. Most likely. The purchase of a pushcart accompanied by an operator agreement appears to satisfy the definition of an investment contract under the *Howey* test: (1) Owen invested money by purchasing the pushcart and agreeing to pay fees under the operator agreement; (2) Outdoor Cafes contemplates a number of investors like Owen (horizontal commonality); (3) Owen is led to expect profits from the sale of muskrat dogs; (4) the return from Owen's investment comes predominantly (if not exclusively) from the efforts of Outdoor Cafes, which is responsible for selecting, training, and supervising the cart operator.

Although Outdoor Cafes might argue that Owen hires the operator, Owen's hiring of the operator is in name only. The operator agreement leaves to Outdoor Cafes all meaningful management decisions related to running the business. Adam's promise of significant returns depends on Outdoor Cafes running the business successfully. Owen is counting on putting money into an arrangement (the pushcart purchase and operator agreement) in which others will manage an enterprise (the pushcart business) that will produce a return on his investment. The arrangement operates as though Outdoor Cafes had set up a new corporation that purchased carts and services from Outdoor Cafes, and Owen had become a shareholder in this new corporation. Disclosure about Outdoor Cafes and its management history and plans will be highly relevant to Owen's investment decision.

c. Standing alone, probably not. This is much more like a typical franchise arrangement; such arrangements generally have been held not to involve the sale of a security. Although the first three *Howey* factors are satisfied (Oprah has invested money, others have invested money, and they expect a profit from their investment), the critical element — that these profits be derived solely or predominantly from the efforts of others — is not met. Oprah is not relying on Outdoor Cafes's management of her investment, and disclosure concerning Outdoor Cafes's history, performance, and plans as a supervisor of pushcart operators would have been largely irrelevant to her decision whether to buy the cart. Although Oprah is expecting Outdoor Cafes's products will sell, her own efforts predominate in determining the carts' success or failure. If Oprah had also been offered an operator agreement, however, the offer (as discussed in Owen's case) would have involved a security. As such, Oprah might be able to seek rescission under §12(1) of a transaction that included the unregistered, nonexempt *offering* of a security.

PART FOUR

The Structure of Corporate Governance

11

Statutory Model of Corporate Governance

More than 200 years ago Blackstone described the corporation as a "little republic." At least in theory, his description is still apt today. The traditional statutory *model* for the corporation prescribes a republican form of governance —

The corporation's *electorate,* the shareholders, elect directors, are entitled to vote on other fundamental corporate transactions (see §12.1), and may initiate bylaw changes, but otherwise do not participate in managing the corporation's business or affairs. In Chapter 12 we discuss the limited role of shareholders in corporate governance.

The corporation's *legislative organ,* the board of directors, is the locus of central management authority. Corporate power flows from the board. In Chapter 13 we discuss the mechanics for selecting directors and board decision-making.

The corporation's *bureaucracy* (or system of internal governance) is structured by the board of directors, and the day-to-day management of the corporation is delegated to officers who are answerable to the board. In Chapter 14 we discuss the ways in which officers can act for and bind the corporation.

In this chapter we provide an overview of the statutory model of corporate governance. As you review this chapter and those that follow, keep in mind that in practice actual governance of modern corporations, both publicly held and closely held, deviates significantly from the model. The governance model is like the speed limits on interstate highways: Most drivers don't seem to follow them, but every driver has to know what they are.

§11.1   Basic Elements of the Corporate Governance Structure

The statutes lay out the scheme of corporate management simply and elegantly:

> All corporate powers shall be exercised by or under the authority of, and the business and affairs of the corporation managed under the direction of, its board of directors. [RMBCA §8.01(b).]
>
> Directors are elected at the first annual shareholders' meeting and at each annual meeting thereafter. [RMBCA §8.03(d).]

The traditional statutory structure for corporate governance has a number of implications:

(1)   The shareholders, even a majority, cannot act on behalf of the corporation — this is left to the board.

(2)   The shareholders, though nominally "owners," exercise control only through the election of directors, approval of fundamental transactions, and amendment of the bylaws.

(3)   The board is not an agent for the shareholders; it has independent status.

(4)   All authority to act for (and to bind) the corporation originates in the board of directors.

(5)   The directors have fiduciary duties to the corporation and the body of shareholders (see Chapter 20).

§11.2   Analyzing the Traditional Model of Corporate Governance

The traditional model, designed for a firm with large capital needs and specialized management, has much to recommend it. It separates the functions of those who provide capital to the business (the shareholders), those who oversee the business (the board), and those who carry on day-to-day business (officers). This specialization of function creates the possibility of greater efficiencies than in an archetypical partnership, where partners have equal management powers and equal capital rights and responsibilities. The corporation can attract specialized capital providers who lack management skills and specialized managers who lack wealth.

To avoid the risk of veto, both the shareholders and the board act by majority rule. While the shareholders have no control over ordinary business decisions, their collective interests are represented by the board, subject to the directors' fiduciary duties. Creditors and others who deal with the corporation are assured that the board (and the board alone) acts for the corporation.

In a number of ways, however, the reality of modern corporate governance diverges from the theoretical model. For both publicly and closely held corporations, the roles assumed by shareholders and directors deviate significantly from the traditional statutory scheme.

§11.2.1 The Reality in Public Corporations

In public corporations (those with many, widely dispersed shareholders and a public market for their shares), shareholder participation in the election of directors is far less fulsome than the model assumes. Shareholders are mostly passive (see Chapter 18). Management nominates a slate of directors and then shareholders mail in proxy cards indicating a vote of yes or no (see Chapters 15 and 19). Public shareholders almost always endorse management's slate. Although this passivity is changing as institutional investors (such as pension funds, mutual funds, insurance companies, and banks that invest money for others) have come to hold a majority of the shares of public corporations, recent shareholder activism in public corporations has not yet undone management control of the proxy mechanism.

In public corporations, the board's role has been largely symbolic. Management — the corporation's senior executives — represent the real locus of power. Management chooses the slate of directors, controls the information directors receive, controls corporate initiatives, and is intimately familiar with the corporation's business. The modern board of directors acts primarily as an adviser to management, as a disciplining force, and as a backstop in times of crisis. Far from being the decision-maker that the statutory model contemplates, the board in a typical public corporation is a "rubber stamp" for management decisions (see §20.3.1). This remains largely true even though most public corporations have a majority of "outside directors" (directors who are not employees of the corporation), most of whom are "unaffiliated directors" (those who have no business dealings with the corporation).

§11.2.2 The Reality in Close Corporations

In closely held corporations (those with few shareholders and no ready market for their shares), things are quite different. (See Chapter 15.) Shareholders in close corporations lack a public market into which to sell their shares and have significant incentives not to leave corporate management in the unfettered hands of directors. The shareholders often rely on the corporation as a source of livelihood and assume a far more active role in the corporation's governance than the statutory model contemplates.

Close corporation shareholders often limit the discretion of the board, retaining it for themselves or specifying by agreement how the corporation will be run (see §16.7). Like partners, they may require that some important decisions be by unanimous consent, and they often provide withdrawal rights comparable to those of partners on dissolution.

12

The Corporate Electorate — The Shareholders' Role in Corporate Governance

According to the traditional corporate structure, the shareholders — the "electorate" of the corporate republic — have a limited role in corporate governance, which they exercise at properly convened meetings. In this chapter we look at the shareholders' governance role under the traditional governance model and the mechanics of shareholders' meetings.

§12.1 The Nature of the Shareholders' Limited Role

Under the traditional statutory model, modified by a few common law glosses, shareholder participation in corporate management is limited to relatively narrow categories of action. The negative implication of the shareholders' limited role is the dominant role of the board of directors.

§12.1.1 Election and Removal of Directors

Shareholders elect directors annually. RMBCA §8.03(d). They can also remove directors before their term expires — for cause or without cause, de-

171

pending on the statute. RMBCA §8.08. The right to control the composition of the board is at the heart of shareholder control rights. (See Chapter 13.)

§12.1.2   Approval of Corporate Transactions

Shareholders have limited powers to approve corporate transactions initiated by the board:

Fundamental corporate changes.   Shareholders have voting rights to approve fundamental corporate changes initiated by management: amendment of the articles of incorporation (RMBCA §10.03), mergers with other corporations (RMBCA §11.03), sale of substantially all the corporate assets not in the regular course of business (RMBCA §12.02), and voluntary dissolution (RMBCA §14.02) (see Chapters 34 and 35). Otherwise, shareholders have voting rights to approve corporate transactions only if the board of directors submits the matter to a shareholder vote or the articles require it.

Conflicting interest transactions.   Shareholders can vote on corporate transactions in which some of the directors have a conflict of interest. RMBCA §8.63 (see Chapter 22). Shareholders can vote to approve the indemnification of directors, officers, or others against whom claims have been brought because of their relationship to the corporation. RMBCA §8.55(b)(4) (see Chapter 25).

§12.1.3   Initiation of Corporate Changes

Shareholders have narrow powers to initiate changes in corporate governance and structure:

Amendment of bylaws.   Historically, shareholders had exclusive power to adopt, amend, and repeal the bylaws. Most modern statutes codify this power. See RMBCA §10.20. Even if the board shares the power to amend the bylaws, whether by statute or in the articles, the board's power is coterminous with the shareholders'. See Official Comment to RMBCA §10.20 ("shareholders always have the power to amend or repeal the bylaws"). Many states do not permit the board to amend bylaws approved by shareholders.

Amendment of articles.   A few statutes permit shareholders to initiate amendments to the articles of incorporation, and others describe the procedure for their adoption without specifying who initiates the amendment. Most statutes, however, vest the initiation power exclusively in the board. See RMBCA §10.03(b).

Furthermore, most statutes do not permit shareholders to initiate other corporate actions even when they are entitled to approve the action. In most states the board must initiate mergers, sales of substantially all assets, and voluntary dissolution — the shareholders are entitled only to approve or reject the board's initiatives. RMBCA §11.03 (merger); RMBCA §12.02 (sale of all assets); RMBCA §14.02 (dissolution).

Nonbinding recommendations. Shareholders can make nonbinding, precatory recommendations about governance structures and the management of the corporation, including matters entrusted exclusively to the board. In public corporations such recommendations are brought as shareholder proposals under Rule 14a-8 (see §19.5). In the leading case on the subject, the court held that shareholders could properly make a nonbinding recommendation that the corporation's former president be reinstated, even though the recommendation had no binding effect on the board. *Auer v. Dressel,* 118 N.E.2d 590 (N.Y. 1954).

What the shareholders *cannot do* under the traditional model is significant. Shareholders cannot act on the ordinary business and affairs of the corporation — including binding the corporation contractually, selecting and removing officers (even for cause), fixing compensation, setting dividend policies, deciding on marketing or production policies, and bringing lawsuits. Shareholders cannot compel or overturn particular decisions by the board unless the board has failed to comply with the corporate statute or the corporation's constitutive documents, or the directors have breached their fiduciary duties.

§12.1.4 Protection of Shareholder Rights

Shareholders can protect these rights by compelling information from the corporation or challenging board actions:

Financial reports. In an unusual departure for state corporate law, the RMBCA requires the corporation to provide to shareholders annual financial information, including an end-year balance sheet, income statement, and statement of changes in shareholders' equity (see §9.2 for accounting description). RMBCA §16.20. The financial information must be audited by a public accountant or include a statement by a corporate official either that the information was prepared on the basis of "generally accepted accounting principles" or that explains any deviations from GAAP. For public corporations, federal securities law already requires the preparation and dissemination of such annual reports (see §19.4.1). For close corporations, however, these reports constitute the only periodic disclosure to shareholders mandated by law.

Inspection of corporate books and records.   Corporate statutes codify shareholders' common law rights to inspect corporate books and records. RMBCA §16.02. Some statutes limit this right to record shareholders (not to the beneficial owners), to shareholders holding a specified percentage of the company's outstanding shares, and to shareholders who have held their shares for a minimum period. Cf. RMBCA §16.02(f) (includes beneficial owners).

Some records, such as the articles of incorporation, bylaws, and minutes of shareholders' meetings, are available as of right. RMBCA §§16.01(e), 16.02(a). Other records, such as board minutes, accounting records, and shareholder lists, are available for inspection only upon a showing of a "proper purpose." RMBCA §16.02(b), (c). Courts have found such a purpose if the shareholder's request relates to the shareholder's interest in his investment. Thus, management must provide a shareholders' list to a shareholder seeking to solicit other shareholders' proxies or to uncover mismanagement but need not if the shareholder seeks information he plans to sell or to give to competitors.

The right to inspect the company's shareholder list is an indispensable tool for proxy insurgents (see Chapter 38). The statutes, however, are often ambiguous about what shareholder information is covered. Some specify only "shareholder list," but do not describe its contents. Many others specify only the relatively useless "stock ledger" list of record shareholders, rather than the more valuable computer-readable information on beneficial ("street name") ownership. See Del. GCL §219(a). The RMBCA calls for a list of shareholders of record and beneficial owners who have on file with the corporation a nominee certificate. RMBCA §§1.40(22), 16.02(b)(3). Judicial interpretation has been mixed. Delaware courts require management to provide only those lists already in existence; there is no duty to compile additional lists. *Hatleigh Corp. v. Lane Bryant, Inc.,* 428 A.2d 350 (Del. Ch. 1981). Some courts outside Delaware, however, have required management to assemble a list of "non-objecting beneficial owners" ("NOBO list") not then in existence. See *Sadler v. NCR Corp.,* 928 F.2d 48 (2d Cir. 1991) (applying New York inspection statute to Maryland corporation).

Enforcement of shareholder rights.   Shareholders may bring *direct* actions against the corporation to enforce the shareholders' rights discussed above, and may bring *derivative* suits to enforce corporate rights when a director, officer, or controlling shareholder has breached a fiduciary duty to the corporation (see §31.1).

§12.2 The Mechanics of Shareholders' Meetings

For the most part, shareholders act by voting at meetings. The mechanics and formalities required for shareholders' meetings are meant to assure the body of shareholders a right of informed suffrage by specifying how meetings are called, the notice shareholders must receive, the number of shares that must be represented at a meeting, and the manner in which votes are counted.

§12.2.1 Annual and Special Meetings

There are two kinds of shareholders' meetings: the annual (or regular) meetings, at which directors are elected and other regular business is conducted (RMBCA §7.01), and special meetings, called in unusual circumstances where shareholder action is required. RMBCA §7.02.

Usually, the bylaws specify the timing and location of the annual meeting. All corporate statutes require an annual meeting, and many permit shareholders to apply to a court to compel a meeting if the annual meeting is not held within a specified period. RMBCA §7.03(a)(1) (within six months of end of fiscal year or 15 months of last annual meeting).

Special meetings must be specially called by the board, the president (if allowed by statute or in the bylaws), shareholders who hold a requisite number of shares (as specified in the statute or bylaws), or other persons designated in the bylaws. RMBCA §7.02.

§12.2.2 Notice

To inform shareholders of what they will be voting on, shareholders entitled to vote must be given written notice of annual and special meetings. In general, the requirements under state law are minimal as to what information must be in the notice. (Compare this to federally mandated disclosure required in proxy solicitations involving public corporations (see §19.4.1).) The notice describes the time and location of the meeting and sometimes summarizes the matters to be considered. RMBCA §7.05.

Shareholders entitled to vote and receive notice. To fix which shareholders may vote, the board sets a *record date* before the shareholders' meeting. RMBCA §7.07 (record date may not be more than 70 days before meeting). Only shareholders "of record" whose shareholding is reflected on the corporation's books as of that date — sometimes referred to as *record owners* — are entitled to notice and to vote.

Whether and how much notice. The nature of the notice required under state law varies according to whether it is for an annual or special meeting. For *annual* meetings at which only directors will be elected and other ordinary matters discussed, it is usually enough that the notice state the date, time, and place of the meeting. RMBCA §7.05. Under some statutes, if any extraordinary matter will be discussed at an annual meeting, notice of the matter must be given. Notice of *special* meetings must specify the purposes of the meeting, as well as the time and location of the meeting. RMBCA §7.05(c).

Window during which notice must be given.   For both annual and special meetings the notice must arrive in time for shareholders to consider the matters on which they will vote, but not so early that the notice becomes stale. Generally, statutes require that notice be given at least ten days, but no more than 50 days, before a meeting. (RMBCA §7.05(a) specifies a 10-60 day window.)

Waiver of defective notice.   Shareholders can waive notice before, at, or after the meeting. RMBCA §7.06. Many statutes provide that attendance at a meeting (other than to object to improper notice) constitutes a waiver of notice. RMBCA §7.06(b).

Effect of defective notice.   If no notice is given to those shareholders who must receive notice or if notice is improperly given and the deficiencies are not waived, the meeting is invalid and any action taken at the meeting is void.

§12.2.3   Quorum

For action at a shareholders' meeting to be valid, the statutes require a quorum typically equal to a majority of shares entitled to vote. RMBCA §7.25(a). Quorum requirements prevent a small faction of shareholders from acting at a shareholders' meeting without the presence of a majority. Some statutes allow the quorum to be reduced in the articles or bylaws to one-third; RMBCA §7.25(a) allows it to be reduced in the articles without limitation.

Once a quorum is established, most statutes provide that it cannot be broken if a faction of shareholders walk out in the middle of the meeting. RMBCA §7.25(b).

§12.2.4   Appearance in Person or by Proxy

Shareholders can appear at a shareholders' meeting, for purposes of a quorum and to cast their votes, either in person or by proxy. RMBCA §7.22(a). A shareholder who acts by proxy gives another person authority to vote her shares on her behalf. The proxy creates an agency relationship. The shareholder (the principal) grants in writing to the proxy holder (the agent) the power to vote her shares. Like any document creating an agency relationship, the proxy can give the proxy holder full discretion or be subject to specific instructions. Generally, the proxy can be revoked by the principal at any time.

(The validity of irrevocable proxies and their use as a control device is taken up in §16.5.) In general, corporate statutes limit the duration of a proxy to 11 months so that shareholders must give a new proxy for each annual shareholders' meeting. RMBCA §7.22(c).

§12.2.5 Voting at Shareholders' Meetings

In general, each share is entitled to one vote. Nonetheless, the articles can change the "one share-one vote" standard and create, for example, super-voting shares or voting caps on any shareholder who holds a specified percentage of shares. See *Providence & Worcester Co. v. Baker*, 378 A.2d 121 (Del. 1977) (upholding charter provision that reduced voting rights to one vote per 20 shares for any shareholder who owned more than 50 shares and capped voting rights for any shareholder who owned more than 25 percent of the company's shares).

For many shareholder actions — such as approval of mergers, sale of assets, or dissolution — a majority of shares *entitled* to be voted must be voted in favor of a proposal — *an absolute majority*. This means abstentions and no-shows effectively count as votes against the proposal. For example, if there are 1000 voting shares outstanding and 800 represented at a meeting, a proposal must garner at least 501 votes to be approved.

Some statutes permit shareholder action by a *simple majority* — that is, a majority of shares represented at a meeting. In our example, a proposal must receive at least 401 votes to be approved. This means abstentions count as votes against the proposal.

The RMBCA takes a slightly different tack. If the articles or corporate statute does not provide for an absolute or simple majority, a proposal is approved if the votes for the proposal are greater than the votes against it — a *plurality*. RMBCA §7.25(c). In our example, the proposal would be approved if 200 votes are cast for and 100 against and 500 abstain. This means abstentions do not count against the proposal.

Voting for directors is handled differently because usually more than one directorship is being voted on. We discuss board elections in the next chapter (see §13.1).

§12.2.6 Action by Consent

Under most statutes, shareholders may act without a meeting by giving their written consent. Action by consent has the same effect as action at a valid shareholders' meeting. Most statutes that allow such a procedure require that the consent of the shareholders be unanimous. RMBCA §7.04(a). But many other statutes, including Delaware's, require only that the consents represent the minimum number of shares that would be required to approve an action if the meeting were actually held. Thus, consent by a majority of shares will suffice.

EXAMPLES

1. Graphic Designs, incorporated in an RMBCA jurisdiction, designs and produces commercial art. Shirley is the majority shareholder and the board's dominant director, but the company president is Buck. Shirley offers her friend Jenny, a commercial artist, a job at Graphic Designs.
   a. If Jenny accepts the offer, is the corporation bound under the agreement?
   b. Shirley, as majority shareholder, instructs the board and Buck to hire Jenny, but they balk. How can Shirley force the board or Buck to follow her instructions?

2. Graphic's five-person board authorizes Buck to fire all of the company's commercial artists and replace them with a computer that will generate graphic designs. Shirley is upset about the board's action.
   a. As majority shareholder, she signs and submits a written consent that purports to remove all the directors. Will this work?
   b. She demands a shareholders' meeting to remove all the directors and Buck. Will this work?
   c. She demands a shareholders' meeting to pass a shareholder resolution that would require the board to undertake a study of the impact on employee morale of replacing human artists with a computer. Will this work?

3. Graphic's articles specify a board of between three and seven directors, the exact number to be "fixed by the board of directors in the bylaws." The current bylaws call for five directors. Shirley wants to change the balance of power on the board at the next annual shareholders' meeting.
   a. She proposes an amendment to the articles that would fix the number of directors at seven, with the vacancies to be filled by the shareholders. Is this proper?
   b. She proposes an amendment of the bylaws that would increase the number of directors from five to seven. Is this proper?

4. Mildred, a minority shareholder of Graphic, is convinced that Shirley's new directors — who have rescinded the computer decision — were unduly influenced by the company's commercial artists. Mildred is considering a derivative suit against the directors.
   a. She wants to inspect the minutes of last year's board meetings. Must the corporation provide the minutes?
   b. She wants to inspect a list of the Graphic shareholders to contact them about joining her suit. Must the corporation provide the list?

c. She wants the board to summarize its reasons for rescinding the computer decision, something the minutes do not do. Must the corporation provide a summary of the board's reasons?

EXPLANATIONS

1a. No. As a shareholder Shirley has no authority either to act on behalf of the corporation or to bind the corporation contractually. Unless the corporation has special governance arrangements that permit shareholders to act as partners (which may have to be stated in the articles), such authority resides solely with the corporation's board of directors. RMBCA §8.01(b).

1b. She cannot. Under the traditional corporate structure, Shirley can elect new directors at the next annual shareholders' meeting (RMBCA §8.03(d)) and hope they will authorize Jenny's employment or appoint a president who will hire her. Shirley might also be able to remove the balking directors and replace them with those of her choosing. RMBCA §8.08. The removal route, however, might be a problem if the articles of incorporation or the statute allow removal only for cause, or if the articles allow only the board to fill vacancies. RMBCA §8.10. (See §13.2.)

2a. No. Like most states that allow shareholder action by written consent instead of by vote at a meeting, the RMBCA requires that the consent be unanimous. RMBCA §7.04.

2b. In part. As the holder of more than 10 percent of Graphic's shares, she can demand a special shareholders' meeting. RMBCA §7.02(a)(2) (demand on corporation's secretary). She must have a proper purpose for the meeting. Removal of directors is a proper purpose, but removal of officers is not. The RMBCA permits shareholders to remove directors with or without cause. RMBCA §8.08(a). The removal and appointment of officers, however, is within the sole discretion of the board of directors. RMBCA §§8.40(a) (appointment by board), 8.43(b) (board can remove officers with or without cause).

2c. No. Some courts have held that shareholders can approve nonbinding, precatory resolutions concerning the management of the corporation. Shirley's resolution, however, is not phrased as a request, but as a demand. This shareholders cannot do. If her resolution had "urged" the board to make the study, it would satisfy the "proper purpose" requirement that courts have implied exists for shareholder resolutions. By linking the computer decision to employee well-being and, arguably, company profitability, the resolution properly relates to the corporation's economic well-being. See *Conservative Caucus v. Chevron Corp.*, 525 A.2d 569 (Del. Ch. 1987) (compelling inspection of shareholders' list for purpose of communicating with shareholders about resolution "request-ing" board to discontinue operations in communist Angola because of potential adverse economic consequences of continued operations).

3a. No. Amendments to articles must be recommended by the board of directors for approval by shareholders. RMBCA §10.02.

3b. Yes. Shareholders have an inherent power to amend the bylaws. RMBCA §10.20. Even though the bylaws state that the power to fix the size of the board rests with the directors, the RMBCA makes the board's power at most coterminous. This a mandatory right that cannot be waived.

4a. Perhaps not. The RMBCA permits shareholders to demand "excerpts from minutes of board meetings" if the demand is made for a proper purpose. RMBCA §16.02(b)(1), (c). Bringing a derivative action — for the benefit of the corporation and the shareholders as a group — would seem to be such a purpose. Nonetheless, her request as currently for-mulated may be too broad in that it goes beyond her interest in chal-lenging the board's rescission of its computer decision. The RMBCA requires that the records be described with "reasonable particularity" and that they relate "directly" to the stated purpose. The board could refuse her demand on this basis.

4b. Perhaps. A shareholder demand to inspect the shareholders' list must be for a proper purpose. RMBCA §16.02(c). Courts have held that the burden to show an improper purpose is on the corporation. The cor-poration — that is, the board and current management — may argue that a shareholders' list is not relevant to bringing a derivative action. Courts, however, have interpreted the proper-purpose test broadly. Un-less Mildred seeks to use the list only to harass or advance her own personal interests, it would be enough if she argued that additional shareholder plaintiffs will help defray the costs of the derivative litigation and add weight to the challenge of the directors' action.

4c. Probably not. Most courts have limited shareholder inspection requests to documents already in existence. The only cases in which courts have compelled management to compile new information was when the in-formation (a list of beneficial owners who did not object to having their identity revealed) was available to management under federal securities law from brokerage firms that are required to maintain and provide lists of NOBO customers. See *Sadler v. NCR Corp.*, 928 F.2d 48 (2d Cir. 1991). To impose a duty to compile or assemble information would go well beyond the limited inspection rights provided by the statute.

13

The Center of Corporate Governance — The Board of Directors

A principal feature of the traditional corporate model is centralized management. In this chapter we summarize the mechanics of central corporate governance: how directors are elected to office, how they can be removed from office, and how action is taken by the board. Many of the statutory rules on the election and functioning of the board are default rules that can be changed in the articles of incorporation or the bylaws.

§13.1 Election of Directors

§13.1.1 Qualifications and Number of Directors

Directors need not be shareholders of the corporation or residents of the state of incorporation or have any other special qualifications. RMBCA §8.02. The statutes require only that directors be individuals (sometimes required to be at least 18 years old) who meet the qualifications (if any) prescribed in the articles of incorporation or bylaws.

The number of directors on the board is specified in the articles or the bylaws. The articles or bylaws may specify a variable range, with the actual number of directors fixed in the bylaws. RMBCA §8.03(c). Many statutes once required a minimum of three directors, but most statutes now permit a board of one director. RMBCA §8.03(a).

§13.1.2   Annual Election by Straight Voting — The General Rule

The general rule is that at each annual shareholders' meeting all directors face election by straight (plurality) voting — the top vote-getters are elected. RMBCA §8.03(d). Under this rule, shareholders holding a majority of the shares can elect the entire board of directors. To illustrate, suppose the articles of AB Corp. authorize five directors and there are two shareholders: Abner owns 51 shares and Byron owns 49 shares. Under the general rule of annual elections and straight voting, all five directors would face election each year, and Abner and Byron would each cast his votes five times for five different candidates. Each of Abner's five candidates would receive 51 votes; each of Byron's five candidates would receive 49 votes. Under straight voting, the top five vote-getters — Abner's slate — are elected directors.

§13.1.3   Cumulative Voting — The Possibility of Minority Representation

To dilute the lopsided advantage that straight voting gives the majority, statutes of some states (and even constitutions of some states) require cumulative voting. In the remaining states, "cumulative voting" is a default term in the statutes that applies if it is included in the articles ("opt-in" statutes) or if not specifically avoided in the articles ("opt-out" statutes). RMBCA §7.28 takes an opt-in approach.

Unlike straight voting, cumulative voting allows minority shareholders to accumulate all of their votes and split them among a few candidates or even to cast all of them for one candidate. This increases the chances of at least some board representation for minority shareholders. Whether required or chosen, however, cumulative voting applies only to shareholders' elections of directors, not to shareholder voting on other matters.

The operation of cumulative voting requires some arithmetic. Suppose that Abner has 70 shares and Byron has 30 shares. In an election of five directors, Abner would have a total of 350 (70 times 5) votes to distribute among his candidates as he chooses, and Byron would have a total of 150 (30 times 5) votes to distribute. If Byron votes intelligently, cumulative voting assures him that at least one of his candidates will be elected. If Byron casts all of his 150 votes for Bernice, there is no way that Abner can prevent Bernice's election. At most, Abner will be able to cast his 350 cumulative votes to elect the four other directors.

Cumulative voting has pitfalls for the unwary. If Abner spreads his votes unevenly or among many candidates, he might find himself electing only three or even fewer directors. Suppose that Abner casts his 350 votes as follows: Agatha (150), Arthur (150), Alexis (20), Andrew (20), and Astor (10). If Byron learns of this, he could catch Abner off-guard by casting his 150 votes as follows: Bernice (50), Bertrand (50), and Beatrice (50). The top five vote-getters would be Agatha, Arthur, Bernice, Bertrand, and Beatrice. By his inept voting, Abner would put only a minority of directors on the board, even though he holds 70 percent of the shares.

How should Abner and Byron plan their strategies? There is a mathematical formula for determining how many shares are necessary to assure the election of a director (or a given number of directors), and thus the optimum way to cast votes. The number of votes necessary to ensure a shareholder the power to elect a given number of directors is provided by a formula:

$$NS = \frac{ND \times TS}{TD + 1} + \text{some fraction (or 1)}$$

where   NS is the number of shares needed to elect the desired number of directors

ND is the number of directors that a shareholder desires to elect

TS is the total number of shares authorized to vote

TD is the total number of directors to be elected

The $\frac{ND \times TS}{TD + 1}$ part of the formula represents the point of equilibrium: A shareholder needs only a fraction more to push her choice over the top; hence the formula's requirement that something be added to this equilibrium figure. Unless the corporation recognizes fractional voting, the number of shares needed must be pushed up to the next whole number, either by rounding up or adding one. In our example, where AB Corp. has 100 voting shares and five directors are to be elected, the formula produces the following results:

Number of directors desired to be elected   *Number shares needed*

Number of directors				
1 director:	100/6 + fraction = 16.67 + fraction	= 17
2 directors:	200/6 + fraction = 33.33 + fraction	= 34
3 directors:	300/6 + fraction = 50 + 1	= 51
4 directors:	400/6 + fraction = 66.67 + fraction	= 68
5 directors:	500/6 + fraction = 83.33 + fraction	= 84

According to this table, Abner's 70 shares assure him of electing at least four directors because he holds more than 67 shares but less than 84. If Abner casts all his votes equally (or nearly so) for four candidates, he is assured of electing four directors. Byron is assured of electing only one director because his 30 shares are greater than 17 but less than 34. Byron must cast all his votes for one candidate to assure representation on the board.

Cumulative voting is not the only way to assure board representation. In close corporations with few shareholders, board representation can be assured by agreement (see §16.2) or classes of stock (see below); in public corporations (more than 500 shareholders), board representation for non-control shareholders is usually a matter of management concession. Cumulative voting often arises in middle-sized corporations having approximately 50 to 500 shareholders.

§13.1.4   Staggered Board — An Exception to One-Year Terms

The articles (and in some states the bylaws) can provide that only some of the directors are to be elected at each annual meeting. RMBCA §8.06 (articles). Under such an arrangement, known as a *staggered board,* the board is divided into groups of directors, each group with a staggered term. For example, suppose a corporation has a 12-person board divided into three groups of four directors each. Each year only four directors are up for election, and each director's term is three years. To ensure that a majority of the board is up for election at least every two years, many statutes specifically require that there be no more than three groups of directors. RMBCA §8.06.

There are a number of reasons for a staggered board, some less laudable than others. First, a staggered board assures greater continuity in board membership from year to year because the directors are not all subject to annual recall at once. Second, a staggered board reduces the number of directors up for election each year, and a majority of shareholders can effectively avoid minority representation on the board if there is cumulative voting. Third, it is more difficult for shareholders (even those holding a majority of a company's stock) to replace the members of a staggered board because only a portion of the board is up for election each year. For this reason, staggered boards (along with limitations on removing directors without cause) often are used by incumbent management to discourage unwanted takeovers (see Chapter 37).

§13.1.5   Classified Boards — Board Representation in the Capital Structure

The articles can specify that certain classes of stock elect their own directors. For example, AB Corp.'s articles might specify that Class A common shareholders elect three directors and Class B common shareholders elect two directors. Classifying the board may be a way of distributing shareholder power. Majority shareholders can also use classifying to undermine a minority shareholder's cumulative voting rights. The majority shareholders can amend the articles to create a new class of stock that allows them to elect a greater proportion of directors than had been the case under cumulative voting. RMBCA §8.04.

§13.2   Removal of Directors

Following the republican notion that legislators are entitled to remain in office during good behavior, the common law allowed shareholders to remove directors only for cause — such as fraud, criminal conduct, gross misman-agement, or self-dealing. Most statutes today give shareholders greater lati-tude to remove directors during their term — with or without cause. RMBCA §8.08(a) (removal with or without cause, unless articles specify otherwise). In addition, some states allow directors to be removed in a judicial proceeding brought by the corporation or by shareholders holding a specified percentage of shares. RMBCA §8.09 (judicial removal for "fraudulent or dishonest conduct, or gross abuse of authority" when in the best interests of the corporation).

§13.2.1   *Procedures for Removal — Due Process Notions*

In those states that allow removal at will by a majority of the shareholders, as well as in those states that allow shareholders to remove directors for cause, due process notions (a vestige of corporate republicanism) continue to require that directors be told of the reasons for removal and have a chance to answer charges. Shareholders must be given specific notice that removal will be considered at a meeting. RMBCA §8.08(d).

§13.2.2   *Removal of Directors Elected by Cumulative Voting*

To prevent majority shareholders from circumventing cumulative voting's promise of minority representation, nearly all state statutes specify that when cumulative voting is authorized, a director cannot be removed if any minority faction, with enough shares to have elected him by cumulative voting, votes against his removal. For example, if 20 shares would have been enough to elect a director under cumulative voting, then he cannot be removed if 20 shares are voted against his removal. RMBCA §8.08(c) (the Official Com-ment indicates that this restriction applies whether removal is with or without cause).

§13.2.3   Filling Vacancies — The Primacy of Shareholders

In general, the board or the shareholders can fill vacancies created by the removal, death, or resignation of directors, or the creation of new directorships. RMBCA §8.10. (Shareholders can exercise this power, however, only at an annual or special shareholders' meeting; see §12.2.1.) Some statutes limit the board's authority to fill vacancies, particularly when directors are removed or new directorships created, on the theory that the board should not be able to usurp the shareholders' power to elect directors.

§13.3   Board Decision-Making

In general, the board acts by majority vote as one body at a directors' meeting after proper notice and at which a quorum is present.

§13.3.1   Board Meetings — Notice and Quorum

Like shareholders, the board meets at both regular and specially called meetings. In general, the bylaws dictate whether, when, and how much notice must be given. RMBCA §8.22(a) (no notice required unless specified in the bylaws); RMBCA §8.22(b) (special meetings require two-day notice unless bylaws specify otherwise). Directors can waive notice in writing and are deemed to have waived notice by attending and not objecting to the meeting. RMBCA §8.23.

Quorum requirements prevent a minority of directors from meeting and taking action that the majority would not have. Unless the bylaws specify a greater number, a quorum exists when a majority of authorized directors are present at a meeting. RMBCA §8.24(a). Some statutes permit the articles or bylaws to specify a reduced quorum, but generally set a floor of one-third of the directors authorized. RMBCA §8.24(b). Many statutes require a quorum at the time the board votes, thus permitting directors to break a quorum and disempower the board by not showing up or walking out during a meeting. RMBCA §8.24(c). In states without such a statute, courts have held that a director who purposefully absences herself from a meeting to prevent a quorum cannot complain if the other directors take action to break the impasse. See *Gearing v. Kelly,* 182 N.E.2d 391 (N.Y. 1962). These cases undermine the use of board quorum requirements as a planning device to give participants in a close corporation a veto power, and dissolution rights, by not attending meetings.

The quorum requirements are relaxed when directors are filling vacancies. Under many statutes a majority of the directors *remaining in office,* even though they represent less than a quorum, constitute a quorum for filling director vacancies. RMBCA §8.10(a)(3).

§13.3.2   Board Action — Majority Voting at a Meeting

Action by directors at a properly convened meeting is generally decided by *majority vote of those present,* unless the articles or bylaws impose a super-majority requirement. RMBCA §8.24(c). Each director has one vote and cannot vote by proxy.

As a general rule, directors cannot vote separately; they must act together as a body at a properly convened meeting. This means that approval of a transaction by individual directors outside a meeting is not binding, even if all of the directors give their consent. Unless there is an exception, failure to comply with the "meeting rule" invalidates any transaction approved by the directors.

The meeting rule, and its lesson for those who deal with a corporation, is illustrated dramatically in *Baldwin v. Canfield,* 1 N.W. 261 (Minn. 1879). King was the sole shareholder of Minneapolis Agricultural & Machinist Association, Inc. (MAMA), whose sole asset was a fairground. King borrowed money from State National Bank, pledging all of his MAMA stock as collateral for the loan. He then arranged to sell the fairground property to Canfield on the condition that King would repay his bank loan and deliver his MAMA stock to Canfield. Without ever meeting, all of MAMA's directors individually and separately signed a deed of trust transferring the fairground to Canfield. His dirty business done, King disappeared with the proceeds from the bank loan and the proceeds from the sale to Canfield. In a suit between the bank and Canfield over ownership of the fairground, the court held that Canfield's deed of trust was invalid because it had not been executed by the directors at a proper meeting. Canfield lost the fairground and his money.

What should Canfield have done? For starters, Canfield should have insisted on receiving the MAMA stock as promised; ownership of the corporation would have assured him title to the fairgrounds. Beyond that, he also should have insisted on seeing the corporate charter and bylaws, as well as minutes of the meeting at which the deed was executed and a certificate from MAMA's secretary stating the minutes' authenticity and accuracy. The meeting rule assures shareholders that board decisions are made collegially at meetings, where there can be group interaction and deliberation. Sociological studies confirm that as to complex problems requiring judgment, the dynamics of a group generally produce better decisions than decisions reached by the same individuals acting separately.

A strict meeting rule has drawbacks. To permit flexible and efficient board action, many statutes now allow boards to take action by the separate consent of directors, provided the consent is unanimous. RMBCA §8.21.

Moreover, many statutes also allow directors' meetings to occur over the telephone or by other means of audio hookups — the next best thing to being there. RMBCA §8.20.

§13.3.3 Delegating Board Functions to Committees

Statutes allow the board to delegate many of the board's functions to committees composed of some (though less than all) of the directors. RMBCA §8.25. Some statutes specify certain functions or powers that cannot be delegated to committees, such as authorizing distributions and share repurchases, issuing shares, approving mergers, amending the articles, amending the bylaws, and making other fundamental corporate changes. RMBCA §8.25(e).

Committees of the board have assumed growing importance, particularly in public corporations. Executive committees act on matters that come up between regular board meetings and often iron out open questions before presentation to the board; the full board in the usual course adopts or ratifies the committee's action. Other standing committees have particular functions: the audit committee reviews the company's financial position with the company's outside auditor; the compensation committee negotiates and sets executive compensation; the nominating committee selects directors to be nominated for election by the shareholders. Often these committees are composed largely of outside directors — directors who are not employees of the corporation — to provide an element of independence in matters where there are potential conflicts between the interests of management (the corporation's top executives) and the interests of shareholders.

A relatively recent phenomenon has been the use of specially appointed temporary committees to deal with particular transactions in which conflicts of interest are likely. Examples include special litigation committees to decide on the corporation's stance toward shareholder derivative litigation against management (see §33.4) and special takeover committees to decide on the corporation's reaction to takeover bids for the company (see §40.2.2).

EXAMPLES

1. Graphic Designs is incorporated in an RMBCA jurisdiction. Its articles of incorporation are silent on the question of how directors are elected. Nine directors sit on Graphic's board.
   a. How are Graphic's directors elected?
   b. Shirley owns 78 of Graphic's 100 shares. Minnie owns the remaining 22. How many directors can Minnie elect under a straight voting scheme?

2. Graphic's articles specify that the corporation's board is to be elected by cumulative voting.

    a. With 22 of 100 shares, how many directors is Minnie assured of electing to the board?

    b. Shirley has heard that Minnie plans to cast her 198 cumulative votes in the following manner: Mary (66), Manny (66), Morton (66). Can Shirley take advantage of this information to increase her representation on the board?

    c. Graphic's board is considering issuing 50 new shares to Percy and reducing the size of the board to seven. How many directors could Percy elect to the seven-person board?

3. Shirley is unhappy with the directors Minnie has elected to Graphic's board. As majority shareholder, she considers some strategies:

    a. Shirley considers eliminating cumulative voting. Can she?

    b. Shirley considers reducing the number of directors on the board to three. What effect will this have on Minnie's cumulative voting rights?

    c. Can Shirley amend the articles to reduce the size of the board to three?

    d. Shirley considers staggering the nine-person board into three groups, each group's members coming up for election once every three years. What will be the effect?

    e. Can Shirley amend the bylaws to stagger the board in this way?

    f. How should Minnie protect her cumulative voting rights against these strategies?

4. Milton, one of the Graphic directors elected by Minnie, has begun a competing graphic design business using secret customer lists he obtained as a director of Graphic.

    a. Before he does further damage, Shirley wants him removed from the board and calls a special meeting for that purpose. If Graphic's articles state that directors can only be removed for cause, can she remove Milton?

    b. At the meeting, Shirley votes her 78 shares to remove Milton, and Minnie votes her 22 shares against removal. Is Milton removed?

    c. Shirley considers other options to remove Milton. What other recourse does she have?

    d. Milton resigns. Graphic's articles state that "The board of directors shall have the authority to fill any vacancies on the board until the next annual election." Shirley calls a special shareholders' meeting to fill the vacancy created by Milton's resignation. Can she?

5. Big Picture, a large commercial advertising firm, has offered a long-term contract to Graphic. The chair of Graphic's nine-person board calls each of the directors on the phone asking them to meet the next day.

    a. Six directors send in written consents approving the contract. Is this action by the board valid?

    b. Four of the directors attend the meeting; three others are patched in on a conference phone call. Is there a quorum?

    c. None of the seven directors objects during the meeting to not having received *written* notice of the meeting. Does lack of written notice undermine the validity of actions taken at the meeting?

    d. Of the seven of the directors present at the meeting, four vote to accept the contract; three oppose it. Is the approval valid?

    e. Halfway through the meeting the three directors on the conference call hang up. The remaining four directors, less than a quorum, approve the contract. Is their action valid?

    f. The three directors call back, and the seven directors appoint a committee consisting of two directors and the company's outside lawyer to negotiate the contract. The committee is given full authority to bind the corporation. The committee negotiates with Big Picture and unanimously approves a contract. Does this have the effect of valid board action?

EXPLANATIONS

1a. Straight voting, each year. Under the RMBCA, unless the articles specify otherwise, all directors are up for election at each annual shareholders' meeting. RMBCA §8.05(b). Each Graphic shareholder may vote for nine director candidates, and the top nine vote-getters are elected. RMBCA §7.28(a) (plurality voting). Cumulative voting and staggered terms apply only if chosen in the articles. See RMBCA §§7.28(c), 8.06.

1b. None. Under a straight voting scheme Shirley and Minnie each will cast their votes nine times for nine candidates. Each of Shirley's nine candidates will receive 78 votes, and each of Minnie's will receive only 22 votes. The nine top vote-getters will be Shirley's slate; Minnie does not have the power to elect any directors.

2a. Two directors. The cumulative-voting formula provides the answer:

$$NS = \frac{ND \times TS}{TD + 1} + \text{some fraction (or 1)}*.$$

Minnie needs —

    11 voting shares to elect one director $\left(\frac{1 \times 100}{9 + 1} + 1\right)$,

    21 shares for two directors $\left(\frac{2 \times 100}{9 + 1} + 1\right)$, and

    31 shares for three directors $\left(\frac{3 \times 100}{9 + 1} + 1\right)$.

Therefore, her 22 shares assure her the ability to elect two directors.

    Under cumulative voting, Minnie will have a total of 198 votes (22

---

    * NS is the number of shares needed to elect the desired number of directors.
ND is the number of directors that a shareholder desires to elect.
TS is the total number of voting shares.
TD is the total number of directors to be elected.

times 9) to distribute among her candidates. If she casts 99 votes for one of her candidates and 99 for the other, there is no way Shirley can cast her 702 votes (78 times 9) so that *more* than seven of her candidates will receive more than 99 votes. At best, Shirley can cast 100 votes for each of seven of her candidates, but she will have only two votes left to cast for her eighth candidate.

2b. Yes. Shirley can distribute her 702 votes among nine candidates, casting 78 votes for each one. Shirley will elect all nine directors in this way — the top nine vote-getters will all be Shirley's candidates. By spreading her votes among three candidates, Minnie dilutes her cumulative voting power.

2c. Two. After the issue, there would be a total of 150 voting shares outstanding. Again, the cumulative-voting formula provides the answer:

$$NS = \frac{ND \times TS}{TD + 1} + \text{some fraction (or 1)}$$

$$= \frac{2 \times 150}{7 + 1} + \text{some fraction (or 1)}$$

$$= 37.5 + \text{fraction}$$

$$= 38$$

Percy's 50 shares would be enough to elect two directors, but not enough to elect three, which would require 57 shares: $3 \times 150/8 + \text{fraction (or 1)} = 56.25 + \text{fraction} = 57$.

3a. Yes. The articles may be amended to delete a provision not required in the articles. RMBCA §10.01(a). Cumulative voting under the RMBCA is an opt-in right and can be removed by action of the board and majority approval of the shareholders.

3b. As a practical matter, it will destroy them. Even though Minnie will be able to cumulate her votes, she will no longer be able to elect a director. According to the cumulative-voting formula, if there are three directors, a shareholder must have 26 voting shares to be assured of electing one director. Minnie's 22 shares are not enough. Notice that a board of four directors would not have done the trick for Shirley. If there are four directors, a shareholder needs only 21 shares to be assured of electing one director. Minnie's 22 voting shares could elect at least one director on a four-person board.

3c. Yes. The effectiveness of cumulative voting is not assured under the RMBCA. Nonetheless, the amendment would seem to "materially and adversely affect" her voting rights, and Minnie may have dissenter's rights to force the corporation in an appraisal proceeding to pay her the fair value of her shares. RMBCA §13.02(a)(4)(iv) (see §36.1.1).

3d. The effect would be similar to reducing the size of the board. Minnie would no longer be assured the ability to elect a director, despite her continuing right to cumulate her votes. Only three directors would come up for election each year, and Shirley would be able to elect all of them.

3e. No. Shirley cannot accomplish this through a bylaw amendment. The RMBCA requires that a staggered board be provided for in the articles. RMBCA §8.06. Even if Shirley were to use her majority power to amend the articles, Minnie may have dissenters' rights. (See the answer to question 3b.) There is, however, no explicit limit on creating a staggered board where it undermines the effectiveness of cumulative voting.

3f. Corporate drafters often include "anticircumvention" provisions in the articles' cumulative voting provisions. These provisions may require, for example, that any changes to cumulative voting rights, the size of the board, or the annual election of all directors be approved by a super-majority vote.

4a. Yes. Milton's misappropriation of the company's trade secrets is not only illegal under state law, but is also a breach of his fiduciary duties (see §24.2). There is cause for his removal.

4b. No. Under the RMBCA, Milton cannot be removed if the number of shares needed to elect in a corporation with cumulative voting are voted against removal. RMBCA §8.08(c). Eleven shares would have been sufficient to elect Milton, $\left(\dfrac{100}{9 + 1} + 1 \right)$, and Milton cannot be removed if eleven (or more) votes are cast against his removal. This means that Minnie can prevent his removal, even though there is cause. Minnie has the power to decide whether Milton's transgressions warrant removal, on the theory that she could re-elect him if she so desired.

4c. Shirley can seek to have Milton removed by judicial order. Under the RMBCA, a 10 percent shareholder can have a director removed if the court finds the director engaged in "fraudulent or dishonest conduct" or "gross abuse of authority or discretion," and that his removal is in the corporation's best interests. RMBCA §8.09. Milton's misappropriation of company trade secrets, particularly if it posed a continuing risk of damage to business, would seem to easily meet this test.

4d. Perhaps. A strong argument can be made that despite the provision in the articles, the shareholders retain their inherent authority to fill vacancies. The provision does not state that shareholders are disempowered or that the board has exclusive authority. RMBCA §8.10 provides that either the shareholders or the board may fill vacancies.

5a. No. In general, directors must act in person. Although action by consent is possible, the RMBCA (and other states that authorize it) require that it be unanimous. RMBCA §8.21. This rule assures the opportunity for minority views to be expressed and for collective decision-making by the directors.

5b. Yes, under the RMBCA. A quorum is present if a majority of the nine-person board is present at a meeting. RMBCA §8.24. Unless the articles or bylaws prevent "presence" by means of audio communication, the three directors on the conference telephone call are considered present at the meeting. RMBCA §8.20(b). The "presence" rule provides the board with greater flexibility in handling emergency matters without the delay, trouble, and expense of a face-to-face meeting.

5c. Yes. Although any notice deficiencies are waived if the directors in attendance failed to object to them at the meeting, the two directors who were not present at the meeting did not waive the notice deficiency. RMBCA §8.23. The purpose of the notice requirements is to assure the representation of all views, and the failure of the two absent directors to waive the notice deficiency undermines the validity of actions taken at the meeting. Nonetheless, if the absent directors give written waivers, which are then filed with the meeting's minutes, the waivers are valid even though given after the meeting.

5d. Yes. There was a quorum at the meeting. Approval is by a majority of the directors present — four of seven. RMBCA §8.24(c). This assures that the board will be able to act, even though some actions may be approved by less than a majority of the authorized directors.

5e. No. According to the RMBCA, a quorum must be present when the vote is taken. RMBCA §8.24(c). This allows directors to break a quorum, giving significance to quorum requirements in determining the balance of power on the board. Some courts have not ascribed this function to quorum requirements and have not allowed directors to complain if they absented themselves or left during a meeting to prevent a quorum.

5f. Perhaps not. Although the board can delegate its functions to a committee, including negotiating and approving a contract, the committee must be composed of directors. RMBCA §8.25. The appointment of a nondirector may render any action by the committee invalid. Nonetheless, it may be argued that the two directors appointed to the committee constituted a proper committee of two, and the board could delegate its decision-making power with respect to the contract to the committee. Viewing the outside lawyer as an advisor to the two directors, the committee action is binding.

14

The Corporate Bureaucracy — Officers' Authority to Bind the Corporation

The board of directors is the locus of power in the traditional model of corporate governance. The authority to act for the corporation resides with the board unless shareholder approval is specifically mandated by statute or in the constitutive documents. This centralizes corporate decision-making in the model's specialized managers and protects shareholder interests against renegade agents.

Corporate law borrows from the law of agency and treats the board as embodying the authority of the corporate principal and the officers (and employees) as agents. Thus, whether the corporation is bound in a particular transaction raises the usual host of agency questions — those of actual, apparent, and inherent authority — with a modern emphasis on protecting outside parties' expectations. This chapter considers the authority of corporate agents to bind the corporation and the extent to which outside parties must inquire into the agent's authority.

§14.1 Corporate Authority

The sources of authority for corporate officers, like those for any agent, exist along a continuum.

§14.1.1   *Express Actual Authority — Formal Board Action*

Corporate authority arises in its clearest form when the board expressly acts at a properly convened meeting. As long as the corporate statute or the corporation's constitutive documents do not limit the board's authority, board action binds the corporation. Most corporate transactions, however, are not expressly entered into by the board of directors. The board usually delegates corporate authority to corporate officers. The board entrusts ordinary corporate matters such as employment agreements, supply and sales contracts, and credit arrangements to corporate officers, who act as the corporation's day-to-day agents. RMBCA §8.41. *Express authority* for officers to bind the corporation can be found in a number of sources: statute (though now rare); articles of incorporation (but not often); bylaws (the most common source for broad descriptions of officers' functions and responsibilities); and board resolutions (which authorize either categories of transactions or specific transactions). The delegation of authority to an officer in one of these sources constitutes corporate consent to the officer binding the corporation. This authority exists whether or not the third party knew about the officer's authority.

Even when an officer's actions are not binding against the corporation when made, the board can create express authority retroactively by ratifying a prior act if the board has the power to authorize the act. Ratification creates the agency relationship and "relates back," so that the prior act, even if by a nonagent, is treated as authorized from the start.

§14.1.2   *Implied Actual Authority — Internal Understandings*

In many instances there is no express authority for an officer to enter into a transaction on behalf of the corporation, yet it can fairly be inferred that the board had implicitly approved the action. How is this inference made? There are two techniques. One is to consider the penumbra of authority that flows from the express authority actually delegated to the officer — such as when a corporate president is authorized to "manage the day-to-day affairs of the business." In such a case, it can be inferred that the board impliedly has given the president broad authority to do anything incidental to the open-ended grant of authority.

The second technique is to look at the board's reaction to other similar transactions as a measure of whether the transaction had been approved impliedly beforehand. In some of these cases, implied authorization is easy to find, such as when the board knows of and acquiesces in an officer's long-standing course of conduct. When the officer engages in this conduct again, it can fairly be said that, considering its prior inaction, the board has already impliedly authorized the conduct. As in cases of actual authority, the corporation is bound even if the third party did not know about this implicit validation of corporate authority.

The difficult cases arise where authority cannot readily be inferred from the officer's express authority and there is no formal ratification of the officer's course of conduct. When is authority for a novel transaction implied? The cases reflect a number of approaches, though it generally is accepted that acquiescence can bind the corporation despite the rule that the board must act at properly convened meetings. Some cases hold that all of the directors must have known about the transaction and done nothing — unanimous acquiescence. Other cases require only a silent majority. In any event, an important consideration in both cases is whether the corporation derived a benefit from the transaction and whether the board waited before repudiating the deal.

Some courts have gone so far as to impute to the board the officers' knowledge and to infer that the board implicitly ratified the transaction if the corporation has accepted the benefits of the transaction. This approach, which disregards board behavior in order to protect third-party expectations, has a strong flavor of inherent authority — that is, authority without regard to actual or apparent corporate consent.

§14.1.3 Apparent Authority — External Appearances

What happens when there is no actual authorization, such as when the board has expressly denied authority to an officer? If the board induces a third party to rely on an officer, even if the officer has no actual authority, the corporation may be bound on a theory of apparent authority. The question of apparent authority often surfaces with respect to what is sometimes (confusingly) described as the "inherent" power of the president to bind the corporation. Early common law flew in the face of the popular assumption that a corporate president has broad "presidential" authority, and third parties often discovered that the validity of their dealings with the corporation depended on internal corporate machinations, not outward appearances. To deal with this unfairness and the inefficiency of forcing outside parties to verify an officer's authority for every transaction, courts began to impose liability whenever the board created the appearance that an officer was authorized to carry out a transaction.

How is the appearance of authority created? Much depends on the corporate officer's position in the corporation. The following describe the general areas of corporate officer's authority and the general assumptions that third parties are entitled to make:

President or CEO. The president (or often in modern usage the chief executive officer) can bind the corporation as to matters in the usual course of business. The president generally cannot bind the corporation as to *extraordinary matters,* which have been held to include the bringing or settling of litigation, offering lifetime employment contracts, and disposing of or mortgaging all the corporation's assets. As to such matters, the outside party is on notice to demand proof of actual authority.

Vice president.   The vice president replaces the president when needed. With the modern proliferation of vice presidents in managerial positions, a vice president can only bind the corporation only as to matters within her area.

Secretary.   The secretary normally does not bind the corporation but merely keeps and certifies corporate records.

Treasurer.   The treasurer normally does not bind the corporation but keeps the corporate books, receives payments, and makes other authorized payments.

Although this describes the general pattern, the authority given an officer in the bylaws or the course of conduct of a particular company's officers may be enough to create the manifestations of authority that an outside party can rely on. Whether or not particular conduct is authorized, the corporation cannot deny the officers' apparent authority.

Often the question of apparent authority will turn on whether the transaction is ordinary or extraordinary. Courts assume the outside party is under a duty to verify authority if the transaction is extraordinary — that is, without apparent business justification or of such importance board approval would seem necessary. In *Lee v. Jenkins Bros.,* 268 F.2d 357 (2d Cir. 1959), the court held that the president's contract promising an employee a pension at age 60, which the court assumed became vested after he worked for a reasonable time, was not "extraordinary" because it neither implicated future managerial policy nor exposed the corporation to significant liabilities. On the other hand, in *Burke v. Bevona,* 931 F.2d 998 (2d Cir. 1991), the court found that a lifetime employment contract was "extraordinary," and in the absence of actual authority the corporation was not bound.

By the same token, the extent of the corporation's business interest in a transaction often determines whether it is ordinary or extraordinary. For example, a copper manufacturer was not bound on its treasurer's unusual guaranty of a loan to a construction company because the manufacturer had at best a tangential interest in the construction company. *General Overseas Films v. Robin International, Inc.,* 542 F. Supp 684 (S.D.N.Y. 1982). But a parent corporation was bound on its president's guaranty of a subsidiary's contract for the printing of its catalogues because the parent stood to gain from the subsidiary's catalogue sales. *Foote & Davies v. Arnold Craven, Inc.,* 324 S.E.2d 889 (N.C. App. 1985).

The theory of apparent authority focuses on protecting the reasonable beliefs of outside parties. Thus, if the third party actually *knows* the officer has no authority, there can be no apparent authority. Likewise, if the third party does not know of a particular corporate course of conduct, the party cannot claim reliance — that is, unknown manifestations of authority cannot create apparent authority. Further, if an officer has expressed doubts about his authority, the third party may be required to verify the officer's actual authority.

You should be careful to distinguish between implied actual authority and apparent authority. The issue of implied authority turns on whether it can be inferred that the board approved the officer's actions and is now trying to weasel out. The third party need not know about the relationship between the board and the officer. The issue of apparent authority, although its proof may overlap with that of implied authority, focuses on whether the board created the appearance to reasonable, reliant third parties that the officer had authority.

§14.1.4 Inherent Authority

Some courts have held that as between the corporation and an innocent outside third party, the corporation receives the greater benefit from the use of agents and thus should bear the risk of an agent acting beyond his authority. Under a theory of *inherent authority,* the corporation is bound regardless of any actual or apparent authority. If verifying authority is costly and there is little reason to protect the traditional exclusivity of the board's authority, courts sometimes find inherent authority even in the absence of actual and apparent authority (as normally understood).

This policy is particularly strong if, for example, the officer who allegedly bound the corporation is also a significant shareholder. In such a case, allowing the corporation to disavow the contract for lack of internal formalities would shift the risk of loss to creditors while only marginally promoting the purposes of central corporate governance.

§14.2 Respondeat Superior — Corporate Liability for Employee Torts

Corporate agents also can bind the corporation in noncontractual settings. If an officer or other employee commits a tort, even though the corporation has not actually or apparently authorized the employee to commit the tort, the corporation is nonetheless bound on a theory of respondeat superior if the employee was acting within the scope of his employment. Fundamental notions of responsibility and risk-shifting akin to those that drive the theory of inherent authority place the burden on the entity for whom the employee was acting rather than on the victimized third party.

EXAMPLES

1. Swamp Acres, Inc. buys and drains swampland for resale. Its president, G. W. Flimm, signs a sales contract to sell Quagacre to Priscilla.
   a. Flimm tells Priscilla that the board has passed a resolution authorizing him to sell Quagacre. Should Priscilla press for more information to make sure the corporation will be bound?
   b. The Swamp Acres board passes a resolution: "President Flimm is authorized to sell Quagacre." Flimm negotiates a sale of Quagacre to Priscilla but does not disclose that he has authority. Priscilla doubts that he does. Is the corporation bound under the contract with Priscilla? If so, on what theory?
   c. As has been his practice, Flimm says he is willing to accept an installment note from Priscilla as consideration for Quagacre. Priscilla does not know of Flimm's past practice. Will the corporation be bound under the installment contract? If so, on what theory?

2. The Swamp Acres bylaws expressly require that all land sales be made with prior board approval. The board revokes its resolution authorizing the sale of Quagacre. Once Flimm had signed a sales contract on his own without board approval, but the board ratified the contract. Priscilla does not know about this, but she relies on Flimm's statement that as president he can sell Quagacre. Is the corporation bound? If so, on what theory?

3. After signing the contract with Flimm, Priscilla learns that the board had never approved the sale as the bylaws required. Priscilla is worried about the contract being honored. What should she do?

4. Flimm decides to hire a sales assistant. He offers the job to W. F. Wiley, who demands that she receive a $20,000 bonus (in addition to her regular commission) for every sale over $1 million. Flimm, who owns a majority of Swamp Acres stock and controls the board, accepts.
   a. Two years later, Wiley sells Sinkacre for $4 million and demands her bonus. Comparable bonuses are unheard of, and the Swamp Acres bylaws specifically state that the president may not offer bonuses to employees without board approval. Is the corporation bound? If so, on what theory?
   b. When the directors hear that Wiley has sold Sinkacre for $4 million, they are elated and authorize payment of the bonus. A few months later, Wiley sells Marshacre for $1.1 million and again demands her special bonus. The board is less enthusiastic about the Marshacre

sales price and refuses to authorize payment. Is the corporation bound? If so, on what theory?

EXPLANATIONS

1a. Yes. Flimm, as an agent of the corporation, cannot create his own authority. Priscilla will want to be sure that the resolution actually was adopted and that it was valid under the state statute, as well as under the corporation's articles and bylaws. In an important transaction with a corporation, third parties often will obtain a copy of the articles from state officials and demand copies from corporate officers of bylaws, relevant resolutions, and minutes of the meetings at which the resolutions were adopted. The third party also will ask that the corporation's secretary certify the genuineness of the bylaws, resolutions, and minutes. If an outside party does this, courts have held that this is enough, and the corporation is bound under a theory of apparent authority even if there was no actual authority. See *In re Drive-In Development Corp.*, 371 F.2d 215 (7th Cir. 1967).

1b. Yes, on a theory of actual authority. Flimm's actual authority does not depend on how things appeared to Priscilla. The corporation will be bound even though Priscilla neither knew of the authorizing resolution and thought Flimm lacked authority. Even though there is no express authority to sell Quagacre to Priscilla, there is implied actual authority. Given the wording of the resolution, it can be inferred that the board did not care who Flimm dealt with.

1c. Probably, under a theory of implied actual authority. The corporation will be bound if it can be inferred from the circumstances that the board viewed the note as adequate consideration or if the board in the past had acquiesced in Flimm's practice of accepting installment notes as consideration. But if the board in the past had expressed its opposition to such consideration, actual authority might be negated.

In either event, when deciding whether actual authority existed, it is irrelevant whether Priscilla knew of Flimm's practice or of the board's reaction to previous sales.

2. Priscilla can argue that Flimm had apparent authority and also that the corporation is bound under the doctrine of respondeat superior for his misrepresentation of authority. However, there is no actual authority, express or implied.

Apparent authority. Priscilla can argue that the board, by naming Flimm as president, created the appearance that he had authority to bind the corporation to contracts in the ordinary course of its business, including sales contracts of corporate property. It is irrelevant that the board had withdrawn actual authority from Flimm to sell Quagacre. Apparent authority exists if such contracts are ordinary for corporate presidents of comparable corporations or for Flimm.

If Priscilla knew that it was the practice that comparable sales contracts be signed by a corporate president, the Quagacre contract is ordinary and within Flimm's apparent authority. Even if there were no such practice, Swamp Acres is bound if the transaction was in its ordinary business — in Priscilla's eyes. This will depend on the nature of Swamp Acres's business, the uniqueness of Quagacre, and the dollar size of the transaction. If Priscilla knew that Swamp Acres was in the business of buying and reselling drained swampland, that property such as Quagacre was easily found, and that the size of the transaction was not substantial for Swamp Acres, the contract would seem ordinary and Flimm's authority apparent. The absence of any of these factors would place Priscilla under a duty to verify Flimm's authority.

Respondeat superior. Priscilla also could argue that Flimm's intentional misstatements carried out in the course of his employment make the corporation liable on a tort deceit theory. Such a theory might be difficult in cases of extraordinary corporate transactions, where the assumption the transaction is so unusual or big that a *reasonable* party would demand verification of corporate authority. That is, reasonable reliance on authority — a necessary element of a deceit action — would be lacking. To protect the integrity of central corporate governance and protect the corporation against renegade agents, third parties are put to the task of verifying authority in extraordinary transactions.

3. She could seek board ratification. Although authority is measured at the time of the transaction, the board can create actual authority by ratifying the sales contract. In a board resolution, express ratification creates express actual authority retroactively.

4a. Perhaps, on a theory of inherent authority. There is neither actual authority (which requires board approval) nor apparent authority (because such a bonus is extraordinary). Nonetheless, as between Swamp Acres and Wiley, it might be argued that Swamp Acres should bear the risk of Flimm's usurpation of authority. The requirement of board approval — presumably to protect shareholders from the actions of rogue officers — is less compelling because Flimm is the majority shareholder.

4b. Probably, on a theory of implied authority from earlier ratification. The board's acceptance of the special bonus in connection with the Sinkacre deal can be seen as an implicit ratification of the bonus contract. The effect of this ratification is as though Flimm had original authority to agree to the special bonus clause. The board cannot now disavow Flimm's exercise of authority.

PART FIVE

Management of the Closely Held Corporation

15

The Control Dilemma in the Close Corporation — An Introduction

The word "corporation" often brings to mind an institution such as General Motors or IBM: a monolithic organization with hundreds of thousands of widely dispersed investors who have pooled their money into a far-flung enterprise with large capital needs run by a corps of professional (and invariably gray-suited) managers. But the advantages of incorporation — in particular, limited liability and the "off the rack" corporate structure — are just as attractive to smaller, less capital-intensive enterprises run by more comfortably dressed entrepreneurs. Small businesses with only a handful of owners have taken advantage of the corporate form, using the same enabling statutes that allow publicly held corporations to incorporate with relative ease. But it is an awkward fit.

In this chapter we introduce the control dilemma faced by participants in a closely held or "close" corporation. In Chapter 16 we consider the various control devices that corporate planners have devised to deal with this dilemma, and in Chapter 17 we discuss how corporate law deals with infighting among close corporation participants.

§15.1   Special Problems in the Close Corporation

The close corporation places the corporate planner on the horns of a dilemma. On one horn, the statutory corporate model calls for majority control, significant power, and discretion in the board of directors, and a relatively limited role for shareholders in the management of the business — the specialized structure typical of a publicly held corporation. On the other horn, the participants in a close corporation will want significantly more control over and protection of their cash and human investments. The planner will discover that such participants will often want to act as an "incorporated partnership" in which they each contribute their money and labor even though (as we have seen in Chapters 11-14) the corporate statutes contemplate a much different organizational structure. Unfettered majority rule and centralized management will often be contrary to their expectations.

Consider the basic differences between a closely held and publicly held corporation.

Close Corporation	*Public Corporation*
(1) a small, tightly knit group of participants (no more than 30 to 50) who often are family members or former members of a small partnership	(1) large number of investors (more than 500) who have no relationship with each other besides their share ownership
(2) active, though informal, participation by nonspecialized investor/owners in managing the business	(2) limited participation by shareholders in the business through proxy voting at formal meetings; active, specialized management by business executives
(3) participants who often look to the corporation for a means of livelihood through payment of salaries or dividends	(3) investors who look for a return on their investment through appreciation in market price and dividend income
(4) no ready market for shareholders to dispose of their shares and sometimes contractual limits on transferability	(4) public trading markets (such as stock exchanges) for shareholders to easily dispose of their freely transferable shares

Perhaps the most significant difference for close corporation shareholders is the limited range of options available if they become disenchanted with the way the corporation is being run or how they are being treated. In a public corporation, disenchanted shareholders have access to reasonably efficient and nearly costless securities markets, such as the New York Stock Exchange, where they can sell their shares — a privilege often called the "Wall Street rule." As a practical matter, this option is unavailable to close corporation shareholders.

Without a public trading market that offers liquidity and price discovery, a disgruntled shareholder has few viable options. The chances of finding an outside buyer are slim because any potential buyer would have to undertake a costly study of the corporation's value and be willing to become stuck himself in the seller's unenviable position. Few investors are willing to accept these uncertainties. If the disgruntled shareholder seeks to sell to the other shareholders, it will often be at an unattractive, forced price. If the disgruntled shareholder seeks judicial protection, she can expect an expensive and drawn-out battle, compounded by corporate law's business judgment rule and its traditional deference to majority control. Greater protection beforehand, preferably built into the corporate structure or in a binding contract, becomes highly desirable.

§15.2 Planning for the Close Corporation

The mission of the attorney for close corporation participants is to create, through careful planning and drafting, control devices that adapt the statutory structure (within limits) to assure that the participants' purposes are accomplished. These control devices can take the form of shareholder agreements, special provisions in the articles and bylaws, and dispute-resolution procedures. The planning challenge requires that the planner be familiar with the available devices and with how corporate statutes and doctrines limit their use.

Over the last few decades, drafters of corporate codes have addressed the close corporation dilemma by adopting special statutory provisions that enable "boutique" close corporations specially structured to meet the needs of their participants. Delaware, for example, offers a special "comprehensive" close corporation statute. Del. GCL §§341-356. (The same ABA committee that adopted the RMBCA also approved a Model Close Corporation Supplement that suggests supplemental provisions for use by close corporations.) Other states, such as California and New York, interweave such provisions throughout their corporate statutes. Recent revisions to the RMBCA add new provisions on shareholders' agreements and buyout remedies.

If the close corporation planner can use these special provisions, her task is much easier. Nonetheless, many corporate codes (even those with special close corporation provisions) continue to reflect a "unified" approach under which all corporations, both closely and publicly held, are governed by the same statutory approach. Although recent judicial trends provide greater tolerance for departures from the traditional corporate model, recognition of the close corporation dilemma is not universal. Beware! The old rule that what is good for the public corporation "goose" is also good for the close corporation "gander" (and what is bad is bad) has remarkable staying power.

EXAMPLES

Three family members decide to go into the pizza business. Bob has some pizzeria experience; his wealthy uncle Rich is willing to invest in the venture; and Bob's cousin Sally has some spare cash and spare time. The three incorporate the business as Pizza Chateau, Inc.

Rich, who knows nothing about pizza, is willing to put up $80,000 and hopes to earn annual dividends equal to at least 10 percent of his investment. Bob has only $5000 to contribute but thinks his pizzeria experience counts for a lot; he is willing to run the business for a steady salary of at least $20,000. Sally, who has $15,000 to invest, is willing to be a part-time bookkeeper.

1. Is Pizza Chateau a close corporation, and, if so, what does this mean for the three parties?
2. Given Rich's expectations, how much control will he want? What about Bob? Sally?
3. If the three parties realign corporate governance and the other corporate attributes to suit their needs, does incorporation assure them limited liability?
4. Would the parties' objectives be accomplished if their shareholdings were proportionate to their capital contributions — 80 percent for Rich, 5 percent for Bob, and 15 percent for Sally?

EXPLANATIONS

1. The corporation is a classic close corporation: Pizza Chateau has only a few shareholders (thus far only three) who have chosen each other and have bargained on the nature of their relationship; two of them are to participate in managing the business and one is counting on it to earn a livelihood; as a practical matter, their investment is not liquid — there is no recognized market for their shares.

2. We can speculate. Rich is an investor of money capital who probably wants to protect his investment. After all, he could have put his money into a bank and earned a safer return. To do this, Rich probably will want some say over the significant matters that affect his investment, although not necessarily over the pizzeria's normal day-to-day operations — *modified central management*. For example, Rich might want to be able to prevent Bob from opening a new restaurant without his permission, although he might not care if Bob adds anchovies to the menu or hires a new delivery driver. Rich also is counting on Bob being the "working partner" and would not want Bob to be able to sell his interest — *restrictions on transferability*. Rich will want some assurances that he will receive steady dividends and that excessive salaries to Bob and Sally will not eat them up — a further *constraint on central management*. And he will want some way to liquidate his investment, perhaps by dissolving the corporation, if he wants to get out — *an exception to corporate perpetuity*.

Bob as manager is investing his human capital; his expectations will be somewhat different from Rich's. He probably will worry that Rich might try to oust him or interfere with running the business. Bob will want an assurance of incumbency and significant management discretion — *an exception to shareholder majority control*. He will also want to be sure he is paid his salary before any dividends are paid — *modified central management*. Like Rich, he might not want the other shareholders to sell to other (unknown) investors without his consent — *a limit on transferability*. Bob probably also will want some way to sell his interest to the corporation or the other shareholders if he decides to get out — *a substitute for a stock trading market*.

Sally is a hybrid capitalist-manager, who will invest both money and human capital. She is a prototypical participant in a close corporation. Her expectations will be a mixture of Rich's and Bob's. Like Rich and Bob, she will want to adjust the traditional corporate attributes of central management, majority shareholder control, free share transferability, and perpetual corporate existence.

3. As a theoretical matter, yes. Unless the corporate veil is pierced (see Chapter 6), neither contract nor tort creditors can hold any of them liable in their roles as shareholders, directors, or officers. Nonetheless, as a practical matter, creditors to a close corporation (such as banks) often will insist on personal guarantees from shareholders. Personal liability will often be contractual.

4. No. Simply incorporating and receiving shares proportionate to their capital contributions could be a governance disaster. Under the traditional structure of central management and majority shareholder control, Rich (as majority shareholder, assuming straight voting) would elect all the directors. The directors would then have the power to decide on how the pizzeria is managed, who is manager, who is bookkeeper, how much and when dividends are paid, and how much is paid in salaries. Neither Bob nor Sal could be assured that their desires would be met. Moreover, under the traditional corporate rule of free share transferability, any of the parties could sell his or her shares, leaving the others with a new unanticipated "partner." Nor does the traditional structure provide any mechanism for any of the parties to withdraw from the business and force the others, or the corporation, to buy his or her interest.

16

Control Devices in the Close Corporation

Various solutions to the control dilemma described in Chapter 15 are available in the close corporation. Each solution deviates from the traditional corporate structure described in Chapters 11-14.

Most of these deviations, or control devices, operate at the shareholder level — supermajority requirements, vote-pooling agreements, voting trusts, additional classes of shares, irrevocable proxies — and their validity generally is easy to assure. Control devices at the management or director level — compensation guarantees, dissolution stipulations, limits on business, dividend policies — present a different story because they may conflict with the statutory norm that the board manages the corporation. Nonetheless, it is not uncommon for both kinds of control devices (though analytically distinct) to be incorporated into a single "Shareholders' Agreement."

In this chapter we consider the more common control devices: their purposes, creation, and validity. Throughout you will notice a tension between (1) the traditional corporate assumptions of centralized management and unfettered majority control and (2) the flexibility sought by incorporated partners to "contract out" of the corporate structure.

§16.1 Supermajority Requirements — Minority Veto Power

One of the simplest ways to modify the control structure of the corporation is to create high quorum and high voting requirements for shareholders' and directors' meetings. Under the traditional corporate model, approval of corporate action follows the same pattern at both the shareholder and board level: There must be a quorum, and there must be approval by a majority of votes present (see §§12.2.3, 13.3).

§16.1.1   Purpose of Supermajority Provisions

Greater-than-majority (or supermajority) quorum or voting requirements give parties in a close corporation *veto power* that they would not have under a system of majority voting. A veto power can exist for specified matters of significance, such as approving mergers, appointing officers, fixing dividends, or issuing new stock. Or it can exist for all matters coming before the shareholders or directors, although this greatly increases the possibility of deadlock when the shareholders or directors (or both) cannot muster a supermajority on anything.

Besides their use as veto devices, supermajority provisions perform a valuable anticircumvention function. They can be (and should be) used to safeguard carefully crafted control rights inserted into the articles or bylaws. Unless a supermajority voting (or quorum) requirement attaches to any change or action that would adversely affect these rights, a majority shareholder (or a coalition of minority shareholders) could easily undo the best laid plans. For example, if charter provisions specify a four-person board and cumulative voting to assure board representation to any 20 percent shareholder, the charter should also specify that these provisions can only be changed through a greater than 80 percent vote. Otherwise, the right of board representation could be eliminated by a simple majority-approved amendment.

§16.1.2   Creation of Supermajority Provisions

Majority action is the rule unless explicitly specified otherwise. Under most statutes supermajority quorum and voting requirements *for shareholder action* must be incorporated in the articles, either when originally drafted or by amendment. RMBCA §7.25(a) and (c); Cal. Corp. §602(a); Del. GCL §216; N.Y. BCL §616. In many jurisdictions, supermajority provisions added by amendment must receive supermajority approval. For amendment of articles, see RMBCA §7.27(b); Cal. Corp. §902(e); Del. GCL §242(b)(4); N.Y. BCL §616. For shareholder amendment of bylaws, see RMBCA §10.21(a); Cal. Corp. §211; Del. GCL §§109(a), 216.

Supermajority requirements *for director voting* may be incorporated in the articles or sometimes in the bylaws if they are not inconsistent with the articles. RMBCA §8.24; Cal. Corp. §307(a); Del. GCL §141(b); N.Y. BCL §709. In addition, if all the parties agree, supermajority requirements can be included in a shareholders' agreement. RMBCA §7.32.

§16.1.3 Validity of Supermajority Provisions

State statutes generally permit supermajority requirements. For shareholder quorum and voting, see RMBCA §§7.27; Cal. Corp. §§602(a), 710; Del. GCL §102(b)(4); N.Y. BCL §616. For director quorum and voting, see RMBCA §8.24; Cal. Corp. §307(a); Del. GCL §141(b); N.Y. BCL §709.

Some earlier cases (their continuing vitality in doubt because of superseding statutory changes) suggest that parties cannot require *unanimous voting* because such a requirement may frustrate regular corporate functioning and create a risk of deadlock. See *Benintendi v. Kenton Hotel*, 60 N.E.2d 829 (N.Y. 1945). For the planner, this is a minor headache. Nonunanimous supermajority provisions can be designed to have the effect of unanimity. For instance, if Rich, Bob, and Sally each take one-third of Pizza Chateau's shares and agree that any matter must be approved by 75 percent of the outstanding votes, the effect is to require unanimity. In addition, the planner can combine unanimous quorum requirements (which cases have upheld) with less-than-unanimous voting requirements for much the same effect. Some statutes specifically allow unanimity requirements if placed in the articles.

One problem with a supermajority *quorum* alone is that to be effective a party must stay away from the meeting to "cast" her veto. If the party shows up at a meeting and is counted for quorum purposes, she might not be able to break the quorum in mid-meeting. See RMBCA §7.25(b); Cal. Corp. §602(b); N.Y. BCL §608(c) (once a share is represented at a meeting, it is present for quorum purposes for the remainder of the meeting); cf. Official Comment to RMBCA §8.24(c) (board cannot act if a director breaks the quorum by leaving during a meeting). Some courts have refused to respect the legitimacy of quorum requirements as a control device. In *Gearing v. Kelly*, 182 N.E.2d 391 (N.Y. 1962), the court said that a director who purposefully refused to attend a board meeting, and was thus prevented a quorum, could not complain when the remaining directors elected a new director without a quorum. The court held that the director could not use the bylaw's quorum provision to deadlock the corporation. A well-reasoned dissent argued, however, that the court should not assist either side in their dispute. Other courts have understood that quorum requirements, though creating a risk of deadlock, can serve as bargained-for "veto" and have invalidated actions taken without a quorum due to the complaining party's absence.

§16.2   Vote-Pooling Agreements — Shareholder Coalitions

Often no one shareholder will have voting control of the corporation's shares in a close corporation. Rather, as in politics, there will be voting coalitions. Shareholders will agree formally or informally to vote their shares as a group to form a voting block sufficient to pass or block initiatives. For example, if Rich, Bob, and Sally each becomes a 33-⅓ percent shareholder in Pizza Chateau and shareholder action is by majority vote, none alone has any meaningful power. But if any two join together, their cabal can block any initiatives by the other and effectively control all matters involving shareholder voting. By pooling their votes on a particular matter or in general, minority shareholders maximize their voting power.

§16.2.1   Workings of a Vote-Pooling Agreement

Vote-pooling agreements are particularly important (and primarily used) in electing directors. Directors generally are elected by straight (plurality) voting unless cumulative voting applies (see §13.1.2). Consider how a pooling agreement might work under both straight and cumulative voting using the facts of the famous case of *Ringling Bros.-Barnum & Bailey Combined Shows, Inc. v. Ringling,* 53 A.2d 441 (Del. 1947). The corporation had seven directors and three shareholders, who held 1000 shares: Mrs. Ringling — 315 shares, Mrs. Haley — 315 shares, and Mr. North — 370 shares.

Straight (plurality) voting.   Under straight voting, the candidates who obtain a plurality of the votes (the top vote-getters) for the open director seats are elected. If Ringling and Haley do not pool their votes, North would elect all the directors. North's seven candidates would each receive 370 votes and be the seven top vote-getters. But if Ringling and Haley pool their 630 votes, together they can *elect all the directors;* their seven candidates would be the top vote-getters.

Cumulative voting.   Under cumulative voting, the number of votes necessary to ensure that a shareholder has the power to elect one or more directors is fixed by formula.* (See §13.1.3.) In our *Ringling Bros.* example, the formula tells us that 126 votes are needed to elect one director, 251 to elect two, and 376 to elect three. Ringling, Haley, and North alone can each elect at most two directors. The seventh director will be elected depending on how the three shareholders split their votes, with North having the best shot at playing

---

* The formula to elect N directors is:

$$\frac{N \times \text{(total number of shares authorized to vote)}}{\text{number of directors} + 1} + \text{fraction (or 1)}$$

his cards right. If Ringling and Haley pool their 630 votes, they can *elect five directors*. (It seems more than an uncanny coincidence that 5 times 126 equals 630.)

$16.2.2 Validity of Vote-Pooling Agreements

In general, shareholder vote-pooling agreements are valid if they relate to a matter on which shareholders may vote. Most statutes require that they be in writing. See RMBCA $7.31; Cal. Corp. $706; Del. GCL $218(c); N.Y. BCL $620. Some statutes specify the maximum duration of the agreement, and a few require some sort of notice of the agreement.

Vote-pooling agreements are governed by regular contracting rules and fiduciary duties applicable to close corporation shareholders. They may not be of indefinite duration; they must be in writing if required by the statute of frauds; they are subject to change only by agreement of all the parties; they may not be for some illegal end; and they may not be oppressive or fraudulent as to other shareholders or creditors (see $17.2).

If the agreement relates to matters the traditional corporate model does not leave to shareholder voting (see $12.1) — such as an agreement limiting the board's management discretion — the agreement may be invalid. When is an agreement related to shareholder matters, as opposed to nonshareholder or management matters? Consider the famous case of *McQuade v. Stoneham*, 189 N.E.2d 234 (N.Y. 1934). Three shareholders of the corporation that owned the New York Giants baseball team (when it still played at the Polo Grounds) agreed *as shareholders* to elect themselves as directors and agreed *as directors* to appoint themselves as officers at specified salaries. The New York Court of Appeals had no problem with the shareholder vote-pooling per se, but it held that the provisions restricting directorial discretion were invalid as a matter of public policy and invalidated the entire agreement, including nonseverable vote-pooling provisions.

$16.2.3 Enforcement of Vote-Pooling Agreements

Generally, vote-pooling agreements are specifically enforceable because of the difficulty in calculating money damages flowing from a loss or diminution of control caused by a shareholder's failure to vote her shares as agreed. See Official Comment to RMBCA $7.31(b).

Enforcement of a vote-pooling agreement should be approached with caution. The problem is illustrated in the *Ringling Bros.* case (see $16.2.1): Two sisters, Mrs. Haley and Mrs. Ringling, each had sufficient shares to elect two directors. To enhance their voting power, they agreed to pool their votes, giving them the power to elect five of the board's seven directors.

Their agreement contemplated they would consult with each other before voting, and a designated arbitrator would resolve any differences on how to vote. At a meeting to elect directors, it became clear that Haley (through her husband) had abandoned Ringling to join the camp of Mr. North, the third shareholder, who was not a party to their agreement. The arbitrator ruled how the sisters were to vote, but the Haleys refused to comply and Ringling sued. Rather than specifically enforce the arbitrator's decision — which would have put three of Ringling's directors and two of Haley's on the board, thus leaving Ringling's directors in a minority — the Chancery Court ordered a new election and presumably a new arbitration.

On appeal, the Delaware Supreme Court went in another direction, away from the agreement. Rather than enforce the arbitrator's decision or call for a new election, it disqualified the shares that the Haleys had sought to vote contrary to the agreement. The effect was nonetheless disastrous for Ringling, who could not pool her votes with those of Haley. Since Ringling had only 315 shares to North's 370, North became the controlling shareholder. Eventually, Ringling was forced to sell out.

Should Ringling have sought a different enforcement mechanism? If the function of the arbitrator was merely to decide on the fifth director, the agreement provided no protection against Haley shifting her allegiance to North. If the arbitrator was supposed to keep control from North — a plausible interpretation given the agreement's history — the agreement's enforcement mechanism was flawed. The Chancery Court's order of a new election may have been an attempt to correct this deficiency by making possible a new, more alert arbitration that would have favored Ringling. But the Supreme Court was not as sympathetic to the drafter's possible carelessness.

EXAMPLES

1. After its incorporation, Pizza Chateau issues 500 shares to Rich and 250 shares each to Bob and Sally. The articles provide for three directors, and at the first meeting the three shareholders elect themselves.

   a. Rich assumes he will have a veto over any corporate matter. Is he right?

   b. Rich assumes he can replace any director who turns on him. Is he right?

   c. To assure each party a veto over management matters, Rich and Bob propose the following bylaw provision: "On any matter that comes before the board, the directors shall act only by unanimous vote." Does this accomplish their apparent objective?

   d. Bob and Sally distrust each other. Each worries that the other might join forces with Rich. Advise them on shareholder supermajority quorum or voting requirements.

2. Draft a provision that will allow each Pizza Chateau director to veto any fundamental corporate change.

3. From the beginning, the parties follow the practice of voting each other to the board. After three years, Rich and Bob have a falling out with Sally, and the two sign an agreement to vote their shares so that they and Rich's trusted friend Ruth are elected to the board. At the next shareholders' meeting, Sally is voted out. She challenges the voting agreement and argues it is precluded by their earlier practice. Is it?

4. The three shareholders patch up their differences and agree in writing to vote their shares to assure that each is elected as director. The agreement has no term. Soon after Sally and Bob propose at a board meeting to open a second pizzeria. Rich objects but is outvoted.

   a. At the next shareholders' meeting, Rich refuses to abide by the pooling agreement. The corporation has cumulative voting, and Rich divides his 1500 votes between himself and his trusted friend Ruth. Bob and Sally cast their votes according to the agreement, 500 votes for Rich and 500 votes each for themselves. Assuming no agreement, who is elected?

   b. Bob and Sally sue to enforce the agreement. Is it valid?

   c. If the agreement is valid, can Bob and Sally have the election set aside and compel Rich to comply with its voting provisions?

5. How might Rich have protected his half ownership interest through a vote-pooling agreement?

EXPLANATIONS

1a. No. As structured, without more, Rich is assured a veto only at the *shareholder level*. No shareholder action can be taken without his shares being represented at a meeting and being voted. See RMBCA §7.25(a) (majority quorum); RMBCA §7.25(c) (voting majority at meeting). At the *board level* no one director can prevent the other two from acting. Rich cannot block Bob and Sally from taking board action: Two directors constitute a majority quorum (RMBCA §8.24(a)), and the board can act by a majority of directors present (again two). RMBCA §8.24(c).

1b. No. If a schism develops on the board, Rich would be powerless to change it. His 50 percent share ownership allows him to block shareholder action but is not enough to initiate action or replace directors. Under a system of straight voting for directors, his 50 percent is not enough to assure the election of his candidates. Under a system of cumulative voting, he would be assured of electing only one director. Rich needs some of Bob's or Sally's votes to control the composition of the board.

1c. Perhaps not. At first blush the provision looks good. It seems to allow any objecting director to block any action by simply not voting, thus preventing unanimity. But the provision may be flawed:

(1) The provision is in the bylaws, and it could be amended or deleted by less than all the shareholders. RMBCA §10.20. Without a supermajority requirement, Rich and Sally could delete it against Bob's wishes. (Notice that the RMBCA anticircumvention requirements applicable to bylaw amendments only apply to changes in quorum or voting requirements for *shareholders*. RMBCA §10.21.)

(2) Without an accompanying high quorum requirement, the unanimity requirement might be empty. If a quorum were a simple majority (two directors), these two directors might vote "unanimously" to take board action at any meeting the other failed to attend. The provision should specify that "unanimous" means a vote by *all* three directors or "all directors in office."

(3) Some courts have viewed unanimous voting requirements with disfavor because they risk deadlock. In some states, a unanimity requirement must be in the articles.

(4) The provision gives a veto to Sally, thus diluting Rich's and Bob's power on the board. The two might best be served by a provision that permits board action only if assented to by the two directors designated as Rich's and Bob's. (A classified board might accomplish this — see §13.1.5.)

1d. Bob and Sally each want their individual 25 percent voting interest to be sufficient to block any shareholder action. A high quorum requirement, such as 80 percent, theoretically would allow either simply not to show up and block any action by the others. But it has two defects. First, once a shareholders' meeting with a proper quorum has started, Bob or Sally might be unable to break the quorum and could then be out-voted. Second, some courts might not enforce the quorum requirement on the theory that a shareholder cannot challenge a quorum defect of the shareholder's own making.

A high voting requirement may be preferable. To avoid questions under earlier cases about the validity of a unanimous voting requirement, a voting requirement of 80 percent of the *outstanding* shares would act as a unanimity requirement. (Notice that if the quorum were a majority, and the voting requirement were 80 percent of the *voting shares present*, it would be possible for Rich and Sally to meet and take action without Bob being able to exercise his veto.)

2. Insert in the articles of incorporation:

Article XX.

In addition to any shareholder approval that may be required, the following corporate actions must be approved by the affirmative vote of at least three-fourths (75 percent) of the directors of the corporation in office: amendments to the articles of incorporation; amendments to the bylaws; dissolution of the corporation; merger or consolidation of the corporation; forced share exchange; sale, lease, mortgage, or transfer of all or substantially all of the corporation's assets; issuance of stock; purchase, redemption, or retirement of the corporation's stock.

This provision operates as a unanimity requirement and cannot be circumvented because it, and the number of directors on the board (which is specified in the articles), can be changed only by approval of the three directors. RMBCA §10.03(b). Further, a director can resign without preventing the remaining two from acting, but it significantly limits corporate flexibility and may invite deadlock.

3. Probably not. Although the parties' vote-pooling practice may have reflected an implicit prior agreement, the agreement was not in writing, a requirement of many statutes authorizing vote-pooling agreements. See RMBCA §7.31(a). Even if a writing were not required by corporate statute, the effect of an unwritten agreement would be subject to traditional contractual rules, such as the statute of frauds and the implication of a limited term. Nonetheless, even if the prior practice did not create a binding agreement, it might have created "reasonable expectations" enforceable as fiduciary duties to Sally. In close corporations, some courts treat fiduciary duties as arising from original understandings (see §20.3.2).

4a. The three top vote-getters are elected: Rich — 1250 votes, Ruth — 750 votes, either Sally or Bob — 500 votes.

4b. Yes. There is little question that vote-pooling agreements for the election of directors are valid. Only if the agreement were subject to a statute imposing specific requirements, such as a maximum term or a notice requirement, or if it were part of any agreement with illegal management restrictions might it be invalid.

4c. Yes. Vote-pooling agreements are specifically enforceable. See RMBCA §7.31(b). The election can be set aside. By virtue of the agreement, Rich is in a minority position on the board, and there is no way he can extricate himself during the term of the agreement.

5. Rich might have sought a board of four directors, to which he could designate two members. The agreement would require Bob and Sally to cast their votes for Rich and his designee. Although this arrangement risks deadlock at the board level, the possibility may be unavoidable if Rich and the other two owners divide control equally.

One problem with a designated director is the director's allegiance to Rich. Although normally the removal of a director requires action by all the shareholders (see §13.2), the agreement could provide for removal and replacement by Rich alone. The agreement could require the other two shareholders to vote their shares to carry out Rich's choice.

§16.3   Voting Trusts — Locking In the Shareholders

Vote-pooling agreements are not self-enforcing. A *voting trust* overcomes this disadvantage. Under a voting trust agreement, a group of shareholders agrees to transfer legal title to their shares to a voting trustee. For a defined period and according to specified instructions, the trustee has the exclusive voting power over the transferred shares. Other attributes of ownership (such as rights to dividends and other distributions) remain with the beneficiaries of the trust — usually the former shareholders. The beneficiaries often take voting trust certificates as evidence of their equitable ownership of the stock.

§16.3.1   Creating a Voting Trust

The requirements for creating a voting trust are straightforward. RMBCA §7.30 is typical:

(1)   Shareholders enter into a written trust agreement setting out the trustee's obligations.

(2)   The shareholders transfer some or all their shares to the trustee. The transfer is normally reflected on the corporation's stock transfer ledger, which shows the trustee as the registered holder of the transferred shares.

(3)   The trust agreement specifies a term, not to exceed ten years. The shareholders can extend the trust by later agreement; the extension binds only those who sign it.

(4)   The trustee prepares a list of trust beneficiaries (who may be different from the shareholders who transferred their shares), together with a description of the shares transferred to the trust. The trustee delivers a copy of this list and the trust agreement to the corporation's principal office.

See also Cal. Corp. §706; Del. GCL §218; N.Y. BCL §621. Generally, a shareholder cannot revoke his transfer to a voting trust. To assure certainty, the prevailing rule is that only the vote of all the beneficiaries of a trust can terminate or amend it during its life.

In general, the powers of the voting trustee are set by contract and depend on the authorizing language of the trust agreement. Where the trust agreement is silent or unclear, courts impose equitable limitations on the trustee's power to take action, such as approving fundamental changes, that damages the corporation's business. In *Brown v. McLanahan*, 148 F.2d 703 (4th Cir. 1945), the court ruled that a trustee could not amend the charter to give voting rights to debenture holders and shift voting power away from the trust beneficiaries, even though the amending power existed in the voting trust agreement. The trustee has fiduciary duties to the trust beneficiaries that transcend the trust provisions.

§16.3.2 Validity of a Voting Trust

Early courts were suspicious of voting trusts and invalidated them because they separated shareholders' voting power and economic ownership interests. Today statutes specifically authorize voting trusts in virtually all jurisdictions. Nonetheless, reflecting the early antipathy, a voting trust that fails to comply with all the statutory requirements risks invalidity.

Unlike a vote-pooling agreement, which in many jurisdictions can be of indefinite duration and may be kept secret, a voting trust must be on file in the corporation's main office and must be for a limited (usually ten-year) term, subject to periodic extension. The voting trust statutes are intended "to avoid secret, uncontrolled combinations formed to acquire control of the corporation to the possible detriment of non-participating shareholders." See *Oceanic Exploration Co. v. Grynberg*, 428 A.2d 1 (Del. 1981).

§16.3.3 Purposes of a Voting Trust

What does a voting trust accomplish that a pooling agreement does not? The principal advantage (and disadvantage) of a voting trust is that it locks the parties into a voting arrangement. There is no need for court-ordered specific performance, as is the case with a vote-pooling agreement. This much greater stability may be sought by creditors (for example, when a corporation is coming out of bankruptcy or receivership) or may be required when a business is divested pursuant to an antitrust decree. See *Brown v. McLanahan*, 148 F.2d 703 (4th Cir. 1945).

A voting trust, unlike a vote-pooling agreement, also permits transferability of *ownership interests* without giving up control. The trust beneficiaries, who usually receive voting trust certificates to evidence their right to share in the corpus of the trust, can transfer their ownership interests without changing the control structure. This may be desirable, for example, for a shareholder who wants to give her children an interest in the company without giving them any voting power. Potential investors, however, perceive this retention of control as a major disadvantage. Investors are leery of buying "power-stripped" certificates or even voting stock if they are locked into a minority position.

§16.3.4   *De Facto Voting Trusts*

Litigants have ingeniously turned the rules on voting trusts against other control devices. A device (particularly a novel one) that locks the parties into a control arrangement giving a third party decision-making authority — thus resembling a voting trust — can be argued to be a disguised or de facto voting trust and invalid because it fails to comply with the duration or publicity requirements. Three cases decided by the Delaware Supreme Court illustrate:

Ringling Bros.-Barnum & Bailey Combined Shows, Inc. v. Ringling, 53 A.2d 441 (Del. 1947):   Two shareholders of a three-person corporation entered into a vote-pooling agreement in which an arbitrator was to resolve any disagreements. When after a disagreement one of the parties refused to comply with the arbitrator's instructions, the other party went to court to seek compliance. The noncomplying shareholder argued that the arbitration procedure operated as a voting trust by separating voting from ownership. The court sidestepped the argument by holding that the agreement technically had not transferred any voting rights to the arbitrator, who had not been given formal power to vote the shares.

Abercrombie v. Davies, 130 A.2d 338 (Del. 1957):   A group of share-holders together holding a majority of shares agreed that eight designated agents would vote their shares under proxies granted for ten years. Voting was to be determined by agreement of seven of the agents or, if seven could not agree, by arbitration. To enforce the agreement the parties endorsed their share certificates and deposited them with the agents. The court held that the agreement was a de facto voting trust because (1) it separated ownership and voting, (2) it transferred voting power irrevocably for a definite period, and (3) its principal purpose was to provide for voting control of the corporation. As a voting trust, it was invalid for not complying with statutory requirements.

Lehrman v. Cohen, 222 A.2d 800 (Del. 1966):   The corporation, owned equally by two families, had two classes of stock that entitled each family to elect two directors to a four-person board. To avoid board deadlock, a third class of stock — which consisted of one share with $10 par value — was entitled to elect a fifth director but had no right to dividends or distributions on liquidation beyond its $10 value. This share was issued to the company's counsel, who eventually joined one of the family camps and was elected as president with a long-term executive employment contract. Unhappy about the internal coup, the other family challenged the third class of stock as a de facto voting trust and illegal because it extended beyond Delaware's statutory ten-year limit. The court applied the *Abercrombie* three-factor test and concluded that the first factor had not been shown because voting rights of the *original* classes of stock had not been divested or separated from ownership, even though the new class had diluted voting power — as usually happens when new stock is issued.

§16.4 Different Classes of Stock — Building Control into the Capital Structure

The control devices we have been discussing attempt to allocate voting power in ways that are *disproportionate* to financial (or equity) interest. Another and straightforward way to do this is to create different classes of shares, each class entitled to elect a specified number of directors. Suppose in Pizza Chateau that Rich is willing to provide 80 percent of the start-up capital on the condition he receives board representation. Bob and Sally are willing to take a proportionally smaller share of profits, provided they control the board. Their desires can be effectuated easily by creating two classes of shares: class A elects one director; class B elects two directors; class A participates in a 4:1 ratio with class B in all corporate distributions. Rich's class A shares choose one director and receive 80 percent of distributions. Bob's and Sally's class B shares choose two directors and receive 20 percent of distributions. The problem is solved.

§16.4.1 Purposes of Classes of Stock

Different classes of shares can serve many purposes:

(1) Board representation — Rich's class A shares elect one director, and Bob's and Sally's class B shares elect two directors.

(2) Super-majority voting — the charter provides that any amendment must be approved by Rich's class A stock.

(3) Nonvoting equity participation — Pizza Chateau has voting common and nonvoting common (each participating equally in any distribution); Rich gets 10 shares of voting common and 70 shares of nonvoting common, and Bob and Sally get 20 shares of voting common.

(4) Limitation on board discretion — the charter specifies that Pizza Chateau's president and vice president must be class B shareholders.

Class voting has its pitfalls. Notice that Rich can circumvent Bob's and Sally's best-laid plans to control the board through class voting if he can remove Bob and Sally as directors. This possibility becomes all the more real if Rich can remove them with *or without* cause (see §13.2). To avoid this, the articles or bylaws might specify that directors elected by class B shareholders can be removed only by shareholders of that class or only by other shareholders for cause.

§16.4.2 Creating Classes of Shares

Different classes of shares, like any equity securities, must be authorized in the articles (see §8.1.1). RMBCA §6.01(c); Cal. Corp. §§203-204, 400; Del. GCL §151; N.Y. BCL §501.

§16.4.3 Validity of Nonparticipating, Nonvoting Classes

Besides its simplicity and ease of enforcement, class voting is advantageous because it is subject to few (if any) of the statutory and common law limitations that continue to dog other control devices. Most states set no limits on creating classes authorized to elect a specified number of directors, authorized to vote only on specified matters, without voting rights, with only limited rights to participate in corporate distributions, or with multiple or fractional voting rights. RMBCA §6.01; Cal. Corp. §400; Del. GCL §151; N.Y. BCL §501.

For example, in *Lehrman v. Cohen*, 222 A.2d 800 (Del. 1966), the Delaware Supreme Court upheld the validity of a new class of stock entitled to elect one director where two existing classes of stock each elected two directors. The deadlock-breaking class of stock consisted of one share, $10 par value, with no right to dividends or distributions on liquidation beyond its $10 value. The court accepted that the new class of stock "became a part of the capitalization" of the corporation, even though its purpose was not to raise capital but rather to resolve control disputes.

§16.5 Irrevocable Proxies — Voting Power "Coupled with an Interest"

Shareholders in the close corporation can also structure control by giving another person (or each other) binding authority to vote their shares — by *irrevocable proxies*. A proxy creates an agency relationship in which the shareholder (the principal) grants in writing a proxy holder (the agent) the power to vote her shares, subject to any shareholder instructions (see §12.2.4). But an ordinary proxy, like most other agency relationships, can be revoked by the principal at any time and for any reason. Under an irrevocable proxy, the shareholder cannot change her mind and revoke the proxy holder's authority to vote her shares. This raises the same "separation of voting and ownership" concerns that fueled the attack on voting trusts, and courts have been reluctant to enforce irrevocable proxies. But the modern trend, reflected in corporate statutes, is to recognize irrevocable proxies that are "coupled with an interest." RMBCA §7.22; Cal. Corp. §705; Del. GCL §212; N.Y. BCL §609.

§16.5.1   Purpose of Irrevocable Proxies

An irrevocable proxy provides a "self-executing" means for the proxy holder to enforce his control interest in the corporation. Pledgees, prospective shareholders, and shareholders who have entered into voting agreements — to give some examples — can be sure with an irrevocable proxy that the shares in which they hold an interest are voted as they want.

§16.5.2   Creating Irrevocable Proxies

What kind of "interest" supports an irrevocable proxy?

Interest in stock.   The most widely recognized interest arises when the proxy holder has an interest in the stock itself — for example, when the proxy holder has an option to buy the stock or lends money to the shareholder who pledges the stock as collateral for the loan. RMBCA §7.22(d)(1), (2); Cal. Corp. §705(e)(1), (2); N.Y. BCL §609(f)(1), (2). This interest supports irrevocability because the proxy holder will in all likelihood vote the shares consistent with the shareholders' and corporation's economic interests.

Economic interest in corporation.   Increasingly, statutes view a proxy as coupled with an interest if the proxy holder has an economic interest in the corporation, even without an interest in the stock itself. Del. GCL §212(c). For example, the holder has agreed to lend money to the corporation or has been induced to become a shareholder (or an employee) in reliance on the other shareholders' granting him an irrevocable proxy. RMBCA §7.22(d)(3), (4); Cal. Corp. §705(e)(3), (4); N.Y. BCL §609(f)(3), (4). This is in line with the general trend toward allowing greater control flexibility in the close corporation. Moreover, the proxy holder's economic interest in the corporation provides an incentive to vote to further the corporation's best interests, and the separation between control and ownership will not be great.

Designated by shareholders.   The hardest case is when the proxy holder has no direct interest in the stock or the corporation but has been designated by shareholders to hold their proxies pursuant to a shareholders' agreement or other control arrangement. See RMBCA §7.22(d)(5) ("party" to a shareholders' voting agreement has sufficient interest); Cal. Corp. §705(e)(5); N.Y. BCL §609(f)(5). In this situation, the proxy holder may have little incentive to vote the proxies to further the corporation's best interests. Voting and economic interests are truly separated. Nonetheless, permitting irrevocability of proxies in shareholders' agreements promotes control flexibility in the close corporation and presumably the shareholders will have protected their economic interests in the agreement.

An irrevocable proxy terminates or becomes revocable when the qualifying interest is extinguished. RMBCA §7.22(f); Cal. Corp. §705(e); N.Y. BCL §609(g).

§16.5.3   Complying with Coupling Requirement

The rule that proxies are revocable unless coupled with an interest has been used as an argument against enforcing control devices that call for voting of shares as an enforcement mechanism. The most famous case was the *Ringling Bros.* case, in which the Delaware courts considered the validity of a vote-pooling agreement that set up an arbitration procedure to resolve voting disputes between two parties (see §16.3.4). When the two parties (who were sisters) reached an impasse and one refused to vote according to the arbitrator's decision, the noncomplying sister argued that the agreement gave the arbitrator an implied proxy, which she could revoke because it was not supported by an interest. The Delaware Supreme Court held that the agreement did not call on the arbitrator to actually vote the shares and the parties had not granted a proxy, revocable or irrevocable.

EXAMPLES

1. Pizza Chateau is a success. Rich wants to give some of his shares to his nephews but does not want them to have control of the business until they are older. Rich owns 500 common shares, Sally 250, and Bob 250. Rich trusts Bob implicitly and is willing to let him continue to make all control decisions. Bob agrees to Rich's suggestion that they consolidate their voting power. What shareholder arrangement will best accomplish their purposes?

2. Rich and Bob consider a voting trust agreement under which Bob has full voting authority over their shares. Each retains a beneficial interest in all dividends and distributions. The agreement has a term of ten years, which is automatically extended another ten years unless either of them objects in writing. Bob sends a copy of the agreement to Sally.

a. Do you see any problems?

b. Rich, although he trusts Bob, is cautious. He wants a provision that Bob can be removed and replaced by another trustee upon the "majority vote of the beneficial interests represented by the voting trust certificates outstanding." Do you see any problems?

3. Rich and Bob decide against a voting trust. Instead, they agree in writing to consult each other on voting their shares. If a dispute arises, they agree to turn over their share certificates to a nonshareholder arbitrator who will vote them and will then return them after voting. Rich and Bob amend the articles to recognize the arbitrator's voting authority, and their share certificates refer to the agreement.

a. Do you see any problems?

b. Is the arrangement consistent with the requirements for a voting trust?

c. Is it relevant that if the parties disagreed they would turn over their shares to the arbitrator?

4. Rich decides to live in Europe for a few years. Bob wants to make sure things will run smoothly while Rich is gone and asks for a proxy to vote his shares. Rich agrees and hands over his share certificates. Two days later Rich has misgivings and signs a three-year proxy appointment form naming attorney Conley as his proxy holder.

a. Who has Rich's proxy?

b. Upon hearing about this turn of events, Bob implores Rich not to leave the fate of the business in the hands of a lawyer. Rich understands and signs a proxy naming Bob during his absence. Who can vote Rich's shares?

c. It turns out that Conley had an interest in Rich's shares. Before leaving the country, Rich had authorized Conley to sell his shares. Conley would earn a commission of 15 percent of the sales price. The proxy appointment form that Rich signed stated the proxy was irrevocable until Rich returned or the shares had been sold. Is Conley's proxy irrevocable?

5. A few years later, Rich returns from Europe, and all proxies end. Rich says that he wants "fluidity." Neither Bob nor Sally knows what he means, and they wonder about Rich's intentions and mental acuity. Rich still controls 500 shares, and each of them controls 250. Worried about deadlocks, the two propose that each shareholder turn over a nominal number of shares to attorney Conley. Rich will transfer two shares, and Sally and Bob one each.

a. The corporation has four directors, elected by cumulative voting. What will be the effect of this arrangement?

b. Can Conley be a deadlock-breaker at both the shareholder and board level, without any ownership interest?

EXPLANATIONS

1. Probably a voting trust. Consider the following advantages and disadvantages of possible arrangements:

   Shareholders' vote-pooling agreement.   Rich and Bob could agree to vote their shares to give Bob a majority of the board, fulfilling their desire that Bob control the business. But this would create difficulties if Rich transfers his shares to his nephews. Although it would be possible to condition their acquisition on being bound under the vote-pooling agreement, the agreement would not be self-enforcing. Bob would have to seek specific performance in court if any of the nephews failed to comply with the agreement's terms. Further, there would be a risk that the nephews could transfer the shares to someone who might escape the condition.

   Different classes of shares.   Rich and Bob could amend the articles of incorporation to create two new class of shares. Rich would receive 500 shares of class R nonvoting common, and Bob would receive 250 shares of class B, with three votes per share. But the arrangement would not fulfill Rich's desire to eventually give his nephews control.

   Irrevocable proxies.   Rich could give Bob a proxy to vote his shares for a specified term. To be certain, the proxy would have to be irrevocable — that is, coupled with an interest. In some jurisdictions, their shareholders' agreement or Bob's interest as a shareholder may be a sufficient interest. Even so, the arrangement might collapse if Rich transferred his shares to others who could revoke the proxy. Under the RMBCA, for example, a transferee (such as one of Rich's nephews or another party taking from them) could revoke if they took their shares without notice of the proxy and if the share certificates did not conspicuously note the proxy's existence. See RMBCA §7.22(g).

   Voting trust.   Rich and Bob could put their shares into a voting trust in which Bob would be trustee. Nothing prevents one of the shareholders from being trustee, and this arrangement would give Bob full control of their collective voting interest. In addition, Rich would be able to transfer his beneficial (nonvoting) interest in the trust — represented by his voting trust certificates — to his nephews without upsetting the control arrangement. A voting trust, recognized by statute, avoids the risks of revocation inherent in a proxy arrangement.

2a. Yes. Rich and Bob may not have complied with the voting trust statute. Disclosure to Sally may not satisfy the requirement of disclosure to the "corporation's principal office." See RMBCA §7.30(a). Such disclosure provides notice of the special control arrangement not only to other shareholders but to directors and officers and possibly creditors.

   In addition, the automatic-extension provision may violate the spirit of the statutory provisions allowing extension after reexamination and voluntary consent by the parties. The RMBCA's requirement that the extension "binds only those parties who sign it" implies that the extension must be accomplished with an additional formality and cannot be automatic. Some statutes make this explicit. Cal. Corp. §706 (extension must be agreed to within two years prior to expiration of original term); Del. GCL §218 (same); N.Y. BCL §621(d) (six months).

2b. No. This provision would undermine some of the certainty for Bob, but there is nothing that prevents the trust agreement from specifying the responsibilities or term of the trustee. Except for limitations imposed by statute, a voting trust agreement can contain any provisions the parties agree to.

3a. Perhaps. It can be argued that the agreement, despite its label, is a de facto voting trust. If so, it is invalid for not complying with the statutory disclosure and ten-year duration rules. See RMBCA §7.30.

Is the agreement a voting trust? A number of jurisdictions specifically state that shareholder agreements should not be construed as being subject to the voting trust requirements. See Del. GCL §218(e). On the other hand, RMBCA §7.31(a) states that shareholder agreements that "provide for the manner in which [shareholders] vote their shares" are not subject to the voting trust provisions. By having their shares voted by another person, Rich's and Bob's agreement might be deemed a voting trust.

The agreement's procedure compares both to the procedure held valid in *Ringling Bros.* and to that held invalid in *Abercrombie* (see §16.3.4). As in *Ringling Bros.,* Rich and Bob have agreed to have an arbitrator resolve their particular voting disputes. But to assure the arbitrator's decision is carried out, the parties have placed voting in the hands of the arbitrator, much as in *Abercrombie.*

3b. Perhaps not. The voting trust requires publicity and limits duration. In this case, publicity does not seem a concern. The parties' agreement is mentioned in the articles and in the share certificates, providing arguably greater disclosure than if it were a properly disclosed voting trust. The agreement, however, has no term. The statutory ten-year limit prevents parties (and the corporation's business) from being locked into a long-term and potentially inefficient arrangement. But the lock-in is far milder than in a voting trust, because the two shareholders need turn over their shares only when a disagreement arises. The permanent lock-in feature inherent in a voting trust (and in *Abercrombie*) is not necessarily present. Even when there is a disagreement, specific enforcement of the promise to turn over the shares might still be necessary (much as in *Ringling Bros.*).

3c. Perhaps. Despite the agreement's arguable consistency with the purposes of the voting trust statutes, the agreement nonetheless has much the same "form" as a voting trust. It contemplates the transfer of shares to be voted by a third party. The Delaware de facto voting trust cases have a distinct air of form over substance. For example, in *Lehrman v. Cohen* the new class of stock had the effect of locking the parties into an indefinite control arrangement not requiring specific performance, but the court held it was not a voting trust (see §16.3.4). As a matter of form, Rich and Bob's agreement is much closer to the *Abercrombie* vote-delegation arrangement than to the nonvoting arbitrator in *Ringling Bros.* or to the new class of stock in *Lehrman v. Cohen*.

The modern statutory trend, however, is that shareholders' agreements are judged by their own standards and specifically seek to negate any argument that the agreement is a de facto voting trust. See RMBCA §7.31; Del. GCL §218(e).

4a. Most probably Conley. Bob's assertion of a proxy has two problems. First, his authority was not in writing, and most statutes require that a proxy, whether or not revocable, be in writing. See RMBCA §7.22(b); Cal. Corp. §§178, 705; N.Y. BCL §609; but cf. Del. GCL §212 (writing not explicitly required). Second, even if an oral proxy were possible, Rich's handing over of the share certificates does not necessarily imply irrevocability. The subsequent written authorization to Conley is a proxy, even though it covers more than one shareholders' meeting. See RMBCA §7.22(c). A subsequent proxy revokes any prior revocable proxies.

4b. Probably Bob. Rich revoked Conley's revocable proxy when he named Bob in writing. Conley's proxy was not irrevocable for two reasons. First, Rich did not intend it to be revocable. Many statutes, including the RMBCA, require that the proxy's irrevocability be conspicuously stated on the appointment form. Second, Conley's proxy could not be irrevocable because it was not coupled with an interest. From the facts, Conley has no interest in the corporation, its shares, or any agreement of the shareholders. There is no assurance that his voting will be consistent with the corporation's interests because he has no economic or contractual incentive to maximize corporate welfare. It is conceivable, for example, that Conley might vote his proxy to create situations that will generate attorney fees from the corporation. Although such conduct might violate his duties as Rich's agent, corporate law does not yet recognize this interest as sufficient to support an irrevocable proxy.

4c. Probably. Conley's interest is probably sufficient under modern views that support irrevocability. This would mean that Rich's attempt to give Bob his proxy was probably a nullity.

Conley's authorization to sell Rich's shares (for a commission) aligns Conley's interests with the corporation's. Although this interest is not enumerated in RMBCA §7.22(d), the RMBCA list is meant to be illustrative, not exhaustive. Official Comment to RMBCA §7.22 (illustration 3). Conley can be expected to vote to further the corporation's interests because his commission is tied to the sales price and thus to the corporation's fortunes. On the other hand, he receives only a percentage of the selling price, and countervailing interests (such as creating opportunities for attorney fees) might weigh more heavily in Conley's voting. Nonetheless, the RMBCA recognizes that others (such as creditors and employees) with potentially mixed interests in the corporation can nonetheless have a sufficient interest to support irrevocability. Arguably, Conley would be as interested in protecting his commission as would a creditor the corporation's solvency or an employee the corporation's viability. Cf. *State ex rel. Breger v. Rusche,* 39 N.E.2d 433 (Ind. 1942) (holding that attorney given proxy and authority to sell shareholders' stock did not have irrevocable proxy, even though he had a right to reimbursement for selling expenses).

5a. The share transfers will have the effect of a new class of shares with the power to break *shareholder* deadlocks between the Rich camp and the Bob-Sally camp. But unlike a nonparticipating class of shares, Conley will participate in any dividends and distributions in proportion to his shares. If the corporation is successful, this ownership interest may exceed the value of Conley's services as a stand-by deadlock breaker. The arrangement will not work to break deadlocks at the board level. Even with 498 of 1000 shares, Rich will still have the power to elect two directors. Deadlocks among the directors remain possible.

5b. Yes. The parties could create a new class of shares that would have one vote on general shareholder matters and the power to elect a new fifth director. If the new class of shares — "class D" (for deadlock-breaker) — were made voting but nonparticipating shares, the parties' purpose would be accomplished. The articles of incorporation would have to be amended to provide for and specify the powers and rights of this new class. Although the validity of such a class of shares may have been questionable once, the ability to create such an arrangement is now generally recognized. See RMBCA §6.01(c).

§16.6   Transfer Restrictions and Liquidity Rights

A significant attribute of many close corporations is a closely knit group of owners. To prevent the intrusion of unwanted outsiders, the owners often agree not to transfer their shares to persons outside the group. But change is inevitable, and absolute restraints on transferability can produce unreasonable hardships. Transfer limits are usually combined with "ways out," such as purchase options or mandatory purchase obligations. These provisions provide liquidity to close corporation shareholders.

§16.6.1   *Purposes of Transfer Restrictions*

Transfer restrictions serve a number of purposes:

(1) They ensure stability in the control and management of the corporation.

(2) They maintain proportionate ownership interests among shareholders and guard against internal coups. For this reason, transfer restrictions often also apply to transfers between insiders.

(3) They ensure that the corporation will satisfy the Subchapter S requirement that it have no more than 35 shareholders (see §2.3.2).

(4) They ensure compliance professional corporation statutes, such as the requirement that only licensed physicians can be shareholders in a professional medical corporation.

(5) They ensure compliance ownership restrictions for regulated businesses, such as the New York Stock Exchange's former prohibition against the transfer of member firms' shares without prior NYSE approval. See *Ling & Co. v. Trinity Savings & Loan Assn.,* 482 S.W.2d 841 (Tex. 1972).

(6) They preserve exemptions under federal (and state) securities laws that prohibit the sale of unregistered restricted securities (see §10.2.2).

§16.6.2   *Creating Transfer Restrictions and Liquidity Rights*

Transfer restrictions typically apply to stock sales, transfers in trust, gifts, and stock pledges. They can be placed in the articles, the bylaws, a shareholders' agreement, or an agreement between the corporation and its shareholders. In some states, any agreement creating transfer restrictions must be filed with the corporation and be available for inspection.

To bind putative transferees — and avoid a "bona fide" purchaser argument — the share *certificates* must note conspicuously that the shares are subject to transfer restrictions. RMBCA §6.27(b); Cal. Corp. §418; Del. GCL §202; UCC §8-204(a). According to RMBCA §1.40(3), a stock legend is conspicuous if printed in *italics,* **boldface,** or contrasting color, or typed in CAPITALS, or underlined. Even if not conspicuous, transfer restrictions are enforceable against any transferee with knowledge. RMBCA §6.27(b); Cal. Corp. §418; Del. GCL §202.

The careful planner must address a host of issues:

• What triggers the restrictions and the purchase provisions?
• Who is subject to the restrictions?

- Who has the option (or obligation) to purchase — the corporation, the shareholders, or both?
- Who participates in the corporate decision to purchase?
- If more than one party is to purchase, in what proportion and order do the purchases take place?
- How is the price for the shares determined (perhaps the thorniest issue) — book value, outside offer, mutual agreement with periodic revision, capitalization of earnings, a formula combining these methods, or an independent appraisal?
- What if the corporation cannot repurchase the shares because of legal capital or solvency impediments (see §9.2)?
- If funding comes from death or disability insurance policies, who pays the premiums?

The planner should keep in mind that shareholders generally will not know beforehand whether they will be "sellers" or "buyers" under the liquidity provisions. Each party usually will consider symmetry to be in his best interests.

§16.6.3 *Validity of Transfer Restrictions*

The general rule, and a significant advantage of the corporate form, is that shares are freely transferable. Even though share transfer restrictions are at odds with the rule, most state statutes recognize their validity. RMBCA §6.27; Cal. Corp. §418; Del. GCL §202. Transfer restrictions must be *reasonable under the circumstances,* an approach that balances two conflicting corporate tenets: free alienability of corporate ownership interests and private corporate structuring to meet the participants' needs. The treatment of various transfer restrictions illustrate this balance.

Flat prohibition. An outright prohibition against *any transfer to any person* likely would be invalid even in a jurisdiction that had adopted a statute authorizing transfer restrictions. But a limited restriction related to some legitimate purpose — such as a restriction in a professional medical corporation limiting transfers only to licensed physicians — would seem enforceable. RMBCA §6.27(d)(4) (restriction limited to designated persons permissible if "not manifestly unreasonable"); Del. GCL §202(c)(4) (same).

Prior approval. Prior-approval restrictions require a shareholder to first obtain approval of the board or other shareholders. Prior approval procedures have been invalidated in a number of cases because consent may be arbitrarily withheld. Some corporate statutes, however, allow prior approval if not manifestly unreasonable. RMBCA §6.27(d)(3); Del. GCL §202(c)(3). These limits are at odds with the notion of the close corporation as an "incorporated partnership." In a partnership, absent contrary agreement, each partner has the power to veto the admission of any new partner. Cf. UPA §18(g).

Purchase option.   First-option provisions require the shareholder (or the shareholder's estate) to first offer her shares to the corporation or the other shareholders *at a specified option price*. Courts have held first options are enforceable. See RMBCA §6.27(d)(1); Del. GCL §203(c)(2). The corporation's decision to refuse a first offer, so that a controlling shareholder can purchase, is a self-dealing transaction subject to fairness review. see *Cash v. Cash Furniture Co.*, 296 A.2d 207 (Vt. 1972).

First refusal.   First-refusal rights obligate the shareholder to first offer her shares to the corporation (or the other shareholders) *at the price and on the terms offered by the outsider*. The difference between a purchase option and a first-refusal right is that the option price is set by agreement, while the first-refusal price is whatever price is offered by the outsider. The outside offer provides significant assurances that the first-refusal price is fair, and courts readily uphold their validity.

Mandatory buy-sell.   On death, withdrawal, deadlock, or other specified contingencies, the shareholder (or the shareholder's estate) is obligated to sell to the corporation or to other shareholders, who in turn must purchase the shares at a specified price. A mandatory buy-sell agreement has advantages for both sides. It assures the shareholder a market for her shares and, if the price is established in good faith to reflect actual value, it helps fix the value of the shares for federal estate tax purposes. It assures the corporation's closed status and provides a way to buy out fractious shareholders. Buy-sell arrangements are valid, provided the corporation has sufficient legal capital to redeem the shares (see §9.2).

In general, the failure of the corporation (or other shareholders) to purchase frees the shareholder to transfer the shares.

There are no statutory or judicial limits on how long transfer restrictions can last. Regular contract rules apply, and shareholders can forsake transfer restrictions by express agreement or by a course of conduct. For example, implied abandonment might be shown if shareholders have failed to object to noncomplying sales by previous shareholders.

EXAMPLES

1. Rich, Bob and Sally agreed when they incorporated Pizza Chateau that none of them would sell their shares to any outsider unless the others first approved the sale. They did not put their agreement in writing.

   a. Rich takes out a bank loan and pledges his Pizza Chateau stock as collateral. If he defaults on his loan, can the bank foreclose on the pledged shares?

   b. If the restriction satisfies the formal requirements, will it be valid?

2. The three parties amend Pizza Chateau's articles to provide: "Any shareholder may withdraw from the Corporation by giving the Corporation ninety (90) days written notice. The Corporation shall be obligated to purchase all of the shareholder's shares." What price provision would you recommend?

3. The parties do not want the buy-sell arrangement to be the exclusive means by which shareholders can sell their shares. Any shareholder can sell her shares to outsiders if the remaining shareholders agree.

   a. How should the parties implement this restriction?

   b. Draft a legend for the share certificates reflecting this transfer restriction.

4. The parties abandon the buy-sell arrangement, but agree to forced redemption by the corporation upon any shareholder's death. Draft a provision.

EXPLANATIONS

1a. Probably. The restriction suffers from two defects. First, it should have been noted conspicuously on the share certificates — a so-called stock legend. Second, even if the "legending" defect is excused because the bank had notice of the restriction, the restriction only covers "sales," not pledges of stock as collateral for a loan. Some courts strictly construe transfer restrictions on the theory that they are restraints on alienation, and many statutes imply that the restrictions must be in writing. Typically, transfer restrictions cover sales, exchanges, assignments, pledges, gifts, bequests, or other transfers.

1b. Perhaps not. The restriction should probably have been less absolute. Allowing any shareholder to veto a transfer threatens stock liquidity, and some courts have invalidated prior-approval restrictions where consent can be arbitrarily withheld. The parties should have specified that prior approval "cannot be unreasonably withheld." Objecting shareholders thus would bear the burden of showing some legitimate business purpose — such as stability in management or preventing opportunistic realignments in share ownership.

2. Any buy-sell price should reflect fair value. At the time the parties agree to a buy-sell agreement, it is unlikely that anyone will know who will be the selling shareholder and who will be the effective buyers. The provision should strike a balance between assuring fair value and assuring that the corporation's going value is not depleted.

There are a number of possibilities, each with advantages and defects:

(1) *A stipulated price subject to periodic revision* has the advantage of mutuality and relative low cost, but it is always possible that the price will not be updated due to oversight or an inability to agree.

(2) *A best-offer price* may reflect an open market valuation of the shares, but it assumes that there has been a best offer and that the offer was made in good faith.

(3) *Book value of the shares* — that is, the per share value of assets minus liabilities — is tantalizingly popular and readily capable of calculation by established accounting methods. It is, however, probably the least accurate measure of the business's value as a going concern: It will reflect fixed value of assets, not earning potential (and goodwill) of the business.

(4) *Capitalization of earnings* measures the earnings potential of the business — what any rational investor will want to know. It depends on determining a discount rate, defining earnings, and making predictions about earnings in the future. Each of these is fraught with potential error. Past earnings are not necessarily a good measure of future earnings. The capitalization calculations usually are made by professional business appraisers (investment bankers) and are expensive, with fees starting at $20,000.

3a. The articles of incorporation, bylaws, or a shareholders' agreement must specify the procedures for prior approval by the other shareholders. In addition, the share certificates must reflect the transfer restriction.

3b. The following legend should be placed conspicuously on all share certificates:

> TAKE NOTICE that the sale, assignment, transfer, or pledge of the shares represented by this Certificate is subject to restrictions contained in the Articles of Incorporation. The Articles restrict the transfer of stock without the permission of the Corporation's board of directors.

For the legend to be conspicuous, the RMBCA requires that a reasonable person against whom it is to operate should have noticed it. The RMBCA suggests some visual devices, such as printing in italics, boldface, or contrasting color, typing in capitals, or underlining. RMBCA §1.40(3).

4. The redemption provision in the articles or bylaws or in a agreement between the shareholders and corporation would bind the corporation and the shareholders:

Redemption upon death.

Upon the death of any shareholder, the Corporation will redeem, to the extent it is legally able, all of the Corporation's shares owned by the deceased shareholder at the time of his death. The deceased shareholder's estate will surrender the certificates representing the shares to be redeemed. The Corporation will redeem the shares at the value fixed by this provision, using insurance proceeds and current liquid assets and, if necessary, by liquidating assets or borrowing funds to the extent permitted by law.

(1) *Life insurance.* The Corporation will acquire, maintain and become the owner of a renewable-term life insurance policy on the life of each shareholder in a face amount equal to $ _____ , which coverage is subject to change as described below. Each shareholder agrees to cooperate fully in causing such a policy (and any amendment) to be issued and maintained.

(2) *Payment of premiums.* The Corporation will pay the premiums on these life insurance policies and will provide proof of payment to the insured shareholders within twenty (20) days before the due date of each premium. If the Corporation fails to pay a premium twenty (20) days before it becomes due, the shareholder may pay the premium and will be reimbursed by the Corporation.

(3) *Share valuation.* The shareholders and the Corporation have valued each of the one thousand (1000) outstanding shares of the Corporation as of the date of this agreement at $ _____ . Each March 1, the Corporation, acting through its board of directors, will recalculate the value of each share. This recalculated value will be reflected in the board minutes. If the board of directors fails to recalculate a value, the last fixed value will remain in effect.

(4) *Insurance coverage.* If in any year the share valuation reflects more than a 20 percent increase in value over the last-fixed value, the Corporation will purchase a proportional amount of additional insurance coverage to reflect the increase in the shares' value. If any shareholder is not insurable at standard rates, the Corporation need not purchase additional coverage.

As with any liquidity right, this redemption provision addresses the trigger (death of shareholder), to whom it applies (the shareholder's estate and the corporation), the limits on the corporation's obligation (legal capital rules), the repurchase procedures (surrender of certificates), the repurchase price (set under a revaluation procedure), the source for payments (insurance proceeds), and assurance of payments (the premium-payment obligations).

§16.7 Restraints on Directors' Discretion — Planner Beware!

Up to this point most of our discussion has been about control devices that affect the *shareholders'* discretion to vote their shares. These devices do not guarantee control over *board* decisions — such as appointing officers, setting salaries, declaring dividends, issuing or repurchasing shares, dissolving the corporation, or limiting the scope of the business.

§16.7.1   Purpose of Management Agreements

For parties to effectively control the management of a close corporation, restraints must be placed on the discretion of the board. These restraints can take many forms:

- contractual agreements by parties (sometimes in shareholders' agreements) to act in specified ways in their capacity as directors;
- contracts with the corporation that effectively disempower the board, such as employment contracts granting an employee significant management discretion; and
- agreements that the shareholders will assume some or all of the powers of the board of directors.

These restraints allow "incorporated partners" to conduct their business as they please. But, as salubrious as they may seem, the restraints run into the corporate tenet and statutory mandate that the corporation's business is to be managed by (or under the supervision of) the board of directors. RMBCA §8.01(b); Cal. Corp. §300; Del. GCL §141(a); N.Y. BCL §701. Any arrangement that restrains directors' discretion is inconsistent with this statutory norm and may undermine expectations of others (nonparty shareholders and creditors) that directors will act flexibly and independently in the best interests of the corporation. As a result, in the absence of statutory authorization, management restraints are perhaps the most problematic of the control devices.

§16.7.2   Validity of Management Agreements

The validity of management agreements depends on the corporate statutes of the state of incorporation. Although older statutes mandated exclusive board management, many modern statutes have special close-corporation provisions that specifically authorize agreements limiting directorial discretion. Cal. Corp. §§158, 300(b) (corporations with no more than ten shareholders); N.Y. BCL §620 (nonpublic corporations); Del. GCL §351 (corporations that file for close corporation status).

The RMBCA, revised in 1991, authorizes shareholders' agreements that govern "the exercise of corporate powers or the management of the business and affairs of the corporation or the relationship among the shareholders, the directors and the corporation." RMBCA §7.32. An agreement is authorized if approved by all the shareholders, whether in the articles or the bylaws or in an agreement signed by all then-current shareholders, and "made known" to the corporation. RMBCA §7.32(b). The expansive new section specifically validates agreements that create alternative governance structures and any others "not contrary to public policy." RMBCA §7.32(a); see Official Comment (section "validates virtually all types of shareholder agreements"). The provision sets the term of an agreement at ten years, unless specified otherwise, and any amendment must be approved by all existing shareholders.

In those jurisdictions that do not have special statutory provisions or where the parties have not properly used them, the validity of restraints on directors' discretion is a matter of common law. Early common law decisions imposed a strict rule that any restraint on the board violates public policy and is unenforceable. Over time cases have adopted an increasingly more relaxed approach, allowing such restraints if: (1) the agreement restraining directors' discretion relates to a close corporation; (2) the agreement does not adversely affect interests of nonparty shareholders or of creditors; and (3) the agreement deviates only slightly from the statutory norm that directors "manage the business of the corporation." This evolution and the operation of the relaxed rules are illustrated in four New York Court of Appeals cases dealing with agreements restraining board discretion.

Manson v. Curtis, 119 N.E. 559 (N.Y. 1918): A majority of the shareholders (though not all) agreed that one of the parties was to be general manager for a year, managing the corporation's business and setting its policy. The court invalidated the provision, along with the rest of the agreement, because by vesting management authority in a single manager it "sterilized the board."

McQuade v. Stoneham, 189 N.E. 234 (N.Y. 1934): The majority shareholder and two other shareholders (though less than all) agreed to keep one another in office as directors and officers and specified their positions and salaries. The court invalidated the entire agreement because its provisions on appointment and compensation usurped the board's function.

Clark v. Dodge, 199 N.E. 641 (N.Y. 1936): The corporation's only two shareholders, Clark and Dodge, agreed that Clark would be general manager with compensation pegged to the corporation's "net income." The court held that the agreement was valid because Clark's promised tenure as long as he "proved faithful, efficient and competent" could harm nobody. The court interpreted Clark's remuneration set at one-fourth of "net income" to mean that he could receive only distributable amounts as determined by the board in its "good faith" discretion. The agreement was viewed as only a slight infringement on the statutory authority of the board.

Long Park, Inc. v. Trenton-New Brunswick Theaters Co., 77 N.E.2d 633 (N.Y. 1948): All the shareholders designated one of themselves as manager with full authority to run the business. The court invalidated the agreement because the directors completely surrendered their powers to the manager.

§16.7.3   Effect of Invalidity and Enforcement

A provision that illegally restrains board discretion is invalid and unenforceable. But what if the provision is part of an agreement that includes other provisions that, standing alone, are perfectly valid? Early cases, reflecting the judicial antipathy toward limits on the board, applied a strict rule against severability, and the whole agreement stood or fell with the provisions restraining directorial discretion. Recent cases, however, reflect the trend toward upholding close corporation shareholders' contracting freedom. Modern courts are more inclined to sever or rewrite troublesome provisions. *Triggs v. Triggs*, 385 N.E.2d 1254 (N.Y. 1978) (refusing to invalidate stock purchase provisions contained in an agreement among less than all shareholders that contained illegal provisions — which the court largely ignored — limiting board discretion); *Galler v. Galler*, 203 N.E.2d 577 (Ill. 1964) (saving an agreement without an express term of duration by inferring that the agreement would operate only as long as one of the parties was living).

Courts have also specifically enforced contractual restraints on directorial discretion. Many of the same arguments supporting specific enforcement of pooling agreements apply because control expectations can generally be vindicated by money damages. Some courts have even specifically enforced employment contracts in close corporations. See *Jones v. Williams*, 39 S.W. 486 (Mo. 1897); *Collins v. Collins Fruit Co.*, 189 So. 2d 262 (Fla. App. 1966).

§16.8   Close Corporation Statutes — Certainty and Guidance for the Planner

Rather than trying to fit "round-shaped" close corporations into the "square" public corporation hole of the general corporate statutes, some states have adopted special "comprehensive" close-corporation statutes. These statutes recognize the special control needs of "incorporated partnerships," and create a special statutory regime for corporations that opt in. Cal. Corp. §158, 300-303; Del. GCL §§341-355. In many respects the RMBCA's recent provisions on shareholder agreements follow the lead of these statutes. Compare Delaware's close corporation statute to the RMBCA:

Opting In. Delaware's statute defines a close corporation as one that has fewer than 30 shareholders of record, whose stock is subject to transfer restrictions, and that has not publicly issued any stock (see Chapter 15). Del. GCL §342. To elect close-corporation status, the articles must originally state (or be amended to state) that the corporation is a close corporation. Del. GCL §§341, 342, 343. In Delaware, an amendment opting into close corporation status requires a two-thirds majority vote. Del. GCL §344. The RMBCA does not have a "close corporation" category, and opting in is not necessary. Nonetheless, any shareholder agreement modifying the control structure must be conspicuously noted on share certificates, much as transfer restrictions. See RMBCA §7.32(c). In addition, the RMBCA requires that the shareholder agreement be approved by all shareholders. RMBCA §7.32(b).

Getting Out. In Delaware, an amendment to the articles voluntarily terminating close corporation status must be approved by a two-thirds majority vote. Del. GCL §346. Close-corporation status terminates when the corporation files the charter amendment or if any condition of close-corporation status is breached. Del. GCL §345. The RMBCA permits amendments to a shareholder agreement only by all shareholders. RMBCA §7.32(b)(2). Further, the agreement ends automatically after ten years, unless the parties agreed otherwise, or if the corporation's shares are traded in a national stock market. RMBCA §7.32(b)(2), (d).

Agreements Restraining Directors' Discretion. In a Delaware close corporation, shareholders holding a majority of voting shares can enter into written agreements that "restrict or interfere with the discretion or powers of the board of directors." Del. GCL §350. In addition, the certificate of incorporation can provide that the business will be managed by the shareholders rather than by a board of directors. Del. GCL §351. The RMBCA provides a more comprehensive list of the kinds of provisions permitted to shareholder agreements but requires that all the shareholders approve the agreement. RMBCA §7.32(a),(b).

Resolving Deadlocks. In Delaware, if the close corporation shareholders manage the business and become deadlocked or if they have the right under the articles to dissolve the corporation, a shareholder may petition the court for the appointment of a custodian — a court-appointed manager. Del. GCL §352. The court also may appoint a provisional director — who is neither a shareholder nor creditor of the corporation — if the corporation is deadlocked. Del. GCL §353 (see §17.2). The RMBCA leaves shareholders to their regular statutory deadlock remedies (see §17.1.3).

Shareholder Responsibility. In Delaware, if the shareholders take over management functions as the statute allows, they assume the duties (including fiduciary duties) of directors. Del. GCL §357(2), (3); *Graczykiowski v. Ramppen,* 477 N.Y.S.2d 454 (App. Div. 1984) (applying Delaware's close-corporation statute to challenge of asset transfer by a managing shareholder). The RMBCA imposes on those vested with management responsibilities "liability for acts or omissions imposed by law on directors." RMBCA §7.32(e).

EXAMPLES

1. How should Pizza Chateau, originally incorporated in an RMBCA jurisdiction, reincorporate as a close corporation in Delaware?

2. Pizza Chateau has three shareholders: Rich 500, with common shares; Bob 250; and Sally 250. Rich and Bob agree that each will vote to assure that each is elected as director and, as directors, they will appoint Bob as general manager at a guaranteed annual salary of $30,000. The agreement has no term.
   a. Is the agreement valid under traditional case law?
   b. Is it valid under the RMBCA?
   c. Is it valid under Delaware's close-corporation statute?

3. All three shareholders enter into a new agreement. They agree to elect themselves to the board and, as directors, to appoint Bob as general manager so long as he "faithfully performs his duties." In addition, Bob will receive an annual salary of $30,000, and annual bonuses equal to 50 percent of profits.
   a. Is this agreement valid under the common law?
   b. Is it valid under the RMBCA?
   c. Is it valid under Delaware's close-corporation provisions?

4. Bob worries about the enforceability of the agreement's employment provisions. He proposes a long-term employment contract with the corporation on the same terms as the shareholder agreement. Is such a contract valid?
   a. Would this employment contract be valid under the RMBCA?
   b. Pizza Chateau hires a nonshareholder, Sam, to manage the business with the same salary and bonus arrangement and subject to the same "faithful performance" provision as applied to Bob. Is this contract valid?

5. The three shareholders want to do as they please. They revise the articles to do away with the board and set up a partnership-type governance structure on which each shareholder can veto any fundamental business changes.
   a. Is the arrangement enforceable under the RMBCA?
   b. Pizza Chateau reincorporates in Delaware, but the new articles inadvertently do not choose close-corporation status. Bob plans to lease

a new store, and Rich vetoes Bob's action as the articles permit. Is the veto provision enforceable?

   c. At the last minute, Sally had voted against the veto provision. Is it nonetheless enforceable under Delaware's close corporation statute?

   d. After a couple years, Sally and Rich are chagrined at how often Bob uses his veto. They vote to amend the articles and delete the veto provision. Can they?

6. Rich, a prudent planner, wants to leave his interest in Pizza Chateau to his young nephews and creates a trust. On death, his shares will be left in trust to his nephews. The trust instrument directs the trustee, Trust Bank, to elect bank officials as directors and to appoint Bob as general manager at a specified salary. If Rich has sufficient shares to elect a majority of the board, is this arrangement valid?

EXPLANATIONS

1. There are two techniques for reincorporation: merger and sale/dissolution. In a merger, the parties form a new Delaware close corporation and merge the existing corporation into it (see §35.2). On merger, the corporate assets and liabilities automatically pass to the new Delaware close corporation, and the original shares are converted into shares of the new Delaware corporation. The RMBCA permits the merger if approved by a majority of the board and of the shares (see §35.2.2).

   In a sale/dissolution, the parties form a new Delaware close corporation and transfer the existing corporation's assets and liabilities by agreement (see §34.2). The original corporation, which receives as consideration shares of the new Delaware close corporation, then dissolves and distributes the Delaware corporation shares to its shareholders. The RMBCA permits the sale and dissolution if approved by a majority of the board and of the shares (see §§34.2.2, 35.3).

2a. Probably not. There are two aspects to this agreement. The first, the agreement among shareholders to elect an agreed-upon slate to the board, is a perfectly valid vote-pooling agreement standing alone. It affects *who* will be on the board, but not *what* the board must decide.

   The other, the agreement among directors to appoint Bob as general manager at a specified salary, is of dubious validity even under modern common law rules. The agreement among less than all shareholders governs the discretion of Rich and Bob as directors, binding them to place management in Bob's compensated hands. Who's hurt? Nonparty Sally and creditors may be hurt because the board would be powerless to do anything if Bob turns out to be a lousy manager. There are no limits on Bob's discretion or on whether the board can act if he becomes incompetent or faithless — the board is "sterilized."

2b. Probably not. The RMBCA provisions authorizing management agreements require agreement among all current shareholders. See RMBCA §7.32(b). Although this defect does not render the agreement invalid, the agreement becomes subject to the common law rules on management agreements. As we have seen, the agreement has a number of faults. Nonetheless, if Sally were aware of the agreement before she invested and there is no showing of harm to creditors, modern courts may be reluctant to invalidate the agreement.

2c. Probably yes. If the corporation has opted into close-corporation status, the shareholders who hold a majority of the shares can agree in writing to take action that "restricts or interferes with the discretion or powers of the board." Del. GCL §350. The agreement is valid "as between parties to the agreement," suggesting that Sally could seek to invalidate the agreement if it adversely affects her interests.

3a. It's now a close question. The vote-pooling agreement is perfectly valid. The management agreement has a number of merits: (1) all shareholders of the close corporation are parties, thus avoiding the problem of injury to nonparty shareholders; (2) the condition requiring Bob's "faithful performance" gives the board some flexibility to deal with Bob's bad management; and (3) the deviation could be characterized as "slight" because the board structure remains and management discretion appears to relate only to a narrow range of issues — the board is not completely sterilized.

But the management agreement has some demerits. There is no assurance that the salary and bonus specified in the agreement will continue to be appropriate under changing circumstances. The board, for example, might at some future time be compelled to abide by the agreement despite outstanding creditor claims or future plans for growth that should get first priority. Cf. *Galler v. Galler*, 203 N.E.2d 577 (Ill. 1964). In addition, the agreement is indefinite, conceivably tying up the corporation beyond the parties' original expectations, although a court might read in an implied duration. Cf. *Galler v. Galler*. On balance, particularly in a jurisdiction with case law or statutory recognition of close-corporation flexibility, the agreement probably would be enforceable.

3b. Yes. The RMBCA specifically permits an agreement among all shareholders that "restricts the discretion . . . of the board," "governs the . . . making of distributions," "establishes the terms . . . of any agreement for . . . services," or "transfers to one or more shareholders . . . authority . . . to manage the business." RMBCA §7.32(a). The agreement must be "made known" to the corporation and conspicuously noted on share certificates.

The agreement does not bind nonparties, see Official Comment to

RMBCA §7.32, and its validity as to creditors and other third parties may depend on making the salary and bonus dependent on the availability of funds. To the extent the board's hands are tied, those persons "in whom such discretion or powers are vested" assume the fiduciary responsibilities of directors. Presumably, Bob acquires fiduciary duties to moderate his compensation if it interferes with others' corporate claims.

3c. Yes. If a statutory "close corporation," the shareholders can "restrict . . . the discretion or powers of the board." Del. GCL §350. The agreement is valid "as between parties to the agreement."

The stockholders assume fiduciary duties by usurping the board's management functions. Under a scheme broader than the RMBCA, Delaware's statute imposes "upon *the stockholders* who are parties to the agreement the liability for managerial acts or omissions which is imposed on directors." Del. GCL §350. The shareholders could be liable in a suit by a trustee in bankruptcy acting for the corporation on behalf of creditors.

4a. Yes, if signed by all the shareholders. A long-term employment contract can raise the same problems as a shareholder agreement that restricts management. Some courts have held that employment contracts of unusually long duration, such as lifetime contracts, are invalid as infringements on the board's discretion. Nonetheless, the RMBCA permits arrangements that restrict board discretion if signed by all the shareholders. RMBCA §7.32(a), (b).

If the shareholders did not all sign, the RMBCA suggests the agreement should be subject to judicial scrutiny since agreements described in §7.32 "can effect material organic changes in the corporation's operation and structure, and in the rights and obligations of shareholders." Official Comment to RMBCA §7.32(b).

4b. Yes, if signed by all the shareholders. Long-term management contracts with third parties suffer the same problem as agreements among shareholders designating one as a manager, if not more so. Such an arrangement locks the board out of management, and the nonshareholder manager (who has no equity position in the corporation) may have less incentive than a shareholder manager to further its best interests. Courts have invalidated long-term management contracts that do not give the board any power of review, even if for cause. *Sherman & Ellis, Inc. v. Indiana Mutual Casualty Co.*, 41 F.2d 588 (7th Cir. 1930); *Kennerson v. Burbank Amusement Co.*, 260 P.2d 823 (Cal. App. 1953).

If all the shareholders signed the contract, it becomes a valid shareholder agreement under RMBCA §7.32(a). If they did not all sign, the issue becomes whether the board retained sufficient supervisory authority. The "faithful performance" provision and an implied term, such as periodic review every five years, would suggest its validity.

5a. Yes. All three approved the change to the articles, which the RMBCA authorizes as an agreement that "governs the exercise of the corporate powers or the management of the business." RMBCA §7.32(a)(8).

5b. Perhaps. The articles' failure to elect close-corporation status is not necessarily fatal to the veto provision's enforceability *as against Bob*. Requiring election in the articles provides notice to all interested parties (shareholders and creditors) of the possibility of special management arrangements. Although Rich's veto rights cannot undermine the third-party lessor's expectations, Bob is bound by them. The statute's publicity requirement was not meant to protect Bob, and he should not be able to hide behind his own failure to properly elect close-corporation status.

A similar issue arose in *Zion v. Kurtz,* 405 N.E.2d 681 (N.Y. 1980). The New York Court of Appeals in a 4-3 decision enforced a shareholders' agreement in a Delaware corporation that gave both shareholders veto power over any new business, even though the corporation had not elected close-corporation status under Delaware law. The agreement could be read to have required this, and the court enforced the veto provision against the party who had failed to effectuate the election. The dissenters argued that the veto provision restrained board discretion and without the public notice by filing the articles the restraint was unenforceable.

5c. Yes. A majority of shares can approve a change to the articles, Del. GCL §242(a). The Delaware close-corporation provisions permit articles to "provide that the business of the corporation shall be managed by the stockholders." Del. GCL §351. Unlike the RMBCA, not all shareholders need agree to such a change in the articles. She and the other shareholders become "subject to all liabilities of directors."

5d. Yes, unless the articles had a supermajority voting requirement. Special management arrangements, like any other contract, are subject to amendment according to the amendment provisions of the contract. In this case, the amendment rules are supplied by the corporate statute, which permits majority-approved changes, unless the parties specified otherwise. See Del. GCL §242 (see §16.1.2).

6. It may depend on the jurisdiction. The trust would restrain directorial discretion as much as, if not more than, an agreement among the directors themselves. Rich's "dead hand" instructions to the trustee cannot be changed except by petition to a court and should be subject to at least the same scrutiny as applies to agreements among directors. See *In re Estate of Hirshon,* 233 N.Y.S.2d 1018 (App. Div. 1962), *modified,* 192 N.E.2d 174 (N.Y. 1963). The instructions to the bank's representatives to appoint Bob appear to be invalid restraints on directorial

discretion. The bank's officials, like directors bound by an agreement among themselves, may discover that voting as Rich has instructed will not be in the best interests of the corporation. Even though the instructions on voting for directors, like a vote-pooling agreement, are themselves valid, there is a chance the offending instructions will not be severed and that the entire trust arrangement will fail. Nonetheless, Delaware's close-corporation statute may permit the arrangement if viewed as a "written agreement among the stockholders of a close corporation holding a majority of the outstanding stock entitled to vote." Del. GCL §350. The RMBCA does not authorize such an agreement unless it was signed by all the shareholders.

17

Dispute Resolution in the Close Corporation

Close corporations, in which owners have significant personal and financial stakes, are breeding grounds for internal squabbles. Without a market in which to sell their interests, minority shareholders are at the mercy of those who control the governance machinery. In this chapter we discuss how corporate law handles close corporate disputes.

§17.1 An Overview

§17.1.1 Freezeouts and Forceouts

To consolidate their control, majority owners can resort to two basic tactics of oppression: battles of attrition — *freezeouts* — and open assaults — *forceouts*. (Together these strategies are sometimes referred to generically as *squeezeouts*.)

Freezeouts, as we use the term, coerce minority shareholders to sell at a low price to, or buy at a high price from, majority or controlling shareholders. To work this coercion, majority shareholders can kick minority owners off the board, remove them from their positions as officers, deny them salaries or other compensation, impose a no-dividend policy, and deny them participation in new stock issues or stock redemptions.

Forceouts are bolder than freezeouts. Majority shareholders can manipulate the fundamental structure of the corporation and forcibly eliminate minority interests. For example, the majority can have the corporation sell its assets to (or merge with) another corporation controlled by the majority, or the majority can recapitalize and amend the articles to eliminate the rights of the minority's shares. We deal with forceout techniques in more detail in Chapter 35, on external organic changes.

§17.1.2 The Squeezeout Dilemma

Squeezeouts expose a fundamental dilemma of the close corporation — such corporations are really partnerships in corporate clothing. The partnership principles of liquidity and coequality run smack into the corporate principles of perpetual existence and majority control.

The traditional corporate model gives significant discretion to the majority to elect directors, appoint officers, declare dividends, set salaries, repurchase shares, and make fundamental changes. Shareholders have rights to sell their shares, but not to the corporation. Although majority control and perpetual existence may be efficient in a public corporation, they produce unfairness in a close corporation, where minority shareholders often count on the corporation for their livelihood and usually have no market to sell their shares.

§17.1.3 A Minority Shareholder's Options

Recall the situation of Pizza Chateau. Suppose that Rich and Bob (with a combined 750 shares) get together and exclude Sally (with 250 shares) from the board, deny her a position as officer, cut off her salary, stop paying dividends, and refuse to redeem her shares. What are Sally's options?

Market Out.   If Sally were a public shareholder, she could sell into a liquid trading market. This option is unavailable, by definition, to close corporation shareholders. A purchaser will not only have to incur the costs of pricing the investment, but will be in the same minority, exploitable position as the seller. For public shareholders the stock trading markets perform the pricing function, and the threat of public shareholders joining together in a takeover or proxy fight disciplines management opportunism.

The only viable "market" for close corporation shareholders is the other shareholders of the corporation. But Sally cannot force Rich or Bob (or both of them as the corporation) to repurchase her shares at a fair price. Corporate law does not create liquidity rights for shareholders unless shareholders enter into a contractual buyout arrangement (by including one in a shareholders' agreement or incorporating it into the articles or bylaws; see §34.1) or unless a state statute provides a special buyout right. (Sally should have planned!)

Dissolution.   If Sally was a partner in a partnership, she could withdraw and dissolve the partnership. UPA §31 (unless agreed otherwise, partnership dissolution occurs upon "express will of any partner"). If her withdrawal was not wrongful, she would be entitled to liquidation of the business and payment in cash of her proportional share. Even if her withdrawal was wrongful, she would receive her share, though without good will and less any damages her dissolution caused. See UPA §38.

In a corporation, a minority shareholder has no power to dissolve the corporation, which requires a board proposal and majority shareholder approval. See RMBCA §14.02. Only if Sally obtains dissolution rights in a shareholder agreement can she liquidate her investment using this route.

Involuntary Dissolution.   Modern corporate statutes provide a minority shareholder with one other option — involuntary dissolution. Sally can ask a court to dissolve the corporation, and she would receive a final distribution after the corporation's assets are liquidated and its affairs are wound up. A court in its discretion may order involuntary dissolution if the shareholder shows one of the statutory grounds:

Board deadlock.   Management is deadlocked — that is, the directors cannot agree and the shareholders have been unable to break the impasse on the board — and the corporation's business is suffering as a result. See RMBCA §14.30(2)(i); Cal. Corp. §1800(b)(2); N.Y. BCL §1104.

Shareholder deadlock.   The shareholders are deadlocked — that is, the shareholders have been unable to elect new directors for a specified period, such as two consecutive annual meetings. RMBCA §14.30(2)(iii); Cal. Corp. §1800(b)(3); N.Y. BCL §1104.

Misconduct.   The majority has engaged in misconduct. The statutes express this in various ways:

- Those in control have acted in a way that is "illegal, oppressive, or fraudulent." See RMBCA §14.30(2)(ii).
- The corporate assets are being "misapplied or wasted." See RMBCA §14.30(2)(iv); Cal. Corp. §1800(b)(4); N.Y. BCL §1104-a.
- Dissolution is "reasonably necessary for the protection" of the complaining shareholder. See Cal. Corp. §1800(b)(5); N.C. GS §55-14-30.

In a minority of states, deadlock is the exclusive ground for involuntary dissolution. In some states, nondeadlock grounds are available only in close corporations. See N.Y. BCL §1104-a.

Fiduciary Challenge.   Sally can also challenge the majority's use of control as a breach of fiduciary duty. Over the last three decades, courts have become more sympathetic to the plight of minority shareholders in close corporations.

Recognizing the "incorporated partnership" nature of close corporations and the absence of a market option for minority shareholders, courts have inferred heightened fiduciary duties of close corporation shareholders.

§17.2   Judicial Protection of Minority Shareholders

Judicial protection for minority shareholders who complain of majority abuse comes in two related forms: involuntary dissolution and fiduciary review.

§17.2.1   Involuntary Dissolution

Before considering this increasingly important option, we should define some terms. *Dissolution* is the formal extinguishment of the corporation's legal life; *liquidation* is the process of reducing the corporation's assets to cash or liquid assets, after which the corporation becomes a liquid shell; *winding up* is the process of liquidating the assets, paying off creditors, and distributing what remains to shareholders (see §34.2.3).

Courts once viewed involuntary dissolution as a drastic remedy. In fact, the Official Comment to RMBCA §14.30 advises courts to be "cautious" in granting dissolution in nondeadlock situations and distinguish between "genuine abuse" and "acceptable tactics in a power struggle." Nonetheless, the usual effect of dissolution on the corporation's business rarely is fatal. Most often a dissolution order acts as a powerful negotiating chip for the minority and forces the majority to buy out the minority (or make other accommodations) on terms favorable to the minority. If the majority fails to offer a fair price or make other concessions, it will lose significant "ongoing concern" value if the corporation is actually liquidated. In other words, a dissolution order usually does not terminate the business; it simply advises the majority to be more accommodating in its negotiations with the minority.

Many recent cases have made involuntary dissolution easier by interpreting the "oppression" and "reasonably necessary for the protection" conditions of the statutes to refer to the *reasonable expectations* of shareholders in the corporation. For example, in *Matter of Kemp & Beatley, Inc.*, 473 N.E.2d 1173 (N.Y. 1984), the court ordered involuntary dissolution on behalf of minority shareholders who had been long-time employees. The court found oppressive the majority shareholders' decision to increase their executive compensation while discontinuing the long-standing practice of distributing earnings as dividends or extra compensation.

Other courts have referred to the parties' original (and sometimes evolving) understandings about salaries, bonuses, dividends, and employment, saying that consideration must be given to whether dissolution is a feasible means of protecting those expectations. *Meiselman v. Meiselman*, 307 S.E.2d

551 (N.C. 1983). In effect, courts have used the dissolution remedy to enforce unwritten agreements by close corporation shareholders who may have been ignorant on how to formally structure their relationship.

Statistical evidence bears out the emerging judicial recognition of implicit dissolution rights in close corporations. Two studies of involuntary dissolution cases from 1960-1976 and 1984-1985 show that there are more involuntary dissolution cases each year and that courts are increasingly willing to order relief, including buyout remedies:

	1960-1976	1984-1985
No relief	27 (50.0%)	4 (10.8%)
Dissolution order	16 (29.6%)	10 (27.0%)
Buyout order	3 (5.6%)	20 (54.1%)
Other relief	8 (14.8%)	3 (8.1%)
Total	54 (100%)	37 (100%)

In recognition of involuntary dissolution as a buyout remedy, the RMBCA was amended in 1991 to permit majority shareholders in a close corporation to avoid dissolution by electing to buy out at "fair value" the shares of a shareholder who petitions for involuntary dissolution. RMBCA §14.34; Official Comment (provision gives majority a 90-day "call" right of minority's shares to prevent strategic abuse of dissolution petition). Purchasing shareholders must give notice to the court within 90 days of the petition and then negotiate with the petitioning shareholder. If after 60 days the negotiations fail, the court can award the petitioner "fair value." If the petitioner had "probable grounds" for relief under the misconduct provisions of the involuntary dissolution statute, the award can include the petitioner's litigation costs (attorney and expert fees).

§17.2.2   Fiduciary Protection

In many instances, the minority shareholder does not want a buyer for his shares but rather wants relief from harmful majority tactics such as the refusal to continue his employment or the adoption of a policy not to pay dividends.

The fiduciary rules borrowed from public corporations offer little solace to frozen out minority shareholders in close corporations. The minority has the burden of showing the majority's actions were motivated by fraud, pique, or self interest — that is, "bad faith." The business judgment rule protects the majority shareholders if they can advance some rational *business purpose* for their actions, so as to negate a finding of bad faith (see §21.2). The focus is on the corporation's interests and not the parties' relationship.

Many earlier courts used the "business purpose" approach to deny relief to minority shareholders who challenged actions they claimed were freezeouts, such as termination of employment or nonpayment of dividends.

Zidell v. Zidell, 560 P.2d 1086 (Or. 1977) (no breach even though corporation had sufficient capital); *Gottfried v. Gottfried*, 73 N.Y.S.2d 692 (App. Div. 1947) (no breach even though majority shareholder had said minority "would never get any dividends because the majority could freeze them out"). If the majority can point to business justifications for its actions, such as expansion plans or personal incompatibility, courts have applied the business judgment rule and have refused to interfere.

This approach is in marked contrast to the rights of partners in a partnership, who are entitled to share in management and profits and owe each other the duties of "utmost good faith and loyalty." Absent a contrary agreement, partners are coagents of each other, have equal management rights, are entitled to an accounting of profits, and cannot be removed without payment of their partnership interest. See UPA §§9, 18, 22, 38. The business justifications propounded by majority partners are irrelevant.

In the last 20 years, there has been a revolution in corporate fiduciary law in close corporations. Increasingly, courts have recognized the illiquidity problems for minority shareholders and have implied partnership-type duties in close corporations. At the same time, courts have fashioned a *direct* cause of action for minority shareholders, abandoning the thesis that corporate fiduciaries owe their duties to the corporation. Minority shareholders can sue (and recover from) controlling shareholders directly, without being subject to the usual impediments of a derivative suit (see Chapters 31 and 32).

In the ground-breaking case of *Donahue v. Rodd Electrotype Co.*, 328 N.E.2d 505 (Mass. 1975), the court stated shareholders in a close corporation have duties of "utmost good faith and loyalty." Suggesting that the majority must provide the minority an "equal opportunity" to participate in corporate benefits, the court compelled the majority to provide the minority plaintiffs an opportunity to redeem their stock on the same terms as had been made available to a controlling shareholder. As a remedy, the court allowed the plaintiffs to choose between rescinding the challenged redemption or participating on the same terms.

Soon after *Donahue* the Massachusetts court retreated from a broad equal opportunity rule. *Wilkes v. Springside Nursing Home, Inc.*, 353 N.E.2d 657 (Mass. 1976). The court concluded that in certain "legitimate spheres" — such as employment matters, declaring dividends, mergers, and dismissing directors — the majority should have discretion to manage the business, even if at the expense of the minority. The court established a balancing test: If the majority shows a "legitimate business purpose" for its action and the minority shows that the objective could have been accomplished in a way less harmful to the minority's interest, then the court must balance the legitimate objective against the practicality of the alternative. In *Wilkes* the controlling shareholders were unable to justify taking the minority plaintiff off the payroll, and the court never reached the balancing test. The court remanded on the issue of the amount of lost wages.

In a close corporation, minority shareholders often will have control rights greater than those of public shareholders. Close corporation opportunism, therefore, can be a two-way street. A minority shareholder who threatens to use her veto power or buyout right to extract concessions from the majority may breach the same implicit promise of good faith to which controlling shareholders are held. Some courts have recognized this and have imposed fiduciary duties on minority shareholders in close corporations. For example, in *Smith v. Atlantic Properties, Inc.*, 422 N.E.2d 798 (Mass. App. 1981), a 25 percent shareholder who had the power to veto the payment of dividends was held liable for tax penalties incurred because of his unreasonable refusal to approve their payment.

EXAMPLES

1. Junior, Robert, and Clifton are in the oil business. Each owns 1000 shares in Lambing Oil, an RMBCA corporation. Since its incorporation 15 seasons ago, the three brothers have run the company on the understanding that each brother would share equally in every aspect of the business. They never reduced their understanding to writing, but each brother has sat on the board, drawn the same salary, and been able to block any action with which he disagreed.

   a. One day Clifton wants out of the business. Can he withdraw and have the corporation dissolved?

   b. Clifton begins to veto all corporate action. He then claims that the board is deadlocked. Will a court order dissolution?

2. Things turn mean. At the next directors' meeting, Junior and Robert remove Clifton as officer and terminate his salary. They say Clifton is a liability because he does not really know the oil business and has never been cut-throat.

   a. Have the controlling shareholders breached a fiduciary duty under traditional fiduciary review?

   b. Have the controlling shareholders breached a fiduciary duty under a *Wilkes* test?

   c. If Junior and Robert breached a fiduciary duty, can the court order them to repurchase Clifton's shares?

   d. Is Clifton entitled to involuntary dissolution?

3. Things turn meaner. Robert and Junior issue to themselves 1000 new shares at $2000 per share, equal to an outside offer they had received (and turned down) to purchase one year before. Robert and Junior make the same offer to Clifton, who they know does not have $500,000 —

the purchase price. They know that Clifton, with his poor credit, cannot borrow the money either. After the issue, Robert and Junior each become 40 percent shareholders, and Clifton 20 percent.

   a. Can Clifton challenge the new issue under a traditional fiduciary test?

   b. Can Clifton challenge the new issue under a *Donahue* approach?

EXPLANATIONS

1a. Probably not. Absent majority "bad faith" or a dissolution agreement, a minority shareholder has dissolution rights only through a petition to the court for involuntary dissolution. Under the RMBCA Clifton would have to show board or shareholder deadlock or misconduct by Junior and Robert. RMBCA §14.30(2). There is no evidence of either. Even if a court were to interpret "oppression" as including frustration of reasonable expectations, there is no evidence that the parties expected they would be obligated to purchase the others' shares. Clifton might argue that the parties' implicit understanding that he could deadlock the corporation entitles him to dissolution rights. But this argument may go beyond the RMBCA, which favors an ongoing business and discourages easy dissolution.

1b. Probably not. Clifton must show two things: (1) he has the power to deadlock the corporation; and (2) he did not violate his fiduciary duties by deadlocking it. It is unclear that Clifton has a veto power, as the shareholders' agreement was never reduced to writing and signed by all the shareholders. Cf. RMBCA §7.32(b); *Dionisi v. DeCampli*, 1991 Del. Ch. LEXIS 111 (July 2, 1991) (reasonable expectations must be reduced to writing if they relate to sale of stock). Even if a court finds that Clifton had "reasonable expectations" in a veto power, it is unclear that the majority's frustration of these expectations would amount to a fiduciary breach or "oppression." Minority shareholders have fiduciary duties not to abuse their control rights. Clifton's self-interested use of his veto undermines his arguments of majority overreaching.

     In a public corporation, Clifton's threat might be perfectly acceptable — public shareholders are said to have the right to do with their shares and vote them as they please. But close corporation shareholders, both majority and minority, lack a market for their shares, and have expectations that the other shareholders will not interfere with mutual advantage.

2a. No. Junior and Robert seem to have legitimate business purposes for their freezeout, undercutting Clifton's claim of "bad faith." So long as they have some support for their doubts about Clifton's services, the court will not interfere in the majority's handling of business.

2b. Perhaps. The *Wilkes* approach balances the majority's expectations of control and the minority's expectations of equal treatment. Robert and Junior have the burden to show a business purpose for their action, such as pointing to particular business problems created by Clifton's lack of expertise. If the court finds the explanation credible and legitimate, Clifton must then show they could have accomplished their objective some other way — for example, by teaching Clifton the oil business and how to be cut-throat. The court would then balance the business purpose against the practicality of the alternative. The alternative may not be practicable, and Clifton might be out of a job and salary under a *Wilkes* test.

2c. Perhaps. Typically, the remedy for a self-dealing breach is rescission. Clifton would be restored to his position, with damages for back pay. But in this case rescission would only perpetuate the parties' animosity and invite further lawsuits or freezeout attempts. Forced redemption would disentangle the parties. Increasingly, courts take an activist role in adjusting the relationships of parties in close corporations.

2d. Probably yes. A petition for involuntary dissolution on the ground of "oppression" is much like a *Wilkes* fiduciary challenge, except that the statutory remedy is dissolution — in effect, a forced buyout. If "oppression" turns on the minority's reasonable expectations, Clifton could point to the Lambing Oil history of coequal sharing and management to support his claim. The majority's justifications for its actions in such a quasi-contract challenge would not be relevant to interpreting the original (and evolving) understandings among the parties continuing their various rights in the business.

3a. No. If the corporation's business has not appreciated significantly in value, the self-dealing issuance of new stock seems to fall within a range of reasonableness. If the majority can proffer some business justification for the issue — raising new capital — the transaction would survive traditional loyalty review. See §22.3.

3b. Perhaps. The *Donahue* "equal opportunity" approach, which applies to a majority's stock transaction, provides minority shareholders equal liquidity rights. The court reserved the question whether it also provides, in effect, preemptive rights. Even if it did, the majority shareholders in this case appear to have provided the minority with an equal purchase opportunity. Nonetheless, under the higher "utmost good faith and loyalty" fiduciary standard *Donahue* creates in close corporations, the majority may have to proffer legitimate business purposes for the issuance. Under the *Wilkes* balancing test, the court will scrutinize the justification and consider the minority's suggestion of less harmful means. Unless there are particularly good reasons for an infusion of equity capital, the majority shareholders are not saved by having "offered" the same deal to Clifton, who they knew could not afford it.

§17.3   Deadlocks

Thus far we have assumed that Sally, our frozen-out minority shareholder, is powerless to use the corporate governance machinery to her advantage. What happens, however, if she has an equity interest or board position sufficient to bring the corporation's business to a grinding halt — to deadlock the corporation? By *deadlock,* we and the corporate statutes do not mean the benign and common situation when the parties are evenly divided and unable to agree on a particular issue. Instead, deadlock is a symptom of fundamental disagreement among shareholders or directors that paralyzes the corporation's business. Virtually nothing can be agreed on; the business either does not run or limps along in suspended animation.

§17.3.1   Environment for Deadlocks

For the planner to guard against deadlock, she must first anticipate how it occurs: an even number of directors on the board, a "neutral director" who resigns or dies, equal division of stock, or the alignment of the parties into two equally powerful camps. For example, assume that Olive and Stanley are each 50 percent shareholders and serve on the board with their friend Max. One day Max resigns, disgusted with their antics. If Olive and Stanley cannot agree on a third director, or anything else, the board will be unable to act and the shareholders unable to break the deadlock. See RMBCA §14.30(2)(i), (iii); Cal. Corp. §1800; N.Y. BCL §1104.

The problem of deadlock raises two questions. First, how should it be handled once it happens? Second, how can it be avoided by good planning?

§17.3.2   Judicial Deadlock Remedies

If the parties did not anticipate deadlocks, recourse is to the courts:

Court-appointed custodians and provisional directors. Many close-corporation statutes authorize courts to appoint custodians and provisional directors. These court-appointed mediators are to continue the business *indefinitely* for the benefit of all the shareholders, both majority and minority, until their differences are resolved. Cal. Corp. §1802; Del. GCL §§352, 353.

Court-appointed receivers. Some statutes authorize courts to appoint receivers on an *interim basis* for a deadlocked corporation that faces imminent dissolution. Cal. Corp. §1803.

Court supervision. The court can retain jurisdiction to protect minority shareholders or to order preliminary injunctive relief (such as salary reductions or an accounting) if there are allegations of misappropriation or other oppressive conduct. Cal. Corp. §§1804, 1806.

Court-ordered involuntary dissolution. The ultimate step is for court-mandated disentanglement through an order of involuntary dissolution. (See the earlier discussion of the requirements for granting involuntary dissolution, §17.1.3).

Other court-ordered relief. The court can order damages, a forced buyout, or payment of salaries or dividends. Cal. Corp. §§1804, 1806.

§17.3.3 *Planning for Deadlocks*

Planners can provide methods to deal with deadlocks once they occur. Some we have already seen; others are new.

Mediation. The deadlocked parties choose a person acceptable to both of them to help resolve their disagreement. The mediator has no power to compel a resolution.

Arbitration. The deadlocked parties agree in a pre-dispute or post-dispute contract to allow an arbitrator to resolve their dispute in a binding decision. An example of a pre-dispute arbitration agreement is found in the *Ringling Bros.* case (see §16.2.3). The Federal Arbitration Act requires enforcement of arbitration clauses in any agreement affecting interstate commerce, and the courts have shown less jealousy to protect their jurisdiction and greater respect for private solutions to their crowded dockets.

Deadlock-breaking director or shareholder. The parties can create a structural tie-breaker. An example of a deadlock-breaking director is found in the *Lehrman v. Cohen* case (see §16.3.4). Whether the parties create a special class of stock or simply transfer a few shares to a mutually acceptable person, the result is a built-in arbitrator.

Voluntary dissolution. The parties can agree to dissolution rights. Many statutes specifically allow the enforcement of preexisting agreements to dissolve. See RMBCA §7.32(a)(7). Although it might seem drastic, dissolution may be the best solution for a paralyzed corporation. As we have seen, in most instances the corporation need not be liquidated or its business wound up when the parties agree to dissolve. Because of the business's value as an ongoing concern, one camp usually will buy out the other camp since liquidation and winding up would destroy an important component of the business's value.

Statutory buyout. A growing number of statutes mandate corporate repurchase at a fair price as a remedy for deadlock and dissension.

RMBCA §14.34 (only in close corporations); Cal. Corp. §1804 (broad remedial powers to avoid involuntary dissolution); N.Y. BCL §1118 (remedy to avoid involuntary dissolution available only in close corporations).

§17.3.4 Validity of Deadlock-Breaking Devices

Negotiated deadlock remedies — many of which work as control devices that take management discretion away from the board — raise the same issues we saw before with restraints on directors' discretion (see §16.7). The problem is illustrated by *Vogel v. Lewis,* 268 N.Y.S.2d 237 (App. Div. 1966), *aff'd,* 224 N.E.2d 738 (N.Y. 1967), where two 50 percent shareholders had agreed to arbitration "in event of a dispute, or difference, arising between them." When a warehouse lease expired and they could not agree on renewing it (because one had a side agreement with the warehouse's owners), the other shareholder sought arbitration. A majority of the court ordered that arbitration proceed, rejecting the obvious restraint-of-board argument. The dissenters, however, thought that the arbitration clause was too broad and that either party could use it coercively to "destroy the business" by insisting on arbitration at the drop of a hat.

EXAMPLES

1. It turns out that Robert, Junior, and Clifton were not the only siblings who inherited Lambing Oil Corporation. A woman named Pamela appears and claims to be their long-lost sister. A probate court accepts her claim and makes her a 25 percent shareholder. With ownership divided equally among the four, Robert and Junior begin to worry that Pamela may join forces with Clifton and deadlock the business.
   a. How might deadlock occur?
   b. The Lambing Oil board has three directors — Robert, Junior, and Clifton. Can Robert and Junior prevent deadlock from occurring?

2. Pamela demands a seat on the board. Robert and Junior want to be accommodating and agree, but they also suggest that the four decide on something to prevent deadlocks.
   a. Clifton suggests a shareholders' agreement under which each shareholder will vote his shares to assure that all four are elected to the board. Does this do the job?
   b. Clifton suggests a voting trust. The trustee will be Clay, the shareholders' stepfather. Does this do the job?
   c. Clifton persists and suggests a shareholders' agreement under which each party will be on the board. In case of a board deadlock, each shareholder will give Clay an irrevocable proxy to vote his or her shares. Clay can then elect a nondeadlocked board. Does this do the job?

d. Clifton does not give up. He suggests that in case of a board deadlock, Clay will arbitrate any difference. He suggests a shareholders' agreement that would assure each shareholder a seat on the board and that allows for any director to "seek arbitration by Clay to resolve any dispute on the board." Does this do the job?

e. Clifton is listening. He suggests that the shareholders create five classes of stock. Each shareholder will hold his or her own class of stock, which will be entitled to elect one director and to receive approximately one-fourth in all corporate distributions. Clay will receive the fifth class of stock, which will be entitled to elect the fifth director and receive 1/100 of all corporate distributions. Does this do the job?

EXPLANATIONS

1a. Deadlock can occur at either the shareholder or board level. At the shareholder level, if the Robert-Junior camp and the Clifton-Pamela camp are unable to agree, there will be no shareholder majority. The result will be that no shareholder action can be taken, and under a system of straight voting no directors can be elected.

Board deadlock is not a necessary consequence of a 50-50 shareholder split. Deadlock among directors depends on the number of directors on the board and whether any directors have disproportionate voting (or veto) powers. If there were three directors — Robert, Junior, and Clifton — when Pamela acquired her 25 percent interest, there is little risk of board deadlock. Assuming that no special voting arrangements apply to the board, deadlock could occur only if one of the three directors were to resign or die and the remaining shareholders and directors were unable to fill the vacancy. Just because one director is always outvoted or the board is occasionally unable to act does not mean the board is deadlocked.

1b. Yes. They could prevent deadlock at the shareholder level by issuing new shares, assuming some are authorized. At the board level, there is little risk of board deadlock. Their presence and voting together at meetings assures that the board will not be deadlocked.

2a. No. The shareholders' agreement avoids the risk of shareholder deadlock. If the shareholders abide by the agreement, they will always be able to elect directors. But a board with an even number of directors invites board deadlock.

2b. Not really. A voting trust eliminates the risk of both shareholder and board deadlock, but there is no assurance that the four shareholders will be represented on the board. Clay, for example, could decide to elect himself and the three brothers to the board, excluding Pamela.

2c. This seems no better than the voting trust. Each shareholder (or camp) risks that Clay will oust him or her from the board. Clay's authority extends beyond resolving the deadlocking issue or issues. In addition, the irrevocable proxy arrangement may not be valid (see §16.5). Some jurisdictions do not recognize the giving of an irrevocable proxy to a party who has no interest in the corporation or its shares. Cf. RMBCA §7.22(d)(5) (valid in a shareholder agreement). Moreover, the granting of voting power to Clay has many of the attributes of a voting trust. If treated as a de facto voting trust, the arrangement must comply with the notice requirements and limits on duration to which voting trusts are statutorily subject.

2d. Clifton is getting warmer. If the management aspects of the agreement are valid, the agreement will help avoid deadlocks using a mechanism agreed to by the parties. The parties will be much more likely to go along with their "own" dispute resolution mechanism rather than one imposed by judicial fiat.

The validity of the agreement may depend on whether the relevant jurisdiction has a statute authorizing deviations from the traditional management model. See RMBCA §7.32(a)(1) (authorizing agreement that "restricts the discretion . . . of the board"). Without statutory guidance, the agreement's validity is less than certain. By allowing Clay to arbitrate "any dispute" without any explicit limits on his authority, it is possible that even a modern court might hold that the mechanism violates public policy and sterilizes the board. As drafted, the mechanism runs a significant risk of abuse by contemplating arbitration whenever any director (perhaps when simply outvoted) considers there to be a dispute and wishes to have it arbitrated. Furthermore, there are no standards under which Clay can conduct the arbitration, and there is little assurance that his interests will be aligned with those of the corporation in general — he has no ownership interest. This detachment is exacerbated by the fact that Clay will not necessarily be abreast of corporate developments when called on to arbitrate disputes.

2e. Clifton seems to be there. The validity of the arrangement seems assured. RMBCA §6.01(c) (see §16.4); *Lehrman v. Cohen* (see §16.3.4). This mechanism assures that Clay will be a permanent deadlock-breaking member of the board. As such, he will be abreast of corporate developments should disputes arise. Furthermore, by participating more than nominally in corporate distributions, he will have an incentive to further the corporation's general interests in resolving those disputes. Perhaps the only problem with the arrangement is that it depends on Clay's continuing to be of good mind and body. The parties should consider procedures for deciding on Clay's successor should he die or become incapacitated. Without more, the parties might unwittingly make one of Clay's heirs (conceivably, one of themselves) the deadlock-breaker.

PART SIX

Shareholder Action in Public Corporations

18

Shareholders' Role in Publicly Held Corporations

Shareholders are often said to "own" the corporation. Although in a close corporation this may accurately describe the majority shareholders' position, in a publicly held corporation this description is at best metaphorical. Stock ownership in public corporations is widely dispersed, and direct shareholder control over corporate affairs is significantly diluted. In public corporations, shareholders are limited to: (1) voting their shares, usually by proxy; and (2) selling their shares, usually on public trading markets.

In this chapter we describe how public shareholders vote and sell their shares. It serves as an introduction to our next chapter, discussing federal proxy regulation (Chapter 19), as well as later chapters on fraud in securities trading regulated under Rule 10b-5 (Chapter 29) and on corporate takeover contests (Chapters 37-40).

§18.1 Shareholder Voting in Public Corporations

§18.1.1 A Glimpse into the Proxy Process

Under corporate law in the United States, equity share ownership generally carries voting rights with it. Shareholders exercise those rights at annual and special shareholders' meetings (see §12.2). But in a public corporation, a proxy solicitation process effectively takes the place of the meeting. Public shareholders need not, and probably will not, attend the meeting to cast their votes. The logistics and expense of bringing together and fitting a public corporation's thousands of public shareholders into one meeting hall help explain the reason for proxy voting. The actual meeting is usually a sparsely attended and predictable (though often showy) event. Under SEC rules, any proxy that a public shareholder returns must be voted according to the instructions on the card.

How does the proxy process work? The solicitation and voting of proxies is usually an annual corporate rite of spring, after the company and its auditors have prepared financial statements for the previous year. After setting the date of the annual meeting, the board of directors selects a "record date" (see §12.2.2) used to identify which shareholders will be entitled to notice and to vote at the meeting. The board then selects its nominees for election as directors and decides which matters to submit for shareholder approval. To solicit proxies, management then sends solicitation materials and proxy cards to shareholders (or their nominees, which act as forwarding agents under procedures set out in SEC rules) so shareholders can authorize the voting of their shares at the annual meeting. Shareholders receive a package a few weeks before the meeting. The package usually includes an annual report, a proxy statement, and a proxy card. The board invariably asks shareholders to return the proxy cards promptly.

At the shareholders' meeting, directors are nominated and resolutions are proposed. Although under state law it may be possible for a shareholder at the meeting to nominate her own slate of directors or propose a resolution, the effort would be futile unless the shareholder had solicited proxies. The votes have already been "cast," in the sense that shareholders have sent in proxy cards instructing how their shares are to be voted.

How does management of a public corporation communicate with its shareholders? Most public shareholders will be beneficial owners, not record owners. This means that investors' shares will actually be owned by a nominee, typically a brokerage firm. The corporation's stock records will show that brokerage firms and similar nominees own a significant percentage of its stock *of record*.

Under SEC rules, management can disseminate proxy materials either to the record owner or to those beneficial owners who do not object to having their nominees furnish their names and addresses (nonobjecting beneficial owners or NOBOs). If management has reason to believe the record owner is acting as a nominee, it must make available enough copies of the solicitation materials so that each beneficial owner will be able to receive and review the information, even though very few actually read it. Depending on the brokerage firm procedures, shareholders will either complete the proxy card and return it themselves or instruct the firm (the record holder) on how to complete it. Under state law, only record holders have formal voting rights.

§18.1.2 History of Public Shareholder Voting

In 1932 a law professor and economics professor (Berle and Means) wrote an influential book, *The Modern Corporation and Private Property,* which systematically identified the separation of corporate ownership and management in public corporations. Berle and Means found that 44 percent of the country's largest 200 companies were under "management control." They explained that stock ownership is widely distributed and no individual or group of shareholders has a sufficient interest to control the company's affairs, management becomes "a self-perpetuating body even though its share in the ownership is negligible."

Central to the Berle and Means thesis of management control was the ineffectiveness of shareholder voting as a control device. In public corporations where shareholders hand over their votes to individuals selected by existing management, proxy voting leaves control in the hands of the board of directors, who thus "virtually dictate their own successors." Although shareholders can replace the existing board of directors by soliciting proxies in support of an insurgent slate of candidates, Berle and Means found proxy contests to be rare.

In reaction to the gloomy Berle and Means story of the separation of management and ownership in public corporations, Congress in 1934 created the Securities and Exchange Commission to, among other things, create a federal proxy voting regime. Despite new SEC rules that required management disclosures and shareholder access to the proxy machinery, shareholders did not leap at the invitation to informed, empowered participation in corporate governance. During the 1950s and 1960s, proxy contests were no more frequent, and insurgents were no more successful; management-sponsored initiatives won and shareholder-sponsored initiatives lost, each by a wide margin. By the 1970s, many academics had come to accept shareholder apathy as insoluble, indeed "rational."

But in the 1980s shareholders began to use their powerful, latent control over managers despite the practical infirmity of their vote. Shareholders' power came from the threat to exit and sell their shares, not from voicing their views through voting. During the takeover boom of the 1980s, shareholder voting served as the linchpin for hostile stock acquisitions and takeovers. Dispersed shareholders began to exercise the power inherent in stock liquidity by selling to one particular buyer, who would consolidate the voting power of the otherwise dispersed shares to replace the board and take over the company. Takeovers and the threat of takeovers provided the discipline that atomistic voting could not.

But as the era of hostile takeovers came to an end, a new era began in the 1990s, during which institutional investors emerged as a powerful new actor in U.S. corporate governance. As Berle and Means had noticed 60 years ago, large shareholders have greater incentives to become informed about management and proxy contests, and are more likely to vote than other shareholders.

Who are these new institutional investors? They are intermediaries that hold large pools of investments for beneficiaries, and include private and public pension funds, mutual funds, insurance funds, bank trusts, and foundation and endowments. Over the last few decades, tax rules have encouraged employers and workers to contribute to pension plans, and individual investors seeking greater diversification have shifted their investments to mutual funds. By 1991 institutional shareholders held 53.8 percent of the nation's $3.6 trillion in equity holdings. (By contrast, in 1981 institutional investors held 38 percent of the $1.5 trillion in U.S. equity holdings.) With over $7.0 trillion in assets, institutional investors today hold unprecedented, concentrated voting power.

Institutional investors have in some dramatic instances been successful in asserting this new power. For example, under pressure from institutional investors, corporate boards of a number of prominent corporations have ousted management, divested businesses, made structural governance changes, and revised dividend policies. The power of the public corporation CEO has wilted, and, as one observer commented, "The once seemingly absolute power of the Top Banana is peeling away."

The story of institutional activism is still young. In the late 1980s and early 1990s, institutional investors used a strategy of confrontation: insurgents in record numbers proposed alternative board slates and initiated proposals for structural reforms to enhance shareholder control. As we approach the mid-1990s, institutional investors seem to be choosing from a variety of nonvoting tactics. Some involve conciliation and quiet diplomacy; others involve public shaming, such as the feared "target list." Recently, "relationship investing" — an established, long-term link with communications between company management and one or more of the larger shareholders — has become popular.

§18.1.3   *Public Shareholder Incentives in Voting*

The emergence of institutional investors as a powerful force in public corporations owes to the voting incentives they have compared to individual public shareholders. For an individual shareholder who seeks management reforms, there is little incentive to try to "collectivize" other shareholders. An insurgent must be prepared to commit significant time, money, and effort to overcome shareholder apathy. Expenses for an insurgent in a contested election have been estimated to range between $5 million and $10 million.

If an insurgent loses, she absorbs the full costs of the contest; she cannot seek contribution from other shareholders or the corporation. If she wins, she may be reimbursed the costs of the contest by the firm, but any gains she creates will be shared with all other shareholders. Her portion of the gains is limited to the percentage — usually quite small — of her shareholding in the firm. In short, she must risk a substantial sum to create gains in which other shareholders will share, even though they have risked nothing. This "free rider" phenomenon leads individual shareholders to do nothing to correct management problems, each shareholder waiting for someone else to incur the costs in hopes of a free ride.

An insurgent's problems are compounded by the "rational apathy" of most small shareholders confronted with competing proxy solicitations. If an individual shareholder holds a small stake in a firm as part of a diversified portfolio, he has little incentive to spend time educating himself about the merits of any given proxy contest. He will perceive (rationally) that the time spent becoming familiar with the contestants and the issues will not be worth any potential gains to his portfolio, even if he votes correctly. It is not surprising, given the information disadvantage of most small shareholders, that they act on a general rule of thumb: vote for or with incumbent managers.

For institutional investors, the incentives are much different. Institutional shareholders have much larger stakes in individual companies, sometimes owning up to 10 percent of the company's shares. Apathy about the corporation's management is not rational, and even though an institutional shareholder must share any gains with all other shareholders, the institution's large share may be worth the effort. In addition, institutional investors cannot easily exercise the "Wall Street Rule" and simply dump their stock when they become dissatisfied, because selling a large block of stock will necessarily drag down the market price of the stock and decrease the selling price.

§18.2 Public Trading of Corporate Securities

The most significant characteristic of a publicly held corporation is a market (or markets) in which shareholders can buy or sell the corporation's securities. The stock trading markets — sometimes known as *secondary markets* — account for about 99 percent of all stock transactions. Only rarely do shareholders buy stock directly from a public corporation on what is known as the *primary market*.

§18.2.1 Functioning of Public Stock Trading Markets

How does stock trading work? Assume your next-door neighbor, Ivan, is like one in every five Americans who individually owns stock in a public corporation. He has decided to buy 100 more shares of EXXON Corp. stock at the prevailing market price, which is listed each day in the newspaper's financial section. How does he go about buying the stock? He probably will call his stockbroker (a salesperson at a brokerage firm such as Merrill Lynch) and give the broker a buy order for his account for 100 shares of EXXON stock at the market price — a *market buy order*. Merrill Lynch can fill Ivan's order in several ways:

(1) Trading on a stock exchange. If the stock is "listed" on a stock exchange — the New York Stock Exchange in EXXON's case — Merrill Lynch (acting as Ivan's agent, or "broker") can relay the order to the "floor" of the exchange where trading occurs. Stock listed on an exchange is offered for sale and purchase by a specialist in the stock, so there is always a seller to match every buyer. Ivan's buy order either will be matched to another's sell order or, if there is none, the specialist will sell the stock himself. Either way, the shareholder is assured that if he wishes to sell, his stock will be bought at the market price. The specialists' market-making role provides liquidity (the assurance of a ready buyer or seller) and prevents erratic price changes. Along the line, Merrill Lynch and the specialist will make their money by charging the buyer and seller commissions for bringing the two together.

(2) Buying on the over-the-counter market. If the stock is not listed on an exchange, Merrill Lynch might be able to fill Ivan's buy order by using a computerized system that quotes available prices from stock dealers (brokerage firms that sell for their own account). The system, known as the National Association of Securities Dealers Automated Quotations System (NASDAQ), is often referred to as the *over-the-counter market*. Most stock available on the OTC is stock not listed on an exchange. Merrill Lynch (acting as a buyer and seller, or "dealer") can use NASDAQ to buy stock for its account and then resell it to Ivan at a mark-up. In the OTC market, some dealers act as market makers, performing much the same role as specialists on exchanges. Orders on the OTC market are placed by telephone rather than being routed to a central exchange. Instead of receiving a commission, Merrill Lynch will make a profit on the difference between what it pays for the stock (the "purchase price") and what it charges Ivan. Although it is a less common arrangement, Merrill Lynch also can act as a broker on the OTC market by purchasing stock from another NASDAQ dealer on Ivan's behalf and collecting a commission for acting as his agent.

(3) Selling from inventory. If it owns EXXON stock, Merrill Lynch can sell Ivan the stock from its own "inventory." Merrill Lynch will make a profit or absorb a loss depending on the price at which it originally bought the stock.

However Ivan acquires his 100 shares of EXXON stock, it is entirely possible that he (like 40 percent of other individual investors and 80 percent of all investors) will never receive certificates for his stock. After the transaction closes — usually a few days after the buy order is executed — Ivan's account with Merrill Lynch will reflect that he owns 100 EXXON shares. He will be the *beneficial owner* of these shares but will not receive share certificates unless he asks for them. Instead, his ownership will be reflected on the books of Merrill Lynch, which will act as his nominee. As Ivan's broker nominee, Merrill Lynch is said to own the stock in its "street name." On EXXON's books (which are kept by a transfer agent — usually a bank) Ivan's beneficial ownership shows up as record ownership by Merrill Lynch.

This "street name" system, though seemingly cumbersome, is actually much more efficient than having Ivan's transaction (and those of thousands of other small shareholders like him) show up on EXXON's transfer agent's books. It is much easier to consolidate the record of these investments on EXXON's books by listing Merrill Lynch as the record owner. Individual investors like Ivan lose very little because, as beneficial owners, they retain the power to decide how their stock is voted and whether it should be sold.

If Ivan becomes disenchanted with his EXXON investment, he can exercise the "Wall Street Rule" and sell his stock by being on the selling end of the transactions we've just described.

§18.2.2 *Efficiency of Public Stock Markets*

It is often said that U.S. public stock trading markets are efficient. What does this mean? Most of the time those who say this mean that the market is "informationally efficient" — that is, that a particular piece of information affects the market price of a company's stock as though everyone had the same information. Simply stated, the information gets impounded in the stock price so that it is as though all investors knew about the information and had agreed on the new price.

What information is impounded? Different kinds of information affect stock prices. When a stock market impounds information about past trading patterns, the market is said to have "weak form" efficiency if investors can't draw charts and guess patterns to extrapolate future prices. A French mathematician noticed at the turn of the century that prices on the Paris stock market exhibited "weak form" efficiency because stock price patterns were completely random, like the Brownian motion of particles suspended in a liquid. There was no way to guess the next move in the price of stock based on past patterns: Stock prices follow a "random walk."

When a stock market impounds all publicly available information, the market is said to have "semi-strong" efficiency. This means that an investor can't beat the market systematically by using public information that affects stock prices — such as information on a company's earnings, competitors' products, government tax policies, changes in interest rates — because the "market" will already have reacted. In fact, a large body of evidence indicates public stock prices for widely followed companies change almost instantly and in an unbiased fashion (neither too much nor too little) in response to new public information. Often formal news of new developments, such as corporate earnings reports or new product announcements, are already old news to public trading markets. It is like a herd of stampeding animals that instantly changes course when a few animals change direction — it as though the herd has a single mind.

How does this efficiency happen? A large number of informed buyers and sellers each trying to make money by outguessing the market create a situation in which new information is almost instantly reflected in a new "consensus" view on the value of the stock — a new stock price. Securities analysts follow the activities of the larger public corporations, hoping to get an informational advantage. Once an analyst identifies a nugget, such as a confirmed rumor of a large dividend, the analyst will immediately have his securities firm or other clients trade. Just a few well-placed analysts, with others following their lead, can drive market prices. Although over time analysts will beat the market a little, they will earn just enough to pay for their effort. Competing analysts doing the same thing will cap trading profits, as illustrated by the fact that mutual funds (which professionally invest money for many small investors) do not on average outperform the market.

One thing the public stock markets are not is perfectly informationally efficient. That is, public stock markets do not impound *all* information that affects stock prices. The proof of this is that corporate insiders can often use their informational advantage to reap significant trading profits. The public stock markets do not have "strong form" efficiency.

Even if the public stock markets exhibit semi-strong efficiency for many U.S. public corporations, this does not mean that the stock markets and stock prices are efficient in allocating capital. That is, just because General Motors is trading at 58 does not mean it is socially desirable that investors pay $58 for General Motors shares. Informational efficiency does not translate into "fundamental efficiency" — it just means that the public stock markets act like a herd of stampeding animals that appear to behave as one organism, not many individuals. Informational efficiency doesn't mean the herd isn't heading over a cliff.

EXAMPLES

1. Ivan has purchased 100 shares of EXXON stock through his broker, Merrill Lynch. What does it mean that Ivan is the beneficial owner of the shares?

2. As a beneficial owner, how is Ivan informed of matters on which EXXON shareholders vote? How does he exercise his voting rights?

EXPLANATIONS

1. Beneficial ownership means that Ivan holds the attributes of owner-ship — the power to decide how the stock is voted and whether it is sold — but is not the shareholder of record on the corporation's books.

Instead, his stock is held in "street name" by Merrill Lynch, which must follow his instructions on voting and disposing of the stock.

2. Even though Ivan is not a record owner of his EXXON shares, EXXON is obligated under SEC rules to ensure that proxy materials are made available to him directly (if Ivan has consented to having Merrill Lynch inform EXXON of Ivan's beneficial ownership) or through Merrill Lynch. Ivan will exercise his voting rights either by filling out a proxy card made available from Merrill Lynch or by instructing Merrill Lynch how to complete the card on his behalf. With respect to routine matters, Merrill Lynch may also cast proxy votes if it does not receive instructions from Ivan.

19

Proxy Regulation

Shareholders of public corporations exercise their control rights primarily — if not exclusively — through proxy voting. State law authorizes shareholders who cannot attend the shareholders' meeting to give another person (usually a member of management) the power to vote their shares to elect directors and approve transactions requiring shareholder approval (see §12.2.4). If the shareholder gives an open-ended proxy, the proxy holder can vote as he sees fit on any matter that comes up at the shareholders' meeting.

As you can imagine, proxy voting creates considerable opportunities for management overreaching. If management can get shareholders to hand over open-ended proxies without informing them of what their shares will be voted on — a common practice before the Securities Exchange Act of 1934 — management effectively wields a shareholder "rubber stamp" for virtually anything it wants. And if management can monopolize the proxy mechanism to prevent shareholders from using it to advance their own proposals or slates of directors, management control becomes virtually airtight. To protect shareholders from these potential abuses, proxy voting is regulated at both the state and federal level, with federal proxy regulation the more encompassing.

§19.1 State Proxy Regulation

§19.1.1 *Authorization of Proxy Voting*

State corporation statutes authorize proxy voting, requiring only that the appointment be in writing and be signed. See RMBCA §7.22. Unless a longer period is expressly provided, proxies are generally valid for 11 months — enough for only one annual shareholders' meeting. RMBCA §7.22(c); cf. Del. GCL §212(b) (three years).

Public shareholders rarely appoint a proxy holder with an interest sufficient to support an irrevocable proxy (see §16.5), and a public shareholder can revoke a proxy if she (1) files written notice with the corporation of an intent to revoke, (2) appoints another proxy holder in a subsequently dated proxy, (3) appears in person to vote, or (4) dies or becomes incapacitated.

Corporate officials are entitled to accept facially valid proxy instruments or to reject instruments whose propriety creates a reasonable basis for doubt. The corporation and its election inspectors are not liable for accepting or rejecting proxies in good faith. RMBCA §7.24(d). The counting and tabulation of proxies is subject to court review.

§19.1.2 State-Mandated Disclosure

State corporate statutes require notice to shareholders concerning the date, time, and place of shareholders' meetings. RMBCA §7.05(a). In most states, the notice for an *annual* meeting need not state the meeting's purposes, describe the matters to come before shareholders, or list the board nominees; a notice for a *special* meeting need only state the meeting's purposes. RMBCA §7.05(b), (c).

Besides the cursory notice requirements for shareholders' meetings, state law does not prescribe the information that public shareholders are to receive when management solicits their proxies. Nonetheless, state courts (particularly in Delaware) have developed a body of case law that prohibits false and misleading statements in any management communication with public shareholders — whether in a proxy solicitation, tender offer, notice of a shareholders' meeting even when proxies are not solicited, or in a notice of a short-form merger for which no meeting is required.

The seminal Delaware case, *Lynch v. Vickers Energy Corp.*, 383 A.2d 278, 281 (Del. 1977), imposes on management a "complete candor" duty that explicitly borrows the framework and materiality standard of the antifraud rules of federal proxy regulation (§19.6). Liability is premised on false or misleading information that "a reasonable shareholder would consider important in deciding whether to [vote]." As is true of federal proxy fraud litigation, challenging shareholders need not show that the alleged misinformation would have changed the outcome of the shareholder vote; it is enough that the challenged disclosure was material. In Delaware, shareholders have used the "complete candor" duty to successfully challenge mergers, reorganizations, and charter amendments. In a variety of conflict-of-interest transactions involving shareholder voting — parent-subsidiary mergers, tender offers by controlling shareholders, and defensive recapitalizations — "complete candor" review has served as a substitute for fiduciary review on the merits.

§19.2   Federal Proxy Regulation — An Introduction

While state law authorizes proxy voting, federal proxy regulation attempts to ensure fair corporate suffrage by requiring that shareholders receive enough information, from management and from other shareholders, to make informed voting decisions. Its goal and theory is "corporate democracy." Federal proxy regulation offers a multi-pronged attack against proxy abuses by management:

SEC-mandated disclosure. Rules of the Securities and Exchange Commission (SEC) require that anyone soliciting proxies from public shareholders must file with the SEC and distribute to shareholders specified information in a stylized "proxy statement." The SEC proxy rules also prohibit fraudulent or misleading proxy solicitations.

No open-ended proxies. The SEC rules attempt to neutralize management's control of the proxy solicitation process by prescribing the form of the proxy card and the scope of the proxy holder's power.

Shareholder access. The SEC rules seek to equalize access to the proxy solicitation process in public companies by requiring management to include "proper" proposals by shareholders with management's proxy materials, though this access is subject to a number of conditions.

Private remedies. The courts have inferred a private cause of action for shareholders to seek relief for violations of the SEC proxy rules, particularly the proxy antifraud rule.

Before dealing with the mechanics of federal proxy regulation, it is useful to consider from whence the rules derive. Section 14(a) of the Securities Exchange Act of 1934 is the open-ended, innocuous culprit:

> It shall be unlawful for any person, by use of the mails or by any means or instrumentality of interstate commerce or of any facility of a national securities exchange *or otherwise,* in contravention of such rules and regulations as the Commission may prescribe as necessary or appropriate in the public interest or for the protection of investors, to solicit or to permit the use of his name to solicit any proxy or consent or authorization in respect of any security (other than an exempted security) registered pursuant to section 12 of this title. (Emphasis added.)

Let's parse. First, the jurisdictional reach of §14(a) is effectively unlimited — the italicized *or otherwise* language means Congress has gone as far as it can under the Constitution. Second, §14(a)'s prohibition applies to proxy solicitations involving securities registered under §12 of the 1934 Act — which means publicly-traded corporations (see §19.3.1). Third, the prohibition applies to proxy solicitations — a relatively broad concept (see §19.3.2). Fourth, the proxy solicitation must comply with SEC rules on filing, disclosure, and distribution of proxy materials (see §19.3.3).

Notice what §14(a) does *not* say — there is no mention of what happens to persons making unlawful proxy solicitations or who can sue them.

§19.3   Reach of the SEC Proxy Rules

§19.3.1   *Public Corporations — Reporting Companies under the 1934 Act*

The proxy rules apply to stock registered under §12 of the 1934 Act. (Registration also compels the company to disclose periodic business and financial information with the SEC.) *Registered* or *reporting* companies fall into two categories. First, companies whose stock is listed on a national stock exchange must register. 1934 Act §12(a). The New York Stock Exchange, for example, permits listing of companies with at least 2000 shareholders and an aggregate market of value of publicly held shares of $18 million. Second, companies must register if at year's end they have more than $5 million in assets *and* at least 500 record shareholders. 1934 Act §12(g); SEC Rule 12g-1 (establishes $5 million threshold). Once *both* the asset and shareholder thresholds are surpassed, the company must register with the SEC within 120 days.

Although it might seem logical that if a corporation falls below either the $5 million asset threshold or the 500 shareholder threshold it should be able to deregister, the SEC rules are not that simple. Registration may be terminated only if: (1) there are fewer than 500 shareholders of record and the company's total assets have not exceeded $5 million as of the end of each of the company's last three fiscal years, or (2) there are fewer than 300 shareholders of record. The SEC believes that once a corporation is registered under §12, thus triggering the full range of federal protection for its shareholders, deregistration should not come easily.

§19.3.2   *Proxy Solicitation*

The federal proxy rules apply only if there is a *proxy solicitation*. Although you might imagine a proxy solicitation as being limited to the formal document that accompanies management's request for shareholders to return a proxy card, the scope of the proxy rules is much broader. SEC Rule 14a-1(l) defines a "solicitation" to include:

- the obvious: the information form accompanying the proxy card that shareholders are asked to sign;
- a request to sign: any request for a proxy, even if a proxy card does not accompany the request;
- a request not to sign: any request to not sign or to revoke a proxy; and
- being sly: any other communication "under circumstances reasonably calculated to result in" shareholders signing, not signing, or revoking a proxy.

The SEC also defines "proxy" broadly to include any action that gives or withholds authority concerning issues on which shareholders may decide — for example, when shareholders give written consents to an action taken without a shareholders' meeting (see §12.2.6). Rule 14a-1(f).

Courts have construed these definitions broadly, leading to protests that the SEC has overregulated communications among shareholders. In 1992, responding to these criticisms, the SEC amended its proxy rules to exempt a variety of communications among shareholders from the rules on filing and distributing proxy statements. We consider how the amended rules will affect certain shareholder activities that prior cases invalidated under the old proxy rules.

Organized shareholder dissent. In *Studebaker Corp. v. Gittlin,* 360 F.2d 692 (2d Cir. 1966), the court held that a proxy solicitation includes any communication to shareholders that asks for action that is *part of a "continuous plan" leading to the formal solicitation of proxies* — a broad notion, indeed. In the *Studebaker* case a shareholder who wanted to initiate a proxy contest to elect a new board sought a shareholders' list under a state law that provided inspection rights only to shareholders holding at least 5 percent of the company's shares. When the dissident shareholder obtained authorizations from 42 other shareholders (whose holdings totaled more than 5 percent) to inspect the list, management sued to block the inspection on the theory that the dissident's request for authorizations constituted an illegal proxy solicitation. The court agreed, pointing out that the definition of "proxy" includes "authorizations," and the dissident group's effort to get inspection authorizations was part of a "continuous plan" intended to end in a formal proxy solicitation. To ensure that shareholders are informed even in the preliminary stages of a voting contest, the court required the dissident group to start again with a proper proxy filing distributed to all solicited shareholders.

The 1992 amendments to the SEC proxy rules explicitly reject the implications of this broad notion of solicitation when nonmanagement shareholders wish to communicate with other shareholders. Under Rule 14a-2(b), the filing, disclosure, and distribution requirements of the proxy rules do not apply to solicitations by persons who do not seek power to act as a proxy and do not furnish or ask for a proxy card. The exemption does not apply to management, director nominees, or those in a control fight with management.

Interestingly, the dissident group in the *Studebaker* case might still have been subject to the proxy rules if the group members intended to act together to vote their shares and, as required of any 5 percent group, filed an SEC disclosure document (Schedule 13D) stating their intent to solicit proxies for the election of directors. See Rule 13d-5(b). (§39.1.)

Public criticism of management.   Management has used the "solicitation" definition to insulate itself from public criticism. In *Long Island Lighting Co. v. Barbash,* 779 F.2d 793 (2d Cir. 1985), the court applied a "chain of communications" theory to hold that a newspaper ad can be a solicitation if motivated to advance a pending insurgency. The ad had been paid for by a public interest group that urged that LILCO be sold to a public power authority and accused LILCO of mismanagement and of raising rates to build an unnecessary nuclear power plant. The ad could be seen as supporting a local political candidate who had succeeded in having a special shareholders' meeting called to consider a sale of the company. The court held that a fact finder could conclude that the ad was "reasonably calculated" to influence shareholders' votes and thus a "solicitation" under the proxy rules, even though the ad did not mention proxies and purportedly addressed matters of "public interest" in a general publication.

To some, this result is absurd, if not a violation of First Amendment free speech rights. The literal breadth of the holding, and the rule's "reasonably calculated" language, could turn every expression of opinion about a public corporation into a regulated proxy solicitation. If so, any person stating an opinion would be required to prepare a proxy statement and mail it to every shareholder being "solicited" — which in the case of public opinion would mean all shareholders.

The amended SEC rules exempt this kind of communication if the speaker neither seeks authority to act as a proxy nor requests a proxy card. Thus, a public interest group — provided it is not aligned with management or acting on behalf of a director nominee or someone seeking control — is under no filing, disclosure, or distribution obligations, although the "solicitation" remains subject to the SEC antifraud rules.

In the amended rules, the SEC has also gone one step further to exclude from the definition of "solicitation" (and thus from the antifraud rules as well) a public announcement by a shareholder on how she intends to vote and her reasons.

§19.3.3   *Mandated Disclosure When Proxies Are Not Solicited*

In some circumstances, such as when a majority of a public corporation's shares are held by a parent corporation, it may be unnecessary to solicit proxies from minority shareholders. Nonetheless, such companies must still file with the SEC and, at least 20 days before the meeting, send shareholders information similar to that required for a proxy solicitation. Reg. 14C and Schedule 14C.

§19.4   Formal Requirements of the SEC Proxy Rules

To enable shareholders to make an informed voting decision, the proxy rules —

- specify disclosure required with (or before) every proxy solicitation;
- specify the form of the proxy card;
- require the preliminary filing of the proxy statement and proxy cards for SEC staff review; and
- prohibit false or misleading proxy solicitations.

§19.4.1   *Mandatory Disclosure in a Proxy Statement*

The proxy rules require that whenever a proxy is solicited that the solicitation be accompanied or preceded by the delivery to the solicited shareholder of a disclosure document known as a *proxy statement*. Rule 14a-3(a). The document must contain information specified in Schedule 14A, which contains a set of itemized instructions on the information required in a proxy statement. The kind of information required depends on who is soliciting the proxy:

Management solicitation.   If management (or, technically, the board of directors) solicits proxies, Schedule 14A requires that management give information about the corporation, the background of all director nominees, management's compensation and conflicts of interest, and any other matters being voted on. If the solicitation is for the annual election of directors, management also must send the corporation's annual report. Rule 14a-3(b). The proxy rules ensure a flow of information from the corporation to shareholders. In fact, for many companies the rules represent the only state or federal regulation that requires periodic corporate communications to shareholders. Cf. RMBCA §16.20 (requiring that shareholders be provided with annual financial statements).

Nonmanagement solicitation.   If a proxy is solicited by persons other than management — such as dissident shareholders or an outside insurgent group — Schedule 14A requires that they tell about themselves, the background of their nominees, and any other matter on which they seek a proxy.

§19.4.2   Form of the Proxy Card

To ensure that shareholders are not asked to give management (or anyone else) a voting carte blanche, the proxy rules specify the form of the proxy card. Rule 14a-4. The proxy card must specify who is soliciting it and the matters to be acted on, and must leave a space for it to be dated. For the election of directors, the card must allow a shareholder to withhold a vote on directors as a group or individually. Under the proxy rules, a proxy cannot be used to elect a nominee if he is not named in the proxy card. Rule 14a-4(d)(1). For other matters, shareholders must be given a chance to vote for or against each matter to be acted on. A shareholder can give her proxy holder discretionary voting power on a matter if the proxy card states in **boldface** type how the proxy holder intends to vote. The proxy holder must then vote in accordance with the instructions.

§19.4.3   The Filing and Distribution of the Proxy Statement

No proxy solicitation can be made unless the solicitor sends (or has already sent) each solicited shareholder a copy of the proxy statement. Any person soliciting proxies must file *preliminary* copies of the proxy statement and the proxy card with the SEC at least ten days before they are sent to shareholders. Rule 14a-6. The SEC staff then reviews and comments on these preliminary materials, giving filers a chance to make changes that conform to the staff's views of what would make disclosure adequate. Management need not make a preliminary filing if the solicitation is routine and relates to nothing more than the election of directors, selection of auditors, or shareholder proposals at an annual meeting. All *final* proxy materials, whether or not required to have been filed preliminarily, must be filed with the SEC at or before the time they are sent to shareholders.

The 1992 amendments to the proxy rules also require that shareholders whose solicitations are exempt because they do not seek proxy authority and do not have a substantial interest in the matter must file a notice with the SEC that attaches all written soliciting materials. Notice is required only of shareholders who own more than $5 million of the shares of a company about which they are communicating.

§19.4.4   Antifraud Prohibitions

At the heart of the proxy rules is the prohibition of any solicitation (written or oral) that is false or misleading with respect to any material fact or that omits a material fact in the solicitation necessary to make statements that are not false or misleading. Rule 14a-9. It is therefore not enough to supply all the information specified in Schedule 14A. The proxy statement must also fully disclose all material information about the matters on which the shareholders are to vote. Rule 14a-9 does not specifically authorize shareholders to sue for false or misleading proxy solicitations. Yet federal courts have inferred a private cause of action, which we discuss in §19.6.

§19.4.5 Exemptions from the SEC Proxy Rules

Exemptions from the proxy rules permit "proxy solicitations" without complying with the filing, disclosure, and distribution requirements of the rules. Some exempt solicitations remain subject to the antifraud provisions —

- solicitations by persons who are not seeking proxy authority and do not have a substantial interest in the matter (Rule 14a-2(b)(1));
- nonmanagement solicitations to less than ten persons (Rule 14a-2(b)(2));
- advice by financial advisors in the ordinary course of their business, provided they disclose any interest in the proxy contest and receive no special fees from others for giving the advice (Rule 14a-2(b)(2)).

Other solicitations are completely exempt from the proxy rules —

- communications by brokers to beneficial owners seeking instructions on how the broker is to vote the owners' shares (Rule 14a-2(a)(1));
- requests by beneficial owners to obtain proxy cards and other information from brokers that hold their shares (Rule 14a-2(a)(2));
- newspaper advertisements that identify the proposal and tell shareholders how to obtain proxy documents (Rule 14a-2(a)(6)).

EXAMPLES

1. Wayne is a shareholder of Video Palace, Inc. (VidPal), which owns and operates a video rental chain. Management has asked VidPal shareholders to give their proxies for management's slate of directors at the next annual shareholders' meeting. An insurgent, Garth, solicits proxies for his alternate slate of directors.
   a. Wayne first returns management's proxy card but then changes his mind and sends in Garth's card. Who has Wayne's proxy?
   b. VidPal management gives notice of the annual meeting but does not disclose that the company's earnings last year fell by over 60 percent. Is this information required under state law?
   c. The VidPal board is think of issuing already authorized stock to Jessica. The issue would bring her holdings to 35 percent, and VidPal

management would own 20 percent. Would VidPal have to solicit proxies at the upcoming meting if it issues this new stock to Jessica?

2. The board does not issue shares to Jessica, and Garth's insurgency fails. As next year's annual meeting approaches, VidPal management begins to plan its proxy solicitation. Consider whether VidPal is subject to the federal proxy rules:

   a. At the end of its last fiscal year, VidPal had assets of $6 million and 650 shareholders of record. The shareholders acquired their shares in a public issue exempt from registration under §3(a)(11) of the 1933 Act — the intrastate offering exemption.

   b. At the end of its last fiscal year, VidPal had assets of $6 million and 400 shareholders of record, many of whom are nominees of beneficial owners. VidPal, in fact, has 650 beneficial owners.

3. VidPal eventually registers its stock under the 1934 Act. Since becoming a reporting company 5 years ago, VidPal has struggled. Its assets have fallen below $4 million.

   a. VidPal management does not want to bother with periodic disclosure and the SEC proxy rules. The company has 700 shareholders of record. Can it terminate its 1934 Act registration?

   b. VidPal repurchases some of its stock, reducing the number of record shareholders to 450. Can VidPal terminate its 1934 Act registration?

   c. VidPal repurchases more stock, reducing the number of record shareholders to 100. Can VidPal terminate its 1934 Act registration and avoid registration indefinitely?

   d. A few years after going private, VidPal makes a large public offering. The company specifies that new stock must be held in street name with a specified list of qualified nominees. This keeps the number of record shareholders below 500. Can VidPal avoid 1934 Act registration in this way?

4. The FBI is investigating several VidPal directors and executives for conspiring to distribute "pirate" videotapes through local VidPal outlets.

   a. Garth sends letters to 15 other shareholders suggesting they begin a derivative suit challenging the directors' actions as a breach of fiduciary duty. Are these letters a proxy solicitation?

   b. Garth also appears on a financial talk show and suggests the directors should step aside until the FBI concludes its investigation. Garth mentions that he is thinking of running his own slate of directors. Are these statements proxy solicitations?

   c. Garth sends letters to 15 other prominent VidPal shareholders and suggests they discuss having a special shareholders' meeting to remove the offending directors "for cause." Garth has enough shares under state law to call the meeting himself, but he will need the votes of the other shareholders in any proxy fight. Are these letters a proxy solicitation?

5. When VidPal's management learns of Garth's activities, the company takes out several newspaper ads claiming that "VidPal only rents properly licensed video tapes" and suggests that "competitors jealous of VidPal's success" have planted false accusations. The ads do not mention Garth or possible shareholder action.

a. Are the ads proxy solicitations?

b. The ads are materially true. Can Garth seek to enjoin further ads?

c. Would the ads violate the proxy rules if the company had already distributed copies of its proxy statement to all shareholders?

d. After filing and distributing its proxy statement, management sends letters to its shareholders stating that Garth's accusations are false and Garth is "trying to tear down the company." Are these letters proxy solicitations?

EXPLANATIONS

1a. Garth has Wayne's proxy if the writing naming Garth bears a later date. On the assumption Wayne did not grant an irrevocable proxy "coupled with an interest" to management, the later-granted proxy revokes the earlier proxy. The election inspector will accept Garth's authority if the writing by Wayne on its face revokes Wayne's prior proxy to management. As proxy holder, Garth will be entitled to cast Wayne's votes at the annual meeting.

1b. Generally, no. Most state statutes do not require more than notice of an annual meeting's location, time, and date. If VidPal is a public corporation, the "complete candor" duty of *Vickers v. Lynch* may require management to disclose material adverse information with its notice and proxy statement.

1c. No proxy solicitation would be necessary. Whether directors are elected by majority or plurality voting, management's slate would be elected if Jessica and management combined their votes. Nonetheless, even when proxies are not solicited, the federal proxy rules require management to file an information statement with the SEC and to distribute it to shareholders entitled to vote. Reg. 14C. This gives shareholders notice of any state rights they may have to challenge the election.

2a. VidPal must register under the 1934 Act and is subject to the proxy rules. VidPal meets the conjunctive test of §12(g) of the 1934 Act: at year-end its assets exceeded $5 million and it had at least 500 shareholders of record.

The exemption from the registration and prospectus delivery requirements of the 1933 Act are irrelevant to the question of whether registration is required under the 1934 Act. The 1934 Act mandates periodic disclosure about reporting companies to facilitate trading in the stock of publicly traded companies; the 1933 Act seeks to provide public investors with information when they invest in a company's offerings of stock.

2b. VidPal is not required to register under the 1934 Act. Unless the company's stock is listed on a stock exchange or the company has previously issued its shares to the public pursuant to a 1933 Act registration statement, it does not become a reporting company under the 1934 Act because it has less than 500 record shareholders at year's end. Beneficial shareholders are not counted for purposes of registration under §12(g). This provides management a readily determinable test for deciding whether registration is required.

3a. No. Although the value of VidPal's assets has fallen below the $5 million threshold for initial registration, SEC rules do not permit termination of registration if the number of shareholders of record exceeds 500, regardless of asset value. The SEC takes the view that public shareholders come to rely on periodic disclosure and SEC proxy regulation, and its rules make "de-registration" difficult.

3b. Perhaps. It depends on how long VidPal's assets have remained below the $5 million mark. Because the number of record shareholders remains over 300 (but below 500), SEC rules permit termination of registration only if year-end assets have not exceeded $5 million for the last three fiscal years.

3c. Yes. This is known as "going private." A company can de-register by stock repurchase, engaging in an issuer self-tender, or structuring a squeeze-out merger. This allows management to avoid the disclosure and proxy rules of federal securities law.

3d. Perhaps not. Under the literal terms of §12(g), it would seem a company just has to keep the number of record shareholders below 500.

A ruse using street-name registration (see §18.2.1) circumvents the purposes of the 1934 Act regulation of public companies. The corporation's beneficial owners will be in need of periodic disclosure and protection from proxy abuses to the same extent as record shareholders. The record ownership requirement was meant to allow management to know with certainty whether it was subject to 1934 Act registration.

As a practical matter, investors may be reluctant to invest in a publicly traded company that avoids the 1934 Act reporting and proxy requirements. Further, brokers and dealers regulated under the 1934 Act may be constrained in participating in the trading of a nonreporting company's securities unless the broker-dealers obtain and make available information about such companies.

4a. Probably not. It is difficult to characterize the letters as being part of a "continuous plan" leading to the formal solicitation of proxies. See *Studebaker Corp. v. Gittlin* (§19.3.2). A derivative suit brought by a shareholder on behalf of the corporation to vindicate a corporate right will not necessarily lead to a proxy contest.

Unless Garth's motives are to use the suit as part of a strategy leading to a proxy solicitation — for example, because the suit will provide free and damaging publicity about the directors — it is unlikely that the letters will be deemed proxy solicitations. To do so would significantly hamper shareholder oversight of management abuse, undercutting the very purpose of the federal proxy rules.

4b. Yes, but they are probably exempt solicitations. Garth's comments seem to be part of a plan leading to a proxy solicitation, and the proxy rules define them to be a proxy solicitation. Nonetheless, the 1992 amendments to the proxy rules exempt solicitations by those who do not seek power to act as a proxy and do not furnish or ask for a proxy card. Rule 14a-2(b). At this point, Garth is just testing the waters for an insurgency and is not asking for proxies. This exemption would not apply, however, if Garth is already a nominee to the board (or is paid by someone who is a nominee) or is a 5 percent shareholder who has declared a control intention.

4c. Yes, and the letters might not be exempt. Garth's letters to his 15 fellow shareholders seem to be part of a "continuous plan" leading to the formal solicitation of proxies. These early communications, without an accompanying proxy statement, may "poison the well" and lead shareholders to join his cause without full information. On the other hand, treating the effort to call a meeting as a proxy solicitation may discourage shareholders such as Garth from taking the first steps to decide whether to exercise their control rights. See *Calumet Industries, Inc. v. MacClure,* 464 F. Supp. 19 (N.D. Ill. 1978) (discussions among shareholders to organize a proxy fight are not a "solicitation" because of the impracticality of preparing a pre-organization proxy statement).

Even if the letters are technically "proxy solicitations," the Rule 14a-2(b) exemption for nonmanagement shareholder communications would apply unless Garth is "seeking the power to act as a proxy." (Nor does the exemption for communications to no more than ten shareholders.) If Garth is asking for shareholder "authorizations" to call a special meeting, the letters may well be nonexempt solicitations. If, however, he is simply asking for preliminary showings of interest — since he already holds enough shares to call the meeting himself — the letters are at most exempt solicitations.

5a. Probably yes. Under a "chain of communications" theory, the ads seem "reasonably calculated" to influence shareholder voting on the removal of the accused directors. The decision to place the ads seems to have been related to Garth's threatened insurgency. Nonetheless, a court might conclude the ads were primarily meant to answer pirating rumors that might have hurt business and to protect the reputations of the directors, rather than to influence shareholder voting. After all, no shareholders' meeting involving the charges had yet been called.

In the end, management's motives behind the ads are determinative. See *Long Island Lighting Co. v. Barbash,* (§19.3.2).

5b. Yes, if they are proxy solicitations. If management did not file a proxy statement and disseminate the statement to shareholders before placing the ads, they can be enjoined for failing to comply with the rule's filing and disclosure requirements. It makes no difference that they are absolutely truthful and well-meaning. As we will see, they can be enjoined either by the SEC or by a shareholder in a private action.

5c. No, unless the ads were false or misleading in some material respect. The proxy rules do not prohibit communications that affect shareholder voting; they mandate that such communications be made only after filing and distributing a proxy statement. This gets the essential information on the table.

5d. Perhaps. The personal attack on Garth may violate Rule 14a-9's prohibition of false or misleading proxy solicitations. To prevent heated and not terribly informative shouting matches, the SEC treats as misleading under the rule "material which . . . impugns character, integrity or personal reputation."

§19.5 Shareholder Initiatives

In a public corporation, where shareholder voting happens through the process of proxy solicitations, shareholder initiatives face enormous obstacles. Shareholders who identify value-producing ideas generally are unwilling to commit the financial resources for massive mailings to other shareholders — their relatively small investment rarely justifies it. Even when they are willing, shareholders must overcome management's domination of the corporate-funded proxy mechanism, including management's control of shareholder information.

The SEC proxy rules attempt to overcome these impediments in two ways. First, management can be compelled to help shareholders communicate with fellow shareholders — at shareholder expense. Second, in limited circumstances management must include "proper" shareholder proposals with the company-funded proxy materials that go to shareholders — at corporate expense.

§19.5.1 The "Common Carrier" Obligation under Rule 14a-7

The federal proxy rules facilitate a shareholder who is willing to pay for the costs of soliciting other shareholders. Under Rule 14a-7 management must mail, either separately or together with the corporation's proxy materials, any shareholder's soliciting materials if the shareholder agrees to defray the corporation's reasonable expenses in forwarding the materials. There is no limit on the length of the materials, nor does the SEC rule specify that management can refuse by objecting to their contents.

Under the rule, management can avoid this "common carrier" obligation by giving the soliciting shareholder a current list of names and addresses of shareholders and any intermediaries. Doing so significantly extends the shareholders' rights under state law to obtain a list of record shareholders for a "proper purpose" (see §12.1). As a practical matter, management is often reluctant to provide the shareholders' list because it can be used for personal solicitations or beyond a shareholder proxy solicitation — such as in a takeover contest.

§19.5.2   Shareholder Proposals under Rule 14a-8

The SEC proxy rules seek to promote shareholder democracy for those shareholders unwilling to bear the expense of a proxy solicitation themselves. Under Rule 14a-8 shareholders can propose their own resolutions through the company-financed proxy machinery at company expense.

The shareholder proposal rule has gone through three developmental stages. During its early history, in the 1940s and 1950s, proponents used the rule to seek changes in corporate governance — proposing such things as mergers and more liberal dividend policies. In the 1970s and 1980s, many proponents came to use the rule as a vehicle for focusing public attention on corporate social responsibility — proposing such things as divestment from South Africa, reduced business with Communist countries, eliminating corporate charitable contributions, protecting the environment, and increasing (or reducing) affirmative action plans. Since 1985, with the advent of institutional shareholder activism, proponents have again focused on governance issues, proposing such things as more outside directors, confidential voting, and elimination of antitakeover devices.

During the rule's first 40 years, shareholder proposals were uniformly unsuccessful. Of the thousands submitted for shareholder vote before 1985, only two were ever approved. Since 1985, however, proposals on governance issues have fared markedly better, occasionally obtaining majority approval and often leading management to make changes to avoid the embarrassment of an adverse vote.

Rule 14a-8 procedures.   Any shareholder who has owned (beneficially or of record) 1 percent or $1000 worth of a public company's shares for at least one year may submit a proposal to management. Rule 14a-8(a)(1). The proposal must be in the form of a resolution (only one) that the shareholder intends to introduce at the shareholders' meeting. Rule 14a-8(a)(4).

Shareholders must submit their proposals in a timely fashion. For an annual meeting, this will generally be at least 120 calendar days before the date that proxy materials were sent for the last year's meeting. Rule 14a-8(a)(3). If the resolution is proper (see below), management must include it in the company's proxy mailing to shareholders. The proponent can include a short supporting statement of up to 500 words to be printed in the company's proxy statement. Rule 14a-8(b). Management's proxy card must give shareholders a chance to vote for or against the proposal. Rule 14a-8(a).

If management decides to exclude a submitted proposal, it must forward the proposal and its reasons for exclusion to the SEC for review. The SEC staff issues a "no-action" letter if the staff agrees with management. Over time this procedure has created a body of SEC "common law" on the meaning of the rule.

Proper proposals.   Rule 14a-8 contains a dizzying list of 13 reasons for management to exclude a shareholder proposal. Management can exclude a proposal if it fits *any* of the categories specified in the rule. The SEC-created exclusions serve a number of purposes: (1) to preserve the state law scheme of centralized corporate decision-making in which shareholders delegate corporate governance to management; (2) to protect the proxy solicitation process from proposals that would interfere with management's usual solicitation efforts; (3) to filter out illegal, deceptive and crackpot proposals.

(1) Proposals that are inconsistent with centralized management.   A number of the exclusions aim at proposals that interfere with the traditional corporate governance structure:

Management can exclude proposals that are not a "proper subject" for shareholder action under state law. Rule 14a-8(c)(1). In *SEC v. Transamerica Corp.,* 163 F.2d 511 (3d Cir. 1947), the court held as proper proposals for shareholder election of independent public auditors, for changing procedures to amend the company's bylaws, and for requiring that a report of the annual meeting be sent to shareholders. Phrasing proposals to be precatory — that is, as advisory suggestions rather than as mandates — further assures their appropriateness under state law. (See *Matter of Auer v. Dressel,* 118 N.E.2d 590 (N.Y. 1954); see §12.1.) Frequently, proposals will ask management to conduct a study or issue a report, without compelling specific action.

Management can exclude proposals that are not "significantly related" to the company's business. Rule 14a-8(c)(5). To be significant, the proposal must relate to operations that account for at least 5 percent of total assets, net earnings, or gross sales. Or the proposal must be "otherwise significantly related" to the company's business. During the 1970s and 1980s, the SEC took a broad view of what is "otherwise significantly related." According to the SEC, matters relating to ethical issues, such as complying with the Arab boycott of Israel or carrying on business in South Africa, could be significant even though not important from a purely financial standpoint. See also *Lovenheim v. Iroquois Brands, Ltd.,* 618 F.

Supp. 554 (D.D.C. 1985) (holding to be "significantly related" a resolution calling for report to shareholders on forced geese feeding, even though the company lost money on goose pate sales, which accounted for less than .05 percent of revenues).

Management can exclude proposals that relate to the "conduct of ordinary business operations." Rule 14a-8(c)(7). The SEC's interpretation of this exclusion has been checkered. In the 1970s and 1980s, the SEC accepted proposals dealing with such things as construction of nuclear power plants and employment discrimination on the theory they do not relate to "ordinary business" because of their economic, safety, and social impact. The SEC's views were strongly influenced by *Medical Committee for Human Rights v. SEC,* 432 F.2d 659 (D.C. Cir. 1970), *vacated as moot,* 404 U.S. 403 (1970), which held management could not exclude a shareholder resolution that Dow Chemical stop selling napalm for use against humans if management's decision to manufacture napalm was motivated by political or moral preferences rather than business considerations. Recently, however, the SEC has reversed course and decided that proposals concerning employment policies (such as equal employment or affirmative action plans) can be excluded as "ordinary business." In *Amalgamated Clothing and Textile Workers Union v. Wal-Mart Stores, Inc.,* 821 F. Supp. 877 (S.D.N.Y. 1993), the court rejected the SEC's new construction of Rule 14a-8 and held a company could not exclude a proposal on EEO policies, which the court considered a topic of "broad social impact."

Management can exclude proposals that relate to the specific amount of dividends. Rule 14a-8(c)(13). This recognizes a fundamental feature of U.S. corporate law, that the board has discretion to declare dividends.

(2) Proposals that interfere with management's proxy solicitation. The rule permits the exclusion of proposals that could interfere with an orderly proxy solicitation:

Management can exclude proposals that relate to the election of directors or officers. Rule 14a-8(c)(8). In this way management can prevent dissidents from "clogging" the company's proxy statement with their own slates of directors.

Management can exclude proposals that are contrary to management proposals. Rule 14a-8(c)(9). Otherwise, the rule would create an open forum in which every shareholder could state a position on any management initiative subject to shareholder vote.

Management can exclude proposals that duplicate another shareholder proposal to be included in the management's proxy materials. Rule 14a-8(c)(11).

Management can exclude "recidivist" proposals that had failed in the past. Rule 14a-8(c)(12). This exclusion covers any proposal dealing "with substantially the same subject matter" as a proposal submitted in the last five years that failed to get 3 percent on its first try, or 6 percent on its second try, or 10 percent after three tries.

(3) *Proposals that are illegal, deceptive, or confused.*   The rule seeks to prevent spurious or scandalous proposals:

> Management can exclude proposals that would require the company to violate any law, including the SEC's proxy rules and, in particular, Rule 14a-9's antifraud prohibition. Rule 14a-8(c)(2), (c)(3). This allows management to exclude proposals that are materially false or misleading.
>
> Management can exclude proposals that relate to any personal grievance. Rule 14a-8(c)(4). This exclusion covers the frequent phenomenon of proposals by disgruntled employees who seek to have the body of shareholders recognize their talents and tribulations.
>
> Management can exclude proposals that deal with matters beyond the corporation's power to effectuate, Rule 14a-8(c)(6), or that are moot because the company is already doing what the shareholder proposes. Rule 14a-8(c)(10).

If a shareholder proposal dances through this minefield of requirements and exclusions, management must include it in the company's proxy statement and proxy card, though management has a chance to object to the proposal and give its reasons for objection. Rule 14a-8(e).

If management fails to include a proposal that is not properly excludable, the proponent can seek an SEC determination under Rule 14a-8(d) that the proxy rules are being violated, or bring an implied private action in federal court to compel inclusion or enjoin management's solicitation as a violation of the proxy rules.

EXAMPLES

1. Garth bought $2000 worth of Video Palace (VidPal) stock two years ago. He recently calculated that the liquidation value of VidPal greatly exceeds its current stock price. Garth wants to bring this to the attention of other shareholders and to propose that the company be liquidated — its assets sold for cash — and the cash distributed to shareholders.
   a. Garth wants to solicit shareholder proxies for a liquidation resolution he plans to present at the upcoming annual shareholders' meeting. Will the company reimburse him for his solicitation expenses?
   b. Garth wants to ask management to include his proposal with the company-funded proxy solicitation. When must Garth make this request?
   c. Garth also plans to submit a four-page attachment to his resolution that explains the advantage of liquidation and blames VidPal management for "destroying shareholder confidence as reflected in the company's below-asset market price." Any problems?
   d. Garth deals with these problems and submits a proposed resolution that the board liquidate the business, dissolve the corporation, and

distribute the proceeds to shareholders. Management objects. What exclusions apply?

   e. How should Garth phrase his proposal to maximize the chances of its being included?

2. Garth's liquidation proposal goes nowhere. As the next annual meeting approaches, he wants to shake up the way VidPal does business. Which of the following would be includable under the shareholder proposal rule?

   a. A proposal offering shareholders an alternative slate of directors — Garth's slate.

   b. A resolution stating the shareholders' desire that management nominate at least two women to the board.

   c. A resolution requesting that the VidPal board prepare a report on an affirmative action plan to create greater diversity in the company's management training program.

   d. A resolution urging the board to adopt a policy that VidPal not rent any "adult" videos. Although such movies account for a small part of VidPal's business, Garth considers them immoral.

3. VidPal management proposes a merger with another video rental chain. Garth wants the merger conditioned on Dixie Video representing that it has never rented "pirated" videos.

   a. Garth makes a proposal to be included with management's proxy solicitation for the merger that would ask for shareholders to approve the merger with this condition. Must management include Garth's proposal?

   b. Garth decides to send his proposal to shareholders and solicits their proxies to vote against the merger unless management conditions the merger on a "no-pirating" representation. He files a proxy statement in proper form with the SEC and mails it to all shareholders. Does VidPal management have a cause of action against him under the proxy rules?

4. VidPal's management is tired of shareholder proposals. So are many of the VidPal shareholders, who have never cast more than 3 percent of their votes for any shareholder proposal. The board proposes, and the shareholders approve, an amendment to the company's charter banning all nonmanagement shareholder proposals unless they are by a shareholder (or group of shareholders) holding more than 10 percent of VidPal's voting shares.

   a. At the next shareholders' meeting, Garth proposes a resolution urging that no executive receive a salary greater than $1 million. He owns enough shares to qualify under Rule 14a-8, but not under the charter provision. Must management include the proposal?

   b. Why don't companies "opt out" of the shareholder proposal rule?

EXPLANATIONS

1a. Almost certainly no. Under state law, the board has no obligation to reimburse shareholders' solicitation expenses — and rarely do. Only if a shareholder gains control of the board and gets other shareholders to ratify reimbursement can the shareholder hope to be reimbursed. Neither Rule 14a-7 nor Rule 14a-8 changes this. Rule 14a-7 merely requires that management provide Garth with a shareholders' list or send his solicitation materials to other shareholders at his expense. Rule 14a-8 does not provide for reimbursement; it only requires inclusion in the company-funded proxy statement of proper proposals by qualifying shareholders who comply with the rule's procedures.

1b. Garth must mail his proposal so that management receives it at least 120 calendar days before the date on which proxy materials were sent out for last year's annual shareholders' meeting. This assumes that this year's meeting is scheduled to fall within 30 days of the date of last year's meeting. Rule 14a-8(a)(3)(i). To avoid any controversy, the SEC recommends proponents send their proposals Certified Mail — Return Receipt Requested.

1c. Garth's proposal is in trouble. He has probably failed to comply with Rule 14a-8's word limit for shareholder proposals, and his statements impugning management's integrity may make the proposal excludable. The rule limits proposals and supporting statements to 500 words — approximately two double-spaced, typewritten pages. Rule 14a-8(b)(1). The rule also allows management to exclude proposals that are contrary to SEC rules, including proxy antifraud Rule 14a-9, which the SEC has said covers "material which impugns character, integrity or personal reputation."

    Management must give Garth 14 days to reduce the length of his proposal. Rule 14a-8(a)(4). SEC staff sometimes permits the proponent of an otherwise includable proposal to save the proposal by deleting the language the staff considers false or misleading.

1d. A number of exclusions may apply. First, the proposal may not be a "proper subject" for action by shareholders under state law. Rule 14a-8(c)(1). Generally, state law requires that sale of substantially all assets and voluntary corporate dissolution be initiated by directors (see §34.2). Although shareholder approval of the sale and dissolution may be necessary, in most states it is not sufficient. The corporate "contract" gives the board the exclusive power to initiate such a change.

    Second, the proposal would require the company to violate state law regarding the process for approving a sale of all the company's assets and corporate dissolution. Rule 14a-8(c)(2).

    Third, the proposal may be seen as relating to "specific amounts of cash . . . dividends." Rule 14a-8(c)(13).

1e. Garth should phrase the resolution to be precatory — a suggestion that the board consider a liquidation/dissolution. The resolution might also call on the board to prepare a report to shareholders on its decision. So, to make his proposal proper, Garth may have to make it toothless.

2a. Excludable. Rule 14a-8 permits shareholders to submit only a resolution, not a slate of directors. Further, the proposal is excludable because it relates to an election to office. Rule 14a-8(c)(8). Although the election of directors is a proper subject for shareholder action, the rule prevents shareholders from interfering with management's orderly operation of the proxy mechanism. If Garth or virtually any other shareholder could propose his own slate of directors, management's proxy statement and proxy card would become unmanageable, jeopardizing proxy voting.

2b. Probably excludable. This resolution is precatory and may be a "proper subject" for shareholder action. Under current SEC interpretation, shareholders may make proposals under Rule 14a-8 that urge the board be composed of "outside" directors or "employee" directors. SEC staff has taken the view that such proposals do not relate to a particular election or nominee and are not covered by the "relates to an election" exclusion of Rule 14a-9(c)(8). Nonetheless, the proposal to nominate a certain number of women may be excludable on the ground that it urges the company to run afoul of antidiscrimination laws. See Rule 14a-8(c)(2) ("Proposal . . . would require registrant to violate any state law or Federal law"). Garth should have urged the board to consider women nominees to the board, without specifying a quota.

2c. Includable, according to *Amalgamated Clothing and Textile Workers Union v. Wal-Mart Stores, Inc.* (§19.5.2). The resolution does not require specific board action, only a report, and deals with a matter of substantial public importance, thus removing it from "ordinary business operations." Rule 14a-8(c)(7).

In a 1992 no-action letter, the SEC took the position that proposals dealing with a company's employment practices are within the company's "ordinary business operations" even when they raise social policy concerns. *Cracker Barrel Old Country Stores, Inc.*, 1992 SEC No-Action LEXIS 984 (Oct. 13, 1992). The court in the *Wal-Mart* case refused to defer to this SEC position because it deviated from an interpretive release that accompanied the (c)(7) exclusion when the SEC adopted it in 1976.

2d. Probably includable. The resolution must walk a narrow line, which this one may. It cannot demand specific board action, an improper subject for shareholder action — the (c)(1) exclusion. It cannot be so broad that it is not significantly related to the company's business — the (c)(5) exclusion. And it cannot be so narrow as to relate to the conduct of VidPal's ordinary business operations — the (c)(7) exclusion.

In other words, the resolution is precatory and avoids (c)(1); it relates to a significant social policy question of "moral" entertainment and may avoid (c)(5); and it is not necessarily a matter that impinges on management discretion and may avoid (c)(7). In general, the SEC and the courts have accepted the propriety of resolutions that propose that the corporation take a particular stand on an issue of ethical importance.

3a. No. This proposal is excludable. It is "counter to a proposal" to be submitted by management at the meeting, here the unconditioned merger — the (c)(9) exclusion. Management has a monopoly over the company-funded proxy mechanism when it makes its own proposals. Moreover, under most state statutes, shareholders have no power to approve fundamental transactions — such as mergers, charter amendments, or dissolution — with conditions, and the proposal is excludable under "proper subject" exclusion.

Even if Garth were willing to pay for the solicitation under Rule 14a-7, management might argue that it need not act as a "common carrier" for proposals that conflict with state law. Unlike Rule 14a-8, however, the "common carrier" requirements of Rule 14a-7 do not offer management any explicit grounds for exclusion or for refusing to provide a shareholders' list.

3b. No. This is the alternative for shareholders who are unable to have their proposals included in the company-funded proxy solicitation under Rule 14a-8. The cost to Garth, however, will be significant. He must pay to print, publish, and mail the proxy statement, as well as for any legal, financial, or public relation fees related to the solicitation. For a large public company, a full-fledged proxy contest costs between $5 million to $10 million.

4a. It depends on whether the SEC proxy rules can be seen to create federal substantive rights or merely provide procedures to exercise rights under state law. Garth's proposal on executive compensation is includable under Rule 14a-8 but not under the company's amended articles.

Many courts have justified Rule 14a-8 on a procedural theory. Without the rule, it would be misleading for management not to disclose shareholder proposals it expects shareholders will raise at an upcoming meeting. The rule provides a procedure for that disclosure. If a shareholder has no right to make a proposal, then presumably the rule does not require that management disclose it.

On the other hand, Rule 14a-8 has over time assumed a life of its own. Many of the exclusion categories — such as for proposals that have failed in the past or are counter to a management proposal or are not significantly related to the company's business — do not find any basis in state law. The SEC, in effect, has created a new substantive right, subject to the agency's list of exclusions. Under this view, companies cannot "opt out" of shareholder access pursuant to Rule 14a-8 any more than they could opt out of the other federal proxy rules.

4b. Management may not be interested in opting out of the shareholder proposal rule for a number of reasons. First, the rule is largely benign. Shareholder proposals, even in this age of increasing shareholder activism, rarely succeed. When they do, they are often precatory and often supported by large institutional shareholders. Second, it might be bad for shareholder relations if management tried to insulate itself from shareholder proposals. Investors might lose confidence in a company whose management tried to cut off shareholder access. Third, an "opt out" might be invalid under state law. Just as shareholders have an implied right to amend the bylaws, courts might well hold that shareholders have an implied (inviolable) right to make proposals at shareholders' meetings. Finally, the shareholder proposal rule may serve as a relatively painless way for activist shareholders to express their business, economic, social, and political views short of seeking government action through the political process.

§19.6   Private Action to Challenge Proxy Fraud

What options does a shareholder have in response to a corporate transaction tainted by management deception?

State fraud regulation — the law of deceit — imposes liability on those who fraudulently misrepresent material facts on which others rely to their detriment. If management accomplished the transaction through a proxy solicitation — often the case for major corporate actions such as charter amendments, mergers, and sale/liquidations (see Chapters 34 and 35) — a deceived shareholder could seek tort relief under state law. This strategy, however, presents a number of pitfalls. State fraud law (though still evolving) might require the shareholder to show —

- the proxy statement contained an actual misrepresentation of fact, not just a deceptive opinion or an omission that made the statement misleading;
- management knew of the misrepresentation or knew that there was no basis for the representations made, and intended shareholder reliance;
- shareholders actually read the proxy disclosures and justifiably relied on them;
- any loss shareholders suffered because of the transaction was related to the misrepresentation, not to extraneous factors.

In a case involving voting by many public shareholders, showing all these elements would often be nearly impossible.

Another option for disappointed shareholders is corporate fiduciary law. As we will see, state law imposes fiduciary duties on management, which shareholders may enforce in a derivative suit (see Chapter 31). But as we will also see, shareholder-plaintiffs often encounter significant impediments in bringing and maintaining derivative suits (see Chapters 32 and 33), and state fiduciary protection is sometimes spotty (see Chapter 21).

The federal proxy antifraud rule offers an attractive alternative. We next take up the questions of who may sue for proxy fraud, what must be shown to establish liability, and what relief is available. As you read through this section, notice the tension federal courts have had to deal with in fashioning a private proxy fraud action. On the one hand, the proxy rules seek to ensure informed shareholder voting and to constrain management through the antiseptic of disclosure; on the other, federal judicial protection of hypothetical shareholder interests in disclosure can interfere with management prerogatives and majoritarian rule — that is, with the normal corporate functioning governed by state law.

§19.6.1   Standing — Implied Private Cause of Action

Remember that §14(a) of the 1934 Act simply prohibits proxy solicitations that do not comply with the SEC's proxy rules. SEC enforcement power is clear enough: §21(d) of the 1934 Act gives the SEC specific authority to enforce its rules in court, including antifraud Rule 14a-9. But Congress never specifically stated who (or if anyone *besides* the SEC) has standing to seek relief for proxy fraud.

The Supreme Court resolved this question in *J.I. Case Co. v. Borak*, 377 U.S. 426 (1964). In a famous (often conclusory) decision, the Court held that a shareholder has an implied right to challenge a corporate transaction approved by a proxy solicitation that violated the SEC antifraud rule. The *Borak* Court used a broad theory that "where there is a wrong the law implies a remedy" and held that shareholders have an implied cause of action under §27 of the 1934 Act to sue for violations of §14(a).

Section 27 is a remarkable source for the Court's implication. By its terms the provision merely gives federal district courts exclusive jurisdiction over actions "to enforce any liability or duty created" under the 1934 Act and prescribes service of process and venue requirements for such actions. The Supreme Court has since held that implied rights arise, if at all, under the 1934 Act's substantive provisions, rejecting §27 as a source. See *Touche Ross & Co. v. Redington*, 442 U.S. 560 (1979).

The *Borak* Court also pointed to §14(a)'s legislative history, which indicated a congressional purpose to protect investors from proxy abuses, and inferred that Congress must have implicitly intended to make private relief available to supplement SEC enforcement. The Court did not look at whether the legislative history or the statutory structure revealed a congressional intent to create a private remedy. Section 14(a)'s legislative history is in fact silent on this point, and the structure of the 1934 Act suggests just the opposite. The Act provides express remedies (subject to specific substantive and procedural restrictions) for specified violations such as market manipulation (one of the charges in *Borak*), short-swing insider trading, and the filing of *intentionally* false or misleading documents on which investors rely. 1934 Act §§9(a), 16(b), 18.

Borak's broad implied-remedy theory has since been rejected by the Supreme Court beginning with *Cort v. Ash,* 422 U.S. 66 (1975), a nonsecurities case, and in more recent cases arising under other provisions of the 1934 Act. The test has become, in essence, whether an implied private action was intended by Congress, taking into account the legislative history, the structure of the statute, and the availability of state remedies. See *Touche Ross & Co. v. Redington,* 442 U.S. 560 (1979) (holding that shareholders have no private action for violation of §17 of the 1934 Act, which requires annual informational filings by stockbrokers with SEC); *Piper v. Chris-Craft Industries, Inc.,* 430 U.S. 1 (1977) (holding that a frustrated bidder lacks standing to challenge tender offer disclosures under §14(e) of 1934 Act). Nonetheless, despite the shakiness of its underpinnings, the *Borak* holding that a federal private action exists for proxy fraud is now entrenched.

§19.6.2   *Federal Proxy Fraud Action*

The proxy fraud action implied in *Borak* is a federal action. As such, it allows challenging shareholders to avoid the substantive and procedural impediments of a fiduciary challenge under state law. By suing under federal law, plaintiffs can avoid state derivative suit limitations (such as posting of security for expenses and demand on directors — see §32.2), limits on fiduciary protection (such as the business judgment rule — see §21.2), and the exclusivity of the appraisal remedy in control transactions (see §32.2).

Under *Borak* a private proxy fraud action can be brought either in the shareholder's own name (as a class action) or in a derivative suit on behalf of the corporation (see Chapter 31). A *federal derivative action* provides a means for shareholder-plaintiffs to recover litigation expenses, including attorney fees, and to avoid state derivative suit procedures. The *Borak* Court justified such an action on the tenuous ground that a federal derivative action would provide relief for damages to the corporation caused by deceptive proxy solicitations. Most state actions challenging disclosure are brought as class actions.

Over the last three decades since *Borak*, the Supreme Court has decided a number of cases that clarify the elements of a federal proxy fraud case — in the early cases opening the federal courthouse door and in later cases leaving it only ajar. Interestingly, the Supreme Court cases to date all have the same factual pattern: a shareholder sues after management arranges a merger or other control transaction accomplished with a false or misleading proxy statement.

Consider the elements of a federal proxy fraud case:

Misrepresentation or Omission of Facts.   Rule 14a-9 specifically regulates a proxy solicitation that "omits to state any material fact necessary in order to make the statements therein not false or misleading." This formulation, which represents an expansion of the traditional common law view that silence is not actionable, invites disappointed shareholders to point to gaps in disclosure.

One important question is whether statements of opinions, motives, and reasons in a proxy solicitation constitute "facts." The common law has traditionally not allowed parties to rely on an adversary's statements of opinion, motives, or reasons concerning a transaction. In *Virginia Bankshares, Inc. v. Sandberg*, 111 S. Ct. 2749 (1991), the Supreme Court held that the board's statement of its reasons for approving a merger can be actionable. Shareholders rely on the board's expertise and the directors' fiduciary duties, and the board's opinions and reasons for a transaction "naturally" can be important to shareholders.

The Court in *Virginia Bankshares*, however, was reluctant to make actionable any misleading opinion or statement of reasons. Concerned that shareholders could use the litigation process to fabricate theories of management's unstated motives, the court held that a statement of opinion, motives, or reasons is not actionable just because a shareholder proves the board did not believe what it said. Imbedded in every opinion are testable statements: (1) the speaker believes his opinion to be correct; (2) the speaker has some basis for making it; (3) the speaker knows of nothing that contradicts it. According to the Court, proving (1) is not enough — a shareholder must also prove (2) or (3). That is, an opinion by the board must both misstate the board's true beliefs and mislead about the subject matter of the statement, such as the value of the shares in a merger.

The *Virginia Bankshares* two-part test seeks to prevent shareholders from using the proxy rules to attack a transaction that, although accompanied by false or misleading opinions or statements of reasons, may nonetheless be fair and thus beyond attack under state fiduciary law. For example, a proxy statement that fails to explain that the company's majority shareholder was seeking a "quick sale" of the company to obtain cash to pay estate taxes is not materially misleading unless the plaintiffs can also show that the sale price was unfair. See *Mendell v. Greenberg*, 938 F.2d 1528 (2d Cir. 1991) (remanded in light of *Virginia Bankshares*).

Materiality. Rule 14a-9 requires that the challenged misrepresentation or omission be "with respect to a material fact." Under the common law, a materiality requirement serves to corroborate the complaining party's claim that she relied on the alleged misinformation in voting her shares. Without some measure of the misinformation's relevance to the transaction, information defects would be an easy pretext to escape bargains that one party finds unfavorable.

In *TSC Industries, Inc. v. Northway, Inc.*, 426 U.S. 438 (1976), the Court defined an omitted material fact as one as to which there is a "substantial likelihood that a reasonable shareholder would consider it important in deciding how to vote." The definition balances the Court's concern that trivial misinformation not be actionable and its concern that a complaining shareholder not have to prove with certainty that the body of shareholders would have voted against the transaction had they been fully informed.

The *TSC v. Northway* test asks what a reasonable shareholder "would" consider important. This requires more proof than if the test were what a reasonable shareholder "might" consider important, a formulation the Supreme Court rejected as improperly suggesting a "mere possibility" of importance. The Court stated that the information must "significantly alter the total mix" of information available. That is, information is not material if it is redundant. The materiality of information also depends on what the shareholders are asked to vote on. In a board election, for example, it would seem "material" that a corporate treasurer nominated to the board's audit committee had been convicted of embezzlement, but the same fact might be irrelevant if the shareholders were being asked to approve a merger.

In *TSC v. Northway* a TSC shareholder complained that the proxy solicitation for a sale/liquidation of the company had failed to disclose that National, the buyer of the assets, controlled the TSC's board. The Court held that the omission was not material because the proxy statement had disclosed that National was a 34 percent shareholder and that five of TSC's ten directors were National nominees. Further information about National's control was superfluous; it would not have altered the total mix of information.

Culpability. Rule 14a-9 is silent on the question, and the Supreme Court has never addressed whether a proxy misstatement must be made culpably. Most lower courts have not required that the party making the misrepresentation knew it was false or misleading. That is, scienter is not required.

Instead, the Supreme Court has suggested that negligent misstatements are enough. *Aaron v. SEC,* 446 U.S. 680 (1980). The few lower courts that have addressed the issue agree. See *Shidler v. All American Life & Financial Corp.,* 775 F.2d 917 (8th Cir. 1985) (no strict liability for incorrectly opining on novel issue of state law); *Gould v. American Hawaiian Steamship Co.,* 535 F.2d 761 (3d Cir. 1976) (outside directors' negligence is sufficient for liability under the proxy rules, analogizing to 1933 Act §11); *Gerstle v. Gamble-*

Skogmo, Inc., 478 F.2d 1281 (2d Cir. 1973) (contrasting Rule 14a-9 with Rule 10b-5).

Nonetheless, the extent of relief available under Rule 14a-9 may vary with culpability. At least one case has imposed a higher fault standard when shareholders have sought damages rather than equitable relief against outside accountants who failed to notice misstatements in the proxy materials. *Adams v. Standard Knitting Mills, Inc.,* 623 F.2d 422 (6th Cir.), *cert. denied,* 449 U.S. 1067 (1980). On the other hand, courts readily grant temporary restraining orders to enjoin meetings on a showing of materiality without any evidence of fault. Rescinding a transaction or imposing damages after shareholders vote may require that management knew, or was negligent in not knowing, that disclosure was inadequate.

Reliance.   Under the common law of deceit, a plaintiff must show that she actually and justifiably relied on the defendant's misrepresentations. Rule 14a-9 is silent on the question. What causal relationship must exist for liability in a federal proxy fraud case? Must complaining shareholders show that they actually read and relied on the alleged misstatements, or that the misstatements had a "decisive effect" on the voting outcome, or that the transaction was unfair and thus shareholders would likely have voted it down?

In *Mills v. Electric Auto-Lite Co.,* 396 U.S. 375 (1970), the Supreme Court rejected these approaches and held that it is enough if the alleged misstatements were material. The Court excused proof of actual reliance, thus eliminating it as an element in a proxy fraud case. The Court said that the materiality test, later refined in *TSC Industries,* embodies a conclusion that the misstatement would have been considered important by a reasonable shareholder and weeds out claims based on trivial or unrelated misstatements.

Causation.   The common law requires that the plaintiff show the defendant's deceit caused her loss. Like the requirements of materiality and reliance, causation seeks to measure whether the plaintiff's loss is linked to the alleged misinformation.

In proxy fraud cases, federal courts have required that the challenged transaction have caused harm to the shareholder — *loss causation.* In a merger, loss causation is relatively easy to show if shareholders of the acquired company claim the merger price was less than what their shares were worth. If, however, shareholders in a merger receive stock in the surviving company and the stock price falls after the merger, shareholders would have to show that the loss in value happened because of the merger, not because of extraneous events.

Federal courts have also required that the proxy solicitation be "an essential link to the accomplishment of the transaction" — *transaction causation.* That is, there can be no recovery if the transaction did not depend on the shareholder vote. In *Mills,* for example, the Supreme Court concluded that transaction causation existed because a proxy solicitation of minority shareholders holding 46 percent of the company's stock was essential to getting the necessary two-thirds approval for the merger.

To illustrate the difference between loss causation and transaction causation, consider a shareholder challenge to a proxy solicitation for a board election that omits information about the company's bribery of foreign officials. This raises two questions. First, did the bribery hurt the corporation or its shareholders? This is a question of loss causation, and shareholders would have to show economic harm to the corporation or shareholders arising from the foreign bribery. Second, even if the bribery caused losses, was the proxy statement (and shareholder voting) an "essential link" in effectuating the bribery? This is a question of transaction causation, and shareholders would have to show the shareholder vote continued or set the bribery into motion. See *Abbey v. Control Data Corp.*, 603 F.2d 724 (8th Cir. 1979), *cert. denied*, 444 U.S. 1017 (1980).

In *Virginia Bankshares*, the Supreme Court considered whether there can be transaction causation when the vote of minority shareholders is not necessary as a matter of state law to accomplish a squeeze-out merger. In the case, the board sought the proxies of minority shareholders, even though the company's parent corporation held 85 percent of the shares and approval of the merger was assured. The plaintiff argued that the board had solicited proxies to accomplish purposes related to the transaction: (1) minority approval improved management's reputation with investors and the omitted information, if revealed, would have shamed the board into acting differently; (2) minority approval insulated the merger from review under Virginia's corporate statute on conflict-of-interest transactions and the omitted information made it less likely that shareholders could sue to block the merger under state law.

On the first so-called shame facts theory, the Court held that the board's desire for a cosmetic vote did not provide the essential link between the proxy solicitation and the merger. Otherwise, the complaining shareholder would be asking a judge to speculate about the board's timidity or boldness. The Court was unwilling to make presumptions about management behavior, as it had about shareholder behavior in *Mills* when it excused proof of individual reliance.

On the second "sue facts" theory, the Court held that even if the board had misled the minority into approving the merger, shareholders were not precluded from challenging the merger in state court, where a shareholder vote obtained through material misinformation would have no validating effect. The Court left open the possibility that disclosure defects might be actionable if they induced shareholders to forgo dissenters' appraisal rights or undermined their ability to challenge the transaction in state court.

Prospective or Retrospective Relief. In *Borak* the Supreme Court also held that relief for a violation of the proxy rules could be either prospective

303

or retrospective. This gives federal courts a broad remedial arsenal: they can enjoin the voting of proxies obtained through proxy fraud, enjoin the shareholders' meeting, rescind the transaction, or award damages.

In fashioning relief, federal courts have inquired into fairness, an inquiry *Mills* purposefully rejected in deciding the question of shareholder reliance. In *Mills* the Supreme Court remanded the case on the question of damages and said "one important factor may be the fairness of the terms of the merger." The Seventh Circuit eventually decided that the merger price was fair and denied the shareholders any relief.

Attorney Fees. In *Mills* the Supreme Court endorsed the awarding of attorney fees, even before a final remedy, to shareholders who successfully prosecute a proxy fraud case. Attorney fees are available on the theory that shareholder-plaintiffs, whether in a class action or derivative suit, are producing a benefit for the body of shareholders. This ruling creates an incentive for an individual public shareholder with a relatively small stake to vindicate shareholder rights under the proxy rules.

EXAMPLES

1. Garth, a VidPal shareholder, is upset with the huge pay package of the company's president, T. V. King. Garth claims it is a waste of corporate assets and that the board violated Rule 14a-9 by not disclosing King's stock options in its most recent proxy statement. He sues in state court claiming federal proxy fraud, state fraudulent misrepresentation, and breach of fiduciary duty. Identify any problems with the suit.

2. Garth sold some of his VidPal shares after he read in the company's proxy materials for the annual board election that "company earnings have been, and will remain, flat for the next two years." At the time, management was secretly buying shares at depressed prices on the open market, and the pessimistic statements turn out to be wrong. Does Garth have an implied right of action under the federal proxy rules?

3. Some of VidPal's directors are under investigation for bribing FBI agents during their investigation of the company's rental of "pirate" videos. The company's proxy statement for the upcoming election of directors does not disclose the investigation.
   a. Does this omission violate the proxy rules?
   b. Garth sues under the proxy rules to enjoin the shareholders' meeting until management distributes a corrected proxy statement. Does Garth have to show that management knew about the bribery investigation?
   c. In his suit to enjoin the shareholders' meeting, does Garth have to prove that a majority of shareholders actually read the proxy statement

and relied on the generally favorable statements about management's board nominees?

4. VidPal enters into a merger agreement under which Dixie Video will acquire VidPal for $50 per share. VidPal shareholders must approve the merger.

   a. The proxy statement recommending the merger fails to disclose that Dixie Video is under indictment for distributing pirate videos and faces potentially staggering fines and civil liability. Garth sues to enjoin the merger under the federal proxy rules. Are Dixie Video's problems material to VidPal shareholders?

   b. At the time of the merger agreement, VidPal has a pending lawsuit against a competing video store chain complaining of unfair competitive practices. The proxy statement for the merger describes the lawsuit and states that damages could exceed $20 million, but "the outcome of the litigation is uncertain." Very soon after the merger, the suit is settled for $30 million. Garth brings a class action on behalf of VidPal shareholders claiming damages under the federal proxy rules. Is the statement about the litigation's uncertainty actionable?

EXPLANATIONS

1. Yes. Federal courts have exclusive jurisdiction over alleged violations of the 1934 Act, including the proxy regulations. 1934 Act §27. Garth must either drop his federal proxy claim from his state complaint or sue in federal court, where the state claims can be asserted under the federal court's pendent jurisdiction. Moreover, the state fraud and fiduciary claims may face a number of procedural and substantive obstacles. To prove fraud, Garth will have to show that the board intentionally misrepresented the president's compensation, that shareholders relied on the board representations, that the shareholders would have voted differently were it not for misrepresentations, and that the compensation caused shareholders a loss. To maintain a derivative suit challenging the directors' fiduciary breach, Garth may have to make a demand on the board or offer an excuse for not making it and perhaps post a bond for defendants' litigation expenses, if his suit is unsuccessful. (§32.2.) He will then have to overcome the business judgment rule that presumes disinterested directors act in good faith, with reasonable care, and in the corporation's best interests. (§21.3.)

2. Probably not. The Supreme Court held in *J. I. Case Co. v. Borak* that a shareholder has an implied right of action to challenge any *corporate transaction* approved by means of a proxy solicitation violating SEC proxy regulations. Garth's losses were not related to the board election, the transaction for which proxies where solicited, and there was no

"transaction causation." The Supreme Court has been unwilling to imply broader rights than those laid out in *Borak* and *Mills*. See *Virginia Bankshares, Inc. v. Sandberg* (§19.6.2).

Nonetheless, Garth may have a perfectly good claim against VidPal's management under 1934 Act §18, which allows shareholders to sue any person who intentionally makes false or misleading statements in filings with the SEC if the statements affected the stock price. Garth may also have claim under Rule 10b-5 under a similar theory (see Chapter 29).

3a. Perhaps. A criminal investigation need not be disclosed, according to the SEC's line-item disclosure requirements. Schedule 14A requires only that the proxy statement disclose that a director "was convicted in a criminal proceeding or is a named subject of a pending criminal proceeding." See Item 401(f), Regulation S-K (required by Item 7, Schedule 14A). Nonetheless, Rule 14a-9 prohibits proxy statements that fail to state any *material* fact necessary to make the proxy statement not false or misleading. Silence is not a defense, but the omitted facts must have been material.

Is there a substantial likelihood that a reasonable shareholder would have considered the bribery investigation important in deciding how to vote on directors? The investigation must have "altered the total mix" of information about the directors, although it need not have been so significant that shareholders necessarily would have changed their vote. Much, therefore, depends on how far along the investigation was. Was it so preliminary or so factually tenuous that no reasonable shareholder would have attached importance to it? The SEC disclosure requirements on pending criminal proceedings assumes shareholders would not want disclosure of mere criminal investigations in which no charges have been brought.

The materiality of the investigation would also depend on how significant the possible charges might be. If the investigation led to indictments and convictions, how much would the company's reputation and business be hurt? Would the company be exposed to liability? If the consequences are serious and indictments probable, the investigation may well be material. See *Basic, Inc. v. Levinson* (§29.3.2) (adopting a "probability-plus magnitude" materiality test for speculative information).

3b. Probably not. The Supreme Court has not decided whether there is strict liability for violations of Rule 14a-9 — the proxy fraud rule. Some cases suggest that to recover damages a shareholder would have to show that management either intentionally concealed the investigation or was negligent in failing to learn of it.

But if (as here) the claim is for injunctive relief, most courts have not required a showing of culpability. A strict liability standard for injunctive claims would seem consistent with the proxy rules' broad purpose to assure fully informed shareholder voting.

3c. No. The Supreme Court in *Mills* recognized that proof of individual reliance would be too burdensome. It is sufficient that the proxy statement contained omissions of material facts.

4a. No. Under the merger, VidPal's assets and liabilities will be absorbed into Dixie Video, and VidPal's shareholders will receive cash. (See §35.2). VidPal's shareholders should be indifferent to the contingent liabilities of the new joint business as long as they receive fair cash consideration for their shares. Dixie Video's problems are not material in this *cash-for-stock* merger.

4b. Perhaps. Garth will have to show that the board's opinion that the lawsuit's "outcome is uncertain" was materially misleading. It is not enough that the recovery by VidPal was larger than the board thought it would be according to the proxy statement. The board's opinion is misleading if (1) management did not believe the outcome was uncertain, but in fact expected a favorable result; and (2) a full and truthful opinion would have affected the ultimate merger price. See *Virginia Bank Shares Inc. v. Saudberg*, 111 S. Ct. 2749 (1991).

Garth will have to show both elements. The timing of the lawsuit's favorable outcome, soon after the merger, suggests that the "outcome uncertain" opinion was misleading boilerplate. Nonetheless, management may have actually been unsure about the litigation's outcome. In addition, the possibility of a large recovery may have been reflected in the merger price, and fuller disclosure would not have affected the price or shareholders' consideration of the merger. *Virginia Bankshares* reflects a reluctance to have judges restructure the terms of a corporate transaction because of tangential disclosure deficiencies.

PART SEVEN

Fiduciary Duties of Management and Controlling Shareholders

20

Corporate Fiduciary Duties — An Introduction

At the heart of corporate law lie duties of trust and confidence — fiduciary duties — owed by those who control the corporate governance machinery to the body of constituents known as the "corporation." Directors, officers, and controlling shareholders have broad obligations to act in the corporation's best interests, principally for the benefit of the owners of the corporation's residual ownership rights. In most instances, fiduciary duties run to equity shareholders as a group; but when the business is insolvent, these duties run to the corporation's creditors. See *Geyer v. Ingersoll Publications,* CITE (Del. Ch. 1992).

Courts, not legislatures, have been primarily responsible for shaping the contours of corporate fiduciary duties. Judicial attempts to balance the need for management flexibility and management accountability have produced vague and shifting fiduciary rules. The American Law Institute has contributed its efforts as well, drafting the Principles of Corporate Governance (see §1.2.4) to articulate and provide guidance on the operation of corporate fiduciary duties. The duties of management have assumed a pivotal role in the debate over the function and responsibility of the corporation in society.

§20.1   The Corporate Fiduciary — A Unique Relationship

§20.1.1   Analogies to Trusts and Partnerships

What is the corporate fiduciary's relationship to the corporation? Early courts analogized the corporation to a trust, the directors to trustees, and the shareholders to trust beneficiaries. But modern courts recognize that the analogy is flawed because of the circumscribed powers and discretion of trustees compared to directors.

The corporation, particularly when closely held, has also been analogized to a partnership. But corporate fiduciaries operate in a system that prizes corporate permanence as well as central management and the discretion it entails. Although some cases have implied partner-like duties for shareholders in close corporations (see §17.1.3), the cases are exceptions to the broad discretion afforded corporate directors.

In the end, the most that can be said is that corporate fiduciaries have a relationship that is unique to the corporation. This relationship arises from the various expectations that corporate constituents, particularly shareholders, have in the maximization of their investment, business risk-taking, and residual control rights.

§20.1.2   A Theory of Fiduciary Duties

The genius of the corporation lies in its specialization of function. Unlike the usual partnership, the corporation allows for the aggregation of capital without capital investors assuming management functions or becoming liable for business debts. Separating functions creates inevitable "agency costs" when investor-owners entrust management functions to a system of central governance in which they retain residual control rights. While generally producing significant efficiencies, this structure creates the possibility that managerial interests will often diverge from and conflict with those of the investor-owners. Underlying the theory of the corporation is the assumption by investors that the costs of inefficient management due to laziness and opportunism are outweighed by the benefits of increased efficiency from operating through specialized manager "agents." Corporate fiduciary rules therefore balance two competing themes:

Management discretion.   The efficiency of specialized central management suggests that those who control the corporate governance machinery should have broad discretion. Removing discretion from managers and giving shareholders significant oversight authority would undermine this premise of the corporate form.

Management accountability. The dangers of entrusting management to nonowners suggest a need for substantial accountability on behalf of management. Without limits on management discretion beyond residual control rights to elect the board and approve fundamental corporate changes, managers might be lazy, faithless, or otherwise abuse their position of control. Management slack or diversion, besides being fundamentally unfair, will ultimately cause investors to lose confidence in the corporate form.

Corporate fiduciary law faces the challenge of distinguishing between those cases calling for judicial abstention and those calling for judicial intervention. In resolving this dilemma, most courts and commentators have accepted a theory of *shareholder wealth maximization*. The theory posits that any fiduciary rule — such as one governing the behavior of directors in the boardroom or directors' use of inside information — must maximize the value of shareholders' interests in the corporation. Under this theory, the corporation's other constituents, such as creditors, employees, and communities in which the business operates, are limited to their contractual and other legal rights. To the extent the nonexpress interests of these other constituents are inconsistent with shareholder interests, shareholder interests prevail.

Despite the theory, close inspection of numerous cases raises doubts about the centrality of shareholder wealth. For example, the case most often cited for the theory of shareholder wealth maximization may actually have turned on nonshareholder interests. In *Dodge v. Ford Motor Co.,* 170 N.W. 668 (Mich. 1919), the Michigan Supreme Court was confronted by the challenge to Ford Motor's decision to discontinue paying a special $10 million dividend, ostensibly to have money to build a smelting plant while actually reducing the price on Ford cars. Minority shareholders holding 10 percent of the company's shares challenged the decision as arbitrary and inconsistent with the fundamental purpose of the business corporation — namely, to maximize the return to shareholders. The court agreed and faulted Henry Ford for reducing the price of cars, and thus the return to shareholders, and for running Ford Motor as a "semi-eleemosynary institution and not as a business institution." The court compelled the payment of the special dividend, but it refused to enjoin Ford's expansion plans on the ground "judges are not business experts."

At first blush, the case seemed to turn on Ford's stated view that Ford Motor "has made too much money, has had too large profits . . . and sharing them with the public, by reducing the price of the output of the company, ought to be undertaken." Nonetheless, much more was happening below the surface. The plaintiff Dodge brothers apparently sought the special dividend to finance their own upstart car company, and Henry Ford's decision to end the special dividend was aimed at forestalling competition, along with the attendant benefits to the consuming public and the Michigan auto industry. The Michigan court's decision to second-guess the product pricing and dividend policies of perhaps the most successful industrialist ever is at odds with the general judicial deference to management, as well as with the Michigan court's specific observation that Ford Motor's great success had resulted from its "capable management."

§20.1.3   Duties of Officers and Other Corporate Agents

Courts have generally imposed on corporate officers and senior executives the same fiduciary duties as those imposed on directors. RMBCA §8.41. In a public corporation, senior executives (as a practical matter) control the corporate governance machinery.

Those employees who are officers in name but have no actual authority, as well as other employees, have traditional duties of care and loyalty as agents of the corporation. In general, corporate fiduciary law — which regulates the relationship between shareholders and management — does not concern itself with these employees.

§20.2   Two Broad Fiduciary Duties — Care and Loyalty

According to the traditional fiduciary analysis, corporate managers owe two duties to the corporation: care and loyalty. The duty of care imposes minimal standards of attentiveness and prudence; it specifies standards for judging the adequacy of corporate decisions when the fiduciary is charged with laziness, although not with a conflict of interest. The duty of loyalty arises when a fiduciary undertakes a transaction that may conflict with the corporation's interests. It imposes stringent standards of fairness in cases of diversion and self-dealing. Each duty describes a set of standards for judicial review of corporate decision-making and fiduciary activities.

§20.2.1   The Duty of Care

The fiduciary duty of care addresses the diligence and competence of managers in performing their decision-making and supervisory functions. The famous business judgment rule presumes that directors (and officers) carry out their functions in good faith, after sufficient investigation, and for acceptable reasons. Courts presume that directors do not breach their duty of care and hold directors liable for care breaches in only a narrow range of cases (see

§21.1.4). Courts have abstained from second-guessing business decisions that appear well-meaning, even when the decisions are flops. This is a risk that shareholders take when they make a corporate investment.

§20.2.2   *The Duty of Loyalty*

The duty of loyalty addresses fiduciaries' conflicts of interests and prohibits fiduciaries from serving their own interests at the expense of the corporation's. Directors, officers, and controlling shareholders breach their duty of loyalty when they divert assets, opportunities, or information of the corporation for personal gain. The diversion can arise in a transaction with the corporation, as well as with another person where the interests of the corporation are at stake. The problem of diversion arises in many ways — avarice can take many forms:

Flagrant diversion.   Diversion can be as simple, and as reprehensible, as a fiduciary stealing tangible corporate assets. This is a plain breach of the fiduciary's duty of loyalty because the diversion was unauthorized and the corporation received no consideration for the asset. Besides being able to disaffirm the transaction as unauthorized (see §22.5), the corporation can sue for breach of fiduciary duty and in tort.

Self-dealing.   Diversion can be masked in self-dealing transactions. When a director or controlling shareholder sells property to the corporation at an excessive price, the effect (from the corporation's standpoint) is the same as if the director or shareholder had appropriated the difference between the fair value of the property and the purchase price (see §22.1).

A parent corporation can breach its duty to the minority shareholders of its partially-owned subsidiary if the parent prefers itself at the expense of the minority. The ultimate form of preferential dealing occurs when the parent squeezes out the minority (in a merger or other transaction) and forces the minority to accept unfair consideration for their shares (see §26.3).

Executive compensation.   When a director or officer sells his executive services to the corporation, diversion can occur if the executive's compensation exceeds the fair value of his services (see Chapter 23).

Taking corporate opportunity.   When a corporate fiduciary seizes for herself a desirable business opportunity that the corporation likely would have taken and profited from, diversion occurs if the fiduciary denies the corporation the opportunity and keeps for herself the profits derived from the opportunity (see Chapter 24).

Trading on inside information.   When a fiduciary knows of confidential corporate information — such as the corporation's impending acquisition of another company — and he buys the target's stock, diversion can occur if the price of the target to the corporation rises because of these purchases. By the same logic, when the fiduciary trades with the company's shareholders using inside information, the fiduciary diverts to himself a gain that may be seen as belonging to the shareholders (see Chapters 28, 29).

Selling out.   A manager who accepts a bribe to sell her corporate office breaches a fiduciary duty of loyalty. Likewise, a controlling shareholder who sells her controlling interest to a new owner, who then diverts corporate assets to herself, can be held liable for recklessly exposing the remaining shareholders to the new owner's looting (see §27.2).

Entrenchment.   A manager who uses the corporate governance machinery or assets to protect the manager's incumbency effectively diverts control from the shareholders to himself (see §40.2). In addition to preventing shareholders from exercising their prerogative to sell control to a new owner, management entrenchment strategies undermine the disciplining effect that robust markets in corporate control have on management slackness and diversion.

There is no uniform standard for judging these conflict-of-interest transactions. In some cases they are flatly prohibited (insider trading), in others they are subject to internal corporate safeguards (executive compensation), and in others they are subject to searching judicial fairness review (squeeze-outs).

§20.3   Fiduciary Duties — Fitting Corporate and Market Realities

§20.3.1   *Fiduciary Duties in Modern Public Corporations*

In public corporations, senior executives (in particular, the company's chief executive officer) generally initiate and control the information, advice, and alternatives available for board review. In general, the board acts as a "rubber stamp" for management initiatives. At most, the directors act as supervisors and monitors of the company's senior executives, to whom broad responsibility to run the business is delegated.

As to normal business matters, the interests of the company's senior executives usually will be closely aligned with those of shareholders. But if the executives of a public corporation mismanage the business, the trading price of the company's stock will fall, making it easier for a takeover in which inefficient management is ousted. It has been argued that the business judgment rule implicitly takes this into account.

When management and shareholder interests diverge, as is the case in self-dealing transactions, outside directors (that is, nonmanagement directors without any employment relationship to the corporation) assume special prominence. Courts have shown an increasing willingness to defer to the "disinterested" judgment of outside directors. Although many have questioned the trustworthiness of their judgment, the chastening possibility of a takeover may dampen some of the concern in a public corporation.

§20.3.2 *Fiduciary Duties in Closely Held Corporations*

In closely held corporations, the corporate participants often have a relationship of special trust. No market exists for their stock, and courts have implied a duty of the participants akin to that of the heightened fiduciary duty of partners. Because in a close corporation the parties will rarely leave matters in the hands of outside directors, courts increasingly have intervened to protect minority participants.

§20.4 Enforcing Fiduciary Duties

Fiduciary duties generally are said to be owed to the corporation, not to particular shareholders, and must be enforced in the name of the corporation. Rarely, however, are fiduciary breaches challenged by the corporation, because those who abused their control of the corporate governance machinery are unlikely to use that control to sue themselves. Instead, fiduciary breaches usually are challenged by shareholders in derivative litigation brought on behalf of the corporation (see Chapter 31). If the corporation is insolvent, fiduciary breaches can be challenged by creditors or a bankruptcy trustee.

21

Duty of Care and the Business Judgment Rule

Corporate law charges the board of directors with the job of managing and supervising the affairs of the corporation, along with specific functions like proposing charter amendments and mergers, declaring dividends, and conducting annual board elections. How well directors perform their functions is measured largely by fiduciary law — specifically by the directors' duty of care.

§21.1 Standards of Care — General, but Misleading, Guidance

In performing their functions, directors (and senior executives) are subject to both statutory and common law standards of care.

§21.1.1 Statutory Standards

Many state statutes codify the standards for directorial behavior. Typical is RMBCA §8.30(a), which requires that directors perform their functions

(1) in good faith,
(2) in a manner they reasonably believe to be in the best interests of the corporation, and
(3) with the care of ordinarily prudent persons in a like position and under similar circumstances.

Under many statutes, officers who have discretionary authority are subject to the same standards. RMBCA §8.42(a).

§21.1.2   Common Law Standards

The articulated common law standards follow much the same pattern as the statutory standards. In *Aronson v. Lewis,* 473 A.2d 805, 812 (Del. 1984), the Delaware Supreme Court stated that the party challenging a business decision has the burden to show the directors failed to act (1) in good faith, (2) in the honest belief that the action taken was in the best interest of the company, or (3) on an informed basis. See also ALI Principles §4.01(a) (adopting essentially the RMBCA formulation). In general, these standards also apply, explicitly and implicitly, to officers. See ALI Principles §4.01(a).

§21.1.3   The Facets of the Duty of Care

Each of the statutory and common law requirements identifies a facet of the duty of care.

Good Faith.   The "good faith" standard has been understood to require that directors (1) not have a conflict of interest, (2) act honestly, and (3) not approve (or condone) illegal activity. Self-interested or fraudulent action is subject to scrutiny under rules that enforce the director's duty of loyalty (see §22.2). Illegality, generally unprotected by the business judgment rule, is subject to heightened judicial scrutiny (see §21.3.1).

Best Interests.   The "best interests" requirement specifies a standard for the *substantive* review of the merits of a director's actions. Under this standard, a board decision or an action by a director must be related to furthering the corporation's interests.

Reasonable Care.   The "ordinary care" and "informed basis" requirements impose on directors a duty of oversight, inquiry, and diligence. It specifies a *procedural* standard that requires directors to have at least minimal levels of skill and expertise, to monitor and supervise management, and to be informed in making decisions. Some statutes require that directors exercise the care that prudent persons would exercise in the management of their "own affairs." Although this requirement would seem to demand of directors greater care compared to the "like position" formulation, there is little to indicate it has affected the results in the cases. The "under similar circumstances" language has been understood to allow a court to take into account the complexity, urgency, and group dynamics of board decision-making.

§21.1.4   The Duty of Care Anomaly — Directors Are Rarely Held Liable

The articulated care standards certainly have a familiar ring: they sound in negligence and tort. One might assume that just as liability regularly follows when negligent driving results in an automobile accident, liability will follow when careless corporate management results in a business failure. There will always be corporations whose new products fail, corporations that miss opportunities to make even greater profits, and corporations that become insolvent — many of these because of well-meaning but imprudent or careless management decisions. Yet in the 150 years during which courts have articulated a directorial duty of care, there have been only a handful of cases in which directors and officers have been held liable for mere mismanagement uncomplicated by illegality, fraud, or conflict of interest. What is really happening?

§21.2   Business Judgment Rule

To understand a director's duty of care is to understand the operation of the famous *business judgment rule*. Rather than providing a formal prescription of a standard of behavior, the rule expresses a judicial "hands off" attitude — a golden rule of corporate law. As explained by the courts, the business judgment rule is a rebuttable presumption that directors in performing their functions are honest and well-meaning, and that their decisions are informed and rationally undertaken. The business judgment rule presumes that directors do not breach their duty of care!

Although the business judgment rule is not statutorily codified, courts have inferred its existence even in states that have adopted statutory care standards. The Official Comment to RMBCA §8.30, for example, explains that "section 8.30 does not try to codify the business judgment rule" and that "[t]he elements of the business judgment rule and the circumstances for its application are continuing to be developed by the courts." For this reason, some commentators have characterized the statutory standards as "aspirational," because their legal effect is profoundly diluted by the business judgment rule.

§21.2.1   How the Business Judgment Rule Operates

The business judgment rule operates at two levels: (1) it shields *directors* from personal liability; and (2) it insulates *decisions* of the board from review — the latter sometimes known as the *business judgment doctrine*. Because the rule's breadth may vary depending on whether damages or injunctive relief is sought, it is useful to distinguish the two aspects of the rule.

The burden of rebutting the business judgment presumption rests on the party challenging a director's actions or board decision. Because of this burden and the obstacles to overcoming the business judgment presumption, claims that directors have breached their duty of care are often dismissed before trial. The rule and doctrine also operate to protect officers and their decisions. ALI Principles §4.01.

§21.2.2   *Justification for the Business Judgment Presumption*

The business judgment presumption has been justified on three basic grounds:

(1) **It avoids judicial meddling.** The business judgment rule (and the doctrine) insulates management risk-taking from judicial meddling and second-guessing. Shareholders expect the board to take business risks — the old adage "nothing ventured, nothing gained" is at the core of why shareholders invest. Corporate statutes reflect this and uniformly specify that corporate management is entrusted to the board of directors.

(2) **It encourages directors to serve.** The business judgment rule (though not necessarily the doctrine) shields well-meaning directors from liability, thus encouraging qualified persons to become directors and to take business risks without fear of being judged in hindsight. Without the rule, directors might not serve or might exercise moribund caution.

(3) **It aligns incentives to comport with shareholder interests.** The business judgment rule (and the doctrine) keeps the myriad of business decisions on which the board acts out of the courtroom and leaves them in the boardroom. Directors and management are likely to have greater business expertise, and their desire to have the business succeed gives them incentives closely aligned with the shareholders' desire that the board maximize the return on their investment. The incentives of judges and derivative suit plaintiffs are loosely consistent and may often be at odds with the interests of the corporation and the body of shareholders.

Some commentators have even suggested that the business judgment presumption should be absolute, eliminating any enforceable care standards. Mismanagement would be subject only to the controls of shareholder voting and the markets. The argument is that if directors make too many mistakes, the corporation's business will suffer, the price of its stock will fall, it will be harder to raise capital, the corporation will become a takeover target or go bankrupt, and eventually management will be replaced. Moreover, if the executives develop a reputation for poor judgment, they will become less attractive candidates in the executive job market.

The operation of markets, so goes the argument, will constrain directors and managers to be diligent and competent. Judges and derivative plaintiff-shareholders, both of whom may sometimes confuse good risk-taking with bad, are a poor substitute for markets operating over time. The argument assumes that markets will operate efficiently and that legal constraints (even though exercised rarely) create more costs than benefits.

§21.2.3 Reliance Corollary — Delegating the Inquiry and Oversight Functions to Others

A corollary to the business judgment presumption and its "hands off" judicial attitude entitles directors to rely on information and advice from other directors (including committees of the board), from officers, and from outsider experts (such as lawyers and accountants). This *reliance corollary* is contained in many statutes and is widely accepted by the courts. See RMBCA §8.30(a). Under some statutes, it also extends to officers. RMBCA §8.42(b).

Particularly in public corporations, directors must be able to rely on information from others. They cannot be expected to learn and know about the full range of the corporation's business. To claim reliance, directors must have read or become familiar with the information or advice and have reasonably believed that it merited confidence.

Directors, however, cannot hide their heads in the sand and claim reliance if they know about something or have suspicions that make reliance unwarranted. RMBCA §8.30(b). For example, a director who knows that corporate earnings have been overstated by management cannot rely on an auditor's opinion that earnings are properly stated. In addition, management directors (who have a greater familiarity with the corporation's business than do outside directors) have a corresponding greater duty to verify information independently. In general, though, the reliance corollary is much more protective than the due diligence and reasonable care defenses available to directors charged with securities fraud (see §§10.3.2, 10.3.3).

§21.3   Overcoming the Business Judgment Presumption

When a challenger asserts liability against a director or challenges a decision of the board, the challenger has the burden of overcoming the business judgment presumption by proving either (1) fraud, illegality, or a conflict of interest; (2) the lack of a rational business purpose; or (3) gross negligence.

§21.3.1 *Fraud, Illegality, or Conflict of Interest*

The director loses the presumption that he was acting to further the corporation's best interests if the challenger shows fraud, illegality, or a conflict of interest.

Fraud. A director who acts fraudulently is liable, and any action tainted by the fraud can be invalidated, regardless of fairness. A director who knowingly or recklessly misrepresents a material fact on which the board or others justifiably rely to the corporation's detriment can be held liable under a tort deceit theory (see §29.2.1).

Illegality. If a director engages in or approves illegal behavior, the prevailing view is that the business judgment presumption is lost even if the director was informed and the action benefited the corporation. For example, directors have been held liable for bribing state officials to protect an amusement park's illegal (and profitable) Sunday operations. *Roth v. Robertson,* 118 N.Y.S. 351 (1909). Courts also have suggested that directors can be held liable for approving bribery of foreign government officials, *Gall v. Exxon,* 418 F. Supp. 508 (S.D.N.Y. 1976), and for approving the dismantling and removal of corporate plants and equipment to discipline unruly employees in violation of labor laws. *Abrams v. Allen,* 74 N.E.2d 305 (N.Y. 1947).

Fiduciary regulation of corporate illegality, however, produces an uncomfortable fit. By making scofflaw directors liable or by enjoining illegal board decisions as a matter of *corporate* law and not as a matter of the substantive law that makes the behavior illegal, the fiduciary duties of directors become a fountainhead for legal norms regulating the corporation. On the one hand, there may be many instances when approving illegal behavior maximizes profits for the corporation; on the other, if knowing illegality were condoned, corporate law would seem to affront the noncorporate norms that make the behavior illegal.

Modern courts have recognized this tension. In *Miller v. AT&T,* 507 F.2d 759 (3d Cir. 1974), shareholders brought a derivative suit challenging AT&T's failure to collect a $1.5 million debt owed it by the Democratic National Committee, a failure the shareholders said violated federal limits on corporate campaign spending. The Third Circuit admitted that under corporate norms the directors' business decision to forgive a debt is normally immune from attack. But the court held that AT&T's failure to collect the DNC debt could be actionable if the shareholders showed that the directors had no "legitimate" business justification, aside from illegally currying political favor, for forgiving the debt. In other words, an illegal purpose alone cannot be a rational business purpose sufficient to trigger the business judgment rule.

The pitfalls of using corporate law to enforce noncorporate legal norms is illustrated by *Miller*. A year after the Third Circuit's decision, the Supreme Court held that shareholders had no implied federal cause of action to enforce federal campaign spending laws. *Cort v. Ash*, 422 U.S. 66 (1975). If the Third Circuit decision has continuing vitality, shareholders could use state fiduciary law to enforce a claim based on a federal law that the Supreme Court has interpreted precludes federal relief for shareholders.

Conflict of Interest. If a director is personally interested in a corporate action, the business judgment presumption shields neither the director from liability nor the board's approval from review. The director's liability and the validity of the action depend on the fairness standards that apply to conflict-of-interest transactions (see §22.3).

What happens to the care standards in a conflict-of-interest case? The courts are silent on this somewhat theoretical point. The ALI Principles suggest that when personal interest taints a transaction, the board's deliberations may be subject to residual care review as well as loyalty review. That is, without the business judgment shield, directors may be liable for breaching their obligations of good faith, reasonable belief, and ordinary care. ALI Principles §4.01(a), comment d. Although it has a certain logic and might allow a plaintiff to tap into an interested director's D&O insurance coverage (see §25.2.2), this approach is found nowhere in the cases and assumes the anomalous possibility that a director interested in a transaction determined to be *fair* to the corporation (a difficult showing) might nonetheless be liable for breaching a less exacting care standard.

§21.3.2 Lack of a Rational Basis

The presumption of the business judgment rule also can be overcome if the action of the directors lacked a "rational" business purpose. The focus is on the merits of the board action or inaction — a substantive review of the challenged decision. When the challenger claims a transaction wholly lacks consideration, the cases often speak of "waste" or "spoliation" of corporate assets. The absence of a rational business purpose powerfully suggests bad faith — that is, a conflicting personal interest, illegality, or deception.

Rational Basis — Any Rational Business Purpose Suffices. How much of a business justification is sufficient?

Under the *rational purpose test,* even board decisions that in hindsight seem patently unwise or imprudent are protected from review and the directors are shielded from liability if the business judgment was not "removed from the realm of reason" (ALI Principles §4.01, comment d, and §4.01(c), comment f) or "improvident beyond explanation." *Michelson v. Duncan,* 407 A.2d 211 (Del. 1979). Only when the board approves a transaction in which

the corporation receives no benefit — such as the issuance of stock without
consideration or the use of corporate funds to discharge personal obligations — have courts found corporate waste. The theme is to protect good-
faith board decisions from judicial second-guessing.

Otherwise, anything goes. If it can be said that the corporation has
received some fair benefit, the matter is entrusted to the directors' judgment.
The cases abound with examples in which courts have forgiven seemingly
patent business folly.

In *Shlensky v. Wrigley*, 237 N.E.2d 776 (Ill. App. 1968), before the
Chicago Cubs joined the rest of major league baseball playing night baseball
games, shareholders challenged the refusal of the Cubs' board to play night
baseball at Wrigley Field. The shareholders claimed that night baseball would
be more profitable and pointed to higher night attendance for the Chicago
White Sox and other teams around the league. Phillip Wrigley, the Cubs'
majority shareholder and dominant member of the board, thought that "baseball is a daytime sport" and that a switch to night baseball would cause the
neighborhood around Wrigley Field to deteriorate. The court granted the
defendants' motion to dismiss, speculating that a deteriorated neighborhood
might cause a decline in attendance or a drop in Wrigley Field's property
value.

In *Kamin v. American Express Co.*, 383 N.Y.S.2d 807 (Sup. Ct. 1976),
the directors of American Express faced the choice of liquidating a bad stock
investment at the corporate level (and taking a corporate tax deduction for
the loss) or distributing the stock to the shareholders as a special dividend,
a taxable event for the shareholders that would have resulted in additional
tax liability of $8 million. Although the choice seemed obvious, the board
opted for the stock dividend, despite shareholder protests. The directors
explained that they were concerned that liquidation would have had an adverse effect on the company's net income figures. The court found the concern
sufficient.

Are actions by a board of directors ever irrational? There is only a small
handful of cases that have found board action so imprudent that the business
judgment presumption is overcome. But under closer inspection, even these
few cases may not be cases of good-faith misjudgment but rather judicial use
of care review when a conflict of interest could be inferred but not proved.
In other words, they may be "safety valve" cases.

The most famous of these cases, *Litwin v. Allen*, 25 N.Y.S.2d 667 (Sup.
Ct. 1940), imposed liability on the directors of Guaranty Trust, a bank affiliate
of J. P. Morgan & Company, for approving stock repurchase agreements
(repos) in the tenuous stock market after the 1929 crash. Under the repos,
Guaranty Trust purchased from Allegheny Corp. convertible 5-1/2 percent
debentures at $100 par, giving Allegheny an option to repurchase the de-
bentures at par in six months. The transaction had the effect of a secured

loan. If Allegheny repurchased the debentures, Guaranty Trust would earn 5-1/2 percent interest for the six months it held the debentures. If Allegheny failed to repurchase (as happened) Guaranty Trust would retain the collateral. The key to the transaction was the solidity of the debentures, which turned out to be victims of the Depression.

The Guaranty Trust directors had guessed wrong that the panic of 1930 had reached its bottom, and the court faulted the directors for approving a transaction "so improvident, so risky, so unusual and unnecessary to be contrary to fundamental conceptions of prudent banking practice." The court imposed liability on the directors, precisely the kind of second-guessing precluded by the business judgment rule. Surely the Guaranty Trust directors, among the most experienced risk assessors in banking, had been inattentive to the repos' risk.

What was happening? Many commentators have explained *Litwin v. Allen* as imposing a higher duty on directors of financial institutions, who were frequent defendants before the era of federal insurance of depositors' accounts. But there may be another explanation. Allegheny was the holding company for the Van Sweringen empire, in which J. P. Morgan & Company was deeply involved. Morgan was interested in buttressing Allegheny's sagging fortunes, and this desire was surely not lost on the Guaranty Trust directors. Although the court agreed that there was no showing of conflict of interest, the court's use of a heightened duty of care overcame this lack of proof. The court used care review, when it actually may have been concerned about a controlling shareholder's self-dealing transaction (see §26.2).

Board Inaction — An Open Question. One significant issue is whether the business judgment rule shields failures of the board to act. The prevailing view is that the board's failure to act — such as a failure to put a monitoring system into place to assure the corporation's compliance with antitrust price-fixing prohibitions — is protected only if the failure was a conscious exercise of business judgment. ALI Principles, comment to §4.01(c). If, for example, a board explicitly considered such a compliance system and decided against it because it seemed unwarranted, such good-faith inaction would be protected by the business judgment rule. See *Graham v. Allis Chalmers Manufacturing Co,* 188 A.2d 125 (Del. 1963) (refusing to holding directors liable for not instituting antitrust compliance program because there were no grounds to suspect it was needed).

According to some court dicta, unconscious inaction is not protected because the business judgment rule only protects the actual exercise of "business judgment." As a practical matter, however, it will be difficult to distinguish between inaction due to the press of other business and that due to sheer inattention.

§21.3.3   Gross Negligence

According to case law, directors who seek the protection of the business judgment presumption must make reasonable efforts to inform themselves. The question whether directors are sufficiently informed can arise in challenges of their supervisory and decision-making functions. In both contexts, the focus is on procedure. Recent courts have said that liability is based on "concepts of gross negligence."

Duty to Monitor.   Directors have oversight and monitoring functions that go beyond their function of making decisions at board meetings. Particularly in public corporations, directors are expected to monitor management, to whom is delegated the authority to run the day-to-day business. The monitoring duty requires directors to inquire into managers' competence and loyalty. A director cannot passively sit by, for example, if she knows that the corporation's treasurer is embezzling money.

Monitoring cases can arise when directors are inattentive either to *mismanagement* resulting from good-faith business mistakes or to *management abuse*. The results in the cases vary depending on which the negligent director failed to notice.

Inattention to mismanagement.   Courts have shown great reluctance to hold directors liable for failing to correct simple mismanagement, even when a director has been completely inattentive to her supervision functions. In *Barnes v. Andrews,* 298 F. 614 (S.D.N.Y. 1924) (Learned Hand, J.), an accommodation director whose "only attention to the affairs of the company consisted of talks with the president [who was a friend] as they met from time to time" was sued after the business failed because of disastrous business decisions by the president. Judge Hand concluded that, although he had technically breached his duty of care, the director could not be held liable because nothing indicated he could have avoided the failure. Learned Hand pointed out that it would be impossible to know if the director could have saved the business or how much of it he could have saved. Even if the inquiry were possible, the business judgment rule teaches that it should not be conducted by judges.

Nonetheless, the Supreme Court of Delaware recently rejected this causation analysis when directors fail to inform themselves in a negotiated sale of the company. In *Cede & Co. v. Technicolor, Inc.,* 634 A.2d 345 (Del. 1993), the court held that when directors breach their duty of care by not becoming sufficiently informed, the directors assume the burden to show that the transaction was nonetheless entirely fair, as to both its terms and the process of approval. That is, once the plaintiff shows a care breach, the causation issue becomes an affirmative defense, not an element of the plaintiff's case.

Inattention to management abuse.   The courts have taken a different view when a director fails to supervise management looting and defalcations. In fact, many of the cases that impose liability on directors for breaching their duty of care — particularly older bank cases — have involved directors who failed to rein in managers who had their hands in the corporate till. Liability in modern cases, many arising from the 1980s S&L scandals, hinges on whether the director knew or had reason to know about the management abuse — in effect, an "abetting" standard. Courts more readily infer knowledge of abuse in the case of management directors.

A modern, although not necessarily illustrative, example of these cases is *Francis v. United Jersey Bank,* 432 A.2d 814 (N.J. 1981). The widow of the founder of Pritchard & Baird, a closely held reinsurance brokerage business, was inactive on the board and knew virtually nothing about the business. Mrs. Pritchard did not read the firm's annual financial statements, which revealed that her sons were misappropriating client funds in the guise of "shareholder loans." The court held her liable for failing to become informed and make inquiries, and inferred that Mrs. Pritchard's laxity was a proximate cause of the losses to the corporation because she could have deterred the sons' illegal misappropriations.

Although *United Jersey Bank* might be understood to imply a duty of directors to inquire whenever management defalcation is possible, most modern cases do not go that far. Instead, inattentive directors are liable only if circumstances indicate they knew of the management diversion. *United Jersey Bank* can be explained by its peculiar facts. The suit was brought by a bankruptcy trustee against the widow and her two sons, the only directors. After her husband died, Mrs. Pritchard had become listless and had started to drink heavily. During the proceedings she died, and the suit proceeded against her estate, whose beneficiaries were presumably her sons. Adding the estate's assets to the bankruptcy pool may explain the court's duty-of-care analysis.

The requirement that directors know or suspect management abuse extends to the duty of directors to monitor management illegality. In *Graham v. Allis-Chalmers Manufacturing Co.,* 188 A.2d 125 (Del. 1963), the court held that the business judgment rule shielded directors who had failed to detect antitrust violations (criminal bid-rigging) by mid-level executives. According to the court, unless the director knew of or suspected the bid-rigging, they were not obligated to install a monitoring system. The Official Comment to RMBCA §8.30(a) reflects the same view: In matters of legal compliance, "the director may depend upon the presumption of regularity, absent knowledge or notice to the contrary."

Informed Decision-Making and the *Trans Union* Case. Many cases say the business judgment presumption only applies to directors whose decisions are informed. The requirement of informed decision-making goes beyond the requirement that decisions be rational. It assumes that diligent board deliberations ensure rational board action.

When are directors uninformed? Until recently, few cases have answered the question. The most famous answer, and perhaps the most important and controversial case of modern corporate law, is *Smith v. Van Gorkom* (the *Trans Union* case), 488 A.2d 858 (Del. 1985). In a 3-2 decision, the Delaware Supreme Court held that there was sufficient evidence to impose liability on the directors of Trans Union Corporation for not having been adequately informed when they approved the sale of the company in a negotiated merger. The case is remarkable: Except for those cases that involve board approval of self-dealing transactions and recent cases involving takeover defenses (see §40.2), no case before or since *Trans Union* has held directors liable (or upset their decision) because they had failed to become sufficiently informed during their decision-making process.

Trans Union's board consisted of five management directors and five eminently qualified outside directors. In 1980 the board approved a friendly cash-out merger at $55 per share, a price that offered shareholders a 40 to 60 percent premium over prevailing market prices. The sequence of events and the board's deliberations, described in great detail in the court's opinion, paint a picture of a CEO (Van Gorkom) who initiated, negotiated, and pushed through the board of directors a merger agreement whose terms may have been one-sided, favoring the acquirer (Pritzker). Shareholders challenged the merger and sought to hold the directors liable on a theory that they had failed to become sufficiently informed.

The court walked through a litany of the board's oversights: The directors had failed to inquire into Van Gorkom's role in setting the merger's terms; they had failed to review the merger documents; they had not inquired into the fairness of the $55 price and the value of the company's significant, but unused, investment tax credits; they had accepted without inquiry the view of the company's chief financial officer (Romans) that the $55 price was within a fair range; they had not sought an outside opinion from an investment banker on the fairness of the $55 price; and they acted at a two-hour meeting without prior notice and without there being an emergency.

The directors argued that despite their oversights they were entitled to rely on Van Gorkom's oral presentation outlining the terms of the merger and on Romans's opinion. But the court held no reliance was warranted: Van Gorkom did not explain that he, not Pritzker, suggested the $55 price; Van Gorkom had not read the merger documents; Van Gorkom did not tell the board that senior management strenuously objected to some aspects of the agreement, including the price; and the directors never questioned Romans about the basis for his opinion.

The *Trans Union* court rejected a number of arguments, any one of which would normally have foreclosed further inquiry under the business judgment rule: The $55 merger price both reflected a significant premium over the then-$38 market price and was within internally calculated leveraged buyout ranges; the directors had no reason to doubt Van Gorkom's assertion of the merger's fairness; the directors had significant business expertise and background knowledge of Trans Union's business; the board's approval was later conditioned on a "test market" during which other offers could be solicited; the board was operating under the time pressure of a Pritzker deadline; and outside counsel had advised the directors that they might be sued for turning away an attractive offer.

What if the board had asked, read, and heard those things it was charged with having failed to? At most, the directors would have learned that Van Gorkom had negotiated on his own initiative a deal with a personal and business acquaintance, had proffered a price during the negotiations at the low end of a credible range of fair value, and had agreed to a merger with some disadvantageous terms that senior management objected to. Even if the directors had been fully informed, as eventually happened at a later meeting when they re-approved the merger, there is little to suggest that they might have extracted a better deal. A fully informed approval surely would have passed the rational basis test. The court's second-guessing of boardroom procedures has been harshly criticized.

What was the *Trans Union* court doing? The case stands alone in holding directors liable for a rational decision as to which there were no allegations of bad faith or self-dealing.

Some commentators have suggested that the Delaware court was simply giving teeth to Delaware fiduciary law, which during the 1970s and early 1980s had come under heavy criticism for being too lax. The Trans Union board's failure to adequately consider the value of the company, including its unused tax credits, provided a convenient target for the court to assert itself.

Others have suggested that, although not alleged, the case had self-dealing overtones: Van Gorkom was reaching retirement age and the merger allowed him to realize an immediate $1.5 million increase in the value of his shareholding. The *Trans Union* dissent pointed out that the majority seemed to believe the directors had been victims of a Van Gorkom-Pritzker "fast shuffle."

Others have pointed out that a board's approval of a merger, which undermines shareholder buy-sell discretion and cuts off the disciplining effect of the markets, should be subject to more stringent review than typical management decisions (see §40.2).

Some commentators have even theorized that the *Trans Union* decision was meant to *promote* board discretion in future takeover cases: After the case, directors who receive an unsolicited offer for their company can put off the unwanted buyer on the ground that Delaware law requires them to take their time to first become fully informed. The *Trans Union* puzzle has not yet been solved.

§21.4　Remedies for Breaching the Duty of Care

If a challenger overcomes the business judgment presumption and shows the board's decision was uninformed or lacked a rational basis, any director who participated in the decision is liable for breaching a duty of care.

§21.4.1　Personal Liability of Directors

If a board action constitutes a care breach, courts have held that each director who voted for the action, acquiesced in it, or failed to object to it becomes *jointly and severally* liable for all damage that the decision proximately caused the corporation. Under most state statutes, a director who attends a meeting at which an action is approved is presumed to have agreed to the action, unless the minutes of the meeting reflect the director's dissent or abstention. RMBCA §8.24(d). Some statutes allow a director who has not voted for the action to register her dissent or abstention by delivering written notice at or immediately after the meeting. RMBCA §8.24(d).

　　Not every care breach creates liability. Many courts require the challenger to show the director's action (or inaction) proximately caused damage to the corporation; other courts permit the directors to negate an inference of harm by showing that the transaction was entirely fair. The proximate cause element takes on particular importance when a care breach is based on directorial inattention. As we have seen, courts have found proximate cause when directors disregard management abuse — itself unprotected by the business judgment rule. But when directors are inattentive to good-faith (but inept) mismanagement, courts have not been willing to make the causal finding.

§21.4.2　Enjoining a Flawed Decision

Courts can also enjoin or rescind board action unprotected by the business judgment doctrine (which insulates from review *board action,* as opposed to individual directors from damages). Because protecting directors from personal liability is not a concern of the business judgment doctrine, some commentators have suggested that it should be easier to enjoin corporate action than to impose personal liability. Nonetheless, courts have not explicitly distinguished between cases to impose personal liability and to enjoin board action.

§21.5　Limitations on Directors' Liability

After the *Trans Union* decision, a perception grew that service as a corporate director had become more risky. Insurance premiums for insurance against good-faith care breaches increased, and there were reports of directors who declined to serve for fear of liability exposure. In response, Delaware and other states enacted protective legislation. The statutes follow three patterns: (1) most (like Delaware) allow charter amendments shielding directors from personal liability for breaching their duty of care; (2) some statutorily mandate a standard of culpability higher than ordinary negligence; and (3) Virginia limits the amount for which a director can be held liable.

§21.5.1   Charter Options

Delaware allows shareholders to amend the corporation's charter to limit directors' *personal liability* for breaches of their duty of care, although directors remain liable for (1) breaches of their duty of loyalty, (2) acts or omissions not in good faith or that involve intentional misconduct or knowing illegality, (3) approval of illegal distributions, and (4) obtaining a personal benefit (such as by insider trading). Del. GCL §102(b)(7).

The RMBCA provides even greater protection to directors. The articles of incorporation can limit a director's liability for money damages to the corporation or shareholders, except liability for (1) the amount of financial benefit he received to which he is not entitled, (2) intentional infliction of harm on the corporation or its shareholders, (3) approving illegal distributions, or (4) an intentional violation of criminal law. RMBCA §2.02(b)(4). None of the "charter option" statutes, however, affects the granting of equitable relief.

§21.5.2   A Heightened Standard of Liability

Some statutes have codified the modern trend that directors are liable (and their decisions subject to review) only on a showing of gross negligence or recklessness. For example, Indiana requires "willful misconduct or recklessness." Ind. Code Ann. §23-1-35(1)(e)(2). The statutes do not permit the corporation to opt out.

§21.5.3   Liability Caps

Virginia combines both types of statutes. Its statute permits damages against directors only in cases of willful misconduct or knowing violations of criminal or securities laws, and then limits the amount of damages to a cap of the director's annual compensation or $100,000, whichever is greater. Shareholders can reduce (but not increase) this cap in the charter or bylaws. Va. Code Ann. §13.1-692.1.

§21.5.4   *The Effect of Statutory Limits on Directors' Liability*

Statutes that limit directors' liability raise some troublesome questions. Is it good policy to allow directors to escape their care responsibilities? Does shareholder approval of these limitations, particularly through proxy voting in a public corporation (see §18.1), provide meaningful assurances that shareholder interests are furthered? And, most important, do the statutes really change the legal norms to which directors are already subject under the business judgment rule?

Some commentators suggest the statutes may be irrelevant because care liability is largely illusory. In the few cases that hold directors liable for carelessness or inattention, the real explanations for liability (such as tacit approval of conflicts of interest) suggest the statutes would not apply. For example, if the Trans Union directors acceded to Van Gorkom's "fast shuffle," they arguably "acted not in good faith" and would not be protected under a Delaware §102(b)(7) charter limitation.

One study, however, strongly suggests that the participants in the stock market think the statutes eviscerate care liability and disserve shareholders. The study found that share prices of companies incorporated in Delaware fell 2.96 percent compared to companies incorporated in other jurisdictions over the months surrounding the effective date of the Delaware "charter option" statute. The study also found that Delaware corporations that adopted a charter limitation experienced a second significant drop in their stock prices. Bradley & Schiapani, The Relevance of the Duty of Care Standard in Corporate Governance, 75 Iowa L. Rev. 1 (1989).

EXAMPLES

1. J. R. Arnolds Tobacco (JRA) is incorporated in an RMBCA jurisdiction. The company, whose shares trade publicly, manufactures and sells cigarettes. It has annual sales of $5 billion and earnings of $800 million. Recently, JRA researchers have developed a "smokeless cigarette." Instead of inhaling tobacco smoke, users inhale powdered tobacco. Charles Edward O'Reilly, JRA's CEO, presents a plan to the board of directors proposing a five-year, $1 billion project to test, develop, and produce the new product, to be named "Chancellor." The board approves the plan.

    a. Sharon, a JRA shareholder, is convinced the plan is a huge mistake. She wants to stop the project. How and on what theory?

    b. Already JRA has spent $10 million developing Chancellor. Sharon wants the directors to refund this money to the corporation. On what theory might she sue the directors?

    c. Assume the Chancellor plan becomes a financial disaster. Without knowing more, what chance does Sharon have of succeeding on either claim?

2. As Sharon delves into the Chancellor project, she learns some things.
   a. A smokeless cigarette is not a new idea. Other major cigarette companies have considered it and uniformly rejected it. No other company has pursued a smokeless cigarette. Would this help Sharon's challenge of the Chancellor project?
   b. When the board met to approve Chancellor, CEO O'Reilly failed to tell the directors that other tobacco companies had considered the idea of a smokeless cigarette and had rejected it.
   c. O'Reilly told the board that consumer tests indicated 40 percent of smokers liked the concept of a smokeless cigarette. He failed to mention that the consumer tests also showed that 50 percent of the smokers who tried a prototype Chancellor said it tasted worse than cardboard and they would rather give up cigarettes than go smokeless. Would this support Sharon's challenge of the Chancellor project?
   d. O'Reilly intentionally misrepresented the consumer test results to promote the project. Does this affect O'Reilly's liability?
   e. J. Belmondo, JRA's vice president for product development and a member of the board, had heard of the results of the consumer tests, and he suspected that O'Reilly was leaving out some information. Is Belmondo liable for the company's losses?

3. Problems for the Chancellor project continue to mount. The Food and Drug Administration says a smokeless cigarette is a "drug" (because of its nicotine content) requiring FDA approval of its safety. At the next board meeting, O'Reilly reports on the FDA determination. Outside legal counsel opines that there is a good chance a court will reverse the FDA, and the board approves a lawsuit. The board does not change the schedule for the Chancellor project, which calls for the ground-breaking in six months of a new $500 million manufacturing plant.
   a. Is the board's failure to revise the schedule protected by the business judgment presumption?
   b. Sharon thinks going ahead with construction while a legal cloud hangs over the project would be the height of folly. On what theory can she challenge the board's failure to revise the schedule?

4. The board decides to continue the project and to choose a construction company by sealed bids. One of the companies expected to bid is ConReilly Inc., which is owned by members of CEO O'Reilly's family, though O'Reilly himself holds no shares. When the board sought bids, there was no indication whether ConReilly would submit a bid or that if it did the board would accept it. Does this affect whether the directors breached their duty of care in continuing the project?

5. The FDA ban on selling Chancellor is upheld in court, but the board accepts a bid and begins construction, hoping to pressure Congress to

act. After one year of construction, Congress still has not acted, and the board finally decides to scrap the project. A state court holds that the board's decision authorizing construction, though itself not illegal, was reckless in the face of the final FDA ban and not protected by the business judgment rule.

a. The minutes of the meeting at which continuing construction was approved reveal the following: director A was absent; director B did not participate in the decision approving continued construction; director C abstained from voting; and the remaining six directors voted to approve continued construction. Which directors can be held liable?

b. All told, the company lost $600 million in its failed "smokeless" experiment. What is the extent of the personal liability of nonparticipating director B, whose abstention or dissent would not have changed the director's approval?

c. Before embarking on the Chancellor project, JRA's articles of incorporation had been amended (pursuant to an authorizing statute) to absolve JRA directors from personal liability to the corporation except when the directors "act in bad faith." Will this provision insulate the directors from liability?

6. During the same meeting at which the board approved construction, the board approved a three-month test market of the new product in cities around the country. Despite the pending FDA ban, Chancellor was sold alongside regular cigarettes. When the FDA ban was upheld in court, the FDA fined the company $50 million for selling an unauthorized drug. The FDA, however, chose not to fine the directors individually.

a. On what theory could a shareholder argue that the directors are liable for the fine because they approved the test market?

b. Is business judgment protection lost because the directors approved smokeless cigarette sales at a time when they were banned by the FDA?

c. Should it make any difference in a shareholders' suit that the FDA chose not to fine the directors individually?

7. In addition to imposing fines, the FDA orders JRA to destroy all remaining Chancellor product in stock. Some of JRA's mid-level executives decide the FDA has gone too far and decide to sell the company's inventory overseas, where the smokeless cigarette is not prohibited. The inventory is shipped to an overseas port "for destruction" but from there is sold. The executives pocket 20 percent of the overseas receipts; the rest is accounted for as cigarette exports. The ruse is exposed, and the FDA fines JRA for violating its order. It is a major embarrassment for the company.

    a. Are the directors liable for failing to put into place a monitoring system that would have exposed the diversion by the rogue executives?

    b. Are the directors liable for failing to put into place a monitoring system that would have assured compliance with the FDA order?

EXPLANATIONS

1a. Sharon might bring a derivative action on behalf of the corporation against the directors. She could claim the directors violated their duty of care to the corporation by approving the plan. RMBCA §8.30(a) requires that directors reasonably believe that their actions are in the best interests of the corporation. Sharon might argue that the plan is improvident and that no reasonable director could believe it would maximize corporate returns. RMBCA §8.30(a) also requires that directors act with the care of an ordinarily prudent person. Sharon might argue that the directors did not have enough information concerning the risks of the Chancellor project.

1b. On the same grounds she sought to enjoin the plan, Sharon might claim that the directors be held liable for any damages caused by their duty-of-care violation. If the directors breached their care duties — because the plan is wasteful or the directors were grossly negligent in approving it — each director who approved it or was at the meeting and failed to object is liable (jointly and severally) for any losses the plan causes the corporation.

1c. Next to none. The board's approval of the Chancellor plan is protected by the presumptions of the business judgment rule, which applies despite the broadly worded standards of RMBCA §8.30(a). The rule insulates the board's decision from attack and shields the directors from liability. Unless Sharon can show (1) that the decision was tainted by fraud, illegality, or a conflict of interest; (2) that the board lacked a rational business purpose for the plan; or (3) that the directors were grossly uninformed in making the decision, courts presume that the directors did not breach their duty of care. Shareholders face dismal odds of proving a care breach.

2a. Probably not. Although industry antipathy to smokeless cigarettes might suggest that directors could not reasonably believe the project was in the best interests of the corporation, the business judgment rule is a formidable shield. To impose on corporate directors the same level of caution exercised by the rest of an industry would kill corporate risk-taking. Directors have wide latitude to experiment — and to fail — without being second-guessed or exposed to liability.

2b. Probably not. Although this information might be of relevance to ordinarily prudent directors, the business judgment rule teaches that courts should not second-guess the process of business decision-making. Directors, of necessity, make decisions on incomplete information, often based on hunches. Lawyers can always dream up inquiries that the directors could have made, but the business judgment rule does not require courtroom-like thoroughness. The rule allows directors to act in an indefinite business world on imperfect information.

2c. Perhaps. If O'Reilly's failure to mention the consumer tests was fraudulent — an intentional misrepresentation of a material fact — Sharon could argue that the board's approval of the Chancellor plan was unprotected by the business judgment presumption. If O'Reilly did not intend to deceive the directors, perhaps because he thought the adverse consumer tests were based on a deficient prototype, the business judgment presumption would apply.

   If Sharon can show fraud, a court could enjoin the Chancellor plan. The directors, however, would be personally liable only if their reliance on O'Reilly's lies was unwarranted. Directors are entitled to rely on information from company officials unless they have reason to know the official is unreliable. The cases on directors' monitoring duties suggest that directors are liable only if they should have known of management fraud or diversion.

2d. Yes. Officers and senior executives are subject to the same fiduciary duties as directors. RMBCA §8.42(a). Presumably, O'Reilly lied for some personal reason and the business judgment rule withdraws its protective presumption.

2e. Not necessarily. If Belmondo doubted that O'Reilly's report was inaccurate, he cannot claim reliance. RMBCA §8.30(c). Further, he might have had a duty to disclose his doubts to the other directors. Even if Belmondo breached a duty of care for not questioning O'Reilly, his liability is not automatic. Under the prevailing judicial approach, Sharon would have to show that Belmondo's silence was a proximate cause of any injury to the corporation. Doing so may be difficult because Belmondo might be able to point to other information that justified the Chancellor project. A court might decide that the inaccurate information about the consumer tests was not a proximate cause of the board's decision and the company's losses.

   In Delaware, however, Belmondo would bear the burden to show his failure to become informed was immaterial because the transaction was nonetheless entirely fair, both on the merits and in the way it was approved. See *Cede & Co. v. Technicolor, Inc.*, 634 A.2d 345 (Del. 1993) (§21.3.3). Under the facts, O'Reilly's deception negates a finding of fair dealing and thus entire fairness.

3a. Probably. The board's inaction appears to be conscious and, as such, is protected by the business judgment rule to the same extent as if the board had formally approved continuation of the plan. Even if the board simply neglected to reconsider the schedule, its inaction and the board's agenda should not be subject to judicial second-guessing — otherwise, derivative suit shareholders and judges could dictate the business agenda for a corporation.

3b. To overcome the business judgment presumption, Sharon would have to show that the board's failure to act on the Chancellor plan either was so improvident as to be beyond explanation or was grossly uninformed. It is unlikely she will succeed.

To show a breach of *substantive* care, Sharon would have to show the board proceeded without a rational business purpose. Any pretext will insulate the board's inaction from attack. For example, with anti-smoking sentiment growing, the board could speculate that a smokeless cigarette would fill an important market niche — there are potentially enormous profits. Moreover, beginning construction immediately will give the company a head start if the FDA, the courts, or Congress eventually allow the product to be sold. A final ban of the product is not certain: The FDA's assertion of jurisdiction might be overturned on appeal; the FDA might eventually authorize the product; Congress might decide to intervene (because of the jobs the plant will provide). A reasonable business person might conclude the *potential* benefits out-weigh the risks — which is enough under the rational basis test.

To show a breach of *procedural* care, Sharon would have to show that the board knew so little it could not have acted rationally. This will be difficult. The JRA board can point out that it knew of the FDA determination and relied on the opinion of counsel that a court might reverse it. Under the business judgment rule, the directors have signif-icant latitude to assess the risks and benefits of a course of action, even if only with sketchy information.

4. Yes. Courts have imposed heightened standards of care in cases that suggest a conflict of interest, even though the conflict is unproved or does not rise to a level that triggers a fairness review. O'Reilly's family ties to ConReilly and the *possibility* that the company would be awarded the contract probably are not enough to subject the board's decision to continue with the Chancellor project to a conflict-of-interest analysis. Nonetheless, a court might require more compelling justifications for allowing the project to go forward than it would in the absence of the ConReilly connection. The broad (and vague) care standards provide a convenient means for courts to adjust their scrutiny as the influence under which the board operates changes.

5a. Each director who was present at the meeting and failed to object or abstain from the action is assumed to have assented (RMBCA §8.24(d)) and may be held jointly and severally liable for the resulting loss suffered by the corporation. Under the RMBCA, therefore, the absent director is not liable, though some common law courts have imposed liability on directors who acquiesce in actions that constitute a breach of the duty of care. The abstaining director is not liable so long as the minutes of the meeting reflect his abstention. The nonparticipating director, however, is liable because he was present. Unless during or immediately after the meeting he delivered written notice of his abstention or dissent (a procedure authorized by the RMBCA), he is assumed to have acquiesced in the action. Finally, all the directors who approved the action are liable. Under the RMBCA, they have no right to dissent or abstain once they have voted for the action.

5b. Subject to statutory caps on director liability, B is jointly and severally liable (along with all the other liable directors) to the corporation for all losses proximately caused by the corporate action recklessly approved by the board — the authorization of construction after the FDA ban was upheld. By failing to dissent, the RMBCA presumes that B assented to the action. RMBCA §8.24(d). But neither B nor the other directors are liable for the full $600 million loss, only that portion attributable to what the court found was a breach of duty.

5c. Not with complete certainty. Although it would seem that because of the charter amendment the directors are not subject to personal liability for reckless imprudence, "bad faith" is a vague concept. It is a short step between finding the directors' action to have been "improvident beyond explanation" and finding that the directors acted in bad faith. Moreover, if the board's actions had self-dealing overtones, bad faith might be found. For example, if ConReilly's construction bid had been accepted by JRA as the winner, the board's obstinacy might be explained as an attempt to keep unneeded construction going for the benefit of the CEO's family.

6a. A shareholder could argue that the directors are liable for failing to act in good faith by approving illegal behavior. Earlier cases accepted this argument. A shareholder also could argue that the directors could not reasonably have believed that the test market was in JRA's best interests and that the business judgment presumption does not apply to their approval of corporate illegality. These arguments assume that corporate law should not provide a shield to those who disregard or flout the law. Imposing liability on directors promotes corporate responsibility.

6b. Not necessarily. Enforcing noncorporate norms in the name of fiduciary regulation highlights the question of using corporate law to enforce other legal requirements. The directors have two potential lines of defense. First, they could argue that their good-faith mistake about the law should be protected as any other good-faith business mistake. If the directors reasonably relied on the advice of counsel that sales during the test market ultimately would not be held illegal, they might be able to claim the protection of the business judgment rule. Directors, they could argue, are liable only for flouting the law and are not guarantors of legality. The business judgment presumption arguably is not overcome unless directors know or have reason to know their action is illegal. Second, the directors could argue that even if they knew the action was illegal, any liability should arise under the norms making the action illegal, not corporate law. If their action was, *from the standpoint of the corporation and shareholders,* taken in good faith, informed, and rational, the business judgment presumption would shield the directors from corporate liability. The corporation (or shareholders in a derivative action) should not be allowed to police noncorporate responsibilities.

6c. It depends on whether illegality should be viewed as a basis for corporate liability. The FDA action is irrelevant if directors can be liable for approving actions that they know or have reason to know are illegal. But if a decision to engage in illegal conduct is treated like any other business decision, the directors could argue that corporate law should not enforce responsibilities not enforced under the governing regulatory scheme. As a matter of corporate law, the directors could argue that they rationally believed the benefits of test marketing outweighed the risk of FDA fines — a business decision. That the directors were acting in good faith in the corporation's best interests is buttressed by the risk of personal FDA fines for approving the illegal sales.

7a. Perhaps. If the directors' failure to detect and prevent the management diversion was because of a failure to establish a monitoring system, under some views the directors are not protected by the business judgment rule. Although a conscious, explicit decision not to monitor might be protected if there were some reason for it, an unconscious failure to monitor might not be. When the issue is the monitoring of a potential diversion, care standards may be less filtered by the business judgment rule and may impose more exacting supervisory obligations. The case for monitoring is certainly strong if there were any indications that it was needed.

7b. Perhaps not. Although the question of monitoring illegality would seem to be the same as monitoring diversion, directors should have greater responsibility *as a matter of corporate law* to assure management integrity rather than corporate legality. Under this view, the directors need to monitor corporate legal compliance only when they know or have reason to know of the illegality. To impose on directors a watchdog function that exceeds their normally conceived function of maximizing shareholder wealth erodes the hands-off philosophy embodied in the business judgment rule.

22

Duty of Loyalty — Self-Dealing Transactions

A director's loyalty to the corporation is most tested when the director is on both sides of a transaction — that is, when the corporation enters into a transaction and the director both has a personal or financial interest in the transaction and is a member of the board of directors that authorizes it. Corporate law's suspicion of self-dealing transactions grows out of two basic assumptions:

Assumption 1: Human nature tells us the director will advance her own interests in the transaction, to the detriment of the corporation.

Assumption 2: Group dynamics will lead the other directors to identify with their interested colleague, even if they do not themselves have an interest in the transaction.

Despite these assumptions, modern corporate law allows self-dealing if it is "fair" to the corporation. Self-dealing transactions are tolerated because they often make business opportunities available to the corporation that are not available from outside third-party sources. That is, self-dealing transactions may sometimes be uniquely beneficial to the corporation. Fairness is a multifaceted concept — a director satisfies her duty of loyalty if the self-dealing transaction meets a mishmash of procedural and substantive tests.

§22.1   The Danger and Forms of Self-Dealing

§22.1.1   The Danger — Unfair Diversion of Corporate Assets

In its most flagrant form, self-dealing on unfair terms is like embezzlement. From the perspective of shareholders and others who have an interest in the corporation, there is little that distinguishes the case of a director who takes $100,000 from the corporate cash drawer and that of the director who sells swampland to the corporation for $102,000 when the land is worth no more than $2,000. Although the sale may appear to be a transaction made in the course of the corporation's business, the diversion is as real as if the director had personally misappropriated the difference between the land's fair value and the purchase price.

§22.1.2   Direct and Indirect Self-Interest

Self-dealing transactions with the corporation — sometimes referred to as *conflict-of-interest transactions* — fall into two broad categories.

   Direct interest.   In its simplest and classic form, self-dealing occurs when a director and the corporation are parties to the same transaction. RMBCA §8.60(1)(i). Examples include sales and purchases of property (including the corporation's stock), loans to and from the corporation, and the furnishing of services by a nonmanagement director such as a lawyer, accountant, or investment banker who sits on the board. (Although a form of self-dealing, the compensation of directors who are executives of the corporation is subject to special treatment, which we discuss in Chapter 23.) The director's conflicting interest creates an inherent risk that the transaction will not be in the corporation's best interests.

   Indirect interest.   The risk that the director will take advantage of the corporation can also arise even when the director is not a party to the transaction. If the transaction is between another person or another entity in which the director has a strong personal or financial interest, the danger of abuse is just as real. The courts generally look through the structure of the transaction to the substance of the director's interest. Self-dealing analysis has been applied to:

Transactions with the director's close relatives: A member of the director's family (or a family trust) enters into a transaction with the corporation. RMBCA §8.60(1)(i), (3).

Transactions with entities in which the director has a significant financial interest: A director of Corporation X is also a significant shareholder of Corporation Y or a partner of Partnership P, and X enters into a transaction with Y or P. RMBCA §8.60(1)(i), (ii).

Transactions between companies with interlocking directors: A director is on the boards of Corporation X and Corporation Y, and X enters into a transaction with Y. The director is self-dealing as concerns both X and Y. RMBCA §8.60(1)(ii). (If X and Y have a parent-subsidiary relationship, the problem of interlocking directors usually is subsumed in the question of a corporation's dealings with a controlling shareholder, which we treat in Chapter 26.)

In each case the other party's self-interest is traced to the director, whose imputed self-interest is assumed to taint the board's decision.

§22.2 Judicial Suspicion of Self-Dealing Transactions

§22.1.1 Flat Prohibition — The Early Rule of Voidability

Early courts accepted that the two basic self-dealing assumptions hold true in nearly all cases. Borrowing from the law of trusts, courts during the latter part of the nineteenth century flatly prohibited self-dealing by directors. Self-dealing was voidable at the request of the corporation, whether the transaction was fair or not. The rule assumed that self-dealing rarely offers the corporation business opportunities not obtainable from other sources and that it is improbable that "disinterested" directors — those who do not have a direct or indirect interest in the transaction — will be immune to the actual and tacit influence of their interested colleagues.

§22.2.2 Substantive and Procedural Tests Replace the Rule of Voidability

For unexplained reasons, the rule of voidability was abandoned at the turn of the century. Since then, courts have articulated a mishmash of substantive and procedural standards to test the validity of the self-dealing assumptions. Procedural fairness tests that focus on the board's decision-making process measure the validity of assumption 2 — that even disinterested directors will accede to interested colleagues. Substantive fairness tests that focus on the terms of the transaction measure the validity of assumption 1 — that the self-interested director will advance her own interests at the expense of the corporation's. Courts have combined these two types of tests into some rough rules:

Substantive fairness plus disinterested board approval. Self-dealing is valid if a court determines the transaction was fair to the corporation *and* if it was approved by a majority of disinterested directors. Both substantive and procedural fairness is required — assumptions 1 and 2 both must be overcome.

Exclusive substantive fairness. Self-dealing is valid if a court determines the transaction was fair on its merits; approval by a majority of disinterested directors is not necessary. Substantive fairness is sufficient — only assumption 1 need be rebutted.

Fairness or disinterested board approval. Self-dealing is valid if a court determines the transaction was fair on its merits *or* if it was approved by a majority of disinterested directors. Either substantive or procedural fairness is sufficient — it is enough if either assumption 1 or 2 is overcome.

Shareholder ratification. Self-dealing is valid if approved or ratified by a majority (or all) shareholders. Approval by disinterested directors is not necessary. Shareholders are trusted to decide that the self-dealing assumptions do not hold in a particular case.

Under the substantive test, the terms of the transaction are evaluated by a reviewing court. Under the procedural test, the board reviews the process by which the board or the shareholders evaluated the terms. Deciding which test (or tests) should apply boils down to a question of who should decide, and under what standard of review, whether the self-dealing transaction was in the corporation's best interests: the board of directors, the shareholders, or a judge?

§22.2.3   *Burden of Proof*

Once a party challenging a transaction has shown a director's conflicting interest, courts generally place the burden to prove the transaction's validity on the party seeking to uphold it. Forcing the challenger to show the transaction's lack of merit or deficiencies in the process of approval would impose a significant impediment to the challenger, inappropriately presuming the propriety of transactions that are presumptively inconsistent with shareholder wealth maximization.

Under process-oriented approaches proposed by the ALI Principles of Corporate Governance and adopted in Subchapter F of the RMBCA (see §22.4), the challenger has the burden to prove the transaction's invalidity when disinterested directors or shareholders have approved the conflict-of-interest transaction. ALI §5.02(b); RMBCA §8.61(b).

§22.2.4   *No Business Judgment Protection*

The conflict that permeates a self-dealing transaction rebuts the usual presumption of the business judgment rule that directors act in good faith (see §21.2). Regardless of which self-dealing standard applies, the business judgment presumption neither shields a self-dealing director from liability nor insulates the board's approval of the transaction from scrutiny.

Courts, however, have drawn a sharp distinction between self-dealing directors and so-called disinterested or independent directors — that is, those directors who have neither a direct nor indirect interest in the transaction and are not dominated by the interested director. The business judgment rule protects from personal liability disinterested directors who approve a self-dealing transaction in good faith (see §21.3.2).

§22.2.5 Self-Dealing by Officers and Senior Executives

In general, officers and senior executives are subject to the same self-dealing standards as directors. See ALI §5.02(a), comment d. Nonetheless, because officers and senior executives generally will be expected to devote themselves primarily, if not exclusively, to the corporation, some cases indicate that such persons' transactions with the corporation are judged under more exacting standards.

§22.3 The "Fairness" Test

When is a self-dealing transaction "fair" to the corporation?

§22.3.1 Nonvoidability Statutes — Inconclusive

Many modern statutes codify the abandonment of the flat prohibition against self-dealing but do not explicitly specify when self-dealing is valid. A good example is Delaware's "interested director" statute. Del. GCL §144. Similar to the former RMBCA §8.31(a), the statute states that a transaction "*shall not be void or voidable solely for the reason*" that a director (or an entity in which the director has an interest) is a party to a transaction with the corporation if:

(1) the material facts are disclosed to the board, and a majority of disinterested directors authorized the transaction; or

(2) the material facts are disclosed to the shareholders, and the shareholders vote to approve the transaction (under some statutes the shareholders must be disinterested); or

(3) a judge determines the transaction to be fair.

Although the disjunctive "or" suggests that the statute creates a "safe harbor" for self-dealing transactions approved after full disclosure by disinterested directors or by a majority of shareholders, most courts have construed the statutes narrowly as merely removing the shadow of automatic voidability. *Fliegler v. Lawrence*, 361 A.2d 218 (Del. 1976); *Remillard Brick Co. v. Remillard-Dandini Co.*, 241 P.2d 66 (Cal. App. 1952). These courts have held that just because a transaction was approved by disinterested directors or shareholders does not displace the court's role to assure the transaction's fairness.

§22.3.2   *"Substantive Fairness" — The Dominant Judicial Standard*

A *substantive fairness standard,* first articulated in the 1940s and generally accepted by the 1960s, is the prevalent *nonstatutory* standard for judicial review of self-dealing transactions. A court will accept a self-dealing transaction's substantive fairness — fairness on the merits — only when it is convinced that the corporation's interests won out over those of the interested director. Under this standard, even if all the directors who approved the transaction were interested or dominated by the interested director, the transaction is valid if a court finds it to have been fair. By the same token, even if fully informed disinterested directors approve the transaction, the transaction's merits remain subject to judicial scrutiny.

Substantive fairness has two aspects. It is first an objective test of whether the self-dealing transaction replicates an arm's-length market transaction by falling into a range of reasonableness. Courts carefully scrutinize the terms of the transaction — principally the price. Second, the transaction must be of particular value to the corporation, as judged by the corporation's needs and the scope of its business. Both aspects of the fairness test involve significant judicial meddling into business matters. *Shlensky v. South Parkway Building Corp.,* 166 N.E.2d 793 (Ill. 1960); see Official Comment to RMBCA §8.61 (Note on Fair Transactions).

Some of the cases and commentators suggest that substantive fairness is a flexible concept that varies with the degree of self-interest. That is, as a director's interest in a self-dealing transaction is more (or less) direct, the level of scrutiny increases (or decreases) concomitantly. For example, transactions between corporations with interlocking directors are subject to less scrutiny than transactions with directors in their personal capacity. The RMBCA reflects this different treatment and subjects transactions between corporations with interlocking directorates to conflict-of-interest analysis only if the transaction is so large that in the normal course it would require board approval. RMBCA §§8.60(1)(ii), 8.61(a).

§22.3.3   *"Procedural Fairness" — The Process of Board Approval*

Despite the prevalence of the substantive fairness standard, the process of approval continues to be relevant. In Delaware, for example, even though the judicial "entire fairness" standard for squeeze-out mergers gives predominant consideration to "fair price," there is also a separate requirement of "fair dealing." *Weinberger v. UOP, Inc.*, 457 A.2d 701 (Del. 1983) (see §26.3.3).

Judicial review of the process of approval examines basic assumption 2 — that directors (even disinterested ones) will accede to their interested colleague. Was the board influenced by the interested director or did it act independently to further the corporation's best interests? In reviewing the process, courts have focused on three procedural elements: (1) disclosure about the transaction to the board, (2) the composition of the board (or committee) that approved the transaction, and (3) the role of the interested director in the transaction's initiation, negotiation, and approval.

Disclosure. Even when courts find self-dealing to be fair on the merits, courts have invalidated the transaction if there was fraud in connection with its approval. Where there is no fraud but only allegations of less than full disclosure, courts have taken a variety of approaches. Some courts have said that full disclosure is a factor bearing on the transaction's fairness; others have required that there be disclosure only of the conflict of interest to put the board on guard; still others have required full disclosure of all material information, including the profit the interested director stood to make in the transaction. Each approach reflects different assumptions about whether full disclosure will give the board a meaningful opportunity to review the merits of the proposed self-dealing transaction and to decline (or negotiate) more favorable terms. See ALI Principles, comment to §5.02(a)(1).

Disinterested Approval. Some courts, applying a less exacting standard of fairness, have treated with deference self-dealing transactions approved by disinterested directors. Other courts have even held that there is a presumption of fairness — and have shifted the burden of proving unfairness to the plaintiff — if the self-dealing is approved by a majority of disinterested directors. The ALI Principles combine both a burden-shifting and modified fairness standard; the new Subchapter F of the RMBCA makes disinterested approval conclusive.

Who is a "disinterested" director? Under most court formulations, a director is disinterested if (1) he is not directly or indirectly interested in the transaction — that is, he has no financial or close family ties to the transaction that would affect his judgment; and (2) he is not dominated by the interested director. Domination is a slippery concept. It means more than being selected by the interested director to serve on the board. Instead, a director is dominated when he acts as requested without independent judgment. *Gries Sports Enterprises, Inc. v. Cleveland Browns Football Co.*, 496 N.E.2d 959 (Ohio 1986) (applying Delaware law).

The ALI Principles define "disinterested director" as one who is neither a party to the transaction nor is indirectly interested (or influenced) in such a way that it can reasonably be expected the director's judgment will be affected adversely. ALI §1.18. New Subchapter F uses an objective test that defines "qualified director" as one who is not a party to the transaction, does not have a beneficial financial interest that would influence the director's judgment, and has no familial, financial, professional, or employment relationship that would influence the director's vote on the transaction. RMBCA §8.60.

Role of Interested Director in the Process of Approval.   Although earlier cases held that negotiation of the deal by the interested director or her participation in the board's decision-making process negated the transaction's validity, many modern statutes and recent self-dealing cases allow the interested director to negotiate, participate, and vote without necessarily undermining the transaction's validity. See former RMBCA §8.31 (replaced by new Subchapter F). An interested director's negotiation or participation, however, may be inadvisable because it may indicate that the interested director dominated the other directors, thus undermining the advantage of disinterested approval.

Many modern statutes facilitate disinterested approval by easing quorum requirements for self-dealing transactions. Some statutes dispense with quorum requirements if the self-dealing transaction is approved by a majority of (but at least two) disinterested directors. See RMBCA §8.62(c); former §8.31(c). These statutes overrule the early common law rule that self-dealing could not be approved unless disinterested directors constituted a quorum of the full board. Other statutes allow interested directors to be counted for quorum purposes, even though they do not participate at the meeting.

§22.3.4   Shareholder Ratification of Self-Dealing Transactions

Courts have shown substantial deference to self-dealing transactions approved or ratified by a majority of informed, disinterested shareholders.

Ratification by a Majority of Shareholders.   Where a majority of the shares are cast by shareholders who neither have an interest in the transaction nor are dominated by those who do, most courts do not require that a defendant show "fairness." Instead, courts generally shift the burden to the plaintiff to show either: (1) the transaction constituted waste — that is, no person of ordinary sound business judgment would say that the consideration was fair (see §21.3.2); (2) the shareholders were uninformed; (3) the transaction was illegal (see §21.3.1); or (4) the transaction was ultra vires because of a prohibition in the articles of incorporation (see §4.2). See *Aronoff v. Albanese,* 446 N.Y.S.2d 368 (App. Div. 1982) (applying waste standard).

This remarkably weaker standard of review assumes that disinterested shareholders, including those in a public corporation, will identify and act in their own best interests. Other courts are unwilling to make the assumption of shareholder autonomy and merely shift the burden of proving unfairness to the party challenging the transaction. *Michelson v. Duncan*, 407 A.2d 211 (Del. 1979); *Gottlieb v. Heyden Chemical Corp.*, 91 A.2d 57 (Del. 1952).

Courts remain suspicious of self-dealing transactions if shareholder ratification is by a majority of shareholders who were interested in the transaction. *Fliegler v. Lawrence*, 361 A.2d 218 (Del. 1976); *Remillard Brick Co. v. Remillard-Dandini Co.*, 241 P.2d 66 (Cal. App. 1952) (leaving burden with defendants to show "intrinsic fairness" of transaction ratified by interested shareholders). Under some conflict-of-interest statutes, including the RMBCA, shares voted by an interested shareholder cannot be counted for purposes of shareholder ratification. RMBCA §8.63(b); former §8.31(d). Nonetheless, many statutes permit a majority of shares held by disinterested shareholders to constitute a quorum. RMBCA §8.63(c); former §8.31(d).

Unanimous Ratification. If self-dealing is ratified unanimously by all the shareholders or by a sole shareholder, courts agree that it cannot be set aside even under a waste standard, so long as there is no injury to creditors. Effective ratification depends on full disclosure to shareholders of the director's conflicting interest.

§22.4 "Safe Harbors" — Informed Approval by Disinterested Directors or Shareholders

Because of the confusing overlap of these substantive and procedural standards, Subchapter F of the RMBCA and the ALI Principles of Corporate Governance adopt *safe harbor tests* to provide greater planning certainty and to assure the validity of self-dealing transactions if properly approved. These approaches question the validity of assumption 2 — that disinterested directors will predictably accede to an interested colleague.

§22.4.1 RMBCA Subchapter F

Subchapter F of the RMBCA provides that a conflict-of-interest transaction is valid if either (1) disclosed and approved by a majority (but not less than two) of disinterested directors, *or* (2) disclosed and approved by a majority (not less than two) of disinterested shareholders, *or* (3) shown to be fair, whether or not disclosed. RMBCA §§8.61-8.63.

The official comments to Subchapter F state that judicial review of an informed decision by disinterested directors would be limited to the "care, best interests, and good faith criteria" of RMBCA §8.30 (see §21.1.1). Nonetheless, the official comments suggest this review may be less deferential than traditional business judgment review, and a court could invalidate a transaction if it determined the terms of the self-dealing transaction "were manifestly unfavorable to the corporation."

Judicial review of shareholder validation, however, is limited to the process of approval: Was there approval by a majority of disinterested shareholders? Did the interested director provide the requisite notice and disclosure of the conflict? Did the interested director notify the company's vote tabulator of the shares he owns or controls? Even when some shareholders vote against the transaction, neither the RMBCA provisions nor the comments suggest the court should engage in any substantive review — such as waste review — if the process was sufficient.

Some commentators have criticized Subchapter F for effectively removing self-dealing substantive review from the courts and placing it in the hands of disinterested directors or passive shareholders. The Subchapter, which was adopted in 1988, has not been well-received in states adopting the RMBCA. As of 1993, only 5 of the 35 RMBCA states have included the subchapter.

§22.4.2 ALI Principles of Corporate Governance

The ALI Principles of Corporate Governance also adopt a safe-harbor approach. The Principles recommend a disjunctive test under which self-dealing is valid if *after full disclosure* (A) a court finds the transaction was fair when entered into, *or* (B) a majority of disinterested directors (not less than two) approved or ratified the transaction, *or* (C) a majority of disinterested shares approved or ratified the transaction. ALI §5.02.

The ALI Principles contemplate a mild judicial review of the substance of a self-dealing transaction validated by disinterested directors. The court must conclude the transaction "could reasonably be believed to be fair to the corporation." ALI §5.02(a)(2)(B). The burden, however, is on the plaintiff to show that disclosure was inadequate, that the approving directors were not independent, or that the transaction fails this watered-down fairness standard.

Unlike the RMBCA, the ALI Principles specify that self-dealing transactions validated by shareholders remain subject to judicial review under a waste standard. Thus, minority shareholders who vote against the transaction can still complain if no reasonable business person would conclude the corporation received fair benefit. (§21.3.2)

According to the ALI Principles, it is also possible for disinterested directors or disinterested shareholders to authorize in advance specified types of self-dealing transactions that can be expected to recur in the company's ordinary course of business. ALI Principles §5.09(a). This standard must be stated in the articles or bylaws or by board or shareholder resolution. ALI Principles §1.36.

§22.5   Remedies for Self-Dealing

§22.5.1   *The General Remedy — Rescission*

As a general matter, an invalid self-dealing transaction is voidable at the election of the corporation — either in a direct action or in a derivative suit. The general remedy is rescission, which returns the parties to their position before the transaction. Normally, the corporation cannot seek to "renegotiate" the terms of the transaction by retaining the transaction's benefits but at a lower price. The theory is that self-dealing transactions may provide value to the corporation, and a director who negotiates a self-dealing transaction should not be exposed to the risk that the corporation use a fairness challenge to renegotiate the deal.

§22.5.2   *Exceptions to Rescission*

A rescission remedy does not always work — such as when self-dealing is also the usurpation of a corporate opportunity, or the property has been resold and is no longer held by the original party. In such cases, the corporation may be entitled to damages instead of rescission.

If a director enters into a transaction with the corporation and the transaction is a "corporate opportunity" that belongs to the corporation, a remedial scheme that forces the corporation to choose between disaffirming the opportunity or accepting it (and forgoing a claim for the director's profits) would allow the director to take a profit that "belongs" to the corporation. In such cases, without rescinding the transaction, the corporation can require that the director account for any profits he has made in the deal.

For example, in *New York Trust Co. v. American Realty Co.*, 155 N.E. 102 (N.Y. 1926), a director of International Paper purchased timberland and, after a few months, resold it to the corporation at a significant profit. Although the transaction was voidable under the then-prevalent "validation plus fairness" test because the director dominated the board, the corporation chose not to rescind. Although the court stated that normally rescission is the exclusive remedy, it held that the director could be liable for his profits on an "agency" (or "corporate opportunity") theory without the transaction being rescinded. By being forced to account for his profits, the director became liable as though he had sold the timberland to a third party — a valuable opportunity of the corporation.

EXAMPLES

1. Last year major league baseball approved two new expansion teams, one in Washington, D.C. The team, to be known as the D.C. Bureaucrats, is incorporated in an RMBCA jurisdiction that has adopted Subchapter F. The largest shareholder is Martha Post (40 percent); the remaining shares are held publicly, mostly by rabid Beltway fans. Martha is the chairman of the board and CEO. She hand-picked the other four directors: Abner (her brother-in-law), Baker (the company's outside counsel), Connor (a prominent Washington bureaucrat), and Duncan (a prominent Washington businessman).

    a. R-E-K Services operates a successful food concession business on the east coast and has submitted a bid to operate the Bureaucrats's food and beverage concessions. Martha serves on the board of directors of R-E-K; Abner is a 25 percent shareholder of R-E-K. Is there any problem if the Bureaucrats accept the R-E-K bid?

    b. The Bureaucrats's bylaws specify that three directors constitute a quorum at board meetings. Martha wants to delegate to Connor and Duncan the decision to accept R-E-K's bid. Will the two be able to conduct a meeting?

    c. Martha calls a meeting to consider the R-E-K bid. Neither she nor Abner attend. Duncan opposes the bid and decides not to attend, either. Can Baker and Connor approve the bid?

    d. Baker and Connor adjourn their meeting to ask Martha for information about other bidders seeking the concession business. Martha attends their reconvened meeting, answers their questions, and votes to approve the R-E-K bid. Baker and Connor also vote to approve. Does Martha's presence and participation at the meeting undermine the board's action?

2. Mitch, a Bureaucrats shareholder who has waited 20 years for baseball in D.C., thinks the R-E-K contract is a sour "sweetheart" deal. R-E-K's three-year contract calls for a flat payment of $2 million per year.

    a. Mitch wants the R-E-K contract invalidated. Assuming the bid was approved by Baker and Connor, who should he sue and what will he have to show?

    b. Mitch discovers that Martha never disclosed to the board that R-E-K had decided that $1.5 million was the lowest price it would accept. Does Martha's failure to disclose R-E-K's reservation price nullify the board's approval?

    c. R-E-K's three-year contract calls for a flat payment of $1 million per year and an additional $50,000 for each 100,000 fans who attend Bureaucrats games during the season. Happieaux Corporation, another well-established food concessionaire and the only other bidder, had bid a flat $2 million per year. The board estimated annual attendance would average more than 2 million fans and chose the R-E-K bid. Is the R-E-K contract valid?

   d. Mitch discovers an internal Bureaucrats study that projects attendance of 1.6 million during the first season, 1.8 million the second, and 2.0 million the third. The study concludes that first year attendance above 2.0 million is possible but unlikely. Martha failed to disclose this study to the board. Does this invalidate the R-E-K contract?

3. A few weeks after the board approves the R-E-K bid, Martha proposes a shareholder resolution to be included in the company's upcoming proxy solicitation. The resolution would ratify the R-E-K contract and declare the shareholders' view that it is "completely fair to the corporation." The company's proxy statement sets forth fully the terms of the R-E-K contract and a statement that management expects annual attendance above 2 million.

   a. Martha owns 40 percent of Bureaucrats stock, and the resolution passes by a bare 55 percent of the outstanding shares. A vocal 30 percent vote against the resolution. What effect does this shareholder ratification have on Mitch's challenge to the contract?

   b. Assume the Bureaucrats articles of incorporation provide:

> Any conflict-of-interest transaction between the Corporation and any director (or entity in which any director is interested) is conclusively valid if approved by a vote of a majority of the outstanding Shares. The Shares of any interested director may participate fully in such a vote.

     Does this affect the outcome of Mitch's challenge?

   c. Assume Martha did not vote and a majority of disinterested shareholders had ratified the R-E-K contract, although their shares did not constitute a majority quorum. Would this vote affect Mitch's challenge to the contract?

4. The court rules that shareholder ratification was defective because the proxy statement failed to disclose Happieaux's bid. The court then rules that the transaction was unfair to the Bureaucrats.

   a. Mitch wants the court to increase the royalties under the contract to at least what Happieaux had offered, which the court agreed was a fair price. Will the court order R-E-K to pay damages?

   b. Mitch also sued Baker and Connor, the disinterested directors who approved the R-E-K contract. Are they liable for the damages the R-E-K contract caused the corporation?

EXPLANATIONS

1a. Yes. The concession agreement could be rescinded as a self-dealing transaction because of Martha's and Abner's conflicting interest in R-E-K. It would seem Abner's 25 percent shareholding in R-E-K creates a "beneficial financial interest" that "would reasonably be expected to influence his judgment." See RMBCA §8.60(1)(i). Martha, because of her position as a director of the other party, has divided loyalties. See RMBCA §8.60(1)(ii). Moreover, if her relationship with Abner is such that she would gain financially because of his R-E-K holdings, she might have a further "beneficial financial interest" that would cloud her judgment. See RMBCA §8.60(1)(i). These interests could lead Abner and Martha as Bureaucrats directors to advance R-E-K's interests at the expense of the Bureaucrats. And their position on the Bureaucrats board raises the possibility that the Bureaucrats directors will accede to their wishes.

1b. Yes. Under RMBCA §8.62(c), as under most modern statutes, there is no quorum requirement if a majority of disinterested directors, but not less than two, approve a self-dealing transaction. The RMBCA and other modern statutes relax the quorum requirement for the approval of self-dealing transactions so that such transactions can be passed on without interested directors having to attend, thus facilitating disinterested review and approval by the board. If Connor and Duncan are disinterested, they would constitute a quorum.

1c. Perhaps. It depends on whether Baker (the company's outside lawyer) and Connor (the outside bureaucrat) are disinterested. If they are, the two of them will be fully capable — as a majority of disinterested directors — to approve the self-dealing transaction, despite Duncan's absence. RMBCA §8.62(a).

Are Baker and Connor disinterested? Even if he does not have a financial interest in the R-E-K deal, Baker would be interested if Martha "dominates" his activities as a director. This involves a factual appraisal of motives and loyalties. As Justice Frankfurter once admonished judges, "[W]e should not be ignorant as judges of what we know as men." If Baker helped structure and negotiate the R-E-K deal for Martha, his impartiality would have to be questioned. Further, if Baker as director normally did as Martha instructed, his independence would be in doubt. Without Baker, Connor (however disinterested she might be) cannot alone approve the R-E-K bid. RMBCA §8.62(a).

1d. No. Like Delaware's "director interest" statute, the RMBCA does not invalidate action by the board just because of the presence or vote of an interested director. RMBCA §8.62(c); Del. GCL §144.

2a. Mitch should bring a derivative action (see Chapter 31) on behalf of the corporation and name the interested directors, Martha and Abner, and the approving directors, Baker and Connor. If he can establish that the approval was flawed or if the directors fail to show the transaction was fair, the corporation can rescind the transaction. The business judgment rule would not apply, and there would be no presumption of validity.

2b. Probably not. The RMBCA safe harbor for self-dealing approved by disinterested directors requires that the interested directors disclose the "existence and nature of their conflicting interest" and all facts known to them about the transaction that an "ordinarily prudent person would reasonably believe to be material" to whether or not to proceed. RMBCA §8.60(4). This duty to disclose *material* information puts the director in the odd position of acting both as a fiduciary and as a self-interested outsider. The RMBCA official comments recognize this and suggest the director need not disclose all material information, but only that information the corporation would normally be able to ascertain before entering an arms' length negotiation. Thus the director need not "reveal personal or subjective information that bears on the director's negotiating position," such as "the lowest price he would be willing to accept."

To require Martha to reveal R-E-K's reservation price (assuming she knows it) would put R-E-K in a less advantageous position than other bidders without interlocking directors. The purpose of the self-dealing statute is to ensure that any conflict-of-interest transaction replicates what the corporation would have obtained in arms' length negotiation — no more.

2c. It depends on the soundness of the attendance estimates. The R-E-K variable price is better than the fixed Happieaux price if the attendance estimates are valid. If the transaction was approved by a majority of disinterested directors, the RMBCA's safe-harbor provision would limit judicial review to whether the attendance assumptions underlying the board's decision to accept the R-E-K bid were "manifestly unreasonable." Were they based on "best case" or "worst case" scenarios? Were they based on the experience of other expansion teams or advance ticket sales in the D.C. market? Were they prepared by Martha or someone uninterested in the R-E-K bid? Although the RMBCA official comments are not clear on the point, the standard of review would appear to be less deferential than under the business judgment rule but more deferential than under the traditional fairness standard.

If the estimates were not manifestly unreasonable, the RMBCA's safe-harbor provisions compel a court to respect the business decision of the disinterested directors. Some cases suggest that this is also the common law approach, even in jurisdictions with only a nonvoidability statute. See *Puma v. Marriott*, 283 A.2d 693 (Del. Ch. 1971) (upholding "independent business judgment" of disinterested directors who initiated and negotiated purchases from company's controlling family). The challenger carries a heavy burden of showing something akin to waste.

2d. Not necessarily. The contract is not protected by the safe harbor for disinterested director approval, but a court may nonetheless conclude it was fair. The RMBCA's safe harbor provision, like the prevailing fairness review, permits judicial inquiry into the process of approval. The *Weinberger* fair dealing approach (see §23.3.3) requires that the process of negotiation and approval of the self-dealing transaction must conform to what would be expected of an independent board. This means the interested director must disclose all *material* information, and the approving directors may neither be interested in the transaction nor influenced by the interested director. If the undisclosed attendance study would have added to information the board had on attendance estimates, it could be expected that Martha would have disclosed it if she were not interested. As such, it is material, and the board's approval does not insulate the transaction from review.

There remains the question, however, whether the transaction was substantively fair at the time it was entered into. RMBCA §8.61(b)(3). It may still be that other higher attendance estimates were more reliable and R-E-K's bid was superior to Happieaux's. It may also be that R-E-K offered superior nonprice terms, such as services offered, concessionaire's upkeep responsibilities, and so on. In short, the transaction was fair if a disinterested board would have accepted the R-E-K bid in an arm's length negotiation. The burden will be on the interested director to show this.

3a. Very little. The resolution was not approved by a majority of shares held by disinterested shareholders. RMBCA §8.62(a), (b) (safe harbor requires majority of qualified shares be cast for transaction; qualified shares are those not owned or controlled by the interested director). In fact, 50 percent of disinterested shares were cast against the resolution and only 25 percent were cast for it. The burden will fall on Martha and the other defendants to show the transaction's fairness.

3b. Perhaps, but only mildly. The RMBCA allows for the articles of incorporation to contain limits on the power of the board and shareholders. RMBCA §2.02(b)(5). But this provision would effectively gut judicial review of self-dealing if the interested director, as here, controls the proxy mechanism or holds a significant block of stock. Just as courts have been unwilling to read statutory provisions such as former RMBCA §8.31(a) as displacing judicial review of self-dealing transactions, there may be judicial reluctance to give such an exculpatory provision full effect. It is possible, as has happened in some cases, that the reviewing court would merely shift the burden of proof to the challenger to show unfairness.

The ALI Principles permit corporate parties to pre-approve self-dealing transactions in the articles, but this dangerous practice is limited to "specified types" of self-dealing transactions that "can be expected to recur in the company's ordinary course of business." ALI Principles §5.09(a). The carte blanche provision in the Bureaucrats articles would not be binding.

3c. Yes. Mitch would have to show some defect in the process of approval. Otherwise, the RMBCA safe-harbor provision treats the shareholder ratification as conclusive without further judicial review even into the transaction's merits. RMBCA §8.63. This is a significant departure from the prevailing judicial approach in such cases either to shift the burden to the challenger or to require a showing of waste.

The failure of the disinterested shareholders to constitute a quorum is not a problem. The RMBCA, like many other statutes, requires only a majority of disinterested shares to constitute a quorum. RMBCA §8.63(c). The failure of Martha to disclose the terms of the competing Happieaux bid or the study estimating attendance would be less than 2 million may be grounds to nullify the shareholder ratification. Like approval by disinterested directors, shareholder approval must be accompanied with disclosure of all *material* facts known to the interested director.

4a. Probably not. The usual remedy for unfair self-dealing is rescission of the transaction. This assures the self-dealing insider that the corporation cannot unilaterally revise the terms of the transaction in a fairness challenge. If the royalties are indeed inadequate, the solution is to rescind the R-E-K contract and for the corporation to find a better contract, presumably with Happieaux. In smaller corporations self-dealing transactions may be uniquely valuable, offering the corporation and shareholders business opportunities not otherwise available on the open market. The rescission-only rule keeps courts out of the business of reforming private arrangements.

4b. Probably not. Since they were not interested in the transaction, they are liable only if they violated their duties of care. If they rationally believed that they were acting in the corporation's best interests and sought information about the R-E-K contract, their liability for approving the contract is shielded under the business judgment rule (see §21.3).

23

Executive Compensation

Despite the relatively searching scrutiny to which courts subject asset transactions between a director and the corporation, courts have shown special deference when the director offers the corporation his executive services. When approved by disinterested directors, executive compensation is subject to business judgment review.

§23.1 Forms of Executive Compensation

Modern executives are compensated *directly* in a number of ways:

Salaries and bonuses. Base salaries and bonuses generally provide compensation for current services.

Stock plans. Stock grants, stock options, and other plans based on stock value create incentives for executive performance in the future; their purpose is to align management and shareholder interests. A *stock grant* by the corporation provides the executive with a shareholding stake in the business but dilutes other shareholders' interests. A *stock option* granted by the corporation gives an employee the option during a specified period to buy a specified amount of the company's stock at a fixed price. If the market price for the company's stock rises, exercising the option becomes highly profitable; if the price falls and the option is not exercised, no shares are issued and the corporation's capital is not diluted. *Phantom stock plans* and *stock appreciation rights* provide similar incentives without the corporation having to issue any stock (or, for that matter, have any stock authorized in the articles). The executive is credited with units on the corporation's books, and the value of the units rises or falls with the market price of the company's stock (including dividends and stock splits). The units' value is not paid until a specified date, such as retirement or death.

Pension plans.   Pension plans and other forms of deferred compensation provide executives with retirement income. Plans that are qualified under the Internal Revenue Code make it possible for the corporation to immediately deduct contributions into the plan, even though the executive is not taxed until later.

Executives are also compensated *indirectly* with fringe benefits (perks), such as expense accounts, company residences, and the use of corporate jets.

§23.2   Judicial Review of Executive Compensation

§23.2.1   *The Dilemma of Scrutinizing Executive Compensation*

Senior executives, particularly in public corporations, have significant sway over board decision-making (see §11.3). The board's setting of executive compensation raises many of the same concerns as are raised in any other self-dealing transaction: (1) The executive predictably will prefer his own interests; and (2) the board will predictably accede to the executive's wishes, at the expense of corporate interests.

But treating executive compensation like any other self-dealing transaction would force courts to place a value on a particular executive's services to the corporation, often without a working knowledge of the corporation or expertise in setting executive compensation. Some commentators argue further that judicial deference is warranted because a labor market in managerial services forces managers to stay honest and, in most large corporations, executive compensation is linked significantly to corporate performance. Others, however, have looked at multimillion dollar executive compensation packages and have questioned the sufficiency of market limits acting alone.

§23.2.2   *Compensation Must Be Authorized*

Like any other transaction with the corporation, executive employment contracts must be properly authorized (see §14.1.1). The articles must authorize the issuance of shares (RMBCA §2.02), and transactions involving the corporation's stock (such as stock grants, options, or repurchases) require board approval. RMBCA §6.24. In public corporations, the board often delegates the task of reviewing and approving executive compensation to a committee of outside directors. RMBCA §8.25(d).

Whether a director interested in his own compensation can be counted for quorum purposes, or vote for his own compensation, raises the same questions as in other self-dealing transactions. Some statutes authorize approval by less than a quorum of directors if at least two disinterested directors approve the compensation.

§23.2.3 Fairness Review Avoided by Disinterested Approval

Executive compensation is not subject to fairness review if the compensation was approved by informed, disinterested directors. The board must be aware of all material information related to the executive's compensation, and the interested executive cannot dominate the board's decision-making (see §22.3.3). Courts have held that "back-scratching" approval — where officer-directors tacitly agree to approve each other's compensation, although each interested executive steps out while his compensation is considered — does not satisfy the requirement of disinterested approval. *Stoiber v. Miller Brewing Co.*, 42 N.W.2d 144 (Wis. 1950). But courts consider approval to be disinterested if nonmanagement (outside) directors or a committee of outside directors make compensation recommendations to the full board, even if the outside directors or committee are less than a quorum of the board and the full board is composed of a majority of inside directors.

In general, it is easier to muster disinterested approval in a public corporation, where outside directors have become the norm, compared to a closely held corporation, where a majority of the board (if not the whole board) will have an employment relationship with the corporation. For this reason, compensation in a close corporation often will be subject to fairness review (see §23.2.5).

Courts are divided on the extent to which approval or ratification by a majority of informed, disinterested shareholders affects judicial review. Some earlier cases dealing with compensation in public companies suggested that shareholder ratification cleanses the transaction and shifts the burden to the shareholder challenger to show waste. *Rogers v. Hill*, 289 U.S. 582 (1933). More recent cases suggest that approval by informed, disinterested shareholders merely "freshens the atmosphere," and the burden falls on the directors to disprove waste. *Gottlieb v. Heyden Chemical Corp.*, 90 A.2d 660 (Del. 1952) ("possible indifference, or sympathy with the Directors, of a majority of the stockholders").

In close corporations, the approval or ratification by a majority of informed, disinterested shareholders stands on firmer ground. ALI Principles §5.03 (placing burden of proof on challenger to show waste if compensation approved by informed, disinterested shareholders).

§23.2.4   The Prevailing Standard — Waste

If executive compensation is approved by disinterested directors, courts invoke the presumptions of the business judgment rule. The challenger must show either that the board was grossly uninformed or that the compensation was a waste of corporate assets — that is, it had *no relation* to the value of the services given and was really a gift. See *Beard v. Elster*, 160 A.2d 731 (Del. 1960) (upholding approval by disinterested directors of stock options in "twilight zone where reasonable businessmen, fully informed, might differ").

The deference given disinterested approval of executive compensation in a public corporation is illustrated by the much-litigated compensation paid the president and five vice presidents of American Tobacco during the Depression. *Rogers v. Hill*, 289 U.S. 582 (1933). Under a bylaw adopted by American Tobacco shareholders in 1912, the executives received annual bonuses based on a percentage of the corporation's net profits above a stated base. As the company prospered, so did the executives. By 1930, with the Depression deepening and America smoking more, the president's annual bonus under the bylaw grew to $842,000 and each vice president's to $409,000. Shareholders challenged the amounts in federal court under federal common law (before *Erie*). Although the amounts were staggering at the time, the Supreme Court gave "much weight" to the shareholders' near-unanimous approval of the bylaw and held that the bonuses could be challenged only if they were shown to be wasteful — that is, only if there was no relation between the bonus amounts and the executive services.

§23.2.5   Fair and Reasonable Compensation

When compensation is not approved in such a way to avoid fairness review, judicial scrutiny is substantial. The court takes over the function of the board (or compensation committee) and assesses whether the challenged compensation is fair and reasonable to the corporation, taking into account: (1) the relation of the compensation to the executive's qualifications, ability, responsibilities, and time devoted; (2) the corporation's complexity, revenues, earnings, profits, and prospects; (3) the likelihood that incentive compensation would fulfill its objectives; and (4) the compensation paid similar executives in comparable companies.

Full-fledged fairness scrutiny has been limited mostly to compensation in close corporations, where boards (or committees) of disinterested directors are the exception. *Wilderman v. Wilderman*, 315 A.2d 610 (Del. Ch. 1974) ("standard for fixing executive compensation is obviously more strict when it is fixed by the recipient himself"). The scrutiny parallels that given executive compensation when the IRS challenges the deductibility of salaries as an "ordinary and necessary business expense."

§23.3 Directors' Compensation

§23.3.1 Directors' Fees

Originally, directors served without compensation; they were rewarded as the value of their shares increased. As public ownership of corporations increased and the shareholdings of directors declined, directors came to be paid relatively modest fees for serving on the board and for each meeting they attended. Today, particularly in large corporations with boards composed of a significant proportion of outside directors, directors' fees have become significant, sometimes totalling up to $100,000 per year.

Directors' fees are treated in much the same way as executive compensation. Fees approved by disinterested directors are subject to review under the business judgment rule. ALI §5.03(a)(2)(B). Fees authorized by disinterested shareholders are reviewable only if they constitute waste. ALI §5.03(c).

§23.3.2 Compensation for Outside Services

Services provided by outside directors (or their firms) to the corporation — such as by lawyers, accountants, and bankers — are treated as self-dealing transactions subject to fairness review. For instance, if a lawyer sits on a board and her law firm provides legal services to the corporation, legal fees must be what would be obtainable in an arm's length relationship and must be for services for which the corporation has a need.

§23.4 Reform Initiatives

In the 1990s executive compensation has become a highly controversial issue of corporate governance. News stories and books have chronicled the exorbitant pay of many American CEOs: In the words of one influential author, "CEOs get paid hugely in good years and, if not hugely, then merely wonderfully in bad years." Graef Crystal, *In Search of Excess: The Overcompensation of American Executives* (1991).

In response to the public outcry against overpaid executives, the SEC in 1992 significantly revised its rules on disclosure of executive compensation in public companies. Reg. S-K, item 402. To provide shareholders (and the financial press) with more understandable presentation of compensation data, the new rules require a series of tables setting forth both annual and long-term compensation as well as the potential value of stock options and stock appreciation rights under various hypothetical assumptions. In addition, the company's compensation committee must report on the corporate performance factors that it used in setting the CEO's compensation. The proxy statement must also show the company's stock performance over the last five years compared to the market as a whole (such as the "S&P 500") and the company's industry peers (such as the "Dow Jones Transportation Average").

Not only has the SEC turned up the heat on compensation committees, but institutional shareholders have also targeted companies with high executive compensation compared to performance. Activist shareholders have used the SEC's shareholder proposal rule to urge compensation reforms (see §19.5.2), and some institutional shareholders have initiated direct discussions with directors on the issue.

In 1993 Congress responded to the public outcry against excessive executive compensation by amending the Internal Revenue Code to cap the deductibility of executive compensation in public corporations at $1 million. IRC §162(m). This limit, which applies only to the corporation's five top-paid executives, does not apply if shareholders have approved the compensation, subject to three requirements: (1) a compensation committee of outside directors must set performance goals; (2) the goals and terms of the compensation plan must be submitted to shareholders for specific approval; and (3) the compensation committee must certify that the goals and terms of the plan have been met prior to payment.

EXAMPLES

1. More Parking Corp. (MP), incorporated in an RMBCA jurisdiction, owns and operates parking garages. Leonard More, the company's founder, is chairman of the board, president of the company, and a 30 percent shareholder. The remaining shares are publicly held; no other shareholder holds more than 5 percent.
   a. More's three-year executive compensation contract is coming up for renewal. The MP board is composed of seven directors: More, three company executives, and three nonmanagement outside directors. Advise the board on how approval of the contract should be handled.
   b. Would you recommend that the board seek to have shareholders ratify the contract?

2. A compensation committee of three outside directors approves a three-year compensation package for More of $400,000 in annual salary and a bonus of 5 percent of net earnings. The committee knows the package is generous. At current earnings levels, More will make $650,000 each year, compared to the $200,000 per year that top executives in the industry are paid.
   a. Cheryl, a long-time MP shareholder, is outraged and wants to challenge More's compensation. She brings a derivative suit. What must she allege?
   b. Is there other action she can take?

3. At More's request, the compensation committee also provided for his retirement. After the three-year contract term, More can retire from the company and receive a guaranteed annual consulting fee of $400,000 a year, whether or not he actually performs consulting services.

    a. Cheryl is even angrier when she learns of the consulting arrangement. Will she succeed if she challenges the consulting arrangement as a waste of corporate assets?

    b. The directors are worried about Cheryl's challenge. How might they change the consulting agreement to bolster its validity?

EXPLANATIONS

1a. Most lawyers advise the board to delegate the task of reviewing and negotiating the contract to a committee of directors, the majority of whom are nonemployee outside directors. This structure will avoid any claim that management directors set his compensation under a "back-scratching" arrangement where each director tacitly agrees to support each other's compensation. The committee should have access to all information about More and the company and should hire its own compensation consultant to provide pay information on comparable executives. To avoid the appearance that he dominated or controlled the committee, it would be advisable that More not be present when the committee deliberates. If approved by informed, disinterested directors, More's compensation will be reviewable only under a forgiving waste standard.

1b. Probably not. Under Delaware law, if board approval is found to have been misinformed or tainted, shareholder ratification serves to shift the burden to the directors to show an absence of waste. If board approval was informed and not dominated by More, submitting the contract for shareholder ratification may at best add weight to the argument that the compensation was related to the value of More's services, and at worst risk a shareholder rebuff. Except for stock plans that require shareholder authorization, modern boards rarely submit executive compensation for shareholder approval.

2a. Cheryl must make allegations that rebut the business judgment presumption — a nearly insuperable standard. She might allege that More dominates the outside directors by virtue of his position as chairman and 30 percent stock owner. "Domination" is a slippery and highly factual standard. Courts have held that generalized allegations of share ownership and position on the board are insufficient. See *Aronson v. Lewis*, 473 A.2d 805 (Del. 1984) (essentially the facts of this problem). Instead, Cheryl would have to show that the directors acted as requested without independent judgment (see §22.3.3).

    Cheryl might also allege that the compensation is a waste of corporate assets — that is, no reasonable business person would say that the compensation had any relation to the services received and that it was in reality a gift. Mere allegations of a discrepancy between the compensation and pay to comparable executives, although sufficient under a fairness standard, would not be enough. The committee (and More) could defend the compensation by pointing to his experience with the company and other possibly unique attributes. Courts are reluctant to become involved in these matters of business judgment.

Even if the directors were not dominated or the compensation was not wasteful, Cheryl might make some last-gasp allegations that (1) the directors were grossly uninformed in setting the compensation; (2) the directors had been deceived; (3) the compensation was specifically forbidden in the articles of incorporation; or (4) the compensation was illegal.

2b. Cheryl might submit a shareholder proposal on executive compensation to be included in the company's proxy statement. Under Rule 14a-8, the proposal cannot demand that the directors set a certain pay but can make precatory (advisory) recommendations or ask for the compensation committee to report on why More's compensation is more than three times higher than those of comparable executives. In 1992, the SEC changed its policy and now considers such shareholder proposals to be includable under the rule.

3a. Probably not. Cheryl would argue that the consulting fee, by its terms, is unrelated to any services. She could assert that there is no assurance More will actually be able to provide the services; there is no indication the corporation will actually consult him; and the services will be of little value and would be available from other sources for less money. Despite these arguments, Cheryl will have an uphill fight. The directors (and More) can argue that his consulting services are unique, that his availability will have great value to the corporation, and that to the extent the consulting contract is seen as a retirement package unrelated to actual consulting services, it is deferred compensation for his three-year employment contract. A similar set of allegations failed to impress the Delaware Supreme Court. See *Aronson v. Lewis*.

3b. The compensation committee could provide that the consulting fee is contingent on More's agreement not to compete with the corporation. The committee should also make clear that the consulting fee is not necessarily related to future services but rather to the noncompete agreement or the three-year contract. Courts have invalidated compensation tied to future services where there was no assurance the services would be performed.

24

Corporate Opportunities and Unfair Competition

The duty of corporate managers to loyally put the interests of the corporation ahead of their own personal interests applies not only to their dealings with the corporation but also to outside business dealings that affect the corporation. Harm to shareholder expectations is just as real when a manager takes away a profitable business opportunity from the corporation or sets up a competing business as when he engages in unfair self-dealing.

But, just as self-dealing is not automatically void, corporate managers (directors and executives) are not flatly prohibited from taking outside business opportunities. Outside opportunities offer managers a means to diversify their own human investment, and a flat prohibition against outside dealings might well lead many managers to shun the corporate form. The *corporate opportunity doctrine* — a subset of the duty of loyalty — balances the corporation's growth expectations and the managers' entrepenuerial interests.

§24.1   The Corporate Opportunity Doctrine

§24.1.1   *Prohibition against Usurping Corporate Opportunities*

The corporate opportunity doctrine supplies corporate law with a deceptively simple rule: A corporate manager (director or executive) cannot usurp corporate opportunities for his own benefit unless the corporation consents. The plaintiff has the burden of proving the existence of a corporate opportunity. The doctrine raises two difficult interpretive issues: (1) When does a business opportunity belong to the corporation and become a "corporate opportunity"? (2) When can it be said the corporation has, or would have, consented to the director taking that opportunity?

§24.1.2   Remedies for Usurping a Corporate Opportunity

A director who usurps a corporate opportunity without consent must share the fruits of the opportunity as though the corporation had originally taken it. Remedies include: (1) liability for profits realized by the usurping manager, (2) liability for lost profits and damages suffered by the corporation, and (3) imposition of a constructive trust on the new business or the subject matter of the opportunity (such as land). Because an outside third party is on the other side of the opportunity, rescission is not available unless the third party had notice of the insider's wrongdoing.

§24.2   Definition of "Corporate Opportunity"

What is a corporate opportunity? The courts have articulated and applied a variety of definitions. Underlying these definitions are two premises:

(1) managers should not compete with the corporation for business opportunities that (in some sense) belong to the corporation — managers should devote themselves to the corporation's business and make corporate profitability paramount; and
(2) managers should not be prevented from developing new businesses — the entrepreneurial spirit should not be squelched without good reason.

It should not surprise you that the courts' attempts to reach a suitable accommodation of these inconsistent premises has led to a variety of vague tests, which have evolved over time.

§24.2.1   Opportunities Developed with Diverted Corporate Assets

A fiduciary cannot develop a business opportunity using assets secretly diverted from the corporation. Requiring the fiduciary to share in any profits derived from the misbegotten business simply enforces the prohibition against misappropriation.

This analysis is clearest when the assets are "hard" assets — such as when a director uses the corporation's cash, property, or employees to set up a business. In such cases, the director is liable whether or not the corporation had an identifiable interest in taking the business opportunity itself and whether or not the business was related to that of the corporation. The real evil is not that the director took an opportunity for himself, but rather that he took something that belonged to the corporation to do it. *Guth v. Loft, Inc.*, 5 A.2d 503 (Del. 1939) (use of corporate funds).

Some courts, however, have only imposed damages on directors who use corporate resources to develop an outside business if the opportunity was not one in which the corporation had an interest or expectancy. See *Lincoln Stores v. Grant*, 34 N.E.2d 704 (Mass. 1941) (refusing to impose constructive trust on competing store that managers set up while still employed by corporation because "company had no interest in or thought of acquiring it").

§24.2.2 Opportunities in Which Corporation Had Existing Interest — Expectancy Test

When the misappropriation is of "soft" assets — such as when the director uses corporate information or the corporation's goodwill to develop a new business — courts have employed an *expectancy test*. Only if the corporation has an existing expectancy in an opportunity or an interest based on preexisting rights is the manager obligated to seek corporate consent before taking the opportunity. The manager's secrecy in taking the opportunity also supports a finding of corporate expectancy, on the assumption the corporation would have asserted its interests had the manager's taking been known. If the corporation has no interest or expectancy, the manager is allowed to exploit the opportunity for himself.

Corporate expectancies need not rise to the level of an ownership interest. For instance, an expectancy exists if the corporation is negotiating to acquire a new business or an executive receives information about a business opportunity in his corporate capacity. Courts have also interpreted the expectancy test to cover opportunities of special or unique importance to the corporation, for which there is a presumed expectancy. For example, a corporation's avowed interest in finding a new headquarters site or in acquiring patents necessary for its business fall within the shadow of the corporation's expectancies.

Aside from the corporate opportunity doctrine, the misappropriation of soft assets may also be subject to other prohibitions. For example, a director who uses customer lists or secret manufacturing processes of the corporation in developing his own business may be liable under state statutes prohibiting misappropriation of trade secrets.

§24.2.3   *Opportunities Related to the Corporation's Existing Business — The Line-of-Business Test*

Modern courts have applied a broader *line-of-business test* to measure the reach of the corporation's interests. Under the test courts compare the new business with the corporation's existing operations. The corporation need not have an existing interest or a special need for the opportunity, or the manager need not learn of the opportunity in his corporate capacity. If the new project is functionally related to the corporation's existing or anticipated business, the manager must obtain corporate consent before exploiting it.

Under the line-of-business test a functional relation exists if there is a competitive or synergistic overlap that suggests that the corporation would have been interested in taking the opportunity itself. Consider the case of *Miller v. Miller*, 222 N.W.2d 71 (Minn. 1974). Miller Waste, a closely held family corporation, was in the waste-reprocessing business. Rudolph Miller, one of Miller Waste's managers, developed a patented lubricator for diesel locomotives and set up his own company for their manufacture. Rudolph's company was supplied with waste products produced by Miller Waste's reprocessing business and competed with Miller Waste in the locomotive lubricator market. The court held that a fact-finder could have found that Rudolph's business was in Miller Waste's line of business.

§24.2.4   *Eclectic Approaches*

Some modern courts have combined the narrower expectancy test and a broader line-of-business test. See ALI Principles §5.05(b). The ALI Principles define a corporate opportunity as a business opportunity that

(1) a director or senior executive becomes aware of in his corporate capacity;

(2) a director or senior executive should know the outside party is offering to the corporation;

(3) a director or senior executive, who became aware of it through the use of corporate information, should know the corporation would be interested in;

(4) the senior executive knows is closely related to the corporation's current or expected business.

Thus, under the ALI Principles *insiders* are subject to line-of-business and expectancy restrictions, while *outside directors* (who have no employment relationship with the corporation) are subject only to expectancy restrictions.

Some courts go beyond the ALI Principles and have added (for good measure) a malleable fairness test to the expectancy/line-of-business tests.

Lewis v. Fuqua, 502 A.2d 962 (Del. Ch. 1985). The fairness test in this context, unlike that for self-dealing, which focuses on the fairness of the transaction to the corporation, focuses on the fairness of holding the manager accountable for his outside activities. Again, *Miller v. Miller,* 222 N.W.2d 71 (Minn. 1974), illustrates. Rudolph and Benjamin Miller had exploited a variety of opportunities for themselves that were closely related to Miller Waste's waste-reprocessing business: They had set up a small-packaging business; Rudolph started a business that manufactured patented lubricators for diesel locomotives using waste filter elements; and they had started a plastics business that used waste cotton cuttings. The trial court found that none of the new businesses were within Miller Waste's line of business, a finding that seems factually questionable. On appeal the court, without upsetting the trial court's findings, held in addition that Rudolph's and Benjamin's taking of the new businesses was not unfair to Miller Waste. The new businesses had benefited Miller Waste by supplying it with a captive market for selling its products; no corporate assets were diverted; there was no secrecy; and Rudolph and Benjamin had continued to work long hours at the waste mill. Thus *Miller v. Miller* in the fairness test served to limit the breadth of the line-of-business test and to insulate the managers from any sharing obligation.

§24.3 Corporate Consent and Incapacity

Even if a court determines that a business opportunity is a corporate opportunity under the applicable test, the manager's obligation to share the opportunity is negated if the corporation either has consented to the taking or was unable to take the opportunity itself.

Some courts have folded the question of corporate consent and incapacity into the question whether the opportunity was a corporate opportunity, placing the burden to show capacity on the corporation. Other cases separate the issues, treating them as defenses to be proved by the usurping manager.

§24.3.1 *Voluntary Consent*

The corporation can voluntarily relinquish its interests in a corporate opportunity by rejecting it. The corporation's rejection, however, is itself a self-dealing transaction because of the conflict between the manager's and the corporation's interests. Some courts subject the corporation's rejection, like the approval of a self-dealing transaction, to fairness review and require a rejection by informed, disinterested directors or shareholders. *Johnston v. Greene,* 121 A.2d 919 (Del. 1956) (see §22.3.3). Some courts have held that informal acquiescence to the taking (particularly in closely held corporations) constitutes rejection, while others have required formal before-the-fact action.

§24.3.2   *Implied Consent*

Many courts also have allowed managers charged with usurping a corporate opportunity to claim that the corporation could not have taken the opportunity because it was financially incapable or otherwise unable to do so itself. Under this approach, it is irrelevant that the manager failed to inform the board. The determination of incapacity is left to the court.

If the opportunity was never presented to the board or the shareholders, courts must speculate on whether the corporation could have taken the opportunity. Claims of financial incapacity illustrate how slippery the argument can become. Even if a manager shows that the corporation lacked the funds to take the opportunity itself, it can always be argued that the corporation could have raised the funds by borrowing money or by issuing new stock; after all, the manager had sufficient access to capital to take the opportunity himself.

Because of the vagaries of such an after-the-fact inquiry, some courts have required that there be a strong showing of incapacity. And a few courts have rejected the incapacity defense on the theory that the determination whether the corporation could have entered into the transaction should be for informed corporate decision-makers. *Irving Trust v. Deutsch,* 73 F.2d 121 (2d Cir. 1934), *cert. denied,* 294 U.S. 708 (1935).

The ALI Principles take an approach that encourages informed, internal decision-making. For a manager to take a corporate opportunity free and clear, (1) the manager must have offered it to the corporation and disclosed his conflicting interest, and (2) the board or shareholders must have rejected it. ALI §5.05. If disinterested directors rejected the opportunity, the board's action is subject to review under the business judgment rule; if rejected by disinterested shareholders, review is under a waste standard; and if the rejection is not disinterested, the court must determine that the taking was fair to the corporation.

In *Klinicki v. Lundgren,* 695 P.2d 906 (Or. 1985), the court applied this offer-rejection approach to the president of a closely held air transportation company who secretly took for himself a contract for a new air charter business. The court refused to consider the president's contention that the company lacked the financial ability to undertake the contract because the opportunity had never been presented to the other participant in the close corporation. Under the ALI Principles, the offer-rejection "safe harbor" is the only harbor.

§24.4   Competition with the Corporation

Competition with the corporation, although often itself the usurpation of a corporate opportunity, is subject to special treatment. In general, managers during their relationship with the corporation may not compete with the corporation unless there is no foreseeable harm caused by the competition or disinterested directors (or shareholders) have authorized it. The prohibition applies whether the competing business is set up during the manager's tenure or was preexisting.

This noncompete duty goes beyond the duties of the corporate opportunity doctrine. A manager with an interest in a competing business that predates his joining the corporation usurps no corporate opportunity but may be liable in damages for continuing to compete. Further, if the manager does not divert assets in setting up a competing business and if the corporation has no existing interest or need to expand, neither the misappropriation nor the expectancy theory prevents a manager from setting up the competing business.

A manager who violates the noncompete duty may be liable in damages for any competitive losses suffered by the corporation, but the manager need not share the competing business unless setting up the business usurped a corporate opportunity. See *Lincoln Stores v. Grant,* 34 N.E.2d 704 (Mass. 1941) (imposing damages, but no constructive trust, on managers who set up competing store while still employed by corporation).

Other theories of liability may also apply to a manager who competes with the corporation: (1) breach of contractual covenant not to compete, (2) misappropriation of trade secrets (such as customer lists or confidential formulas), or (3) tortious interference with contractual relationships if the manager induces the corporation's customers or employees to follow him.

EXAMPLES

1. Gusto Bottlers, Inc. is the authorized bottler of Gusto Cola on the Atlantic seaboard. The corporation is owned and operated by the Garret family. A few years ago, Ruth Garret (the company's founder and largest shareholder) brought her unemployed brother Garth into the business. He is now president and chief executive officer. Garth has often said, "I owe everything to Ruth." Ruth recently learned that Garth has set up a chain of dessert shops that has been very profitable.

   a. Ruth is distressed and thinks Garth should be forced to share the shops' profits with Gusto. She thinks that Garth set up the dessert shops with loans that Gusto guaranteed, under Garth's unauthorized signature. Must Garth share his profits? Under what theory?

   b. As things turn out, Ruth got the facts wrong. Garth set up the dessert shops on his own time and with his own money, without using the company's credit. Gusto had no plans to diversify into the dessert business. Can Garth be forced to share his profits?

   c. Ruth points out that from the beginning the understanding of the Garret family was that "everyone would pitch in and everyone would be taken care of." Does it make any difference that Gusto is a closely held corporation?

2. Gusto managers have been considering installing new lights at the company's bottling plant. Sally Garret (Ruth's niece and supervisor of the plant) has drawn up a lighting design, which she plans to submit to the board.

   a. Before Sally submits her plan, Garth receives a letter from Dustri-lite, an industrial lighting company that is going out of business and liquidating its inventory. Without telling anyone, Garth uses his own money to buy a shipment of lighting fixtures. When the board approves Sally's plan, Garth resells the fixtures to Gusto at the prevailing market price. Must Garth share his profits? Under what theory?

   b. Would it make any difference if Garth had disclosed the Dustri-lite offer to Gusto's board and the board had at first turned down the offer?

3. Gusto's sales have fallen recently, and some of the company's bank lenders have expressed concern to Garth about the company's ability to repay its outstanding loans.

   a. Garth, who is swimming in cash because of the success of his dessert shops, decides to get the banks off Gusto's back. He believes that Gusto's credit is basically sound, and is willing to buy Gusto's loans from the banks at a deep discount. If he does, could he be forced to share this discount with Gusto?

   b. Garth believes that the banks would not have been willing on principle to allow Gusto to renegotiate its debt. Does this affect Garth's duties?

   c. Garth claims that everyone else at Gusto knows about the banks' nervousness and has done nothing. Does this affect Garth's duties?

4. Garth reads in the newspaper that Tanfa Beverages, a bottler of fruit-flavored sodas in California, is going out of business. Gusto Bottlers has no plans to expand out of the Atlantic region, but Garth calls Tanfa's president, who confirms the company is for sale.

   a. Garth wants to buy Tanfa for himself without disclosing his purchase to Gusto. Can he?

   b. Garth figures Gusto lacks the funds to buy Tanfa. Does this affect his duties?

   c. Garth buys Tanfa and convinces his cousin, Jack Garret (Gusto's promotional director), to leave Gusto and work for Tanfa. Do you see any problems?

EXPLANATIONS

1a. Yes, under a misappropriation theory. Garth's unauthorized use of Gusto's credit is as much a diversion of assets as if he had misappropriated money. Thus, Garth's use of Gusto's credit to set up the dessert shops imposes on him a duty not to take the opportunity, regardless of whether

Gusto had any interest in opening dessert shops itself or whether the shops were related to Gusto's existing soft drink business. Some courts, however, would limit Gusto's recovery to the damages resulting from Garth's unauthorized use of the company's credit. See *Lincoln Stores v. Grant* (§24.2.1). This approach could lead to the anomalous result that Garth would escape liability because Gusto has not yet had to pay on its guarantee.

1b. It seems unlikely. Garth's dessert business is not a "corporate opportunity" under any of the definitions applied by the courts. (1) A misappropriation theory does not apply: Garth diverted no Gusto assets in setting up his business. (2) Gusto had no expectancy: There is no indication Gusto had an interest in or needed to enter the dessert business, and Garth started the business on his own time, presumably with information he derived from outside Gusto. (3) The business opportunity was not within Gusto's "line of business": The dessert shops are not functionally related to the business of bottling and selling soft drinks; there is no overlap in raw materials, production, and marketing. Even if Gusto's charter permitted it and Gusto had the financial means to expand into dessert shops, the line-of-business test does not treat every profitable business as within a corporation's expansion potential. It must be closely related to the company's existing or contemplated business. (4) Garth's new business did not compete with Gusto for customers, suppliers, employees, or assets.

1c. Perhaps. Ruth could argue that Garth has a duty not to take the opportunity because of the special expectations in this close corporation. The argument parallels the "reasonable expectations" argument that courts have increasingly come to accept in close corporation freezeout cases (see §17.1). If in this family business the participants had a "share and share alike" understanding — that a business opportunity available to any of them would be made available to the family corporation — a court might apply broader notions of corporate expectancy and line of business. That is, the corporate opportunity doctrine provides a default rule that the parties have some leeway to contract around. The ALI Principles, for example, permit corporate participants to establish a "standard of the corporation" that permits the taking of specified corporate opportunities without further disinterested approval. ALI Principles §5.09. By the same token the corporation, just as it sometimes obtains noncompete promises, could expand the definition of what constitutes a corporate opportunity. Even if a court were to give significance to the family's "share and share alike" understanding, it should also consider Garth's entrepreneurialism and his desire to diversify his human capital by branching into new businesses.

2a. Yes, under an expectancy theory. The Dustri-lite opportunity was an existing expectancy of Gusto because of Sally's plans for new lighting at the plant. Given his secrecy and prescience to buy the right fixtures, it seems clear that Garth knew about her plans. It makes no difference that the board had not yet approved Sally's plans or that Gusto's interest was not based on preexisting rights (such as a Dustri-lite contract with Gusto). Even though Gusto could not legally preclude Garth or anyone else from purchasing the fixtures, Gusto's plans were far enough along to impose on Garth a duty not to take the opportunity. In these circumstances, a line-of-business theory would not work because buying lighting fixtures is not part of Gusto's bottling business. The line-of-business test does not compel Garth to get permission to become a lighting fixture marketer.

You might have noticed also that Gusto could have sought damages from Garth on a self-dealing theory because he sold the fixtures to the corporation (see §22.5). Although the transaction's price might have been the fair market price, a court could characterize it as procedurally unfair — particularly if Garth failed to disclose how much he stood to profit when he made the sale. In such a case, the self-dealing remedy of rescission would be inadequate; courts have held that damages under a corporate opportunity theory are appropriate.

2b. Yes, if the board had been informed of Sally's lighting plans. Under most judicial approaches, the informed and disinterested rejection by Gusto's board of the opportunity relinquishes the corporation's claim to it, freeing Garth to take it for himself. Garth would have to disclose not only the terms of the Dustri-lite offer but also Sally's lighting plan and his intentions if the board turned down the offer. Further, for the directors to be considered disinterested, Garth could not dominate the board's decision-making (§22.3.3).

3a. Perhaps. Garth's purchase of the debt would mean that Gusto would owe him 100 percent principal and interest under its loans, even though Garth had paid less than 100 percent for these rights. Gusto could use an expectancy theory to characterize Garth's purchase of its discounted debt as a corporate opportunity and compel Garth to share the profits from his refinancing of the debt. Even if Gusto had not expressed an interest in financing its debt, Gusto could argue that, like any business, it has an ongoing interest in repurchasing its own securities or obligations at a discount because of their "unique value" to the corporation.

On the other hand, Garth could argue that he was simply assuming Gusto's credit risk from the bank. There is nothing to indicate Gusto could have refinanced its debt with a lender other than Garth. It would be unfair to Garth to share any profits, because his purchase of Gusto's debt meant only that he would bear any losses if Gusto did not repay on schedule. His argument would be buttressed if Garth, not the banks, initiated the idea of refinancing or repurchase of the debt.

3b. Perhaps. If the banks had been unwilling to sell back their loans to Gusto at a discount, Gusto would lack the corporate capacity to take the opportunity itself. The question of Gusto's capacity is one that some courts treat as an element of whether there existed a corporate opportunity. If Garth could show that the banks would not have dealt with Gusto, his loan purchase might not be treated as a corporate opportunity. This forces a court to speculate on something that never happened, placing the corporation at a disadvantage to rebut the banks' after-the-fact statements about not giving discounts to borrowers. Because of this, the modern judicial trend (reflected in the ALI Principles) is to compel the manager to seek corporate rejection. If the banks are truly unwilling to give Gusto the opportunity, Gusto's disinterested participants will reject the opportunity. Under current doctrine, Garth walks a dangerous line by not seeking formal corporate rejection.

3c. Perhaps. Garth might be able to characterize Gusto's inaction as an implied rejection of the opportunity to refinance its debt. Some courts have treated acquiescence as rejection of an opportunity. Nonetheless, the approach of other courts, and of the ALI Principles, is to avoid speculation about corporate capacity. Under the ALI Principles, for example, the opportunity must be offered to the corporation and rejected by the board or shareholders. ALI §5.05(a)(2). To meet the standards of the business judgment rule, it appears rejection by the board must be by formal action; shareholder action must be taken at a meeting. This approach may not make much sense in a close corporation, such as Gusto, where the corporate participants may act casually without corporate formalities.

4a. Probably not. The Tanfa opportunity may be a corporate opportunity for Gusto under a line-of-business theory. Although the corporation has no present plans to expand into the West Coast market, the line-of-business test does not depend on actual expectancies. Although the two bottlers do not sell in the same markets, Tanfa is in the same business as Gusto. Gusto's acquisition of Tanfa would create significant new opportunities for expanding Gusto's existing business: It would provide new products for Gusto's current markets and open a new market for its existing products.

An expectancy theory would not work because Gusto has no current expansion plans, and Garth did not learn of Tanfa's interest in his corporate capacity. Nor would a competition theory work because there is no current marketing overlap between Tanfa and Gusto.

4b. Perhaps. It depends on whether a court would accept Garth's incapacity defense or whether the court would require disclosure to the board. Some courts would allow the defense, even though the opportunity was never presented to the corporation. The burden of proving financial incapacity may be a difficult one for Garth because it might have been possible for Gusto to have raised the money by corporate debt or equity financing. The argument that financing was unavailable will ring hollow because Garth was able himself to have afforded the acquisition.

Some courts, and the ALI Principles, have rejected the incapacity defense. Under their approach, corporate incapacity must be decided by fully informed, disinterested directors or shareholders. Under this approach, however, Garth need not offer to lend money to the corporation so it can make the acquisition.

4c. Yes, on three possible grounds: (1) Whether or not the acquisition of Tanfa is a corporate opportunity, Jack's continued employment with Gusto might be seen as one. Gusto could argue it has an expectancy that Jack stay with Gusto (particularly if he is under contract) and that his services have special value to Gusto. By hiring him away, Garth has usurped a corporate opportunity. (2) Tanfa is now competing with Gusto, and Garth, as a fiduciary of Gusto, is under a broad duty not to harm Gusto competitively. (Notice that this may conflict with his duties to Tanfa and force him to cut his ties to one or the other.) Garth can compete with Gusto after he resigns from his positions. (3) If Jack is under contract, Garth may have tortiously interfered with Gusto's contractual relationship by wooing Jack away.

25

Indemnification and Insurance

Becoming a corporate director or officer in our litigious society is a risky proposition. To encourage people to accept such positions and then to take good-faith risks for the corporation without fear of personal liability, corporate statutes allow (and sometimes require) the corporation to indemnify directors and officers against liability. Directors' and officers' (D&O) liability insurance supplements this protection. Indemnification and insurance are in addition to liability insulation provided directors under the business judgment rule (see §21.2) and authorized by recent liability limitation statutes (see §21.5).

§25.1 Indemnification — Reimbursement by the Corporation

What is "indemnification"? It is simply the corporation's promise to reimburse the director for litigation expenses and personal liability if the director is sued because she is or was a director. (Indemnification of officers and other corporate agents is similar and is discussed below in §25.1.5.) In general, indemnification applies when the director is or was (or is threatened with being made) a defendant in any civil, criminal, administrative, or investigative proceeding. A director's indemnification rights continue even after she has left the corporation.

Open-ended indemnification can fly in the face of directorial accountability imposed under corporate law and other noncorporate regulatory schemes. For example, if a director can with impunity make false disclosure to investors or approve the illegal dumping of toxic chemicals and be confident

381

that the corporation will reimburse her if she is ever sued and held liable, the deterrent effect of personal liability under the securities laws and the environmental laws will be significantly diluted. If the corporation can indemnify grossly negligent or interested directors who breach their fiduciary duties to the corporation, the compensation and deterrence goals of fiduciary liability are effectively nullified.

Because of indemnification's potential to frustrate other policies, a director's right to indemnification and the power of the corporation to indemnify depend on (1) whether the director was successful in defending the action, and (2) whether an unsuccessful director can justify her actions.

§25.1.1 Mandatory Indemnification for Successful Defense

If a director is sued and defends successfully, the corporation is *obligated* under all state statutes to indemnify the director for litigation expenses, including attorney fees. RMBCA §8.52 (unless limited by the articles of incorporation); Cal. Corp. §317(b); Del. GCL §145(c). The right of the successful director to claim repayment of expenses is available whether the suit was brought on behalf of the corporation or by an outside party.

A director's right to mandatory indemnification raises two issues: (1) When is a defense successful? (2) Can there be mandatory indemnification for a partially successful defense?

Success — "On the Merits or Otherwise."   The statutes uniformly require indemnification when the defendant is successful "on the merits," such as when the suit is dismissed for lack of evidence or on a finding of nonliability after trial. RMBCA §8.52; Cal. Corp. §317(d); Del. GCL §145(c). Under most statutes, success also can be on procedural grounds — when success is "otherwise" — such as when a suit is dismissed because the plaintiff lacks standing or the statute of limitations has run. RMBCA §8.52; Cal. Corp. §317(b); Del. GCL §145(c). A director, however, is not deemed successful if the claim is settled out of court.

Indemnification "to the Extent" Successful.   Some statutes require indemnification "to the extent" the director is successful, and the corporation must reimburse the director's litigation expenses related to those claims or charges she defends successfully. Del. GCL §145(c). In *Merritt-Chapman & Scott Corp. v. Wolfson,* 321 A.2d 138 (Del. 1974), the Delaware Supreme Court interpreted a statute that required indemnification if the director was successful "in defense of any claim, issue or matter therein" as requiring indemnification for partial success. In the case, a director charged with five criminal offenses pleaded "no contest" to one on the condition the others were dropped. The court held he was entitled to indemnification as a matter of right for the litigation expenses related to the charges that were dropped.

This interpretation permits undeserving directors to settle or plea bargain away most of the claims against them and become entitled to indemnification for the bulk of their litigation expenses. For this reason, some statutes make mandatory indemnification "all or nothing" and limit it to defendants who were "wholly successful." RMBCA §8.52; Cal. Corp. §317.

§25.1.2   Permissive (Discretionary) Indemnification for an Unsuccessful Defense

Indemnification is not automatic when a director becomes liable because of a court judgment, an out-of-court settlement, or the imposition of penalties or fines. Instead, indemnification of an unsuccessful director's liability and expenses is discretionary. The director may be indemnified only if the corporation or a court decides, subject to specified criteria. Under modern statutes the ability of the corporation to indemnify depends on whether the action was brought by a third party or was brought on behalf of the corporation.

Permissive Indemnification in Third-Party Actions.   A director must be deserving to be entitled to indemnification in an action brought by a third party, such as when the EPA sues for illegal dumping or investors claim securities fraud.

Indemnification criteria.   Many statutes permit corporate indemnification arising from third-party actions only if certain criteria are met:

(1)   The director acted in good faith — that is, the director did not know her conduct was illegal and did not act for improper personal gain. RMBCA §8.51(a)(1); Cal. Corp. §317(b); Del. GCL §145(a).

(2)   The director reasonably believed her actions were in the corporation's best interests or, under some statutes, if she acted in an unofficial capacity (such as a representative to a trade association) in a manner not opposed to the corporation's best interests. RMBCA §8.51(a)(2); Cal. Corp. §317(b); Del. GCL §145(a).

(3)   The director in a criminal proceeding had no reasonable cause to believe that her actions were unlawful — a standard that goes beyond whether she acted in good faith. RMBCA §8.51(a)(3); Cal. Corp. §317(b); Del. GCL §145(a).

Often the findings implicit in a final court judgment (or administrative order) against a director will be inconsistent with a finding that the director satisfied these criteria. A director increases her chances of permissive indemnification by settling or plea-bargaining claims against her. Most statutes cooperate and state that a judgment, order, settlement, or no-contest plea is not conclusive as to whether the director meets the criteria for indemnification. RMBCA §8.51(c); Cal. Corp. §317(b); Del. GCL §145(a).

Coverage. A director sued in a third-party action may be indemnified for reasonable litigation expenses and any personal liability arising from a court judgment, an out-of-court settlement, or the imposition of penalties or fines. RMBCA §§8.51, 8.50(3), (4); Cal. Corp. §317(b), (c)(2), (c)(3); Del. GCL §145(a), (c).

Procedures. Many statutes specify that the determination whether a director meets the criteria for permissive indemnification must be made by (1) directors who are not parties to the proceeding or (2) shareholders. RMBCA §8.55(b); Cal. Corp. §317(e); Del. GCL §145(d). Some statutes also permit a committee of nonparty directors to make this determination or allow the board (or a committee of the board) to name a special, independent legal counsel to determine if the director meets the criteria, though not the actual amount the corporation must pay. RMBCA §8.55(b)(3), (c); Del. GCL §145(d).

Exclusivity of case-by-case procedure. Many statutes require a specific, case-by-case determination that the director is entitled to permissive indemnification. RMBCA §8.55. Under these statutes it is not enough that an employment agreement or the bylaws contain a blanket indemnification clause. Nonetheless, other statutes permit the corporation to indemnify directors under provisions in the bylaws or in a contract even though the statute does not contemplate it. Cal. Corp. §317(g); Del. GCL §145(f). The indemnification procedures applicable under these extrastatutory provisions govern, provided they are consistent with public policy. Some statutes, however, make the statutory grounds for indemnification controlling. Indemnification under the articles or bylaws, by resolution of the shareholders or the board, or in a contract is invalid if inconsistent with the statute. RMBCA §8.58.

Permissive Indemnification in Actions by or on Behalf of the Corporation. Most statutes do not allow the corporation to indemnify a director "adjudged liable" to the corporation if the action is brought by the corporation itself or by shareholders in a derivative action on behalf of the corporation (see §31.1). RMBCA §8.51(d)(1); Cal. Corp. §317(c)(1); Del. GCL §145(b). Allowing indemnification would create the absurd situation where a culpable director would pay the corporation with one hand and the corporation would reimburse the director with the other. This circularity would gut the effectiveness of directorial accountability.

Nonetheless, the corporation can indemnify a director who *settles* a suit by or on behalf of the corporation for her litigation expenses if she meets the criteria for permissive indemnification. RMBCA §8.51(e) and Official Comment (indemnification of unsuccessful director's litigation expenses "applies only to settlements since all indemnification is prohibited . . . in cases where a director is 'adjudged' liable to the corporation").

Court-Ordered Indemnification. Even if the corporation refuses to (or cannot) indemnify a director under its discretionary authority, some statutes allow a court to order indemnification. There are three approaches:

(1)   In some states, the court can order indemnification if the director "is fairly and reasonably entitled to indemnification in view of all the relevant circumstances." Del. GCL §145(b). This approach allows for indemnification (of expenses and liability) of an unsuccessful director who does not meet the criteria of permissive indemnification or becomes liable to the corporation.

(2)   The RMBCA uses the same standard as Delaware. RMBCA §8.54. But if the director is adjudged liable to the corporation or is adjudged to have acted for personal gain, the court can only order indemnification of the director's expenses. RMBCA §8.54(2).

(3)   In other states, the court can order indemnification only if the director meets the criteria for permissive indemnification.

§25.1.3   Advancement of Litigation Expenses

Even if the corporation must reimburse a director for litigation expenses after a successful defense, the promise of indemnification may be empty if the director cannot pay for a full defense out of his own pocket. For this reason, most statutes allow the corporation to advance litigation expenses during the proceeding. RMBCA §8.53; Cal. Corp. §317(f); Del. GCL §145(e). When the advances are made, it will not be known whether the director ultimately will be successful or be entitled to permissive indemnification, and the statutes impose varying conditions for advancing expenses.

The RMBCA takes a case-by-case approach: (1) the director must affirm his good faith belief that he would be entitled to permissive indemnification; (2) the director must undertake to repay the advances if he is not entitled to indemnification; and (3) those who determine whether to make the advance (nonparty directors, shareholders, or special legal counsel) must know of nothing that would preclude indemnification. RMBCA §8.53(a). Some other statutes do not require a case-by-case determination, and advances can be made if required in the articles, the bylaws, or a contract. Del. GCL §145(e).

Under the RMBCA, a director need not give security for his repayment obligation. To avoid discriminatory treatment against directors of modest means, the corporation can accept the repayment obligation "without reference to the [director's] financial ability to make repayment." RMBCA §8.53(b).

§25.1.4 *Exclusivity of Statutory Indemnification*

The RMBCA makes the statutory indemnification provisions and procedures exclusive. Indemnification pursuant to the articles of incorporation, the by-laws, or an agreement is permitted only to the extent consistent with the statute. RMBCA §8.58.

Other statutes explicitly permit extrastatutory indemnification. Cal. Corp. §317(g); Del. GCL §145(f). Cases suggest such indemnification is possible if consistent with "public policy." Among other things, this means that the corporation cannot indemnify a director for liability to the corporation (because of the circularity problem).

§25.1.5 *Indemnification of Nondirectors*

In general, the corporation may indemnify nondirector officers, employees, and agents to the same extent as directors. RMBCA §8.56; Cal. Corp. §317; Del. GCL §145. Indemnification of officers (though not others) is mandatory to the same extent as if the officers were directors.

§25.2 Insurance

Corporate statutes permit the corporation to buy insurance to fund its own indemnification obligations and to fill the gaps in coverage left by corporate indemnification, principally when a director is liable to the corporation in a derivative suit.

§25.2.1 *Insurance Covering Corporation's Obligations*

Indemnification is a form of insurance provided by the corporation to its directors, officers, employees, and other agents. The corporation can meet its indemnification obligations, statutory or extrastatutory, either by acting as a self-insurer or by purchasing insurance from outside insurance companies.

§25.2.2 *Insurance Covering Liability of Directors and Officers*

To supplement indemnification and to cover liability to the corporation, the corporation also can purchase liability insurance for its directors and officers — *D&O insurance*. Premium payments for such policies constitute additional compensation to the executive and are authorized either as such or by specific statute. RMBCA §8.57; Cal. Corp. §317(i); Del. GCL §145(g). Many statutes authorize the purchase of insurance, even if it covers expenses and liability the corporation could not indemnify. RMBCA §8.57; Cal. Corp. §317(i); Del. GCL §145(g). Although it might seem anomalous that the corporation can indemnify indirectly through insurance what it is prohibited from indemnifying directly, the theory is that the director could have herself bought insurance and it should not make any difference that the corporation compensates her by paying her premiums.

Usually, the corporation submits the D&O application and pays the premiums in the name of the insured executives. D&O policies typically cover any liabilities or defense costs arising from the executive's position with the corporation. The policies, however, exclude coverage for improper personal benefits (such as self-dealing), actions in bad faith (including dishonesty), illegal compensation, libel or slander, knowing violations of law, and other willful misconduct. Many policies also exclude coverage for fines and penalties (including punitive damages), regardless of the executive's intentions. The effect of the exclusions is to make D&O insurance sometimes less encompassing than indemnification by the corporation.

EXAMPLES

1. Jones, a shareholder of Trans Combo Corporation, sues the company's directors for failing to approve a merger for $55 per share with the Harmon Group at a time the company's stock was trading at $38. Jones brings a derivative suit claiming the board failed to become informed about the bid and for failing to negotiate harder. Jones seeks damages, jointly and severally, from the directors. Assume Trans Combo is incorporated in an RMBCA jurisdiction. The Trans Combo board appoints a committee composed of directors who recently joined the board and whom Jones did not sue. The committee is authorized to decide all indemnification issues.

    a. The director-defendants consider settling with Jones for $62 million — $5 per share. Will Trans Combo have to reimburse them?

    b. The defendant-directors ask the committee to advance them money to pay for their mounting attorney fees. Some of the directors cannot afford to pay for a defense. Can the committee decide to have the corporation pay the defendants' litigation expenses?

    c. The litigation committee is convinced that all the directors acted in good faith and with the best interests of the company in mind. The committee nonetheless chooses not to advance the directors' litigation expenses. Can it do that?

    d. The committee believes that if the directors go to trial, the maximum recovery would be $3 per share. Could the committee then decide

to have the corporation reimburse the director-defendants for this liability?

e. The defendant-directors receive a settlement offer. Are there any disadvantages to taking it?

f. The directors go to trial and are found liable for having rejected the
merger without sufficient information but are not liable for failing to
negotiate further. The defendant-directors seek repayment of their
expenses related to their successful defense of the disclosure claim.
Are they entitled?

2. The directors pay the settlement amounts. Old Trans Combo had pur-
chased a typical directors' and officers' insurance policy from Concord
Insurance Company. The policy period covers the claim brought by
Jones.

a. Can the directors seek indemnification for the settlement payments
from the insurance company?

b. Does the D&O insurance policy also cover the directors' litigation
expenses?

c. Orkin, Trans Combo's CEO, lied to the directors about the worth
of the merger. He wanted to avoid the merger, no matter what. Can
Orkin seek indemnification under the D&O policy?

3. The Trans Combo directors get a second chance. The Harmon Group
again offers $55 a share, and this time the directors accept the offer.
Trans Combo merges into New Trans Combo, a Harmon subsidiary.
There is no pleasing Jones, who brings a class action in which he claims
the directors were uninformed of the company's value, which he says is
at least $65 per share.

a. The directors again want to settle. Are the directors entitled to statutory indemnification from New Trans Combo?

b. The bylaws of Old Trans Combo stated that each director is entitled
to indemnification if he acted "in good faith with a reasonable belief
his conduct was in the best interests of the corporation." Can the
directors compel New Trans Combo to make good on this promise
and pay for their settlement?

c. New Trans Combo is willing to pay for the settlement. Is there a
problem of circularity?

4. When the Harmon Group approached Trans Combo the first time about
a merger, Orkin secretly bought Trans Combo stock on the market.
After the board turned down the merger, he held on to the stock and
later made a hefty premium with the merger. The SEC sued him for
insider trading (see §29.5) but was unable to show liability.

a. Must New Trans Combo pay Orkin's defense costs?

b. If New Trans Combo indemnifies Orkin, can it make a claim under
Old Trans Combo's D&O insurance policy?

5. New Trans Combo hires Orkin to run the company. Orkin wants an indemnification agreement before he accepts. Draft one.

EXPLANATIONS

1a. No. If the directors settle, they would not have been successful "on the merits or otherwise," and statutory indemnification would not be available as of right.

1b. Probably. Under RMBCA §8.53, the corporation may advance a director's litigation expenses if —

(1) He affirms his good-faith belief that he is entitled to permissive indemnification under the statutory standard of conduct — that is, when he rejected the merger he acted in good faith (not dishonestly or with a conflicting interest) and reasonably believing it was in the corporation's best interests.

(2) He undertakes to repay all advances if it turns out he is not entitled to indemnification. Even though some of the directors may never be able to repay these advances, the RMBCA permits the committee to accept their undertaking "without reference to financial ability to make repayment." RMBCA §8.53(b).

(3) A proper decision-maker determines it knows of nothing that would preclude indemnification. Advancing expenses, like indemnification for liability, is a form of self-dealing. The RMBCA requires that any discretionary decision to pay (or advance) expenses or to indemnify a director be made by a disinterested decision-maker: nonparty directors, a committee of the board, a special legal counsel, nonparty shareholders. RMBCA §8.55(b). If a quorum of the board consisting of nonparty directors cannot be obtained, the board may compose a committee of at least two nonparty directors — the case here. In approving the advance, the committee need not conduct a special investigation that the director would meet the standard of conduct. Official Comment to RMBCA §8.53.

1c. Yes. Advances of expenses are discretionary, and the corporation is under no statutory obligation. Unless the directors have nonstatutory rights in the corporation's articles or bylaws or in an indemnification agreement, the statute limits mandatory indemnification to directors who are "wholly successful." Court-ordered indemnification under the RMBCA is not available for advances of expenses. If the directors are not successful, they may ask a court to order the corporation to indemnify them.

RMBCA §8.54. They would have to show that they are "fairly and reasonably entitled to indemnification in view of all the relevant circumstances." A court may make this finding if the directors did not satisfy the statutory standard of conduct. For example, the directors might show that the committee was acting out of spite and it was in the corporation's best interests for them to litigate the question of a director's duty to investigate merger proposals.

1d. No. Although indemnification is available for all liability arising because "an individual . . . is or was a director," indemnification is not available after a derivative suit in which directors are "adjudged liable to the corporation." RMBCA §8.51(d)(1). Otherwise, the corporation would be collecting from the directors in the suit and repaying them through indemnification. The deterrent and compensation purposes of derivative litigation would be frustrated.

1e. Yes. If they settle, the directors will not be "adjudged liable" and may be entitled to indemnification — if they meet the standard of conduct. Further, a settlement suggests less than a judgment of liability that the directors acted in bad faith or without a reasonable belief that they were acting in the best interests of the corporation. See RMBCA §8.51(c) (settlement is not determinative that director did not meet standard of conduct). This means that, to resolve an intracorporate dispute, the corporation may end up paying both the shareholder-plaintiff's expenses (see §31.1.3) and the director-defendants' expenses. The RMBCA, however, limits indemnification to the payment of the directors' litigation expenses. RMBCA §8.51(e). This avoids any circularity problem for settlement payments.

1f. No. The RMBCA requires that the directors be "wholly successful." RMBCA §8.52. Even though the directors' decision not to negotiate may have been proper and the defense of the claim in the corporation's interest, the RMBCA seeks to prevent mandatory payments to possibly undeserving defendants. Remember permissive indemnification may be available.

2a. Yes. D&O coverage extends to suits brought by or on behalf of the corporation. Typically, policies cover the directors for acts or omissions in their capacities as directors or by reason of their status as directors. They exclude coverage for claims of personal profit, deliberate fraud, criminal acts, unauthorized compensation, short-swing trading profits, or failing to maintain insurance. That is, breaches of a director's duty of care will typically be covered.

2b. Yes. D&O policies typically cover defense costs. Some policies contemplate that the insurance company will conduct the defense and require that the insured directors turn over litigation to the insurance company.

2c. No. D&O coverage, like all other insurance, excludes coverage for willful, knowing, or fraudulent acts.

3a. No. In the merger, the surviving corporation assumes all the liabilities of the Old Trans Combo, including any statutory indemnification obligations it would have had. See RMBCA §11.06(a)(3). Unless the directors are "wholly successful," they have no statutory indemnification rights.

3b. Probably not. The RMBCA, unlike Delaware's statute, does not permit extrastatutory indemnification unless it is consistent with the statute. The directors could not have enforced the indemnification bylaw against Old Trans Combo because it did not call for a determination that the directors had met their standard of conduct by a disinterested decision-maker. RMBCA §8.51(a). It might be argued, nonetheless, that since a new set of shareholders (the Harmon Group) will bear the costs of any payments by New Trans Combo, this is not a self-dealing transaction, and it would not be inconsistent with the statutory scheme for an *outsider* to reimburse the directors if the directors had met the standard of conduct. This argument, however, would put New Trans Combo in the position of having a greater indemnification obligation than did Old Trans Combo.

3c. No. In this class action, the directors will be liable to the Old Trans Combo shareholders, not to the surviving corporation. New Trans Combo's payment to the directors will have the effect of the Harmon Group paying additional consideration for the merger. There is no problem of circularity.

4a. Perhaps. New Trans Combo acquires the indemnification obligations of Old Trans Combo in the merger. See answer 3a above. The RMBCA, however, is not entirely clear about whether a company's mandatory indemnification obligations cover defense costs in an insider-trading case.

Mandatory indemnification applies to "any proceeding to which [the director or officer] was a party because he is or was [a director or officer]." RMBCA §§8.52, 8.56. Orkin could argue that the SEC sued him for misusing inside information that he acquired *because* of his insider position. The statute's provisions on permissive indemnification, which allow indemnification in cases other than "conduct of official capacity," suggest that an insider's indemnification rights extend beyond corporate functions. See RMBCA §8.51(a)(2). See *University Savings Association v. Burnap*, 786 S.W.2d 423 (Tex. App. 1990) (indemnification of director who successfully defended against tipping liability).

Some of the considerations that justify indemnification argue for finding the statute covers Orkin. Indemnification seeks to align the incentives of directors and officers with the risk-taking preferences of shareholders. So does stock ownership. Directors and officers may be reluctant to acquire shares if their service on the board may expose them to liability if they trade in the company's shares. To encourage share ownership by directors, an indemnification scheme allowing indemnification for trading in those shares makes sense.

4b. Perhaps. Unless the D&O policy has a nonassignment clause, its coverage passes to New Trans Combo in the merger. Typically, D&O policies reimburse the company's indemnification of directors' liability or expenses pursuant to statute, contract, charter, or bylaw provision. D&O policies often exclude coverage for claims under §16(b) of the Securities Exchange Act of 1934, the short-swing profits provision. See §30.2. That is, insurance does not allow an insider to preserve his illegal trading profits. In this case, however, the director is not claiming a return of profits, and the exclusion would not seem to apply.

5. An indemnification contract might read as follows:

> This confirms the agreement between you and New Trans Combo (Corporation) concerning indemnification.
>
> 1. *Indemnification.* The Corporation indemnifies you in your capacity as officer and director (or either) of the Corporation to the full extent permitted by law.
>
> 2. *Notice.* You will notify the Corporation in writing of any proceeding (whether threatened, pending, or completed) with respect to which the Corporation might be required to provide indemnity. You will provide this written notice within ten (10) business days after first becoming aware that you may be, are, or were a party to such a proceeding. The notice will describe the proceeding and your status in the proceeding and will attach any documents filed in the proceeding. If you fail to provide timely notice, the Corporation will not be obligated to indemnify you with respect to that proceeding.
>
> 3. *Defense and advancement of funds.* Unless independent counsel determines that the Corporation is not obligated to provide indemnity, the Corporation will: (a) defend and settle at the Corporation's expense any claims against you in your capacity as officer or director of the Corporation; and (b) pay any fines, judgments, and amounts in settlement in connection with claims against you in your capacity as officer or director of the Corporation. You will cooperate fully in any defense or settlement undertaken by the Corporation. If it is ultimately determined that you are not entitled to indemnity with respect to payments or expenses (including attorneys' fees) incurred by the Corporation, then you will reimburse the Corporation for these amounts.
>
> 4. *Insurance.* The Corporation will purchase and maintain director and officer liability insurance in the face amount of [typically $1 million] on your behalf under a standard such policy. If at any time after the first year of coverage you conclude that this coverage is inadequate, you will notify the Corpora-

tion. If the Corporation does not adjust coverage to your satisfaction, you may request that independent legal counsel (to be paid by the Corporation) review the adequacy of the coverage. Counsel's evaluation will be binding.

5. *Nonexclusivity and subrogation*. Your rights to indemnification and to advances under this agreement are not exclusive of any other rights to which you may be entitled. To the extent the Corporation has paid amounts under this agreement and you are also entitled to payment from any other person, the Corporation will be subrogated to any claim that you may have for such payment.

6. *Duration, governing law, severability*. This agreement will terminate on the later of (a) ten (10) years after you cease to be a director or officer of the Corporation, or (b) the final disposition of any pending proceeding as to which you have a right of indemnification under this agreement. This agreement is governed by [RMBCA jurisdiction] law. The provisions of this agreement are severable. This agreement is binding on and will inure to the benefit of the Corporation's and your heirs, personal representatives, successors, and assigns.

New Trans Combo Corp.

By: _____

Accepted:

_____

26

Responsibilities of Controlling Shareholders

Corporate fiduciary duties impose responsibility on those who control the governance mechanisms of the corporation. Although the board of directors has governance authority, ultimate control rests with the shareholders. Any shareholder who can exercise the power of the body of shareholders — a *controlling shareholder* — effectively runs the corporation. A controlling shareholder, who chooses the board of directors and can approve fundamental changes, has significant latitude to act to the detriment of minority shareholders. This potential for control abuse has led courts to impose fiduciary duties on controlling shareholders that parallel those of directors.

In this chapter we discuss how courts scrutinize transactions between controlling shareholders and the corporation. In the next chapter we consider the obligations of shareholders who sell control.

§26.1 Who Are Controlling Shareholders?

A controlling shareholder, whether an individual or a parent corporation, has enough voting shares to determine the outcome of shareholder voting. Directors are usually chosen by majority vote, and any shareholder who can put together a majority of votes wields effective control. In close corporations, this may require a shareholding of more than 50 percent — a majority shareholder. In a public corporation with widely dispersed shareholders, it may be enough to own as little as 20 percent and have the support of incumbent management — a dominating shareholder. ALI §1.10(b) (presumption of control with 25 percent shareholding).

§26.2   Dealings between the Corporation and Controlling Shareholders

Dealings between a controlling shareholder (for simplicity's sake, the parent) and the corporation (the subsidiary) raise many of the same conflict-of-interest concerns as do dealings between a director and the corporation. For a parent and its subsidiary, multiple sources of conflict exist: Executives of the parent often serve on the board of the subsidiary; parent executives often dictate the subsidiary's policies; and the parent, by definition, has a controlling shareholding position.

§26.2.1   Dealings with Wholly Owned Subsidiaries

If there are no minority shareholders, the parent has virtually unfettered discretion to do with the corporation as it — the controlling shareholder — pleases. Duties exist only to creditors and, to a limited extent, future minority shareholders. As we have seen, promoters cannot enter into unfair self-dealing transactions to the detriment of future creditors or shareholders (see §5.3), and shareholders are liable for siphoning corporate funds at the expense of creditor claims (see §6.2). But if these interests are not implicated, there is no conflict when a parent corporation deals with its wholly owned subsidiary.

§26.2.2   Dealings with Partially Owned Subsidiaries

Dealings between a parent and its partially owned subsidiary create risks of control abuse:

Dividend policy.   The subsidiary declares dividends to a cash-strapped parent at the expense of internal expansion. Or the subsidiary adopts a no-dividend policy to force minority shareholders to sell to the parent.

Issuance of shares.   The subsidiary issues the parent stock at less than fair value, thus diluting the minority's interests.

Parent-subsidiary transactions.   The subsidiary enters into contracts (with the parent or related affiliates) on terms unfavorable to the subsidiary, effectively withdrawing assets of the subsidiary at the expense of the minority.

Usurpation of opportunities.   The parent (or other affiliates) takes business
opportunities away from the subsidiary (see Chapter 24).

When must the parent answer to the minority? Corporate statutes provide little guidance. Some conflict-of-interest statutes by their terms cover
transactions when a director has a relationship to another corporation — the
usual situation in parent-subsidiary dealings. But the statutes either fail to
provide conclusive standards of review, see former RMBCA §8.31, or explicitly exclude parent-subsidiary transactions from their reach. RMBCA
§8.60(1) (official note stating that parent-subsidiary transactions are to be
dealt with "under the rubric of the duties of a majority shareholder").

Courts have wavered on the degree of scrutiny applicable to parent-
subsidiary dealings.

Ordinary Business Dealings.   Most courts, including those of Delaware,
view with sympathy the argument that controlling shareholders should get
something for their control position. Parent-subsidiary dealings in the ordinary course of business are subject to fairness review only if the minority
shows the parent has preferred itself at their expense. If so, the courts presume
the parent dominates the subsidiary's board and places the burden on the
parent to prove the transaction was "entirely fair" to the subsidiary (see
§26.3.3 below). See ALI §5.10 (burden on parent unless approved by disinterested directors). But if there is no preference, the transaction is subject
to business judgment review, and the minority must prove that the dealings
lacked any business purpose or that their approval was grossly uninformed.

The dichotomous treatment of parent-subsidiary dealings is illustrated
in *Sinclair Oil Co. v. Levien*, 280 A.2d 717 (Del. 1971). Minority shareholders
of Sinven, a partially owned (97 percent) Venezuelan subsidiary of Sinclair
Oil, challenged three sets of parent-subsidiary dealings:

1. Sinven's high-dividend policy.   The minority alleged that Sinclair had
imposed on Sinven a dividend policy that depleted the subsidiary. The court
held that the policy did not prefer Sinclair because Sinven's minority shareholders received their proportionate share of all dividends. In the absence of
preferential treatment, the shareholders had the burden to show that the
policy was not protected by the business judgment rule, which they failed
to do.

2. Sinclair's allocation of projects to other affiliates.   The minority claimed
that Sinclair allocated industrial projects to its wholly owned subsidiaries, to
the detriment of partially owned Sinven. The court held that the projects
were not corporate opportunities of the subsidiary, and the parent was under
no obligation to share them with Sinven.

3. Sinven's failure to enforce contracts with other Sinclair affiliates.   The
minority claimed that Sinven's nonenforcement of contracts for the sale of
oil products to Sinclair affiliates preferred the affiliates to Sinven's detriment.

The court treated the nonenforcement as self-dealing and held that Sinclair had failed to show that nonenforcement was fair to Sinven.

The key in each instance was whether the minority shareholders could show a clear parental preference detrimental to the subsidiary. The *Levien* test assumes the propriety of parent-subsidiary dealings, a departure from the traditional rule that fiduciaries have the burden to show the fairness of their self-interested dealings (see §22.2.3). The burden is on the minority shareholders to show that the dealings were *not* those that might be expected in an arm's length relationship, rather than on the parent to show that they were.

Exclusion of Minority.   Many courts hold controlling shareholders to a higher standard when they use control in stock transactions to benefit themselves to the exclusion of minority shareholders. In the leading case, the court imposed on the controlling shareholder the burden to prove that a stock transaction that excluded minority shareholders was justified by a "compelling business purpose." *Jones v. H. F. Ahmanson & Co.,* 460 P.2d 464 (Cal. 1969). United Savings & Loan was controlled by Howard Ahmanson, who had made the S&L a great success. But the S&L's shareholders were unable to capitalize on the success because of the thin market for their shares. Although publicly held, the S&L had less than 7000 outstanding shares, which traded at $2400 per share. As a result, few investors were interested in buying and few shares were available for sale, even though S&Ls were then the darlings of the stock markets.

To remedy this, Ahmanson set up a holding company, United Financial, which exchanged its stock for his and his friends' S&L shares — all told, 85 percent of the S&L shares outstanding. United Financial's shares became widely traded, creating a lucrative market for Ahmanson's majority interest in the S&L. The plaintiff, a minority shareholder who was not allowed to participate in the exchange, argued that Ahmanson should have created a market for all the S&L shareholders by splitting the S&L stock on a 250-for-1 basis. Ahmanson argued that he and the other favored shareholders had an unfettered right to do as they pleased with their shares, and that the exchange had not affected the plaintiff's interest in the S&L, which remained unchanged.

Writing for the court, Justice Traynor rejected Ahmanson's argument and held that controlling shareholders have fiduciary duties to minority shareholders. Even accepting (as the plaintiff conceded) that Ahmanson had caused no harm to the corporation, Traynor said that controlling shareholders cannot use their control to benefit themselves to the detriment of the minority. Ahmanson violated a duty to the minority by creating a market from which the minority shareholders were excluded without a compelling business purpose. The court required that the minority shareholders be given an opportunity to exchange their S&L shares for a proportionate number of holding company shares.

Other courts have used this analysis to invalidate stock redemptions and conversions that prefer controlling shareholders. For example, in *Zahn v. Transamerica Corp.*, 162 F.2d 36 (3d Cir. 1947), a corporation had two classes of common shares, class A and class B. The class B shares held voting control. The class A shares, which were entitled in liquidation to twice as much as class B shares could be redeemed by the corporation at any time for $60. The controlling shareholder had the corporation redeem all of the minority's class A shares and then liquidate the corporation's assets, which had recently tripled in value. The result was that the controlling shareholder received the lion's share of the company's liquidation value. The court reasoned there was "no reason" for the class A redemption except for the controlling class B shareholder to profit. In a subsequent opinion, the court upheld a recovery to the class A shareholders based on the liquidation value they would have received if they had exercised their rights to convert their class B shares into class A shares. See *Speed v. Transamerica Corp.*, 235 F.2d 369 (3d Cir. 1956).

Approval by Disinterested Shareholders.   Just as shareholder ratification insulates directorial self-dealing from review (see §22.3.4), approval by a majority of informed, disinterested shareholders insulates a parent-subsidiary transaction. If the parent discloses the conflict and the terms of the transaction, the transaction is subject to review only under a waste standard. That is, a challenger must show there was no rational business justification for the transaction. ALI §5.10(a)(2).

Remedies.   Remedies for improper parent-subsidiary dealings are the same as those for self-dealing by directors (see §22.5). Rescission is the general remedy, unless rescission does not provide adequate compensation — such as when a parent usurps the subsidiary's corporate opportunities — or rescission is no longer possible.

When a controlling shareholder engages in transactions in the corporation's stock to the detriment of the minority, courts recognize a direct action by minority shareholders and order either equal treatment or recovery based on what the minority would have received absent the breach.

§26.3   Squeeze-out Transactions — Eliminating Minority Interests

The early view was that controlling shareholders could vote their shares as they pleased. Modern courts, however, place significant restrictions on the controlling shareholder's ability to structure transactions and vote their shares to eliminate minority interests.

Eliminating minority interests is of particular importance in corporate takeovers. After acquiring a voting majority, an acquirer (whether in a friendly or unfriendly takeover) will often want to consolidate control to use corporate assets to repay their takeover debt and eliminate minority shareholders in a back-end squeeze-out merger.

§26.3.1   The Mechanics and Conflict of a Squeeze-out

A controlling shareholder can force out minority shareholders and acquire 100 percent control in a number of ways:

Squeeze-out merger.   The parent and subsidiary agree to a merger under whose terms the subsidiary's minority shareholders receive cash (a cash-out merger) or other consideration for their shares, and the parent retains its shares and becomes the sole shareholder (or acquires the subsidiary as a new division).

Liquidation.   The subsidiary sells all of its assets to the parent (or an affiliate) and then dissolves and is liquidated. Minority shareholders receive a pro rata distribution of the sales price.

Stock split.   The subsidiary declares a reverse stock split (such as 1 for 2000) that greatly reduces the number of outstanding shares. If no minority shareholder owns more than 2000 shares, all minority shareholders come to hold fractional shares, which are then subject to mandatory redemption by the subsidiary as permitted under some state statutes.

These transactions present a clear conflict of interest. In each instance the parent will want to pay the minority shareholders as little as possible for their shares. The minority is particularly vulnerable because the parent both controls the subsidiary's board *and* generally has sufficient voting power to approve any merger or dissolution over the minority's opposition. Despite the potential for abuse, these transactions present an opportunity for important efficiencies. By eliminating minority shareholders, the parent can use the subsidiary's assets as it pleases, it can consolidate the businesses for tax and accounting purposes, it can avoid reporting costs under the Securities Exchange Act of 1934 (see §19.3.1), and the subsidiary becomes a more attractive merger candidate. In short, the subsidiary may be worth more if wholly owned.

§26.3.2   Business Purpose Test

A squeeze-out terminates the minority shareholders' investment without their consent. Some courts require that the transaction not only be fair but that

the parent also have some business purpose for the merger other than eliminating the minority. *Coggins v. New England Patriots Football Club, Inc.*, 492
N.E.2d 1112 (Mass. 1986); *Alpert v. 28 Williams Street Corp.*, 473 N.E.2d
19 (N.Y. 1984).

The business purpose test has been widely criticized as weak and easily
manipulated. It imposes little substantive protection for minority shareholders because management can always create a record of avowed purposes for
the squeeze-out, such as greater operational or financial efficiencies, accounting simplicity, or tax advantages. At most, the business purpose requirement
may sometimes distinguish between those squeeze-out mergers motivated by
pique and those that create some general gain.

In 1983 the Delaware Supreme Court did away with the business purpose requirement in Delaware on the grounds that (1) it provides no meaningful protection beyond that afforded by the "entire fairness" test (see
§26.3.3 below), and (2) shareholders in Delaware have expanded appraisal
rights (see §26.3.3 below). *Weinberger v. UOP, Inc.*, 457 A.2d 701 (Del.
1983), *overruling Singer v. Magnavox Co.*, 380 A.2d 969 (Del. 1977).

§26.3.3   *Entire Fairness Test*

In Delaware squeeze-out mergers are subject to a two-prong *entire fairness
test. Weinberger v. UOP, Inc.*, 457 A.2d 701 (Del. 1983). The test focuses
on the fairness of both the transaction's price and the process of approval.

Fair price.   The *Weinberger* court characterized *fair price* as the prepon-
derant consideration and liberalized Delaware's valuation methods for determining fair price in the context of a merger. It rejected the exclusivity of
the *Delaware block method,* which gave a particular weight to historic earnings
per share, asset value per share, and market price, and then added them
together to produce a share price. Instead, the court held that valuation must
take into account all factors, including discounted cash flow. The *discounted
cash flow method,* generally used by investment bankers in valuing companies,
looks at the company's anticipated future cash stream and then, after making
assumptions about interest rates, figures how much cash would be needed
today to replicate that stream. The present cash value represents how much
the business is worth.

Fair dealing.   The *Weinberger* court described *fair dealing* as relating to
"when the transaction was timed, how it was initiated, structured, negotiated,
disclosed to the directors, and how the approvals of the directors and the
stockholders were obtained." The court strongly recommended an independent negotiating committee of outside directors of the subsidiary to act
as a representative of the minority shareholders.

In *Weinberger,* minority shareholders of UOP challenged a cash-out
merger at $21 per share initiated by the parent, Signal. The court faulted the

procedures by which the merger had been initiated, negotiated, and approved — principally Signal's failure to disclose to UOP's outside directors or shareholders a feasibility study prepared by two of UOP's management directors, who were also executives of Signal. The study concluded that a price of $24 per share would have been a "good investment" for Signal. The court also found other deficiencies: Signal had initiated and structured the merger; there were no meaningful negotiations with UOP's outside directors; and the shareholders were not told that an investment banker's fairness opinion on the $21 price was based on a hurried and cursory review of the company. In all, the merger failed the fair dealing test, and the court remanded for the Chancery Court to reconsider whether the $21 price was fair and to order appropriate relief in view of the procedural unfairness of the merger.

Since *Weinberger* the Delaware Supreme Court has clarified some aspects of the entire fairness test:

(1)   The parent must disclose internally prepared valuations (and its reservation price) only if they are prepared by directors or officers of the subsidiary. *Rosenblatt v. Getty Oil Co.*, 493 A.2d 929 (Del. 1985). Only when executives have overlapping roles must the parent show its cards.

(2)   Negotiation by a team of the subsidiary's outside directors significantly buttresses procedural fairness, particularly when the directors are well-informed and negotiations are "adversarial." *Rosenblatt*. This is so even though the outside, nonmanagement directors are chosen by the parent.

(3)   Overwhelming approval by minority shareholders, after full disclosure, also buttresses procedural and price fairness. *Rosenblatt*. For this reason, it is advisable to condition the merger on approval by a specified majority of minority shareholders, even though their approval is not required.

(4)   If supported by an outside fairness opinion and asset valuations by outside experts, the share price paid minority shareholders can be calculated using the old Delaware block method. Valuation based on discounted cash value is not exclusive. *Rosenblatt*.

(5)   A squeeze-out merger, although the share price is within a range of fairness, may not be timed by the parent to avoid a contractual obligation to pay a higher price. *Rabkin v. Philip A. Hunt Chemical Corp.*, 498 A.2d 1099 (Del. 1985). The merger cannot blatantly advance the parent's interest at the expense of the minority shareholders' — a lingering business purpose analysis.

To date, *Weinberger* and its progeny have not addressed to what extent the parent must share with the minority shareholders any gains (such as financial, operational, or tax gains) created by the merger.

§26.3.4 Remedy in Squeeze-outs

The traditional remedy for unfair self-dealing — rescission of the transaction — often is not possible in a squeeze-out. A squeeze-out fundamentally changes the corporate structure, and returning the corporation and its shareholders to their prior position may be impractical.

Minority shareholders are not necessarily entitled to recover damages. *Weinberger* held that dissenters' appraisal rights (see Chapter 36) are normally the exclusive remedy when a squeeze-out merger is challenged on the basis of price. But when a merger is challenged on the basis of fraud, misrepresentation, self-dealing, deliberate waste, or palpable overreaching, the *Weinberger* court stated that appraisal would not be exclusive. See also RMBCA §13.02, Official Comment (appraisal is exclusive unless the transaction is "unlawful or fraudulent" — which includes violation of corporate law on voting or of the articles, deception of shareholders, and a fiduciary breach). This seems to mean that appraisal is exclusive only when price is challenged but not when there is a challenge of procedural fairness or the adequacy of disclosure.

EXAMPLES

1. Yankee Air, incorporated in an RMBCA jurisdiction, operates a passenger and cargo airline with its main hub in Atlanta. Yankee Air is a wholly owned subsidiary of Yankee Holdings, and most of Yankee Air's directors are officers of Holdings. Holdings owns a number of other subsidiaries in a wide range of industries. One of them, Yankee Shipping, operates a commercial shipping business in the United States and abroad. Under a contract with Shipping, Yankee Air provides air transportation services at rates significantly below those available from other airlines.
   a. Is the shipping contract subject to challenge?
   b. Yankee Air soon becomes insolvent because of the burdensome shipping contract with Shipping. Can Yankee Air's creditors hold Holdings liable on a self-dealing theory?

2. Yankee Holdings decides to expand Yankee Air's operation into new markets, but Holdings does not have enough capital. Yankee Air issues common stock to public investors to fund the expansion. After the public issue, Holdings holds 80 percent of Yankee Air's outstanding stock. The Yankee Air board, composed mostly of Holdings's officers, remains unchanged.

   Yankee Air acquires all of its aircraft under long-term leases with Holdings. Under the arrangement, Holdings becomes the owner of the aircraft, arranges for financing, and charges Yankee Air above-market rates for leasing the aircraft. Yankee Air nonetheless becomes highly profitable and issues a large stock dividend because Holdings needs cash.

    a. Is the leasing arrangement subject to challenge?

    b. The dividend is legally permissible but weakens Yankee Air's ability to expand further. Is the dividend subject to challenge?

3. Holdings ends its forced-leasing policy and allows Yankee Air to acquire aircraft from other companies. Yankee Air purchases aircraft and earns investment tax credits (ITCs) when it makes the purchases. (ITCs entitle their holder to reduce corporate income tax by the amount of the credit.) Holdings and Yankee Air agree to continue filing a consolidated tax return, which allows a parent corporation to include the income, deductions, and credits of any 80 percent subsidiary in a single consolidated return. Holdings files a consolidated return, and Yankee Air's ITCs reduce Holdings's total tax liability by $10 million. Yankee Air did not have any taxable income itself and under the tax law could not have used the ITCs itself.

    a. Under the majority approach to parent-subsidiary business dealings, must Holdings share this tax savings with Yankee Air? To what extent?

    b. Under the judicial approach toward preferences taken by controlling shareholders, must Holdings share the ITCs' value with Yankee Air? To what extent?

    c. Which approach is appropriate in this case?

    d. The prospectus that Yankee Air minority shareholders received when they invested said that Holdings would continue to file a consolidated tax return and that Holdings might use ITCs generated by Yankee Air in its consolidated return. Does this make any difference in deciding whether Holdings must share?

4. Frances is a director and officer of Yankee Air, as well as a director of Holdings. She learns that Lone Star Airways is selling a number of once-profitable air routes at bargain prices, and she suggests to Charles, the Holdings CEO, that the Yankee group should buy the routes. Charles agrees and is confident that the new routes would be highly profitable for Yankee Air. Holdings proposes a merger with Yankee Air in which minority shareholders will receive $50 per share. (Yankee Air's shares had been trading at $40.) Frances is the only one on Yankee Air's board who knows the reason for the squeeze-out is to profit fully if the Holdings group acquires the Lone Star routes. Which of the following will help insulate the merger from review in a challenge by a minority shareholder:

    a. Holdings does not disclose its interest in the Lone Star routes to the Yankee Air board or shareholders.

    b. The Yankee Air board forms a committee of outside directors to consider the merger. The committee hires its own outside lawyer and investment banker to advise it.

    c. The committee asks First Lynch Securities to opine whether $50 is a fair price for Yankee Air's shares, based on *current* earnings projections using a discounted cash flow analysis.

    d. The committee concludes it will be easier for a combined Holdings-Yankee Air entity to attract financing than would the current partially owned structure. The committee recommends the merger.

    e. The Yankee Air board conditions the merger on the approval of a majority of the minority shares, although without disclosing the possibility that Yankee Air might buy the Lone Star routes.

5. Holdings and Yankee Air take all these actions, and the Yankee Air shareholders approve the merger. Mildred, a minority Yankee Air shareholder, sues in court on behalf of Yankee Air shareholders (except those who did not vote for the merger and have sought appraisal).

    a. Who should be the defendants?

    b. What must the defendants show to withstand this challenge?

    c. Mildred seeks to have the merger rescinded. Is the court likely to rescind?

    d. The minority shareholders did not seek appraisal but claim that the $50 price was unfair. They say that Yankee Air, with the possibility of obtaining the Lone Star routes, was worth at least $65 per share. Is the court likely to award $15 in damages? On what theory?

EXPLANATIONS

1a. No. Who is hurt and who would attack it? Yankee Air has no minority shareholders, and its board is controlled by its parent, Holdings. Although the shipping contract is self-dealing by Holdings, it is not subject to fairness review. One of the benefits of complete ownership is the flexibility of the parent to choose profit centers — in this case Yankee Shipping.

1b. Perhaps. Under a theory that fiduciaries' duties to the corporation encompass duties to creditors that may be asserted on corporate insolvency, the creditors (or their representative) could claim a breach of Holdings's duty of loyalty to Yankee Air. In effect, the claim would be that Holdings was enriching itself at creditor expense through self-dealing. Whether the self-dealing was unfair may turn on whether Holdings disclosed to creditors its arrangements with Yankee Air (see §22.3.3). If the self-dealing was undisclosed to creditors, Holdings might also be held liable on a "piercing the corporate veil" theory (see §6.2.2).

2a. Yes. Minority shareholders of Yankee Air could bring a derivative suit challenging the arrangement as a breach of Holdings's fiduciary duty to Yankee Air and its minority shareholders.

    The arrangement is also a conflict-of-interest transaction because of the indirect interest of the Yankee Air directors. See RMBCA §8.60.

The directors predictably may be expected to further the interests of their employer, Holdings, at the expense of Yankee Air's minority shareholders. The RMBCA reflects the prevailing judicial approach and conceives of parent-subsidiary dealings as raising a conflict between the parent's and subsidiary's interests, not as a conflict involving the subsidiary's directors. This approach presumes that the subsidiary's directors will be dominated by the parent and that the parent's interests will be theirs.

2b. It depends. On its face, the declaration of dividends did not prefer Holdings because minority shareholders also received their pro rata share. Nonetheless, the parent may have put its cash needs ahead of the subsidiary's expansion potential. Should the dividends be characterized as a parental preference or as a business decision protected by the business judgment rule? The RMBCA is silent on the question.

Under the prevailing judicial approach, the board's declaration of dividends is subject to loyalty review only if the challenger shows the parent was motivated to prefer itself at the expense of the minority shareholders. This is a difficult showing in our case because the minority shareholders shared pro rata in the distribution, and it is unclear that the subsidiary's business was necessarily hurt by the parent's high-dividend policy.

If the challenger can characterize the transaction as a parental preference, Holdings would have the burden of showing a compelling business purpose for declaring the dividends. This may be difficult because there are suggestions that Yankee Air would have been better off with access to the internally generated capital. In the end, though, the minority faces a difficult burden to show the dividends preferred the parent.

3a. Probably not. Arguably, Holdings did not prefer itself to the detriment of minority shareholders because the ITCs in Yankee Air's hands were of little or no value — Yankee Air did not have enough taxable income to have used the ITCs. Tested under the business judgment rule, the ITC-sharing by Yankee Air passes muster if the subsidiary received some consideration for the ITCs. (The ITCs have some value because they could conceivably be used in the future under IRS carryforward rules, which allow credits that are unusable in one year to be used in future years when there exists taxable income, or if Yankee Air were sold to a company able to use the ITCs.) The calculation of a present value for this future, speculative value would be left to the discretion of the Yankee Air board. The prevailing approach allows a parent corporation to exploit its control position.

3b. Probably, to the extent of the tax savings value to Holdings. Under the preferential treatment analysis, the court strictly protects the subsidiary's and minority shareholders' interests. Arguably, a consolidated tax return and Yankee Air's ITCs had a value to Holdings of $10 million, the amount of the tax savings. Under this approach, a court would require a showing of a "compelling business reason" for Yankee Air giving up the ITCs, without receiving their value to Holdings. Unless the uncompensated sharing were shown to be necessary to Yankee Air — to keep Holdings as a source of future below-market financing, for instance — the court probably would require that Holdings pay full value. This approach attaches little significance to Holdings's control position, and the parent must treat the subsidiary virtually as an outside party.

3c. The "control preference" test. The more deferential business dealings test applies to transactions with the corporation that the controlling shareholder could also have effected with an outside party. The control preference test applies when the controlling shareholder uses control in a way unavailable to it in third-party transactions. The Yankee Air ITCs were not available to Holdings except through its control position.

3d. Yes. If minority shareholders knew of this ITC-sharing policy and their shares were priced accordingly, it is difficult to argue Holdings preferred itself at the minority's expense. The minority's knowing purchase (and pricing) of Yankee Air shares has the same effect as after-the-fact ratification. If *current* shareholders know of this policy and the market prices the company's shares accordingly, it is as though the shareholders ratified the policy unanimously. The policy is not even subject to waste review.

4a. Does not insulate. In general, the parent need not disclose its motives and purposes. Parent's management has fiduciary duties to the parent's shareholders to achieve a favorable transaction, consistent with the parent's fiduciary duties to the subsidiary's minority shareholders. Nondisclosure in this case, however, creates two problems. First, it would be procedurally unfair if a director of the subsidiary knew of the parent's interest in the Lone Star routes and failed to disclose these to the Yankee Air board and shareholders. *Weinberger.* Second, the parent cannot use control to prefer itself. Although it is unclear whether the Lone Star routes are corporate opportunities of Yankee Air, that possibility seems to be behind Holdings's desire to consolidate its control. Holdings should be prepared to disclose this interest and pay for the potential value it creates for Yankee Air.

4b. Helps insulate. If Yankee Air's minority shareholders are represented by outside directors — who are neither executives of Yankee Air nor directors or executives of Holdings — a court might treat the merger as an arm's length transaction. See *Weinberger.* As such, Holdings would have no obligation to reveal its cards unless forced to do so during the negotiations. The outside directors acting as a separate committee are well-advised to hire outside counsel and an investment banker, neither of whom should have any preexisting relationship to Holdings or Yankee

Air. The outside directors should be unhurried and fully inform themselves about, among other things, options for Yankee Air in the future, including adding new routes.

4c. Might help insulate. The opinion gives the committee objective information on fair value. The discounted cash flow method provides a valuation of a company's cash-generating worth. It anticipates a future earnings stream and calculates how much cash today would be necessary (making some assumptions about future interest rates) to generate that same stream. The Delaware courts now accept this as a legitimate, although not exclusive, means of valuing a company. Nonetheless, the opinion may not be valuable if it does not include the future potential value of new air routes. The investment banker's failure to consider this potential future cash flow would undermine the reliability of the opinion.

4d. Not help insulate. The committee should be considering the fairness to minority shareholders. It is not acting for Holdings. Whatever Holdings's business purposes, the committee must act as arm's length negotiator on behalf of Yankee Air's minority shareholders.

4e. Not help insulate. In general, conditioning the merger on approval by a majority of the minority shareholders — that is, more than 50 percent of the public shareholders (who own 20 percent of the stock) — ratifies the self-dealing transaction, *if the shareholders are fully informed*. In this case, the failure to disclose the potential value to Yankee Air of possible new routes undermines the value of minority ratification. Although Holdings need not discuss its plans, Yankee Air must discuss its material plans. Frank's knowledge of the possibility compels him and the Yankee Air board to disclose this material information.

5a. Holdings, as controlling shareholder, and the directors of Yankee Air. The cases place principal responsibility with the controlling shareholder to ensure entire fairness to the minority shareholders. In addition, the cases indicate the corporation's board has significant responsibilities in representing minority interests in the transaction.

5b. The RMBCA is unclear. A squeeze-out merger is a conflict-of-interest transaction in which minority shareholders are treated differently from the controlling shareholder. The minority receives the consideration (cash or other securities) specified in the merger agreement, and the controlling shareholder retains its equity ownership or acquires the subsidiary as a new division. The RMBCA does not address what standard applies to such transactions. Nonetheless, most courts permit such transactions, provided they are fair to the minority. Under an entire fairness standard, the defendants would have to show the price was fair and the dealings were fair. This would be difficult if Holdings failed to disclose its interest in acquiring the Lone Star routes. Nondisclosure would affect price fairness and taint any negotiations if Frank withheld this information from Yankee Air.

5c. No. Undoing the transaction would involve forcing shareholders to repurchase their shares at the merger price and rescinding any postmerger transactions between Holdings and Yankee Air. Rescission after the merger would probably be unworkable.

5b. Perhaps, on a disclosure theory. The RMBCA states that appraisal is exclusive unless unlawful or fraudulent. RMBCA §13.02 (see §36.3). If the court invalidates the merger as fraudulent, out-of-pocket damages that compensate shareholders for the difference between the "value" of their shares and the merger price is the usual fraud remedy. In this case, if the shares were worth $65 at the time of the merger, factoring in the possibility of the Lone Star routes, recovery would be $15.

27

Sale of Control

Corporate control is a valuable commodity. Shareholders who have control can minimize the risk that management's interests will diverge from theirs and use the assets of the corporation as they choose. But with control also comes responsibility to other corporate constituencies. In this chapter we discuss the duties that corporate law places on sellers of control.

§27.1 Sale of Office

Directors and officers are strictly prohibited from selling their offices for personal gain. *Rosenfeld v. Black,* 445 F.2d 1337 (2d Cir. 1971), *cert. dismissed sub nom. Lazard Freres & Co. v. Rosenfeld,* 409 U.S. 802 (1972). Corporate offices are not the incumbents' to sell. Officers are answerable to the board, and directors are answerable to the shareholders. As fiduciaries, corporate managers are bound to perform their functions under the terms of their appointment.

§27.2 Limitations on Sale of Controlling Stock

§27.2.1 Control Premium

The value of control is not always reflected in the trading price of corporate shares. Normally, individual shares cannot alone affect control, and their trading price does not fully reflect the latent control potential they carry. When a buyer seeks to amass enough shares to gain a voting majority, control value attaches itself to the shares. The difference between the value of shares with only latent control rights and their value as a means to achieve voting control is referred to as a *control premium.*

How is the control premium measured? Assume that Publix (a public corporation) has 10 million shares outstanding that trade at $50 per share. If Kendall owns 3 million shares, how much are his shares worth? They are probably worth more than $50 per share because a 30 percent shareholder of a company whose other shares are widely dispersed will generally have effective, working control. If Barbara wanted to buy Kendall's stock, she would have to pay extra for the control that attaches to his block of stock — let's say $240 million ($80 per share) for all of Kendall's shares. The control premium is the $90 million difference between the sales price and the market price of his block, or $30 per share.

§27.2.2   *The No-Sharing Rule*

The general rule is that shareholders can sell their shares at whatever price they can get, including at a premium not available to other shareholders. Controlling shareholders need not share the premium that their control block commands. *Zetlin v. Hanson Holdings, Inc.,* 397 N.E.2d 387 (N.Y. 1979). Some commentators have criticized this no-sharing rule and have urged an "equal opportunity" rule under which all shareholders would share pro rata in any control premium. Some commentators argue that control should be viewed as an "asset" of the corporation, and each share's equal ownership interest entitles it to participate equally in any increment in corporate value. Berle, The Price of Power: Sale of Corporate Control, 50 Cornell L.Q. 628 (1965). Others argue that if the buyer pays a premium because she believes control is more valuable in her hands than in the incumbents', the buyer will be willing to pay the same premium for all the shares. See Andrews, The Stockholder's Right to Equal Opportunity in the Sale of Shares, 78 Harv. L. Rev. 505 (1965).

Opponents of an equal opportunity rule argue that it would result in fewer beneficial control transfers and cause inefficient management to remain entrenched. The rule would increase the cost of buying control because the buyer would have to pay a control premium to all shareholders, not just to the holder of the control block. The buyer might be unable or unwilling to buy all the shares or to get financing. An equal opportunity rule would also dilute the value of control held by existing controlling shareholders, for which they may have already paid a premium. These commentators argue that minority shareholders would on balance prefer a rule that would result in efficient new management, even at the expense of not sharing in any control premium. Easterbrook & Fischel, Corporate Control Transactions, 91 Yale L.J. 737 (1982). Recent studies indicate that prices of minority shares rise in a public corporation after the sale of control, even when the control buyer does not later purchase the minority shares. See ALI Principles §5.16, note 1.

Nearly all courts have rejected the equal opportunity rule, primarily on the grounds that equal sharing would effectively require that any purchase of control be by means of a tender offer to all the shareholders and would discourage beneficial takeovers. Nonetheless, an equal opportunity rule of sorts now exists for acquiring control in publicly held corporations. Under federal tender offer rules applicable to public corporations (see §39.2), a transaction that meets the "tender offer" definition must be open to all shareholders — the "all holders" rule. 1934 Act Rule 14d-10(a)(1). Each shareholder must also be paid the highest price paid any other tendering shareholder — the "best price" rule. 1934 Act Rule 14d-10(a)(2).

§27.2.3 *Exceptions to No-Sharing Rule*

To discourage harmful transfers of control, courts recognize exceptions to the general rule of shareholder autonomy. See Elhauge, Triggering Function of Sale of Control Doctrine, 59 U. Chi. L. Rev. 1465 (1992). Controlling shareholders cannot sell in three situations:

Sale of Office.   Often the seller of a control block will promise, as part of the sale, the seriatim resignation of his directors, with each vacancy filled by the buyer's directors. Without such a promise, a control buyer would have to pay for a special shareholders' meeting to elect his new board or wait to buy until the next annual shareholders' meeting, or risk a large investment until his board is seated.

Courts treat a "board succession" promise as a prohibited sale of office in only two narrow cases: The challenger shows either: (1) the buyer did not acquire working control and could *not* have elected his own slate, *Essex Universal Corp. v. Yates,* 305 F.2d 572 (2d Cir. 1962); or (2) the sales price exceeds the premium the control block alone commands, suggesting part of the price included the sale of office. *Perlman v. Feldmann,* 219 F.2d 173 (2d Cir. 1955) (J. Swan, dissenting).

Some commentators have argued shareholders (not judges) should decide whether the buyer acquired "working control" when the buyer acquires less than 50 percent of the voting shares. In such cases, they argue, the buyer should demonstrate his working control at a shareholders' meeting to elect new directors. Courts, however, have not imposed this burden, and in no reported case has a buyer of control failed to have his board elected at the next shareholders' meeting.

Usurpation of Corporate Opportunities.   Some cases hold that a controlling shareholder cannot convert an offer made to the corporation into one to the shareholder. If the control buyer offers to deal with all the shareholders on an equal basis — such as by proposing a merger or the purchase of all the corporation's assets — the controlling shareholder cannot divert the "corporate opportunity" to himself. Some courts look at the seller's failure to disclose the offer to the corporation (that is, to the disinterested directors), and others focus on how the buyer presented his offer.

Sale to "Looters."   A controlling shareholder may not sell control if the seller has reason to suspect the buyer will use control to harm the corporation and the shareholders left behind. If the control seller suspects the buyer will loot the corporation by stealing corporate assets or engaging in unfair self-dealing transactions, the seller becomes liable for any damages caused by the buyer, including any damage to the corporation's earning power. Recovery to the corporation is not limited to the control premium the seller received.

When does a controlling shareholder have a reason to suspect the buyer is a looter? Looters do not often reveal their intentions. Courts accept that the selling shareholder is not a guarantor of the probity of the buyer — too strict a duty discourages transfers of control. Instead, most courts require the seller to investigate the buyer's intentions only when circumstances raise a reasonable suspicion that looting will follow the sale. *Gerdes v. Reynolds,* 28 N.Y.S.2d 622 (Sup. Ct. 1941); *DeBaun v. First Western Bank & Trust Co.,* 120 Cal. Rptr. 354 (Cal. App. 1975). Although actual knowledge of the buyer's purposes is not necessary, if circumstances surrounding the sale are suspicious and the seller fails to investigate or his investigation confirms the suspicions, the seller becomes liable for any losses to the corporation.

What circumstances create danger signals?

The price is too good.   Although a high price may merely reflect the buyer's view that the corporation is worth more in his hands than in those of incumbent management, an excessive premium should cause suspicion, particularly if the corporation's assets have a readily ascertainable market value. For example, if the buyer offers $8 million for a 60 percent interest in a closed-end investment fund that holds liquid marketable securities worth $10 million, the only explanation for paying $8 million for an interest worth $6 million is that he expects to extract the difference by looting the company.

The buyer cannot afford the company.   If the buyer buys control on credit and will use assets or earnings of the company to repay the debt, the seller should be on guard if the company's assets and anticipated earnings will be insufficient to repay the debt.

The buyer is dishonest or hurried.   If the buyer shows himself to be dishonest, the seller should make further inquiries. See *Harris v. Carter,* 582 A.2d 222 (Del. Ch. 1990) (even if sellers relied on misrepresentations to their detriment). In addition, if the buyer shows little interest in the company's business and urges that the transaction be closed quickly, the seller may be required to investigate the buyer's motives.

The buyer has a bad business reputation. If the seller knows the buyer has significant debts, outstanding liens against his other businesses, and fraud judgments against him, the seller should suspect that the buyer does not worry about how he makes his money. *DeBaun v. First Western Bank & Trust Co.*, 120 Cal. Rptr. 354 (Cal. App. 1975).

§27.2.4   *The Meaning of Perlman v. Feldmann*

The overlap of the sale-of-control limitations is illustrated by the famous, much-dissected case of *Perlman v. Feldmann*, 219 F.2d 173 (2d Cir. 1955). Feldmann, who controlled 37 percent of the shares of Newport Steel, sold his shares for $20 per share — a two-thirds premium over the then-market price of $12. A minority shareholder brought a derivative suit claiming that Feldmann had sold a corporate asset: Newport's control over steel supplies during the Korean War's steel shortage, when steel prices were controlled and access to steel supplies commanded a premium. Feldmann had invented a way to skirt the price controls (known in the industry as the "Feldmann Plan") by having buyers make interest-free advances to obtain supply commitments. The buyer (Wilport), a syndicate of steel end-users, sought access to Newport's steel supplies free of the Feldmann Plan. The court held that Feldmann had breached a fiduciary duty to the corporation because his control sale sacrificed the favorable cash flow generated by the Feldmann Plan. The court held Feldmann accountable to the minority shareholders to share his premium.

What was the theory of the case? The answers span the range of limits placed on control transfers:

Sale of office. After Wilport bought Feldmann's control shares, Feldmann and the rest of the board resigned and installed Wilport's nominees. The court agreed that the price Wilport paid for Feldmann's shares was a fair one, negating any inference that Wilport had paid Feldmann to sell his office.

Denial of "equal opportunity" to share control premium. Although the Second Circuit's opinion contains broad statements about the duties of fiduciaries, the court's focus on the loss to the corporation of the gains created by the Feldmann Plan undermines this broad reading of the case. Other courts, including state courts in Indiana whose law the Second Circuit was purporting to interpret, have rejected this broad holding.

Sale to looter. Wilport wanted control to have a supply of steel free of the Feldmann Plan prepayment terms — that is, it planned to engage in self-dealing at controlled "below-market" prices. Feldmann no doubt knew this. The Second Circuit rejected arguments that gray market pricing under the Feldmann Plan was unethical and concluded that Wilport had taken a corporate asset by discontinuing Newport's gray market profits. Nonetheless, Newport's minority shareholders on balance benefitted from the sale, as measured by post-sale increases in their share prices. That is, the loss of gray market pricing was offset by the vertical integration with Wilport or its more efficient management. Wilport was at worst a beneficent looter.

Taking of corporate control opportunity.   There was evidence that another purchaser had originally approached Feldmann to merge with Newport, a transaction through which all the shareholders would have shared in any control premium. Feldmann rejected this offer and soon after sold to Wilport.

Although the minority shareholders sued derivatively on behalf of the corporation, the Second Circuit allowed the minority shareholders to recover in their own right. Recovery by the corporation of Feldmann's premium would have allowed Wilport to recoup part of the premium it paid Feldmann for control (see §31.1.2).

§27.2.5   Disclosure Duties

Controlling shareholders who know of an impending control offer and buy shares from minority shareholders cannot misrepresent their reasons for buying. Likewise, when controlling shareholders purchase or sell minority shares in a face-to-face transaction, they have a fiduciary duty to reveal any material information — a disclose-or-abstain duty (see §28.2). Under Rule 10b-5, controlling shareholders also have a disclose-or-abstain duty when trading on public markets (see §29.5). But a controlling shareholder who fails to tell minority shareholders that he is selling for a premium is not liable to shareholders who neither bought nor sold and thus lack standing to sue. *Blue Chip Stamps v. Manor Drug Stores*, 421 U.S. 723 (1975); *Birnbaum v. Newport Steel Corp.*, 193 F.2d 461 (2d Cir. 1952), *cert. denied*, 343 U.S. 956 (1952).

EXAMPLES

1. Foamex manufactures foam for use in furniture. Stella, the corporation's founder, owns 40 percent of Foamex's stock. Stella is getting on in years and has left management to her son-in-law Carl, the company's CEO

and a 5 percent owner. There are 700 other shareholders, for whose stock there is a thin public trading market. Foamex stock has been trading at $20 a share.

    a. Boyerhill, a large furniture manufacturer and Foamex's largest customer, wants to buy the company. Boyerhill offers to buy Carl's stock at $50 per share if he and the rest of the board resign and install Boyerhill's directors. Would the election of Boyerhill's nominees be valid?

    b. Carl rebuffs Boyerhill, which then approaches Stella to buy her 40 percent block for $30 a share. What obligations does Stella have before selling?

2. Boyerhill had originally approached Carl suggesting that Boyerhill acquire Foamex in a merger at a price of $25 million — $25 per share. Carl told Stella about the offer. Stella thought the price was too low. Carl rejected Boyerhill's offer.

    a. Soon afterward, Stella suggested to Boyerhill that she would be willing to sell her 40 percent block at $30 per share — $12 million. Stella points out that this would be less expensive than Boyerhill acquiring control in a $25 million merger. Do you see any problems?

    b. Would it make any difference if Carl had informed the board of Boyerhill's merger offer and the board had turned it down because the price was too low?

    c. A court holds Stella liable for selling her shares after Boyerhill had offered to share the control premium with all the shareholders in a merger. Stella sold her shares for $12 million; in a $25 merger she would have received $10 million; and when she sold the aggregate then-current market value was $8 million. What is the appropriate remedy?

3. Soon after buying Stella's 40 percent block, Boyerhill buys Carl's 5 percent holding. Boyerhill paid Carl $30 per share on the condition that Carl would use his best efforts to have the other members of the board resign and install Boyerhill's slate of directors.

    a. Shawn, a Foamex shareholder, challenges Carl's sale. On what theory?

    b. Evaluate the merits of Shawn's challenge.

4. After installing its own board, Boyerhill increases its foam purchases from Foamex and takes volume discounts not available to other Foamex customers or in the industry. This pattern is not new. Boyerhill has bought control positions in other suppliers to obtain supply discounts. Stella knew about Boyerhill's past practices. Shawn calculates that these discounts reduce Foamex's annual earnings by $2 million.

    a. Shawn sues Stella. On what theory?

    b. Does Shawn have recourse against anyone else?

    c. A court finds Stella liable. To whom and for how much?

EXPLANATIONS

1a. No. Carl has sold his corporate office. Carl's 5 percent shareholding is insufficient to give his shares any meaningful control, particularly since Stella owns a controlling 40 percent block. The premium over market that Boyerhill was willing to pay for Carl's shares can only be explained as consideration for Carl's promise to use his influence on the board to help install Boyerhill's slate of directors. A shareholder could challenge the validity of the board's filling of vacancies.

1b. None, unless she suspects Boyerhill will loot the company. Shareholders have significant autonomy to decide whether or not to sell their shares, and the duty to investigate is triggered only when there is reason for the seller to be suspicious. Are there any apparent danger signals here? The 50 percent control premium hardly triggers suspicion — courts have approved control sales with premiums of up to 300 percent. Boyerhill's status as a Foamex customer does not necessarily imply future supply arrangements will be unfair self-dealing. Unless Stella had some reason to suspect that this was Boyerhill's plan — for example, if Boyerhill needed to cut its foam costs significantly to stay competitive — Stella would be under no obligation to investigate or to refrain from selling her shares.

2a. Yes. Stella's sale of her control block may be viewed as the usurpation of a corporate control opportunity. A merger would have meant equal sharing of any control premium. Although an equal-sharing rule may generally discourage corporate takeovers, when the buyer (as here) is willing to deal with all the shareholders, little would seem to be lost by enforcing a sharing requirement. Nonetheless, a control opportunity rule reallocates part of the control premium to the other shareholders and dilutes the value of a controlling shareholder's control block. The rule would put Stella in the untenable position of rejecting the transaction or putting the merger to a shareholders' vote and voting against it. Modern courts are not inclined to force sharing just because the buyer originally suggested a sharing transaction. Only if the seller engages in insider trading or fraudulently buys minority shares to resell to the buyer do the courts impose a sharing obligation.

2b. Perhaps. Arguably, the board's rejection of the merger opportunity freed Stella to take the opportunity herself. But the board's rejection, like that of other corporate opportunities, should be subject to fairness scrutiny as a conflict-of-interest transaction if Stella anticipated selling her control block. Was the board sufficiently disinterested, independent, and informed? See §22.3.

Even if the board's rejection would fail a fairness test, the question remains whether fiduciary law should force the sharing of a control premium whenever a buyer presents a control transfer as a sharing transaction. Forcing a controlling shareholder to seek board approval and giving minority shareholders another grounds for challenge chills control transfers. The no-sharing rule reflects a view that courts should intervene only when the transfer increases the risks of control abuse or frustrates minority expectations. The no-sharing rule assumes that normally control transfers are beneficial and that minority shareholders prefer a facilitative rule.

2c. Sharing with the minority, even though the normal remedy for a fiduciary breach is recovery by the corporation. Requiring Stella to pay her control premium (or a portion of it) to the corporation would produce a windfall for Boyerhill, indirectly refunding it the control premium it had paid for Stella's shares.

   The failure to share breached a duty to the minority shareholders, and any remedy should be tailored to address the theory of liability. There are two possible theories: (1) an "equal sharing" theory based on Stella's taking the control premium, a corporate opportunity; (2) an "improper rejection" theory based on her blocking the merger. Under an "equal sharing" theory, Stella would be liable for 60 percent of the premium to the other (60 percent) shareholders. This was the remedial approach in *Perlman v. Feldmann* (see §27.2.3). Stella's control premium was $4 million (the difference between her sales price and their aggregate trading value), suggesting a $2.4 million recovery for the other shareholders — $4 per share. Under an "improper rejection" theory, the loss to the minority shareholders of the blocked merger was $5 per share (the difference between the merger price and the market price).

3a. Sale of office. Carl's sale is prohibited if Shawn can show that Boyerhill did not obtain working control or Carl's premium ($10 per share over market) included a payment to relinquish his office. If so, Shawn can seek to have Carl share his premium.

3b. Shawn has a difficult challenge. Although a 5 percent block could not alone command a control premium, a 5 percent *incremental* block might have been of particular importance to Boyerhill, a 40 percent shareholder. The additional 5 percent would make it virtually impossible for the public shareholders to form an effective dissident block — it would take 91 percent of the public shareholders to outvote a 45 percent Boyerhill. On the other hand, the most significant impediment to Boyerhill exercising effective control is not Carl's 5 percent share ownership but Carl's incumbency and the board's control of Foamex's proxy machinery. Nonetheless, courts are reluctant to accept the obvious: A "board succession" promise has value to a control buyer and forms part of the bargain. Only if there is some suggestion Boyerhill has bought the board's replacement to abuse its control should a court intervene.

4a. Sale to a looter. There are two issues: (1) Did Boyerhill's self-dealing transactions constitute looting? (2) If so, did Stella have reason to suspect that Boyerhill would engage in them?

Boyerhill's self-dealing purchasing appears to be on terms unfair to Foamex — they do not fall into a range of what would be expected in arm's length transactions (see §22.3.2). Yet, overall, Boyerhill's ownership may not cause losses to Foamex. Looting liability is limited to the losses the new owner causes the company.

Even if Boyerhill is a looter, Stella is liable only if there were circumstances that created a suspicion Boyerhill planned to engage in unfair self-dealing. Although Stella should have known Boyerhill planned to increase its purchases from Foamex, Stella had no apparent reason to suspect the purchases would be on unfair terms. Stella was under no duty to investigate whether purchases from other Boyerhill-controlled companies were on unfair terms unless there were suspicious circumstances.

4b. Yes. He can also sue Boyerhill as controlling shareholder, on a self-dealing theory (see Chapter 22).

4c. Stella will be liable to the minority shareholders on a pro rata basis for their losses, not limited by the control premium Stella received. (Recovery in a derivative suit would indirectly reimburse Boyerhill.) These losses could well exceed (and if the looter does what it intended, should exceed) any control premium. Stella would be liable not only for the actual losses from the self-dealing (here $2 million a year) but also any losses to Foamex's earning power (consequential damages).

PART EIGHT

Dealings in Securities

28

Common Law Prohibitions on Insider Trading

Insider trading has captured a great deal of popular attention. From press accounts, it would seem to be among the most contemptible of corporate behavior. Remarkably, state corporate law turns a blind eye to insider trading on public stock markets. The law of insider trading is largely federal — an offshoot of securities antifraud Rule 10b-5 under the Securities Exchange Act of 1934.

In this chapter we discuss the nature of insider trading and consider its relatively limited regulation under state fiduciary law. In Chapter 29 we discuss the broader regulation imposed by Rule 10b-5, and in Chapter 30 we consider the federal remedial scheme under §16 of the 1934 Act applicable to short-swing trading profits by designated insiders.

§28.1 An Introduction to Insider Trading

§28.1.1 Classic Insider Trading

In the paradigm case of insider trading, a corporate insider trades (buys or sells) shares of the corporation using material, nonpublic information obtained through the insider's corporate position. For example, if Boris Ivansky, the CEO of MACO Inc., learns in his capacity as CEO that the company is about to obtain an important government contract and he secretly begins to purchase MACO stock, he engages in insider trading. This trading deprives shareholders who sell before the contract is made public of a hefty increase in the value of their shares. Ivansky has taken advantage of his position to benefit himself at the expense of MACO's shareholders.

The risk of insider trading arises whenever an insider has access to information that is not known to other stock traders (nonpublic information) and that is likely to affect stock prices once it is disclosed (material information). Armed with this information, the insider will be tempted to use it for personal advantage and exploit this advantage, whether the information is good or bad. If it is *good news* and the stock price goes up after it becomes public knowledge, the insider can make a profit by buying stock from shareholders. (An insider can garner an even greater profit by purchasing options to buy the shares in the future.) If it is *bad news* and prices will fall, the insider can make a profit by selling to unknowing investors. (An insider who does not own shares can accomplish the same thing by selling for delivery in a few days, known as "selling short," or by purchasing options to sell the shares in the future.)

§28.1.2   *Misappropriation of Information — Outsider Trading*

An insider also can exploit an informational advantage by trading in *other* companies' stock. If the insider learns through his corporate position that his company is about to do something that will affect the value of another company's stock, trading on this material, nonpublic information can also be profitable. For example, if Ivansky learns that MACO is about to acquire Bullseye and he secretly purchases Bullseye stock, he has "misappropriated" inside information. This trading deprives Bullseye's shareholders who sell before announcement of the acquisition of the hefty premium offered by MACO. In a real sense this is "outsider trading" because Ivansky was an outsider from the perspective of the Bullseye shareholders; if he violated any confidence, it was MACO's.

Although classic insider trading and trading based on misappropriated information often are grouped together under the rubric of "insider trading," the theory for liability in each case is different from the other. In fact, state fiduciary law has developed almost exclusively in the context of classic insider trading. Federal jurisprudence under Rule 10b-5, federal mail, and wire fraud statutes have grappled with both insider and outsider trading.

§28.2   State Fiduciary Law on Insider Trading

What are the duties under state law of insiders who exploit their informational advantage by trading on material, nonpublic information? State law provides a relatively narrow range of answers.

§28.2.1   Fraud or Deceit — Limited Tort Liability

Traditional tort law rules against fraud and deceit apply when:

- The insider affirmatively misrepresents a material fact or omits a material fact that makes his statement misleading. (There is a duty to speak in a relationship of trust and confidence.)
- The insider knows the statement is false or misleading or, under evolving notions, recklessly disregards the truth.
- The other party actually and justifiably relies on the statement.
- The other party is harmed as a result.

Restatement (Second) of Torts, §§525, 526, 537, 538. These elements are important because the regulation of insider trading (both federal and state) derives from them.

Tort liability is easily avoided if the insider simply keeps silent. In a public corporation, this is easy to do. For example, if CEO Ivansky knows that MACO is about to declare a special dividend, he can avoid the deceit prohibition simply by buying stock in an impersonal trading market without saying anything. Even if Ivansky is said to have a special duty to disclose, the absence of privity means there is no causal link between Ivansky's purchases and particular shareholders' sales. It would be nearly impossible for selling shareholders to prove they had actually relied on Ivansky's silence.

Early state courts, accepting the argument that corporate fiduciaries owe duties to the corporation and not to individual shareholders, imposed liability in insider trading cases only on a showing of actual deceit. This is *caveat emptor* — it creates no more duty than that which a used car salesperson owes her customers.

§28.2.2   Special Facts Doctrine

An insider trading rule that merely prohibits fraud fails to recognize an insider's special status as a fiduciary. State courts have recognized the problem, and the prevailing view has become that insiders have a diluted duty to individual shareholders to disclose their inside information or abstain from trading. Silence is not a defense. In face-to-face transactions — as distinguished from transactions on stock trading markets between anonymous traders — courts have developed a *special facts rule* under which neither affirmative misrepresentations nor actual reliance need be established.

The special facts rule is nonetheless limited. The following must be shown:

- The insider (an officer or director) purchased from an existing share-holder — sales by insiders to nonshareholder investors in the case of "bad news" are not covered.
- The insider was in privity with the selling shareholder — there must be a face-to-face transaction or something approximating it.
- The insider knew of a highly material corporate event, such as the impending sale of significant corporate assets or the declaration of a special dividend.
- Secrecy was critically important to the sale, and it seems clear that the shareholder would not have traded had she known the information.

Special facts cases have usually involved concealment of the insider's identity and sympathetic plaintiffs, such as widows.

A good illustration and the source of the special facts rule is *Strong v. Repide,* 213 U.S. 419 (1909), in which the Supreme Court applied general federal common law on insider trading. (The case arose when such things were possible before *Erie Railroad v. Tompkins*.) In the case, Repide (the company's majority shareholder and general manager) was negotiating a sale of corporate property to the Philippines government when he bought another shareholder's stock. To hide his identity, Repide used an intermediary to buy stock from the shareholder through her agent. The Court accepted that the agent would not have sold had he known that Repide was the buyer. After the Philippines deal went through, the stock increased in value tenfold. The Court held that Repide's position as majority shareholder, director, and negotiator, along with his affirmative concealment, were "special facts" that supported rescission of the stock sale.

§28.2.3 Strict (Kansas) Rule

A handful of state courts have expanded the special facts rule to impose a duty to disclose material, nonpublic information in any face-to-face trans-action; "special facts" need not be present. The theory is that insiders who acquire such information do so in their corporate capacity and cannot exploit their advantage at shareholder expense. This stricter approach has its origin in a Kansas case and hence is known as the *Kansas rule*. In *Hotchkiss v. Fischer,* 16 P.2d 531 (Kan. 1932), the court said that in direct negotiated purchases there is a "relation of scrupulous trust and confidence." A corporate president had told a widow, who was undecided whether to sell her shares or wait for a dividend, that he was not sure whether a dividend would be declared. The president bought the widow's shares for $1.25 per share, and a week later the board declared a $1.00 dividend, a possibility the president knew about. The president was held liable. Although the facts of the case fall into the special facts mainstream, the broad language of "scrupulous trust and confidence" has been seen as imposing a higher disclose-or-abstain duty. The "Kansas rule" has been rejected in some jurisdictions.

§28.2.4   Limitations of Special Facts Doctrine and Kansas Rule

Although the special facts and Kansas rules take some of the bite out of the limited deceit rule, they have two significant shortcomings.

"Bad news" insider trading.   The rules assume purchases from existing shareholders on the basis of undisclosed "good news." A number of courts have refused to impose liability when an insider dumps stock on nonshareholder investors using inside "bad news."

Trading on stock markets.   The rules require privity. When insider trading occurs on an anonymous stock trading market, state courts have shown great reluctance to impose a disclose-or-abstain duty. A good example is *Goodwin v. Agassiz,* 186 N.E. 659 (Mass. 1933), where the court held that insiders who purchased their company's stock on the Boston Stock Exchange could not be held liable under a special facts test. The insiders had access to a geologist's theory that, if valid, indicated the possibility of valuable copper deposits on property owned by the company. The court found two main problems with imposing liability. First, the court said the insiders had a fiduciary duty to the corporation, not to individual shareholders. Assuming there was no harm to the company when the insiders traded on corporate information, the court held that the insiders were not liable as fiduciaries. Second, privity between buyer and seller does not exist in anonymous trading on a stock exchange, and there will be insurmountable practical problems of how disclosure would be made when information (such as a geologist's theory) becomes material, and how to line up sale and purchase transactions to determine which shareholders are entitled to recover and how much.

The same analysis has been applied in Kansas rule cases, with the result that the traditional state rules have been irrelevant to insider trading in public corporation stock.

§28.3   Liability to the Corporation for Insider Trading

In an attempt to overcome these gaps in the common law, the New York Court of Appeals in *Diamond v. Oreamuno,* 248 N.E.2d 910 (N.Y. 1969), held that insiders who had dumped their stock after learning nonpublic bad news about the company's earnings could be *liable to the corporation* in a derivative suit. The court responded in two ways to the objection that no harm to the corporation had been shown. First, no harm need be shown. As between the insiders and the corporation, just as between an agent and his principal from whom the agent receives confidential information, the corporation "has a higher claim to the proceeds derived from the exploitation of the information." The insider cannot unjustly enrich himself. Second, the court inferred that the insider trading might have caused harm to the corporation by damaging the company's reputation and thus the marketability of its stock — though this need not be proved. The court analogized its novel approach to §16(b) of the Securities Exchange Act of 1934, which allows the corporation in a direct or derivative suit to recover short-swing trading profits from insiders (see §30.2). The court, however, doubted the adequacy of federal remedies. No relief was available under §16(b) because trading had occurred outside that section's six-month window, and, according to the court, Rule 10b-5 raised unresolved questions on defining the class entitled to recover, the measure of damages, and the allocation of recovery. (As we will see, these 10b-5 issues are today somewhat clearer. See §29.5.)

The *Diamond v. Oreamuno* approach in effect assumes nonpublic inside information is a corporate asset that cannot be used by insiders to their advantage even if the corporation suffers no pecuniary harm. Other courts have rejected the assumption. In *Freeman v. Decio,* 584 F.2d 186 (7th Cir. 1978), the Seventh Circuit predicated corporate recovery for insider trading on a showing that the corporation "could have used the information to its own profit." For example, if the corporation were about to buy its own stock in the market, any purchases by insiders would be in direct competition with (and raise the price to) the corporation. See *Brophy v. Cities Service Co.,* 70 A.2d 5 (Del. 1949). The Seventh Circuit analogized this weaker version of insider-trading liability to usurping corporate opportunities. Other courts have rejected the *Diamond v. Oreamuno* approach outright. *Schein v. Chasen,* 313 So. 2d 739 (Fla. 1975); cf. ALI §5.04 (adopting unjust enrichment approach, with the additional gloss that the corporation, or the shareholders as a group, can authorize or ratify insider trading if in the corporation's interest). Although the *Diamond v. Oreamuno* approach offers a practical solution to the limits of the traditional insider trading rules, it has some strange and troubling implications.

Windfall to nontrading shareholders.   Shareholders who held on to their shares during the insider trading receive a windfall if the corporation recovers. In the case of insider trading on good news, the losers are the shareholders who sold their shares at deflated prices: They do not share in the corporate recovery at all. In the case of insider trading on bad news, the losers are the investors who bought the stock at inflated prices: They recover only to the extent the corporate recovery increases the value of their stock — at most a partial recovery.

Possibility of multiple liability.   Corporate recovery also creates for the insiders the possibility of double liability. In addition to being liable to the corporation, the insiders may be liable under Rule 10b-5 to contemporaneous traders and for penalties up to three times their trading profits (see §29.5). Although the *Diamond v. Oreamuno* court suggested this problem could be handled by interpleader, there will be jurisdictional, notification, and class certification difficulties.

Despite these deficiencies, the ALI Principles view a corporate recovery better than no rule at all. ALI Principles §5.04 (prohibiting insiders from using material nonpublic information concerning the corporation to advance their pecuniary interests, whether or not such use harms the corporation).

§28.4   Liability for Outsider Trading under State Law

Until now the cases we have seen talk only about insiders exploiting their informational advantage by trading *in their company's shares* — classic inside trading. Very few state cases involve allegations of trading *in other companies' shares* using "misappropriated" information — outsider trading. Nonetheless, outsider trading may violate state trade secret laws and the antifraud provisions of state "blue sky" laws, as well as the principle that agents are duty-bound to keep their principals' secrets in confidence. See ALI Principles §5.04.

EXAMPLES

1. Elbert, a chemist of BIM Corp., has conducted preliminary tests on a superconductive material at room temperatures. If the tests can be confirmed, it will be a huge scientific breakthrough with enormous commercial potential. Adelle, BIM's CEO, learns of the tests and sends a memo to all who know of them urging complete secrecy. BIM's stock is publicly traded, and its stock price eventually doubles when BIM confirms the tests and discloses the discovery.

    a. Before Elbert's tests were confirmed, BIM's board offered Adelle options to buy the company's stock. Adelle accepted without telling the board of Elbert's tests. Is Adelle liable to the corporation under state law?

    b. Before Elbert's tests were confirmed, Adelle purchased BIM stock from Columbia Employees Pension Trust, one of BIM's major institutional shareholders. Adelle used a broker, who did not disclose for whom he was purchasing. Is Adelle liable to CEPT under a fraud theory?

    c. Is Adelle liable to CEPT under state corporate law?

    d. After Elbert's tests were confirmed but before they were made public, Adelle purchased BIM stock through her broker, who filled the order on a stock exchange. Shareholders who sold at about the time of Adelle's purchases seek to recover from her the profits they would have made if they had not sold. Can they under state common law?

    e. Still before public disclosure, Elbert (who is neither a director nor officer of BIM) purchased BIM stock from fellow employees who do not know of the discovery. He says nothing to them, and they do not ask. Is Elbert liable under state common law to these shareholders?

2. Let's turn the tables. Assume BIM publicly announced Elbert's tests before they were confirmed. The price of BIM's stock rises dramatically. Elbert then tells Adelle the announcement was premature. The tests appear to have been a fluke and cannot be reproduced. When BIM issues a public disclaimer, the price of its stock plummets to preannouncement levels.

    a. Before BIM disclaimed the original announcement, Adelle sold her stock under a corporate stock repurchase program. She did not tell the board or anyone else that the announcement had become misleading. Is Adelle liable to the corporation under state law?

    b. Before BIM disclaimed the original announcement, Adelle sold her entire shareholding to Mutual of Columbia, a major insurance company, through various brokers who did not disclose for whom they were selling. Is Adelle liable to MOC under state common law?

    c. Before BIM disclaimed the original announcement, Elbert (who is neither a director nor officer of BIM) bought put options as soon as he realized the original tests were flukes. Can any of those on the other side of these transactions recover under state common law?

    d. Elbert prepared the original announcement of the superconductivity material knowing that his preliminary tests were flukes. Elbert bought options, as above. Is he liable to the parties on the other side of these transactions under state common law?

EXPLANATIONS

1a. Probably. Adelle has a fiduciary duty to the corporation not to use her position to harm the corporation. Although she did not misrepresent anything, deceit law imposes a duty to speak on those in a relationship of trust and confidence. Further, her silence in the *face-to-face* negotiations fits the special facts test. The discovery had enormous potential value, and it is likely the board would have reconsidered its decision when it approved the options.

1b. Probably not. CEPT probably will be unable to show all the elements of fraud — there were no affirmative misrepresentations, and CEPT did not actually rely on Adelle's silence. CEPT did not know it was buying from Adelle and thought it was selling at a good price. Although evolving fraud standards impose a duty to disclose in a confidential relationship — requiring disclosure to an employer or a client — state fraud law has not yet expanded to cover a corporate insider's relationship to shareholders.

1c. Perhaps. It depends on whether the state accepts the strict Kansas rule or only the more limited special facts doctrine. Both tests cover dealings outside of impersonal trading markets, and neither requires affirmative misrepresentations. Nonetheless, the "materiality" requirements are different. Under the special facts doctrine, Elbert's preliminary tests must constitute unusual or extraordinary information that, if disclosed, would cause a reasonable shareholder to act differently. This may be hard to show because the tests had to be confirmed, and a reasonable shareholder might view the preliminary tests as flukes. The strict Kansas rule is less deferential. It is enough that the information would have been important to the shareholder's decision to sell. In view of the enormous potential value of the discovery, Adelle's duty of "scrupulous trust and confidence" probably would require her not to trade without first disclosing the tests and their potential implications. In either case, since CEPT's losses can readily be attributed to Adelle and are equal to her gains with respect to the sold stock, there are none of the problems of imposing liability for trading on impersonal trading markets.

1d. No. State fraud law requires some misrepresentation, absent in this case of impersonal market trading. Moreover, identifiable privity is required under the special facts doctrine and the strict Kansas rule. The absence of face-to-face dealings will preclude these shareholders from recovering from Adelle. Notice that the *Diamond v. Oreamuno* corporate recovery approach also leaves them in the cold because any recovery goes only to the corporation.

1e. No. Although state fraud law prohibits silence by those in a confidential relationship, it is unlikely that Elbert's coworker relationship would be enough. Courts have applied the special facts and strict Kansas rules only to officers and directors. Thus, even though Elbert as an employee has a fiduciary relationship to the corporation, he does not have a state fiduciary relationship to fellow coworkers or shareholders.

2a. Probably. Just as a fiduciary cannot buy from the corporation on the basis of undisclosed "good news," the fiduciary cannot sell to the corporation on the basis of undisclosed "bad news." Elbert's inability to confirm the original tests would seem to be material under both the special facts rule and the Kansas rule.

2b. No. There was no affirmative misrepresentation or confidential relationship, and hence no fraud under state law. Further, liability under a special facts or strict Kansas rule is premised on the fiduciary's relationship to existing shareholders. Adelle's sale to a nonshareholder investor leaves MOC unprotected under traditional state law.

Even if corporate recovery were available under a *Diamond v. Oreamuno* theory, BIM's recovery would only indirectly and partially compensate MOC to the extent the recovery increases the value of MOC's shares.

2c. Probably not. Under a put option, Elbert receives a contractual right to sell BIM stock to the option sellers in the future at a predetermined price (the *strike price*). If the strike price is higher than the market price on the strike date — which will certainly be the case once the "bad news" is announced — Elbert will profit either by selling cheap stock or (as is more common) by simply having the other party buy back the commitment at the difference between the lower market price and the higher strike price. There are options markets on which these arrangements can be made.

There are a number of impediments for option sellers to recover. Fraud law requires some affirmative misrepresentation, and here there was none. Corporate fiduciary rules require that there have been some semblance of privity — there was none. Further, because options traders are not shareholders of the corporation, even *Diamond v. Oreamuno* recovery may be unavailable because the disappointed traders were not past or present shareholders.

2d. Yes, under a fraud theory. Fraud law does not require privity; it is enough that Elbert knowingly made an affirmative misrepresentation intending that others rely, that the option sellers actually and justifiably relied, and that they were damaged as a result. Assuming the option sellers knew of the BIM announcement — which is likely — they have a good chance to recover. State corporate law, however, provides little help. None of the options sellers was trading in the capacity of a BIM shareholder.

Rule 10b-5

Corporate law regulates securities transactions in a variety of ways. State corporate law requires that shares be issued for proper consideration (see §8.1.3), limits when the corporation can repurchase shares (see §8.1.2), and superimposes fiduciary rules on securities transactions (such as mergers and restructurings) that are unfair to minority shareholders.

State corporate law, however, does not mandate that buyers and sellers of securities be on an equal informational footing. Federal law has assumed that task. The Securities Act of 1933 imposes expanded antifraud liability in the issuance of securities and specifies disclosure by issuers in a public distribution of securities. SEC rules under the Securities Exchange Act of 1934 impose disclosure requirements in trading markets, the most important of which is the securities antifraud Rule 10b-5.

In this chapter we consider Rule 10b-5: its background, scope, usefulness, and specific elements. We also discuss 10b-5's high-profile use as the principal weapon against insider trading.

§29.1 An Introduction to Rule 10b-5

Rule 10b-5 has aptly been described as "the judicial oak which has grown from little more than a legislative acorn." Its origins were humble. In 1942, faced with reports of a company president buying his company's stock while making pessimistic statements about company earnings, the SEC sought to fill a gap in its regulatory authority. The antifraud provisions of the 1933 Act prohibit fraudulent *sales* of securities, but there is no specific prohibition against fraudulent *purchases*. Using the catch-all authority of §10(b) of the 1934 Act, which authorizes the SEC to promulgate rules prohibiting "any manipulative or deceptive device or contrivance . . . in connection with the purchase or sale of any security," the SEC filled the "purchase" gap.

The language of Rule 10b-5, unchanged since its promulgation, comes from §17 of the 1933 Act. The rule prohibits *any person*, in connection with a purchase or sale of *any security*:

(1) to employ any device, scheme, or artifice to defraud;
(2) to make any untrue statement of a material fact or to omit to state a material fact necessary in order to make the statements made, in light of the circumstances under which they were made, not misleading; or
(3) to engage in any act, practice, or course of business which operates or would operate as a fraud or deceit upon any person.

§29.1.1   The Rule's Content

Some preliminary points are in order:

- The *"manipulative or deceptive device or contrivance"* language of §10(b) is different from the Rule 10b-5 language. Courts have interpreted the enabling statute to be narrower. The §10(b) limitation governs, and courts have come to treat the phrasing of the 10b-5 prohibitions as largely irrelevant.
- Rule 10b-5 protects both investors who purchase and shareholders who sell. Both the statute and the rule apply to *sales and purchases*, which the 1934 Act broadly defines to include "acquisitions" and "dispositions." See 1934 Act §3(a)(13), (14).
- Both the statute and the rule apply to *any security* transaction. It does not matter whether the securities are those of a public reporting company (whose securities are listed on a national stock exchange or registered under §12 of the 1934 Act) or whether the corporation is closely held.
- The statute and the rule apply to fraud *in connection with* security transactions — a broad concept that regulates false or misleading statements that affect securities trading. Rule 10b-5 applies to *any person*, whether or not the speaker himself trades.

§29.1.2   The Rule's Jurisdictional Reach

The jurisdictional requirement of §10(b) and Rule 10b-5 — the use of facilities of interstate commerce or the mails — raises what is essentially a nonissue. Rarely will a securities transaction *not* use the mail or interstate facilities at some point. The 1934 Act treats *intrastate* phone calls to involve the use of a facility of interstate commerce. 1934 Act §3(a)(17). If the transaction involves a check (which must be cleared) or a letter (for example, to transfer shares on the corporation's books), the mail will be used. It is difficult to imagine a securities transaction that does not involve interstate facilities or the mail.

§29.1.3 SEC Enforcement and Implied Private Actions

Under §21 of the 1934 Act, the SEC can sue to enjoin violations of its rules, including Rule 10b-5. Courts allow the SEC to seek broad equitable remedies where injunctive relief is insufficient. *SEC v. Texas Gulf Sulphur Co.*, 401 F.2d 833 (2d Cir. 1968), *cert. dismissed*, 394 U.S. 976 (1969) (ordering the establishment of a fund from which protected shareholders could recover from insider traders). The SEC can also recommend that the Justice Department institute criminal action, a common occurrence in insider-trading cases.

It is now beyond question that Rule 10b-5 implies a private cause of action. In *Kardon v. National Gypsum Co.*, 73 F. Supp. 798 (E.D. Pa. 1947), the first case to recognize a private 10b-5 cause of action, the court held an insider liable for misrepresenting that the business was not going to be sold, when in fact the insider knew it was about to be sold at a substantial profit. See also *Superintendent of Insurance v. Bankers Life & Casualty Co.*, 404 U.S. 6 (1971) (confirming existence of private action). Originally, courts justified an implied private action on a broad tort theory that where there is a legal wrong, there must be a private remedy — a theory since rejected by the Supreme Court (see §19.6.2). Nonetheless, an implied private 10b-5 action can be justified as a supplement to SEC enforcement and as a means for enforcing §29 of the 1934 Act, which makes void any contract that violates the Act's rules, including a fraudulent securities transaction that violates Rule 10b-5.

As we will see, only actual purchasers or sellers may sue for damages under Rule 10b-5 (see §29.4.2). In addition, if a corporation is the victim of a securities fraud, shareholders may sue derivatively under Rule 10b-5 on behalf of the corporation. There is, however, *no privity requirement* — that is, the defendant need not have traded with the plaintiff and in fact need not have traded at all to be liable (see §29.3.4). Even if it does not itself trade on the basis of the deception, a corporation that makes false or misleading statements in a prospectus, an annual report, a press release, or other public medium can be liable under Rule 10b-5.

§29.2 Rule 10b-5 — An Overview

Suppose that Liz tells Simon, a shareholder of MEGA Industries, that the company is about to lose a great deal of money on a new product when Liz has reason to believe the product will be phenomenally successful. Simon sells his shares, and when news of the product's success is made public, he wants to sue.

§29.2.1   Rule 10b-5 Fraud Elements

By its terms Rule 10b-5 does specify the elements a plaintiff must show to be entitled to relief. The Supreme Court has looked to §10(b), the source for the SEC's 10b-5 authority, for clues. Since the mid-1970s the Supreme Court has insisted that Congress meant "fraud" when it said "any manipulative or deceptive device or contrivance" in §10(b), and the Court has interpreted Rule 10b-5 to bear a strong resemblance to its common law forbearer.

As interpreted, the elements for 10b-5 liability are remarkably similar to those for the common law tort of fraud or deceit:

(1) Material misinformation.   The defendant affirmatively misrepresented a material fact, or failed to state a material fact that made his statement misleading, or remained silent in the face of a fiduciary duty to disclose a material fact.

(2) Scienter.   The defendant knew or was reckless in not knowing of the misrepresentation and intended the plaintiff to rely on the misrepresentation.

(3) Reliance.   The plaintiff relied on the misrepresentation. In cases of omitted information or trading transactions on impersonal trading markets, courts infer reliance under Rule 10b-5 from the omission's materiality or dissemination of the misinformation in the trading market.

(4) Causation.   The plaintiff suffered actual damages as a result. Courts use a variety of theories to measure damages under Rule 10b-5, including an out-of-pocket theory derived from common law deceit. Unlike the common law, Rule 10b-5 does not make punitive damages available.

These elements act as sieves that gauge whether the plaintiff's losses should be laid at the feet of the party who supplied the claimed misinformation.

§29.2.2   More on Rule 10b-5's Advantages

Return to our problem of Liz and Simon. If Simon sold his shares to Liz, his chances of recovering his loss are good whether he proceeds under state law or Rule 10b-5. If Liz was an officer or director of MEGA, Simon also has a fiduciary claim (see Chapter 28). Why then would defrauded securities traders (and their lawyers) use Rule 10b-5 rather than state law?

Procedural Advantages.   A Rule 10b-5 claim must be brought in federal court (1934 Act §27), where a plaintiff has a number of procedural advantages: State derivative suit requirements do not apply (see Chapter 32), even if the action is brought as a derivative claim; federal discovery may be broader; §27 of the 1934 Act authorizes worldwide service of process and broad venue; there is no diversity-of-citizenship requirement and state claims may still be brought as pendent claims.

Substantive Advantages.   Rule 10b-5 also has a number of substantive advantages. In our example, Simon would probably fare poorly under state law if Liz was not an insider and her misrepresentations were not express or if Liz had not purchased from Simon in a face-to-face transaction. For example, if Liz was a corporate officer who predicted poor product sales to throw off competitors and Simon had bought on a stock exchange, he might find little solace under state law.

Some Caveats.   Despite 10b-5's advantages, some recent developments have begun to shift securities fraud litigation to state courts. Civil dockets in many federal district courts are woefully crowded; some state blue sky antifraud provisions broadly cover deceptive *offers*, in addition to purchases and sales; some state provisions also cover *negligent* misrepresentations, dispensing with the 10b-5 scienter requirement; and state blue sky laws generally provide for recovery of attorney fees.

   Rule 10b-5 does not establish a limitations period. Instead, the Supreme Court has used the short limitations period of the 1934 Act's express remedial provisions. A 10b-5 action must be brought within three years after the challenged violation and within one year after the discovery of the facts constituting the violation. *Lempf, Pleva, Lipkind, Prupis & Petigrow v. Gilbertson*, 111 S. Ct. 2773 (1991). The Court rejected the prior approach of many circuits to borrow the typically longer limitations period for fraud actions in the state where the deception had taken place. After *Gilbertson*, Congress passed legislation to allow plaintiffs whose cases had been dismissed under the uniform three-year/one-year limitations period to reinstate their actions if the action had been filed before *Gilbertson* and if it was not time-barred under the limitations period then applied in the relevant circuit. 1934 Act §27A.

§29.3   Rule 10b-5 — The Basic Elements

§29.3.1   *Misinformation*

It is often said that Rule 10b-5 prohibits "false or misleading" statements. Not only are outright lies prohibited; so are half-truths. Even if a statement is true, it can be actionable if it omits related material information that makes the statement misleading. Rule 10b-5 also prohibits false impressions that manipulate the price of a company's stock. Artificial market activity has the same effect as false statements about the company and its securities. For example, if MEGA is about to issue new stock and management initiates a secret purchase campaign to raise the price of MEGA's sagging stock, this activity creates the misleading impression of market interest. It is as though MEGA had issued a false press release announcing higher earnings and induced demand for its stock that otherwise did not exist.

In addition, silence can violate Rule 10b-5 if the defendant has a duty to disclose because of a relationship of trust and confidence with the plaintiff. For example, bank employees who failed to tell shareholders they could sell their shares for higher prices in a resale market, instead of the primary market offered through the bank, breached their duty to disclose. The bank acted as transfer agent for the shareholders' corporation and thus had a relationship of trust. *Affiliated Ute Citizens v. United States*, 406 U.S. 128 (1972).

§29.3.2 *Materiality*

Not all misinformation is actionable. To make sure the misinformation is not a pretext by the plaintiff to shift his trading losses, materiality is a requirement for actions under Rule 10b-5. The Supreme Court has held that a fact is material if there is a substantial likelihood that a reasonable investor *would* (not *might*) consider it as altering the "total mix" of information in deciding whether to buy or sell. *Basic Inc. v. Levinson*, 485 U.S. 224 (1988). See also *TSC Industries Inc. v. Northway, Inc.*, 426 U.S. 438 (1976) (articulating same test for omissions in proxy statements) (see §19.6.3). If disclosure of the information would affect the price of the company's stock, it is material.

A slippery materiality question arises when corporate managers disclose corporate information, particularly information about merger negotiations, that may be significant to shareholders and investors. In any corporate disclosure, there will be a tension between the value of secrecy and the value of disclosure. Secrecy may be important, for example, to keep merger talks alive or to keep competitors off-guard. On the other hand, prompt and full disclosure fosters informed investment decisions and creates confidence in stock trading markets. The lower courts and the SEC have floundered on the issue. *Greenfield v. Heublein, Inc.*, 742 F.2d 751 (3d Cir. 1984) (corporation does not violate Rule 10b-5 when it makes "no corporate developments" statement during takeover negotiations if management did not know of anything that would explain unusual market activity); *In the Matter of Carnation Co.*, 1934 Act Rel. No. 22214 (SEC 1985) (corporation violates Rule 10b-5 when uninformed press officer issues "no corporate developments" press release during ongoing acquisition negotiations of which he was not aware).

In 1988 the Supreme Court clarified when corporate developments are material. In *Basic Inc. v. Levinson*, the Court said that if a significant corporate development is "certain and clear," the corporation must disclose. But when its occurrence is speculative, as is true with merger negotiations, the test of materiality must balance the probability that the event will occur and its anticipated magnitude in light of the company's total activity. When the corporation speaks, it must speak truthfully about material information. The Court rejected a bright-line test that merger negotiations are material only when the parties have reached an "agreement in principle" on the merger's price and structure. The Court said such a test (1) paternalistically assumes that shareholders cannot appreciate the uncertainty inherent in merger negotiations and (2) will necessarily be over-and under-inclusive.

The *Basic* Court distinguished the questions of materiality and duty to disclose. Just because corporate information is material does not mean the corporation has a duty to disclose it. The corporation can remain silent during merger negotiations unless it has a duty to update prior misleading reports or to disclose trading by corporate insiders. The SEC has incorporated this idea in its periodic disclosure rules, which exempt the disclosure of confidential merger negotiations — even if they are material. Sec. Act Rel. No. 6835 (May 18, 1989).

§29.3.3 Scienter

To establish a violation of Rule 10b-5, a private plaintiff must prove — just like in a state fraud action — the defendant's *scienter*, a "mental state embracing intent to deceive, manipulate, or defraud." *Ernst & Ernst v. Hochfelder*, 425 U.S. 185 (1976). In *Hochfelder*, an accounting firm *negligently* failed to audit the company's accounts, which would have revealed that the company president had induced investors to put money into nonexistent escrow accounts and then had pocketed the money himself. Defrauded investors claimed the accounting firm's negligence enabled the fraud. The Court rejected the argument, previously accepted by several lower courts, that negligence was enough under Rule 10b-5. It based its holding not on the language of Rule 10b-5, which actually supports such a construction, but instead on the enabling "manipulative or deceptive device or contrivance" language of §10(b).

This culpability threshold is the same whether the suit is brought by the SEC or a private plaintiff, and whether the suit seeks injunctive relief or damages. *Aaron v. SEC*, 446 U.S. 680 (1980) (scienter required in SEC injunctive action). In *Hochfelder*, the Court left open the question whether recklessness — where actual intent cannot be proved, but the circumstances indicate that the defendant should have known of the misrepresentations — might be enough to satisfy the culpability standard. The lower courts have uniformly accepted a recklessness standard. Although some courts have implied that recklessness includes unknowing (but gross) inattention, most lower courts have interpreted it to mean that the misrepresentation was so obvious that the defendant must have known of it. Under this prevailing view, recklessness exists when the circumstances strongly suggest actual knowledge or intentional deceit.

§29.3.4 *Reliance and Causation*

In a common law fraud action, the misrepresentation must be causally linked to the defendant's actions (the reliance requirement) and to the defendant's loss (the causation requirement). In securities fraud cases, the *reliance* requirement weeds out cases where the deception did not make any difference in the investor's buy-sell decision. The *causation* requirement, like proximate cause in tort law, weeds out those cases where the stock trade was not "responsible" for the investor's loss.

Reliance.   Courts treat reliance as an element of a Rule 10b-5 case but have significantly relaxed the requirements of proof. In cases of nondisclosure or of misrepresentations on trading markets, courts presume reliance. Nonetheless, if it can be shown that the plaintiff actually did not rely — because he would have purchased anyway or because he actually knew of the misrepresentation at the time of his transaction — there can be no Rule 10b-5 liability.

Nondisclosure.   In a case of nondisclosure — whether involving an open-market or face-to-face transaction — courts dispense with proof of reliance if the undisclosed facts were material. *Affiliated Ute Citizens v. United States,* 406 U.S. 128 (1972) (no reliance need be shown when bank employees in face-to-face transactions failed to disclose stock's value or the bank's position as market maker in stock). The materiality of the undisclosed information means a reasonable investor would have considered it important. To require proof of reliance in such cases would impose a nearly insuperable burden on plaintiffs to prove they relied on something not said.

Fraud on market.   In a case of false or misleading statements on a public trading market — a so-called *fraud on the market* — courts have created a rebuttable presumption of reliance. *Basic Inc. v. Levinson,* 485 U.S. 224 (1988) (plurality decision). The theory is that those who trade on public trading markets rely on the integrity of the stock's market price. In an open and developed stock trading market, the market price — according to the efficient capital market hypothesis — reflects all public information about a company's stock, and investors implicitly assume the price reflects true information. If a misrepresentation artificially inflated (or deflated) the market price and thus operated as a "fraud on the market," courts infer that investors who rely on the price as reflecting true value have relied on the misrepresentation. If the truth had been disclosed, investors would not have traded at the prevailing nondisclosure price. In *Basic Inc. v. Levinson,* the Supreme Court said a defendant can rebut the presumption of reliance and avoid the "fraud on the market" theory by showing that the challenged misrepresentation did not in fact affect the stock's price or that the plaintiff would have traded regardless of the misrepresentation.

Face-to-face misrepresentations. In a misrepresentation case involving a face-to-face transaction, reliance must be shown. But in keeping with Rule 10b-5's liberal remedial purposes, some courts have crafted a "reasonable reliance" test that requires only that the plaintiff show (1) he was aware of the misrepresentation, and (2) it was *in a general sense* material, even though the plaintiff did not subjectively rely on its veracity.

Causation and damages. A 10b-5 plaintiff must show two kinds of causation to recover. *Transaction causation* requires the plaintiff to show that "but for" the defendant's fraud, the plaintiff would not have entered the transaction or would have entered under different terms — in effect, a reliance requirement. *Loss causation* requires the plaintiff to show that the fraud produced the claimed losses to the plaintiff — in effect, a proximate cause requirement. If the investor's loss is due to extraneous causes, such as a general decline in the economy, Rule 10b-5 does not impose liability.

Private 10b-5 plaintiffs have a full range of equitable and legal remedies. Section 28 of the 1934 Act, which states that the plaintiff's recovery cannot exceed actual damages, specifies the only limitation.

The courts have adopted various damages theories. To illustrate, assume that Liz announces publicly that sales of a heralded new product of MEGA Industries will be disappointing. At the time MEGA's stock is trading at $25; after the false bad news it falls to $20. (Experts later opine the stock's "value" at the time was $27, given the product's true potential.) Simon sells to Liz at $20. When rumors begin to circulate that Liz's announcement was unduly negative, the stock price rises, and Liz sells at $28. Then MEGA discloses the product's true success, and its stock price jumps to $31. When Simon sues Liz, the market price is $33. What remedies are available to Simon?

Rescission. In a face-to-face transaction, rescission allows the defrauded plaintiff to cancel the transaction. If the plaintiff sold, he gets his stock back; if he bought, he returns the stock and forces the seller to return the purchase price. In our example, if Liz had not sold the stock she bought from Simon, Simon could force her to resell for $20, producing for Simon an instant paper gain between the rescission price and $33 (the current market price) — $13.

Rescissionary (disgorgement) damages.   If the stock has been resold and rescission is not possible, rescissionary damages replicate cancelling the transaction. A defrauded seller recovers the buyer's profits (the difference between the price at which the defendant bought the stock and the price at which the defendant resold it). A defrauded buyer can recover from the seller his losses (the difference between the price the plaintiff bought the stock for and the price at which the plaintiff resold it). In our example, Liz would disgorge her profits — the difference between $20 (the price Liz bought the stock for) and $28 (the price at which she sold it) — $8.

Cover (or "conversion") damages.   Cover damages, like those in a tort conversion action, restore the plaintiff to his original position absent the fraud. They are the difference between the price at which the plaintiff purchased or sold and the price at which the plaintiff could have sold or repurchased once the fraud was revealed. The theory assumes the plaintiff must cover (by selling or reinvesting) to mitigate his losses. In our example, Simon would recover the difference between $20 (the price at which he sold) and $31 (the market price once the fraud was revealed) — $11.

Out-of-pocket damages.   This is the most common measure of damages in Rule 10b-5 cases. The plaintiff claims the difference between what he actually purchased or sold the stock for and its "value" at the time. This does not take into account any posttransaction changes in price. In our example, if the court accepted the experts' opinion on "value," Simon could recover the difference between $27 (the stock's but-for value when he sold) and $20 (his actual price) — $7. Valuing stock is often speculative, and some courts have used the change in price at the time of disclosure as a measure of the difference between original cost and value. In our example, this would be the difference between $28 (the predisclosure price) and $31 (the post-disclosure price) — $3.

As the different amounts of recovery in our example indicate, which theory the court accepts may make a big difference in the amount of recovery. No one theory is always advantageous to the plaintiff because the relative differences between transaction price, resale price, and market price can vary, and with them the relative recovery under each theory. Courts may decide to use the theory advanced by the plaintiff or one that best fits the pattern of the transactions, that best serves the goal of compensating defrauded traders, or that best deters the challenged behavior.

In one significant respect, Rule 10b-5 is less advantageous than a state fraud claim. The "actual damages" limitation of §28 of the 1934 Act means no punitive damages can be awarded.

§29.3.5   *Fraud Must Be "in Connection with" the Securities Trading*

Rule 10b-5 requires that the false or misleading statements be "in connection with" the trading of securities. Courts have interpreted this requirement broadly to include any fraudulent scheme that includes a securities transaction. In *Superintendent of Insurance v. Bankers Life & Casualty Co.*, 404 U.S. 6 (1971), the Court held that a complex scheme to misappropriate the assets of an insurance company violated Rule 10b-5, since it was accomplished by deceiving the board to authorize the sale of some of the company's securities — namely, $5 million of U.S. Treasury bonds — without receiving equal consideration. The Court held that the fraudulent scheme was "in connection with" a securities transaction.

In addition, courts have interpreted the broad "in connection with" language to mean that there is no requirement of privity in a Rule 10b-5 action. Although private plaintiffs must have been purchasers or sellers to seek damages, there is no requirement that the defrauding defendant traded with the plaintiff or with anyone else. Thus, corporate statements — such as press releases and annual reports — reasonably calculated to influence the investing public are actionable under Rule 10b-5, even if the corporation did not itself trade in the market or profit from the deception. *Basic Inc. v. Levinson*, 485 U.S. 224 (1988).

§29.4   The Limits of Rule 10b-5 — Pruning the Oak

In a series of decisions beginning in the mid-1970s, the Supreme Court has sought to prune the reach of the Rule 10b-5 oak.

§29.4.1   *The Scienter Requirement*

In 1976 the Supreme Court rejected the argument that negligence could be actionable under Rule 10b-5 and instead required that the plaintiff prove the defendant's scienter. *Ernst & Ernst v. Hochfelder*, 425 U.S. 185 (1976). Although a scienter requirement increases the burden on 10b-5 plaintiffs, it also limits the defendant's defenses. Before *Hochfelder* the negligence standard had been a two-edged sword. Some lower courts had allowed defendants to assert an affirmative defense that the plaintiff had not been reasonably diligent in noticing the misrepresentation. The idea was that when neither party knew of the misrepresentation, any loss should fall on the more culpable party. Since *Hochfelder* lower courts have allowed a due diligence defense only if the plaintiff acted recklessly with the same degree of culpability as the defendant in failing to uncover the misrepresentation. The defense is limited because defendants generally are in a better position to have known of the fraud.

§29.4.2   *Purchaser or Seller Standing*

In 1975 the Supreme Court held that only actual purchasers or sellers may recover damages in a private action under Rule 10b-5. *Blue Chip Stamps v. Manor Drug Stores,* 421 U.S. 723 (1975). Even if a misleading statement leads persons not to buy (or not to sell) a security — with results as damaging as if the person had been induced to trade — there is no 10b-5 liability.

In *Blue Chips Stamps* an antitrust consent decree called for the reorganization of a trading stamp company. The decree required the reorganized company to offer its shares at a discount to retailers harmed by the prior anticompetitive activities. Management had an incentive to discourage the retailers from purchasing. One of the retailers, who decided not to buy, later sued and sought damages on the theory that the prospectus offering the stock was intentionally too pessimistic. Speaking for the Court, Justice Rehnquist said that the language of §10(b) and the 1934 Act's definitions did not cover "offers" to sell, but only actual "sales or purchases." He found telling that for nearly 25 years Congress had failed to act in the face of consistent application of the doctrine articulated in *Birnbaum v. Newport Steel Corp.,* 193 F.2d 461 (2d Cir.), *cert. denied,* 343 U.S. 956 (1952), that nonpurchasers do not have Rule 10b-5 standing (the so-called *Birnbaum* doctrine). Justice Rehnquist then launched into a diatribe against Rule 10b-5 litigation in general. He speculated that an indeterminate class of nonpurchasers would bring vexatious litigation to extract settlements and in the process disrupt business and abuse the discovery process. In addition, liability could be staggering if nonpurchasers could claim they would have purchased had disclosure been less discouraging.

Blue Chip Stamps leaves open the question whether the purchaser-or-seller standing rule extends to injunctive relief. Lower courts have said that the *Birnbaum* doctrine only applies to private damages actions because there is no problem of speculative or runaway liability in an injunctive action. Nonetheless, the *Blue Chip Stamps* Court's reading of the language and the history of the statute and the concern about vexatious strike-suit injunctive actions by an indeterminate class of plaintiffs, the *Birnbaum* rule may extend to injunctive actions, too.

§29.4.3   *Deception Requirement*

In 1977 the Supreme Court held that Rule 10b-5 regulates only deception, not unfair transactions or breaches of fiduciary duties. *Santa Fe Industries v. Green,* 430 U.S. 462 (1977). Even though shareholders claiming corporate mismanagement or a breach of fiduciary duties may find federal securities litigation more attractive than state litigation, Rule 10b-5 does not cover allegations of corporate mismanagement unless the shareholder can point to inadequate disclosure or manipulation of stock prices through deception.

In *Santa Fe* a parent company merged with its majority-owned subsidiary (see §35.2.3) after giving minority shareholders notice of the merger and an information statement that explained their rights to a state appraisal remedy. The parent stated that a valuation of the subsidiary's assets indicated a $640 per share value, even though the parent was offering only $125 per share, an amount slightly higher than a valuation of the subsidiary by the parent's investment banker. The Court held that unless the disclosure had been misleading (which plaintiffs did not claim was the case) no liability could result. An unfairly low price could not amount to a fraud.

The holding in *Santa Fe* has led to the inventive question whether Rule 10b-5 applies to failure to disclose unfairness: Can there be 10b-5 liability for failing to disclose that a particular transaction is unfair or constitutes a breach of fiduciary duties? Claiming such a failure is a clever attempt to get to federal court on what is essentially a state claim.

It would seem that *Santa Fe* precludes such claims. First, they are essentially state fiduciary claims dressed up in federal disclosure clothing. The ruse is transparent, and *Green* makes clear that Rule 10b-5 is not a source of federal fiduciary law. Second, even if the directors in some abstract sense "deceived the corporation" by failing to disclose the transaction's unfairness, it is unclear that disclosure would have changed anything because the directors might still have approved the transaction.

Nonetheless, several lower courts have upheld a "fraud on the corporation" claim. In the leading case, *Goldberg v. Meridor,* 567 F.2d 209 (2d Cir. 1977), *cert. denied,* 434 U.S. 1069 (1978), the Second Circuit accepted that minority shareholders could bring a derivative action on behalf of the corporation (see §31.1), claiming that the company's directors had failed to disclose the unfairness of certain self-dealing stock transactions between the corporate parent and the corporation. The *Goldberg* court focused on a press release to minority shareholders that failed to mention the inadequacy of the transactions' consideration. The court's theory was that if noninterested directors or minority shareholders could have used the disclosure to disapprove or enjoin the stock transactions under state law, the disclosure would be material to the corporation in making its "decision" to enter into the transaction. The theory is limited to fiduciary breaches in connection with securities transactions.

§29.4.4 *No Aiding and Abetting Liability*

Often the principal perpetrators of a securities fraud, such as corporate officers or the selling brokers, are judgment-proof. Not surprisingly, defrauded securities traders have sought to extned 10b-5 liability to secondary participants, such as accountants and lawyers, who assisted in the fraudulent transaction.

In 1994 the Supreme Court rejected aiding and abetting liability under Rule 10b-5. *Central Bank of Denver v. First Interstate Bank of Denver,* — U.S. — (1994). In a 5-4 decision, the Court read the "manipulative or deceptive" language of §10(b) to require that 10b-5 defendants engage in actual fraudulent behavior, not merely collateral assistance. The Court pointed out that none of the other express private causes of action of the 1934 Act impose aiding and abetting liability and that such liability has never been widely accepted under tort law. Even though lower courts since 1966 had widely assumed 10b-5 aiding and abetting liability, the Supreme Court concluded that Congress had never approved these cases and suggested that Congress should remedy the problem if the Court's reading was in error.

§29.4.5   *Rule 10b-5's Continuing Vitality*

Not all of the Supreme Court's recent 10b-5 cases have cut back on the reach of 10b-5 liability.

In 1993 the Court accepted the existence of a right to seek contribution among parties jointly liable under Rule 10b-5. *Musick, Peeler & Garrett v. Employers Ins. of Wausau,* 115 S. Ct. 2085 (1993). The Court noted that Congress has recognized a judicial authority to shape 10b-5 liability and that other express antifraud provisions of the 1934 Act explicitly permit parties who become liable to recover contribution from others who would have been liable if they had also been sued.

In 1985 the Court held that Rule 10b-5 applies to stock sales in a sale-of-business transaction, even though the purchaser is not investing as a shareholder but buying the business outright. *Landreth Timber Co. v. Landreth,* 471 U.S. 681 (1985). Rejecting a *sale of business doctrine,* the Court read Rule 10b-5 literally to apply to any purchase or sale of securities, including the sale of a business structured as a 100 percent stock sale.

In 1983 the Court held that even though a claim against an accounting firm could have been brought under §11 of the 1993 Act (the prospectus liability provision), an action under Rule 10b-5 was proper. *Herman & MacLean v. Huddleston,* 459 U.S. 375 (1983). The Court rejected the suggestion in other decisions concerning implied private actions that specific liability schemes negated an inference of broad implied remedies.

EXAMPLES

1. Last year BIM Corp. (whose common stock is publicly traded) issued preferred stock to a group of institutional investors in a private placement exempt from registration under the 1933 Act. BIM is now experiencing financial problems — its annual revenues have dropped from $400 to $300 million, and it has discontinued paying dividends on the preferred

stock. One of the investors, Lucre Life Insurance Company, thinks the offering circular describing the preferred stock was misleading.

   a. Does Lucre Life have standing to bring an action under Rule 10b-5?

   b. Lucre Life is worried about delays in federal court. Can it sue in state court?

2. The offering circular stated: "BIM is committed to superconductivity research and has spent over $30 million on this research in the last two years."

   a. In fact, BIM had spent only $27 million. Is there 10b-5 liability?

   b. The offering circular failed to mention that BIM's superconductivity research is a long shot and there is no assurance it will produce results having any commercial value. Is there 10b-5 liability?

3. BIM's offering circular falsely stated the company had been awarded a large government contract. In fact, the company was hoping to receive it, but its bid lost. Jane, BIM's outside attorney who prepared the offering circular, had an inkling that BIM had not actually been awarded the contract.

   a. Assuming the offering circular was materially false, can Lucre Life sue Jane under Rule 10b-5?

   b. Jane sent a letter that urged Lucre Life to buy BIM stock although she did not mention or know the status of the contract award. Can she be liable?

   c. Lucre Life did not read the portion of the offering circular mentioning the contract award. There is no organized market in BIM's preferred shares. Can it recover under Rule 10b-5?

   d. Lucre Life bought its stock at $100. After it learned that BIM had lost the bid, it sold at $75. Assuming liability, how much can Lucre Life recover?

4. Lucre Life settles its lawsuit. Soon afterward, BIM research scientists conduct preliminary tests on a metallic ceramic that indicates superconductivity at room temperatures. If true, the discovery would be an enormous breakthrough with great commercial value.

   a. Must BIM issue a press release disclosing the tests?

   b. In the week after the tests, there is an unusual amount of trading activity in BIM's common stock, which rises in price from $50 to $60. A *Wall Street Journal* reporter calls John, BIM's president, and asks if he can explain the recent price rise. John does not believe there has been insider trading and doesn't want to say anything. What should he do?

   c. BIM's management wants to put an end to media speculation and issues a press release stating that "there are no corporate developments that would explain the unusual recent market activity in BIM's stock." Does this violate Rule 10b-5?

   d. How should the press release have been drafted?

5. Sharon sells her BIM stock when the price falls after the press release. Eventually, BIM issues another press release confirming its preliminary research and its stock price rises. But Sharon no longer owns BIM stock.

    a. BIM never purchased or sold its stock in connection with the press release. Can Sharon sue BIM under Rule 10b-5?

    b. Sharon was never aware of the first misleading press release, and BIM argues her decision to sell was unrelated to it. Can Sharon show she acted in reliance on the press release?

6. Sharon becomes interested in BIM again after the second press release confirming the superconductivity tests. She asks her broker, Conway, whether she should buy. Conway's brokerage firm is buying BIM stock, and Conway tells Sharon a self-serving lie that BIM is about to announce the tests were flukes. Sharon does nothing.

    a. Can Sharon sue her broker under Rule 10b-5?

    b. Does Sharon have any other recourse?

7. BIM owns a fast-food chicken subsidiary, Captain Broiler. BIM's management considers selling BIM's 100 percent stake in Captain Broiler to Polly Farms. Management's decision is made easier when Polly Farms gives each member of BIM's top management a new luxury car. BIM's board approves the sale.

    a. BIM announces the sale to its shareholders and states "the transaction is consistent with the corporation's long-term strategy." The announcement does not mention the luxury cars. Has management violated Rule 10b-5?

    b. After the purchase, Polly Farms realizes that BIM's management had significantly overstated Captain Broiler's past earnings. Can it sue under Rule 10b-5?

    c. The sale was consummated in January 1993; Polly Farms realized the earnings were overstated in May 1993; it sued BIM in January 1995. Did Polly Farms sue in time?

EXPLANATIONS

1a. Yes. Lucre Life has standing as a purchaser of securities, even though they are not traded on a public trading market.

1b. Not under Rule 10b-5. Jurisdiction over 10b-5 claims is exclusively in federal court. If the action were brought in federal court, any state fraud or blue sky claims could be brought as pendent claims. Suing in federal court may provide some procedural and substantive advantages that may encourage the defendant to settle. In addition, many securities lawyers perceive federal judges to be more sophisticated in securities matters.

    Nonetheless, Lucre Life could sue in state court on a theory of common law fraud or under state blue sky provisions similar to Rule 10b-5. Substantive state law may not be much different from Rule 10b-5 and in some states may be broader.

2a. Probably not. The only representation was the $3 million discrepancy between stated and actual research expenditures. A 10 percent discrepancy in research expenditures for a company with $400 million in revenues would not seem material. Lucre Life would have to show it is substantially likely a reasonable investor would have considered the $3 million discrepancy important in deciding to invest at the offering price.

2b. Probably not. It seems unlikely a reasonable investor, particularly an institutional investor in the preferred stock offering, would have understood BIM's statement that it was "committed to superconductivity research" as suggesting the company expected commercial successes. The "no assurance" caveat would not have added to the overall mix of information available to the investors.

3a. Not unless Jane herself engaged in fraudulent behavior, such as by making false or misleading statements on which investors relied. Jane may not be liable under Rule 10b-5 on an aiding and abetting theory based solely on her assistance in the transaction. See *Central Bank of Denver v. First Interstate Bank of Denver* (§29.4.4). Moreover, Jane's silence is not actionable unless she had a fiduciary relationship with Lucre Life that obligated her to speak. This would not be the case if she was acting as an attorney for BIM, the seller.

3b. Perhaps. By sending the soliciting letter, which failed to mention the true status of the contract award, Jane became a primary participant in the fraud. Even though she did not know her letter was misleading, she may be liable on a recklessness theory. Courts have inferred scienter when the circumstances suggest that the misrepresentation was so obvious that the defendant must have known about it.

3c. Perhaps. Reliance is an element of a 10b-5 action, and Lucre Life must show it acted on the basis of the circular's false statements concerning a government contract. This will be difficult because the plaintiff never read this part of the circular. Nor is there an open, developed, efficient market that sets the price for the preferred stock, undermining for the plaintiff a traditional "fraud on the market" theory of reliance. Nonetheless, Lucre Life might argue that it relied on the private placement market. Some courts have accepted the argument that a plaintiff establishes reliance if it can show a new offering would not have been marketed at all if the investors had known the true facts. That is, Lucre Life could argue it relied on the other institutional investors' decision to buy. This theory nearly excuses reliance in any issuance of stock, and some courts have limited the theory to fraud that was "so pervasive that it goes to the very existence" of the securities on the market. *Ross v. Bank South, N.A.,* 885 F.2d 723 (11th Cir. 1989), *cert. denied,* 110 S. Ct. 1924 (1990).

3d. Lucre Life has a number of remedial theories to choose from; its choice may depend on which defendant it seeks to recover from. If the plaintiff seeks to recover from BIM, a rescission theory avoids issues of valuation and posttransaction losses. It compensates Lucre Life for losses it would not have incurred but for the fraud (its theory of liability) and prevents unfair enrichment by BIM. Lucre Life can support a rescission theory by pointing to §29(b) of the 1934 Act, which states that any "contract made in violation" of any rule under the statute is void. Rescissory damages in this case would be the difference between $100 (the purchase price) and $75 (the price at which Lucre Life later sold) — $25.

A rescission theory does not fit as well for Jane, the soliciting attorney. Jane was not the seller and was not unjustly enriched; heavy damages might overdeter her conduct. A cover theory — which assumes the plaintiff sells once the fraud is revealed — does not fit the facts well because there was no market into which the plaintiff could sell or to measure the effect on price when the fraud was revealed. An out-of-pocket theory, the traditional theory for fraud damages, would allow Lucre Life to recover the difference between the purchase price and what the price would have been had the disclosure been adequate. This will require Lucre Life to prove the "true" value of the preferred stock as of the time of its purchase. Recovery will probably be less than $25.

4a. No. Rule 10b-5 does not require disclosure of all material information. Only if BIM has a duty to speak is silence actionable. A duty might arise in a few ways: (1) BIM bought or sold its own shares; (2) BIM was aware of insider trading; (3) BIM had a duty to correct an earlier statement that had become inaccurate; (4) BIM had a fiduciary duty to its shareholders.

BIM's fiduciary duty to disclose arises only if the value of secrecy to rational profit-maximizing shareholders is greater than the value of disclosure — a decision protected by the business judgment rule. BIM's management could decide secrecy is in the shareholders' overall best interests for competitive or any other business-related reason. An evaluation of BIM's disclosure duties turns on general, rather than individual, shareholder wealth maximization.

4b. "No comment." The Supreme Court in *Basic Inc. v. Levinson* took the view that this would be tantamount to silence. Absent a duty to speak, silence is not actionable. Although some might view a "no comment" answer to be tacit confirmation of undisclosed material information, the Supreme Court suggests companies can create a reputation for discretion, whether or not there are material developments. The president might well say, "We have a corporate policy not to comment on market trends or rumors."

4c. Yes, if the preliminary tests were material. Whenever a company makes a statement about material information, it cannot be false or misleading. BIM's management might argue the press release is essentially true because management thinks the tests have been kept secret and does not know why there has been unusual trading activity. On similar facts, the Supreme Court in *Basic Inc. v. Levinson* rejected this sophistic argument.

A "no developments" statement suggests management does not know of information that would be of interest to the market, which is misleading if the tests are material. To judge the materiality of the tests requires balancing the probability of a superconductivity breakthrough (which may be low because the tests were preliminary) and the breakthrough's significance to the corporation (which is extremely high). See *Basic Inc. v. Levinson* (§29.3.5). The "probability plus magnitude" test suggests it is substantially likely that reasonable shareholders would consider the tests relevant to their buy-sell decisions. This conclusion is bolstered if the recent price increases related to rumors about superconductivity research. It would indicate that superconductivity information is relevant to trading and pricing of BIM's stock.

4d. The release should have made clear the tests are preliminary, have not been confirmed, and might never be confirmed:

> BIM's research scientists have conducted tests on a metallic ceramic that suggests superconductivity at temperatures of up to 75° Fahrenheit (24° Celsius). The tests have not been confirmed by the company or by independent researchers. It is possible that they cannot be duplicated and that the test results were due to some cause other than superconductivity.

The release must walk a fine line. If it is overly pessimistic, some shareholders may sell, be disappointed, and sue. If it is overly optimistic, some investors may buy, be disappointed, and sue.

5a. Yes. A private purchaser (or seller) of securities has an implied right of action under Rule 10b-5. Further, there is no privity requirement if the challenged misstatements were made "in connection with" stock trading. BIM should have known that shareholders and investors would rely on its press release.

5b. Yes. In a face-to-face transaction, Sharon would have to show that she actually knew of the press release and that she sold because of its bad news. When trading occurs in an impersonal stock market, courts relax the reliance requirement and accept a "fraud on the market" theory. *Basic Inc. v Levinson* (see §29.3.5). Under this theory, a public company's stock price is set by available public information and those who trade rely on the integrity of the market. If there is fraud, the stock price impounds the misinformation, and those who trade rely on the misinformation as though they had known of it. BIM would have the burden to rebut the presumption by showing a break between the misinformation and Sharon's trading: (1) BIM's stock is not widely followed, and misinformation is not necessarily reflected in its stock price; (2) securities traders already knew of the preliminary tests, the press release notwithstanding; (3) Sharon would have traded even if the price had been different or she had known the press release was false.

6a. Not for damages. *Blue Chip Stamps* makes clear that as a nonseller Sharon cannot sue under Rule 10b-5, even though she relied on the broker's fraudulent statement. If she seeks equitable relief — such as an injunction requiring the broker to state its market position in BIM stock when advising clients — some lower courts would permit her to maintain a 10b-5 action. Her injunctive action does not threaten heavy damages based on speculation whether, or how much, she would have sold.

6b. She can always sue under state fraud law. Moreover, federal courts have used Rule 10b-5 to develop duties of professionalism applicable to securities brokers. Under the so-called shingle theory, a broker who hangs out his shingle for business implicitly represents that he offers fair and honest service. By virtue of the relationship of trust and confidence to their customers, brokers have a duty of professionalism that includes providing customers with full information. Sharon could use Rule 10b-5 to state a theory of professional wrongdoing.

7a. Probably not. Even though Sharon did not trade, she has standing to sue derivatively under Rule 10b-5 on behalf of the corporation if the corporation was deceived when it entered into a securities transaction. *Goldberg v. Meridor* (see §29.4.3). To make a "fraud on the corporation" claim, she might argue that BIM's management failed to disclose to the corporation (namely, the independent directors or shareholders) that the sale to Polly Farms was a breach of their fiduciary duties. This failure prevented the board or shareholders from blocking the sale of the subsidiary. The theory has a couple of defects. First, courts outside the Second Circuit might not tolerate use of Rule 10b-5 to state what is essentially a state fiduciary claim — a federalism concern. Second, Sharon would have to show that the board or the shareholders could have taken alternative action, such as a state fiduciary claim, to block the sale. Some courts have required a showing of management abuse that would clearly justify state remedies. In this case, it is not clear that the Polly Farms transaction was unfair to the corporation and that the board or shareholders would have acted differently, despite the bribes to BIM management.

7b. Yes. The sale of the subsidiary was structured as a sale of stock, and Rule 10b-5 applies. Even though Polly Farms essentially bought the subsidiary's business, its purchase of 100 percent of the stock constitutes a securities transaction covered by Rule 10b-5. See *Landreth Timber Co. v. Landreth* (see §29.4.5). If BIM had sold the subsidiary's assets, there would be no sale of securities and Rule 10b-5 would not apply. In deciding how to structure the sale of a business, planners should take into account potential fraud liability (and protection) under Rule 10b-5.

7c. No. The Supreme Court has inferred a one-year/three-year statute of limitations in 10b-5 actions. Although Polly Farms sued within three years after the fraudulent transaction, it did not sue within one year of discovering the facts (misstated earnings) constituting the fraud.

§29.5   Rule 10b-5 and Insider Trading

We are now prepared to tackle the most difficult task to which Rule 10b-5 has been put — insider trading. As we have seen, state common law on insider trading has been of limited use (see §28.2), and, as we will see, §16(b) of the 1934 Act applies only to a restricted group of insiders who trade in their company's stock during a narrow six-month window (see §30.3).

Defined simply and perhaps simplistically, *insider trading* is the buying or selling of stock by those who exploit an improper informational advantage. "Insider trading" generically describes two kinds of trading: (1) classic insider trading occurs when a corporate insider *trades in his corporation's stock* on the basis of material, nonpublic information obtained in his corporate capacity; (2) outsider trading occurs when an insider misappropriates such information *to trade in another corporation's stock*. A trader with inside information can realize gains whether the information is "good news" or "bad news" (see §28.1).

There are a number of persons who can gain from trading on inside information, and the rules vary for each group:

- *insiders,* who obtain information because of their corporate position — directors, officers, employees, or controlling shareholders of the corporation;
- *constructive insiders,* who are retained temporarily by the corporation — such as accountants, lawyers, and investment bankers;
- *tippees* to whom the insider reveals (or tips) the information — the *tipper* may be an insider or a tippee of the insider;
- *sub-tippees,* who are tipped by a tippee, and so on; and
- *strangers* who have no relationship to the insider or the corporation but who overhear the information.

There are a number of theories for federal regulation of insider trading. First, insider trading is basically unfair to those who trade without access to the same information available to insiders and others "in the know" — a "fairness" rationale. The legislative history of the 1934 Act, for example, reflects congressional concern about "abuses" in trading by insiders. Second, insider trading undermines the integrity of stock trading markets, making investors leery of putting their money into a market in which they can be exploited — a "market integrity" rationale. A fair and informed securities trading market, essential to raising capital, was the ultimate purpose of the 1934 Act. Third, insider trading exploits confidential information of great value to its holder — a "business property" rationale. Those who trade on confidential information reap profits without paying for their advantage and undermine incentives to engage in commercial activities that depend on confidentiality.

§29.5.1   Duty to "Abstain or Disclose"

Rule 10b-5 prohibits securities fraud. No person, whether or not trading in securities, may misrepresent material facts that are likely to affect others' trading decisions. This duty is meaningless to insider trading, which happens not by means of misrepresentations but rather by silence.

Some early courts held that just as every securities trader has a duty not to lie about material facts, anyone "in possession of material inside information" must either abstain from trading or disclose the information to the investing public — an *abstain-or-disclose duty*. *SEC v. Texas Gulf Sulphur*, 401 F.2d 833 (2d Cir. 1968), *cert. dismissed*, 394 U.S. 976 (1969). But a "parity of information" or "equal access" rule of insider trading goes too far. Strategic silence is different from outright lying. To impose an abstain-or-disclose duty on everyone with nonpublic material information — however obtained — would significantly dampen the enthusiasm for trading in the stock market. Capital formation might dry up if investors were prohibited from exploiting their hard work, superior skill, acumen, or even their hunches. Investors would have little incentive to buy securities if they could not use perceived informational advantages.

Trading by Insiders — A Fiduciary Duty to Disclose.   In the early 1980s, the Supreme Court provided a framework for the abstain-or-disclose duty. *Chiarella v. United States*, 445 U.S. 222 (1980); *Dirks v. SEC*, 463 U.S. 646 (1983). Treating Rule 10b-5 as an antifraud rule, the Court held that an insider has a duty to disclose when the other party is entitled to disclosure because of a relationship of trust and confidence — a fiduciary relationship. The Supreme Court thus anchored federal regulation of insider trading on a presumed state fiduciary duty of insiders to the corporation's shareholders — even though state corporate law has largely refused to infer such a duty in impersonal trading markets (see §28.2).

In *Chiarella v. United States,* defendant Chiarella was employed in the composing room of a financial printer that printed confidential takeover documents for corporate raiders. Chiarella figured out the identity of some of the takeover targets and bought stock in the targets, which he sold at a profit when the raiders made their bids. The Supreme Court reversed Chiarella's criminal conviction under Rule 10b-5. It held that Rule 10b-5 did not impose a "parity of information" requirement and that merely trading on the basis of nonpublic material information did not trigger a duty to disclose or abstain. Chiarella had no duty to the target shareholders with whom he traded because he had no fiduciary relationship to the *target companies or their shareholders*. (The Court decided that Chiarella could not be convicted for trading on information misappropriated from his employer because that theory was not presented to the jury.)

In *Dirks v. SEC,* a securities analyst, Dirks, learned of an insurance company's massive fraud and imminent financial collapse from Secrist, a former company insider. Dirks passed on the information to his firm's clients, which dumped their holdings before the scandal became public. The Court held that Dirks was not liable because Secrist's reasons for revealing the scandal to Dirks were not to obtain an advantage for himself. For Secrist to have tipped improperly, the Court required a fiduciary breach — which the Court assumed would mean the insider had gained some direct or indirect personal gain or a reputational benefit that could be cashed in later. In the case, Secrist had exposed the fraud with no expectation of personal benefit, and Dirks could not be held liable for passing on the information to his firm's clients.

The Implications of "Duty" Analysis.   The *Chiarella* and *Dirks* "duty" analysis leads to the following 10b-5 rules:

Strangers.   A stranger with no fiduciary relationship to the corporation or its shareholders has no duty to disclose or abstain simply because he is in possession of material, nonpublic information. *Chiarella.*

Fiduciaries (insiders and agents) who trade.   Insiders have an abstain-or-disclose duty while in the possession of material, nonpublic information obtained in their fiduciary position and in which the corporation has a confidentiality interest. *Chiarella.* This duty extends to *constructive insiders* who have a direct or indirect agency (fiduciary) relationship to the corporation. For example, an employee of an accounting firm that is an agent of the company is a constructive insider. Some courts, perhaps erroneously, have extended this concept to *temporary insiders* who acquire inside information in an arm's length, nonfiduciary business relationship. *SEC v. Lund,* 570 F. Supp. 1397 (C.D. Cal. 1983).

Tippers.   Insiders and others who knowingly pass on improper tips are liable as participants in insider trading. A tipper is liable for transmitting material, nonpublic information if she knows (or should know) it is confidential and came from an insider who anticipated some direct or indirect personal benefit from the disclosure. *Dirks.* The tip is improper if the insider anticipates reciprocal benefits — such as when the insider sells the tip, gives it to family or friends, or expects the tippee to return the favor. The tipper can be held liable even though she does not trade, so long as a tippee or sub-tippee down the line eventually does.

Noninsider tippees and sub-tippees.   Those who do not have a fiduciary relationship to the corporation inherit the insider's abstain-or-disclose duty if they knowingly trade on improper tips. *Dirks.* A tippee is liable for trading after obtaining material, nonpublic information that he knows (or has reason to know) is confidential and came from an insider who anticipated some direct or indirect personal benefit from the disclosure. The abstain-or-disclose mantle passes only if the insider's original tip was a breach of a fiduciary duty. Overhearing a conversation between insiders in a crowded restaurant, for example, would not create tippee liability because the insiders do not anticipate any personal gain from their indiscretion. See *SEC v. Switzer,* 590

F. Supp. 756 (W.D. Okla. 1984) (holding that eavesdropper is not liable for trading after overhearing CEO tell his wife the company might be liquidated).

Satisfying the Disclosure Duty.   An insider may trade on inside information by first disclosing the information. An insider who plans to trade on a public trading market must wait (some have suggested 24 to 48 hours) for the information to be disseminated in the market through wire services or publication in the financial press. *SEC v. Texas Gulf Sulphur Co.,* 401 F.2d 833 (2d Cir. 1968), *cert. denied sub nom. Coates v. SEC,* 394 U.S. 976 (1969).

§29.5.2   Outsider Misappropriation

One issue not resolved in *Chiarella* and *Dirks* is whether stock traders are liable under Rule 10b-5 for misappropriating information and trading in the stock of *other* companies to which they have no relationship and to which they owe no fiduciary duties. The *Chiarella* theory of a disclosure duty based on a fiduciary relationship with the *other parties to the transaction* does not work in this setting.

In *Carpenter v. United States,* 484 U.S. 19 (1987), the Court split 4-4 on the question whether Rule 10b-5 encompasses a misappropriation theory. The case involved a *Wall Street Journal* reporter, Winans, who tipped information from upcoming stories in a column he wrote called "Heard on the Street." Without using any nonpublic information, the column reported on companies and invariably affected the companies' stock prices. The newspaper had a policy of keeping the identity of the companies confidential, apparently to protect the appearance of journalistic integrity. Winans was convicted for misappropriating the advance information and tipping it to a friend and a broker, even though the *Wall Street Journal* had no interest in the trading. The Court's split 4-4 decision had the effect of affirming the conviction but carried no precedential value.

In 1988 Congress endorsed *civil* misappropriation liability in the Insider Trading and Securities Fraud Enforcement Act. Under new §20A to the 1934 Act, contemporaneous traders may sue inside traders, tippers, and their controlling persons for violating Rule 10b-5's insider trading prohibitions. The 1988 Act's legislative history makes clear that this express private right of action is intended to allow "recovery by plaintiffs who were victims of misappropriation." The 1988 Act thus overturns earlier cases that had denied recovery to target shareholders who traded at about the same time as those who used misappropriated information concerning takeover plans.

Lower courts, principally the Second Circuit, have adopted the misappropriation theory in *criminal* cases. An insider who uses secrets misappropriated from his company (or principal) to trade in other companies' stock is seen as "defrauding" his company. The theory makes sense if the company plans to trade or bid for the stock of the other company in which the insider trades. See *Newman v. United States,* 664 F.2d 12 (2d Cir. 1981), *cert. denied,* 464 U.S. 863 (1983) (upholding tippee's criminal liability for buying stock of target after being tipped of bidder's takeover plans by employee of bidder's investment banker).

Criminal Liability for Mail and Wire Fraud.   In *Carpenter v. United States,* 484 U.S. 19 (1987), the Supreme Court deftly sidestepped the misappropriation quagmire by affirming in an 8-0 decision a *Wall Street Journal* reporter's conviction (discussed above) under federal mail and wire fraud criminal statutes. The Court held that the newspaper had a "property" interest in keeping the "Heard on the Street" column confidential prior to publication, and that the reporter's breach of his confidentiality obligation defrauded the newspaper. Although the Court's decision raises disquieting issues about criminal liability for breaching an employment stipulation, it is now clear that trading on misappropriated information is subject to criminal penalties.

§29.5.3   *Rule 14e-3 — Misappropriation of Tender Offer Information*

Soon after the *Chiarella* decision, the SEC applied the misappropriation theory to trading in connection with a tender offer. Using its authority under §14(e) of the Williams Act (see §39.2.4) — which allows the SEC to regulate "fraudulent, deceptive, or manipulative acts or practices, in connection with any tender offer" — the agency prohibited trading by those with inside information about a tender offer. 1934 Act Rule 14e-3. The rule prohibits trading during the course of a tender offer by anybody (other than the bidder) who has material, nonpublic information about the offer that he knows (or has reason to know) was obtained from either the bidder or the target. There is no need under Rule 14e-3 to prove that a tipper breached a fiduciary duty for personal benefit.

The Second Circuit considered the difference between 10b-5 and 14e-3 liability in *United States v. Chestman,* 947 F.2d 551 (2d Cir. 1991) (en banc). Chestman was a stock broker who learned of an impending tender offer from Loeb, the husband of the niece of the company's controlling shareholder, who had agreed to sell his control block prior to the tender offer. When Chestman traded on this information and tipped his clients, the government prosecuted him under Rule 10b-5 and 14e-3. The Second Circuit agreed that Rule 14e-3 was a valid exercise of the SEC's §14(e) rulemaking power and affirmed Chestman's 14e-3 conviction. The court, however, held that Chestman could not be convicted under a 10b-5 misappropriation theory because Loeb did not have a fiduciary duty to his family not to disclose confidential information. The family did not depend on Loeb to serve its interests, and, absent a fiduciary breach, there could be no 10b-5 liability.

§29.5.4   *Remedies for Insider Trading*

Insider traders are subject to a host of sanctions and liabilities. (It is no wonder that law firms tell new lawyers not to trade on clients' confidential information.)

SEC Injunction and Disgorgement.   The SEC may seek to enjoin insider trading (assuming it is likely to recur) and seek a court order that the insider trader or tipper disgorge any trading profits. *SEC v. Texas Gulf Sulphur Co.,* 401 F.2d 833 (2d Cir. 1968), *cert. denied sub nom. Coates v. SEC,* 394 U.S. 976 (1969) (ordering establishment of fund from which shareholders and other contemporaneous traders could recover from insider traders and tippers).

Civil Liability to Contemporaneous Traders.   In an impersonal trading market, it is unclear who is hurt by insider trading and how much. Shareholders and investors who trade at the same time as an insider presumably would have traded even had the insider fulfilled his duty and abstained. If, however, the theory is that insider trading is unfair to contemporaneous traders, recovery should be equal to the traders' contemporaneous trading "losses," which typically would be significantly greater than the insider's gains. If the theory is that insider trading undermines the integrity of trading markets, recovery should be disgorgement of the insider's trading gains to the market as a whole. If the theory is that insider traders pilfer valuable commercial information, recovery should be based on the losses to the owner of the confidential information.

Congress has addressed the issue and has adopted a recovery scheme that borrows from both the unfairness and market integrity rationales. Under the Insider Trading and Securities Fraud Enforcement Act of 1988, only traders (shareholders or investors) whose trades were contemporaneous with the insider's can recover. The act limits recovery to the disgorgement of the insider's actual profits realized or losses avoided, reduced by any disgorgement obtained by the SEC under its broad authority to seek injunctive relief. 1934 Act §20A. Courts generally have followed the same disgorgement theory. See *Elkind v. Liggett & Meyers, Inc.,* 635 F.2d 156 (2d Cir. 1980). Disgorgement recovery will often exceed plaintiffs' "losses," and plaintiff claims are prorated.

Civil Liability to Defrauded Parties.   Owners of confidential information can bring a private action under Rule 10b-5 only if they were actual purchasers or sellers of securities. *Blue Chip Stamps v. Manor Drug Stores,* 421 U.S. 723 (1975). Courts allow a "defrauded" company to recover if it suffered trading losses or was forced to pay a higher price in a transaction because the insider's trading artificially raised the stock price. *FMC Corp. v. Boesky,* 673 F.2d 272

(N.D. Ill. 1987), *remanded,* 852 F.2d 981 (7th Cir. 1988) (holding tippee not liable for trading on misappropriated information concerning company's impending recapitalization plan because company lost nothing in the recapitalization). Although some commentators have proposed corporate recovery *on behalf of shareholders,* courts have insisted on a corporate (not shareholder) injury for there to be corporate recovery.

Civil Penalties.   To buttress the SEC's inherent enforcement powers, Congress passed the Insider Trading Sanctions Act of 1984. The Act authorizes the SEC to seek a judicially imposed civil penalty against traders and tippees who violate Rule 10b-5 or Rule 14e-3 of up to three times the profits realized (or losses avoided) in insider trading. 1934 Act §21A. The penalty, which is paid into the federal treasury, is in addition to other remedies, thus making it possible for an insider or tippee to disgorge his profits (in a private or SEC action) *and* pay the treble-damage penalty.

In the Insider Trading and Securities Fraud Enforcement Act of 1988, Congress added more deterrent bite by extending civil penalties to employers and others who "control" insider traders and tippers. 1934 Act §21A. Controlling persons are subject to additional penalties up to $1 million or three times the insider's profits (whichever is greater) if the controlling person knowingly or recklessly disregards the likelihood of insider trading by persons under its control. Broker-dealers that fail to maintain procedures protecting against such abuses may also be subject to such penalties if their laxity substantially contributed to the insider trading.

Insider trading, cloaked as it is in secrecy, is difficult to track down. The stock exchanges have elaborate surveillance systems to alert officials if trading in a company's stock moves outside preset ranges. When unusual trading patterns show up or trading occurs before major corporate announcements, exchange officials can ask brokerage firms to turn over records of who traded at any given time. The exchanges conduct computer cross-checks to spot "clusters" of trading — such as from a particular city or brokerage firm. An Automated Search-and-Match system, with data on thousands of companies and executives on such things as social affiliations and even college ties, assists the exchanges. If the exchanges see something suspicious, they turn the data over to the SEC for a formal investigation. The SEC can subpoena phone records and take depositions, sometimes promising immunity to informants. To encourage informants the 1988 Act grants the SEC authority to pay bounties to anyone who provides information leading to civil penalties. The bounty can be up to 10 percent of the civil penalty collected. 1934 Act §21A(e).

Criminal Sanctions.   The Insider Trading and Securities Fraud Enforcement Act of 1988 also authorizes heavier criminal penalties for violators. 1934 Act §32(a). Congress increased maximum criminal fines for violations of the 1934 Act from $100,000 to $1,000,000 ($2,500,000 for nonindividuals), and jail sentences from five years to ten years.

EXAMPLES

1. BIM Corp. is a publicly traded corporation. Elbert, a BIM chemist, has conducted preliminary tests on a material that is superconductive at room temperatures. If the test results can be confirmed, it will be a huge scientific breakthrough with enormous commercial potential. Adelle, BIM's CEO, learns of the tests and sends a memo to everyone in the company who knows of them urging their complete secrecy. When Elbert's test results are confirmed and made public, BIM's stock price doubles.

   a. Before Elbert's results are confirmed, BIM's board offers Adelle options to buy BIM stock. Adelle accepts but without telling the board of Elbert's tests. Is Adelle liable to the corporation under Rule 10b-5?

   b. Before Elbert's results are confirmed, Adelle purchases BIM stock on the stock market. Is Adelle liable under Rule 10b-5?

   c. Before Elbert's results are confirmed, Elbert (who is neither a director nor officer of BIM) purchases BIM stock on a stock market. Is Elbert liable under Rule 10b-5?

2. After the tests are confirmed, Elbert tells Jane (a physicist who works for another research company) of the superconductivity breakthrough.

   a. Before public disclosure, Jane buys BIM stock. Is she liable under Rule 10b-5?

   b. Elbert reveals his tests to Jane in the hope of similar insider trading scoops, but he does not trade himself. Is he liable under Rule 10b-5?

   c. Elbert and Jane discuss the future of superconductivity while riding in a limousine on their way to a science conference. Mickey, the limo driver, overhears their conversation and the next day purchases BIM stock. Is Mickey liable under Rule 10b-5?

3. Before public disclosure of the superconductivity breakthrough, Adelle discloses it to Dwight (the president of Third Federal Bank) to obtain a loan for BIM to build a new manufacturing plant. Adelle asks Dwight to keep the information secret.

   a. Dwight calls his broker and buys BIM stock. Is Dwight liable under Rule 10b-5?

   b. Dwight tells his wife, Wanda, over dinner that BIM's stock price is "probably going to go through the ceiling." Wanda buys BIM stock. Is Dwight or Wanda liable under Rule 10b-5?

   c. Tina, a corporate spy, breaks into Third Federal's offices and rifles the files to find the BIM loan application. She buys BIM stock. Is Tina liable under Rule 10b-5?

4. BIM's board decides to buy Ovid Corporation, a commercial builder, to gain the expertise to build new manufacturing plants to produce superconductive materials. BIM negotiates a merger with Ovid.

    a. Before BIM announces the merger, Adelle purchases Ovid stock through her broker. Is Adelle liable under Rule 10b-5? Under Rule 14e-3?

    b. Ovid shareholders who sold during the period between Adelle's trading and eventual disclosure of the merger sue Adelle to recover the gains they would have made if they had not sold. Is Adelle liable to the shareholders under Rule 10b-5?

    c. Adelle makes $100,000 in trading profits by buying Ovid stock. What is her maximum liability?

    d. BIM purchases Ovid stock before announcing the merger. Is BIM liable to Ovid shareholders under Rule 10b-5?

    e. Adelle attends a stock analysts' meeting. She announces that BIM will manufacture its new superconductive material. Adelle does not say whether BIM will build a manufacturing plant or mention Ovid. One of the analysts, Tom, figures out that BIM must build and is likely to buy Ovid. Tom tells some of his clients, who buy Ovid stock. Is Tom liable under Rule 10b-5?

EXPLANATIONS

1a. Yes, if the preliminary tests are material. Adelle has a fiduciary relationship to the corporation and, under Rule 10b-5, has a duty to "abstain or disclose" when trading on material, nonpublic information with the corporation. *Chiarella.* An insider trading case under Rule 10b-5 must also satisfy the fraud elements of materiality and scienter:

    Materiality. The information about the preliminary tests is material if a reasonable investor would consider it important to a buy/sell decision. Under the "probability plus magnitude" test of *Basic Inc. v. Levinson,* the magnitude of superconductivity is demonstrated by the later jump in BIM's stock price. The probability that the preliminary tests would seem high, particularly if there is insider trading on the basis of the information.

    Scienter. Adelle accepted the options with scienter because she knew of the tests.

    Normally, in trading involving nondisclosure, the Supreme Court dispenses with a showing of reliance. *Affiliated Ute Citizens v. United States.* In this face-to-face transaction, Adelle might nonetheless rebut the assumption of reliance by showing that the corporation (acting through an independent board) would have offered the options even had it known of the inside information.

1b. Yes, almost certainly. Adelle's abstain-or-disclose duty extends to shareholders and investors in BIM's stock. *Chiarella.* Although materiality would seem to be an issue, it rarely is in insider trading cases. If the insider considered the information significant to his buy/sell decision, it is almost certain that a court will conclude that a reasonable shareholder would also.

1c. Yes, for the same reasons Adelle is liable. Rule 10b-5 applies to any insider with a fiduciary (or agency) relationship to the corporation. Elbert, an employee-agent of BIM, is treated in the same way as Adelle.

2a. Perhaps, depending on Elbert's motives. If Jane knows (or has reason to know) that the information came from an insider, that it was confidential, and that the insider had tipped for some personal or reputational benefit, Jane is liable as a tippee. *Dirks.* A significant issue is whether Elbert disclosed the breakthrough for personal gain or for some non-personal corporate reason. If he expected reciprocal stock-trading tips or reputational gain, the tip violated Rule 10b-5 if Jane had reason to know those were his motives. If, however, Elbert revealed the breakthrough for business reasons, such as to discuss the scientific aspects of the discovery, Jane is under no confidentiality obligation. Jane's liability thus hinges on Elbert's motives — a deficiency of the *Dirks* approach, but part of federal insider trading law.

2b. Yes. Elbert is liable as a tipper because he gave the tip in breach of his fiduciary duty for an improper personal benefit — reciprocal tips. Even though Elbert did not trade himself, a tipping insider is liable for placing confidential nonpublic material information in peril of abuse. *SEC v. Texas Gulf Sulphur* (see §29.5.1). Under this aiding-and-abetting theory, nontrading tippers are jointly and severally liable to the same extent as their trading tippees. See 1934 Act §20A(c).

2c. Perhaps, although not as a tippee. If Elbert did not anticipate a personal gain from his discussion, there was no breach of duty, and a tippee (or an eavesdropper) could not be liable. Nonetheless, Mickey might be liable on a misappropriation theory. If Mickey worked for a limousine company that expected complete discretion of its employees, he could be liable for breaching his employer's expectation of confidentiality. See *United States v. Carpenter* (see §29.5.1).

3a. Yes, under a misappropriation theory. Adelle provided Dwight with information on the superconductivity tests on the condition that the bank keep it confidential. Dwight, in effect, misappropriated this information *from the bank*. If the bank has a policy against employees using confidential customer information — which seems nearly certain — Dwight would be liable on a misappropriation theory. The theory protects confidential business information and assures stock trading markets that trading cannot happen with purloined information.

Notice that Dwight was neither a tippee not a constructive insider of BIM. He was not a tippee because Adelle expected no personal gain from the disclosure and breached no duty when she provided it. She supplied the information so the corporation could get a loan. Moreover, the bank was not an agent of BIM, and Dwight could not be a constructive insider. Unlike investment banking firms that provide takeover advice, commercial lenders typically deal with borrowers on an arm's length basis. Borrowers do not entrust commercial banks with discretionary authority or depend on them to serve their interests. To say that there is a fiduciary relationship of trust and confidence would stretch state fiduciary law beyond its current limits. See *United States v. Chestman* (§29.5.3).

3b. Both are. Tipper and tippee liability is the same in an outsider misappropriation case as in an insider trading case. If (as discussed in the prior answer) Dwight is under an abstain-or-disclose duty because of his position at the bank, he cannot tip the information. Wanda is liable as a tippee if she knew (or had reason to know) that Dwight received the information from the bank, that it was confidential to the bank, and that Dwight gained some personal benefit (such as a share of her trading profits) by disclosing it to her. She is liable as tippee, and he as tipper, for any trading gains.

3c. No. Rule 10b-5 liability hinges on a fiduciary relationship, and there is none here. Tina is not a fiduciary to either BIM or Third National Bank. Although insider trading prohibitions may protect confidential business information, liability is not as broad as the theory. Compare *SEC v. Cherif,* 933 F.2d 403 (7th Cir. 1991), *cert. denied,* 112 S. Ct. 966 (1992) (liability of former employee who used magnetic identification card to gain access to secret information on pending takeovers).

4a. Yes under Rule 10b-5, but not Rule 14e-3. Adelle misappropriates BIM's undisclosed merger plans to trade in Ovid's shares — a case of outsider trading. In the legislative history to the Insider Trading and Securities Fraud Enforcement Act of 1988, Congress indicated its understanding that Rule 10b-5 encompasses a misappropriation theory. 1934 Act §20A. Trading on BIM's confidential information may harm BIM, whose deal with Ovid may well depend on the value of Ovid's shares. Adelle did not violate Rule 14e-3, which concerns trading on information about a tender offer. Unless the corporate acquisition was accomplished through a public offer to buy shares, the broad misappropriation theory of Rule 14e-3 does not apply.

4b. No, only shareholders who traded "contemporaneously" with Adelle. The Insider Trading and Securities Fraud Enforcement Act of 1988 provides an explicit private right of action to contemporaneous traders against misappropriators. 1934 Act §20A. At one time courts saw the misappropriation theory as protecting the confidences of the outside company, here BIM, and Rule 10b-5 did not protect trading shareholders, such as Ovid's. The 1988 Act rejects this view. Liability, however, is not tied to the period during which the misappropriator failed to disclose, but rather to the period of the misappropriator's trading.

4c. There is no maximum. Adelle can be liable for her trading profits in a disgorgement proceeding by the SEC or in a restitution suit by contemporaneous traders — maximum $100,000. See 1934 Act §20A. In addition, she can be liable for civil penalties of up to three times her trading profits — maximum $300,000. 1934 Act §21A. She can also be liable for any losses to BIM if it had to pay more for the merger — no maximum. Finally, she can be subject to criminal fines — up to $1,000,000. All for a $100,000 trading gain!

4d. No. There is no trading in breach of a fiduciary duty. See *Chiarella* (§29.5.1). BIM has not misappropriated any information. Any interest in the confidentiality of the information concerning the Ovid merger belonged to BIM. BIM is merely exploiting its informational advantage, based on its own plans, and has no abstain-or-disclose duty.

4e. No. Tom has no fiduciary relationship to Ovid and could not acquire an "abstain or disclose" duty from this source. Tom is not a tipper of information misappropriated from BIM. He has no fiduciary relationship with BIM, and he was not a sub-tipper because Adelle's revelation was not for a personal gain and breached no fiduciary duty. See *Dirks* (§29.5.1). Did Tom not misappropriate confidential information from his brokerage firm — namely, the information that Ovid was a likely merger partner? Although the brokerage firm could have used this information to its advantage, it is unlikely the firm has a policy against analysts disclosing their analysis. In fact, Tom's job is probably to do precisely what he did. The Supreme Court in *Dirks* recognized the crucial role securities analysts play in disseminating information to the market. In a similar vein, the legislative history of the Insider Trading and Securities Fraud Enforcement Act of 1988 indicates that the Act is not intended to interfere with those functions. H.R. Rep. No. 100-910, at 19 (1988).

30

Section 16(b) — Disgorging Short-Swing Profits

The profits from insider trading tempt those who control public corporations to manipulate stock prices so they can buy when the price is artificially low and sell when the price is artificially high. Section 16(b) of the Securities Exchange Act of 1934 deters insider manipulation in public corporations and encourages control persons to acquire long-term interests in such corporations. The section requires specified insiders to report their trading in their company's securities and allows the corporation to recover from these insiders any short-swing trading profits.

§30.1   Coverage of §16

Section 16 only applies to trading in the stock of a corporation that has a class of stock registered under §12 of the 1934 Act (see §19.3.1). In effect, §16 applies to trading in the securities of any *public* corporation, whether or not the traded securities are subject to §12 registration. For example, if a company's common stock is subject to 1934 Act registration but its bonds are not because there are fewer than 500 bondholders of record, trading by insiders in the unregistered bonds is subject to §16's reporting and disgorgement rules.

Section §16's short-swing trading provisions only apply to directors, officers, and 10 percent shareholders (those who *beneficially own* more than

10 percent of any class of a public corporation's equity securities). To facilitate the policing of insiders' short-swing trading, §16(a) requires a report by directors, specified officers, and 10 percent shareholders. The report, which must be filed with the SEC and any stock exchange that lists the company's securities, discloses the amount of securities held by the insider and the price paid in any purchase or sale. Updating reports must be filed at the end of each month in which there are any changes in the insider's holdings. Failure to file subjects the insider to penalties. Section 16(b), limited to trading in public corporations during a narrow six-month window, is narrower than Rule 10b-5. Yet, by reaching any trading during the six-month window, whether or not based on material inside information, §16(b) is also broader than Rule 10b-5.

§30.2   Disgorging Short-Swing Profits under §16(b) — The Mechanical Test

§30.2.1   *Strict Liability for Insider Profits Made within Six Months*

Section 16(b) imposes automatic, strict liability on any director, officer, or 10 percent shareholder who makes a profit (as defined) in short-swing trans-actions within a six-month period. No proof of intent or scienter is required. Recovery is to the corporation, and suit may be brought either by the corporation or by a shareholder in a derivative suit.

The mechanical short-swing profit rules are both overly broad and overly narrow. They cover innocent short-swing trading that occurs without the use of inside information or any manipulative intent, yet they do not cover abusive insider trading that occurs outside the six-month window or by those who are not insiders specified under §16.

§30.2.2   *Operation of the Mechanical Disgorgement Rules*

There are four basic points to keep in mind in determining whether disgorgement is available:

Match any transactions that produce a profit.   Section 16(b) liability is predicated on the matching of any purchase with any sale, regardless of order, during any six-month period in which the sales price is higher than the purchase price.

No offset is necessary.   There is no need to offset any losses — that is, any purchases and sales in which the sales price is lower than the purchase price need not be matched and can be disregarded.

Officer or director status must exist at either end.   For officers or directors (but not 10 percent shareholders), it is enough that the person was an officer or director at the time of either purchase or sale but not necessarily both. The theory is that the officer or director had access to inside information and could manipulate the price of the stock.

Shareholder status (10 percent) must exist "immediately before" both ends.   For 10 percent shareholders, it is necessary that the person have held more than 10 percent *immediately before* both transactions that are to be matched. *Reliance Electric Co. v. Emerson Electric Co.,* 404 U.S. 418 (1972) (holding that the shareholder must hold 10 percent or more before matching *sale*); *Foremost McKesson Inc. v. Provident Securities Co.,* 423 U.S. 232 (1976) (holding that shareholder must hold 10 percent or more before matching *purchase*). The different treatment of 10 percent shareholders is based on an exclusion in §16(b) of "any transaction where [the] beneficial owner was not such both at the time of the purchase and sale, or the sale and purchase, of the security involved." The rationale is that 10 percent shareholders are less likely to have access to inside information or to control mechanisms than directors or officers; their insider status and presumed access to inside information and the company's control mechanisms must exist at both ends of the matching transactions.

§30.3   Special Interpretive Issues

The literal terms of §16(b) are inflexible, sometimes too harsh and other times too lenient. To accomplish the rule's purpose to discourage abusive insider trading, courts have interpreted the section's significant terms — *director* and *officer, beneficial ownership,* and *purchase* and *sale* — to introduce reasoned analysis into the otherwise mechanical disgorgement rules.

§30.3.1   Directors and Officers

Courts have interpreted §16(b) to bring into its reach persons and entities who do not fall within the literal definition of *officer* or *director* but who are functionally equivalent for purposes of insider access.

Functional Officers.   For purposes of §16(b), an officer is any employee who has a position in the corporation that gives her access to confidential inside information that is not freely circulated. An official title may help identify these persons but is not determinative. *Merrill, Lynch Pierce Fenner*

& Smith, Inc. v. Livingston, 566 F.2d 1119 (9th Cir. 1978) (holding that a brokerage firm's "vice president" was not officer for §16(b) purposes because his title was merely honorary in recognition of sales accomplishments and did not reflect access to inside information).

Deputization.   Courts have developed a *deputization theory* for entities represented on the board of directors of a corporation in whose stock they trade. For example, suppose that Henrietta is a managing partner (an investment banker with a securities trading department) of Trout Brothers and that she also sits on the board of Bullseye Corp., the subject of takeover speculation. If Trout Brothers purchases 5 percent of Bullseye's stock, §16(b) by its literal terms does not create any short-swing trading exposure: Trout Brothers is neither a 10 percent shareholder nor a director, and Henrietta is not the beneficial owner of Trout Brothers's holdings (see §18.2). Nonetheless, there should be concern that Trout Brothers will use Henrietta as its conduit of inside information.

Under the deputization theory, Henrietta is treated as Trout Brothers's "deputy" and any Trout Brothers transactions in Bullseye stock are brought under the short-swing profit rules. The scope of the deputization theory is unclear. Under one view, Trout Brothers is treated under §16(b) as a "director" if Henrietta (1) represents its interests on the Bullseye board and (2) actually passes along inside information to Trout Brothers. See *Blau v. Lehman,* 368 U.S. 403 (1962) (entire partnership not liable as an insider merely because one of its members was a director in a corporation in whose stock the partnership traded based on public information). Some courts have taken a broader view, suggesting Henrietta need not have actually passed along inside information if she had "responsibility" for the challenged stock transactions. See *Feder v. Martin-Marietta Corp.,* 406 F.2d 260 (2d Cir. 1969), *cert. denied,* 396 U.S. 1036 (1970) (company liable under §16(b) when its president represented company's financial interests on target's board, was ultimately responsible for company's financial investments, and was in a position to pass along inside information).

§30.3.2   Ten Percent Beneficial Owners

In general, beneficial ownership under the 1934 Act depends on whether a shareholder has the power either to dispose of securities or to vote them (see §18.2). Section 16(b) liability, however, proceeds on a different and broader theory of beneficial ownership. According to the SEC, a person is a beneficial stock owner if she receives the benefits of ownership. See *Whiting v. Dow Chemical Co.,* 523 F.2d 680 (2d Cir. 1975) (finding beneficial ownership when shares were for the joint benefit of husband and wife). This means spouses and other family members normally will be deemed beneficial owners of each other's stock for §16(b) purposes.

§30.3.3   *Unorthodox Transactions*

Usually whether a stock transaction constitutes a matchable purchase or sale under §16(b) is not an issue. But when the stock transaction is *unorthodox* — such as when shares are acquired in a merger or in an option transaction — the courts have been willing to inquire into whether the transaction should be treated as a matchable "sale" or "purchase" for purposes of §16(b). The SEC also has promulgated extensive (and very technical) rules that exempt certain transactions — such as redemptions, conversions, and transactions involving employee benefit plans — where the risk of insider abuse is minimal. 1934 Act Rules 16b-1 through 16b-11.

The Supreme Court has held that an unorthodox transaction by a hostile bidder (and 10 percent shareholder) in a takeover contest is not a matchable sale if there is no evidence of abuse of inside information. *Kern County Land Co. v. Occidental Petroleum Corp.,* 411 U.S. 582 (1973). Occidental made a successful tender offer for 20 percent of Kern County's stock and became a 20 percent shareholder. Concerned about Occidental's intentions, Kern County management found a white knight, Tenneco, which agreed to buy Kern County in a merger. Under the merger terms, "Old Kern" merged into a wholly-owned Tenneco subsidiary and became "New Kern." In the merger, Old Kern shareholders received Tenneco preferred stock in exchange for their stock. To buy Occidental's good will, Tenneco granted Occidental an option to sell its Tenneco preferred (after the merger) at a premium. Occidental agreed not to oppose or vote on the merger, and the remaining Old Kern shareholders approved. Occidental, along with the other Old Kern shareholders, then received Tenneco preferred stock for their Old Kern stock.

Was there a "sale" that could be matched with the tender offer "purchases"? The plaintiff argued there were two: (1) the option granted to Occidental — granted within six months of the original purchases, though exercisable after the six-month period; and (2) Occidental's exchange of New Kern stock for Tenneco preferred stock in the merger, which occurred within the six-month period. In other contexts, the receipt of consideration in a merger has been treated as a sale under the federal securities laws. See 1933 Act Rule 145 (requiring prospectus disclosure for securities issued in a merger). Nonetheless, the Supreme Court decided that Occidental had not "sold" its Old Kern stock in the merger because the transaction was involuntary and the relationship between Occidental and Kern County's management was hostile. Likewise, there was no evidence of abuse of inside information in the granting of the option, which was granted to buy Occidental's acquiescence in the merger.

But when it is possible that inside information has been abused, the granting of an option has been treated as a "sale." In *Bershad v. McDonough,* 428 F.2d 693 (7th Cir. 1970), McDonough and his wife had purchased more than 10 percent of Cudahy's stock, and McDonough became a director. Within six months of these purchases, the McDonoughs granted another company, Smelting Refining, an option to purchase the bulk of their Cudahy stock. McDonough then resigned from Cudahy's board, and Smelting Refining placed its representatives on the board. Under the option agreement, the McDonoughs placed their Cudahy shares in escrow. Smelting Refining exercised the option more than six months after their original purchase. The court held that the granting of the option was a matchable "sale" because it could lend itself to inside speculation.

EXAMPLES

1. BIM Corp. has one class of common stock, which is registered under §12 of the 1934 Act. Dorothy is a director of BIM. For each of the following situations, what is Dorothy's disgorgement liability under §16(b)?

   a. Dorothy purchases 100 shares of BIM stock on February 1 at $10 per share and sells on August 2 at $15. BIM's stock price rose because it was awarded a large government contract on April 1, which Dorothy knew about when she bought.

   b. Dorothy buys 200 shares on July 1 at $5, sells 200 shares on February 1 of the next year at $15 per share, and then purchases 300 shares on May 1 at $10 per share.

   c. Dorothy buys 100 shares at $10 on February 1, buys another 100 shares at $20 on March 1, sells 100 shares at $12 on April 1, and sells another 100 shares at $15 on May 1.

   d. Dorothy buys 180 shares on February 1 at $10, sells 150 shares on May 1 at $15, and then sells another 100 shares at $18 on June 1.

   e. Dorothy becomes a director on March 1. Prior to this, on February 1, she had purchased 100 shares at $10 per share. She purchases 100 shares at $12 on April 1 and sells 100 shares at $15 per share on June 1.

   f. Dorothy purchases 100 shares at $10 per share on February 1. She becomes a director on March 1 and resigns as director on May 1. She sells 100 shares at $15 per share on May 2. Dorothy had purchased in February at $10 knowing of confidential, nonpublic developments that would raise the price in May.

2. Cheryl is an investor with a keen interest in BIM. She is neither a director nor officer of BIM.

   a. Over four years, Cheryl accumulates 9 million (9 percent) of BIM stock. On February 1 she buys 5 million additional shares at $15 per share, bringing her holdings to 14 percent. On May 1 she sells all of her 14 million shares at $20 per share. What is Cheryl's §16(b) liability?

   b. After selling all her BIM stock last year, Cheryl decides to acquire control of the company by making open-market purchases and a tender offer. She is prepared, however, to sell her holdings if another bidder offers a good price. Advise Cheryl on how to purchase and, if the opportunity presents itself, sell her stock without becoming subject to §16(b) liability.

3. Cheryl does not take your advice. Instead, she buys 11 percent of BIM's stock in December and then buys an additional 9 percent on March 1, bringing her holdings to 20 percent. She then enters into negotiations with BIM's management and on July 20 agrees to have the corporation repurchase all her stock.

   a. The repurchase agreement calls for closing on the repurchase to occur on October 1, outside the six-month window that opened on March 1. Under §16(b), can Cheryl's March purchases be matched with her July agreement?

   b. If the closing had occurred on August 1 — at a slightly lower price — does your answer change?

4. After selling back her shares, Cheryl and her husband, Charles, each begin buying BIM stock. By November, each owns 6 percent of BIM's stock. In January, Charles purchases additional shares at $40 per share, bringing his holdings to 9 percent. In March of the same year, Cheryl sells some of her shares at $45 per share, bringing her holdings to 3 percent. Is either liable under §16(b)?

5. The management of MACO Corp. decides to "greenmail" BIM by threatening a hostile tender offer. MACO, which has no shareholding in BIM, will buy a significant block of BIM stock on the open market and then announce a tender offer. MACO management expects BIM's management to offer to buy MACO's shares at a premium.

   a. Otto, an officer of MACO, sits on BIM's board. Is there a possibility of §16(b) liability in MACO's plans?

   b. MACO has Otto resign from the BIM board. MACO then becomes a 10 percent shareholder in January and in February purchases 200,000 more shares. BIM management reacts by offering its shareholders a capital restructuring in which they will receive a package of cash and preferred stock. This will require an amendment of BIM's charter. MACO supports the restructuring, and its votes for the charter amendment prove decisive. After the June restructuring, MACO makes a significant profit. Is MACO liable under §16(b)?

EXPLANATIONS

1a. Dorothy has no disgorgement liability under §16(b) because her trades did not occur within six months. Under §16(b) it is irrelevant whether Dorothy had any confidential, nonpublic information about the government contract when she made these trades. She may be liable, however, under Rule 10b-5 (see §29.5).

1b.

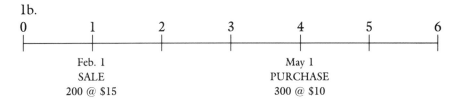

Feb. 1
SALE
200 @ $15

May 1
PURCHASE
300 @ $10

$1000. Lower-priced purchases are matched with higher-priced sales occurring within six months. Only the February sale and May purchase can be matched; the July purchase is outside the six-month window. The disgorgement formula operates regardless of the order of the transactions as long as the sale price is higher than the purchase price. In this case, only 200 shares match, and Dorothy is liable to disgorge $1000 in profits (200 shares times $5).

1c.

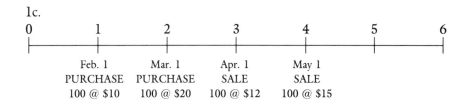

Feb. 1
PURCHASE
100 @ $10

Mar. 1
PURCHASE
100 @ $20

Apr. 1
SALE
100 @ $12

May 1
SALE
100 @ $15

$500. Matching the February purchase and the May sale produces the highest gain — $500 (100 shares times $5). There is no need to offset any losses, and the $800 loss generated by matching the March purchase and the lower April sale can be disregarded. Even though Dorothy lost a net $300 during the six-month trading period — she purchased 200 shares for $3000 and sold 200 shares for $2700 — she is subject to disgorgement liability. The §16(b) crude rule of thumb assumes that her February and May transactions were based on inside information or short-swing market manipulations.

1d.

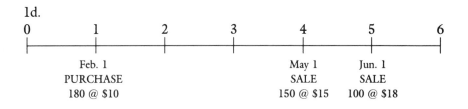

Feb. 1
PURCHASE
180 @ $10

May 1
SALE
150 @ $15

Jun. 1
SALE
100 @ $18

$1200. First match the transactions that produce the greatest gains (100 shares — February and June) and then any other transactions that produce gains (80 shares — February and May). The combined recoverable profits are $1200 (100 times $8 plus 80 times $5).

1e.

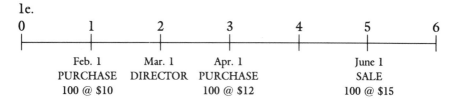

0   1   2   3   4   5   6

          Feb. 1   Mar. 1   Apr. 1   June 1
          PURCHASE   DIRECTOR   PURCHASE   SALE
          100 @ $10   100 @ $12   100 @ $15

$500. Although an April-June match produces a gain, a February-June match produces a higher gain. This is possible under §16(b) because Dorothy was a director at one end of the match, the June transaction. Dorothy's liability is $500 (100 shares times $5).

1f.

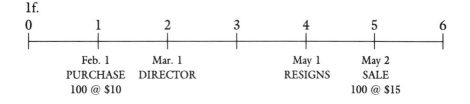

0   1   2   3   4   5   6

          Feb. 1   Mar. 1   May 1   May 2
          PURCHASE   DIRECTOR   RESIGNS   SALE
          100 @ $10   100 @ $15

Dorothy is not liable under §16(b). There is no sale and purchase to match because Dorothy was not a director at the time of either trade. Nonetheless, Dorothy may be liable under Rule 10b-5 for trading on material nonpublic information she received in her capacity as a director (see §29.5).

2a.

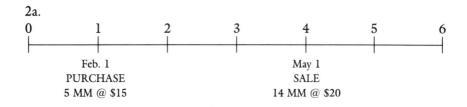

0   1   2   3   4   5   6

          Feb. 1   May 1
          PURCHASE   SALE
          5 MM @ $15   14 MM @ $20

Cheryl is not liable under §16(b). The February purchase cannot be matched because Cheryl was not a 10 percent shareholder *immediately prior* to it. Shareholders must have "inside" status — that is, hold more than 10 percent of the shares — immediately before each transaction to be matched. This differs from the rule for directors and officers and is based on an assumption that shareholders are less likely to have access to inside information and thus the ability to manipulate prices.

2b. Cheryl should buy only 9.9 percent of BIM's outstanding shares on the open market. The purchase that brings her above 10 percent should be in one fell swoop — such as in a tender offer (see §37.1). In this way, none of her purchases will occur when she is a 10 percent shareholder, and none will be matchable. Cheryl can sell without any §16(b) liability. The assumption in *Kern County* (see §30.3.3), decided by the Supreme Court in 1973, that tender offer purchases that bring a shareholder's holdings above 10 percent are matchable, was explicitly rejected by the Supreme Court in *Foremost McKesson* in 1976 (see §30.3.2).

If Cheryl makes any matchable purchases while a 10 percent shareholder, she should sell her stock in chunks, not all at once. In this way, only those sales that she makes while she is a 10 percent shareholder are matchable. Once her holdings fall to 10 percent or less, any further sales are not matchable. This limits her §16(b) exposure.

3a. Probably not. Can the July 20 agreement be characterized as a "sale" for purposes of §16(b)? Management's apparent hostility to Cheryl suggests she had no access to corporate information or control, and there would be little purpose in imposing short-swing liability. Such liability would effectively allow the corporation to renegotiate the repurchase price.

3b. Probably. There would then be a traditional purchase and sale within six months. Nothing in the language of §16(b) suggests that there are exceptions to the disgorgement rules if the evidence strongly suggests the absence of inside abuse. Although the August closing would seem for financial purposes to be equivalent to an October closing, §16(b) may elevate the form of the transaction over its substance.

4. Yes, probably both. Are Cheryl and Charles treated as a single beneficial owner and their individual 6 percent holdings combined? If so, Charles's January purchases can be matched with Cheryl's March sales for a recoverable profit — together they beneficially owned more than 10 percent immediately before each transaction. If not, neither Cheryl nor Charles can be liable because neither individually surpassed the 10 percent threshold.

According to the SEC and some courts, under §16(b) their holdings must be aggregated if they share in the financial benefits of ownership, the usual case in a family. Unless their spousal relationship does not involve sharing of benefits, Cheryl and Charles will be deemed the beneficial owners of each other's shares, making them liable for their short-swing profit on the January and March transactions.

5a. Yes. MACO might be treated as a Bullseye director under a "deputization" theory because Otto, an officer of MACO, sits on Bullseye's board. If MACO is "deputized," any gains in its short-swing trading would be subject to §16(b) disgorgement. To show deputization, Otto must have represented MACO on the board. In addition, it might be necessary to show some (or all) of the following: Otto was "controlled" by MACO; Otto was ultimately responsible for deciding about MACO's acquisitions of Bullseye stock; Otto had access to inside Bullseye information; and Otto actually passed such information on to MACO. Although requiring a showing of actual access or actual passing of inside information might seem inconsistent with §16(b) strict liability, deputization is meant to achieve the underlying §16(b) purposes of deterring and compensating for the abuse of inside information. A deputization test requires a showing of actual or probable abuse.

5b. Perhaps, though it is hard to say. Although the February and June transactions are matchable because MACO was a 10 percent shareholder before each one, it could be argued that the June transaction was not a "sale" for purposes of §16(b). Arguably, the June restructuring was involuntary — that is, its timing was not of MACO's making — and MACO's relationship to BIM was such that it is unlikely any confidential information was passed to MACO. See *Kern County* (§30.4.3).

There are, however, two significant differences between this case and the situation in *Kern County*. First, MACO supported the restructuring. This should not make a difference if the choice of how BIM responded to the takeover threat was not MACO's and there was no passing of insider information. Second, BIM's management may have had reasons to pass inside information to MACO. It is possible that the restructuring was negotiated with MACO — just as was the option in *Kern County*. If so, BIM's management might have found it useful to pass inside information to MACO to assure the success of the restructuring. Nonetheless, even if BIM passed inside information, it may well have been "good news" to encourage MACO's support. Because all the MACO shareholders shared in the restructuring premium, the abuse would not have harmed them.

PART NINE

Shareholder Litigation

31

Shareholder Litigation

Two remedies are available to shareholders to vindicate their interests in the corporation. Shareholders can sue in their own capacity to enforce their rights as shareholders (a direct action), and they can sue on behalf of the corporation to enforce corporate rights that affect them only indirectly (a derivative action). How one characterizes the suit affects a number of things: who pays for litigation expenses, who recovers, what procedures apply to the shareholder-plaintiff, and whether the suit can be dismissed by the corporation.

In this chapter, we describe the nature of the derivative suit and how it differs from a direct suit. Derivative litigation is subject to significant procedural impediments, which we discuss in Chapter 32. Derivative suits are unique in that courts often allow others besides the plaintiff to decide the fate of the litigation; we discuss dismissal of derivative suits in Chapter 33.

§31.1 The Nature of Derivative Litigation

The derivative suit is the primary means by which shareholders hold directors, officers, and other fiduciaries accountable. It is equity jurisdiction's ingenious solution to the dilemma created by two inconsistent tenets of corporate law — namely: (1) corporate fiduciaries owe their duties to the corporation, not to individual shareholders, and (2) the board of directors manages the corporation's business, which includes bringing lawsuits to ensure compliance with duties owed the corporation.

Derivative litigation breaks the stranglehold the board would otherwise hold over fiduciary accountability. If the board's virtual monopoly of central corporate governance extended to litigation decisions, management's fiduciary duties to the corporation would be virtually meaningless. It would be the rare case that managers would choose to sue themselves.

479

§31.1.1   The Concept — Two Suits in One

In a derivative suit, shareholders sue on behalf of the corporation to enforce rights of the corporation. It is in effect two suits in one. In theory, the shareholder (1) sues the corporation in equity (2) to bring an action to enforce corporate rights. Although the modern derivative suit is treated as one action, the historical notion of two suits survives. The corporation is an indispensable party and is made a nominal defendant. The corporation (that is, the board of directors and management) is also allowed to compel the derivative suit plaintiff to comply with various procedural requirements (see §32.2).

Viewing a derivative suit as two suits in one produces an important procedural effect: The right to a federal jury trial exists if the corporation would have been entitled to one had it brought suit — generally when the suit seeks damages. *Ross v. Bernhard,* 396 U.S. 531 (1970). (Many states have different jury trial systems; in Delaware, for example, the chancery court hears all corporate law cases without a jury.)

§31.1.2   All Recovery to the Corporation

Derivative litigation enforces corporate rights, and any recovery in derivative litigation generally runs to the corporation. The shareholder-plaintiff shares in the recovery only indirectly, to the extent her shares increase in value because of the corporate recovery. The shareholder-plaintiff also benefits indirectly by the deterrent value of successful derivative litigation or when equitable relief forbids or undoes harmful behavior.

Sometimes corporate recovery does not compensate those injured by the wrongdoing because the corporation is no longer in existence or corporate recovery would produce a windfall for new owners. Courts in these circumstances have allowed recovery by injured shareholders in proportion to their holdings. See *Perlman v. Feldmann,* 219 F.2d 173 (2d Cir. 1955) (see §37.2.3); *Donahue v. Rodd Electrotype Co.,* 328 N.E.2d 505 (Mass. 1975) (see §17.1.3). The ALI Principles of Corporate Governance suggest that when derivative litigation involves a close corporation, a court may exercise its discretion to allow direct shareholder recovery, provided the corporation is not exposed unfairly to multiple claims, creditors are not materially prejudiced, and the recovery can be fairly distributed. ALI §7.01(d).

§31.1.3   Reimbursement of Successful Plaintiff's Expenses

Why would a shareholder, particularly a shareholder in a public corporation with a typically small, indirect stake in any recovery, undertake the trouble and expense of a derivative suit? The answer is simple and troubling: reimbursement of the plaintiff's attorney fees. Contrary to the prevailing American rule that each litigant bears his own expenses, the universal rule in derivative litigation is that the corporation pays the successful plaintiff's litigation expenses, including attorney fees. RMBCA §7.46(1) ("if . . . the proceeding has resulted in a substantial benefit to the corporation"). The theory is that the plaintiff (and her attorney) produced a benefit to the corporation, and they should be reimbursed for their effort.

Effect of Rule. The engine driving the derivative suit in public corporations is the plaintiff's attorney — a "bounty hunter" for the corporation whose fees are contingent on an award by the court or in a settlement. There is a perception that the attorney is the real plaintiff in interest: He has the greatest stake in the outcome because he stands to gain the most; he often brings the possibility of a lawsuit to the shareholder-plaintiff's attention. The attorney usually runs the litigation, and he decides on when and whether to settle — often depending on the amount of attorney fees provided under the settlement offer. Corporate law deals with this alarming reversal of the client-attorney roles by placing procedural requirements on the bringing and settlement of derivative litigation (see §32.2).

Method of Calculation. Attorney fees in derivative litigation generally have been calculated using either a *percentage-of-recovery* method or a *lodestar* method. Under the percentage-of-recovery method, the attorney receives a percentage of the corporation's recovery, varying between 15-35 percent depending on the size of the recovery. Under the lodestar method, fees are based on the number of hours spent on the suit multiplied by the prevailing rate for similar legal work by an attorney of comparable experience and stature; this amount then may be adjusted upward or downward depending on the quality of work, the novelty of the issues, and the original likelihood of success. The lodestar method, unlike the increasingly used percentage-of-recovery method, creates an incentive for protracted litigation and discourages reasonable, prompt settlement.

§31.1.4 The Derivative Suit Plaintiff — A Self-Appointed Representative

In a derivative suit, the plaintiff-shareholder chooses herself as a representative for the corporation. The possibility that the plaintiff will conduct the litigation for her own gain without serving the interests of shareholders as a group is evident. A shareholder (and her attorney) may bring a derivative suit solely as a nuisance to extract a settlement benefiting primarily them. Courts and statutes have imposed on the derivative suit plaintiff a duty, akin to that of a fiduciary, to be a faithful representative of the corporation's and the other shareholders' interests. See Fed. R. Civ. P. 23.1 (shareholder-plaintiff must "fairly and adequately represent the interests of the shareholders or members substantially similarly situated in enforcing the right of the corporation").

§31.1.5 *Res Judicata — Preclusion of the "Corporation" to Relitigate*

In a derivative suit the shareholder-plaintiff sues on behalf of the corporation, and the corporation is bound by any judgment or settlement. Neither the corporation nor a subsequent derivative suit plaintiff can bring a suit based on claims that were raised in a derivative suit. By the same token, if the corporation itself has already litigated or settled in court a claim in good faith, res judicata prevents a shareholder from bringing a derivative suit making the same claim.

§31.2 Distinguishing between Derivative, Direct, and Class Action Suits

A shareholder may also sue in her personal capacity to enforce her rights as a shareholder — a direct action. Unlike a derivative suit, a direct action is not brought on behalf of the corporation. To avoid the host of procedural requirements that apply to derivative suits, shareholders will often seek to characterize their suit as a direct action. For example, if state law requires that derivative suit plaintiffs post security for the defendants' expenses (see §32.2.3), the characterization of the suit as derivative or direct may decide its viability as a practical matter.

§31.2.1 *Some Examples of Direct Suits*

In many cases, the characterization is straightforward. Direct suits are those in which shareholders seek to enforce rights arising from their share ownership, including suits:

- to challenge the denial or dilution of voting rights, such as when substantially all the corporation's assets are sold without shareholder approval (see §35.3);
- to compel payment of dividends that were declared but not distributed;
- to enjoin ultra vires actions (see RMBCA §3.04);
- to challenge fraud on shareholders in connection with their sale, purchase, or voting of securities (see §§10.3, 19.1, 29.1);

- to compel dissolution of the corporation (see §34.2);
- to compel inspection of shareholders' lists, or corporate books and records (see §12.1);
- to challenge corporate restrictions on share transferability (see §16.6); and
- to require the holding of a shareholders' meeting (see §12.2).

Derivative suits, on the other hand, are characterized by claims of a breach of fiduciary duties by directors, officers, or controlling shareholders — duties owed to the corporation. For example, suits that ask a director to account for profits when he usurped a corporate opportunity or that challenge executive compensation as corporate waste are derivative suits.

§31.2.2 Claims Having Both Direct and Derivative Attributes

Some shareholder suits are difficult to characterize. For example, while most courts have characterized a suit to compel the payment of dividends as direct, see *Cowin v. Bresler*, 741 F.2d 410 (D.C. Cir. 1984), some have characterized the suit as derivative. See *Gordon v. Elliman*, 119 N.E.2d 331 (N.Y. 1954).

Sometimes the facts may suggest both a direct and a derivative claim. In such a case, the shareholder's choice on how to plead governs. For example, a wrongful refusal by management to provide a shareholders' list to a shareholder for a proxy fight may violate not only the shareholder's rights to inspection but also management's fiduciary duties to the corporation. The shareholder may bring the claim as either a direct action seeking inspection or as a derivative action to enjoin management's entrenchment, or both. See ALI Principles §7.01(c).

The shareholder's characterization of the suit, however, is not controlling. A shareholder cannot escape the procedural restrictions of a derivative suit simply by claiming that she was directly injured when the value of her shares fell as a result of a breach of a duty to the corporation. *Armstrong v. Frostie Co.*, 453 F.2d 914 (4th Cir. 1971).

But careful pleading can help. If a shareholder can characterize a transaction as diluting voting power, for example, even though the transaction may also be a fiduciary breach, the suit is direct. In *Eisenberg v. Flying Tiger Line, Inc.*, 451 F.2d 267 (2d. Cir. 1971), a shareholder challenged a corporate reorganization in which shareholders of an operating company became, after a merger, shareholders of a holding company. The corporation sought to require the plaintiff to post security for expenses, a derivative suit requirement (see §32.2.3). The court, however, held that the action was direct because the reorganization deprived the shareholder of "any voice in the affairs of their previously existing operating company."

§31.2.3   Class Actions — A Direct Suit Brought in a Representative Capacity

When a shareholder sues in his own capacity as well as on behalf of other shareholders similarly situated, the suit is not a derivative suit but a class action suit. In effect, all the members of the class have banded together through a representative to bring their *individual direct suits* in one large direct suit.

Some of the procedural rules applicable to class actions — such as that the class action plaintiff be representative of the other shareholders' interests and that any settlement be approved by the court — also apply in derivative suits. See Fed. R. Civ. P. 23. They assure that shareholders are well-represented and that the judicial process is not abused by nuisance plaintiffs.

A class action, however, does not interfere with the prerogatives of central corporate governance, and many requirements that apply to derivative suits do not apply to class actions. For example, in a class action the plaintiff need not post security for the defendants' expenses (see §32.2.3) or make a demand on the board of directors before bringing suit (see §32.2.4). Class actions, however, have their own impediments, such as requirements that plaintiff-representatives bear the expense of providing notice to members of the class.

EXAMPLES

1. Ten years ago, Consolidated Engines (a major public corporation) acquired Digital Engineering in a merger. H. Russell Thoreau, Digital's principal shareholder, received 2 percent of Consolidated's common stock, and he was informally assured a seat on Consolidated's board for as long as he held the stock. Last year Thoreau and Consolidated's chairman had a falling out. The board decided to repurchase Thoreau's 10 million shares for $90 a share at a time when the stock was trading at $80 — a $100 million premium to Thoreau.

   a. Abe Pomerantz, an attorney with broad experience representing shareholders, brought the repurchase to the attention of Pam Walden, a long-time shareholder of Consolidated. Under what procedure can Walden seek to have the repurchase rescinded?

   b. Walden (through her lawyer, Pomerantz) sues to rescind the repurchase or, in the alternative, to hold the directors liable for Thoreau's $100 million premium. Walden owns exactly $4000 (.00001 percent) of Consolidated's stock. How much can she hope to recover?

   c. Consolidated's directors offer to settle Walden's derivative suit by promising not to repurchase any more shares from Thoreau. The corporation, however, will recover nothing in cash. Can Pomerantz expect any fees?

2. Settlement negotiations fail. Thoreau offers to repay 10% of the premium he received from Consolidated. The Consolidated board seizes the opportunity: It authorizes a suit against Thoreau, which is then settled under the terms of his offer, and approved by a court.

   a. Can Walden continue her suit?

   b. Is there another course open to Walden?

   c. When Pomerantz hears of Consolidated's settlement, he is outraged. He has spent a significant amount of time preparing the derivative suit for trial. Can Pomerantz seek attorney fees?

3. Some of Consolidated's senior executives propose a management buyout (see §35.2). Under the terms of the buyout merger, Walden and all other shareholders would receive $80 for their shares.

   a. Walden thinks $80 is inadequate. The proxy materials seeking shareholder approval of the going-private transaction fail to disclose that Consolidated's board considered the company was worth at least $100 per share. Walden wants to enjoin the merger. What kind of suit would you advise?

   b. Walden brings both direct and derivative claims. The board agrees to settle by amending its proxy materials and paying Walden $500,000, on the condition that she dismiss all her claims. Are there any problems if Walden accepts?

   c. The shareholders approve the merger. Walden amends her complaint to claim damages. The court holds the directors liable for being grossly negligent in approving the merger at $80 per share. What is the appropriate remedy?

EXPLANATIONS

1a. Walden can bring a derivative suit on behalf of the corporation alleging that Consolidated's directors breached their fiduciary duties to the corporation. The theory might be that the repurchase wasted corporate assets (see §21.3.2), lacked a reasonable relation to the threat of Thoreau launching a proxy fight or other takeover attempt (see §40.2.3), or constituted self-serving entrenchment (see §40.2.1). The suit would be subject to daunting derivative suit requirements: demand on the board, possible shifting of fees, dismissal by the corporation.

   Walden might be able to characterize her suit as a direct action if the repurchase was an illegal distribution under an insolvency or balance sheet test (see §§9.2, 9.3). Otherwise, the transaction did not dilute Walden's voting rights (to the contrary, it concentrated them) or otherwise affect her rights as a shareholder. Just because the corporation's assets are depleted, the indirect injury to Walden's interest does not allow her to sue in her own capacity.

1b. Nothing. In a derivative suit, any recovery runs to the corporation. Walden can only hope to increase the value of her shares to the extent corporate recovery increases general share value. There is an exception to this approach. Shareholders can recover directly if the corporation is closely held or no longer in existence, or recovery would not redound to the benefit of contemporaneous shareholders indirectly injured. None of these, however, applies to Consolidated.

1c. Yes. Pomerantz can expect attorney fees either as part of the settlement or as ordered by the court in its approval of the settlement, even though the corporation recovered nothing. Studies show that attorneys in settlement of shareholder suits involving public companies receive fees 90 percent of the time, even though only 55 percent of the settlements have monetary recovery.

Under a lodestar method for computing his fees, Pomerantz's billable hours would be multiplied by a reasonable hourly rate, which because of his experience and stature would be at the upper end of the range. This amount then might be adjusted upward, given Pomerantz's success in the face of the business judgment rule's teaching that courts normally defer to valuations by the board. The percentage-of-recovery method would not apply.

2a. Probably not. A derivative suit is brought on behalf of the corporation, and the corporation's settlement is binding (res judicata) on Walden in her suit challenging the Thoreau repurchase. Unless she can show fraud or a fiduciary breach that would justify vacating the judgment, she cannot continue her suit.

2b. A fiduciary challenge. Walden might be able to challenge the directors' decision to enter into the settlement as a breach of their duty of care or loyalty. This derivative claim may be difficult because of the business judgment rule. Unless Walden can show that the board was interested (because of an entrenchment motive) or failed to become informed about the settlement's terms, the board has discretion to make rational litigation decisions.

2c. Perhaps. Pomerantz might argue Walden's suit goaded the Consolidated board to act. In derivative litigation, shareholder-intervenors may recover their expenses and the fees of their attorneys if their efforts contributed to the recovery or settlement. Pomerantz could argue that Walden's suit brought the excessiveness of the repurchase price to the board's attention, and the board's out-of-court settlement (like a successful derivative suit settlement) should be seen as resulting from her suit and his efforts.

3a. Walden can choose between a direct suit, a derivative suit, or a suit with both direct and derivative claims. She has a direct claim under federal proxy rules: The corporation failed to adequately disclose the terms of the merger. Rule 14a-9 of the Securities Exchange Act of 1934. (See

§19.6.) This claim may also be brought as a derivative claim. (See §19.6.2.) Walden also has a derivative claim that the board's approval of this self-dealing, going-private merger and its deception about the merger price violates the executives' and the board's fiduciary duties (see §26.3). Walden maximizes her leverage by bringing both claims in one suit. If she does, she must sue in federal district court, which has exclusive jurisdiction over federal proxy claims.

3b. Yes. It is unclear why Consolidated is offering to pay $500,000 to Walden. The payment does not seem to be related to her direct claim, because the merger has not been approved and Walden has suffered no loss. Nor can the payment be tied to the derivative suit, because any recovery in such a suit is to the corporation. Rather, the payment appears to be a bribe for her to dismiss the derivative claims. Although such a payment is perfectly acceptable in an individual direct action, it is not in a derivative suit. The court is unlikely to approve a settlement of the derivative claim in these circumstances (see §36.2.5).

3c. Shareholder recovery, whether the claim is seen as derivative or direct. If the claim is direct, as was the case in *Smith v. Van Gorkom* (see §21.3.3), the shareholder class members would recover in proportion to their shareholdings. The claim might be characterized as direct because the directors' approval of the merger caused the shareholders' interest to be converted from one of share ownership to a cash payment right. To the extent the suit challenged the board's disclosure, it would also be direct. If the claim is seen as derivative, the normal rule is that defendant directors (or their insurers) pay the corporation. In this case, this would result in payment to New Consolidated, the surviving corporation that acquired all the rights of Consolidated after the merger (see §35.2). New Consolidated is controlled by new owners (the management team), and any corporate recovery would not remedy the injury to the body of shareholders who received an inadequate price for their shares. An exception to the rule of corporate recovery in derivative litigation is called for: Pro rata recovery by former shareholders would produce a correct result.

32

Procedural Restrictions on Derivative Litigation

The derivative suit is an essential tool for enforcing management accountability. It is also subject to abuse. To address the risk that the derivative suit plaintiffs represent corporate interests poorly or not at all, a variety of procedural requirements seek to filter out abusive and improvident derivative litigation.

§32.1 The Distorted Incentives Created by Derivative Litigation

Derivative litigation allows self-appointed shareholders to become champions of corporate rights, but the incentives of the derivative suit plaintiff and defendant may produce results at odds with corporate interests:

- The plaintiff may be indifferent to the outcome of the litigation. Any recovery will be to the corporation, and the plaintiff's financial interest in the corporation will often be insignificant.
- The plaintiff's case is largely in the hands of her attorney, whose fees are usually contingent on payment in a settlement or an award by the court. The attorney is indifferent to the outcome, as long as it includes adequate attorney fees. The attorney may prefer protracted litigation over a settlement, particularly if fees are calculated under a lodestar method.

- The individual defendants (typically directors or officers of the corporation) usually will prefer settlement rather than trial. Settlement increases the possibility that the defendant's expenses, as well as amounts paid in settlement, will be indemnified by the corporation or covered by insurance (see Chapter 25).
- The corporation (the board of directors) often will be influenced by the interests of the individual defendants.

These realities of derivative litigation invite evil-hearted plaintiffs. Some shareholders may be tempted to bring suit to coerce a settlement based on the suit's nuisance value — the infamous *strike suit*. The history of corporate law is spiced with colorful stories of "strike suit artists" who have led long and lucrative careers as gadfly derivative suit plaintiffs. Derivative litigation also creates a potential for well-meaning but faint-hearted plaintiffs, who are unwilling to pursue a meritorious claim because of the incentives to settle.

Derivative litigation also threatens the integrity of the judicial process. By using the courts to bring vexatious litigation, strike suit plaintiffs waste and abuse judicial resources. Nonetheless, derivative litigation provides the means for enforcing fiduciary duties, and corporate statutes attempt to distinguish between the meritorious and the strike suit.

§32.2   Procedural Requirements

A variety of procedural requirements attempt to weed out strike suits.

§32.2.1   *Plaintiff's Verification of Complaint*

Some statutes require that the plaintiff verify the complaint. See Fed. R. Civ. P. 23.1. The requirement provides a basis for applying sanctions for perjury against those who fabricate charges in a strike suit. It is not necessary, however, that the plaintiff have personal knowledge or comprehend the specific factual allegation in the complaint as long as the plaintiff reasonably relied on her lawyer's investigation and advice. *Surowitz v. Hilton Hotels Corp.*, 383 U.S. 363 (1966).

§32.2.2   *Plaintiff Standing — Contemporaneous and Continuing Equity Ownership*

Contemporaneous Ownership.   Most statutes require that the plaintiff have been a shareholder when the wrong occurred — the *contemporaneous* *ownership requirement.* RMBCA §7.41(1). The requirement is meant to assure that the shareholder did not buy her shares to buy a lawsuit. The ALI Principles urge an exception to the requirement when an undisclosed wrong (such as a pattern of waste) was continuing when the plaintiff acquired her shares. See ALI §7.02(a)(1). A logical extension of the contemporaneous ownership rule is that the corporation itself cannot sue for wrongdoing that occurred before a change in ownership — the *vicarious incapacity rule* or *corporate incapacity rule.* If ownership changes, the corporation's new owners should not be able to cause the corporation to sue former managers (or shareholders) for wrongs committed before control changed hands because the new owners would lack capacity under the contemporaneous ownership rule to bring a derivative action. To allow the corporation to recover would produce a windfall for the new owners, whose purchase price presumably took into account any losses caused by the earlier wrongs. *Bangor Punta Operations, Inc. v. Bangor & Aroostook Railroad Co.,* 417 U.S. 703 (1974). The theory does not work as neatly when the recovery would benefit others besides the new owners, such as when the new owners hold less than 100 percent of the stock or when a corporate recovery would benefit creditors. Some jurisdictions, including Delaware, reject the vicarious incapacity rule and allow recovery by the surviving corporation. See *Lewis v. Anderson,* 477 A.2d 1040 (Del. 1983).

Continuing Interest. Some statutes require that the plaintiff continue to be a shareholder when suit is brought and then through trial — the *continuing interest requirement.* Cf. RMBCA §7.41 (no continuing ownership requirement; plaintiff must "fairly and adequately" represent corporate interests). The continuing interest requirement tests the genuineness of the plaintiff's intentions. Delaware courts recognize a narrow exception when the plaintiff ceases to be a shareholder after a fraudulent or illegal merger. *Lewis v. Anderson,* 477 A.2d 1040 (Del. 1983). The ALI Principles broadens the exception to allow a plaintiff to continue her derivative action after a merger if the action was pending at the time of the merger or if the plaintiff is best able to vindicate the shareholders' interests. ALI Principles §7.02(a)(2).

Equity Interest. Most statutes give equity (common and preferred) shareholders standing to bring a derivative suit to protect their residual interests in the corporation against management abuse. Some cases have also allowed holders of options or convertible securities, and creditors of an insolvent corporation, to protect their ownership interests and assert derivative claims. The RMBCA limits derivative suit standing to equity shareholders and beneficial owners; it excludes option holders and convertible debtholders. RMBCA §7.40(2). Some statutes, however, require that the plaintiff be a record owner, not merely a beneficial owner.

Multiple Suits Making Same Claims.   Often different shareholder-plaintiffs (and lawyers) will bring more than one derivative suit concerning the same transaction. If each suit makes essentially the same claims, allowing all to proceed would produce a wasteful and potentially confusing overlap. Courts will want to choose which shareholder should be the leading representative. Toward this end, courts have broad discretion to dismiss redundant derivative suits, to consolidate derivative suits brought in the same court, to stay proceedings in one suit to await a board investigation or the outcome in another suit, and to transfer proceedings (in federal cases) to other courts. See ALI Principles §7.06 (stay pending board review or resolution of "related action").

§32.2.3   Shifting the Expense of Frivolous Litigation to the Plaintiff

Many statutes provide for shifting the defendants' litigation expenses, including attorney fees, to the plaintiff. This discourages unfounded derivative claims and compensates defendants who must defend strike suits. Under the RMBCA, the court may order fee-shifting if the plaintiff commenced or maintained the suit "without reasonable cause or for an improper purpose." RMBCA §7.46(2). This standard forces derivative suit plaintiffs to tread cautiously; the normal standard for recouping expenses based on a claim of frivolous prosecution is more demanding and requires a showing of malicious intent or fraud. Cf. RMBCA §13.31 (in appraisal proceeding, expenses may be shifted to shareholder-dissenter who acted "arbitrarily, vexatiously, or not in good faith").

A once common but now very infrequently used requirement in many states allowed the court to require the plaintiff to post security (pay a bond) for the defendants' litigation expenses as a condition of maintaining the action. The court would act on a motion of the corporation or the defendants. A security-for-expense requirement often had a lethal effect on derivative litigation. The cost of posting security and the risk of having to pay the amount that the bond secured usually outweighed any gain a shareholder-plaintiff might hope for in the suit. Most modern statutes reject this requirement as going too far in limiting fiduciary accountability. See ALI Principles §7.04(c).

Many of the security-for-expenses statutes exempted shareholders with a specified percentage of ownership (such as 3 percent or 5 percent) or a minimum dollar amount ($25,000 or $50,000). The exemptions assumed that most strike suits are brought by shareholders with small holdings and presumably little real concern for the corporation's interests. Shareholder-plaintiffs would try to avoid the security-for-expense requirement by bringing direct actions (see §31.2) or actions under federal law, such as Rule 10b-5 (see §29.2).

§32.2.4 Demand-Pleading Requirement — the Exhaustion of Internal Remedies

Many statutes require that the derivative plaintiff's complaint state with particularity her efforts to make a demand on the board to resolve the dispute or the reasons she did not make demand. Del. GCL §23.1; Fed. R. Civ. P. 23.1. By their terms, these statutes neither require the plaintiff to make a pre-suit demand on the board nor specify the effect that should be given the board's response. Nonetheless, many courts (including in Delaware) have interpreted the statutes to make demand mandatory, unless it would be futile (see §33.3). The demand-pleading requirement allows the court to ascertain whether the board could have acted on the demand. *Aronson v. Lewis,* 473 A.2d 805 (Del. 1984).

Some courts, however, have interpreted the demand-pleading statutes to require only a statement describing the plaintiff's efforts (or non-efforts) to make a demand. This informs the other parties and the court, but there is no substantive effect if the plaintiff fails to make a demand. In many instances, a pre-suit demand would forewarn defendants of an impending suit, giving them an opportunity to take evasive actions. If a shareholder could not bring an action until the board had acted on her demand, the board would be able to put the suit into suspended animation.

Many recent statutes explicitly impose a demand requirement and force a shareholder contemplating a derivative suit to make a demand on the board first. Under the RMBCA, the shareholder must wait for 90 days before filing suit unless the board rejects the demand or the corporation would be irreparably injured by waiting. RMBCA §7.42. The demand requirement gives the board (even if the directors are named defendants) a chance to take corrective action and avoids the difficult question whether demand is excused. See also ALI §7.03(b) (recommending a universal demand requirement unless it would irreparably injure the corporation).

These different approaches do not answer what substantive effect should be given to the board's rejection of a demand or its refusal to bring a suit. Also unanswered is whether the board (or a committee of the board) can act on behalf of the corporation to dismiss the litigation. The demand-pleading requirement is inextricably linked to the question of who can decide the fate of derivative litigation. We discuss these issues and the dismissal of derivative litigation in Chapter 33.

§32.2.5 Court Approval of Settlement — The Clean Solution

The principal danger of derivative litigation is the potential for abusive settlements. Unlike normal litigation in which an arm's length compromise agreed to by plaintiff and defendant provides the best measure of the suit's worth, derivative litigation provides no such assurance. In a derivative suit the interests of the corporation — on whose behalf suit is presumably brought — may not be represented by *any* of the parties.

Most statutes deal with this problem head on and require judicial approval before a derivative suit can be settled, discontinued, or dismissed. RMBCA §7.45; Fed. R. Civ. P. 23.1. The proponents of the settlement have the burden to show it is fair and reasonable to the corporation.

To decide whether to approve the settlement, the court has broad discretion to consider:

(1) the terms of the settlement, including recovery by the corporation (or other relief) and any reimbursement of expenses (including attorney fees) to the shareholder-plaintiff and to the individual defendants; and

(2) the outcome that might have resulted from a trial, discounted by

- the inherent uncertainty of litigation,
- the costs caused by the delay of trial,
- additional litigation expenses that the corporation might be required to pay the plaintiff,
- additional indemnification payments to the defendants if they are successful or if indemnification is determined to be appropriate,
- disruption of business and possible negative publicity because of trial, and
- increased insurance premiums if recovery at trial is higher than in settlement.

Because the proponents' reasons for supporting the settlement may diverge from general corporate and shareholder interests, many statutes require the court to notify nonparty shareholders and solicit their comments. RMBCA §7.45; Fed. R. Civ. P. 23.1. In a public corporation, where such a notice-and-comment procedure would be tantamount to an expensive proxy solicitation, the court may request comments from a sampling of shareholders or solicit comments through published notice.

By their terms, these settlement procedures apply only to derivative litigation. An argument can be made, however, that they should apply whenever the corporation on its own initiative settles claims out of court that might have been brought or already were pending in a derivative suit. An out-of-court settlement by the corporation raises doubts about the parties' incentives in much the same way as a derivative suit settlement. In *Wolf v. Barkes,* 348 F.2d 994 (2d Cir.), *cert. denied,* 382 U.S. 941 (1965), the Second Circuit rejected this argument even though the corporation's out-of-court settlement purported to resolve fiduciary claims involving management stock options that were pending in a derivative suit. Judge Friendly explained that management flexibility should not be impeded in settling corporate claims and that the out-of-court settlement would not necessarily preclude the shareholder's continuing her derivative claims. The shareholder could still attack the settlement as unfair self-dealing, fraudulent, or wasteful. But under this analysis, a corporation's out-of-court settlement is subject to less stringent review than when the same claims are settled in a derivative suit.

§32.3 Derivative Litigation in Federal Courts

§32.3.1 Diversity Jurisdiction

In federal diversity action, there are two principal issues: (1) Is the corporation a plaintiff or a defendant for assessing the parties' citizenship? (2) What rules govern the proceeding — state or federal?

Corporation is a defendant. The Supreme Court has held that even though shareholders technically bring derivative suits on behalf of the corporation, the corporation should be treated as a defendant for purposes of federal diversity jurisdiction if it (or, more precisely, its management) is antagonistic to the claim. *Smith v. Sperling,* 354 U.S. 91 (1957). A further requirement under Fed. R. Civ. P. 23.1 is that the suit not be brought collusively to avoid "complete diversity" requirements. For example, if a North Carolina corporation wished to sue a North Carolina supplier for breach of contract (no diversity of citizenship), a Virginia shareholder of the corporation could not collude with management to bring a derivative action based on diversity by naming the corporation as nominal defendant and the North Carolina supplier as real defendant.

State derivative suit requirements are substantive. Courts have held that state procedural requirements are "substantive" under the *Erie* doctrine. This means that even though not imposed by federal Rule 23.1, state conditions such as the security-for-expense requirement apply in derivative actions brought under federal diversity jurisdiction actions. *Cohen v. Beneficial Industrial Loan Corp.,* 337 U.S. 541 (1949).

§32.3.2 Federal Actions

Actions brought in federal court on behalf of the corporation claiming violations of federal law are subject to federal, not state, procedures. The Supreme Court has held that derivative suits may be brought for alleged violations of Rule 10b-5 (the general securities trading antifraud rule) and Rule 14a-9 (the proxy antifraud rule) of the Securities Exchange Act of 1934 if the fraud was perpetrated on the corporation. *Superintendent of Insurance v. Bankers Life & Casualty Co.,* 404 U.S. 6 (1971) (Rule 10b-5); *J. I. Case Co. v. Borak,* 377 U.S. 426 (1964) (Rule 14a-9). In such cases, the procedural requirements of Rule 23.1 apply, but state procedural requirements — such as state security-for-expense requirements — do not. Nonetheless, the

Supreme Court recently said that when there are gaps in federal securities law that bear on the allocation of power in the corporation, federal law should incorporate the law of the state of incorporation. *Kamen v. Kemper Financial Services, Inc.*, 111 S. Ct. 1711 (1991). Thus, in a derivative suit brought under the federal Investment Company Act for the breach of fiduciary duties by a mutual fund's investment adviser, demand on the board serves to allocate corporate governance between the board and individual shareholders and, absent contrary federal policies, must be determined by reference to state law. The Court rejected the lower court's argument that a universal demand requirement makes good policy sense and should be adopted as a matter of federal common law.

EXAMPLES

1. Protox Corporation, a public company incorporated in Delaware, issues options on 400,000 shares of its common stock to Paula Paleau, the outgoing CEO and chair of the board. The options entitle Paleau to buy Protox shares at $30 (the current market price) at any time for the next five years.

   a. Lois Schneider, a longtime Protox shareholder, is outraged. She brings a derivative suit in federal district court in Maryland claiming that the directors breached their fiduciary duties. Delaware does not have a security-for-expense requirement, but Maryland does. Is Schneider subject to Maryland's security-for-expense requirement?

   b. Believing the security-for-expense requirement applies, Schneider looks for other shareholders to join her so their aggregate shareholdings will exceed the Maryland threshold of $50,000. Schneider finds three such shareholders, but none owned their shares when the board granted Paleau's stock options. Maryland does not have a contemporaneous ownership requirement. Can Schneider bring her federal diversity action?

   c. Is there any way for Schneider to avoid this tangle of derivative suit requirements?

2. After discovery, Paleau agrees to settle Schneider's claims and to return half of the stock options granted her.

   a. Schneider's complaint had sought a return of all the options. Can the court approve the settlement?

   b. Under the terms of the settlement, the corporation agrees to pay Schneider's attorney $500,000 for his representation. Is the court bound by the parties' agreement on attorney fees?

3. While the federal court in Maryland is reviewing the settlement, shareholders file two more derivative actions challenging the stock options, one in state court in Virginia and the other in federal district court in California.

    a. What becomes of these later actions?

    b. What will be the effect on them of a court-approved settlement of Schneider's claim?

    c. The plaintiff in the Virginia case filed his suit hoping that a successful resolution of the Maryland suit would automatically allow him to claim attorney fees in his suit. Are there any risks in this scheme?

4. Protox has become the subject of takeover speculation, and the board approves contracts for top executives that promise three years' worth of compensation if they are ever forced to leave the company after a change in ownership (commonly known as "golden parachutes"). One year later, Protox is bought in a leveraged buyout by RKK Partners, which, after a cash-out reverse subsidiary merger (see §35.2.5), becomes Protox's 100 percent parent.

    a. The new Protox board fires some Protox executives, but RKK chafes at its subsidiary paying for their golden parachutes. Can RKK bring a derivative suit challenging the contracts?

    b. RKK has the new Protox board initiate a suit against the old directors for awarding the golden parachutes. Can Protox assert these fiduciary claims?

    c. Schneider, who owned Protox shares when the board approved the golden parachutes, believes RKK paid less because of the contingent golden parachute liability. Can she bring a derivative suit challenging the golden parachutes?

EXPLANATIONS

1a. Perhaps not. Schneider's action is brought in Maryland federal court based on diversity jurisdiction. *Erie* requires that the district court apply the substantive rules of Maryland, including its choice-of-law rules. In a case involving substantially the same facts, the Supreme Court has held that a security-for-expense requirement is substantive and must be applied in diversity actions. *Cohen v. Beneficial Industrial Loan Corp.*, 337 U.S. 541 (1949).

    Although this analysis would seem to require the court impose Maryland's security-for-expense requirement, closer analysis leads to the opposite conclusion. Remember the security-for-expense requirement (like other derivative suit requirements) has two purposes: to protect corporate interests and to prevent abuse of the judicial process. In this case, Maryland has no reason to be concerned about either. Protox is a Delaware corporation, and to the extent that the security-for-expense requirement assures that corporate interests are well-represented in derivative litigation, this is a concern of Delaware corporate law, which does not impose such a requirement on its shareholder-litigants. Moreover, suit is brought in federal court, and to the extent that the security-for-expense requirement protects courts from abuse of their process, that is a concern of the federal district court, whose rules (specifically Rule 23.1) do not impose a security-for-expense requirement. *Cohen* may have been wrongly decided.

1b. No. The three new shareholders, although their combined holdings exempt the plaintiffs from the security-for-expense requirement, are not contemporaneous owners. Rule 23.1 protects against abuse of judicial process in federal court and imposes such a requirement in derivative actions brought in federal court, even though Maryland would not. Schneider is caught in a patchwork of federal and state rules.

1c. Perhaps, though she needs more facts. Schneider can avoid the security-for-expense requirement by bringing a direct action against the corporation under state law. Direct claims are not subject to derivative suit procedural requirements (see §31.2). For example, she could make a direct claim if the options were not properly authorized or if they required shareholder approval. In addition, Schneider can avoid state derivative suit requirements by bringing a federal securities claim — whether direct or derivative. For example, she might bring a federal derivative suit claiming that Paleau had violated Rule 10b-5 if she failed to disclose the options were without consideration (see §29.3).

2a. Yes, if the court determines that the settlement is fair and reasonable to the corporation. In making this determination, the court will weigh the terms of the settlement against the probable outcome of the case had it gone to trial, offset by the delay, expense, and inherent uncertainty of a trial particularly when the board's grant may be protected by the business judgment rule.

2b. No. Again the issue is whether this aspect of the settlement is "fair and reasonable." Whether the attorney fees are related to the outcome and represent a fair valuation of services is largely within the discretion of the court.

3a. It depends on how the courts exercise their discretion. Since derivative suit plaintiffs sue on behalf of the corporation, subsequent derivative suits may be dismissed, consolidated with the original suit, transferred to another court, or stayed pending the outcome of the original suit. Although the Virginia state court cannot consolidate or transfer the new case, it can dismiss or stay it. The federal court in California can dismiss or stay the case, or transfer it to the federal court in Maryland for that court to decide its disposition.

3b. The settlement would have a res judicata effect and bar the continuation of any other suit based on the same claims (see §31.1.5).

3c. Yes. Many statutes permit the court to shift fees against derivative suit plaintiffs. Even if the Maryland suit succeeds, the defendants in the Virginia suit could argue that the "me too" plaintiff brought it for an "improper purpose." See RMBCA §7.46(2). Fee-shifting deters suits brought for their nuisance value.

4a. Perhaps not. If RKK was not a shareholder when the directors awarded the golden parachutes, the contemporaneous ownership requirement would bar RKK from pursuing a derivative claim. Although RKK might argue that the payments constitute a "continuing wrong" to the corporation, RKK's purchase price was in all likelihood discounted to take into account the contingent golden parachute obligations. If so, any recovery by RKK would be a windfall.

Even if RKK owned some shares before the buyout and was a contemporaneous owner, a court might apply the same theory to deny a recovery to RKK or might decide the recovery should be shared pro rata by pre-buyout shareholders. See ALI Principles §7.01(d) (applying this analysis in context of closely held corporation). It would be an important factual question whether RKK figured its potential golden parachute obligations in its buyout price.

4b. Perhaps not. Protox may be barred by the vicarious incapacity rule from bringing a suit that RKK, its only shareholder, could not bring derivatively. (See the previous answer.) Any recovery by Protox would produce a windfall for RKK if it had already discounted Protox's value to take into account the contingent golden parachute obligations. Nonetheless, some jurisdictions allow the surviving corporation (at the behest of new owners) to pursue existing fiduciary claims, and this contingent benefit is sometimes taken into account in deciding on the purchase price.

4c. Perhaps, depending on the jurisdiction. If the jurisdiction does not have a continuing interest requirement, a former shareholder who was a contemporaneous owner would have standing if she fairly and adequately represented the corporation — or, here, all former shareholders after the merger. RMBCA §7.41.

If the jurisdiction has a continuing interest requirement, Schneider could argue an exception to the requirement. Unless cashed-out shareholders could sue the former directors for pre-merger wrongdoing, their overreaching would go undeterred and the shareholders' loss uncompensated. See ALI Principles §7.02(a)(2) (allowing former shareholder to bring a post-merger derivative suit with pro rata recovery). The only question is whether Schneider is best suited to represent the other former shareholders.

Under Delaware's strict "continuing interest" rule, Schneider could not maintain a derivative suit after the cash-out merger. At most, she could bring a direct action if the merger was illegal or was accomplished by fraud. See *Lewis v. Anderson* (§32.2.2). The strict Delaware approach assumes the buyer has paid the former shareholders for the right to sue for management abuse. If RKK chooses not to pursue this claim, the claim would be lost.

33

Dismissal of Derivative Litigation — Finding a Corporate Voice

In theory, a shareholder's derivative suit is brought on behalf of the corporation. The "corporation" should have a voice in deciding whether the suit is brought and, once brought, whether maintained. But who should speak for the corporation? There are a number of possible voices: the individual shareholder-plaintiff, the shareholders as a group, the board of directors, a committee of the board, and a court.

In this chapter, we consider the extent to which courts listen to each of these speakers in deciding whether to dismiss derivative litigation. The issue is who should decide the relative merits and worth of derivative (fiduciary) litigation. As you review the variety of approaches to identifying a trustworthy corporate voice, consider the incentives of each speaker.

§33.1 The Self-Appointed Derivative Suit Plaintiff

Derivative suits are potentially subject to abuse by shareholder-plaintiffs (see §32.1). A derivative suit plaintiff, although purporting to step into the corporation's shoes and to represent general corporate interests, may in fact be representing his own inconsistent interests. To prevent abuse of the judicial process and to maintain the integrity of central corporate governance, derivative suit plaintiffs are subject to a variety of procedural rules (see §32.2).

In addition, corporate law increasingly instructs judges to listen to other voices in deciding the fate of a shareholder's derivative suit.

§33.2　The Unwieldy Body of Shareholders

Derivative suits represent the principal means by which shareholders enforce fiduciary accountability to the corporation. In theory, allowing the group of shareholders to decide the fate of derivative litigation would overcome the risk of abuse and disincentives of individual shareholder-plaintiffs. But requiring a demand on shareholders and allowing a majority of shareholders to refuse to sue would create a number of problems:

- In public corporations, requiring such a demand would effectively compel an expensive and burdensome proxy contest before suit could be initiated. It would effectively kill derivative litigation against all but the clearest and most costly fiduciary breaches.
- Shareholders as a group, particularly in a public corporation, may lack the incentives to evaluate properly the relative costs and benefits of derivative litigation. Shareholders might approve suits that are not in the corporation's best interests and disapprove others that are.
- Allowing a majority of shareholders to refuse to litigate would permit majority ratification of fraud, self-dealing, or waste. In a public corporation, management's control of the proxy machinery would make majority refusal of doubtful legitimacy. In a close corporation, majority refusal would predictably gut fiduciary protection for the minority.

Most statutes do not require a demand on shareholders. RMBCA §7.42; ALI §7.03(c); cf. Fed. R. Civ. P. 23.1 (pleading requirement). Moreover, in those states where shareholder demand is required, courts have excused it when the derivative plaintiff alleges a wrong (such as waste) that cannot be ratified by a majority of shareholders or demand would be extremely burdensome because of the number of shareholders. See *Mayer v. Adams,* 141 A.2d 458 (Del. 1958).

§33.3　Board of Directors — The Voice of Central Corporate Governance

The board's power to speak for the corporation in a derivative suit is linked to the ability of the directors to act on a shareholder's demand. Before we consider the various judicial and statutory approaches, consider the mixed signals from corporate law. On the one hand, the business judgment rule assumes the board has wide discretion to make business decisions, including litigation decisions. The directors, more than shareholders or judges, are in a better position to evaluate whether a claim has merit, whether it is consistent with corporate interests, and whether corporate resources (money and personnel) should be used to pursue it. If there is no conflict of interest, the board's incentives will predictably be closely aligned with general corporate interests.

On the other hand, if the corporate claim involves charges of a fiduciary breach against a member of the board, an officer, or a controlling shareholder, corporate law questions the board's ability to be impartial. Even directors who were not involved in the alleged wrongdoing and are not themselves being sued may be solicitous of fellow directors who have been sued. Structural bias on the board because of personal, professional, and social ties may create pressure for directors to act in ways inconsistent with general corporate interests. A similar bias may also motivate directors' actions when the suit is against senior executives or controlling shareholders, with whom the directors have similar ties. Nonetheless, courts and statutes increasingly assume that the board may be a better voice for the corporation than self-appointed shareholder plaintiffs.

§33.3.1 Demand Required Unless Futile

Under the prevailing judicial approach, the board of directors can decide the fate of derivative litigation if a pre-suit demand on the board is required (see §32.2.4). If the board responds to a demand by refusing to act or by settling the charges, its response (or non-response) receives deferential review under the business judgment rule (see §21.2). A shareholder-plaintiff must show that the board's response to the demand was self-interested, dishonest, illegal, or insufficiently informed. In general, a demand-required claim is a lost claim.

If demand is excused because it would be futile for the shareholder to bring the matter to the board, the directors have no power itself to block a derivative suit or seek its dismissal. Their voice is silenced. The assumption in a demand-excused case is that it is unlikely the board could be objective in considering the merits of the suit. Allowing a tainted board to make litigation decisions would be tantamount to allowing an accused to decide whether to pursue his own prosecution. *Clark v. Lomas & Nettleton Finance Corp.*, 625 F.2d 49, 53-54 (5th Cir. 1980), *cert. denied*, 450 U.S. 1029 (1981) (vacating settlement on ground that board cannot compromise a derivative claim against its members).

The approach can be shown with a diagram:

DEMAND-REQUIRED — — — — — > Board Decides Fate of Claim, Subject to Review under Business Judgment Rule

DEMAND-EXCUSED   — — — — — > Claim Goes Forward; Board Cannot Dismiss

When is demand excused? The courts have taken a variety of tacks:

Board's objectivity in doubt.   A few courts have said that demand on the directors is excused when it would be unlikely to "prod them to correct a wrong." *Lewis v. Curtis,* 671 F.2d 779, 786 (3d Cir.), *cert. denied,* 459 U.S. 880 (1982). This is shown if a majority of the directors approved or acquiesced in the challenged transaction, or other facts suggest the board would not respond to the demand independently and objectively. *Barr v. Wackman,* 329 N.E.2d 180 (N.Y. 1975).

Board is tainted.   Some courts excuse demand only if the shareholder-plaintiff shows that a majority of the current board is either personally interested in the challenged wrongdoing or dominated by the wrongdoer. Under this view, a director's approval of the challenged transaction is not enough to establish personal interest or domination. Further, the shareholder-plaintiff cannot create a disqualifying personal interest simply by suing a majority of the directors; courts have rejected this bootstrap argument. See *Lewis v. Graves,* 701 F.2d 245 (2d Cir. 1983).

Shareholder has strong case.   Other courts excuse demand if the challenged transaction was on its face improper. Otherwise, the shareholder's demand is at the board's mercy if it is weak or lacks factual support.

The Delaware two-part test.   The Delaware Supreme Court has adopted a two-part test for Delaware corporations. *Aronson v. Lewis,* 473 A.2d 805 (Del. 1984). Demand is excused if the shareholder-plaintiff can state with particularity facts that create a reasonable doubt on two scores: (1) doubt that a majority of the directors on whom demand would have been made are disinterested and independent, AND (2) doubt that the challenged transaction was protected by the business judgment rule — by showing a conflict of interest or grossly uninformed decision-making. To make this two-part showing, the plaintiff must point to specific facts (before discovery) that tend to show *both* that the board is now untrustworthy to respond to the demand *and* that the underlying transaction was improper. Even if the plaintiff can show the board is self-interested or dominated, demand is required unless the plaintiff can allege specific facts raising doubts about the validity of the challenged transaction. Likewise, even if the plaintiff has a good case, demand is required unless the plaintiff can show a majority of the current directors are disqualified to respond.

As applied, the *Aronson* test casts a heavy shadow on derivative litigation. For example, in *Aronson* the plaintiff challenged a compensation package that the board approved on the retirement of the company's chair and 47 percent shareholder. The court said that just because the defendant owned a controlling block of the company's stock and had selected all the directors did not create a "reasonable doubt" concerning the directors' independence. Further, the court held that the alleged facts failed to make out a claim of waste, even though the plaintiff alleged that the defendant performed "little or no service" and would be compensated whether or not he was able to perform.

In Delaware, once a shareholder makes a demand, she cannot bring a derivative suit unless she can show the board's rejection was wrongful — that is, it was not made in good faith after a reasonable investigation. *Spiegel v. Buntrock,* 571 A.2d 767 (Del. 1990). The effect of a demand is to place the fate of the derivative suit in the hands of the board, and a shareholder who makes a demand cannot later assert that demand should have been excused. *Levine v. Smith,* 591 A.2d 194 (Del. 1991).

§33.3.2 Universal Demand

The RMBCA avoids the demand-required/demand-excused question by making demand a precondition for suit in all cases. RMBCA §7.42. A shareholder wishing to file suit must make a demand and then wait 90 days — unless the board rejects the demand or waiting would result in irreparable injury to the corporation. See also ALI §7.03 (requiring demand in every case, except when "irreparable injury" would result).

After the 90-day waiting period, the shareholder may bring a derivative suit but must plead with particularity that either the board's rejection of the demand was not disinterested or the rejection was not in good faith or not informed. (This is substantially less burdensome than Delaware's approach.)

After suit is brought, the board can move for dismissal if independent directors constitute a quorum (at least a majority of the board — see RMBCA §8.24) and a majority of independent directors determine in "good faith" and after a "reasonable inquiry" that maintaining the suit is not in the corporation's best interests. RMBCA §7.44(a), (b)(1). The statute defines "independence" much the same as have the courts. A director is not disqualified merely because he is named as a defendant, was nominated or elected to the board by defendants, or approved the challenged transaction. RMBCA §7.44(c).

§33.3.3 Demand as Pleading Requirement

Some courts have rejected the idea that the fate of derivative litigation should turn on whether or not demand is required. These courts treat demand as a pleading requirement and subject any request for dismissal of a derivative suit (including one made by the board) to searching judicial review. See *Alford v. Shaw,* 358 S.E.2d 323 (N.C. 1987).

§33.3.4   *Demand and Dismissal in Federal Court*

If a derivative claim is brought under federal law, the demand and dismissal rules are governed by the law of the incorporating state, unless its application would be inconsistent with federal policy. *Burks v. Lasker,* 441 U.S. 471 (1984). The Supreme Court recently rejected use of a universal demand standard in federal securities derivative litigation because the demand requirement bears on the allocation of power in the corporation, a matter on which federal law normally defers to the law of the state of incorporation. *Kamen v. Kemper Financial Services, Inc.,* 111 S. Ct. 1711 (1991).

State rules governing shareholder litigation, however, must also be consistent with federal policy. In *Daily Income Fund, Inc. v. Fox,* 464 U.S. 523 (1984), the Supreme Court held that no demand could be required before a shareholder brings a suit against a money market fund's investment advisor under §36(b) of the Investment Company Act of 1940. Refusing to characterize such a suit as "derivative," the Court decided that Fed. R. Civ. P. 23.1 did not apply. The Court pointed out that §36(b) was a remedial provision meant to assure that mutual fund investors can challenge unfair compensation in investment advisor contracts, which are often rife with conflicts of interest.

§33.4   Special Litigation Committees

During the 1970s, boards of directors responded to a spate of derivative lawsuits challenging foreign bribery by corporate officials and other illegal corporate activities with an ingenious device. The board, whose members were usually named as defendants for permitting or failing to stop the illegal activities, appointed a special litigation committee (SLC) of disinterested (often recently appointed) directors to determine whether the derivative suit should go forward. The committee, often assisted by an outside advisor, investigated the charges and prepared a (usually voluminous) report. The committee invariably recommended that the suit not be pursued further and then sought dismissal of the suit.

During the 1970s and early 1980s, SLCs gained popularity. Typically, the board would give the committee full power to make litigation decisions for the corporation (see §13.3). The committee usually was comprised of directors who had not participated in the challenged transaction and hence could not be named as defendants. The SLCs showed a remarkable disposition for director defendants: In no reported case has an SLC continued the suit against a colleague.

Academic commentators questioned whether an SLC should be treated as a trustworthy, independent voice for the corporation and pointed out that research on group dynamics suggested committee members would be subject to implicit pressure to dismiss charges against a fellow director. See *Lewis v. Fuqua*, 502 A.2d 962 (Del. Ch. 1985) (holding a committee member not to be independent because he was a director when the challenged actions took place, was named as a defendant, had political and financial dealings with the company's dominating CEO, and was president of a university that had received significant contributions from the CEO and the company).

Courts have responded to SLCs in a variety of ways:

§33.4.1 Business Judgment Review

The first cases during the 1970s uniformly held that an SLC's recommendation to dismiss litigation was like any other corporate business decision, despite the self-interested taint of the board that had appointed the committee. Unless the plaintiff could show that the committee's members were themselves interested or did not act on an informed basis, the committee's recommendations were entitled to full judicial deference under the business judgment doctrine (see §21.2). *Gall v. Exxon Corp.*, 418 F. Supp. 508 (S.D.N.Y. 1976); *Auerbach v. Bennett*, 393 N.E.2d 994 (N.Y. 1979).

Under this approach, after a committee investigates the claims made by the plaintiff, it can recommend dismissal of the litigation for any of a variety of reasons: The suit would undermine employee morale and waste employee time, litigation expenses would exceed any possible gain, the suit would create bad publicity for the company, the underlying claim lacks merit, the corporation might be required to indemnify a successful defendant, and so on. Some commentators criticized this business judgment deference as sounding the death knell for derivative litigation, and the approach has eroded.

§33.4.2 Lack of Power

A few courts have held that if the board lacks the independence to itself dismiss derivative litigation, it cannot establish an SLC with the power to do what it cannot. That is, if the board is disabled, so too is any committee chosen by the board. *Miller v. Register & Tribune Syndicate, Inc.*, 336 N.W.2d 709 (Iowa 1983). Nonetheless, the trial judge could appoint a special panel to make recommendations to the court on whether the derivative litigation should proceed. See ALI §7.12; RMBCA §7.44(f).

§33.4.3   *Heightened Scrutiny (Demand-Excused Cases)*

In Delaware, when demand on the board is excused as futile, the courts listen to the SLC but regard any recommendation to dismiss with great suspicion. In *Zapata Corp. v. Maldonado,* 430 A.2d 779 (Del. 1981), the Delaware Supreme Court agreed there might be empathy and even "subconscious abuse" by members of the committee asked to pass judgment on fellow directors. The court established a two-part inquiry into whether an SLC's recommendation to dismiss would be followed:

Part 1. The defendants must carry the burden of showing the committee members' independence from the defendants, their good faith, reasonable investigation, and the legal and factual bases for the committee's conclusions. If there is a genuine issue of material fact as to any of these counts, the derivative litigation proceeds.

Part 2. Even if the SLC's recommendation passes this first stage of inquiry, the trial judge may apply his own "independent business judgment" as to whether the suit should be dismissed. This second inquiry is far more intrusive even than the fairness test applicable to self-dealing transactions. It recognizes that judges are particularly adept (in fact it is generally their job) to evaluate the merits of litigation and that judicial incentives to further the interests of the corporation are perhaps stronger than those of an SLC.

At first blush, the two-step *Zapata* inquiry seems to be a remarkable departure from earlier cases that applied a forgiving business judgment presumption to SLC recommendations. But in Delaware, the *Zapata* test applies to SLC recommendations only in demand-excused cases. Three years after *Zapata,* the Delaware Supreme Court significantly limited the decision's importance by making demand a requirement in a large number of cases. In *Aronson v. Lewis,* 473 A.2d 805 (Del. 1984) (see §33.3.2), the court held that demand is excused only if the shareholder can state particular facts that call into question both the trustworthiness of the current board *and* the validity of the challenged action. Under *Aronson,* structural bias is not presumed but must be established with specific facts.

§33.4.4   *Heightened Scrutiny (Regardless of Demand Requirements)*

Some courts subject SLC dismissal recommendations to heightened scrutiny whether demand on the board is required or excused. Under this approach, the trial court independently evaluates the suit's merits, giving some (but not presumptive) weight to the SLC's recommendation. *Joy v. North,* 692 F.2d

880 (2d Cir. 1982), *cert. denied,* 460 U.S. 1051 (1983); *Alford v. Shaw,* 358 S.E.2d 323 (N.C. 1987); see also ALI §7.08.

For example, in *Alford v. Shaw,* the North Carolina Supreme Court focused on the court's supervisory function in derivative litigation under the state's demand-pleading statute (see §32.2.4). The court concluded that the statutory requirement that the plaintiff plead his demand efforts could not be read to require different levels of judicial scrutiny depending on whether demand was required or excused. Further, under the statute, the trial judge could not disregard shareholder interests by relying blindly on the SLC's recommendations. Just as settlement of derivative litigation is subject to court review, so is dismissal.

§33.4.5 *Measured Scrutiny (Universal Demand)*

Under the RMBCA, an SLC (of at least two independent directors) may seek dismissal of derivative litigation after a shareholder has made the obligatory pre-suit demand. If the committee was appointed by a majority of independent directors, the RMBCA requires the court to dismiss the action under the same standards as board dismissal: The SLC determines in "good faith" and after a "reasonable inquiry" that maintaining the suit is not in the corporation's best interests. RMBCA §7.44(a), (b)(2). The same definition of "independence" applies: A director is not disqualified merely because he is named as a defendant, was nominated or elected to the board by defendants, or approved the challenged transaction. RMBCA §7.44(c).

§33.4.6 *SLC Dismissal of Federal Derivative Claims*

When a derivative suit involves federal claims — such as under the federal securities laws — the Supreme Court has accepted as a matter of federal law that an SLC can dismiss the litigation, provided dismissal is consistent with federal policy. In *Burks v. Lasker,* 441 U.S. 471 (1979), a shareholder brought a derivative action against several directors of a mutual fund and its investment advisor claiming violations of the Investment Company Act of 1940. The fund had purchased commercial paper of the Penn Central railroad just before it became insolvent. An SLC investigated the allegations that the directors and investment advisor had breached their duty of care. The SLC decided litigation was not in the fund's best interests and sought dismissal. The Supreme Court upheld the dismissal. It held that the suit on behalf of the fund was governed by the law of the state of the fund's incorporation, provided state law is not inconsistent with federal policy. In the case, the Court held that the 1940 Act did not forbid termination of nonfrivolous claims, and thus dismissal was not inconsistent with federal policy.

EXAMPLES

1. Owing-Indiana (O-I), a widely-held public corporation, is incorporated in an RMBCA jurisdiction. The company manufactures glass containers. Last year O-I's board of directors unanimously approved a $5 million loan to Glass Advocates Committee (GAC), a political action committee set up to fight a state referendum to ban disposable soda bottles. GAC was organized by Frank Norenza, Jr., the son of O-I's CEO, Frank Norenza, Sr. There have been allegations that GAC is spending most of its funds compensating its organizers. The GAC loan is now delinquent, and O-I has done nothing. Dottie Sweet, a long-time O-I shareholder, wants O-I to collect the loan, and she asks you for litigation advice.

   a. Must Sweet first make a demand on the shareholders?

   b. Must Sweet first make a demand on the board?

   c. What strategy do you recommend to Sweet: Should she make a demand on the board first, or should she bypass the board and file a suit?

2. Kerning Glass, another glass container manufacturer, is incorporated in Delaware. Its board also approved a loan to GAC, which is now delinquent. Phil Sativa, a long-time Kerning shareholder, wants Kerning to collect. He also asks you for litigation advice.

   a. Must Sativa first make a demand on the shareholders?

   b. Must Sativa first make a demand on the board?

   c. What litigation strategy do you recommend to Sativa?

3. Sweet and Sativa make demand on their respective boards, and the boards do nothing. After waiting three months, each shareholder files a derivative suit naming the respective board's directors. After a cursory presentation by the company's inside attorney, who says the suit is "no more than the machinations of another gadfly shareholder," each board moves to have the suit dismissed.

   a. Under the RMBCA, how will the court respond to the O-I board's request?

   b. Under Delaware law, how will the court respond to the Kerning board's request?

4. After Sweet files her complaint, the O-I board considers appointing an SLC to investigate the claims of the complaint. This will avoid any questions about the role of Norenza, Sr.

   a. What should the board do to maximize the binding recommendations of the committee?

   b. What should the committee do to maximize the chances that its recommendations will be listened to?

   c. The SLC issues a report recommending that Sweet's complaint be dismissed. Is the recommendation binding on the court?

EXPLANATIONS

1a. No. The RMBCA has no requirement of a demand on shareholders.

1b. Probably. The RMBCA imposes a universal requirement that a complaining shareholder exhaust internal remedies by making a pre-suit demand on the board. RMBCA §7.42. Sweet can avoid making demand if there would be irreparable injury by waiting for the board to act during the 90-day waiting period. Sweet might argue that the ongoing dissipation of funds by GAC makes it increasingly unlikely the corporation could sue to recover the loan. Unless she sues immediately, the corporation will not necessarily be made whole with damages against GAC or its directors, or from D&O insurance. A demand is required even though the GAC loans might be characterized as a director conflict-of-interest transaction. See RMBCA Subchapter F (§22.4). The universal demand requirement gives even nonindependent directors an opportunity to reconsider their position and saves the time and expense of litigating the demand issue.

1c. She must make a demand, unless she can show irreparable injury. The RMBCA largely moots the question of the best strategy, and eliminates most threshold litigation about whether the shareholder chose the correct strategy. Proceedings on the question of demand will often be complex but collateral to the merits of the claim. The Official Comment to RMBCA §7.42 contemplates that cases in which demand will be excused will be "relatively rare."

2a. Probably not. Although the Delaware statute requires that the plaintiff plead her efforts to make a demand on the shareholders or give the reasons why she did not, courts have largely read this demand requirement out of the statute in public corporations. If the shareholder can show such demand would be extremely expensive or delay the action, or if the wrong is nonratifiable, courts have not excused demand on shareholders.

2b. Not necessarily. Delaware case law permits a shareholder to bring a derivative suit and argue that demand was excused as futile. Under *Aronson v. Lewis,* Sativa would have to plead particular facts that created reasonable doubts about the directors' lack of a direct personal interest or their domination by an interested director, and about the validity of the loan and its forgiveness.

Even though it may be illegal for a corporation to forgive a political loan — see §21.3.1 — and thus the board's action might not be protected by the business judgment rule, demand would not be excused unless Sativa created doubts about the directors' disinterestedness or independence. Given the Delaware courts' reluctance to infer these doubts, Sativa would probably have to show more to avoid making a demand.

2c. Sativa should file suit, not make demand. In Delaware, a shareholder who makes a demand concedes that a majority of the board has the requisite disinterest and independence to respond to the demand and decide the fate of the shareholder's claim. That is, a demand on the board concedes the corporate voice to the board.

If Sativa makes a demand, he can continue his claim only if he shows the board's response to the demand — whether inaction or settlement of the claim — was not protected by the business judgment rule. That is, he would have to show the board was grossly uninformed or lacked any rational basis for its response. If Sativa files suit and argues demand was excused, he must plead particular facts to create the two-part doubts of *Aronson v. Lewis* (see previous answer). This will be difficult in the case of Kerning, since there is no indication that any of the directors have a personal interest in the loan or its forgiveness.

3a. The court must dismiss the suit if a majority of the board is independent and sought dismissal in good faith after a reasonable inquiry. RMBCA §7.44. Under the doctrine of res judicata, the GAC loan controversy would then be precluded from further judicial review in any court.

If the court determines a majority of the board was independent, judicial review approximates that under the business judgment rule. That the O-I directors were named by Norenza, Sr. or have been named as defendants does not necessarily cause them to not be independent. The burden will be on the shareholder to show the board acted insincerely or without sufficient information. The Official Comment clarifies that the board need not engage outside counsel or advisors if it has knowledge of the pertinent facts or reasonably relies on others. The board could dismiss if it honestly and reasonably believed Sweet was "another gadfly shareholder."

3b. If demand was required, the court will dismiss the action unless Sativa can show that the board's decision to dismiss was grossly uniformed or irrational, thus not protected by the business judgment rule. If demand was excused, the board's dismissal request will have no effect. Demand excusal carries with it the assumption that the board lacks the independence to make a dismissal request.

4a. The committee should be composed of directors who have no connection to the loan approval — because they either did not participate in the decision or were elected afterward. The committee should be given full power to bind the corporation; its recommendations should not be subject to review or approval by the board.

4b. The committee must create the appearance that it has fully investigated the charges of the plaintiff's complaint. It should conduct a discovery-like investigation: Hire a prestigious (unaffiliated) special counsel such as a retired judge or law professor, interview relevant people, review documents, and seek other knowledgeable and expert advice. The committee should carefully document its investigation and the basis for its recommendations.

4c. Probably. If a majority of the whole board was independent when the SLC made its recommendation, Sweet would have the burden to overcome a business judgment presumption and show the SLC members acted insincerely or without adequate information. Even if a majority of the whole was not independent but the committee members were, the SLC has the power to seek dismissal but would have the burden to show its recommendation is protected by the business judgment rule.

The RMBCA's approach largely disregards the problems of structural bias on the board. Nonetheless, it is possible that judges will review dismissal requests with greater scrutiny than under the normal business judgment rule. Just as a court has authority to consider the merits of the derivative suit when it approves a settlement, judges may feel inclined to delve into the SLC's "no sue" decision. See *Alford v. Shaw* (see §33.4.4). Judicial scrutiny of the SLC's independence or its deliberations would recognize the self-interested motives of the possible voices in a derivative suit. This would be consistent with the logic in demand-required cases of the two-step *Zapata* test (see §33.4.3) and judicial rejection of the *Auerbach v. Bennett* business judgment rule approach (see §33.4.1).

Judicial scrutiny of the SLC recommendations assumes, as does the second step of the *Zapata* test, that inevitably judges will exercise their own "business judgment" concerning the litigation's merits to the corporation. Although some have argued that such decisions are not significantly different from ordinary business decisions and should not be left to judges, a strong argument can be made that judges are particularly capable to make judgments about the expected value of litigation and often are called on to make business judgments when considering the substantive fairness of self-dealing transactions.

PART TEN

Organic Changes

34

Internal Organic Changes — Charter Amendments, Recapitalizations, and Dissolution

Charter amendments, recapitalizations, corporate combinations, and dissolutions — often referred to as *organic changes* — each effect a fundamental change in the corporation. An organic change fundamentally alters shareholders' rights, and corporate law interposes a variety of protections.

In this chapter, we consider *internal* organic changes that affect only the corporation. In Chapter 35 we consider *external* changes in which two (or more) corporations are combined. Finally, in Chapter 36 we look at the *appraisal remedy,* a protective "opt out" procedure sometimes available to shareholders who dissent from these changes.

§34.1 Amendments to Articles of Incorporation

Modern corporate law's philosophy of majority rule extends to charter amendments. Unlike partners, who must unanimously approve any change in the partnership agreement (UPA §18(h)), individual shareholders have no vested rights in the corporate "contract." Minority shareholders are powerless to block a change to the articles of incorporation.

§34.1.1   Power to Amend the Charter — Majority Rule

Modern corporate statutes permit amendment of the articles of incorporation so long as the new provision (or deletion) could have been part of the articles as originally adopted. RMBCA §10.01(a).

No vested rights in corporate "contract."   By authorizing charter amendments, state incorporation statutes undercut any argument that shareholders have vested contract or property rights in the corporation. The statutes implicitly reserve the majority's power to change the corporate "contract"; shareholders can have no expectations of immutability.

Most legislatures also specifically reserve the power to change the corporate contract by amending the corporate statute. See RMBCA §1.02. This reservation is of constitutional dimension. In *Dartmouth College v. Woodward,* 17 U.S. (4 Wheat.) 518 (1819), the Supreme Court held that New Hampshire's legislature violated the Constitution's contract impairment clause when it amended the charter of Dartmouth College to change the name of the college, increase the number of trustees, and create a board of overseers with powers superior to the trustees'. The amendment, the Court held, breached the vested rights arising under an actual contract between the state and the corporation. In a concurring opinion, Justice Story suggested that states could have avoided the problem by statutorily reserving the power to amend the charter, a suggestion universally adopted in modern incorporation statutes. RMBCA §10.01(b).

Limitations set in articles.   The articles themselves may limit the board's and shareholders' amendatory powers. Supermajority provisions or special procedural requirements can protect shareholder, and sometimes management, interests (see §16.1). For example, the articles can specify that any amendment to provisions requiring the payment of specified dividends be approved by at least three-fourths of the outstanding shares.

§34.1.2   Mechanics for Approving Charter Amendments — Shareholder Protection

Charter amendments, like other organic changes, can fundamentally change the corporation. Corporate law gives shareholders three layers of protection: (1) the board must (generally) initiate the amendment, (2) a majority of the shareholders must then approve it, and (3) in some circumstances, dissenting shareholders may force the corporation in an appraisal proceeding to redeem their shares for cash.

Board Approval.   Most states require that any amendment to the articles must be proposed by the board; shareholders cannot initiate the amendment. RMBCA §10.03(b)(1); Del. GCL §242(b)(1). A few states, however, allow either the board or a specified percentage of shareholders to propose the amendment.

This first layer of protection gives the board the first crack at safeguarding the interests of shareholders and other corporate constituents. Board approval is subject to fiduciary review. Absent a showing of bad faith, self-interest, or gross negligence, the board's decision is protected by the business judgment rule (see §21.3).

Shareholder Approval.   Approval by a shareholder majority provides the second layer of protection. Most statutes require approval by a majority of outstanding voting shares (an absolute majority). Cal. Corp. §902(a); Del. GCL §242(b)(1). The RMBCA requires an absolute majority for voting groups with appraisal rights and a simple majority for all other voting groups. RMBCA §10.03(e).

Shares with voting rights (such as common stock) are entitled to vote on any amendment to the articles. Some statutes require separate approval by each class of stock that is entitled to vote. RMBCA §§10.04(e)(1). Under the RMBCA, nonvoting shares are entitled to vote if the amendment would "materially and adversely affect" the rights of shares of the class. RMBCA §§10.04, 13.02 (changes to preferential, redemption, preemptive, voting rights). Class voting, or voting by groups, ensures that the majority cannot run roughshod over a minority whose interests are specially affected. For example, if the board proposed to authorize a new class of preferred shares with rights senior to all other shares, the amendment would have to be approved by an absolute majority of voting common shares and an absolute majority of each existing class of preferred shares (voting or nonvoting).

In addition, the board can add to shareholder protection by conditioning the proposed amendment on a specified vote. For example, the board can require approval by a specified supermajority or by a specific category of shareholders. RMBCA §10.03(c).

Appraisal Rights.   Some state statutes allow dissenting shareholders to *opt out* of the change — in certain circumstances — by forcing the corporation to pay cash for the appraised fair value of their shares (see §36.1.1). RMBCA §13.02(a)(4). Under the RMBCA such rights exist only if the amendment would materially and adversely affect the rights of a particular class of shareholders.

Many state statutes do not provide for dissenters' appraisal rights in the case of charter amendments. Cal. Corp. §1300; Del. GCL §262(a).

§34.1.3 *Recapitalizations*

One important use of the charter-amending power is to alter the corporation's capital structure. Changes in the rights, privileges, powers, and immunities of corporate securities — such as a conversion of common stock into a package of cash and debt securities or a conversion of preferred stock with dividend arrearages into common stock — may be in the interests of the corporation as a whole. A recapitalization supplies a flexible tool for adjusting the corporation's financial direction, sometimes making new financing possible or offering shareholders an improved package of rights. Recapitalizations also create significant potential for abuse, and all the protections applicable to charter amendments are available.

A recapitalization also can be accomplished by merger (see §35.2): A shell subsidiary is set up, the corporation is merged into it, and shareholders receive a new package of securities in the surviving corporation. In *Bove v. Community Hotel Corp.*, 249 A.2d 89 (R.I. 1969), a preferred shareholder sought to enjoin a merger that had the effect of converting preferred stock (and its accrued, but unpaid, dividends) into common stock. The shareholder argued that if the recapitalization had been accomplished by an amendment to the articles, state law governing charter amendments would have required unanimous approval by the preferred shareholders. The merger statute required that only two-thirds of the preferred shareholders approve. The court accepted the board's choice of form and upheld the merger.

§34.2   Dissolution

Dissolution is the ultimate organic change. Although dissolution results in the death of the corporation, it does not necessarily mean the death of the business. Because of its going-concern value, the business (meaning its assets) usually will be sold intact, and dissolution simply serves as a redistribution device that follows the sale of assets to an outside party or to a shareholder faction. In dissolution, shareholders receive a pro rata share from the proceeds of the sale.

§34.2.1   Defining Some Dissolution Terminology

Dissolution terminology is often confusing. *Dissolution* is the formal extinguishment of the corporation's legal life. *Liquidation* is the process of reducing the corporation's assets to cash or to liquid assets, after which the corporation becomes a holding shell. *Winding up* is the whole process of liquidating the assets, paying off creditors, and distributing what remains to shareholders.

§34.2.2   The Process of Approval — Shareholder Protection

Dissolution, like charter amendments, is subject to majority rule. Absent oppression or deadlock, individual shareholders generally cannot terminate the corporation. Likewise, individual shareholders cannot force the corporation's continuance.

Voluntary dissolution is subject to only two levels of protection: (1) approval by the board, and (2) approval by shareholders — usually by an absolute (as opposed to simple) majority. RMBCA §14.02(c); Del. GCL §275. State statutes provide no appraisal rights on the theory that all shareholders are being treated equally, and allowing some shareholders to demand cash would interfere with the winding-up process.

§34.2.3 The Process of Winding Up — Creditor Protection

In the winding-up process, the corporation must pay all known claims. Unknown claims, such as contingent tort claims, may be brought under some statutes against the dissolved corporation. RMBCA §14.07 (claims allowed for five years after notice of dissolution); Del. GCL §278 (claims allowed for three years after dissolution). If the corporation does not retain sufficient assets after the distribution, some statutes permit the claimant to seek satisfaction from former shareholders. Under the RMBCA, each shareholder is obligated to pay a pro rata share of the claim, up to the amount distributed to the shareholder in dissolution. RMBCA §14.07(d)(2). If creditors' claims cannot be satisfied against the dissolved corporation or its former shareholders, claimants may assert their claims against the entity that acquired the business's assets under the successor liability doctrine (see §35.4.2).

EXAMPLES

1. MEGA Motors is incorporated in Delaware. Times have been tough in the auto industry, and the company has not paid dividends in the last two years, including those due on its 200,000 shares of nonvoting cumulative preferred stock. The arrearages on the preferred total $4.8 million; the stock has fallen in value and is trading at $60. The MEGA Shareholder Revitalization Committee, a group of common shareholders, proposes to amend the articles so that future dividends on the preferred shares would be paid in common stock (using a formula based on the common's market value when dividends are declared). Preferred arrearages would be cancelled by paying 1.37 common shares for each share of preferred. By eliminating the preferred arrearages and future cash drain, new financing is possible.

   a. Can the SRC do this?

   b. The MEGA board submits the SRC proposal for a shareholder vote. Some preferred shareholders object. Is the amendment possible?

   c. MEGA has sufficient authorized common shares to pay arrearages under the plan and to pay dividends in the form of common stock well into the future. Which shareholders must approve the plan?

     d. Some of preferred shareholders object to having their rights to cash payments changed into rights to noncash common stock. Can they prevent their rights from being usurped?

2. The MEGA board proposes a charter amendment to authorize an additional 50 million shares of common stock to finance a major project to develop an electric car. There are 200 million shares of common outstanding.

     a. At the shareholders' meeting, 140 million shares are represented and 90 million approve the amendment. Has it passed?

     b. MEGA's shareholders vote against the new shares, apparently believing that electric cars have no future. Management, however, is convinced of the value of the project. The board approves a MEGA subsidiary to develop an electric car. To finance the project, the subsidiary will issue 50 million shares. Is this permissible?

3. Five years ago Jerry, a compulsive tinkerer, designed an automotive "thermal ignition system," which replaces spark plugs in internal combustion engines. Jerry incorporates Tinker Corp. in an RMBCA jurisdiction and sells common stock to a few friends, while keeping a majority of the stock himself. His idea turns out to be a major engineering breakthrough, and the value of Tinker soars. Jerry wants to get rid of his friends. Jerry dissolves Tinker. The board sells all of its assets to JRS Combustion, a corporation wholly owned by Jerry. The minority Tinker shareholders receive $400 per share, based on a sales price of $1 million for the assets.

     a. Is such a transaction possible?

     b. Can Jerry's friends block his plan under the statutory dissolution procedures?

     c. Jerry's friends believe they have not received a fair price for their shares. Can they seek a judicial appraisal of their shares?

     d. Can Jerry's friends attack the transaction?

EXPLANATIONS

    1a. No. Under Delaware's statute, as well as most other statutes, the board must initiate any charter amendment. Del. GCL §242(b)(1). In theory, this assures that the board will look out for interests of all corporate constituencies, including minority shareholders and creditors. The board's action is subject to fiduciary review; shareholders' proposals may not be. But the effect of requiring board approval is to hold shareholders hostage. Some statutes do allow shareholders to initiate charter amendments, if the amendment is permissible, on the theory that the risk of board tyranny outweighs the risk of shareholder majority tyranny.

    1b. Yes. The amendment calls for payment of stock dividends, which is permitted under Delaware's statute and could have been inserted in the articles originally. Del. GCL §242(a) (see §3.1.1). Further, the amendment can be approved by a majority of outstanding shares entitled to vote on the amendment. Objecting shareholders have no vested rights in a static corporate structure and cannot stand in the way of the majority will. Minority shareholders in some jurisdictions, although not in Delaware, have the right to dissent and seek a cash appraisal of their shares. Otherwise, they must accede to majority rule, provided the board and any controlling shareholders discharge their fiduciary duties.

1c. MEGA's common shareholders and preferred shareholders, each group voting separately. Delaware's statute requires approval by shares with voting rights whether or not their interests are affected (the common stock) and by any nonvoting shares that are "adversely" affected by the amendment (the preferred stock). Del. GCL §242(b)(2). First, class voting by common shareholders secures their right to protect any "upstream" changes that affect their residual interests. Second, class voting by preferred shareholders protects them against unilateral changes by common shareholders that frustrate their investment expectations.

1d. Probably not. In most jurisdictions, including Delaware, preferred shareholders are not assured payment of dividends and thus have no contractual or vested right to payment. Del. GCL §170. (A few states, however, treat preferred dividends in much the same way as interest on debt, requiring their payment without any discretion in the board.) In Delaware, only if dividends have been declared do preferred shareholders have a right to payment. The failure of MEGA's board to pay dividends, though giving preferred shareholders cumulative rights if dividends are ever declared, does not create a right to payment. Shareholders' contingent rights, however, can be changed by majority rule.

2a. No. An absolute majority of the *outstanding* common shares (at least 100 million and 1) must be voted for the amendment. Del. GCL §242(b)(1). The Delaware requirement of an absolute majority is more burdensome than that of the RMBCA and other statutes, which authorize approval upon the vote of a majority of the shares represented at a proper meeting (a simple majority). RMBCA §§7.25(c), 10.03(e)(2). The nonvoting preferred shareholders are not entitled to vote on this amendment because it does not adversely affect their interests. The additional common shares (like the existing common shares) do not have rights superior to the preferred shares.

2b. Probably. The limitation in MEGA's articles on issuing new shares does not apply to the subsidiary. As long as the board satisfied its duties of care and loyalty in setting up the subsidiary — which the business judgment rule makes likely — any limitation on raising money would have to be inferred from MEGA's articles.

A challenging shareholder might argue that the shareholders' rejection of the board's original plan imposed an implicit limit *in the articles* on any financing for the electric car project. But this reads too much into the shareholders' vote. The statutes specify that the charter can be amended only through a formal board proposal and shareholder approval. If shareholder rejection of a board initiative could create de facto charter limitations, there would be great uncertainty about the effect of shareholder rejection. Moreover, de facto limitations would usurp the role of board as initiator and undermine board flexibility. In a public corporation (such as MEGA) where board initiation protects shareholders from minority opportunism, a contrary rule would undermine the power of the board — a power delegated by shareholders. Implying such limits in a close corporation, however, may be appropriate to protect the participants' reasonable expectations (see §17.2.1).

3a. Yes. Dissolution requires a board proposal and approval by a majority of shareholders. RMBCA §14.02.

3b. No. Jerry has a majority of the shares and approval is inevitable. The minority shareholders have no vested right to retain an interest in the corporation.

3c. No. In a dissolution, shareholders have no appraisal rights. See RMBCA §13.02(a). This prevents dissenting shareholders from seeking a preferred position compared to other shareholders during the winding-up process. Furthermore, if dissenters could pursue an appraisal remedy, they would be entitled to a cash payment of fair value before the remaining shareholders receive their pro rata distribution of the corporation's liquidated assets. In theory, the liquidated value of the shares should be identical to their fair value.

3d. Yes. The dissolution and the liquidation of Tinker's assets are self-dealing transactions. The board and Jerry (as controlling shareholder) have the burden to prove the transactions' fairness. If the sold assets were undervalued, the minority shareholders will be able to rescind the transaction or have Jerry pay fair value (see §22.3.2).

35

External Organic Changes — Corporate Combinations

Corporate law supplies a variety of techniques for combining the businesses of two (or more) corporations under one management. Although the many techniques can be made to produce a functionally identical result, the choice of technique can have important implications. The choice affects the protections available to shareholders, taxation of each corporation and its shareholders, and the form and liabilities of the resulting entity. As in any complex system of rules where different paths lead to the same goal, gamesmanship is at a premium.

In this chapter, we consider the corporate "game rules" for structuring a corporate combination. We do not address the tax rules, although they are crucial in how the game is played. Furthermore, we make only passing reference to the fiduciary and disclosure protections that the various structures implicate. No analysis of a corporate combination is complete without considering these additional constraints.

§35.1 The Combination Choices — Some Basics

Suppose that Alpha Corp. wants to buy a closely held business, Sigma Inc. Alpha has enough authorized stock or cash to buy Sigma, and Sigma's shareholders are amenable. How might the transaction be structured?

Statutory merger.   Sigma could be merged into Alpha. In the merger, Sigma would be absorbed into Alpha and would disappear as a separate entity. Alpha would issue its shares or pay cash to the Sigma shareholders. (In the nomenclature of the Internal Revenue Code, this is an *A reorganization*.)

Asset acquisition.   Alpha could buy all the assets of Sigma. Alpha would issue stock or pay cash to Sigma for the assets; Sigma as an entity would remain unaffected by the sale. In the normal case, however, Sigma would be dissolved after the sale and Sigma's assets (the cash or stock Alpha paid for Sigma's business assets) would be distributed to its shareholders on a pro rata basis. (Under the IRC, this is a *C reorganization*.)

Stock acquisition.   Alpha could buy a controlling block of Sigma shares from Sigma itself (if there is sufficient authorized but unissued stock) or from some or all of the Sigma shareholders. Alpha would exchange its stock or pay cash for the shares, and Sigma would become a subsidiary of Alpha, although Sigma (as an entity) would be unaffected by the transaction. (Under the IRC, this is a *B reorganization*.)

In each case, the practical effect of the transaction is identical: Alpha pays consideration (directly or indirectly) to the Sigma shareholders to acquire control of Sigma's business.

In this chapter, we discuss the two combination techniques — statutory mergers and sales of assets — for which corporate law has traditionally afforded shareholders (and other corporate constituents) specific protections. Acquisition of control through stock purchases from shareholders, whether through open market transactions or by means of a tender offer, is subject to federal securities regulation (see Chapters 10, 39) and state takeover legislation.

§35.2   Mergers and Consolidations

In a *statutory merger,* the acquiring corporation absorbs the acquired corporation, the acquired corporation disappears, and the acquiring corporation becomes the surviving corporation. Below we diagram a stock-for-stock merger in which Sigma merges into Alpha and Alpha issues its shares to Sigma's shareholders as consideration.

A *consolidation* is closely related to the statutory merger. In a consolidation, two or more existing corporations combine into a new corporation and the existing corporations disappear. The same rules that apply to mergers also apply to consolidations. Below we diagram a consolidation of Alpha and Sigma into New Alpha, with shareholders of both corporations receiving shares in New Alpha as consideration (see next page).

Sigma Merger into Alpha

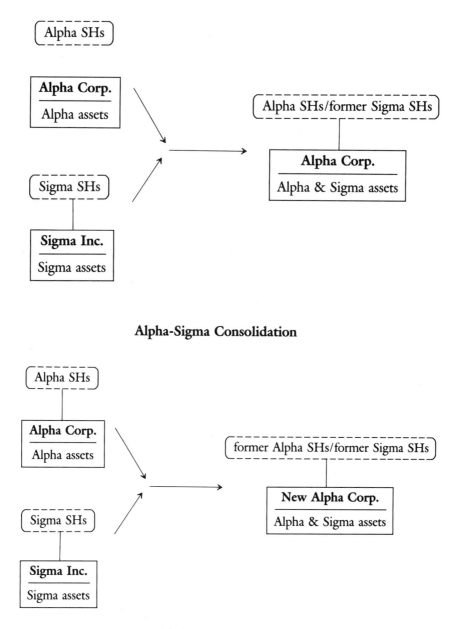

Alpha-Sigma Consolidation

Notice that a consolidation can also be accomplished using a statutory merger procedure: (1) Alpha creates a shell subsidiary — New Alpha; (2) Alpha, Sigma, and New Alpha enter into a tripartite merger agreement; (3) in the merger, Alpha and Sigma are absorbed into New Alpha, the new surviving corporation; (4) the shares of Alpha and Sigma are converted into New Alpha shares. For this reason, the RMBCA and some modern statutes do not offer a consolidation procedure.

§35.2.1 Effect of a Merger — Complete Absorption

In a merger, the surviving corporation steps into the shoes of the acquired corporation when the required document is filed at the appropriate state office. RMBCA §11.05 (articles of merger); Cal. Corp. §1103 (agreement of merger); Del. GCL §251(c) (certificate of merger). By operation of law, the surviving corporation becomes the owner of all the acquired corporation's assets, becomes subject to all its liabilities, and is substituted in all pending litigation. Compared to other corporate combination techniques, this complete absorption is a unique characteristic of a statutory merger.

Historically, this absorption theory also extended to the treatment of the acquired corporation's shareholders, whose shares had to be converted into shares of the acquiring-surviving corporation. Nearly all modern statutes do away with this requirement and allow consideration to be paid in the form of securities of the acquiring corporation (or any corporation), cash, property, or a combination of these. RMBCA §11.01(b)(3); Cal. Corp. §1101; Del. GCL §251(b).

§35.2.2 Statutory Protections in a Merger

A statutory merger carries with it three layers of protection: board approval, shareholder approval, and appraisal rights.

Board Initiation.   The board of each constituent corporation initiates the merger by adopting a document known as a *plan of merger*. The plan outlines the terms and conditions of the merger (including how shareholders will vote on it) and the consideration that shareholders of the acquired corporation will receive. RMBCA §11.01(b); Cal. Corp. §1101; Del. GCL §251(b). Under some statutes, the merger plan may also amend the articles of the acquiring-surviving corporation. RMBCA §11.01(c); Cal. Corp. §1101; Del. GCL §251(b). Fiduciary and federal disclosure rules provide additional glosses to this first layer of protection:

Fiduciary protection.   In approving a merger, the directors are bound by their fiduciary duties (see Chapter 20). If the merger is with a controlling shareholder (parent corporation) or otherwise involves a conflict of interest, the merger is subject to review as a self-dealing transaction (see §26.3).

Disclosure protection.   The issuance of stock in a merger is a "sale" under the federal securities laws. See Rule 145, Securities Act of 1933. Shareholders who receive publicly traded shares for their stock are entitled to prospectus disclosure and antifraud protection under the federal securities laws (see Chapters 10, 29).

Shareholder Approval. After board adoption, the plan of merger must generally be submitted to the shareholders of each corporation for their separate approval. RMBCA §11.03(a); Cal. Corp. §1201; Del. GCL §251(c). This second layer of protection is supplemented by "complete candor" under state law and federal proxy rules for voting in a public corporation (see §19.2).

At common law, shareholders' approval of a merger had to be unanimous, but modern statutes have done away with this vestige of the vested rights theory. Dissenting shareholders are bound by the will of the majority. Originally, most statutes required two-thirds approval of all outstanding shares to approve a merger. Now most statutes require only a majority of all outstanding voting shares — an absolute majority. RMBCA §11.03(e); Cal. Corp. §§152, 1201; Del. GCL §251(c).

If a corporation has more than one class of voting stock outstanding, many statutes require separate approval by each voting class. RMBCA §11.03(e); Cal. Corp. §§152, 1201. Rejection of the merger by any voting class or group means that the merger is not approved. Under many statutes, nonvoting stock also has a right to vote as a group on the merger if the stock would be substantially affected by the merger. RMBCA §11.03(f)(1). A few statutes even require approval by each voting and nonvoting class, regardless of the merger's effect. Delaware, however, requires approval only by voting shares, even if other nonvoting classes of stock are adversely affected by the merger. Del. GCL §251 (vote by "majority of outstanding stock . . . entitled to vote thereon"). Nonvoting shareholders have fiduciary protection and appraisal remedies.

Approval by the shareholders of the *acquired* corporation is always required, on the theory that their interests are fundamentally altered in a merger. This not always the case for the *acquiring* corporation's shareholders. When a big firm absorbs a smaller one, the effect on the *acquiring* corporation may be minimal, not justifying the expense and trouble of shareholder approval. Most statutes exempt the *acquiring* corporation from obtaining shareholder approval in a whale-minnow merger:

(1) the articles of the surviving corporation are unchanged (other than a name change);

(2) the acquiring corporation's shareholders continue to hold the same number of voting shares as before the merger; and

(3) the merger does not dilute the voting and participation rights of the acquiring corporation's shareholders by more than 20 percent. In other words, the number of shares (whether the shares have rights to vote or to participate in distributions) outstanding after the merger does not exceed by more than 20 percent the number of shares outstanding before the merger. RMBCA §11.03(g); Del. GCL §251(f).

The New York Stock Exchange listing rules parallel the RMBCA rule and require listed companies to obtain shareholder approval before issuing more than 20 percent of their stock, even if the stock is already authorized.

Appraisal Rights.   Shareholders cannot opt out of a merger and retain their original investment. For this reason, all state statutes grant dissenting shareholders entitled to vote on the merger a right to receive the appraised fair value of their shares in cash. RMBCA §13.02(a)(1); Cal. Corp. §1300(a); Del. GCL §262. This remedy is the third layer of protection. Dissenters' appraisal remedies, which sometimes also arise with respect to other organic corporate changes, are discussed in Chapter 36.

§35.2.3 Short-Form Merger of a Subsidiary into its Parent

When a parent corporation owns 90 percent or more of a subsidiary, many corporate statutes allow the subsidiary to be merged into the parent without approval by shareholders of either corporation. RMBCA §11.04; Cal. Corp. §1110(a); Del. GCL §253. Only approval of the parent's board of directors is required.

The rationale for the streamlined, short-form procedure is that approval by the subsidiary's board and the subsidiary's shareholders is preordained, and the parent's shareholders will not be materially affected because the parent already holds at least a 90 percent interest in the subsidiary. Minority shareholders of the subsidiary are protected by the fiduciary rules applicable to the parent as a controlling shareholder (see §26.3) and by appraisal remedies, which statutes automatically grant minority shareholders in a short-form merger. RMBCA §13.02(b)(2).

§35.2.4 Merger of Corporations Incorporated in Different States

The merger of a domestic and a foreign corporation (see §3.2.2) presents a metaphorical problem: How can two "creatures" each created and defined by a different state's law become a new "creature" defined by only one law? State statutes deal with this problem parochially. Nearly all statutes authorize the merger of a domestic and foreign corporation and allow the surviving corporation to be a domestic corporation. But the statutes maintain the purity of the "creature" metaphor: Each corporation is bound by the statutory merger requirements of its jurisdiction. Cal. Corp. §1108(b); Del. GCL §252. That is, shareholder protection in a merger is defined by the corporate law of the incorporating state.

§35.2.5   *Triangular Merger (and Compulsory Stock Exchange)*

Absorption by merger may not always be desired. In many instances, the acquiring corporation will want to keep the acquired firm's business incorporated separately, held as a wholly owned subsidiary. This may be necessary to comply with antidiversification requirements in regulated industries, such as banking or insurance. It may also be desirable to insulate the parent from the subsidiary's liabilities or to keep the acquired business separate if the parent plans to sell it in the future. Neither a statutory merger nor a sale of assets accomplishes this result. Nonetheless, the statutory merger technique can fill the bill with a *triangular merger*. Consider the following series of transactions:

A.   Alpha sets up a new wholly owned subsidiary — Merger Sub. Alpha capitalizes Merger Sub with its shares or other assets (such as cash). In return, Merger Sub issues all of its shares to Alpha.

B.   Merger Sub enters into a plan of merger with Sigma under which Merger Sub will be the surviving corporation.

C.   After the merger of Sigma into Merger Sub, Sigma's shareholders will receive as consideration either Alpha stock or other assets that Merger Sub received when Alpha capitalized it.

D.   After the merger, Alpha continues as the sole shareholder of the surviving Merger Sub, which might adopt a new, more descriptive name like Alpha-Sigma, Inc. as part of the plan of merger.

Sketching out this series of transactions reveals the triangle namesake of this combination technique, also often called a *reverse subsidiary merger*:

Target Merged into Merger Sub

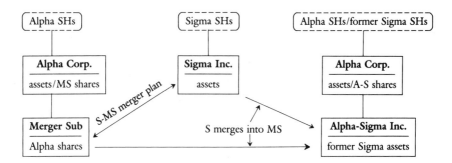

The triangular technique has many possibilities. Consider a *forward triangular merger* in which Merger Sub merges into Sigma, which becomes the surviving corporation:

Merger Sub Merged into Target

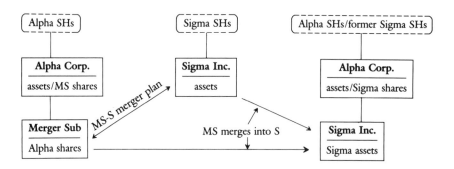

Compulsory Share Exchange.   Some states have adopted a more direct procedure for accomplishing the same result as a triangular merger. In a *compulsory share exchange,* the acquiring corporation can force the target's shareholders to exchange their shares for consideration offered by the acquirer. Shareholders of the acquired corporation enjoy the same protections as they would in a triangular merger: The target's board must first approve the exchange, a majority of the target's shareholders must then approve it, and dissenters have appraisal rights. If the exchange is approved, all the target's shareholders receive the consideration offered by the acquirer. RMBCA §11.02.

§35.2.6   Squeeze-Out Merger

As you can see, the statutory merger technique offers dizzying possibilities. One use, which has nothing to do with combining separate businesses, allows a controlling shareholder to rid itself of minority shareholders in what is known as a *squeeze-out merger.* (This is sometimes less accurately referred to as a *freeze-out merger.*) Squeeze-out mergers are often the second step in a hostile takeover, once a bidder has successfully purchased a controlling interest by means of a tender offer (see §§26.3, 37.1).

In a squeeze-out merger, the parent corporation merges into a wholly owned subsidiary created for the merger. The plan of merger calls for disparate treatment of the parent and minority shareholders. The parent receives the surviving subsidiary's stock while the remaining shareholders receive other consideration, such as cash or nonvoting debt securities. A squeeze-out merger in which the minority shareholders receive cash is referred to as a *cash-out merger*:

Minority Shareholders Cashed Out

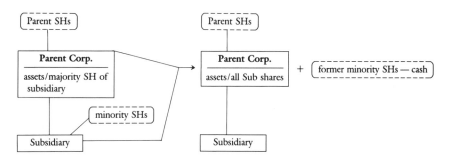

Squeeze-out mergers are subject to the three layers of protection that apply to every merger and, in particular, to the self-dealing rules that apply to corporate transactions with controlling shareholders. In Delaware, for example, squeeze-out mergers are subject to review under an "entire fairness" test that requires fair-dealing and a fair price in the merger. *Weinberger v. UOP, Inc.,* 457 A.2d 701 (Del. 1983).

§35.3 Sales of Assets

A corporation's business is no more than the sum of its tangible and intangible assets, and control can be transferred by selling all of the corporation's assets. Suppose Alpha buys all of Sigma's assets, giving Alpha stock as consideration:

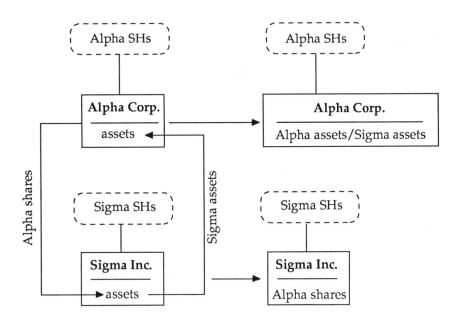

§35.3.1   The Effect of a Sale of Assets

After selling all or "substantially all" of its assets, the corporation's existence does not automatically terminate. Instead, it becomes a shell or holding company whose only assets consist of the sales proceeds. Only after paying its liabilities and distributing the remaining sales proceeds to the shareholders pro rata can the corporation then dissolve (see §34.2).

Unlike a merger, an asset acquisition does not automatically substitute the buying corporation for the selling corporation. Creditors, suppliers, lessors, employees, and others who deal with the selling corporation may have to consent to a substitution. But if consent is given, a sale-of-assets transaction can be structured to have much the same effect as a merger:

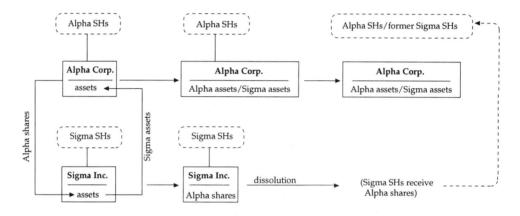

§35.3.2   Statutory Protections in a Sale of Assets

Most state statutes treat the sale of all or substantially all of the corporate assets (not in the usual or regular course of business) as an organic change and impose the same three layers of protection applicable in a merger: board approval, shareholder approval, and (in many instances) dissenters' appraisal rights. RMBCA §12.02; Cal. Corp. §1001 (no appraisal rights); Del. GCL §271(a) (no appraisal rights). (If substantially all the assets are sold in the *regular course of business* — such as a real estate holding company that regularly sells all its inventory — the transaction is treated like any other business transaction, and only board approval is required. RMBCA §12.01(a).)

Under many statutes, including the RMBCA, the protection in a sale of assets is similar to that for a statutory merger. But there are differences:

- No statutes require approval by the shareholders of the buying corporation.

- All statutes require shareholder approval for asset transactions between parent corporations and their subsidiaries, unless the parent owns 100 percent of the subsidiary's shares.
- A few statutes do not provide dissenters' appraisal rights in a sale of assets.

These differences sometimes determine which combination technique to use — a merger or a sale of assets.

§35.3.3 Conditions for Triggering Protection

Whether the three layers of protection apply to any given asset sale depends on two questions: (1) Is the transaction a "sale"? (2) Does the sale involve "substantially all" the assets?

"Sale" of assets. Any transaction that is extraordinary and fundamentally affects corporate ownership and use of the corporation's assets is a "sale" that triggers the three layers of protection. Most statutes, however, do not treat a pledge, a mortgage, or a deed of trust covering all or substantially all the assets to secure debt of the corporation as a triggering "sale." RMBCA §12.01(a)(2).

"Substantially all" assets. When a corporation sells less than all its assets outside the ordinary course of business, the three levels of protection apply only if "substantially all" were sold. Under the RMBCA, "substantially all" means "nearly all" — this avoids insiders' circumventing shareholder approval and appraisal remedies by holding back an insignificant part of the assets. Official Comment to RMBCA §12.01.

Courts in other jurisdictions have construed "substantially all" to provide significantly more protection to shareholders. In *Gimbel v. The Signal Companies, Inc.,* 316 A.2d 599 (Del. Ch.), *aff'd per curium,* 316 A.2d 619 (Del. 1974), the Delaware Chancery Court adopted a disjunctive qualitative-quantitative test. Under the test, a sale that is either quantitatively vital to the company's operations or qualitatively substantial to its existence and purpose must be approved by the shareholders. In the case, a parent corporation sold its energy subsidiary — which accounted for 41 percent of the total net worth, 26 percent of the assets, and 15 percent of the earnings of the conglomerate parent. The court held that the subsidiary was neither *quantitatively* nor *qualitatively* substantial, even though it had once been the bedrock of the parent's business. There was thus no requirement that the parent's shareholders approve its sale. Cf. *Katz v. Bergman,* 431 A.2d 1274 (Del. Ch. 1981) (shareholder approval required for sale of subsidiary that accounted for 45 percent of total net sales and 51 percent of parent's assets).

§35.4   De Facto Merger and Successor Liability Doctrines

As we have seen, a corporate combination can be structured in a number of functionally identical ways, each often affecting the protections available to shareholders and creditors. An asset acquisition, for example, can be structured to have much the same effect as a merger and yet avoid some of the shareholder approval and appraisal rights otherwise afforded the merging corporation's shareholders. An asset sale can also be structured so that creditors' claims do not pass to the acquiring corporation.

§35.4.1   De Facto Merger Doctrine

Under the judicially created *de facto merger doctrine,* a handful of courts have interpreted the statutory merger provisions to give shareholders in functionally equivalent asset sales the same protections available in a statutory merger. If the asset sale has the effect of a merger, shareholders receive such merger-type voting and appraisal rights. In *Farris v. Glen Alden Corp.,* 143 A.2d 25 (Pa. 1958), Glen Alden acquired the assets of List in a stock-for-assets exchange approved by both companies' boards and by List's shareholders. The transaction doubled the assets of Glen Alden, increased its debt sevenfold, and left its shareholders in a minority position. To protect the Glen Alden shareholders' expectation of "membership in the original corporation," the court recast the asset acquisition as a merger and enjoined the transaction for failing to give the Glen Alden shareholders the voting and appraisal rights that they would have had in a statutory merger.

The use of the de facto merger doctrine to imply shareholder protection not explicitly provided by statute has been widely criticized. In the modern corporation, shareholders have no assurance that the corporation's business, its capital structure, or the number of shareholders will remain stable. In fact, modern shareholders purchase their shares with the expectation (and often the hope) that there will be control transfers. Most courts that have considered the issue have refused to imply merger-type protection *for shareholders* when the statute does not provide it. *Hariton v. Arco Electronics, Inc.,* 182 A.2d 22 (Del. Ch. 1962), *aff'd,* 188 A.2d 123 (Del. 1963). In fact, in many states where courts have used a de facto merger analysis, the legislature has later abolished the doctrine by statute. See 15 Pa. CSA §1904; Iowa BCA §496A.68.

§35.4.2   Successor Liability Doctrine

In a statutory merger, all the outstanding claims pass to the surviving corporation. In an asset acquisition, however, none of the liabilities are transferred unless the parties agree. This makes a sale of assets significantly more advantageous than a merger for the buying-successor corporation, if the seller is willing to retain some or all of the liabilities.

Courts have fashioned a *successor liability doctrine* by imposing liability on the buying corporation (or another successor down the chain) when the claims were unknown or contingent at the time the assets were sold. Courts use the doctrine to provide a source of compensation for tort claimants (particularly products liability victims) and apply it even when the buyer disclaimed assumption of such claims. The successor liability doctrine is sometimes (confusingly) referred to as an aspect of the de facto merger doctrine, but the two are distinct: The former protects involuntary creditors; the latter protects shareholders. Some courts that have rejected the de facto merger doctrine on behalf of shareholders have suggested there might be successor liability on behalf of tort victims. *Heilbrunn v. Sun Chemical Corp.*, 150 A.2d 755 (Del. 1959).

Courts that impose successor liability often refer to: (1) the plaintiff's inability to seek relief against the original owner; (2) the buying corporation's ability to assume a risk-spreading role (such as through insurance); and (3) the continuity of the original business after the sale of assets. See *Ray v. Alad Corp.*, 560 P.2d 3 (Cal. 1977); *Turner v. Bituminous Casualty Co.*, 244 N.W.2d 873 (Mich. 1976) (successor liable if it continues to manufacture product line of seller).

Other courts have been less sympathetic to successor liability claims and have required that there be a continuity in the business, management, assets, and shareholders of the selling corporation and that the selling corporation dissolve and liquidate after the buyer assumed known liabilities — in other words, a transaction with all the characteristics of a stock-for-stock merger. See *Niccum v. Hydra Tool Corp.*, 438 N.W.2d 96 (Minn. 1989).

EXAMPLES

1. JRS Combustion, incorporated in an RMBCA jurisdiction, holds method patents for a "thermal ignition system." The system is a technological breakthrough that promises to eliminate spark plugs in auto ignitions and virtually eliminate auto pollution while allowing vehicles to burn almost any kind of fuel. MEGA Motors, a public Delaware corporation, wants to acquire JRS.

   a. MEGA proposes to acquire JRS by paying JRS shareholders a package consisting of $600 in cash and ten shares of MEGA common stock (worth $400) for each JRS share. Can this be done by means of a statutory merger?

   b. MEGA is most interested in the JRS patents. As a matter of corporate law, what documents will transfer the patents when MEGA merges with JRS?

c. Jerry (a 25 percent JRS shareholder and its board's dominant member) has reservations about MEGA's proposal, but the other JRS shareholders may be interested in a merger. Should MEGA negotiate with them?

2. MEGA overcomes Jerry's objections. The boards of MEGA and JRS consider various merger plans:

a. JRS shareholders will receive $1000 cash. JRS has 10,000 voting shares outstanding. Shareholders holding 3000 shares say they object to the cash consideration, which will create a taxable transaction, and they will not go to the meeting. Shareholders holding 2500 shares say they will attend and vote against the merger. But they will be outvoted by shareholders holding 4500 shares, who say they will vote for the merger. Is the merger in trouble?

b. JRS shareholders will receive a package of cash and MEGA stock. MEGA will issue 2 million shares of already authorized common stock as consideration for the merger. This will increase the number of MEGA's total outstanding shares to 22 million. Must MEGA shareholders approve the merger?

c. JRS shareholders will receive 4 million MEGA shares. To authorize additional shares, MEGA will amend its certificate of incorporation pursuant to the merger plan. If two-thirds of MEGA's shares are represented at the shareholders' meeting on the merger and 51 percent vote to approve the merger, will the merger be approved?

d. MEGA will pay cash; the merger will affect neither MEGA's articles nor the number of its outstanding shares. To buttress its validity, the merger plan calls for the approval by at least 75 percent of the MEGA shares represented at a shareholders' meeting on the merger. If 12 million of MEGA's 20 million shares outstanding are represented at the meeting, how many must be voted for the merger?

3. For tax reasons, MEGA wants to purchase all of JRS's assets instead of acquiring JRS in a negotiated merger. (This will give it a higher basis in JRS's assets, increasing tax depreciation.) In addition, MEGA wants to hold the JRS assets in a separate subsidiary so it can easily resell the business in the future.

a. Can a sale-of-assets transaction be structured to accomplish these purposes — that is, to have the effect of a triangular merger?

b. JRS will sell all its assets to MEGA, but MEGA expressly will not assume any contingent liabilities. JRS will be dissolved after the sale, and its shareholders receive pro rata consideration. After the transaction, if a patent infringement suit is brought against MEGA for claims that arose when JRS operated the business, will MEGA be liable?

c. MEGA will purchase all of JRS's assets in exchange for 4.5 million already authorized MEGA shares. MEGA also will assume all of JRS's liabilities. Is approval by MEGA shareholders required?

4. In addition to its patents and its research facilities, JRS also owns a significant tract of prime commercial real estate on which the facilities sit. The land, deeded to the company by the founder, Jerry, has been used as collateral for loans to finance the thermal ignition research. Although licensing of the thermal ignition patents accounts for nearly 90 percent of the company revenues and earnings, the land represents approximately 50 percent of the value of the company's assets.
   a. Is shareholder approval required if the JRS board agrees to sell the thermal ignition assets but not the land?
   b. Would the result be different if JRS were incorporated in Delaware?

EXPLANATIONS

1a. Yes. The authority for the merger comes from both Delaware law and the RMBCA. Delaware law authorizes MEGA to merge with a foreign corporation and for MEGA to be the surviving corporation. Del. GCL §252. The RMBCA authorizes JRS to merge with a foreign corporation. RMBCA §11.07. Under both statutes, consideration for the merger can include securities, cash, or other property — whatever is specified in the plan of merger. RMBCA §11.01; Del. GCL §251.

1b. In the normal case, all that is necessary is a plan of merger and the filing of merger documents with the respective states' secretaries of state. RMBCA §11.05 (articles of merger); Del. GCL §252(c) (certificate of merger). As a result of the merger, MEGA steps into JRS's shoes. Corporate law provides that MEGA automatically acquires all of JRS's assets, including its patents. The complete substitution of the acquiring corporation for the acquired is a significant, and unique, characteristic of a statutory merger.

   For some regulatory and licensing purposes, the merger alone cannot transfer ownership. In fact, federal patent law requires that patent assignments be explicit, even in the case of a statutory merger. A further written assignment would thus be necessary to transfer the patents from JRS to MEGA.

1c. Not really. The boards of both corporations must approve the merger before submitting it to their shareholders. The merger will go nowhere unless the JRS board is interested.

2a. Yes. An absolute majority of all JRS's outstanding voting shares must approve the merger — that is, at least 5001 shares. RMBCA §11.03(e) (requiring "a majority of all the votes entitled to be cast on the [merger] plan"). A simple majority of the shares represented at the meeting will not be enough. Shares not voted at the meeting count as votes against the merger.

2b. No. Delaware's statute, like those of most states, requires approval by shareholders of the acquiring corporation only if the merger is significant.

Del. GCL §251(f). The statute uses certain factors to identify a merger that is significant to the acquiring corporation. Satisfying any one factor triggers a requirement of shareholder approval. But in MEGA's case, none of the factors applies: (1) The merger plan does not amend MEGA's charter; (2) the rights of MEGA's outstanding shares will not be changed by the merger; and (3) the number of shares of common stock outstanding after the merger (22 million) will not exceed by more than 20 percent the number of shares before it (20 million). Del. GCL §251(f). Although the merger will dilute the equity and voting interests of MEGA's common shareholders, the dilution will not be significant. The Delaware statute views shareholder approval in this case to be an unnecessary and costly bother because the merger will be relatively inconsequential to MEGA and its shareholders.

2c. No. MEGA's shareholders must approve the merger because the charter will be amended. In Delaware, this requires approval by a majority of MEGA's outstanding stock entitled to vote — an absolute majority. Del. GCL §151(c). It is not enough if the merger is approved only by a simple majority — a majority of those at the meeting.

2d. The answer is 9 million — three-fourths of the shares represented at the meeting. The problem is tricky. Although approval by a majority of the outstanding shares — 10 million and one shares — generally sets a minimum for a merger plan (Del. GCL §251(c)), MEGA is exempted in this case by Del. GCL §251(f) (see answer 2b). The three-fourths approval condition, authorized by Del. GCL §252(b), supplies the relevant voting requirement.

This problem illustrates the possibility that approval by a simple supermajority (in this case three-fourths of the shares at the meeting) may not constitute approval by an absolute majority of the outstanding shares. For example, if 12 million of MEGA's 20 million shares are represented, approval by 9.5 million would be enough to satisfy the condition but would not be a majority of the total outstanding shares.

3a. Yes. The following steps will do it:

(1) MEGA creates a wholly owned subsidiary, J-Sub, and capitalizes it with the consideration it will use to buy JRS's assets;

(2) JRS's board and shareholders approve the sale of all the assets;

(3) J-Sub purchases all of JRS's assets, assumes all of its known and contingent liabilities, and is substituted in any pending litigation;

(4) J-Sub pays JRS with the consideration it received from MEGA, which can be any consideration that would have been permitted in a merger;

    (5) JRS's board and shareholders approve a plan of dissolution (at the same time they approve the sale of assets);

    (6) JRS pays any creditors who did not accept the substitution; and

    (7) JRS's only assets (the consideration from J-Sub) is distributed to its shareholders pro rata.

This structure, however, has some critical and unavoidable differences from a merger. Unlike a merger, the constituent corporations must obtain consent to the substitution from creditors, suppliers, lessors, employees, and others who deal with the corporation. The documentation will be very different. In a sale of assets, all the transferred assets and assumed liabilities must be identified. A bill of sale transfers personal property, and deeds must transfer any real property.

3b. Perhaps. Although MEGA did not assume this liability contractually, a court might use the successor liability doctrine to treat the sale of assets as a statutory merger. MEGA would be deemed to have stepped into JRS's shoes and assumed its liabilities. The question of successor liability often comes up in products liability litigation. MEGA may satisfy some of the factors courts have identified in finding a succession of interest: the continuity of JRS's business after the sale, and the plaintiff's inability to seek relief against the original patent claimant or its shareholders. Other courts, however, have shown hostility to liability rules that discourage control transfers that put assets into higher-valuing hands. The successor liability doctrine seeks to balance the goals of protecting claimants and providing corporate-contractual certainty. For example, if the patent plaintiff had purposely desisted from suing until the asset sale, the goal of protecting the patent would seem less compelling than that of certainty.

    It is important to remember that JRS's shareholders might also be held liable on the infringement claim. Under the RMBCA, unknown claims (and known claims not properly discharged) may be asserted up to five years after dissolution and recovered from each shareholder to the extent of the shareholder's pro rata liquidating distribution. RMBCA §14.07 (see §34.2.3).

3c. Probably not. Even though the transaction would have required approval by MEGA shareholders if structured as a merger — because the 4.5 million shares put it over the 20 percent threshold of Del. GCL §251(f) — no approval of the acquiring corporation is necessary when it purchases assets. This is an instance in which the structure of the corporate combination will affect the degree of shareholder protection. Some courts, however, have held that when an asset acquisition is functionally equivalent to a merger, statutory merger protections — in particular, appraisal remedies — are available under the de facto merger doctrine. This activist construction of the merger statutes has not found favor in Delaware, where MEGA is incorporated. Delaware courts have shown little willingness to imply additional protections not found in the statute.

4a. Probably no — under the RMBCA, which applies to JRS's sale. According to the Official Comment to RMBCA §12.01, the term "substantially all" is synonymous with "nearly all." Shareholder approval cannot be avoided by holding back a few inconsequential assets. But otherwise, the *qualitative* productivity of the assets sold does not appear to be relevant. Even though the thermal ignition assets are the company's principal source of revenue and cash flow value, the RMBCA treats this as irrelevant. Shareholder approval is not required because retaining the land does not appear to be a pretext for avoiding shareholder protection, and JRS is not selling "nearly all" its assets.

4b. Probably yes. Under Delaware's disjunctive qualitative-quantitative test, shareholder approval would probably be required because the sale is *qualitatively* substantial to the corporation's existence and purpose. That is, shareholders should regard their investment as fundamentally changed when the high tech JRS is converted into a holding company. Under Delaware's approach, quantitative substantiality is not necessary if the sale is qualitatively substantial. The Delaware test thus gives shareholders greater protection than does the RMBCA's narrow quantitative test.

36

Dissenters' Appraisal Rights

Corporate law empowers the majority to approve organic changes over the objections of the minority. Majority rule gives the corporation needed flexibility to adjust to new conditions. It can also be an instrument of oppression, forcing minority shareholders to accept an inadequate price for their shares or locking them into a restructured investment that they neither contemplated nor desire.

To protect against these possibilities and compel those contemplating organic changes to avert dissension, all corporate statutes provide an appraisal remedy that allows dissenters in certain circumstances to "opt out" of majority rule. The appraisal remedy gives minority shareholders the right to dissent and to insist on being paid the "fair value" of their shares in cash.

§36.1 The Appraisal Remedy — Protection against Majority Tyranny

§36.1.1 *Appraisal in Organic Changes*

The statutes specify who may assert dissenters' rights and in which fundamental transactions:

- Shareholders entitled to vote on a merger or consolidation. RMBCA §13.02(a)(1); Cal. Corp. §1300(a); Del. GCL §262(a). This means that shareholders of the acquiring corporation in a "whale-minnow" merger, who are not entitled to vote, do not have appraisal rights. See Del. GCL §262(b)(1).

- Shareholders entitled to vote on a compulsory share exchange. RMBCA §13.02(a)(2).
- Shareholders entitled to vote on a sale of assets. RMBCA §13.02(a)(3); Del. GCL §262(c) (only if provided in charter).
- Under many statutes, shareholders whose interests are significantly affected by an amendment to the articles of incorporation (such as in a recapitalization). RMBCA §13.02(a)(1); Del. GCL §262(c) (only if provided in charter).

Generally, dissolution does not trigger appraisal rights, on the theory that all shareholders receive a pro rata distribution and appraisal claims would disrupt the winding up process. Many statutes permit both record and beneficial shareholders to dissent and seek appraisal. RMBCA §§13.02, 13.01(7). Yet, to avoid confusion, some statutes give dissenters' rights only to record shareholders. *Cede & Co. v. Technicolor, Inc.*, 542 A.2d 1182 (Del. 1988).

§36.1.2   *"Market Out" Exception in Public Corporations*

Some statutes, most notably in Delaware, do not provide appraisal rights in a stock-for-stock merger if shares of the corporation are traded on a public stock market — a publicly traded corporation. Cal. Corp. §1300(b)(1) (no appraisal if prior to merger corporation's shares listed on national securities exchange or traded in the over-the-counter market); Del. GCL §262(b)(1), (b)(2) (no appraisal if constituent corporation's shares listed on a national securities exchange or held by more than 2000 shareholders of record and shareholders receive stock in publicly traded corporation). Nonetheless, appraisal rights exist in a stock-for-cash merger when the publicly traded shares are acquired wholly or partially for cash. Del. GCL §262(b)(2).

The theory for this "market out" exception is that a shareholder who is unhappy with the change in her investment and who would prefer cash can simply sell in a public trading market at a price the market has determined is fair. Otherwise, such dissenters could interfere with organic changes by forcing the corporation to bear the additional and unnecessary expense of redeeming their shares for cash in an appraisal proceeding.

The "market out" exception assumes the market price is a good approximation of "fair value." The RMBCA rejects the Delaware approach because the market does not always reflect "true value." The drafters gave some examples: the market may be "demoralized"; some shareholders may hold "restricted securities" (see §10.2.2); some shareholders may hold large blocks that a thin market could not absorb; or the market may already reflect price depreciation in anticipation of the organic change. Official Comment to RMBCA (1978). See Cal. Corp. §1300(b) (allows dissent by shareholders holding restricted securities or at least 5 percent of the outstanding stock).

§36.2 The Appraisal Proceeding

§36.2.1 Procedures — A Deck Stacked against Dissenters

Appraisal procedures vary widely from state to state. Dissenting shareholders must strictly comply with these complex procedures, which often are stacked against them. In non-RMBCA jurisdictions, such as Delaware, appraisal procedures typically require the following:

Preserve right to appraisal. Before the shareholders' meeting on the organic change, the corporation sends shareholders notice of their appraisal rights. Shareholders who want to dissent must give the corporation written notice of their intent before the meeting. Shareholders must vote against, or at least not vote for, the proposed change.

Exercise right to appraisal. After the effective date of the organic change, the corporation must notify shareholders of their appraisal rights. Within a specified number of days, dissenters must accept the terms of the change or tender their shares to the corporation and demand payment. Dissenters must then bring an appraisal action in court and initially bear all their litigation expenses. Dissenters do not receive payment until finally ordered by the court. Dissenter's expenses (such as attorney and expert fees) can only be charged against the value of the appraised shares and cannot be recovered from the corporation.

Contested appraisal proceedings may drag on, leaving dissenting shareholders in a twilight zone. After tendering their shares, dissenters lose their status as shareholders; the shares neither receive dividends nor appreciate in value during the pendency of the appraisal proceeding. Payment of fair value must await final court order. The dissenter must bear all costs of litigation unless the court charges the dissenter's expenses against the pool of recovery.

The RMBCA attempts to make appraisal a more realistic option. If the dissenting shareholder preserves her dissenter's rights, demands payment, and tenders her shares, the corporation *must* promptly pay the dissenter the corporation's estimate of fair value (RMBCA §13.25) and then must attempt to settle any asserted shortfall. RMBCA §§13.28, 13.30(a). Court appraisal is a last resort only if the shareholder views the corporation's payment to be inadequate and negotiations fail. If the dissenter's payment demand remains unsettled for 60 days, the corporation must commence a judicial appraisal proceeding and initially bear court and expert costs. The court may also order the corporation to pay the dissenters' attorney fees if it failed to act in good faith or to comply with the appraisal procedures.

§36.2.2   "Fair Value" — The Slippery Problem of Valuing the Firm

Dissenters also face the risk that the court will undervalue the firm and its shares. Generally, valuation does not take the effect of the organic change into account when assigning share value. Courts generally attempt to determine value as of the date of the shareholders' vote. The RMBCA, however, looks to the shares' value immediately before the corporate action is taken.

Valuation Based on Past Performance.   The problem of valuing the corporation arises in many contexts, and there is no simple method. In appraisal proceedings, appraisers traditionally have determined fair value on the basis of the firm's past performance:

Market price.   One valuation factor is the price at which the corporation's shares were trading (if a market exists) or at which they could have been sold to a willing buyer. Less weight is given market price in the case of thinly traded shares, although unusual trading in a deep market before the transaction may justify discounting this factor.

Past earnings.   Earnings value, or "investment value," seeks to measure the earning capacity of the corporation based on its previous earnings record. Average annual earnings are computed and then capitalized by applying a multiplier, which is determined according to the business conditions and the type of business involved. *Beerly v. Department of Treasury,* 768 F.2d 942 (7th Cir. 1985), *cert. denied,* 475 U.S. 1010 (1986) (fixing multiplier on basis of price-earnings ratios for sales of minority stock blocks in comparable companies).

Book value.   The firm's book value is the excess of historical-valued assets over liabilities (see §9.2.2). Book value does not reflect the ongoing earnings from the business. Courts use it only when valuation based on earnings is unreliable.

Liquidating value.   A firm's liquidating value is the amount for which the corporation's marketable assets could be sold for cash. It may fail to take into account the firm's value as an ongoing business.

Going-concern value.   A firm's going-concern value is an eclectic valuation that combines all the elements reasonably related to value, including market price, earnings and dividends, asset value, and the nature of the enterprise. See *Tri-Continental Corp. v. Battye,* 74 A.2d 71 (Del. 1970).

Recognizing the slipperiness of each of these concepts, Delaware courts in the past have used a "block" method. Under this method the appraiser assigns an arbitrary weight to various values and then adds them up to get a weighted value. For example, a Delaware court valued a conglomerate in a depressed stock trading market by weighting assets 45 percent, average earnings 40 percent, and market price 15 percent. *Tannetics, Inc. v. A. I. Industries,* 5 Del. J. Corp. L. 337 (Del. Ch. 1979). The computations looked like this:

Type of Valuation	Appraisal Amount		Weight Given		
Asset Value	$100	×	.45	=	$45
Earnings Value	$120	×	.40	=	48
Market Price	$ 75	×	.15	=	11.25
Appraisal (Fair Value)				=	$104.25

Valuation Based on Future Earnings. Most of the above techniques fail to recognize that shares, like any other investment, are valuable because they represent a promise of *future* income. In *Weinberger v. UOP, Inc.,* 457 A.2d 701 (Del. 1983) (see §26.3.3), the Delaware Supreme Court held that the "block" method would no longer be exclusive. Instead, the appraiser may now look to elements of future value, provided they are susceptible of proof.

The most widely used method of valuation in the financial community is *discounted cash flow.* Under this method, the present value of expected future cash flows is calculated using a discount rate to take into account the time value of money. Consider the following simplified illustration. Suppose a firm's earnings prospects are as follows: There is a 10 percent chance that annual earnings will be zero, a 50 percent chance they will be $10 million, and a 40 percent chance they will be $20 million. The expected value of annual earnings based on weighting the different possible outcomes is as follows:

	Expected Value	Earnings Probability		
Scenario #1	$0	.10	=	$0.0
Scenario #2	$10	.50	=	$5.0
Scenario #3	$20	.40	=	$8.0
Expected Value			=	$13.0

If we assume that the firm's expected earnings of $13.0 million per year will continue into the foreseeable future, it is possible to calculate the value of this cash flow. If the interest rate on no-risk, long-term U.S. Government bonds is 10 percent, the discounted value of the firm's cash flow is $130 million. That is, an investor would be willing to pay $130 million for the firm's cash flow potential because the risk-free alternative — investing the same amount in U.S. Government bonds — would produce $13 million annually. To a risk-neutral investor, the firm's cash flow over time has the same value as $130 million in cash today. Since a firm (like any other investment) has value depending on the return it provides to investors over time, this calculation represents the value of the firm.

In Delaware the company's earnings potential after a merger, as long as this is not speculative, can also be taken into account. *Weinberger v. UOP, Inc.* ("elements of future value, . . . known or susceptible of proof as of the date of merger and not the product of speculation, may be considered"). Other statutes, however, exclude "appreciation . . . in anticipation of the merger." *In re Valuation of Libby, McNeil & Libby,* 406 A.2d 54 (Maine 1979).

§36.3   Exclusivity of Appraisal

Faced with an organic change, a dissenting shareholder has two options: (1) challenge the action as fraudulent or unfair and seek rescission (or rescissionary damages), or (2) seek an appraisal. Does the existence of an appraisal remedy foreclose a challenge of the transaction?

§36.3.1   *Price or Process Fairness*

The question of appraisal's exclusivity turns on whether minority shareholders should be able to undermine the majority will. On the one hand, if a dissenter considers the transaction to be unsound, limiting her protection to appraisal will protect her financial interest. But if there was abuse in the approval process (such as deception of shareholders or fiduciary overreaching), it can be argued that unfair manipulation of the process should not be shielded because of the appraisal option.

States are divided on whether appraisal is the only remedy. Some statutes explicitly make appraisal exclusive, and courts have denied shareholders' attempts to set aside the transaction. Nonetheless, in Delaware a shareholder may challenge a transaction, even if appraisal is possible, if (1) approval of the transaction was obtained fraudulently; (2) the transaction breached a fiduciary duty of fair dealing; or (3) the transaction did not comply with formal approval requirements. *Weinberger v. UOP, Inc.* (see §26.3.3). A number of statutes adopt this latter approach. RMBCA §13.02(b) (appraisal is exclusive unless "action is unlawful or fraudulent with respect to the shareholder or the corporation"). See also Cal. Corp. §1312 (appraisal is exclusive unless shareholder vote was insufficient or transaction involved self-dealing); N.Y. BCL §623(k) (appraisal remedy does not preclude equitable relief).

§36.3.2   *Nonappraisal Remedy*

If a shareholder can challenge the process of approval of an organic change, what should be the remedy if the process is unfair? Arguably, the appropriate remedy is to undo the transaction because a damages award would be tantamount to appraisal without the normal appraisal procedures. In many instances, however, rescission may impose a significant burden, particularly where the challenge is resolved long after the transaction has closed. For this reason, some courts have accepted the possibility of rescissory damages — damages based on the value of the shares if the transaction had been originally rescinded — to compensate shareholders for unfair dealing or an inadequate price. *Weinberger v. UOP, Inc.* (see §26.3.3).

§36.3.3 Effect of Choice

Courts generally treat as binding a shareholder's choice to accept the transaction's terms, to seek appraisal, or to challenge the process of approval. Permitting tandem proceedings — a fiduciary challenge and appraisal — can lead to seemingly inconsistent results. For example, after Shell Oil entered into a $60 squeeze-out merger of minority shareholders, a Delaware court in an appraisal proceeding found the shares were worth $71.20, while another Delaware court said that minor disclosure deficiencies resulted in damages of $2 — a price of $62. Justifying the difference, the court hearing the disclosure challenge said that the dissenting shareholders in the appraisal proceeding faced greater burdens (loss of use of money, long duration, uncertain outcome, bearing own litigation costs) than the shareholders challenging disclosure in a class action. See *Smith v. Shell Petroleum, Inc.*, 1990 LEXIS Del. Ch. 190 (Nov. 26, 1990).

EXAMPLES

1. JRS Combustion, incorporated in an RMBCA jurisdiction, has agreed to merge into MEGA Motors, a Delaware corporation. Both JRS's and MEGA's shareholders must approve the merger. Under the terms of the merger JRS shareholders will receive MEGA common stock as consideration. MEGA's stock is traded on the New York Stock Exchange; JRS's stock is all held privately.

   a. Since announcement of the merger, MEGA's stock price has fallen, apparently in reaction to the news. Many of MEGA's employees hold restricted stock, which they cannot sell on a trading market (see §10.2.2). Do MEGA shareholders have appraisal rights?

   b. Many of the JRS shareholders are also executives of the company. Do JRS shareholders have appraisal rights?

   c. MEGA wants to plan for the contingency of appraisal. When will MEGA know how many shareholders are dissenting and how much they are seeking?

   d. MEGA is worried about contingent appraisal rights. How can it limit its exposure?

2. All of the JRS shares are represented at the shareholders' meeting on

the merger. The shareholders approve the merger by a thin margin: 502 shares for, 498 against.

   a. Jessica is a JRS shareholder who has preserved her dissenters' rights. Some votes were cast by proxy for the merger and she questions their validity. Should she challenge the merger or seek appraisal?

   b. MEGA promised Jerry (JRS's founder) a position with MEGA after the merger. Dissenters claim that JRS's directors were dominated by Jerry and approved a lousy deal. They claim if the directors had fulfilled their fiduciary duties, shareholders would have received $25 million more for their shares. Can the dissenters challenge the merger price as unfair?

EXPLANATIONS

1a. No. MEGA is subject to Delaware's appraisal statute, which does not create appraisal rights with respect to a stock-for-stock merger if the constituent corporation's shares are traded on a national stock exchange. Del. GCL §262. Delaware rejects that a "demoralized market" might not reflect fair value and assumes that holders of restricted shares discounted the value of their shares to reflect their lack of liquidity and appraisal rights. MEGA shareholders who hold restricted shares have no choice but to accept the merger terms if approved by the majority, unless they can show a defect in the process of approval.

1b. Yes. The RMBCA which provides appraisal for shareholders who are entitled to vote on a merger, governs appraisal for JRS shareholders. RMBCA §13.02. There is no distinction between management and nonmanagement shareholders. Appraisal provides a "base floor" for the price of all shareholders.

1c. MEGA acquires all of JRS's appraisal obligations after the merger. Before the merger the RMBCA provides MEGA with information only about the number of shareholders who might demand payment and appraisal. Before the shareholders' meeting, shareholders who notify JRS of their intent to dissent need not make a demand for payment. Under the RMBCA, the corporation first learns its *potential* appraisal liability when dissenters demand payment after the merger. This will happen within 30 to 60 days after shareholders receive notice of the merger, which MEGA must send at least 10 days after the merger. RMBCA §13.22(b). In effect, MEGA will not know for two to three months after the merger. Even then, it may be possible that a court will value the shares for an amount greater than that sought by the aggregate of dissenters.

1d. MEGA can make sure the merger is fair. One reason for appraisal is to induce corporations engaged in fundamental transactions to ensure a fair price. A fair price in the merger will discourage dissenters who risk receiving an appraised value that is lower than the merger price. In addition, MEGA can condition the merger on approval by a supermajority of JRS shareholders, such as two-thirds or three-fourths. MEGA can also condition the merger on receiving less than a specified number of dissenters' notices.

2a. Jessica has a choice. She can challenge the merger for failing to comply with voting requirements — that is, it was not approved by the requisite majority. RMBCA §13.02(b). The appropriate remedy is rescission of the merger, not damages. If the challenge can be resolved quickly enough to undo the transaction without hardship to other shareholders or third parties, damages should not be available because of the speculative nature of valuing the lost voting rights. Even if Jessica wants only a better price, the voting challenge has some advantages and disadvantages. Challenging the transaction exposes MEGA to a rescission remedy — easier for a close corporation than a public corporation — which could force MEGA to pay a higher merger price to all shareholders. To avoid this, MEGA may be more willing to settle on favorable terms with Jessica. Even if she must settle for rescissory damages, they should reflect what her shares would be worth had the merger not been approved — fair value.

There is, however, one disadvantage in a voting challenge. Whether Jessica brings the action as a derivative or direct claim, she will not be entitled to payment of attorney and expert fees (if at all) until the end of the litigation. Under the RMBCA, the corporation must bear the ongoing expenses of court appraisal, and Jessica may ultimately be able to seek payment of her expenses under a more relaxed standard than would apply in a direct action.

2b. Probably not. The RMBCA by its terms allows a dissenter to bypass appraisal and challenge the transaction only if the transaction was "unlawful or fraudulent." RMBCA §13.02(b). The Official Comment explains that a minority dissenter should not be able to interfere with majority will because the minority "considers the change unwise or disadvantageous." Nonetheless, the Official Comment recognizes the appropriateness of challenges to a transaction "in violation of a fiduciary duty." Does this include a "fair price" breach? In *Weinberger v. UOP, Inc.* (see §26.3.3), the Delaware Supreme Court held that appraisal was the exclusive method for challenging the price in a cash-out parent-subsidiary merger with self-dealing overtones. The RMBCA Official Comment cites *Weinberger* with approval, suggesting that an appraisal proceeding is the exclusive method for challenging price unfairness under the RMBCA. This gives shareholders who are unhappy with price, but not those who approved the merger, a remedy that will enforce a price floor under their shares.

PART ELEVEN

Takeover Contests

37

Takeover Contests — An Introduction

We have finally reached the pinnacle of corporate law — the hostile corporate takeover. It culminates our inquiry into the regulation of the shareholder-management relationship and raises fundamental questions about the vitality of shareholder control rights, the responsibilities of the board of directors, the functioning of securities trading markets where control can be purchased, and the appropriate role of the corporation in the economy and in society.

It has been said that a hostile corporate takeover is the most regulated of all commercial transactions, a conclusion borne out by the importance, complexity, and uncertainty of the law in this area. Our treatment of the subject, which has engaged voluminous attention by academics and members of the corporate bar, is by necessity an overview.

In this chapter, we describe the mechanics of a takeover and the issues that arise. In Chapter 38, we discuss regulation of proxy contests; in Chapter 39, federal regulation of tender offers; and in Chapter 40, takeover defenses.

§37.1 The Hostile Choices — Proxy Contest or Tender Offer

Hostile takeovers are the exception. Most control changes occur in negotiated "friendly" acquisitions. The management of two corporations bargain over terms, structure, and future management. When they reach an arm's length deal, they present it to the shareholders of the acquired (and sometimes the acquiring) company for approval (see §35.2.2). If the two managements cannot agree, the matter usually ends.

But when the corporation is publicly held, a persistent suitor who fears being rebuffed can go over the heads of an unwilling management and court the shareholders directly. An outsider seeking control has three options:

Option 1: **Proxy Contest**. The suitor can appeal to the shareholders' hearts by soliciting their proxies to oust the incumbent board and to install the suitor's slate of directors — a *proxy contest*. The suitor (or *insurgent*) must convince shareholders that they will be better off under new management. If the insurgent fails, it will have little to show for the effort.

Option 2: **Tender Offer**. The suitor can appeal to the shareholders' wallets by seeking to buy a controlling block of shares at above-market prices. To reach dispersed public shareholders quickly and minimize the risk of falling short, the suitor (or *bidder*) will publicly offer to buy shares at a premium above the market price on the condition that a sufficient number are submitted (tendered) within a specified period — a *tender offer*. Acquiring voting control in a successful tender offer, unlike winning a proxy contest, gives the bidder a majority equity position and the assurance of control.

Option 3: **Combined Proxy Contest-Tender Offer**. The suitor can solicit proxies to replace the board, on the promise that the suitor will make a tender offer after the new board removes any takeover impediments installed by the old board. This *two-step bid* is more costly than a straight tender offer but may be the only way to acquire equity control in the face of an entrenched board.

In the 1980s, most suitors chose a hostile tender offer over a proxy contest. A tender offer provided an element of surprise and a greater chance of succeeding than a proxy contest, along with the certainty and opportunities inherent in immediate equity control. If a bidder failed to acquire control — often when another bidder or management offered shareholders a better price — the unsuccessful bidder could nonetheless profit if it held stock in the target. Bidders often acquired an early "toehold" position in the target's stock to compensate for their trouble of identifying and pursuing a good target.

In the early 1990s, hostile takeover activity fell off significantly. There have been many explanations. After many shaky deals at the end of the 1980s, financing has not been as available for new deals; there are far fewer "good buys" that can be restructured profitably; state antitakeover laws passed in the late 1980s add significant expense and uncertainty to hostile bids; and state courts have given incumbent boards significant latitude to resist outsiders. Nonetheless, as of 1994, there has been an increase in takeovers (some hostile) in industries in flux — such as banking, medium-size manufacturing, telecommunications, and entertainment. The battle between QVC and Viacom for Paramount illustrates that the hostile takeover activity of the 1980s was not a passing aberration.

§37.2 A Garden-Variety Takeover Drama

During the 1980s, takeovers assumed nearly mythical proportions. They produced the largest private transactions in history ($25.7 billion for Kravis, Kohlberg & Roberts's 1988 acquisition of RJR Nabisco), and they restructured the landscape and mentality of corporate America. Their disconcerting complexity, often played out in the news headlines, made the dramas seem beyond any but the most sophisticated critic's comprehension. Nonetheless, the actors in these dramas, their roles, the conventional parts and scenes, the script devices, and the range of outcomes became somewhat standardized.

To acquaint you with the dynamics and vocabulary of a takeover, we present the story of a garden-variety takeover drama: the 1987 takeover battle for Burlington Industries, the nation's largest textile producer.

Act I, Scene 1
The Bidder Identifies the Target

In 1987 Burlington was a publicly traded company listed on the New York Stock Exchange, with 27.3 million shares of common stock outstanding. At the beginning of the year, the stock was trading at around $40 a share; the company's aggregate market value was about $1.3 billion. Like most public corporations, Burlington was incorporated in Delaware. Its principal operations and corporate offices were in North Carolina.

A number of factors, discernible from publicly available information, suggested Burlington's attractiveness as a takeover target. The ratio of its stock price to book value was 1:1, its net sales (in a turbulent textile market) had fallen only a modest 3.2 percent annually during the previous five years, its cash flow was running at 8 percent of sales, and its debt to equity ratio was about 4:5. In short, Burlington was a company with a strong asset base, a relatively low debt burden, and a strong cash flow. As with any other potential target, there were a number of likely bidders for Burlington: companies in the textile business, conglomerates looking for diversification opportunities, and investment firms set up to find profitable takeover targets.

In Burlington's case, two of these likely bidders joined forces. Dominion Textiles (Canada's largest textile firm) and Asher Edelman (a financier who had created a fortune and a reputation taking over companies) pooled together their cash, raised money from outside sources, and agreed to take equal equity positions if the takeover succeeded. Like other raiders, they would become surrounded by a host of takeover professionals — lawyers, investment bankers, public relation experts — each of whom would receive enormous fees.

Usually, a bidder must make do with available public information and rumors, but in the Burlington takeover bid, Dominion became interested in Burlington only after receiving inside information from a former, disgruntled

Burlington executive. These contacts gave Dominion important confidential information about the value of Burlington's assets, but eventually would be the "smoking gun" that would be a bid-killing "show stopper" for the Dominion-Edelman group. The pitfalls for a bidder are many.

Act I, Scene 2
The Bidder Lines Up Financing

In February 1987, Dominion's board formally decided to explore the possibility of taking over Burlington. During the 1980s' takeover binge, raising cash was not a serious obstacle. Dominion had a number of financing options, some of them of very recent vintage. These financing techniques made it unnecessary for a bidder itself to have cash to buy the target. "Bootstrap" cash could actually come from the target! Investment bankers had devised a number of ways to use *the assets of the target* to finance the takeover:

Two-tier buyout. During the early 1980s, many bidders structured their takeovers in two stages — a *two-tier buyout*. In the first stage, the bidder would acquire voting control (51 percent of the stock) with a "front-end" cash tender offer. In the second stage, the bidder would use a "back-end" squeeze-out merger to avoid minority shareholders and to gain full control over the target's assets. The minority shares remaining after the first stage typically were converted into high-risk, high-yield subordinated debt instruments — aptly called *junk bonds*. Front-end cash came from the bidder's own internally generated resources and sometimes from bank financing; funds to repay the junk bonds come from the target's cash flow. If cash flow was insufficient, the bidder would supplement it by selling parts of the target's business — a *bust-up takeover*.

Two-tier buyouts were structurally coercive. By announcing that the back-end consideration would be worth less than that of the front-end, the hostile bidder pressured target shareholders into tendering so they would be sure to share in the front-end cash. Consequently, the bidder greatly increased its chances of acquiring a majority equity position and later single-handedly accomplishing the second stage of the deal. The front-end thus assured the success of the back-end, and vice versa. During the mid-1980s, the structural coercion of a two-tier bid was used to justify a variety of takeover defenses (see §40.2) and state antitakeover legislation (see §40.4).

Any-and-all cash offers. By 1987 the two-tier bid had become obsolete. The success of takeovers had led to the creation of huge investment pools, and most bidders could buy all of a target's stock in cash. This cash came from a variety of sources: (1) the bidder, (2) takeover cash pools held by investment bankers, (3) takeover firms and their cash pools (such as Kohlberg, Kravis & Roberts), (4) private financiers (such as Asher Edelman), and (5) interim bridge loans from banks. Bridge loans, in particular, have made it possible for the bidder to offer to buy all the stock in cash — an *any-and-all cash tender offer*. Once the bidder acquires control, any remaining shares are cashed out in a back-end merger. The banks' bridge loans are then repaid from the proceeds of newly issued junk bonds and long-term, syndicated bank loans, both of which are collateralized by the target's cash flow and assets. Insufficient cash flow is supplemented by selling off parts of the business.

Financing for the Edelman-Dominion bid came from Shearson Lehman Brothers (its takeover pool) and an international banking group headed by the First National Bank of Chicago and the Royal Bank of Canada. The three joined in raising $2 billion in cash.

Act I, Scene 3
The Bidder Quietly Acquires a Foothold

At the same time financing was being arranged, the Edelman-Dominion group began buying Burlington stock on the market. These purchases were made through various brokers under different account names in an effort to mask them. A hostile bidder typically acquires such a silent equity cushion for a number of reasons. Before the takeover bid is announced, stock is available at bargain prices compared to what the bidder will have to pay once the target is "in play." In addition, this equity cushion protects the bidder against the significant risk that management will rebuff the hostile bid by offering shareholders a more lucrative option. If this happens, the bidder can itself accept the management offer, so that the sale of the previously purchased shares will compensate the bidder for its effort.

On April 24, ten days after passing the 5 percent threshold and as required by federal securities law, the Edelman-Dominion group disclosed to the SEC and the stock market that it had acquired 7.6 percent of Burlington's stock (representing an investment of about $100 million) and that it planned a takeover. As usually happens, the market price of the target's stock jumped almost instantly, moving from $54 on April 23 to $59 on April 27.

Act II, Scene 1
The Bidder's Tender Offer Officially Puts the Target in Play

Soon after revealing the toehold, Edelman proposed to meet with Frank Greenberg, Burlington's president and CEO, to discuss a negotiated transaction at $60 per share. A negotiated transaction, although sometimes more protracted and uncertain, gives the bidder more information about the target and avoids the risk of a successful defense. As often happens, Greenberg never responded to this "bear hug."

On May 6, the Dominion-Edelman group made a $67 cash tender offer to buy any and all of Burlington's shares, thus bringing the group's total purchase price to $1.5 billion. Although the group needed only 43 percent more to gain control, open-market purchases were not a real option. Once a company becomes a takeover target, shareholders generally will hold out and wait for a higher price. Their hand must be forced in a tender offer, which makes an above-market price available only if shares are tendered within a specified period. Nor was a partial front-end loaded bid for 43 percent of the stock a wise option. By this time, hostile bidders had largely stopped using front-end-loaded offers because of the takeover defenses such offers could invite.

In its tender offer filings, the Edelman group announced that it would sell unspecified parts of Burlington's business if it gained control of the company. The Edelman group would later raise its bid to $72 and then to $77.

Act II, Scene 2
The Arbs Amass Stock and Take Center Stage

As rumors of a bid for Burlington began to circulate, confirmed by the Edelman group's disclosure of its 7.6 percent toehold, the composition of Burlington's shareholders began to change dramatically. Securities speculators known as *risk arbitragers* (or *arbs*) became significant purchasers. They bought stock hoping to make money on the difference between the trading price and the price for which the shares would eventually be sold — whether to the Edelman group, to another bidder, or even back to the company. With the announcement of the Edelman tender offer, the arbs' buying began to drive the market price toward the tender offer price.

As usually happens, individual and institutional shareholders, faced with the choice of selling in an increasingly attractive market or holding in the hope that the tender offer would succeed, began to peel away. For some institutional shareholders, such as pension funds and bank trust departments, the decision to sell was compelled by their fiduciary duties to their beneficiaries.

The arbs, who often may end up holding 60 percent to 70 percent of the target's stock, perform the important function of assuming the risk that the tender offer may fail. They are natural allies of the bidder, in whose success they are keenly interested. The arbs also signal the bid's strength. For example, if trading prices languish, it is a sign that the arbs think the bid will fail; if trading prices rise above the tender offer price (as sometimes happens), it is a sign the arbs think the bid will be raised or bettered.

Act III, Scene 1
The Target Management Defends

Immediately upon hearing of Edelman's stake, Burlington's Greenberg began to plan a defense strategy for "his" company. The Burlington board approved the hiring of two investment bankers and an outside law firm to advise it on antitakeover strategies.

During the 1980s, management's financial and legal counsel devised a mind-boggling variety of reactions and defenses to hostile bids. Not only was the defensive arsenal potent and extensive, but its argot was colorful and vivid:

Revise the corporate governance structure.   The board can be staggered, thus delaying any change in the its composition; the charter can be amended to require supermajority approval of mergers and other corporate combinations; the charter can be amended to require a fair price (at least equal to the tender offer price) in any back-end transaction. These moves (sometimes known as *shark repellents*) are often taken in advance of a bid and may require shareholder approval. They make any attempt to change control more drawn out and expensive.

Revise the capital structure.   The target can offer to repurchase its stock for cash or, as is often the case, a package of new equity and debt securities (an *issuer self-tender*); the target can buy its stock on the open market from arbs and others who have accumulated blocks of stock in response to the possibility of a takeover (a *market sweep*); the board can give shareholders the right to buy the target's (or the bidder's) stock at huge discounts if the target is ever combined with the bidder (a *poison pill*); the board can allow shareholders to redeem at a set price any shares not purchased in the tender offer (*lollypop rights*); the board can issue new debt with *poison pill puts* that allow debtholders to compel the target to redeem the debt at attractive prices if there is ever a takeover; the board can issue new debt with covenants restricting the target's ability to take on new debt after a takeover or to combine with the bidder in the first place. These changes to the capital structure, most of which can be effected without shareholder approval, return equity to shareholders or create new debt (or both), thus making the target less financially attractive to potential acquirers.

Alter the shareholder mix.   An issuer self-tender can decrease the holdings of fickle shareholders and increase the proportion held by shareholders loyal to management; the target can issue stock to an investor friendly to management (a *white squire*) or to an *employee stock ownership plan (ESOP)* whose shares are voted by trustees or employees sympathetic to management; the board can grant a stock *lockup* that promises stock to a favored bidder at bargain prices. These changes increase the proportion of shareholders sympathetic to (or controlled by) management.

Find a palatable bidder.   Management can induce a favored bidder (*white knight*) to bid for or merge with the target on an understanding that management will not be replaced; management can mount (alone or with investment partners) its own bid for the target, often financed with debt (a *management leveraged buyout* or *management LBO*); the target can concede the white knight a *no-shop clause* that precludes the target from soliciting or giving information to other bidders and assures the white knight that it will not be a *stalking horse* for other bids. Each strategy increases the likelihood that management will be retained.

Buy new businesses or sell existing businesses. The board can grant an *asset lockup* that gives a white knight the option to buy parts of the target's business at bargain prices; the board can sell or option a *crown jewel,* stripping away the most desirable part of the target's business and undercutting the reason for a takeover; the target can buy new businesses or properties that create antitrust or banking regulatory problems for the bidder (and may increase the target's debt). These *scorched earth defenses,* none of which require shareholder approval, make the target less attractive from a business or regulatory standpoint.

Accelerate or increase management's employment benefits. The board can grant senior management *golden parachutes* that assure severance payments (which for tax reasons are usually set at three times their salary) if there is a takeover; the board can make pension and stock plans subject to contingent vesting if a takeover succeeds. These arrangements increase the costs of a takeover and soften the blow if one succeeds.

Buy out the bidder. The target can pay *greenmail* by buying the bidder's shares at a premium. Sometimes the target will require a greenmailer to enter into a *standstill agreement* obligating the greenmailer not to acquire more shares for a specified period. This, at least temporarily, ends the threat.

Attack the bidder. The target can sue the bidder for violating antitrust merger guidelines, margin rules, securities disclosure law, and state takeover legislation; the target can turn the table and begin a tender offer for the bidder (the *Pacman defense*). These attacks add to the confusion and may undermine confidence in the bidder.

As was typical, Burlington's management chose a multipronged defense. On May 11, based on the advice of its investment bankers, the board recommended that Burlington's shareholders reject the initial $67 offer as inadequate. The board also announced that it might seek control of Dominion — the involuted Pacman defense. The board also announced that the company would commence an $80 self-tender for up to 30 percent of Burlington's shares (8 million shares) and that it was considering a restructuring to benefit the remaining shares.

Meanwhile, management had begun a search for a white knight. On April 29, Greenberg had preliminary discussions with Morgan Stanley (an investment bank with its own access to takeover financing) about a leveraged buyout (LBO) in which current management would be retained. The board approved giving Morgan Stanley confidential information, and on May 20 agreed to a merger agreement. As was often true in the 1980s, Morgan Stanley found that since the bidder group could line up financing, so could Morgan Stanley. On May 26, it commenced an any-and-all tender offer for $76 in cash — a total bid of $2.4 billion. (The company's self-tender was made contingent on the Morgan Stanley bid failing.) Morgan Stanley gave informal assurances to some of Burlington's executives that they would be equity participants in the new private company. Morgan Stanley later raised its offer to $78, which turned out to be the winning bid.

Burlington's board also authorized a lawsuit attacking the Dominion-Edelman group. The suit, brought in federal district court in North Carolina on April 29, claimed that the group had made its bid using inside information in violation of Rule 10b-5 (see §29.5). The suit also challenged a Dominion-Burlington combination as illegal under the merger guidelines of the federal antitrust laws.

The Edelman group responded with its own lawsuit. It claimed that Burlington had failed to disclose management's equity participation in Morgan Stanley's buyout. It also claimed that the board violated its fiduciary duties by approving the merger agreement with Morgan Stanley without allowing the Edelman group a chance to participate in an auction for the company.

Act III, Scene 2
The Target's Management Turns to the State Legislature for Help

Burlington's management also turned to the political process for help. Arguing that a Dominion-Edelman takeover would cost North Carolina jobs, taxes, and community support, management importuned the North Carolina legislature to pass laws discouraging the hostile Dominion-Edelman bid. The legislature acted promptly. On April 23, it passed a fair-price statute effectively requiring any bid for Burlington to satisfy a pricing formula. N.C. Gen. Stat. §§55-75 to 55-79. On May 13, it passed a control-share statute that limited the voting rights of any hostile bidder whose acquisition of control had not been approved by the board or by the other shareholders. N.C. Gen. Stat. §§55-90 et seq.

As it turned out, the big guns were unnecessary for Burlington. Nonetheless, the heavy artillery of state antitakeover legislation has assumed great importance in the retrenchment of takeover activity in the 1990s. Delaware's 1988 takeover law, for example, fundamentally altered the bidding strategy for Delaware-incorporated firms (see §40.4.2).

Act III, Scene 3
The Unraveling of the Battle

In response to the Morgan Stanley offer, the Edelman group on May 28 raised its bid to $77 per share — $2.5 billion. But the resolve of the Edelman group was beginning to fray. In late May, it disclosed that it had reduced its holdings in Burlington from 13.4 percent to 12.3 percent.

On June 5, the federal district court in North Carolina enjoined the Dominion-Edelman group from continuing its bid because it had misused inside information. Sensing victory, Morgan Stanley raised its bid to $78 per share on June 10 — $2.7 billion. On June 25, Morgan Stanley acquired control when nearly 80 percent of the shares were tendered into its $78 offer. Later in the summer, Morgan Stanley bought out the remaining shareholders in a back-end merger. Burlington's management received a 37 percent interest in the new "private" company.

Act IV
The Denouement

The battle for Burlington was remarkable in one significant respect: The hostile bidder lost. But its effect on Burlington was not insignificant. As things turned out, management restructured the company's businesses in much the same way that the Edelman group would have. After the LBO, management cut worldwide jobs from 43,000 to 24,000, closed one-third of the company's plants, and embarked on a two-year corporate sell-off program to raise $900 million. The takeover battle had simply been over who would make Burlington leaner.

To reduce labor costs and compensate employees with stock, the company in 1989 issued 35.5 percent of its shares to an employee stock ownership plan (ESOP), which took on a $112 million debt for the shares. The per-share purchase price of $38 was four times greater than Morgan Stanley had paid for its stock two years before. In fact, Morgan Stanley had invested a total of $46 million in cash for its voting shares, while receiving $87 million in fees for advising management in the LBO and for selling the junk bonds to finance the deal. Later it would collect an additional $33 million in fees to help Burlington divest some of its businesses and adjust its capital structure. In 1990, however, Morgan Stanley handed full control over to Burlington's management and the ESOP by exchanging all of its voting shares for nonvoting preferred stock.

By 1992, Burlington had reduced its debt to $1.8 billion, but its debt burden was still greater than the company's cash flow could bear and resulted in annual losses that approached $100 million. To avoid bankruptcy, the company "went public" again in 1992 and issued 83 percent of its stock (57 million shares) to public investors for a capital infusion of $800 million. The public offering reduced the proportionate equity interest of management and the ESOP. Within a year after going public, Burlington again became profitable.

Burlington's management also fared well in the restructured company. Frank Greenberg, Burlington's CEO, stayed on to oversee the company's restructuring, in the process earning stock and other bonuses worth in excess of $8 million. In 1992, his salary of $1.8 million was the highest reported salary in the industry. In addition, he and other Burlington executives continue to hold a significant percentage of Burlington shares.

Burlington was among many companies in the U.S. textile industry to go through an LBO or other restructuring in the 1980s. As a result of heavier debt levels, textile companies were forced to concentrate on their core businesses, often making significant investments to meet emerging competition from outside the United States. As the dust clears from the turbulent 1980s, the U.S. textile industry is more profitable than it ever was — with record profits in 1992 of $2.1 billion — and many industry analysts believe the industry emerged as one of the most efficient and technologically advanced of all U.S. industries.

What happened to Asher Edelman? He was not discouraged by his defeat. On the very day in 1987 that Morgan Stanley completed its merger, Edelman announced his plans to buy Foster Wheeler for $888 million, and one month later he bid $965 million for Telex Corporation. In addition, Edelman created quite a stir when he proposed to teach a course at Columbia Business School in which any student who came up with a worthwhile takeover target would receive an "A" and $100,000.

Perhaps the most salient feature of the Burlington takeover was that litigation proved to be both the wild card and the trump card. Although somewhat at a loss in the face of the titanic dimensions of takeover battles, courts have been pivotal and volatile in deciding on the legality of bidding maneuvers and takeover defenses. Excellent lawyering was at a premium.

§37.3 An Epilogue — Is the Takeover Phenomenon Healthy?

One thing that is clear about the Burlington takeover, and virtually every other recent takeover, is that shareholders gain handsomely. It has been estimated that during the 1980s, takeovers increased net shareholder wealth by more than $200 billion. In the late 1980s, takeover premiums over prevailing market prices ranged from 50 percent to over 100 percent.

Why were bidders willing to pay such princely premiums? There are a number of explanations, some focusing on the particular characteristics of the bidder and others on the nature of takeovers. Some of these explanations suggest that takeovers are beneficial:

The disciplining hypothesis. The bidder, such as a "financial" acquirer who borrows money against the target's cash flow, thinks a new management team will operate the business more profitably than incumbent management. Shareholders reap the unexploited value of their investment (or at least part of it) when the business is transferred to more efficient hands. Economists argue that this disciplining extends even to firms that are not taken over. In these firms, the takeover threat forces management to run the business in a way that keeps stock prices high and discourages takeover attention. Hostile takeovers in the 1980s often occurred in industries in decline, where managers had put resources to wasteful use (such as in the broadcast and oil industries), and in industries in which managers failed to adjust quickly to rapid market, regulatory, or technological changes (such as the textile and airlines industries).

The synergy hypothesis.   The target's business has unique synergistic value to the bidder. The value of the combined firms — such as a vertically integrated manufacturer and retailer — exceeds the independent sum of the two. In the early 1990s this has been a frequent explanation for "strategic" acquisitions of companies in related industries or in complementary markets in the same industry. The $9.8 billion acquisition in 1994 of Paramount (entertainment) by Viacom (telecommunications) offers a good illustration. Shareholders share the value of this more efficient allocation of resources.

The market myopia hypothesis.   The stock markets undervalue the long-term prospects of certain firms. This undervaluation, particularly in cyclical industries such as oil, allows astute buyers to pay shareholders more than investors on the stock markets are willing to.

Other explanations suggest takeovers are bad:

The empire-building hypothesis.   The bidder (or more precisely its management) prefers control over large companies because executive prestige and compensation are often tied to company size, not necessarily to profitability. Shareholders of the target receive some of the spoils of this empire-building; shareholders of the bidder subsidize the frolic.

The goring hypotheses.   The shareholders' gain is at the expense of other stakeholders of the target — employees, creditors, customers, and taxpayers. Streamlining the target's business costs jobs and leads to lower wages; increased leverage forces existing creditors (such as bondholders) to subsidize the takeover; takeovers that combine competing businesses concentrate market power and force customers to pay higher, noncompetitive prices; replacing equity with debt reduces the target's tax burden — because interest is deductible, while dividends are not — and forces other taxpayers to pick up the slack; cuts in long-run research and development after a takeover reduce American competitiveness and hurt everyone; increased leverage puts firms in a precarious position, with little margin for error in an economic downturn.

So the hypotheses go. Empirical evidence tends to support an eclectic answer. Each hypothesis has some support, some more than others. Studies show that, on balance, leveraged buyouts and restructuring have achieved efficiency gains by causing managers of debt-heavy companies to focus on the "bottom line" and redeploy assets to their most productive uses.

Synergy, which was used to explain the conglomeration of U.S. business during the 1950s and 1960s, does not explain the *deconglomeration* of the 1980s. Studies show that merged firms in the 1980s have experienced returns that are 10 percent less than the returns for comparable independent firms. Smaller, specialized firms may be better at competing in today's global, fluid market than larger, diversified firms.

Although many have questioned the stock market's ability to value firms since the October 1987 stock market "correction," when stock prices on the New York Stock Exchange fell more than 30 percent in a week, the markets do seem to take into account a firm's long-term prospects. Studies show that firms with high research and development expenditures were actually less vulnerable to takeovers and that stock prices rise on announcements of increased R&D spending.

The loss of jobs (and lower wages) in some industries seems to be more the result of broad-based economic change than an effect of takeovers. Studies show that layoffs are as frequent in companies that have not been taken over as in companies that have been. An example is the auto industry, where there have been no takeovers but unprecedented layoffs. In addition, some studies show that, on the whole, existing bondholders are not worse off because of takeovers, although there are a number of individual exceptions.

The loss in tax revenues resulting from interest deductibility does not fully account for takeover premiums, nor does it take into account the taxes on capital gains when shareholders receive takeover premiums. The evidence indicates that takeovers have a neutral (or even positive) effect on R&D spending. Overall debt-equity ratios are not at record levels, and in 1985, for instance, they actually declined. The defaults on junk bonds during the late 1980s turned out to be a transitory phenomenon, and junk bond returns in the 1990s have been higher than returns on equity investments. That is, former shareholders achieved higher returns when they moved up the priority ladder to become junior bondholders.

One significant element that the takeover debate often disregards, however, is the drain caused by takeover transaction costs. Billions of dollars were paid in loan commitment fees, investment advisory fees, and legal fees. It was argued that the takeover binge was consuming the talents of America's best and brightest. Even as takeovers are again on the rise in the 1990s, this drain continues. As proof, you have just finished reading this chapter.

38

Proxy Contests

A proxy contest in a public corporation pits incumbent management against an insurgent challenger in a fight for the hearts (and votes) of the shareholders. Each contestant offers its own slate of board candidates, making its pitch in proxy solicitations and advertisements. At stake is representation on the board and control of the corporation.

Proxy voting is regulated at both the state and federal levels. As we saw in Chapter 19, federal proxy rules under the Securities Exchange Act of 1934 govern the timing, content, and veracity of proxy solicitations in a public corporation. State law empowers proxy voting and voting by consents, and authorizes the board to manage the corporate voting machinery, subject to state fiduciary limits.

In this chapter, we summarize the federal proxy rules as they apply to proxy contests and discuss state fiduciary regulation of management defensive tactics in a proxy fight.

§38.1 The Insurgent's Uphill Battle in a Proxy Contest

Insurgents face a number of obstacles in a proxy contest:

(1) **Shareholder passivity**. Chances are that any shareholders who are dissatisfied with current management already have exercised the "Wall Street rule" and have sold their shares. Current shareholders are often those who have decided to stay the course with incumbent management.

(2) **Limited access**. *Insurgent shareholders* have limited access to other shareholders. Access to the company's list of shareholders under state law may often require court action (see §§12.1, 19.5). The federal proxy rules give management the choice of whether to

569

provide an insurgent with a shareholders' list or mail the insurgent's proxy materials at the insurgent's expense. Rule 14a-7 (see §19.5.1).

(3) **No corporate reimbursement.** Insurgents must fund their own voting campaign, while management may use corporate funds. Corporate reimbursement is available only to successful insurgents.

Lately, however, some of these obstacles may be on the wane. Institutional shareholders will often support management changes rather than try to sell their large blocks at a loss. The SEC has made it easier for shareholders to communicate with each other without being subject to the proxy filing and distribution rules. Furthermore, in the face of tender offer impediments (see Chapter 40), bidders have resorted to two-step proxy contest-tender offers to acquire control, and activist shareholders have used threats of proxy contests to catalyze greater management responsiveness.

The number of proxy fights for board control nearly tripled in the 1980s, compared to the 1960s and 1970s. The annual average of contests for board control rose from 5.6 during the 1960s and 1970s, to 15.7 during the early 1980s, to 30.0 during the late 1980s. Insurgents have also been increasingly successful. In the early 1990s, insurgents seeking board control enjoyed a success rate well above 50 percent, compared to a 20 percent success rate during the 1960s and 1970s.

§38.2   Federal Regulation of Proxy Contests

The federal proxy rules regulate voting in public corporations (see Chapter 19). As applied to proxy contests, these rules require:

- **Filing and distribution.** Both the incumbent board and any insurgent soliciting proxies must file specified information with the SEC before distributing proxy materials to shareholders. Rule 14a-6 (see §19.4.3). Organizing an insurgent group runs the risk of itself being considered a solicitation, as to which the filing and distribution requirements apply (see §19.3.2).
- **Disclosure.** Participants in the insurgent's solicitation must disclose their identity, their interest in the company's securities, any financing arrangements, their participation in other proxy contests, and any understandings about their future employment with the company. Rule 14a-11 (see §19.4.1).
- **Antifraud prohibitions.** Any information or accusations in the proxy materials are subject to the proxy rules' prohibition against materially false or misleading solicitations. Rule 14a-9 (see §§19.4.4, 19.6).

In addition, if an insurgent group is composed of shareholders who together own more than 5 percent of the public company's equity stock, disclosure of group status, stock holdings, financing, and plans is required under the 1934 Act (see §39.1). Currently, under §13(d) of the 1934 Act, disclosure must be made within ten days of the group's agreement to act together to affect control.

§38.3   State Fiduciary Regulation of Proxy Contests

State corporate statutes delegate to the board the function of managing the corporation's proxy machinery: setting annual and special meetings, specifying a record date for voting, establishing the size of the board, creating notice requirements for insurgent slates, offering its own slate of directors, setting the agenda for the meeting, and soliciting shareholder proxies.

In addition, the board has wide latitude over shareholder voting. Without formal shareholder approval, the board can unilaterally dilute shareholder voting blocks and structure transactions to avoid shareholder approval rights. The board can also initiate charter amendments that change the voting structure — such as staggered boards, elimination of consent procedures, and supermajority voting requirements. An incumbent board's use of the corporate governance and voting machinery to defend itself in a voting contest raises serious conflicts of interest. The courts' response has been ambivalent.

§38.3.1   Corporate Funding of the Proxy Contest

As a general matter, the corporation bears the normal costs of an uncontested proxy solicitation. To ensure a quorum of shares at the shareholders' meeting, management uses corporate funds to pay for preparing, printing, and mailing the proxy materials. In an uncontested proxy solicitation, management and shareholder interests coincide.

But when an insurgent opposes management, corporate payment of the incumbents' proxy solicitation expenses presents a clear conflict. In a contested election, there is little risk that there will be insufficient proxies to constitute a quorum. The greater risk is that management will use the company-funded proxy machinery to entrench its incumbency at shareholder expense.

Courts have dealt with this conflict by avoiding it. In the leading case, *Rosenfeld v. Fairchild Engine & Airplane Corp.*, 128 N.E.2d 291 (N.Y. 1955), the court held that unless it is clear that management was out to protect its incumbency at shareholder expense, management may use corporate funds to pay for its proxy battles. Under this approach, corporate funding is proper if the voting contest relates to corporate "policy" rather than to a "purely personal" quest for control. Since any control fight can be cast as a question of how the corporation should be managed, not who should do it, all incumbent expenses are payable — and, in practice, are paid — by the corporation.

The obverse, the funding of a successful insurgent's proxy expenses, has been dealt with in much the same way. If the proxy contest was over "policy" rather than "personality" and shareholders approved the disbursement, the corporation may reimburse the successful insurgent. See *Rosenfeld*. In practice, however, this happens only when the insurgent wins the control fight, and shareholders end up funding both sides in the campaign.

§38.3.2   *Board Manipulation of the Governance Machinery*

Management may also try to fend off an insurgent by using the corporate governance and voting machinery. Courts have treated any manipulation by the board of the voting process as inequitable — a presumptive breach of fiduciary duty. Unless the board can articulate a "compelling justification" for its action, courts intervene to protect "established principles of corporate democracy":

- The board cannot advance the annual meeting date if it would burden insurgents in a pending proxy contest. *Schnell v. Chris-Craft Industries,* 285 A.2d 437 (Del. 1971).
- The board cannot postpone the annual meeting date if opposing proxies already gathered by an insurgent would expire by the time of the meeting. *Aprahamiam v. HBO & Co.,* 531 A.2d 1204 (Del. 1987).
- The board must waive a bylaw that would have required a prospective insurgent (but not management) to give notice of its slate of directors after certain incumbent directors learned they would not be renominated. *Hubbard v. Hollywood Park Realty Enterprises,* 1991 Del. Ch. LEXIS 9 (1991).
- The board cannot create bylaws that impose waiting periods, advance-notice requirements, inspection and record-date procedures for shareholder action by written consent if they unnecessarily delay the effect of action. *Allen v. Prime Computer, Inc.,* 540 A.2d 417 (Del. 1988); *Datapoint Corp. v. Plaza Securities Co.,* 496 A.2d 1031 (Del. 1985).

The courts have also nullified board actions that do not manipulate the voting process if they interfere with the opportunity of shareholders to vote:

- The board cannot issue new stock meant to dilute an insurgent who has started or is threatening a proxy fight. *Condec Corp. v. Lunkenheimer Co.,* 230 A.2d 769 (Del. Ch. 1967).
- The board cannot increase the board size and fill the resulting vacancies to nullify a pending consent solicitation. *Blasius Industries v. Atlas Corp.,* 564 A.2d 651 (Del. Ch. 1988).

- Management must compile for the insurgent a list of shareholders who do not object to being solicited, even though such a list does not exist. *Sadler v. NCR Corp.,* 928 F.2d 48 (2d Cir. 1991).

Nonetheless, the courts have been ambivalent (even contradictory) in enforcing fiduciary duties in other voting situations. Courts have permitted the board significant latitude to take preemptive actions prior to an insurgency or in response to two-step proxy contests/tender offers:

- The board, before an insurgency, may adopt bylaws that require shareholders to give advance notice of their candidates to the board. *Stroud v. Grace,* 606 A.2d 75, 93 (Del. 1992).
- The board may issue shares to an employee stock ownership plan (ESOP) in the face of a threatened two-step proxy contest/tender offer, even though the issuance (along with other defenses) would give the board voting power over 34 percent of the company's shares. *Shamrock Holdings v. Polaroid,* 559 A.2d 257 (Del. Ch. 1989).
- The board may adopt a poison pill plan (see §40.2.3) that prevents an insurgent/bidder in a two-step proxy contest/tender offer from forming an insurgent group. *Stahl v. Apple Bancorp, Inc. (Stahl II),* 1990 Del. Ch. LEXIS 121 (Aug. 9, 1990).

In like vein, courts have been reluctant to question the validity of "shark repellent" charter amendments, initiated by the board and approved by a majority of shareholders before an insurgency. Even though such amendments hamper insurgencies and studies show that they lead to a loss in share value, courts have upheld charter amendments that impose supermajority voting, staggered boards, aggregation caps on voting power, board-size provisions, and elimination of written consent procedures. *Providence & Worcester Co. v. Baker,* 378 A.2d 121, 124 (Del. 1977) (voting cap on any shareholder with more than 25 percent of company's shares).

Courts have also interpreted "shark repellent" provisions against shareholders. For example, in *Centaur Partners, IV v. National Intergroup, Inc.,* 582 A.2d 923 (Del. 1990), the court interpreted a staggered board provision to prevent an insurgent from proposing a bylaw amendment that would have increased the size of the board from 9 to 15 directors and thus given it immediate control of a 15-person staggered board. The court assumed the bylaw amendment was governed by the charter's ambiguous condition that "to amend, repeal, or adopt any provisions inconsistent with" the staggered board provision required an 80 percent shareholder vote. Although the insurgent did not propose to do away with the staggered board, the court assumed the bylaw change would conflict with "continuity in the board of directors," and the court read the charter to give the board sole power to change its size.

EXAMPLES

1. Conanstand Partners is an investment firm that buys large blocks of stock in companies whose assets it believes are under-utilized or mismanaged. After buying a strategic stake, Conanstand urges the target's management to make the company more profitable or to face a takeover. Usually, target management restructures the business as suggested, although occasionally another company acquires the target in a cash tender offer. Either way Conanstand garners a handsome profit. Recently, Conanstand identified a target: Gillick Industries, a publicly traded corporation that manufactures shaving products. Gillick has a pattern of strong revenues, good customer base, and a surprisingly low price/earnings ratio.

   a. Conanstand contacts investment bankers and institutional investors to ask whether they think a proxy contest would succeed. Are these discussions legal?

   b. At the time of these discussions, Conanstand holds 2 percent of Gillick's common stock. The institutional investors it has contacted together hold more than 15 percent of Gillick's stock. Must these discussions be disclosed?

2. Conanstand acquires 6 percent of Gillick's shares and announces it will seek to put four directors on Gillick's 12-person board. In its proxy solicitation, Conanstand says it wants Gillick's management to put the company up for sale.

   a. Gillick's management responds by placing newspaper advertisements in major newspapers questioning the foreign composition of Conanstand's investor group, with the ads asking: "The Conanstand Group — Who Are They Really?" Gillick's management suggests that a shadowy foreign billionaire heads the group. In fact, Conanstand is composed entirely of U.S. investors and pension funds. Can Conanstand stop management's misinformation campaign?

   b. Conanstand also mounts its own newspaper campaign, stating that Gillick has entered into standstill agreements barring various potential acquirers from acquiring control of Gillick for up to ten years. As it turns out, Conanstand is mistaken — all of the standstill agreements have expired. Will Gillick be successful if it sues?

3. As the election nears, Gillick's management worries that arbitrageurs that have been buying Gillick stock are receptive to Conanstand's arguments. Gillick's bylaws specify that the annual shareholders' meeting will be held on the first Tuesday of May.

   a. The Gillick board amends the bylaws to set the record date for the annual shareholders' meeting as of March 1, four weeks earlier than the current bylaws specify. Recent purchasers will not be able to vote. Can Conanstand challenge the board action?

    b. Gillick management follows through on a pre-insurgency plan to place 25 percent of Gillick's stock in a newly created ESOP. A voting trustee will vote this stock according to employee instructions. Can Conanstand challenge the issuance to the ESOP?

    c. Conanstand thinks that, one way or another, its insurgency will have a salutary effect on Gillick. It wants to be reimbursed for its reasonable expenses in the proxy solicitation. Can it demand reimbursement?

4. Conanstand wins its four seats to the board. The new Conanstand board decides that the corporation should sell some of its less profitable operations over the next few years — not quite what Conanstand had hoped for. Can Conanstand demand the board sell the company, as the shareholders wanted?

EXPLANATIONS

1a. Probably, even though Conanstand has not filed or distributed any disclosure documents. There are two arguments: (1) the contacts are not proxy solicitations; (2) even if treated as proxy solicitations, they are exempt under recent SEC rule changes.

Interpreting the SEC proxy rules, courts have characterized communications that are part of a "continuous plan" leading to a formal solicitation of proxies as proxy solicitations. See *Studebaker Corp. v. Gittlin* (see §19.3.2). Nonetheless, courts have recognized the necessity for some leeway in allowing preliminary discussions leading to the formation of an insurgent group. In this case, Conanstand does not yet know whether the discussions will lead to a proxy contest, and there seems little risk that the institutional shareholders with which Conanstand is talking will be irremediably swayed by these early discussions.

Even if the contacts are proxy solicitations, SEC rules exempt this kind of communication from the proxy filing and distribution requirements if Conanstand neither seeks authority to act as a proxy nor requests a proxy card. Rule 14a-2(b)(1). (The "solicitations" nonetheless remain subject to the SEC antifraud rules.) Further, the contacts are also exempt from the filing and disclosure requirements if they involve fewer than ten shareholders. Rule 14a-2(b)(2) (see §19.4.5).

1b. Perhaps. It is possible to view Conanstand and the contacted investors as a "group" for purposes of the 5 percent shareholding disclosure requirements of §13(d) of the 1934 Act. As we will see, this depends on whether the shareholders (whose holdings exceed 5 percent) can be said to have reached an understanding to affect control of the corporation (see §39.1.2). Disclosure on Form 13D may be required even though the discussions do not amount to "proxy solicitations" or are exempt from the proxy rule's filing and distribution requirements.

2a. Probably. Rule 14a-9 of the proxy rules prohibits any solicitation that is materially false or misleading (see §19.4.4). Is the makeup of Conanstand "material"? It seems substantially likely that a reasonable shareholder would consider important who is behind Conanstand and might be unwilling to support Conanstand if there were some indication of an international plot to plunder the company. See *TSC Industries v. Northway, Inc.*, 426 U.S. 438 (1976) (see §19.6.3). On the other hand, reasonable shareholders may not care about Conanstand's makeup, because what is most relevant are the merits of Conanstand's desire to have Gillick management sell the company. Nonetheless, Gillick management's apparent belief that shareholders would find Conanstand's composition important to their voting decision would seem to make the information material.

The federal proxy rules give Conanstand a private cause of action. Before the election, Conanstand could seek an injunction, including corrective disclosure. Even after the election, a court might order a new election if Conanstand lost.

2b. Probably. The existence of standstill agreements, if true, is material because it indicates that Gillick management is attempting to insulate the company from a takeover, to the detriment of shareholders. Reasonable shareholders considering how to vote would consider it important that management tends toward entrenchment. If Gillick only seeks corrective disclosure, it is probably irrelevant whether Conanstand's mistake was intentional or innocent. To protect the shareholders' franchise, the mistake should be corrected. If Gillick seeks damages, it may have to show Conanstand's misstatement was intentional or negligent and that the shareholders or the company suffered some loss as a result. Loss causation may be hard to show, because even if Conanstand is successful in placing its four directors on the board, they will remain in the minority.

3a. Yes. Like other corporate statutes, the RMBCA contemplates that the board has the power to control the voting process. RMBCA §10.20(a) gives the board power to amend the bylaws, and RMBCA §7.07 specifies that the record date is the date set in the bylaws, provided it is at least 70 days before the meeting — which this is. But the board's action, even if authorized, may violate the directors' fiduciary duties. The effect of the "surprise" record date is to dilute the voting power of the arbs. By taking an action with no apparent business justification except to thwart a pending shareholder insurgency opposed by management, a court may well find the directors acted inequitably in breach of their fiduciary duties. Courts have found "compelling justifications" for board manipulation of the voting process only in the narrow case when the board had already agreed to sell the corporation and the insurgency might upset the sale.

3b. Yes, but it's a closer question. Conanstad can argue that the ESOP is an entrenching device that dilutes the voting power of existing shareholders and makes the insurgency more difficult. In similar cases, courts have assumed employee-shareholders are more likely to side with current management, since employees faced with the choice of jeopardizing their jobs or a better retun on their ESOP investment would opt for job security. See *Shamrock Holdings v. Polaroid*, 559 A.2d 257 (Del. Ch. 1989) (hostile bidder with plans to sell the company "will inevitably raise concerns about job security").

The board might rebut this argument on two grounds. First, the issuance of stock to the ESOP is not necessarily entrenching since the plan trustee must vote the ESOP shares as employees direct, and nothing prevents employees from voting with the insurgent. Delaware's anti-takeover statute, for example, does not count ESOP shares as being management-controlled if the shares are subject to confidential pass-through voting. Del. GCL §203(a)(2)(ii) (see §40.4.2). Second, the board can argue that heightened *Schnell-Blasius* review should not apply to a transaction planned outside the context of a voting contest. In *Polaroid*, for example, the court reviewed an ESOP issuance under a lower *Unocal*-proportionality standard of review (see §40.2.3) because it was in response to a hostile tender offer rather than the bidder's later proxy solicitation. In our example, the board could argue that the ESOP issuance, which was in the works before the voting insurgency, should be treated like any other business decision. The board could readily justify the ESOP issuance as a way to increase employee productivity and loyalty, easily passing muster under a business judgment review. The question in our example would be whether the ESOP issuance really related to a preexisting corporate plan or was meant to dilute the pending insurgency. See *AT&T v. NCR Corp.*, 761 F. Supp. 475 (S.D. Ohio 1991) (invalidating ESOP created during pending control contest).

3c. No. An insurgent has no right to reimbursement unless the board authorizes it. As a practical matter, Conanstand can hope to be reimbursed only if it acquires control and the shareholders ratify payment of expenses that the insurgent already incurred. Since the proxy fight is over a policy issue — whether the corporation should be sold — the shareholders may approve reimbursement of the successful insurgent. Otherwise, the matter lies in the discretion of the *incumbent* board.

4. No. Victory in a proxy fight can be fleeting. Unless the insurgent places a majority on the board, the directors are under no obligation to institute the insurgent's "platform." Without a majority, the most that the insurgent can hope for is that the directors will exercise their business judgment to adopt the insurgent's agenda and that the increase in share

value will justify the effort for the insurgent. For this reason, insurgents rarely seek less than majority representation on the board. Further, to provide shareholders with a tangible reason to vote for the insurgent, recent insurgents often propose a recapitalization plan or tender offer that promises an immediate increase in share value. Although proxy fights in the 1960s and 1970s were often waged by former managers seeking to regain their positions, recent insurgents rarely wage proxy fights merely to gain a long-term management position.

39

Federal Securities Regulation of Tender Offers

The buying of control blocks in nonnegotiated transactions is not a new phenomenon. The 1950s and 1960s witnessed a wave of corporate conglomeration, much of it hostile. Federal proxy rules applied when shareholders had to vote to approve a negotiated transaction (see §19.2), and the 1933 Act's prospectus disclosure rules applied if any securities were exchanged in a tender offer (see §10.1). But no federal securities regulation applied to buying a *control block for cash,* whether by means of open-market purchases or a tender offer.

To plug this regulatory gap, Congress passed the Williams Act in 1968. The Act, which added provisions to the Securities Exchange Act of 1934, applies to public corporations whose stock is registered under §12 of the 1934 Act (see §19.3.1). The Williams Act:

- mandates disclosure for stock accumulations of more than 5 percent of a target's equity securities so the stock market (and the target's management) can react to the possibility of a change in control;
- mandates disclosure by anyone who makes a tender offer for a company's equity stock so that shareholders can make informed buy-sell-hold decisions; and
- regulates the structure of the tender offer so that shareholders are not stampeded into tendering.

The legislative history of the Williams Act contains statements that the legislation was not intended to favor either bidders or management. Rather, it was meant to benefit shareholders by giving them the means to evaluate takeover bids and by assuring a level playing field in the takeover game.

§39.1   Disclosure of Foothold Position

Any person (or group) that acquires beneficial ownership of more than 5 percent of a public corporation's equity securities must file a disclosure document with the SEC. 1934 Act §13(d).

§39.1.1   *Schedule 13D Disclosure — 5 Percent Shareholders*

The filing, known as a Schedule 13D, must disclose (1) the acquirer's (and any group member's) identity and background, (2) the source and the amount of funds for making the purchases, (3) the number of the target's shares held by the acquirer, (4) any arrangements that the acquirer has with others concerning shares of the target, and (5) the acquirer's purposes for the acquisition and his intentions with respect to the target. A Schedule 13D must be filed within ten days after the 5 percent threshold is passed. This gives an acquirer a ten-day window during which to buy stock on the open market before having to signal that the company may be in play.

§39.1.2   *Schedule 13D Disclosure — 5 Percent Groups*

If persons who collectively hold more than 5 percent agree to act together for the purpose of affecting control, they (as a group) become subject to the §13(d) reporting requirement. Even if the group does not acquire more shares, their *agreement* triggers the reporting obligation. Rule 13d-5(b)(1); *GAF Corp. v. Milstein*, 453 F.2d 709 (2d Cir. 1971).

§39.2   Federal Tender Offer Rules

Seeking control through open market purchases is problematic — rarely will enough shareholders be willing to sell at market for a bidder to acquire a control block. A tender offer forces the question. The bidder greatly increases its chances of acquiring a control block by publicly offering to buy a specified number of tendered shares during a specified period at a premium over prevailing market prices. A tender offer operates much like a retailer's "weekend clearance sale at never-again prices."

Any tender offer for a public corporation's equity securities that would result in the bidder holding more than 5 percent of the target's securities is subject to both disclosure requirements and substantive rules governing the terms of the offer. 1934 Act §14(d). In effect, this covers all public tender offers. Federal tender offer regulation seeks to ensure that shareholders have sufficient information about the offer and adequate time to evaluate the offer, so they are not unfairly pressured into tendering their shares.

§39.2.1 Tender Offer Disclosure

The bidder must file a disclosure document with the SEC on the day it commences the tender offer. The document, known as a Schedule 14D-1, must include the same information as Schedule 13D, along with information about the tender offer, past negotiations between the bidder and the target, the bidder's financial statements (if material), any regulatory requirements that may be applicable to the bid, and any other material information.

The target must cooperate in distributing the bidder's tender offer materials to shareholders by choosing either to mail the materials to shareholders (at bidder expense) or to furnish the bidder a current shareholders' list. Rule 14d-5.

§39.2.2 Mandated Opportunity to Evaluate Disclosure

Besides requiring disclosure, the SEC tender offer rules depart from the general disclosure-only philosophy of federal securities regulation by prescribing how a third-party tender offer must be carried out. Many of the rules expand the minimum levels specified in the statute. The current rules (as of 1993) require:

Open for minimum 20-day period.   The tender offer must be left open a minimum of 20 business days. Rule 14e-1. If any change is made in the offered price or the percentage of shares being sought, the offer must be left open for an additional ten days after the change.

Shareholder withdrawal at any time.   Shareholders can withdraw their shares (revoke their tenders) at any time while the tender offer is open. Rule 14d-7.

All-holders rule.   The tender offer must be open to all shareholders of the same class and not exclude any shareholders from tendering. Rule 14d-10(a)(1).

Best-price rule.   Each shareholder must be paid the best price paid to any other shareholder. Rule 14d-10(a)(2). If different consideration alternatives are provided (such as a choice of cash or debentures), each shareholder must be allowed to choose. Rule 14d-10(c)(1).

Pro rata purchase (if partial tender offer is oversubscribed). When the bidder seeks only a portion of all the shares (a partial tender offer) and shareholders tender more shares than the bidder seeks, the bidder must purchase from the tendered shares on a pro rata basis. 1934 Act §14(d)(6). For example, if the offer is for 50 percent of the target's stock and 75 percent of the shares are tendered, the bidder must purchase two-thirds (50/75) of each shareholder's tendered shares (disregarding fractions) and then must return the unpurchased shares. Rule 14d-8.

No outside purchases. The bidder cannot purchase outside the tender offer while it is pending. Rule 10b-13.

To make sure shareholders hear the other side of the story, target management must make a statement responding to the offer within ten business days after the tender offer commences. Rule 14e-2. The management statement, on Schedule 14D-9, can either oppose or support the bid, take a neutral position, or take no position at all. Whatever its response, management must give its reasons.

§39.2.3   Parity — Regulation of Issuer Self-Tenders

As we have seen, an issuer may defend against a hostile tender offer by buying back its own stock. This increases the proportion of friendly shareholders or burdens the target with unattractive debt, or both.

The Williams Act authorizes the SEC to promulgate rules regulating tender offers by targets — *issuer self-tenders*. 1934 Act §13(e). In general, the SEC rules regulate self-tenders in much the same way as third-party tender offers, imposing both disclosure requirements and substantive regulation that mirror the rules for third-party offers. Rule 13e-4. Self-tender regulation (as of 1993) differs significantly from third-party regulation in only two respects:

Outside purchases allowed. The issuer may purchase stock outside the terms of its self-tender. Open-market purchases, whether part of an ongoing corporate repurchase program or part of a defensive strategy, are not subject to the prohibition applicable to third-party tender offers. If the purchases are made while another tender offer is pending, SEC rules require only disclosure. Rules 13e-1.

Cooling-off period. For ten days after a self-tender terminates, the issuer is prohibited from making any purchases. Rule 13e-4(f)(6). This prevents an issuer from starting a tender offer, withdrawing it, and then purchasing stock in the resulting depressed market.

§39.2.4   Regulation of Deception (But Not Unfairness)

The Williams Act also contains a broadly worded antifraud provision. Section 14(e) prohibits any false or misleading statement, as well as any fraudulent, deceptive, or manipulative act, in connection with any tender offer or any solicitation for or against tenders. Although §14(e) is modeled on Rule 10b-5, it does not contain the "sale or purchase" language of the latter, suggesting that nontendering shareholders and nonpurchasing investors who lack standing under Rule 10b-5 may be protected by §14(e).

In *Schreiber v. Burlington Northern, Inc.,* 472 U.S. 1 (1985), the Supreme Court held that §14(e)'s prohibition against "manipulative acts" regulates only deception in connection with a tender offer and cannot be the basis for challenging a tender offer's substantive fairness. In the case, Burlington Northern withdrew its hostile tender offer and substituted a friendly tender offer with terms less favorable to shareholders. Shareholders claimed that the target's management had been bought off and therefore that the second tender offer was unfair and "manipulative." As it had with respect to Rule 10b-5 (*Santa Fe Industries v. Green;* see §29.4.3), the Court held that full disclosure, not regulation of corporate mismanagement, is the sole objective of §14(e).

Insider trading during a tender offer: Rule 14e-3.   Using its authority under §14(e), the SEC has prohibited trading by those with inside information about a tender offer. Rule 14e-3. The rule prohibits trading during the course of a tender offer by anybody (other than the bidder) who has material, nonpublic information about the offer that he knows (or has reason to know) was obtained from either the bidder or the target. There is no need under Rule 14e-3, unlike under Rule 10b-5, to prove that a tipper breached a fiduciary duty for personal benefit.

A 10b-5 reminder.   Disclosure in connection with stock trading during a takeover is regulated under Rule 10b-5's broad antifraud prohibitions (see §29.2). In the takeover context, Rule 10b-5 has two significant effects. First, it regulates the issuer's disclosure of merger negotiations, such as when an unsolicited acquirer privately proposes a merger (a "bear hug") or during a target's discussions with a white knight or a management LBO group (see §29.3.2). Second, it regulates insider (and outsider) trading on the basis of material, nonpublic confidential information about takeover plans, whether or not they include a tender offer (see §29.5).

§39.2.5   Unorthodox Tender Offers — High-Pressure Open Market Purchases

The term *tender offer* is not defined in either the Williams Act or the SEC rules. This is usually not a problem. An orthodox tender offer is easy to recognize: A bidder publicly announces an offer to buy a specified number of shares at a premium within a specified period, subject to specified terms. But problems arise when a purchase program involves the same kinds of high-pressure tactics that led to the passage of the Williams Act. By their nature, such programs cannot comply with the SEC tender offer rules, such as the minimum 20-day open period and the "all holders" rule.

Does a purchaser engage in an *unorthodox tender offer* when it imposes a deadline on a select group of shareholders or publicly announces an open-market purchase program for a specified number of shares? The cases have taken a variety of approaches. Some courts have held that a tender offer occurs only when solicited shareholders lack information and are subjected to coercive pressure akin to that of an unregulated tender offer. In *Hanson Trust PLC v. SCM Corp.*, 774 F.2d 47 (2d Cir. 1985), a bidder terminated its tender offer and, on the same day, purchased 25 percent of the target's stock in a series of five privately negotiated transactions and one open-market purchase. The Second Circuit, focusing primarily on the five negotiated purchases from institutional investors and arbitragers, held that the sellers had not been publicly solicited, that they were securities professionals aware of the essential facts concerning the target, and that they were not coerced to sell because the bidder bought at the market price without imposing any contingency that a specified number or percentage be acquired and without imposing any time limits. Accordingly, the court found the bidder's purchases did not constitute a tender offer.

Other courts, and the SEC, have articulated an eight-factor "taste" test that describes the ingredients of an orthodox tender offer and seeks to gauge how orthodox the challenged purchase program tastes. Under the test, a "tender offer" exists if there is (1) active and widespread solicitation of public shareholders (2) for a substantial percentage of the target's shares (3) at a premium price above market (4) where the offer is firm and nonnegotiable, (5) contingent on a fixed number of shares being tendered, and (6) open for a limited time. All of this (7) subjects offerees to pressure to sell their stock and (8) usually results in rapid, large accumulations of the target's shares. *SEC v. Carter Hawley Hale Stores, Inc.*, 760 F.2d 945 (9th Cir. 1985).

Courts have been reluctant to subject open-market purchases to the tender offer rules, unless the purchaser publicizes its purchase plans or makes a general solicitation that coerces shareholders to sell. Even without such coercion, it is possible to buy a large block of stock after arbitragers have begun to acquire stock in reaction to a tender offer. Known as a *street sweep*, this technique can be used to buy an effective control block (30 percent to 40 percent) virtually overnight. Although the SEC in 1987 proposed to prohibit unregulated purchases of 10 percent or more of a target's stock after a tender offer is made for the stock, the proposed rules proved unnecessary, because state antitakeover statutes have made it infeasible for a purchaser to acquire control in a street sweep. The Delaware statute, for example, imposes a three-year moratorium on any back-end transaction unless the acquirer buys 85 percent of the target's shares — a virtual impossibility in a street sweep.

§39.3 Standing to Sue for Williams Act Violations

Although §21 of the 1934 Act explicitly authorizes the SEC to enforce the Williams Act in federal court, none of the act's provisions expressly creates a private cause of action. Nonetheless, lower courts have inferred implied private actions under the Williams Act, although there have been three main sticking points: (1) Do bidders and management have standing? (2) Can damages be awarded? (3) What kinds of injunctive relief are proper?

§39.3.1 Standing to Represent the Shareholders

Courts have held that shareholders, for whom the Williams Act was passed, have standing to challenge violations of the Act. Commentators have pointed out that §14(e) does not mention "sale or purchase" and have suggested that standing extends to nontendering shareholders and nonpurchasing investors, subject only to the usual requirement that they show materiality, reliance, causation, and damage (see §29.3).

The question of standing for the combatants — the bidder and the target — has been more difficult. Courts have been ambivalent about standing for bidders and targets because the combatants' interests will often be at odds with shareholder interests. Nonetheless, courts have accepted standing for bidders and targets to the extent they represent shareholder interests.

§39.3.2 Damages

Lower courts, buttressed by approving Supreme Court dictum, have awarded damages to shareholders injured by Williams Act violations. See *Osofsky v. Zipf*, 645 F.2d 107 (2d Cir. 1981) (approving shareholder recovery under a benefit-of-the-bargain theory). The Supreme Court, however, has held that a frustrated bidder cannot sue under §14(e) for damages arising from fraudulent statements made by the target in opposing the bidder's tender offer. *Piper v. Chris-Craft Industries, Inc.*, 430 U.S. 1 (1977).

§39.3.3 Injunctive Relief

The Supreme Court has held that a target cannot sue to disenfranchise a bidder unless the traditional showing for injunctive relief — irreparable injury — has been made. *Rondeau v. Mosinee Paper Corp.*, 422 U.S. 49 (1975).

Some lower courts have denied standing to targets seeking to disenfranchise bidders or to force them to divest their holdings. Most lower courts, however, have allowed bidders and targets to seek less burdensome relief, such as corrective disclosure and interim standstill injunctions.

§39.3.4 *The Williams Act's Effect on Takeovers*

Despite the protestations of the Williams Act drafters that the legislation was meant to be neutral, assuring protection of shareholders without favoring management or bidders in a takeover fight, some commentators have criticized the Act as having a pro-target bias. In fact, studies indicate that in the years immediately after the Act was passed in 1968, takeover premiums increased from 32 percent to 53 percent, while the frequency of takeovers declined. By imposing disclosure and timing impediments on bidders, without limiting the defensive arsenal of the target, some have argued that the Act actually tilts the playing field in favor of the target. During the mandated pendency of a tender offer, management has the opportunity to mount a defense whose substantive terms are not within the purview of the Williams Act's antifraud prohibitions.

EXAMPLES

1. Raider Partners is an investment firm engaged in the leveraged buyout of companies. Its dominant partner, Ernest Krass, has identified a takeover possibility: Target Industries, Inc., a consumer products manufacturer with a pattern of strong cash flows, widely respected brand names, and a low debt-equity ratio. Target has one class of common stock, which is traded on the New York Stock Exchange. No shareholder holds more than 5 percent of its stock, which has been trading in the range of $40-45 per share.

   a. Raider develops a takeover strategy and, without disclosing its takeover purpose, begins making purchases of Target stock on the NYSE surreptitiously through a number of brokers. Krass acknowledges privately that if Target shareholders were to know of Raider's plans it is unlikely any would be willing to sell at prevailing prices. Is Raider under an obligation to disclose these purchases?

   b. After acquiring 4.9 percent of Target, Krass decides to test the waters for a $65 takeover. He asks First Phillie (FP), a leading investment banking firm, whether FP would be willing to sell into a $65 tender offer for Target. FP's arbitrage department has been following Target with great interest and already holds 2 percent of its stock. FP says that $65 would be acceptable and FP probably would sell. Does Raider have to report this contact?

2. By the time the §13(d) ten-day window closes, Raider acquires 11 percent of Target. It discloses in its Schedule 13D that "Raider is considering its options, including gaining control of Target." Soon after this, trading in Target stock increases dramatically and the price rises to $55. Arbitragers soon hold most of Target's stock.

Krass has a plan for pushing Raider's holdings above 50 percent: (1) First Phillie (acting as broker for Raider) will have its reps call 30-40 arbs and institutional investors to ask whether they would be willing to sell privately; (2) the reps will call on a Friday afternoon at 2:00 P.M. without revealing for whom they are calling, saying only that they are soliciting others in the same way; and (3) the reps will ask each investor to sell at $60 per share and will require an answer by 5:00 P.M., after the NYSE closes. Is this market sweep legal?

3. Krass decides against a market sweep and instead considers a tender offer. He outlines his tender offer proposal and asks you to point out any problems with each of its following elements:

a. Any shareholder will be allowed to tender, although Raider will buy only 75 percent of Target's stock (bringing its total holdings to 86 percent).

b. The offer will be open on a first-tendered, first-purchased basis until the 75 percent threshold is reached.

c. Consideration will be $65 cash or $70 in subordinated notes of Target, at the option of each tendering shareholder, provided that no more than 50 percent of those tendering choose cash.

d. The offer will be open for 20 business days, and tendering shareholders can withdraw their shares during the first 7 business days after the offer.

e. Raider announces in its Schedule 14D-1 that the offer will be followed by a back-end squeeze-out merger (see §26.3) in which the remaining shares will be acquired for $65 in subordinated notes of Target — less than the consideration being offered shareholders in the tender offer.

f. Raider will disclose its plans in Schedule 14D-1 as follows: "If the offeror succeeds in gaining control of Target, it will study Target's business operations and prospects and after such examination may implement an alternative plan of operations."

g. Raider will disclose in Schedule 14D-1 that both during and after the tender offer it may purchase shares on the open market at prevailing prices.

h. Raider will not buy any shares pursuant to the tender offer unless Target's board redeems its poison pill and Raider is able to obtain a commitment to sell junk bonds to finance the deal.

4. Raider makes a properly structured $65 tender offer for 40 percent of Target's stock. Target's management thinks that the price is too low and

that Raider is merely trying to coerce Target to buy out Raider's interest at a premium (greenmail). Management proposes a restructuring in which the corporation will take on new debt and repurchase 50 percent of its shares for $75 cash per share. To frustrate Raider's greenmail plans, the issuer self-tender excludes Raider from tendering.

    a. Raider wants to have the issuer self-tender enjoined for violating the federal tender offer rules. Does the exclusionary tender offer violate the rules?

    b. Does Raider have standing to challenge the self-tender as a violation of the rules?

EXPLANATIONS

    1a. No, as long as Raider's holdings do not exceed 5 percent of Target's common stock. The Williams Act requires disclosure of open-market purchases only when a person (or group) acquires beneficial ownership of more than 5 percent of a class of registered equity securities. 1934 Act §13 (d). Further, no disclosure is required under Rule 10b-5 because Raider has no fiduciary relationship with Target or its shareholders and developed its purchase plan on its own (see §29.5.1).

    1b. Perhaps. If Raider and FP are members of a group for purposes of §13(d), their holdings must be aggregated to determine whether the 5 percent threshold is exceeded. Courts have interpreted §13(d) to contemplate the existence of a group without any of its members making any additional stock purchases. If Raider and FP agreed to hold, acquire, or dispose of their Target stock for purposes of affecting control in Target, §13(d) requires that they report their identity, their holdings, their intentions, and their arrangement within ten days after their agreement. Was FP's statement that FP probably would sell at $65 such an agreement? On the one hand, it could be argued that FP did not commit to sell to Raider or to otherwise further Raider's takeover plans — there had been no agreement to affect control. On the other hand, FP's implicit commitment to sell its 2 percent into a $65 tender offer meant that, effectively, Krass could count on acquiring a total of 6.9 percent of Target's stock — the 5 percent trigger had been reached and Target shareholders are entitled to information about the possibility of a takeover. Much would depend on how firm FP's commitment to sell was.

    2. Perhaps not. If it is a tender offer, it violates a number of the federal tender offer requirements — namely, the filing of a Schedule 14D-1, an open period of at least 20 business days, withdrawal rights for tendering shareholders, and equal treatment of all shareholders.

        At first blush, the plan seems to be an unorthodox tender offer. It contemplates coercing precisely the kind of "stampede mentality" that led to the enactment of §14(d). The plan's attractiveness is that it coerces the professional investor-solicitees into selling quickly, without detailed information about the bid or about who is making it. The plan anticipates that they will be put in the position of believing they must sell or lose any opportunity for a control premium. Further, the solicitees will not have the benefit of a 20-day period to evaluate the company, Raider's offer, and management's response. A very similar open-market pressure tactic was held to be a tender offer. See *Wellman v. Dickinson*, 475 F. Supp. 783 (S.D.N.Y. 1979).

More recent cases, however, suggest a different result. If sophisticated professional investors did not actually feel pressured to sell (for example, because they had evaluated Target and believed the price would remain high even if Raider succeeded in buying a significant bloc), some recent cases suggest that Krass's plan would not be a tender offer. Applying the manipulable eight-factor test also might lead to a conclusion that there was no tender offer: (1) There was no public solicitation; (2) there was no premium over market; (3) the offer was not contingent on a specified tender; and (4) the sophisticated offerees may not have been subjected to significant pressure. In the end, the answer turns on how a court views whether consenting, sophisticated investors need the protection of the tender offer rules and whether the orthodoxy (and egalitarian philosophy) of a regulated tender offer should be imposed on all hostile takeovers.

3a. No problem. Partial tender offers are possible under the tender offer rules. The All Holders Rule requires only that the tender offer be to all shareholders. If the offer is oversubscribed, the pro rata rules require that the bidder buy from each shareholder in proportion to the ratio of the number of shares sought and the number of shares tendered.

3b. Problem. The Pro Rata Rules specify how shares are to be purchased if the tender offer is oversubscribed. Buying shares on a first-come, first-served basis pressures shareholders to make ill-considered, rushed decisions, which is the main evil addressed by the tender offer rules. Although the open withdrawal rights provided for by the SEC rules largely ameliorate the problem of a first-come, first-served tender offer, the statute nonetheless requires pro rata purchases.

3c. No problem. The bidder can offer alternative forms of consideration and condition the tender offer in any way that does not violate the tender offer rules.

3d. Problem. Although the statute contemplates that shareholders may withdraw tendered shares (in the normal case) only for the first 7 business days of the offer, SEC rules expand withdrawal rights through the entire period the offer is open. To prevent fraudulent, deceptive, or manipulative tender offers, the SEC has required that the tendering period be at least 20 business days. 1934 Act rule 14e-1.

3e. No problem. There is no requirement that all the shares be acquired pursuant to a tender offer. In fact, there will always be some shareholders who fail to tender into even the most generous tender offer because of stubbornness, lack of initiative, loyalty to management, or ignorance. If Raider acquires control (usually a condition of the tender offer) and wants 100 percent ownership (particularly if it contemplates self-dealing transactions to pay off the takeover debt), it can accomplish this in a back-end merger. As far as the federal tender offer rules are concerned, nontendered shares (as well as shares returned if the partial tender offer is oversubscribed) can be squeezed out in a merger for whatever consideration Raider decides to pay — as long as there is disclosure. The Best Price Rule does not apply to the merger, nor does §14(e) require that the price or other terms of the merger be fair, as long as nothing false or misleading is said about the merger during the tender offer. The only significant constraints on Raider are the state fiduciary rules applicable to controlling shareholders in a squeeze-out merger.

3f. No problem. If this is true and not misleading, the tender offer rules do not require the bidder to have full plans in place. In fact, recent courts have held that it is not even necessary for the bidder to have its financing for the offer lined up when it commences a tender offer, as long as this is disclosed.

3g. Problem. Third-party bidders are prohibited from making purchases during the tender offer. Rule 13d-10. This keeps a bidder from starting a low-priced tender offer that artificially depresses the stock price and then buying at the manipulated price. Currently, third-party purchases are not prohibited after the tender offer ends. Unlike issuers that are subject to a 10-day cooling-off period after a self-tender, third-party bidders are required to disclose the possibility of such purchases only if they are material to shareholders deciding to tender.

4a. Technically, yes. The All Holders Rule requires that every tender offer (including a self-tender) be made to all shareholders (Rule 14d-10 (a) (1)), and Target's is not. The SEC has justified the rule on two grounds. First, it comports with the equal treatment philosophy of §14(d), a philosophy based on the assumption that equality means fairness. Second, without the rule, bidders could pressure the excluded group to sell to the included group while avoiding the disclosure and substantive requirements of the tender offer rules. Excluded shareholders wishing to participate indirectly in the premium would not receive disclosure, would sell on a first-come, first-served basis and would have no withdrawal rights. These justifications for the rule, however, may not be as persuasive when the excluded shareholder group (Raider) is a bidder. The All Holders Rule effectively undercuts Target's ability to respond to a perceived greenmailer with a self-tender. The rule would allow Raider to extract a premium at the expense of tendering shareholders, who would be forced to share their premium under the Pro Rata Rules. Although excluding Raider may pressure it to give up the fight and sell to included shareholders, the Williams Act's pro-shareholder philosophy may not be concerned by the bidder's plight. Furthermore, the All Holders Rule may tilt the playing field against issuers by denying them the exclusionary self-tender strategem.

4b. Perhaps not. Raider's exclusion benefits tendering shareholders, who need not share their self-tender premium with Raider. Because only Raider is excluded, it can be argued that Raider's challenge would not further the shareholder-protection purpose of the Williams Act. In *Piper v. Chris-Craft* (see §39.3.2), the Supreme Court held that a bidder could not recover damages for a violation of the tender offer rules. In the case, recovery to the bidder would have come at the expense of shareholders who allegedly had been deceived. Nonetheless, Raider might assert standing in its capacity as a shareholder. Denying Raider standing would effectively keep it from recouping a part of its bidding expenses by the sale of its shares at a premium, thus removing one of the important cushions that soften the financial risk of launching a takeover bid. As a result, shareholders in general would be hurt if takeover bids were to become more expensive — a tilting of the playing field against bidders that the Williams Act regime is supposed to avoid.

40

Takeover Defenses

More than any other regulating device, a hostile takeover exposes management to shareholder control. Not surprisingly, managers of public corporations have invoked a number of protections to blunt the force of the freewheeling market in corporate control: disclosure and timing constraints imposed under the Williams Act, firm-specific takeover defenses, and state antitakeover legislation.

As we have seen, the Williams Act offers at most porous protection, requiring of the bidder only full disclosure and some patience (see Chapter 39). The real protections lie in firm-specific takeover defenses and generic state antitakeover statutes. These protections are the subject of this chapter.

§40.1 The Dilemma of Takeover Defenses — The Proper Role of the Target's Board

Management of the corporation and control of the corporation's governance machinery reside with the board of directors. The propriety of takeover defenses thus turns on how one views the proper role for a board of directors whose shareholders are presented with a tender offer that management opposes. Simply put, should the board be passive and not interfere or should it be active and resist?

§40.1.1 The Passive/Active Debate

Strong arguments can be made on both sides of the passive/active debate.

The Passivity Thesis. A hostile bidder premises its bid on ousting incumbent management if the bid succeeds. Thus hovers the omnipresent specter of a conflict of interest: Shareholders will want to receive premium offers, while incumbent management will have an ineluctable self-interest in opposing hostile bids. The predictable motive of management to perpetuate the lucre, power, and prestige of control — the entrenchment motive — suggests that the target board should not be allowed to use corporate resources to interpose obstacles. Empirical data indicates that targets that successfully repulse hostile bids do not recoup the bid's forgone value for their shareholders; target managers overestimate how good a job they can do. Although some defensive tactics are not preclusive and may extract stronger bids, the prospect of their use will dissuade many bidders from bidding at all and will crimp the disciplining effects of a robust market in corporate control. The board should be passive.

The Activist Thesis.   Despite the potential for conflicts of interest, the board is in a unique position to use the corporate governance machinery and assets to represent shareholder (and nonshareholder) interests. That is, the board can negotiate on behalf of dispersed public shareholders and represent otherwise voiceless nonshareholder constituents. Without a bargaining agent, shareholders may be pressured into accepting a first, inadequate, ill-timed, or coercive bid. Without the ability to act in the best interests of all corporate participants, the board cannot fulfill its mediative role. Measured defensive tactics can drive away weak or destructive bids, induce better bids, buy time to find other bidders or company-sponsored alternatives (such as restructuring and stock repurchases), or otherwise assure fair treatment of corporate constituents. Empirical studies suggest that compared to a passive board, a bashful board — one that resists at first but eventually allows the takeover — increases shareholder gains. Moreover, the board can protect nonshareholder constituents — such as creditors, employees, customers, and communities — against bidders that may have no regard for them. The board should be active.

§40.1.2   *The Independence of Outside Directors*

The passive/active debate turns in large measure on how we view the relationship of management and the board. The passivity thesis assumes that the directors' interests — whether because the directors also fear losing their positions or because of a built-in bias for management — will be closely aligned with management interests. The activist thesis assumes a more independent board, an assumption that has some plausibility. The boards of public corporations often are composed of a majority of nonmanagement outside directors whose financial stake in the company is relatively small. In recent cases, these outside directors have sometimes shown remarkable independence. A good example is the $25 billion takeover of RJR Nabisco, in which outside directors chose a third-party bid over a "substantially equiv-alent" management bid.

§40.1.3   The Board's Duties to Other Constituents

The passive/active dilemma also turns on whether we think the board should have social responsibilities to constituents other than shareholders. If we conclude that the board's perspective in a takeover should be limited to shareholder wealth maximization, a passivity thesis makes sense. But if we conclude that the board should (and would) consider a takeover's effect on nonshareholder constituents — such as employees, creditors, suppliers, cus-tomers, and communities — an activist role becomes appropriate.

Recent state statutes attempt to resolve this question by authorizing the board to take into account nonshareholder constituencies in a takeover, as well as other corporate contexts. Pennsylvania's statute is typical:

> In discharging [their] duties, directors of a business corporation may . . . consider . . . the effects of any action upon . . . shareholders, employees, suppliers, customers and creditors of the corporation, and upon communities in which offices or other establishments of the corporation are located.

See Pa. BCL §1715. These so-called constituency statutes are intended to insulate the board's decision to defend actively against unwanted takeover bids. It is significant that Delaware does not have such a statute.

Although to date none of the constituency statutes has ever been tested in court, some commentators view them as a fundamental shift in the U.S. corporate paradigm of shareholder wealth maximization. These commenta-tors have argued that the statutes should be read to permit nonshareholder constituents to enforce their extracontractual expectations in court, and others have argued that courts should reject (and in fact increasingly have rejected) the notion of shareholder primacy. Other commentators see the statutes as doing no more than restating current law, which permits the board to take into account nonshareholder constituencies if shareholder interests are not adversely affected. Yet other commentators view the statutes as a cynical attempt by management to justify their entrenchment.

§40.2   State Fiduciary Law — An Evolving Response to the Takeover Dilemma

State law determines the propriety of takeover defenses. The Supreme Court has made clear that current federal securities law requires only disclosure, not management fairness to shareholders (see §39.2.4). Under state law, takeover defenses raise two issues: (1) Does the board have the *power* to adopt the defense? (2) More important, can the board adopt the defense without violating its *fiduciary duties* to the corporation and the shareholders? Analysis of the first issue is sometimes interesting, but usually pedestrian; we discuss it at §40.3.

The important question is how corporate fiduciary law resolves the takeover dilemma. The answer: rather clumsily. The traditional fiduciary model is dichotomous and points in opposite directions. On the one hand, defensive tactics involve an inherent conflict of interest; traditional loyalty-fairness standards would subject them to strict scrutiny (see Chapter 22). On the other hand, defensive tactics offer potentially unique value, and the board is in a unique position to act on behalf of dispersed shareholders and other constituents; traditional care-business judgment rule standards would subject them to deferential review (see Chapter 21). It should not surprise you that judicial responses to the takeover dilemma have been contradictory.

§40.2.1 The Original Approach — The Dominant-Motive Test

Courts initially dealt with the takeover dilemma by a judicial sleight of hand. To ascertain whether an entrenchment motive lurked behind a takeover defense, courts adopted a process-oriented standard. The courts accepted defensive actions if the incumbent board could point to a "reasonable investigation" (preferably by outside directors) into a plausible business purpose for the defense — thus showing the *absence* of an entrenchment motive. The challenger then had the difficult task to prove that the dominant motive for the board's action was entrenchment.

Using the dominant-motive analysis, courts readily accepted almost any business justification for defensive tactics. All the target board needed to do was identify a policy dispute between the bidder and management. In the case credited with originating the dominant-motive analysis, *Cheff v. Mathes,* 199 A.2d 548 (Del. 1964), the target board paid greenmail to an acquirer who had threatened to take control and do away with the company's anachronistic direct-sales marketing. The court upheld the defense because the board had investigated the threat that the acquirer posed to "the corporation in its current form" and because the buyout premium paid to the acquirer reflected a reasonable price for a control block. In *Panter v. Marshall Field & Co.,* 646 F.2d 271 (7th Cir.), *cert. denied,* 454 U.S. 1092 (1981), the dominant-motive test reached its zenith. In the case, the target board embarked on an acquisition program and filed an antitrust lawsuit to drive away a bidder that had offered shareholders a 75 percent premium over market. The court noted with favor that seven of the ten-member board were outside directors and accepted the board's justification to "build value within the company" and to protect against a merger whose antitrust problems were the board's own doing. In other words, a thinly disguised policy of entrenchment could be used to justify almost any defensive tactics.

The dominant-motive analysis met a storm of academic criticism during the early 1980s. Commentators decried the sophistry of the analysis and the misuse of the business judgment rule in the takeover context. Given the unavoidable conflicts of interest and the board's structural bias for management, the effect of the traditional analysis was virtually to remove takeover defenses from fiduciary review. It left shareholders at the board's mercy and insulated entrenched management from the discipline of the market in corporate control.

§40.2.2 An Intermediate Procedural Approach — Heightened Duty of Care

One judicial response to the dominant-motive test has been to impose heightened standards of deliberative care in takeover fights. Requiring directors to probe into the business and financial justifications for takeover defenses — thus putting teeth in the *reasonable* investigation standard — dissipates the misplaced protection extended by the business judgment presumption.

In *Hanson Trust PLC v. ML SCM Acquisition, Inc.*, 781 F.2d 264 (2d Cir. 1986), the Second Circuit applied New York law to invalidate two "crown jewel" lockup options conceded to a management LBO group by the target board during the final stages of a heated takeover fight. The options, which allowed the management group to buy two of the company's prime divisions at deep 20 percent to 30 percent discounts if any other bidder acquired a control block, ended the bidding contest. The court concluded that the outside directors' deliberations on whether to grant the options revealed a predisposition toward management. The directors had failed to ask whether the lockup prices were fair, whether the management bid was in fact superior to the hostile bid, or how exercising the options would affect the company.

The heightened due care standard has led target directors, on the advice of their lawyers, to carefully orchestrate the appearance of procedural integrity. A common technique has been for the board to form a special takeover committee, composed of outside directors with no business affiliations to the target. The committee hires its own investment banker, meets at length to carefully review documents and listen to advice, and sometimes sets up procedures for negotiating with management and other bidders. Throughout, the directors rely heavily on the orchestra conductor — the committee's lawyer.

§40.2.3   *An Intermediate Substantive Approach — Proportionality*

Another judicial response to the takeover dilemma has been to adopt inter-mediate *substantive* standards — between intrinsic fairness and rational basis. The Delaware Supreme Court formulated the most important test in *Unocal Corp. v. Mesa Petroleum Co.*, 493 A.2d 946 (Del. 1985). Under the two-prong *Unocal* test (1) the board must reasonably perceive the bidder's action as a threat to corporate policy — a threshold dominant-purpose inquiry into the board's investigation, and (2) any defensive measure the board adopts "must be reasonable in relation to the threat posed" — a proportionality test. If the defensive reaction fails either prong, the court assumes that management entrenchment motivated the defensive tactic.

During the last decade the Delaware courts have defined the contours of the *Unocal* test. First, the test eliminates the presumption that defensive tactics are *not* motivated by entrenchment. Instead, the Delaware courts have assumed a skeptical agnosticism in the active/passive debate. For example, directors who advance their own interests by preferring a management bid that insulates directors from liability cannot claim a mantle of propriety. Yet the courts have upheld defensive tactics if the board articulates reasons tied to shareholder welfare.

Second, the courts say the paramount concern is shareholder welfare. No longer is it sufficient for directors to argue that "protecting the enterprise" justifies any defensive tactic. Interests of creditors, employees, and other constituents are relevant only if they coincide with maximizing shareholder interests.

Third, the "threat" justifying the target's reaction is a malleable concept, encompassing anything inconsistent with shareholder welfare. The board may react to a bid whose structure is coercive, or to noncoercive bids that it considers to be underpriced, or to a bidder who proposes to bust up the business if the bust-up possibility threatens shareholder welfare.

Fourth, any reaction must be proportional to the threat, with propor-tionality judged from an objective standpoint. Preemptive actions taken in anticipation of yet unknown takeover threats may be more sweeping than reactions to an identified threat during a bidding contest; defenses to a coercive front-end loaded bid may be stronger than reactions to a noncoercive any-and-all bid; and responses to a noncoercive fair bid should be neutral, at most offering shareholders a genuine alternative or carrying forward pre-existing plans.

Finally, the board has a duty to seek the "best value" for share-holders, which may include the duty to auction the company to multiple bidders, when a transaction will result in a change of control or a break-up of the company. During an auction the board cannot prefer one bidder over another, except to extract significantly better bids. The board must be informed and must act impartially to maximize shareholder value when the board considers a bid's fairness, feasibility, financing, legality, and risks, as well as the bidder's reputation and proposed business plans for the company.

Unocal and its progeny illustrate these five points.

Unocal Corp. v. Mesa Petroleum Co., 493 A.2d 946 (Del. 1985). The court announced its heightened proportionality test but applied it to uphold Unocal's decisive and brilliant defense against T. Boone Pickens of Mesa Petroleum. The Unocal board responded to a Pickens front-end loaded 42 percent tender offer with its own self-tender (a debt-for-equity restructuring) that excluded Mesa from participating. Applying its new two-step test, the court held that the board (composed of a majority of outside directors) had sufficiently investigated the coercive nature of the Pickens bid by consulting with outside investment bankers and lawyers. The court viewed the exclusionary aspect of the self-tender as justified to dissuade greenmail and to proportionally increase share value for the remaining shareholders.

Moran v. Household International, Inc., 500 A.2d 1346 (Del. 1985). The court upheld a poison pill rights plan approved in advance of a specific takeover bid. Such plans have become a favorite among defense tactics, with over a majority of large public companies adopting them by the end of the 1980s. Poison pills are designed to compel a bidder to negotiate with the board and ostensibly to assure shareholders and other corporate constituents fair treatment. Their operation is convoluted, resembling a corporate Rube Goldberg device.

How does a poison pill rights plan work? Under the *Household* plan (a prototype for later plans), the board issued one right for each common share outstanding. As issued, the rights were essentially worthless, entitling a shareholder to buy preferred stock at prices far in excess of current market value — that is, stock "out of the money." The real impact of the rights arose if any acquirer bought 20 percent or more (or made a tender offer for 30 percent or more) of the company's shares. After this first trigger, the board would have ten days to redeem the rights for a nominal amount. If the target failed to take this antidote, the rights became poison and the acquirer would be in great peril. Any back-end transaction with tainted acquirer, such as a merger or sale of assets, activated a second trigger in which the target would swallow the plan's poison. What is the poison? Each right would become exercisable and its holder would be able to purchase $200 worth of the acquirer's or the target's securities (depending on the structure of the back-end transaction) for $100. (A flip-in plan entitles the holder to buy discounted *target* securities and sensibly excludes the tainted acquirer from participating; a "flip-over" plan entitles the holder to buy discounted *acquirer* securities.) The Household board hoped this potential dilution would force any potential bidder to negotiate with the board, which held the redemption antidotes, before beginning a hostile takeover.

The *Household* court held that in adopting the plan, the board was properly concerned with the coercive nature of potential front-end loaded tender offers and of the effect that the threat of a bust-up takeover has on company morale. The poison pill plan, the court summarily concluded, was a reasonable response to these threats because it established the board's preeminent negotiating position. The court left for another day the question of how the board could use this ingenious tool in the midst of a takeover battle.

After *Household* the Chancery Court held that the board may have a fiduciary duty under *Unocal* to redeem poison pill rights in the face of a noncoercive, any-and-all cash tender offer. *City Capital Associates v. Interco,* 551 A.2d 787 (Del. Ch. 1988). The Delaware Supreme Court later rejected these lower-court decisions and held that the board has significant discretion to decide whether a bid poses a "threat to corporate policy and effectiveness." *Paramount Communications, Inc. v. Time Inc.,* 571 A.2d 1140 (Del. 1990).

Revlon v. MacAndrews & Forbes Holdings, 506 A.2d 173 (Del. 1986). The court invalidated an asset lockup option conceded by Revlon's board to Forstmann Little, a white knight bidder. The board had granted the option to Forstmann to induce it to submit a higher bid in response to a hostile takeover bid by Pantry Pride. The option, which effectively killed a bidding contest for Revlon, would have allowed Forstmann to acquire two of Revlon's most desirable divisions at significant discounts from their appraised value if another bidder acquired more than 40 percent of Revlon's shares.

The board defended its preference for Forstmann because Pantry Pride proposed a bust-up takeover and the lockups were necessary to induce a higher Forstmann bid. The *Revlon* court did not focus on the board's deliberations concerning this perceived threat, but rather on the reasonableness of the lockup response. Although the court said that a board could seek to frustrate a bust-up takeover, it held the board must assume the role of an auctioneer once such a takeover becomes inevitable. The board failed in this duty because the lockup option to Forstmann effectively ended the auction for "very little actual improvement in the final bid."

The *Revlon* court was also concerned that the directors were co-opted when Forstmann promised to support the market price of notes that the board had issued during an earlier stage of the takeover fight. Noteholders angry about the falling price of their notes had threatened to sue the directors, and the Forstmann bid provided a convenient way for the directors to extricate themselves from their troubles. The court held that the board could not prefer the noteholders, whose rights were fixed by contract, at the expense of shareholders.

Ivanhoe Partners v. Newmont Mining Corp., 535 A.2d 1334 (Del. 1987). The court began to reverse direction, upholding an entrenching standstill defense on the ground that it assured the target's "independence." Newmont's management was caught between two threats. Ivanhoe Partners, a T. Boone Pickens outfit, had bid for 42 percent of Newmont's stock but had not made a *firm* commitment with respect to the remaining shares — a potentially coercive front-end loaded offer. Newmont's management also feared the company's largest shareholder, Gold Fields, whose standstill agreement with Newmont had terminated when Pickens's holdings exceeded 9.9 percent. Newmont's board steered between the dual threat by (1) declaring a special $33 per share dividend to finance a Gold Fields street sweep that brought its holdings to 49.7 percent, and (2) entering into a revised ten-year standstill agreement that limited Gold Field's board membership to 40 percent.

The court accepted the Newmont response in a surprising way: "[T]he Newmont board acted to maintain the company's independence and not merely to preserve its own control." Taken literally, the court's analysis seems to return to the heyday of the dominant-motive test, in which entrenchment masked as independence can justify any defensive reaction. Nonetheless, two factors temper this reading of the case. First, the court seemed impressed that Gold Fields had been pleased with Newmont management — the corporation's "independence" did not entrench an inefficient management. Second, the defense defeated a coercive Pickens bid and prevented a potentially unfair back-end Gold Fields transaction.

Mills Acquisition Co. v. Macmillan, Inc., 599 A.2d 261 (Del. 1989). The court invalidated a lockup agreement, granted during a purported auction of the target, to an LBO group led by Kohlberg, Kravis & Roberts (KKR) in which management had a 20 percent ownership stake. The court held that when management has an interest in a bid and oversight by outside directors is lacking, the auction process must withstand rigorous scrutiny under the "intrinsic fairness" loyalty standard. The auction failed to meet this high standard: It had been conducted by management's hand-picked financial advisor (Wasserstein, Perella & Co.); Wasserstein rejected out-of-hand a substantially increased bid by the third-party bidder (Robert Maxwell); and Wasserstein refused to negotiate with Maxwell; Wasserstein imposed unnecessarily short bidding deadlines and deliberately misled Maxwell. The court pointed out that nothing justified this hostility toward Maxwell, who had shown a willingness to operate the company as a going concern. The unfairness of the auction process was further compounded by a series of improper tips to KKR from both Wasserstein and the target's CEO. The tips revealed the price and structure of Maxwell's first bid and suggested how KKR should improve its final bid. The court held that the board could not rely on Wasserstein's advice that KKR's bid justified conceding it a lockup agreement.

Paramount Communications, Inc. v. Time Inc., 571 A.2d 1140 (Del. 1990). The court sought to resolve when the *Revlon* auction duty is triggered and whether under *Unocal* a target can block an unsolicited (but attractive) cash bid. Many have read the court's decision as a significant retrenchment in the judicial scrutiny given takeover defenses.

In 1984 Time began exploring ways to expand from publishing and cable TV into entertainment production. Time identified Warner Communications (films, records, and Bugs Bunny) as a potential target, and in 1990 Time and Warner agreed to a stock-for-stock merger. Two weeks before the Time and Warner shareholders were to approve the merger, Paramount announced a $175 (and later a $200) cash offer for Time's shares, conditioned on the merger not happening. Convinced that the Time shareholders would turn down the merger to take Paramount's bid, Time and Warner restructured their deal so that Time would buy 51 percent of Warner's shares in a lucrative tender offer. Time would take on significant debt to finance the purchase, and Time's shareholders would be prevented both from voting on the restructured Time-Warner combination and from taking the Paramount offer.

The court rejected the argument that the Time-Warner combination constituted a change in control that triggered the *Revlon* auction duties. The court stated that *Revlon* duties are triggered generally when a target initiates an active bidding process or seeks a "breakup of the company," either unilaterally or in response to a hostile bid. Because the Time-Warner combination would not result in a breakup and ownership would remain with public shareholders, no change of control occurred. Curiously, the court did not tie an auction duty to whether management was interested in the bidding, as had been the case in *Revlon* and *Macmillan*.

The court also held that Time's outside directors could decide, without violating *Unocal*'s proportionality standard, to restructure the Time-Warner combination to prevent shareholders from voting on it. The court accepted the directors' findings that Paramount's offer was inadequate and that Time shareholders might have been ignorant about the strategic benefit of combining with Warner or confused by the timing of the Paramount bid. These "threats" justified the board's taking the decision away from the shareholders. The court noted that in any event the combination was not final: Paramount or another bidder could still bid for the $30 billion combined entity.

Paramount Communications Inc. v. QVC Network Inc., — A.2d — (Del. 1994). After a hiatus, the Delaware Supreme Court revisited the question of the board's duties in a takeover and outlined an invigorated judicial approach to takeover defenses in control transactions.

In the case, Paramount found itself in much the same position that Time had four years earlier. After its unsuccessful bid for Time, Paramount had continued looking for other media/communications companies and in mid-

1993 began serious discussion with Viacom, whose cable-TV systems and channels (MTV, Nickelodeon, and Showtime) offered a natural outlet for Paramount's entertainment holdings. In September the two companies agreed to a merger in which Paramount shareholders would receive a combination of cash and Viacom stock — worth about $69 per share. To facilitate and sweeten the deal, the Paramount board amended the company's poison pill to permit the merger with Viacom and granted Viacom a stock lockup, a termination fee, and a no-shop promise.

Within days of the merger announcement, QVC (a company with a TV-cable home-shopping network) proposed a competing two-step bid consisting of an $80 cash tender offer for 51 percent of Paramount's shares and a second-step merger with like-valued QVC stock. QVC conditioned the tender offer on invalidation of the stock lockup (which by then had become worth $200 million).

Viacom countered by raising its offering price to $85 per share, and QVC responded with a $90 bid. Showing remarkable disdain for the QVC interest, the Paramount board refused to modify the preferences for Viacom on the assumption that the QVC offer was "illusory."

QVC challenged the board's inaction as a breach of fiduciary duty. On review, the Delaware court pointed out that in a control change "the fluid aggregation of unaffiliated shareholders" sell their voting control to a single buyer and give up forever their voting leverage. The court held that in such circumstances the board has a duty to evaluate the alternatives and seek "the best value reasonably available" for the public shareholders' control premium. This evaluation, the court stated, is subject to enhanced judicial scrutiny both of the decision-making process and of the "reasonableness" of the board's actions. Seeking to clarify *Revlon* and *Time-Warner,* the court said the duty to seek "best value" — the *Revlon* duty — arises not only when the company initiates a bidding process or when its break-up is inevitable, but also when there will be a change in control.

Applying this heightened standard of review, the court then had little difficulty in concluding that the Paramount board had failed miserably in fulfilling its "best value" duties. The court faulted both the process and the substance of the board's actions: the board's approval of the potentially "draconian" provision of the Viacom stock lockup, its reluctance to modify the takeover defenses and negotiate with QVC, its uninformed belief that the QVC bid was "illusory," and its stubborn commitment to a strategic alliance with Viacom.

In response to this decision, the Paramount board conducted an open auction for the company that Viacom eventually won when 90 percent of the Paramount shareholders tendered their shares to Viacom. Viacom's winning bid consisted of $107 in cash for 50.1 percent of the stock; in a second-step merger shareholders received Viacom stock guaranteed to reach a specified price level within three years of the merger.

§40.2.4   A Fairness Review — Ascribing Interest to Outside Directors

Some courts have chosen a loyalty, instead of a modified care analysis, in the takeover context. Rather than impose a heightened due care duty or proportionality requirement, these courts have readily imputed entrenchment motives to outside directors, thus triggering a fairness review. In *Edelman v. Fruehauf, Inc.*, 798 F.2d 882 (6th Cir. 1986), the Sixth Circuit applied Michigan law to invalidate a management leveraged buyout approved by a committee of outside directors. The court viewed a no-shop provision and concessions to the buyout group as evidencing a preference for management. It treated the outside directors "as interested parties" and reviewed the committee's failure to conduct equal-access "open bidding" under a loyalty fairness standard. The committee's actions failed this demanding review, even though the committee had negotiated a substantial increase in the buyout price, from $44 to $48.50.

In *Dynamics Corp. of America v. CTS Corp.*, 794 F.2d 250 (7th Cir. 1986), the Seventh Circuit applied Judge Posner's version of Delaware law to invalidate an exclusionary poison pill intended to drive away a partial tender offer that the target board (composed of a majority of outside directors) considered inadequate. Judge Posner stated that management's inherent conflict of interest is not cured by using outside directors:

> [N]o one likes to be fired; whether he is just a director or also an officer. The so-called outsiders moreover are often friends of the insiders. And since they spend only part of their time on the affairs of the corporation, their knowledge of those affairs is much less than that of the insiders, to whom they are likely therefore to defer.

Posner dissected the poison pill, which entitled the target's shareholders to buy a package of common stock and debentures at a 75 percent discount upon any hostile 15 percent acquisition. Posner doubted that the bid was really inadequate and, even if low, that the pill's dilutive effect on the bidder and risk to the company's solvency were worth the additional consideration to shareholders. He also concluded the pill was premature and too costly a reaction to the risk of a disadvantageous back-end transaction.

Under a loyalty analysis virtually every takeover defense becomes suspect. The intrusive fairness test would require the board to show the defense would clearly maximize shareholders' gains, such as by offering shareholders a fair (not just competitive) price, by creating an open auction, or by establishing a mechanism that the shareholders would likely have chosen collectively themselves.

§40.3 The Board's Power — A Mild Revival of the Ultra Vires Doctrine

In most instances the power of the board to adopt a takeover defense is not an issue. The usual defensive tools — such as issuing stock, selling assets, repurchasing stock, or compensating management — unquestionably are all within the board's powers. But if the articles of incorporation limit such action or the capital structure is manipulated in novel ways, some early courts used the *ultra vires doctrine* (see §4.2) to limit the board's power to defend.

In response to early poison pill plans, federal courts interpreted state law to invalidate poison pills for violating the statutory requirement that all shares of a class have equal rights. (Flip-in poison pills, to ensure their dilutive effect, deny the hostile acquirer the right to buy stock at a discount after a back-end transaction.) See *Asarco, Inc. v. Court,* 611 F. Supp. 468 (D.N.J. 1985) (applying New Jersey law); *Minstar Acquiring Corp. v. AMF, Inc.,* 644 F. Supp. 1252 (S.D.N.Y. 1985). Soon after, state legislatures specifically authorized exclusionary poison pill plans. N.J. BCA §14D:7-7(3); N.Y. BCL §4603(a)(2).

EXAMPLES

1. Raider Partners, a takeover firm with an investment pool for buying companies, has identified a takeover possibility: Target Industries, a Delaware corporation. Raider's dominant partner, Ernest Krass, calls Target's CEO, Phess Mackerel, and offers to buy Target in a negotiated transaction for $75 cash per share. Krass threatens a hostile tender offer if Target refuses. The Target board meets to consider Krass's "bear hug." There are ten directors on the board: three are management directors, two are outside directors whose firms have significant dealings with Target (a bank and law firm), and five are nonaffiliated directors (CEOs and political types).
   a. What should the board do?
   b. Can the board reject the bear hug?
   c. Must the Target board deal with Krass, such as by meeting with him or by asking for more information about his offer?
   d. Last year, Target's shareholders adopted a charter amendment authorized by Del. GCL §102(b)(7) (see §21.5.1), absolving the directors from liability unless (among other things) they fail to act in good faith. Can directors be held personally liable for rejecting Krass's $75 offer?

2. The Target board stonewalls the Krass overture. Raider then makes a cash tender offer at $80 per share for 51 percent of Target's shares. Target's investment banker, Trout Brothers, opines that the $80 price is fair but not acceptable — it could be higher.

    a. Can the board defend at all?

    b. Would your answer be different if Raider had made an any-and-all $80 cash tender offer?

    c. Could Target's board respond to a $80 any-and-all offer by adopting a poison pill?

    d. Can the board justify blocking the takeover?

3. In the meantime, CEO Mackerel and other members of Target management have been shopping the company, looking for a white knight. They have met with a number of investment firms, but only the firm of Sturgeon Manly (SM) is interested. Sturgeon Manly proposes an $85 buyout: It would finance the acquisition using some of its own cash, floating junk bonds to be repaid out of Target's cash flow, and selling some of Target's assets. Senior Target management (including the management board members) would receive 10 percent of the new company's equity; and Target would continue to be run by current management. SM says it needs an answer in two days.

    a. The board wants to accept the SM proposal. Under what standard will its decision be reviewed?

    b. What should the board do to ensure that its acceptance will be reviewed favorably in court?

    c. Target's board forms a special takeover committee, and its members consider the SM offer at a day-long meeting. Mackerel explains that management had discussed bids for Target with 15 other companies, but none (except SM) had shown an interest in bidding. Trout Brothers, Target's long-time investment banking firm, opines that SM's $85 price is fair and adequate and that SM should be able to arrange financing for its bid. If the committee accepts the SM bid, without notifying Raider, would the decision survive review?

    d. The committee contacts Krass and explains that SM has made a $85 bid. It asks Krass to submit Raider's best offer in a week, and makes the same request of SM. SM bids $93 (a package of $50 cash and new Target securities it values at $43) on the condition that Target enter into a binding merger agreement and provide SM an asset lockup. SM also promises that it will not sell more than 25 percent of Target's assets after acquiring control and not fire more than 10 percent of Target's senior management. Raider's bid is for $90, a package of $60 cash and Target securities it values at $30. Raider makes no promises on what it will do with the company. Can the committee accept the SM offer?

EXPLANATIONS

1a. The board should consider the offer, although it probably need not begin negotiations with Raider. Under *Unocal,* the board may refuse

Raider's bear hug, provided that the directors conduct a reasonable investigation and identify a threat to shareholder welfare in Krass's offer. This investigation, under the due care standards articulated in *Smith v. Van Gorkom* (see §21.3.3), should delve into the $75 price, the timing of the offer, the effect of the offer on the company, regulatory issues, Krass's intentions, Raider's financing, and the ultimate price Raider may be willing to offer.

The board should seek the advice of a lawyer who specializes in takeovers and the opinion of an investment banker concerning the fairness and adequacy of a $75 price, as well as the company's fair value. At this point, the board probably need not compose a special takeover committee, particularly because a majority of the board is composed of outside directors and because the interests of the shareholders and management are not yet clearly at odds. As a tactical matter, composing such a committee may evidence management's and the board's nervousness about the company's exposure to a takeover.

The board must also consider the company's disclosure obligations concerning this potentially material information under the federal securities laws, particularly Rule 10b-5 (see §29.2). To be safe, it should not make any public statements that would trigger a full disclosure obligation.

1b. Almost certainly. The *Unocal* test does not require board passivity. Both *Newmont Mining* and *Time-Warner* make clear that the board need not put the company into play or set up an auction in response to every takeover bid. If the directors are able to identify a material deficiency in Krass's offer, Delaware courts have permitted boards to reject such overtures as a proportional response.

The directors can reject the offer on a number of grounds: The offer does not reflect the company's fair value; it is poorly timed; it would adversely affect other corporate constituents (and indirectly diminish shareholder value), might never be consummated, and is illegal (perhaps under the antitrust laws); or a higher value could be attained in a bidding contest. A fundamental tenet of the *Unocal* test is that the board's proper role is as a negotiator. Just saying no would seem a perfectly acceptable negotiating tactic.

1c. Probably not, although it may be advisable to do so. The *Unocal* reasonable investigation obligation would seem to require that the board have some basis for concluding that a threat existed. If the board is unable to conclude that the price is unfair, a meeting with Krass might serve to provide ammunition for rejecting the offer. In addition, the board can call Krass's bluff by proposing nonbinding negotiations on the condition that Raider enter into a standstill agreement, which would prohibit it from making a hostile bid for a specified period.

1d. Perhaps. Implicit in the answers above has been an assumption that the board will be predisposed to reject the unsolicited offer. Although it seems clear that §102(b)(7) was intended to absolve directors from liability for good-faith breaches of their duty of care — as in *Smith v. Van Gorkom* — the meaning of the good-faith exception is far from clear. It could be argued that directors who blindly accede to management's entrenchment wishes do not act in good faith. The Delaware Supreme Court hinted that blind obeisance to management involved in an LBO could constitute a breach of a duty of loyalty. *Mills Acquisition Co. v. Macmillan, Inc.,* 599 A.2d 261 (Del. 1989). Even though the corporation has adopted a charter amendment pursuant to §102(b)(7), directors still face substantial liability exposure in takeover battle.

2a. Emphatically yes. Because the tender offer is not for any-and-all shares, it is structurally coercive. Shareholders will feel pressured to tender because of the structure of the bid. To be sure to participate in the front-end cash and avoid the uncertainty of a back-end transaction once Raider acquires control, a rational shareholder will tender. Led by the decision in *Unocal* and confirmed in *Newmont Mining,* the Delaware courts make clear that the board can assume a very active posture when the threat is a structurally coercive offer.

2b. Probably, although *Time-Warner* suggests that the board retains significant discretion to just say no. Even though an any-and-all bid is not structurally coercive, shareholders face the dilemma of whether $80 is the best price they will get for selling control or whether they should wait. *Paramount v. QVC* suggests that the board has a heightened duty to assure "best value" whenever shareholders would give up voting control in a takeover. Although the Delaware courts allow the board to assume a role as negotiator and use a poison pill or other device to place it in the negotiator's seat, the proportionality test by its terms gives the board less room to maneuver when confronted with a structurally noncoercive bid. At the least, the board must justify any defense on price grounds and be able to point to an informed judgment that other alternatives offer better value.

2c. Probably. Modern poison pill plans force the bidder either to negotiate with the board or to withdraw. If triggered, they create a financial dilution of the successful acquirer's interest that makes the acquisition prohibitive in the first place. For this reason, bidders condition their bid on the board redeeming the pill's rights or on a court invalidating the pill.

Although *Time-Warner* held that a board could retain a poison pill even in response to an any-and-all bid in order to protect an existing transaction, *Paramount v. QVC* narrowed the holding and made clear that the board has little leeway to erect defenses when shareholders face competing bids seeking to buy control of them. Some argued that one reason for the falloff in hostile takeovers in the early 1990s was the Delaware court's apparent willingness to permit poison pill plans. Many see the Delaware court's decision in *Paramount v. QVC* as heralding a new acceptance of hostile bids.

2d. Some commentators have criticized Delaware's lax fiduciary standards, which allow the board to take upon itself the paternalistic role of deciding for the shareholders whether an offer's timing and price are fair or not. The theory of the corporation rests on the efficiency of separating the capital-providing and management functions; specialization maximizes the gain for both investors and managers. Under the theory, timing and price issues are investment issues properly left to corporate investors, not managers. If there is no structural coercion, allowing the board to take such a role assumes that there is disparity in the information available to management (and board) and to the shareholders. Presumably, management will want to convince shareholders of the inadequacy of the bid and disclose whatever supporting information it has available, such as that the corporation is on the verge of unparalleled success because of an as-yet unannounced new product. If after this disclosure shareholders remain unconvinced, to allow the board to persist in its role as their protector would be to accept that the board knows better about investment valuation and hold-sell decisions than the investors themselves.

Nonetheless, the argument can be made that management will be hampered in convincing shareholders that the price is not adequate or that the timing is poor because their arguments often will depend on intuition and soft information whose disclosure may run afoul of federal securities disclosure rules. Moreover, recent studies suggest that management does better at forecasting future results than do shareholders or stock markets. Despite the danger of management's self-serving beliefs concerning value, the Delaware courts take the approach that an independent board still has a valuable function as a collective actor for the shareholders. An activist role also gives the board leeway to act on behalf of nonshareholder constituencies, which the board in *Time-Warner* ostensibly did when it sought to preserve Time's "editorial integrity in journalism."

3a. Delaware's *Unocal* standard applies in the control context, unless the plaintiff shows that the board's dominant motive was entrenchment or some other self-interest. Target management's participation in the SM bid would seem to make the transaction a classic case of self-dealing, but the Delaware courts have not automatically reviewed board responses to management-backed bids under a loyalty-fairness standard. See *Revlon; Mills Acquisition* (§4.2.3). This puts management bids on comparable footing with nonmanagement bids — as long as the board is independent, management does not dominate the decision-making process, and the board's motives are not self-interested.

3b. To strengthen the case of its disinterestedness, the board should either act without the management directors present, which in Target's case it can do and still keep a quorum, or compose a special takeover committee. Acting as a board, however, raises one problem: Two of the directors are affiliated outside directors (Target's banker and outside lawyer) and are presumably interested in the continuation of Target's business relationship with their firms. A court might later say that these two were not independent because they were incapable of exercising independent judgment. But without these two, the board could not muster a quorum. A special takeover committee composed of some or all of the remaining five directors should be formed, and it should pursue its own independent course, with its own counsel and financial advisors.

3c. No. The committee's approval of the SM bid probably would fare poorly under both prongs of the *Unocal* test. Under the reasonable investigation test, the committee's reliance on Trout Brothers is questionable. Trout Brothers has an interest in maintaining its relationship with Target management. The committee should have sought the advice of a nonaffiliated investment banker in addition to or instead of Trout Brothers. Further, the committee failed to consider whether Raider might be willing to raise its bid or whether negotiations with SM might lead to a higher bid. See *Paramount v. QVC*. The committee must consider all available options, with the help of expert counsel. Further, according to *Smith v. Van Gorkom,* the board must become fully informed even if it means demanding an extension of the bidder's deadline. The committee cannot hide behind the two-day SM deadline.

In addition, the committee's approval would not satisfy its "best value" duties as laid out in *Paramount v. QVC*. Expanding on *Revlon* and *Time-Warner,* the Delaware court in *Paramount v. QVC* imposed auction-type duties when public shareholders sell their control to a buying group. Thus, in our case, since the shareholders will be selling their control to SM, the committee must assure itself that the shareholders will receive "best value" from SM. When there are two bidders, each offering comparable terms, the Delaware court suggests that the board must play the bidders off each other. In an auction, approval of the SM bid without soliciting further interest from Raider would seem unreasonable (that is, disproportionate to the threat that SM might withdraw its bid and leave shareholders only with the lower Raider bid). Given the ways of bidding for takeover targets, it is nearly certain that Raider or SM may be willing to go higher. The committee is duty-bound to consider all possible alternatives.

3d. Possibly. By setting up a bidding process, the committee is subject to the "fair auction" standards of *Revlon*. The first question is whether the

SM offer is better than the Raider offer from the shareholders' standpoint. Although SM's offer is facially superior to Raider's, it may not be valued that way by shareholders. The committee must investigate the value of the securities and the ability of each bidder to pay, principally by consulting with an outside investment banker.

If the committee comes to believe that the SM offer's price is better than the Raider offer, it cannot agree to the lockup until there is reason to believe that further bidding is unlikely. If there is a substantial risk SM or Raider, or both, will drop out if asked to bid again — a question that will require informed judgment by the committee — the committee may be able to grant the lockup as the final "gavel-falling" step in the auction. At some point, the committee should be able to declare a winner and give the winner some certainty that its victory will not be snatched away. The question, which will possibly be subject to judicial second-guessing, is whether the lockups were necessary to extract a final, best bid. *Mills Acquisition* makes clear that lockups cannot be granted if there is bias in the auction process.

If, however, the committee is told that the price of SM's offer is not superior to the Raider offer's price, the committee may be able to consider SM's promise not to engage in a full-flung bust-up merger. Normally at this point in the auction process, the committee cannot take into account nonshareholder interests to the extent they conflict with shareholder interests. The restriction on SM's ability to sell off assets and fire management is to protect management, employee jobs, supplier and customer relationships, and perhaps communities. Nonetheless, if shareholders continue to have an investment interest in the company — which would happen under both bids — stakeholder morale will be related to shareholder interests. The committee could take into account SM's promise in valuing the SM bid.

§40.4 State Antitakeover Statutes — Protection for Whom?

State antitakeover legislation complements firm-specific defenses and has assumed great importance in takeover contests. The legislation eliminates the uncertainty of firm-specific defenses and transforms the validity of takeover defenses into a political and constitutional question rather than a common law fiduciary one. Since 1987, when the U.S. Supreme Court accepted the constitutionality of antitakeover statutes that apply to companies incorporated in the regulating state, state legislatures have accepted the Court's invitation to regulate the market in corporate control. *CTS Corp. v. Dynamics Corp. of America*, 481 U.S. 69 (1987). Today most states, including Delaware, have enacted antitakeover legislation.

The political history of 1980s antitakeover legislation has been interesting. Most of the statutes were drafted by management or pro-management lobbies, not by the typical bar committees of corporate lawyers and academics that draft state corporate codes. In the late 1980s legislatures passed antitakeover statutes with surprising quickness, sometimes in less than a week, responding to widely held fears that hostile takeovers hurt the local economy and the local tax base. Management entrenchment desires overlapped with legislative concern for jobs, suppliers, customers, factories, communities — in short, a concern for protecting the status quo. But to fit the statutes into the constitutional niche fashioned by the Supreme Court, the legislative rhetoric and substance revolved around protecting shareholders from coercion and the collective action problem.

§40.4.1 History — Three Generations

The history of state antitakeover statutes can be divided into three phases, each phase transition marked by a Supreme Court decision:

First Generation.   After the 1968 passage of the "neutral" Williams Act, most states moved to regulate tender offers as part of their "blue sky" regulation of stock transactions. These early antitakeover statutes applied broadly to public corporations either incorporated in the state or with significant contacts in the state. They generally imposed precommencement notice and administrative hearing requirements that significantly impeded hostile tender offers.

In 1982, the Supreme Court held Illinois's first-generation antitakeover statute unconstitutional. *Edgar v. MITE Corp.*, 457 U.S. 624 (1982). The statute applied to corporations incorporated in Illinois as well as to non-Illinois corporations that had their principal offices in Illinois or at least 10 percent of their capital "represented within" the state, if at least 10 percent of the shares sought in the tender offer were held by Illinois residents. The statute imposed a 20-day preannouncement waiting period and allowed for potentially indefinite administrative review of the tender offer for fairness.

A plurality of the *MITE* Court further concluded that the delays allowed by the statute were preempted by the Williams Act's carefully balanced disclosure scheme. A bare majority of the Court held that the statute violated the "dormant" commerce clause because the statute's burden on out-of-state tender offers outweighed any state interest in disclosure and shareholder protection.

Second Generation.   After *MITE,* courts invalidated many of the first-generation statutes. States responded by enacting a second generation of statutes that purported to regulate corporate internal affairs rather than impose blue sky disclosure regulation. These statutes, which were generally less burdensome, tended to apply only to domestic corporations (incorporated in the state) and imposed price or voting conditions that purported to address the evil of coercive tender offers. Many commentators, practitioners, and judges doubted their constitutionality.

But in 1987, the Supreme Court upheld the constitutionality of a second-generation Indiana statute. *CTS Corp. v. Dynamics Corp. of America*, 481 U.S. 69 (1987). The statute, which applied only to corporations incorporated in Indiana with significant Indiana shareholdings, required that disinterested shareholders (excluding the bidder and management) vote collectively to approve the voting rights of any bidder who sought to acquire a controlling interest in the corporation. That is, until the body of shareholders voted to enfranchise, the bidder's "control shares" would not carry voting rights. The Court held that the statute's requirement of a shareholder vote was not inconsistent with the Williams Act as it did not interfere with the bidding process and that it comported with the traditional power of states to regulate the internal affairs of domestic corporations.

Third Generation.   Encouraged by *CTS*, states have tightened their second-generation statutes or have adopted new variants. Some of these are modeled on the Indiana statute, while others go beyond it.

§40.4.2   *Current Antitakeover Statutes*

The third-generation statutes fall into a number of categories:

Control Share Statutes.   An example is the Indiana statute upheld in *CTS*. Control share statutes allow the body of shareholders (but excluding the bidder and management) to decide on the bidder's fate. Under some statutes, the bidder can acquire "control shares" only if other shareholders approve; under others, the bidder acquires voting rights for these shares only if the other shareholders approve. A bidder becomes subject to this rite of initiation when its total shareholdings exceed one of three specified "control" thresholds (usually 20 percent , 33 percent, and 50 percent). Under the statutes, the bidder must give notice and the board must set a date for a shareholders' meeting (usually no more than 50 days after the notice) to decide on the bidder's fate. Control share statutes are ostensibly meant to protect against coercive tender offers by authorizing collective shareholder action.

Business Combination (or Moratorium) Statutes.   A bidder who acquires a specified stock position (such as 15 percent) cannot for a moratorium period (such as three or five years) enter into a back-end transaction with the corporation *unless* (1) the board and a majority (or supermajority) of the other shareholders approves the transaction; or (2) the bidder acquired control in a tender offer for a significant majority of the stock (such as 85 percent); or (3) the original board of directors had approved the bidder's acquisition. The statutes are meant to give shareholders a greater chance to share in the control premium and to give the board enhanced negotiating leverage.

The Delaware Statute.   In 1988 Delaware passed a moratorium statute applicable to all public corporations incorporated in Delaware. Del. GCL §203. Under the statute, any person who acquires 15 percent or more of a Delaware corporation's stock (an "interested shareholder") is disabled for the next three years from effecting any merger or business combination, *unless* (1) the board of directors has approved the business combination before the triggering 15 percent acquisition; (2) the interested shareholder crosses the 15 percent threshold in a transaction (tender offer) in which it acquires at least 85 percent of the company's stock, presumably at a highly favorable price — the 85 percent excludes shares held by management and management-controlled ESOPs; or (3) the business combination is approved by the board and two-thirds of the shares held by other shareholders.

The Delaware statute can be avoided in a number of ways. The statute itself specifies some of them: (1) the bidder can negotiate a deal with incumbent management; (2) the bidder can make a sweet tender offer for 85 percent of the company's stock; (3) the bidder can propose a sweet back-end transaction that will gain two-thirds minority support; and (4) the bidder can wait out the three-year moratorium. In addition, the bidder can mount a proxy contest for board control and, if successful, have the new board approve the bidder's proposed business combination. The Delaware statute is not mandatory, and a corporation can opt out of it after a one-year waiting period.

Fair Price Statutes.   The fair price statutes, predecessors of the business combination statutes, prohibit back-end transactions after a bidder acquires control unless the bidder pays a fair price or the transaction is approved by one of the methods described above. "Price fairness" is usually defined by a formula that assures shareholders a price at least equal to that paid in the front-end acquisition of control. Fair price statutes are meant to prevent front-end-loaded tender offers and acquisition programs. New York adopted a moratorium-fair price statute in 1986. N.Y. BCL §§1600-1613.

Appraisal Statutes.   Appraisal statutes go one step beyond the fair price statutes and give shareholders a right to force the bidder (after acquiring a triggering block) to buy their shares for cash at a formula price specified in the statute. The cash-out right exists whether or not the bidder plans a takeover. The statutes are meant to assure all shareholders a fair price for their shares.

Nonshareholder Constituency Statutes. Many states have also adopted "constituency statutes" along with specific antitakeover statutes. These statutes allow directors to consider the effect of a takeover bid on nonshareholder stakeholders, such as employees, suppliers, and communities. Although not yet tested in court, they ostensibly allow directors greater latitude in structuring and justifying takeover defenses.

Under virtually all of these statutes, the current board has the power to opt out of the statutory scheme or to avoid the statute's coverage with respect to a particular bidder. Without exception, the antitakeover statutes apply only to public companies.

§40.4.3   The Constitutionality of Third-Generation Antitakeover Legislation

The Supreme Court's analysis of the Supremacy Clause (Williams Act preemption) and dormant Commerce Clause in *CTS* provides a blueprint for analyzing the constitutionality of the third generation of state antitakeover statutes.

Preemption. Absent an explicit congressional preemptive intent, federal law preempts a state statute only if compliance with both the federal and state regulatory schemes is physically impossible or if state law frustrates the purpose of federal law. In *CTS,* the Court pointed out that a bidder could comply with both regimes because the Indiana statute's mandate of a shareholder vote within 50 days after the triggering acquisition was consistent with the Williams Act rules, which require only that tender offers be open for at least 20 business days (see §39.2.2).

The Court then held that the Indiana statute did not frustrate, and in fact was consistent with, the purposes of the Williams Act. The Court understood the Williams Act's purposes to provide shareholders with disclosure and with an opportunity to consider the information in making their buy-sell decisions during a takeover. The Court held that the Indiana statute's procedure for collective shareholder action did not interfere with these purposes. Instead, the Court stated, the statute's inhibition of coercive bids was consistent with the Act's shareholder-protection purpose. The Court cavalierly dismissed the argument that the Indiana scheme's 50-day waiting period impeded hostile bids, to management's advantage. The Court said that the Williams Act does not guarantee a perfectly level playing field, and the Court accepted the traditional power of states to authorize procedures, such as staggered boards and supermajority shark repellents, that protect management.

Commerce Clause. Even in the absence of congressional action, the Supreme Court has interpreted the Commerce Clause as prohibiting state regulation that places a discriminatory, inconsistent, or excessive burden on interstate commerce. The *CTS* dormant Commerce Clause analysis, like the preemption analysis, assumed that the Indiana statute was meant to protect shareholder welfare. The Court did not address the political history of state antitakeover statutes to favor in-state management, jobs, and the local tax base.

The Court dismissed the argument that the Indiana statute discriminated against bidders, who usually are out-of-staters, because the statute on its face treated all bidders identically. The statute's application only to corporations incorporated in Indiana avoided any possible interstate burden created by inconsistent state regulations. As to whether the burden on the national market in corporate control exceeded Indiana's interests, the Court assumed that the statute was meant to protect shareholders from coercion. The statute's restrictions on the bidder's voting rights, the Court held, simply regulated the "internal affairs" of a domestic corporation, a power historically resting in state hands. The court declined to involve itself or other federal courts in the debate on the costs and benefits of takeovers.

EXAMPLES

1. The state of Utopia has a Control Share Acquisition Act modeled after the Indiana control share statute upheld by the Supreme Court in *CTS Corp. v. Dynamics Corp. of America*. Even though Target Industries is incorporated in Delaware, the Utopia statute applies to Target because (1) at least 50 percent of its fixed U.S. assets are in Utopia and at least 50 percent of its U.S. employees are residents of Utopia, (2) it has more than 500 shareholders, of whom more than 10 percent are Utopia residents, and (3) its principal office is in Utopia. Raider Partners is worried about the effect of the Utopia statute on its bid for Target.
   a. What will be the effect on Raider of having to comply with the Utopia statute?
   b. Assuming the statute's validity, can Raider avoid the statute?

2. Raider cannot afford to make a bid for Target under the Utopia statute. The statute will require that it keep its tender offer open beyond the minimum 20-day period required by federal law. Raider makes an any-and-all tender offer and assures shareholders the same price in any back-end merger after the tender offer is completed. It then challenges the Utopia statute's constitutionality.
   a. How is the Utopia statute different from the Indiana statute upheld in *CTS*?
   b. Do these differences affect the Utopia statute's constitutionality under a preemption analysis?
   c. Do these differences affect the Utopia statute's constitutionality under a dormant commerce clause analysis?

EXPLANATIONS

1a. Once Raider acquires a triggering percentage of Target's shares (20 percent, 33 percent, or 50 percent), all of the shares that exceed the threshold (control shares) are stripped of voting rights. The voting rights can be restored if Target's remaining shareholders approve the enfranchisement. Raider can seek a special shareholders' vote on the question in a meeting that must occur no later than 50 calendar days after the bid. This is about three weeks after Raider could have purchased the shares under the SEC tender offer rule that imposes a minimum open period of 20 business days (about four weeks). 1934 Act Rule 14e-2 (see §39.2.2). The effect is to chill hostile takeovers of corporations covered by the statute. The 50-day waiting period creates great uncertainty for bidders. Even if a majority of shareholders tender their shares, the bidder will not know whether it bought control until the shareholders' meeting. The additional delay imposes significant additional financing costs and risks that the deal may not be approved or may be blocked during the extended waiting period by some firm-specific defense. In the takeover game, time and risk are money.

1b. Perhaps. Bidders can deflect some of the risks of the statutory 50-day waiting period and shareholder vote. The Supreme Court in *CTS* suggested a bidder could make its bid contingent on shareholders giving their consents or proxies when they tender. The Court observed that in all likelihood the *record date* for the shareholders' meeting will fall before the bidder could have purchased its shares under federal rules, anyway. In addition, others have suggested that a bidder could purchase shares but retain an option to resell them if the results of the meeting were unfavorable — in effect making the tender offer contingent on the shareholders' vote. Others have suggested the bidder could use the statute to compel a shareholders' meeting at which it could replace the board, and the new board could then enter into a friendly negotiated deal.

2a. The Utopia statute is different in one constitutionally significant way: It is extraterritorial — it applies not only to domestic corporations but also to foreign corporations having significant contacts with the state. Utopia cannot justify the statute to carry out its historic role of defining the attributes of corporations incorporated in the state.

2b. Probably not. Utopia's statute does not interfere with the process by which tender offers are made. Compliance with the timing, disclosure, best price, and proration requirements of the Williams Act regime remains unaffected. Nonetheless, Raider might argue that the statute's extraterritoriality and its application to any-and-all bids frustrate the Williams Act purpose of shareholder protection in takeovers.

Extraterritoriality. The statute's extraterritoriality arguably conflicts with the Williams Act because it exposes a bidder to potentially irreconcilable or overlapping *state* requirements, a burden that may offend the Williams Act's philosophy of an even playing field for bidders and Target management. If the Utopia and Delaware antitakeover statutes both apply, Raider may well have to make a tender offer for 85 percent of Target's stock (to avoid the Delaware statute) and wait 50 days for voting rights (to gain control under the Utopia statute). Nonetheless, the Supreme Court in *CTS* did not seem concerned about the burden on the bidder as long as the burden could be seen as furthering shareholder protection and not significantly undermining the bidding process. In this case, if Delaware's statute can be seen as preventing bust-up bids, the additional burden of complying with it would not seem to be preempted under the deferential *CTS* analysis. In other words, Utopia might well have passed a statute combining the elements of a control share statute and moratorium statute. Even though compliance might impose additional costs on Raider, which would have to carry financing commitments for a longer time and on more shares, *CTS* did not seem concerned with regulatory costs unless they actually interfere with the bidding process.

Application to any-and-all bids. Raider's bid assures all shareholders an equal price and is less coercive than the partial bid that was at issue before the Court in *CTS*. According to the *CTS* Court, one of the principal justifications for the Indiana statute was that it protects shareholders against structurally coercive bids. It is unlikely, however, that the Court would probe the strength of the state's interest in regulating an any-and-all bid. For purposes of preemption analysis, it is enough that the Utopia statute does not undermine the bidding process and that it serves the ostensible purpose of reducing collective action problems that shareholders face in any bid. After *CTS,* the extent to which a state antitakeover statute favors management over bidders does not seem significant.

2c. Probably. The "extraterritorial" Utopia statute creates the possibility of inconsistent state regulation and is probably unconstitutional under the dormant Commerce Clause.

Extraterritoriality. In *CTS,* the Supreme Court made much of the Indiana statute's regulation of the "internal affairs" of *domestic* corporations. The Utopia statute undercuts the well-established corporate law doctrine that the state of incorporation regulates corporate shareholder-manager relationships, which would include such matters as shareholder voting rights and business combinations involving controlling shareholders. The doctrine provides certainty and stability and is taken as a given in securities trading markets and markets in corporate control. Since *CTS* a number of lower courts have struck down extraterritorial antitakeover statutes. Nonetheless, the Utopia statute applies only to those foreign corporations with most of their assets and employees in the state, minimizing the possibility of inconsistencies. Bidders will have to comply with, at most, two statutes. In this case, Raider can comply with both the Delaware and Utopia antitakeover statutes by bidding for 85 percent of Target's shares and waiting out the 50-day period. It might be argued that except in cases of actual or probable inconsistency — that is, where the bidder is unable physically to comply with both at the same time — the Commerce Clause should not be understood as interfering with state prerogatives to define corporate relationships. Nonetheless, this interpretation of the dormant Commerce Clause is at odds with the Supreme Court's apparent desire in *CTS* to avoid federal involvement in such fine questions of corporate governance. *CTS* preserves the incorporation-based system of corporate ordering in the United States.

Application to any-and-all bids. The Utopia statute's regulation of any-and-all bids presents less of a problem. The *CTS* Court made clear that it would not engage in a balancing of the burden of the regulation on interstate trading markets and the putative local benefits of a state's antitakeover statute. As long as the Utopia statute's regulation is related to some theory of shareholder protection, the deference to state corporate law is controlling. Although the statute may in fact discourage bids to protect the local status quo, its economic folly does not make it unconstitutional. See *CTS* (Justice Scalia, concurring).

Index

Acquisitions. *See* Corporate combinations
Action by consent, shareholders, 12.2.4
American Law Institute (ALI)
  corporate governance project, 1.2.4
  corporate opportunities, 24.2.4
  director self-dealing transactions, 22.4.2
Antitakeover statutes. *See also* Takeovers,
    defenses
  as defense mechanism, 40.4
Appraisal rights
  exclusivity, 36.3.1
  "fair value," 36.2.2
  market-out exception, 36.1.2
  organic changes, 36.1.1
  procedures for dissenters, 36.2.1
Arbitration, deadlocks in close corpora-
    tions, 17.3.3
Articles of incorporation. *See also* Incorpora-
    tion; Organic changes
  amendments, 34.1
  amendment procedure
    board initiation, 12.1.3, 34.1.2
    shareholder approval, 34.1.2
  contents of articles, 3.1.1
  "shark repellants", 37.2, 38.3.2
Authority. *See* Officers

Balance sheet test. *See* Corporate distribu-
    tions
Beneficial owners (beneficial shareholders)
  appraisal rights, 36.1.1
  derivative suits, 32.2.2
  disclosure of 5 percent ownership, 19.5.2
  inspection rights, 12.1.4
  proxy disclosure, 19.4.5
  proxy voting, 18.1.1
  "public corporation," definition of, 19.3.1
  public stock markets, 18.2.1
  shareholder proposals, Rule 14a-8, 19.5.2
Board of directors. *See* Directors
Business judgment rule. *See also* Duty of care
  generally, 21.2
  dismissal of derivative action, 33.4.1
  *Graham v. Allis Chalmers Manufacturing
    Co.*, 21.3
  justifications, 21.2.2
  presumption, 21.3
  rebutting presumption
    conflict of interest, 21.3.1
    fraud, 21.3.1
    gross negligence, 21.3.3

  illegality, 21.3.1
  irrational, 21.3.2
  reliance corollary, 21.2.3
  rule versus doctrine, 21.2.1
  *Smith v. Van Gorkom (Trans
    Union)*, 21.3.3
Bylaws
  governance structure, 3.1.4
  "proper proposals," 19.5.2
  shareholder amendment, 12.1.3

Class actions. *See* Shareholder litigation
Classified board. *See* Directors
Closely held corporations
  classified boards, 16.4
  close corporation statutes, 15.2, 16.8
  deadlocks, 17.3
  director compensation, 23.3
  executive compensation, 23.2.4
  fiduciary duties, 17.2.2, 20.3.2
  freeze-outs, 17.1.1
  involuntary dissolution, 17.2.1
  irrevocable proxies, 16.5
  management agreements, 16.7
  piercing corporate veil, 6.2.1
  special problems, 15.1
  squeeze-outs, 17.1.2
  supermajority requirements, 16.1
  transfer restrictions, 16.6
  vote pooling agreements, 16.2
  voting trusts, 16.3
Conflicting interest transactions. *See* Self-
    dealing transactions
Consolidations. *See also* Corporate combina-
    tions
  definition, 35.2
Controlling shareholders. *See* Shareholder,
    Controlling
Control person. *See also* Shareholder, con-
    trolling
  sale of control, 27.2
  sale of securities, 10.2.4
Control premium. *See* Sale of control
Control Shares.
  See Antitakeover statutes; *See* Sale of con-
    trol
Corporate combinations. *See also* Mergers;
    Sale of assets; Squeeze-out transac-
    tions
  consolidations, 35.2
  mergers, 35.2

Corporate combinations (*continued*)
  sale of assets, 35.3
  short-form merger of subsidiary into
      parent, 35.2.3
  squeeze-out merger, 35.2.6
  triangular merger, 35.2.5
Corporate distributions
  capital distributions, 9.1.2
  contractual limits, 9.3
  dividends, 9.1.1
  equitable subordination doctrine, 7.2
  equity insolvency test, 9.2.1
  limits on corporate distribution
    balance sheet tests, 9.2.2
    equity insolvency test, 9.2.1
  nimble dividends, 9.2.2
  redemption, 9.1.3
  repurchase, 9.1.3
  stated, paid-in capital, 9.2
  stock dividends, 9.2.2
  stock splits, 9.2.2
Corporate finance. *See* Debt financing;
    Equity securities
Corporate gifts. *See* Ultra vires doctrine
Corporate governance
  ALI Corporate Governance Project, 1.2.4
  board of directors, 11.1
  closely held corporation, 11.2.2
  publicly held corporations, 11.2.1, 18.1
  shareholders, 11.1, 12.1
  traditional model, 11.2
Corporate opportunity doctrine
  ALI Principles of Corporate
      Governance, 24.2.4
  competition with corporation, 24.4
  defenses
    consent, 24.3
    corporate incapacity, 24.3
  definition, 24.2
  remedies for taking, 24.1.2
  sale of control, 27.2.3
  tests
    diversion, 24.2.1
    expectancy, 24.2.2
    line of business, 24.2.3
Corporation
  as "person"
    constitution, 1.3
    regulatory schemes, 7.1.1
  basic characteristics
    central management, 1.1.1, 12, 13, 18.1
    free transferability of shares, 1.1.1, 18.2
    limited liability, 1.1.1, 6.1
    separate entity, 1.1.1, 7.1.1, 14
  corporate statutes, 1.2.2
  financial structure, 8.3
  history, 1.2.1
  incorporation, 3.1-3.2
  perspectives
    contractarian, 1.1.3
    traditionalist, 1.1.3
Corporation by estoppel. *See* Promoters
Cumulative voting. *See also* Staggered board
  electing directors, 13.1.3

Debt financing
  debt-equity ratio, 8.2.2
  debt securities, 8.2.1
  leverage, 8.2.2
  priority over equity, 8.2.5
  tax advantages, 8.2.2
De facto corporation. *See* Promoters
De facto merger. *See* Mergers
De jure corporation. *See* Promoters
Demand requirement. *See also* Derivative
    actions
  generally, 32.2.4
  federal litigation, 33.3.4
  futility exception, 33.3.1
  pleading requirement, 33.3.3
  universal demand, 33.3.2
Derivative actions. *See also* Shareholder
    litigation
  contemporaneous ownership require-
    ment, 32.2.2
  corporate incapacity rule, 32.2.2
  demand requirement, 32.2.4
  dismissal of derivative actions
    board recommendation, 33.3
    demand requirement, 33.3
    federal litigation, 33.3.4
    special litigation committee, 33.4
    Zapata Corp. v. Maldonado, 33.4.3
  federal procedures, 32.3
  frivolous suits, 32.2.3
  settlement, 32.2.5
Director liability. *See also* Duty of care; Duty
    of loyalty; Insider trading
  breach of fiduciary duty
    corporate opportunity, 24.1.2
    duty of care, 21.4, 21.5
    sale of control, 27.2.3
    self-dealing, 22.5
  charter exculpation, 21.5.1
  corporate distributions, 9.4
  indemnification of, 25.1
  insurance, 25.2
Directors. *See also* Business judgment rule;
    Corporate opportunity doctrine;
    Duty of care; Duty of loyalty;
    Insider trading; Rule 10b-5; Self-
    dealing transactions
  compensation, 23.3
  disinterested, 22.4, 23.2.3
  election of, 12.1.1, 13.1
    classified board, 13.1.5
    cumulative voting, 13.1.3
    proxy contests, 38.3
    qualification, 13.1.1
    staggered board, 13.1.4
    straight voting, 13.1.2
  filling vacancies, 13.3
  liability. *See* Director liability
  "meeting rule," 13.3.2
  ratification of officers' actions, 14.1.1
  removal of, 13.2
Disclosure. *See also* Securities; Rule 10b-5
  insider trading, duty to abstain or
    disclose, 29.5.1

mergers, 35.2.2
proxy solicitations. *See also* Proxies
  SEC proxy rules, 19.2
  state law, 19.1
  sale of control, 27.2.5
Discounted cash flow
  valuation of corporation, 36.2.2
Dismissal of derivative actions. *See* Derivative
  actions
Dissenter's rights. *See* Appraisal
  rights
Dissolution. *See also* Closely held corporations; Organic changes
  involuntary, 17.2.1
  voluntary, 34.2
Dividends. *See also* Corporate distributions
  cash, 9.1.1
  nimble, 9.2.2
  stock, 9.1.1, 9.2.2
  stock, 9.2.2
Dominant-motive test
  takeover defenses, 40.2.1
Due diligence. *See also* Securities
  defense to securities fraud, 10.3.2
Duty of care. *See also* Business judgment
  rule; Fiduciary duties
  duty to become informed, 21.3.3
  duty to monitor, 21.3.3
  elements of duty of care, 21.1.3
  rational basis test, 21.3.2
  remedies for breach
    charter exculpation, 21.5.1
    director liability, 21.4.1
  RMBCA §8.30, 21.1.1
  Smith v. Van Gorkom (Trans
    Union), 21.3.3
Duty of loyalty. *See also* Fiduciary duties;
  Self-dealing transactions
  controlling shareholders
    partially owned subsidiaries, 26.2.2
    squeeze-out transactions, 26.3
  directors and officers
    competition with corporation, 24.1
    corporate opportunities, 24
    executive compensation, 23
    indemnification, 25.1
    self-dealing transactions, 22
Duty to abstain or disclose. *See also*
  Rule 10b-5
  insider trading, 29.5.1

Earned surplus. *See* Corporate distributions
Enterprise liability. *See* Piercing the corpo-
  rate veil
Entire fairness test. *See also* Shareholder,
  controlling
squeeze-out mergers, 26.3.3
Equitable subordination doctrine. *See also*
  Corporation
  protection of creditors, 7.2
Equity insolvency test. *See also* Corporate
  distributions
  RMBCA §6.40(c)(1), 9.2.1

Equity securities. *See also* Common stock;
  Dividends; Issuance of equity
  securities; Preferred stock
  common stock, 8.1.3
  dividends, 8.1.2, 8.1.3
  preferred stock, 8.1.3
  rights on dissolution, 8.1.2, 8.1.3
Executive compensation
  disinterested director approval, 23.2.3
  fair-and-reasonable standard, 23.2.5
  forms of compensation, 23.1
    pension plans, 23.1
    salaries/bonuses, 23.1
    stock plans, 23.1
  judicial review, 23.2
  waste standard, 23.2.4
Expectancy test. *See also* Corporate opportunity doctrine
  corporate opportunities, 24.2.2

Fairness test, self-dealing transactions, 22.3
Federal corporate law, 1.2.5
Federal courts, derivative actions, 32.3
Fiduciary duties. *See also* Duty of care; Duty
  of loyalty
  generally, 20.2
  closely held corporations, 20.3.2
  controlling shareholders, 26.2
  duty of care, 20.2.1
  duty of loyalty, 20.2.2
  duty to disclose, 29.3.2
  promoters, 5.3.1
  proxy contests, 38.3.2
  public corporations, 20.3.1
  theory of fiduciary duties, 20.1.2
  trading in securities
    liability to corporation, 28.3
    misappropriation, 29.5.2
    Rule 10b-5, 29.5.1
    state law, 28.2
Fraud-on-the-market theory. *See also* Rule
  10b-5
Rule 10b-5, causation
  requirement, 29.3.4
Freeze-outs and force-outs. *See also* Closely
  held corporations; Corporate
  combinations; Squeeze-out transactions
  close corporations, 17.1.2
  mergers, 35.2.6
Fully paid and nonassessable shares. *See*
  Issuance of equity securities

Incapacity, corporate opportunity
  defense, 24.3
Incorporation
  articles, 3.1.1
  filing, 3.1.3
  foreign corporations, 3.2.2
  incorporators, 3.1.2
  internal affairs doctrine, 3.2.1
  state of incorporation, 3.2

Index

Indemnification
    director and officer liability
        insurance, 25.2.2
    directors, 25.1
    mandatory, 25.1.1
    nondirectors, 25.1.5
    permissive, 25.1.2
Insider trading. *See also* Short-swing
        profits
    generally, 28.1
    misappropriation, 28.1.2, 28.4, 29.5.2
    Rule 10b-5
        duty to abstain or disclose, 29.5.1
        fiduciary duty, 29.5.1
        mail and wire fraud, 29.5.2
        outsider misappropriation, 29.5.2
        remedies, 29.5.4
        Rule 14e-3, tender offers, 29.5.3
        tippers and tippees, 29.5
    state fiduciary law, 28.2
        bad news trading, 28.2.2
        fraud or deceit, 28.2.1
        Kansas rule, 28.2.3
        liability to corporation, 28.3
        limits, 28.2.4
        special facts doctrine, 28.2.2
    under federal law, 29.5.4
Inspection of corporate records
    common law basis, 12.1.4
    proxy disclosure, 19.1.1, 19.4.1
Insurance, director and officer
        liability, 25.2.2
Internal affairs doctrine, incorpor-
        ation, 3.2.1
Investment contracts, definition of
        security, 10.4.2
Involuntary dissolution, closely held
        corporations, 17.2.1
Issuance of equity securities
    authorized, 8.1.1
    board liability, 8.1.4
    fully paid and non-assessable
        shares, 8.1.3, 8.1.4
    par value shares, 8.1.4
    preemptive rights, 8.1.2
    shareholder liability, 8.1.4
    watered, bonus and discount stock, 8.1.4

Joint ventures, compared to other organiza-
        tional forms, 2.2
Jury trials, derivative actions, 31.1.1

Limited liability company
    liability of participants, 2.2.4
    life span, 2.2.1
    management, authority to bind and
        control, 2.2.2
    taxation, 2.2.5
    transfer of ownership, 2.2.3
Line of business test, corporate
        opportunities, 24.2.3
Looting, sale of control, 27.2.3

Market-out exception. *See* Appraisal
        rights
Mediation, deadlocks in close corpora-
        tions, 17.3.3
Mergers. *See also* Consolidations; Proxies
        contests; Sale of assets; Sharehold-
        ers, controlling
    appraisal rights, 35.2.2, 36.1.1
    de facto merger, 35.4.1
    fairness review, 26.3
    fiduciary protections, 35.2.2
    merger of corporations in different
        states, 35.2.4
    shareholder approval, 35.2.2
    short-form merger of subsidiary into
        parent, 35.2.3
    squeeze-out merger, 26.3, 35.2.6
    statutory mergers, 35.2
    successor liability doctrine, 35.4.2
    triangular merger, 35.2.5
Misappropriation (outsider trading)
    confidential information, 28.1.2, 28.4
    remedies, 29.5.4
    Rule 10b-5, 29.5.2
    tender offer information, 29.5.3

Nimble dividends, 9.2.2. *See also* Corporate
        distributions
No-sharing rule, sale of control, 27.2.2

Officers
    actual authority (express and im-
        plied), 14.1.1
    apparent authority, 14.1.2
    extraordinary transactions, 14.1.2
    inherent authority, 14.1.3
    ratification by board, 14.1.1
    respondeat superior, 14.2
    self-dealing transactions, 22.2.5
Organic changes. *See also* Dissolution;
        Merger; Sale of assets
    amendments to articles, 34.1
    appraisal rights, 34.1.2
    charter amendments, 34.1.1
    dissolution, 34.2
    recapitalizations, 34.1.3

Paid-in capital (stated capital). *See* Corporate
        distributions
Parent corporation. *See* Shareholder,
        controlling
Parent-subsidiary transactions. *See also* Share-
        holder, controlling
    mergers, 35.2.3
    self-dealing, 26.2
Partnerships
    authority to bind and control, 2.2.2
    general, 2.1
    liability, 2.2.4
    life span, 2.2.1
    limited, 2.1

Index

limited, with corporate general
    partner, 2.3.2
taxation, 2.2.5
transfer of ownership, 2.2.3
Par value shares, 8.1.3. *See also* Issuance of
    equity securities
Pension plans. *See* Executive compensation;
    Takeover defenses
Perlman v. Feldmann, sale of
    control, 27.2.4
Piercing the corporate veil
    active participation, 6.2.7
    closely held corporations, 6.2.1
    commingling of assets, 6.2.5
    corporate formalities, 6.2.4
    deception, 6.2.8
    involuntary creditors, 6.2.1
    multiple incorporation, 6.2.2
    traditional factors, 6.2
    undercapitalization, 6.2.6
    Uniform Fraudulent Transfer Act
        (UFTA), 6.3.1
    Walkovsky v. Carlton, 6.2.3
Poison pills
    proxy contests, 38.3.2
    takeover defense, 37.2, 40.3
Promoters
    corporation by estoppel, 5.2.2
    de facto corporation, 5.2.2
    defective incorporation, effect of, 5.2
    de jure corporation, 5.2.1
    fiduciary duties, 5.3.1
    liability for pre-incorporation
        contracts, 5.1
    self-dealing by promoter, 5.3
Proportionality test. *See* Takeover
    defenses
Proxies. *See also* Proxy contests
    authorization, 12.2.4, 19.1.1
    definition of "solicitation," 19.3.2
    federal proxy regulation, 19.2
        disclosure requirements, 19.3.3, 19.4.1
        proxy card, form of, 19.4.2
        registered or reporting
            companies, 19.3.1
    proxy fraud
        elements, 19.6.2
        fraud action, state, 19.1.2
        implied cause of action, federal, 19.6.2
    shareholder proposals
        company-funded, 19.5.2
        "proper proposals," 19.5.2
        Rule 14a-8, 19.5.2
        shareholder-funded, 19.5.1
    state proxy regulation, 19.1
    takeovers, 37.1
Proxy contests
    corporate funding of management
        proxies, 38.3.1
    federal proxy regulation, 38.2
    fiduciary duties, 38.3.2
    "poison pills," 38.3.2
    shareholder passivity, 38.1
    "shark repellant" charter amendments

generally, 37.2 (Act III, Scene 1)
    fiduciary duties, 38.3.2
    state regulation, 38.3
Public offerings. *See* Securities

Ratification, shareholder. *See also* Share-
    holder, controlling
    self-dealing transactions, 22.3.4
Rational basis test, business judgment
    rule, 21.3.2
Recapitalizations, 34.1.3. *See also* Organic
    changes
Record date, shareholders entitled to
    vote, 12.2.2
Record owners (record shareholders). *See also*
    Beneficial owners; Shareholders
    appraisal rights, 36.1.1
    derivative suits, 32.2.2
    disclosure of 5 percent ownership, 19.5.2
    inspection rights, 12.1.4
    proxy voting, 18.1.1
    public corporation, definition, 19.3.1
    shareholder proposals, Rule 14a-8, 19.5.2
    shareholders entitled to vote, 12.2.2
Res judicata, derivative actions, 31.1.5
Restricted securities, 10.2.2. *See also*
    Securities
Rule 10b-5
    advantages over state law, 29.2.2
    deception requirement, 29.4.3
    elements of violation, 29.2.1
    fraud on the market, 29.3.4
    "in connection with" requirement, 29.3.5
    insider trading, 29.5
        duty to abstain or disclose, 29.5.1
        fiduciary duty, 29.5.1
        mail and wire fraud, 29.5.2
        outsider misappropriation, 29.5.2
        remedies for insider trading, 29.5.4
        Rule 14e-3, tender offers, 29.5.3
        tippers and tippees, 29.5
    negligence standard, 29.4.1
    sale-of-business doctrine, 29.4.4
Rule 14a-8. *See also* Proxies
    shareholder proxy initiatives, 19.5.2
Rule 14e-3, misappropriation of tender offer
    information, 29.5.3

Sale of assets. *See also* Mergers
    definition of "sale" of, 35.3.3
    description, 35.3
    statutory protections, 35.3.2
    "substantially all" requirement, 35.3.3
Sale of control
    control premium, 27.2.1
    disclosure duties, 27.2.5
    no-sharing rule, 27.2.2
    Perlman v. Feldmann, 27.2.4
    sale of office, 27.1
    sale to looters, 27.2.3
    usurpation of corporate
        opportunities, 27.2.3

Schedule 13D. *See* Tender offers
Securities
 definition of "security," 10.4.1
 efficiency of public stock markets, 18.2.2
 NASDAQ, 18.2.1
 over-the-counter market, 18.2.1
 public trading, 18.2
 stock exchanges, 18.2.1
Securities Act of 1933. *See also* Securities
  offerings
 disclosure requirements, 10.1
Securities Exchange Act of 1934. *See also*
  Short-swing profits
 section 16(b), 30
 short-swing trading, 30.1
 tender offers, 39.1-39.3
Securities offerings. *See also* Debt financing;
  Equity securities
 civil liability under 1933 Act, 10.3
 control person, 10.2.4
 damages, section 11, 10.3.2
 due diligence defense, 10.3.2
 exemptions from registration, 10.2
 federal regulation, 10
 investment contracts, 10.4.2
 postdistribution market trading
  exemption, 10.2.4
 private offerings (private placement)
  exemption, 10.2.2
 registration of public offerings, 10.1.1
 Regulation D, 10.2.2
 rescission, for fraud, 10.3.3
 rescission, section 12(1), 10.3.1
 restricted securities, 10.2.2
 Rule 144, 10.2.4
 Securities Act of 1933, 10.1
 small offering exemptions, 10.2.3
 underwriters, 10.2.4
Self-dealing transactions (conflict of interest)
 generally, 22.1
 ALI Principles of Corporate Governance, 22.4.2
 approval by disinterested board or shareholders, 22.4
 burden of proof, 22.2.2
 fairness test, 22.3
  procedural fairness, 22.3.3
  substantive fairness, 22.3.2
 officers, 22.2.5
 remedies for self-dealing, 22.5
 shareholder ratification, 12.1.2, 22.3.4
 Subchapter F, RMBCA, 22.4.1
 voidability of, 22.2.1
Shareholder, controlling. *See also* Sale of
  control
 approval by disinterested shareholders, 26.2.2
 business purpose test, 26.3.2
 dealings with partially owned
  subsidiaries, 26.2.2
 dealings with wholly owned subsidiaries, 26.2.1
 definition of, 26.1

 entire fairness test, 26.3.3
 exclusion of minority, 26.2.2
 remedy in squeeze-out transactions, 26.3.4
 squeeze out transactions, 26.3
 Weinberger v. UOP, Inc., 26.3.3
Shareholder litigation
 class actions, 31.2
 derivative actions, 31.1, 31.2
 direct actions, 31
 plaintiff-shareholder, 31.1.4
 res judicata, 31.1.5
 right to jury trial, 31.1.1
Shareholder meetings
 action by consent, 12.2.4
 annual and special meetings, 12.2.1
 notice, 12.2.2
 quorum, 12.2.3
 record date, owners, 12.2.2
 vote by proxy, 12.2.4
Shareholder passivity. *See* Proxy contests
Shareholders. *See also* Appraisal rights;
  Proxies; Shareholder litigation;
  Shareholder meetings; Shareholder
  voting
 appraisal rights
  generally, 36
  mergers, 35.2.2
 disclosure of 5 percent ownership, 19.5.2
 inspection rights, 12.1.4
 limited liability, 6.1
 plaintiff in derivative action, 33.1
 "public corporation," definition of, 19.3.1
 role in corporation, 11.1-11.2, 12.1
  amending articles, 12.1.3
  amending bylaws, 12.1.3
  approval of conflicting interest
   transactions, 12.1.2
  approval of fundamental corporate
   changes, 12.1.2
  initiation of corporate changes, 12.1.3
 shareholder equity, 9.2.2
 shareholder litigation
  direct actions, 12.1.4
 shareholder proposals, Rule 14a-8, 19.5.2
 voting by proxy, 12.2.4, 18.1.1
  in public corporations, 18.1
 shareholders entitled to vote, 12.2.2
Shareholder voting. *See also* Shareholder
  meetings
 history of, 18.1.2
 mechanics of, 12
 proxy process, 18.1.1
Shark repellant charter amendments. *See*
  Proxy contests
Short-swing profits
 disgorgement rules, 30.2.2
 merger and option transactions, 30.3.3
 Securities Exchange Act of
  1934 §16, 30.1
   directors and officers under, 30.1, 30.2.2
   shareholders under, 30.2.2
 strict liability, 30.2.1

Smith v. Van Gorkom, 21.3.3. *See* Business judgment rule
Sole proprietorship, 2.1
Solicitations, definition, 19.3.2. *See also* Proxies
Special facts doctrine, insider trading, 28.2.2
Special litigation committee. *See also* Derivative actions
  dismissal of derivative litigation, 33.4
Squeeze-out transactions
  close corporations, 17.1.2
  liquidation, 26.3
  squeeze-out mergers, 26.3
  stock splits, 26.3
Staggered board, 13.1.4. *See also* Directors, election of
Stated, paid-in capital. *See* Corporate distributions
Statutory mergers. *See* Mergers
Stock redemption, repurchase. *See* Corporate distributions
Straight voting, electing directors, 13.1.2
Subchapter F, RMBCA. *See also* Self-dealing transactions
  conflict of interest transactions, 22.4.1
Successor liability doctrine, mergers, 35.4.2
Supermajority voting requirements, closely held corporations, 16.1

Takeover defenses
  antitakeover statutes, 40.4
  board's power to adopt, 40.3
  dominant-motive test, 40.2.1
  fairness review, 40.2.4
  fiduciary law, 40.2
  outside directors, 40.1.2
  poison pills, 40.3
  proportionality test, 40.2.3
  role of target board, 40.1
  types of, 37.2 (Act III, Scene 1)
    asset lockups, 40.2.3
    employee stock ownership plans, 40.4.2
    golden parachutes, 37.2
    greenmail, 40.2.1
    issuer self-tenders, 39.2.5
    leveraged management buyout, 40.2.3
    market sweep, 39.1.1, 39.2.5
    poison pill, 40.2.3
    shark repellants, 38.3
    white knights, 40.2.3
  ultra vires doctrine, 40.3
Takeovers. *See also* Takeover defenses; Tender offers; Proxy contests
  arbitraguers, 37.2 (Act II, Scene 2)
  bidders, 37.2 (Act I, Scene 1)
  bust-up takeovers, 37.2 (Act I, Scene 2)
  evaluation of takeover, 37.3
  financing, 37.2 (Act I, Scene 2)
  foothold investment, 37.2 (Act I, Scene 3), 39

junk bonds, 37.2 (Act I, Scene 2)
proxy contests, 37.1, 38
tender offers
  generally, 37.1
  antifraud action, 39.2.4
  any-and-all, 37.2 (Act I, Scene 2)
  definition, 39.2.5
  disclosure, 39.2.1
  issuer self-tender, 39.2.3
  substantive requirements, 39.2.2
target
  generally, 37.2 (Act I, Scene 1)
  putting in play, 37.2 (Act II, Scene 1)
Williams Act
  effect on takeovers, 39.3.4
Target company. *See* Takeovers
Taxation
  avoiding double taxation, 2.3.2
  flow-through vs. corporate double tax, 2.1
  limited liability companies, 2.3.2
  limited partnership with corporate general partner, 2.3.2
  subchapter S election, 2.3.2
Tender offers. *See also* Takeovers
  deception, 39.2.4
  disclosure of 5 percent holding, 39.1
  disclosure requirements, 39.2.1
  federal tender offer rules, 39.2
  issuer self-tenders, 39.2.3
  open market purchases, 39.2.5
  Schedule 13D, 39.1.1
  takeovers, 37.1
    damages recovery, 39.3.2
    injunctive relief, 39.3.3
    standing, 39.3.1
  unorthodox tender offers, 39.2.5
  Williams Act
    generally, 39.2.3
    effect on takeovers, 39.3.4
Tippers and tippees
  Rule 10b-5, liability for insider trading, 29.5

Ultra vires doctrine. *See also* Takeovers
  common law origins, 4.1.1
  corporate gifts, 4.4
  distinguishing from corporate duties, 4.3
  modern doctrine, 4.2
Uniform Fraudulent Transfer Act
  applied to piercing corporate veil, 6.3.1

Valuation of corporation. *See also* Appraisal rights
  "block" method, 36.2.2
  discounted cash flow, 36.2.2
Vote pooling agreements, closely held corporations, 16.2
Voting trusts, closely held corporations, 16.3

Index

Walkovsky v. Carlton. See Piercing the
    corporate veil
Waste standard, executive
    compensation, 23.2.4
Watered stock. *See also* Issuance of equity
    securities

equity securities, 8.1.3
Weinberger v. UOP. See Shareholder, controlling
Williams Act. *See also* Tender offers;
    Takeovers
generally, 39
effect on takeovers, 39.3.4